THE CHIEF EXECUTIVE

THE CHIEF EXECUTIVE

LOUIS W. KOENIG

Harcourt, Brace & World, Inc.

NEW YORK / CHICAGO / BURLINGAME

TO

Juliana, Fred, and David

Acknowledgments

___

My views on the chief executive have undergone the perceptive scrutiny of students in my university classes on the American Presidency. The progress of this book has benefited from Virginia Canfield's indispensable ability to develop typed copy from difficult hand drafts. I am grateful to my wife, Eleanor White Koenig, for unfailing understanding and encouragement, and to my mother, the late Pauline Graef Koenig, who despite severe illness heroically performed several necessary tasks. I am also grateful to the public affairs program of the Ford Foundation and the research fund of the New York University Graduate School of Arts and Science for contributions toward the expenses of this book.

LOUIS W. KOENIG

Washington Square North
New York University
New York City
July 11, 1964

Contents

═══

THE CHIEF EXECUTIVE

CHAPTER

1

Perspectives on Presidential Power

PRESIDENT John F. Kennedy, according to Theodore Sorensen, his valued counselor, was a man "subject to moods" and at times discouraged by his inability "to get everything done as quickly as he would like to get it done." The source of Kennedy's discouragement was the far-stretching chasm between the ideal of a vigorous, creative Presidency he envisaged in his gallant 1960 campaign and the reality of the complicated, restraint-bound, frustrating office he discovered after his inauguration. The Presidency of John Kennedy's campaign speeches was the office that would "get this country going again," an organ of bold leadership in a fast-changing world, the mover and shaker of legislation fit for the urgent, controversial problems of the day.

In a press conference of June 27, 1962, with his term nearing its midpoint and the end, therefore, of a span that ordinarily is the most fruitful part of a Presidential tenure, Kennedy indulged, with the reporters' encouragement, in an off-the-cuff evaluation of his official experience, all the more candid because it was spontaneous. He acknowledged, with a tinge of sadness, that even with a one-third majority in both houses of Congress, he lacked, as he put it, a "working majority." Even though Democrats at the time outnumbered Republicans 263 to 174 in the House of Representatives and 64 to 35 in the Senate, with one Republican vacancy, he could not command sufficient support from his own party nor wean away enough Republicans to move difficult bills through Congress and onto the statute books. The President was goaded into his notice of a lack of a "voting majority" by the fact that a week before his press conference his farm bill had been lost in the House, with forty-eight Democrats voting against it. "We should realize," he told the reporters, "that some Democrats have voted with the Republicans for twenty-five years, really since 1938, and that makes it very difficult to secure the enactment of any controversial legislation."

The President on that June day looked to the approaching November Congressional elections with hopes that the Democratic Congressional majority might be increased. Kennedy did not get his "working majority," but fared better than most Presidents, whose Congressional strength traditionally sags in midterm elections. Although the new totals of 258 Democrats and 177 Republicans in the House meant a net Democratic loss of four seats, the President enjoyed a net gain of three Representatives who promised to support his program. In the Senate the Democrats gained four seats. In the House, where the President's troubles were greatest, he still required between ten and forty Republican or Southern Democratic votes on controversial issues. A year after the election and a year and a half after the press conference, when the tragedy of his assassination struck, Kennedy still was deprived of legislation he deemed important—public school aid, civil rights legislation, medical care for the aged, the establishment of a cabinet-level urban affairs department, the barring of arbitrary use of literacy tests as qualifications for voting, the establishment of standby authority to lower taxes, the withholding of taxes on dividend and interest income at the source, and the permanent strengthening of the unemployment insurance system. Kennedy's principal victory in nearly three years of office, and probably the only one that deserves to be called major, was the Trade Expansion Act of 1962. The balance of political power between the White House and Congress in the Kennedy years was so even that the President could not with any certainty secure the controversial legislation he wanted and the country needed. The President and the nation were the victims, in the phrase of James MacGregor Burns, of "the deadlock of democracy."

President Kennedy's frustrations were not confined to the domestic scene. Conflict and rejection often blocked him from achieving his purposes in foreign affairs. His plans for United States and multi-national control of nuclear weapons were spurned by the French. He proposed to reduce United States troops in Europe and Berlin, but the allies refused to fill the vacuum with their own forces, so he resigned himself to the status quo. He put to work a State Department group to make a fearless review of the policy toward Red China, but after the study was reported, Kennedy, staring political reality full in the face, put the project aside. "We live in a world," Sorensen said, in explanation of Kennedy's moods, "which is full of setbacks to the hopes of a man who has a good many ideals, who would like to make a contribution during the short time he's on the scene. So he's bound to have his moments of discouragement."

As President, Kennedy labored mightily and often brilliantly against the obstacles. He was "in the thick of the battle," as he promised in the campaign he would be, pressing legislators for their votes, arguing and pleading with Allied leaders and taking his message to their peoples, campaigning unstintingly to increase the number of Congressional Democrats, breasting the torrent of executive business with his extraordinary command of fact and deep involvement in decision, instilling vitality and urgency into administrative effort, and rallying around him a staff whose outstanding competence bears comparison with that of any Presidency. Yet when the record of the late President is compiled and weighed, the gulf between the Presidency he hoped for in 1960 and the Presidency he attained is striking. Kennedy—the contours of historical judgment are already emerging—will be remembered more for the ideals and innovative methods he brought to the great office than for achievement in program and policy. The Presidency and its world were something less than responsive to his commanding talent and high purpose. "Has your experience in the office matched your expectations?" Kennedy was asked in 1962 in a year-end interview. "Well, I think . . . the problems are more difficult than I had imagined they were," he replied. The Presidency, for which he had so long and so skillfully campaigned, in no little way let him down.

◊

AS MUCH as if not more than most American chief executives, Kennedy was the victim of the chasm between the Presidency as it appears, or is imagined, and the Presidency of reality. The imagined Presidency is vested in our minds with more power than the Presidency really has. The real Presidency is what the Presidency effectively is in the present, what it can do in a given situation. The imagined Presidency is a euphoric impression of its past, present, and future, and is grounded partly in reality and partly in fancy. It exaggerates the office's strength, encouraged by the substantial power it actually possesses, the prestige built in its past, and the pomp that surrounds it. The imagined Presidency underestimates the limitations of power and environment the office suffers. It equates past Presidential success, the nation's might, and expectations of how the world should go, with available Presidential power.

The chief executive of the world's most advanced technological nation, which produces 40 per cent of the world's wealth and sustains a military establishment of unsurpassed destructive capabilities, is bound to bask in an aura of reflected power, no matter what the inherent power of his office may be. Our view of what the Presidency can do is shaped by what it has done. It is an office whose finest triumphs are better remembered than its failures. It is a gallery of our heroes: Washington launching the republic despite economic weakness and foreign hostility; Andrew Jackson asserting union against nullification and implanting political and economic democracy; Abraham Lincoln leading the union through the crucible of civil war; Theodore Roosevelt, Woodrow Wilson, and Franklin D. Roosevelt raising high the banner of economic and social reform; and Wilson and the second Roosevelt triumphing in two wars. The Presidency is a place where men faced with horrendous challenge have achieved unexpected growth and responded with unexpected effectiveness. Lincoln, James K. Polk, and others, held in poor esteem when they took up their duties, grew enormously in stature after brief exposure to the trials of office. "Go thou and do likewise," we are ready to instruct any present incumbent.

The Presidency appears all the more imposing because it is the center of our expectations. Just as he is to the Sioux Indians, the President is in a sense the Great Father to us all. We look to him because he has unlimited power to make proposals for action. He can, if he chooses, espouse any cause, from simplified spelling to the soil bank, and whatever he says will be heard and noticed. The one figure in our public life elected by and responsible to a national constituency, he better than anyone can bring problems forward, define the possible solutions, and advocate the one most likely to achieve the chosen end. But woe to him if trouble does not fade and the clouds do not roll back. He often will fail because some of us expect him to do things he cannot do: to maintain a posture of victory in any war the country is associated with, to secure from the investment of foreign aid a return of friendship and loyalty, and to organize an administration of invariable efficiency. The President cannot extract conformity with United States objectives with absolute success from traditional allies whose wealth, and therefore independence, is on the rise. He cannot, merely by his own acts, keep the economy whirring at high speed, puncture ballooning unemployment, and fasten tight the lid on inflation. He cannot, by a wave of his hand, assure Americans a life of peace, contentment, and security. He does not, as Sidney Hyman has suggested, "have God's autonomous powers to make mountains without valleys as the mood strikes him." The difference between what some of us imagine the Presidency to be and what it really is leads to disappointment, frustration, and attack.

The appearance of Presidential power is enhanced by the color and pageantry of the office, the adaptation to American needs of the monarchical principle. The President reigns as well as rules. Like the flag, he is the symbol of national unity, a focal point of loyalties, and the ceremonial chief of the nation. He approaches with the accompaniment of "Hail to the Chief"; he decorates war heroes, dedicates parks and post offices, and performs prodigious social feats on the scale of Theodore Roosevelt who on New Year's Day in 1902 shook hands with eight thousand people.

The appearance of Presidential power is increased by the sweeping appreciations that are accorded it, like Harry S. Truman's when he declared that "The Presidency of the United States of America has become the greatest and most important office in the history of the world." Its might is inherent in the epithets sometimes flung at Presidents in mid-tenure like "that man in the White House" Franklin D. Roosevelt and "Mad Tom" Jefferson. The appearance of power glows more strongly when a hero-figure like Dwight D. Eisenhower and a hero-glamour-figure like Kennedy occupy the White House. The appearance of power is conveyed in Eisenhower's astounding electoral victory margin of 9.5 million votes in 1956 and by the equally astounding popularity of John Kennedy, whose ratings in the public opinion polls at times outdid those of his predecessor. But mere popularity, both those Presidents would testify, does not achieve policy.

The appearance of the Presidency as an office more powerful than it really is has led to ill-advised attempts to reduce its presumed effectiveness by drastic surgery. One of the most menacing of these attempts has succeeded, the Twenty-Second Amendment, adopted in 1951, which was hawked with cries that it was imperative to prevent the President from becoming a dictator, even though no such dictator had appeared in the long experience of the American Presidency. In actuality, as public discussion made clear, the amendment was a reflection upon Franklin D. Roosevelt, who was driven by the urgencies of World War II into accepting, and by no means willingly, an incumbency of four terms. The amendment is a tragedy whose full dimensions are yet to be known; it badly inhibits the President's power in his second term and shifts the balance in the legislature's favor.

Spurred by the success of the Twenty-Second Amendment, the foes of Presidential power launched the Bricker amendment, also of the 1950's. Appearing in its long career in several forms and pushed by tireless promoters, the amendment would in effect have prevented the chief executive from making treaties and executive agreements with foreign governments. It would have largely shut down the Presidency in foreign affairs. Other amendments are floated periodically by those afflicted with the high fever of the imagined Presidency. They propose to limit income tax assessments to 25 per cent, to transfer federal welfare functions to the states, and other such things, all of which either directly or indirectly could do the Presidency great harm.

The glory and power of the Presidency have been a favorite theme of those who, over the decades, have been charged with the task of introducing the chief executive on great occasions to make an address. Former President William Howard Taft recalled one day in a lecture at Columbia University how those who formerly presented him, by way of exalting the occasion, frequently cited him as one "who exercised greater governmental power than any monarch in Europe." This of course was a day when monarchs still were thriving. Taft declared to his university audience,

> I need hardly point out the inaccuracies of this remark, by comparing the powers of the President of the United States with those of the rulers of countries in which there is not real popular legislative control. The powers of the German Emperor, of the Emperor of Austria, and the Emperor of Russia are far wider than those of the President of the United States.

◇

THOSE who introduced President Taft on the public platform were confused by the difference between the appearance and the reality of Presidential power. The real Presidency exists in a world of circumscribed powers whose limits are becoming increasingly confining. That the Presidency should be a tightly limited office was part of its original conception. Distrustful of power and fearful of tyranny, the Founding Fathers instilled the principles of checks and balances and separation of powers into the Constitution. The arrangement of the executive and Congress, as Woodrow Wilson put it, reflected "the Whig Theory of political dynamics, which was a sort of unconscious copy of the Newtonian Theory of the universe." Neither Congress nor the executive was to become the dominant force, but each shared the power of the other, whether making laws, appointments, or treaties, and each therefore could check the other's assertion.

From the beginning and throughout Presidential history, the chief executive has been able to maintain no important policy, domestic or foreign, without Congressional support in the form of laws and money. Neither is there any dependable way under the Constitution in which the President can bring Congress to provide this wherewithal against its will. A complex of forces that prompts Congress to resist or oppose the President much of the time prevails. Because the method of electing the President differs from the method of electing Congress, their constituencies, concerns, and viewpoints differ. The President and Vice President alone are chosen by the nation. Senators and Congressmen, in contrast, are essentially local officers responsible to the voters of a single state or Congressional district. Congress does not choose the President and is therefore not beholden to him, and cannot be bullied by him. Only once in four years are the President and members of the House of Representatives elected simultaneously, and even on that occasion only one-third of the Senate is elected. At the President's midterm the House and another one-third of the Senate are chosen, usually with local issues predominating. The outcome more often than not worsens the President's own party support in both Congressional houses. At no point in his four-year span does the President face a Senate wholly elected during his tenure, owing to the Senate's six-year-term and system of staggered elections. Presidents come and go, but the most powerful legislators—the chairmen of the standing committees—stay on, often rolling up tenure of a third of a century and more.

The likelihood is that a President who seeks legislation promoting social and economic reforms, as Kennedy did, will face a hard wall of opposition from the legislative leaders of his own party. These are the committee chairmen who have risen by seniority because they come from "safe" districts, which are situated chiefly in Southern or rural Northern areas. Both areas tend toward conservative outlooks and therefore produce conservative legislators. Theodore Roosevelt, advancing the reforms of his Square Deal, had to work principally through conservative Senators Eugene Hale and Nelson Aldrich in the Senate and Speaker "Uncle Joe" Cannon in the House, who "distrusted anything that was progressive." "We succeeded in working together," Roosevelt wrote of their relationship, "I pushing forward and they hanging back," not a promising juxtaposition, on its face, for cooperative endeavor. Speaker Cannon's estimate of his dealings with Theodore Roosevelt is an admirable indication of the President's common plight in legislative relations. "He was a good sportsman," said Cannon, "and accepted what he could get so long as legislation conformed even in part to his recommendations."

Although the Founding Fathers did not foresee political parties, their rise has in no significant way hampered the intended effect of checks and balances. Parties are not a dependable force for cooperation between the legislative and executive branches. The party functions effectively as a national organization only once every four years, when control of the White House is at stake. Otherwise, the party is a confederation of largely autonomous state and local organizations, where sectional cleavages and factional differences are commonplace. The President, in fact, invests much time maintaining unity between the squabbling factions. The President and the legislators, although they wear the same party label, are nominated by different party organizations as well as being chosen by different electorates, an arrangement hardly conducive to unity. There is no known common standard of party loyalty, and no party caucus, as in Great Britain, which joins the executive with the legislators of his party in the enterprise of an accepted policy program. Indeed the Presidency and Congress may simply be vantage points of the party's rival factions. Thus Eisenhower in the Presidency was faced with an array of standing committee chairmen, holders of the supreme legislative policy posts, who were identified overwhelmingly with the Taft wing of his party, which had fought his nomination unremittingly. Eisenhower may have beaten Robert Taft for the nomination, but Taft got the enormous consolation prize of the United States Congress.

The President is checked by the opinion of the people in general or, when they organize, by their opinion as pressure groups. American pressure groups possess enormous economic, ethnic, and sectional diversity. What pleases the Democratic Italian voters of New York may be anathema to Democratic Negro voters of Los Angeles or Democratic Protestants of the Middle West. A policy that delights Republican hard-money bankers in New York may disgruntle Republican wheat farmers in Kansas. The President has the Solomon-like task of mediating between the groups with all their hopes and fears, of weighing the political situation as a whole, and of safeguarding the public interest. He is both a great and good engine of the aspirations of the groups and a brake upon them when they seek too much at the expense of the nation and other groups. The relationship is also, to a degree, reciprocal. A President, particularly a Democratic President, must pay heed to groups that because of their voting power function as veto groups. Pressuring for new advantage and meaning to keep gains already achieved, they weigh and criticize his plans and act according to their lights. He earns their votes only if they judge him to be sufficiently the vehicle of their purposes. Among Lyndon Johnson's earliest callers after his accession to the Presidency were the leaders of organized labor and Negro civil rights groups, the two veto groups on whose favor his political future most depends.

◇

IMPRESSED from his own full and intimate knowledge of the limitations the chief executive toils under, Harry S. Truman once observed, "The principal power that the President has is to bring people in and try to persuade them to do what they ought to do without persuasion. That's what I spend my time doing. That's what the powers of the President amount to." Given the interdependence of its powers, the Presidency is an intensive experience in practical politics. To lead, to win support, to achieve, the President must practice with skill and ardor the arts of political persuasion. Woodrow Wilson noted before taking up the Presidency, "We have all been the disciples of Montesquieu, but we have also been practical politicians." The President must woo, cajole, threaten, and even wage war on party leaders, legislators, and chieftains of the veto groups. He must bring the several parts of government and the private groups into harmonious effort to accomplish shared objectives. He alone in our political life can do it.

George Washington discovered the necessity for practical politics promptly upon taking up the Presidential office. The new government, he wrote, was to be one "of accommodation as well as a government of laws." The President's political means cover a wide gamut: blandishments, favors, bargains, compromises, and the assertion, when necessary, of naked pressure. Herbert Hoover, aiming to secure tariff reform legislation, met with the legislative leaders and made public appeals. When these proved unavailing, he granted a rare recognition by entertaining Senator William E. Borah alone at dinner to woo him, and, varying his attack, dispatched a sharp message to Senator Reed Smoot, who was guiding the bill in the Senate: "No flexible tariff, no tariff bill." Again failure on both counts, whereupon Hoover entertained all the Republican leaders at breakfast, but without success. When he learned that the House-Senate conference committee had watered down the flexible provisions nearly to the point of drowning them, Hoover responded with equal ferocity. "I wrote out the provision I wanted," he said. "I sent word that unless my formula was adopted the bill would be vetoed. The result was a complete victory."

To get his controversial measures enacted, whether in foreign or domestic affairs, the President, because of the unreliability of his own party, must build a special coalition for his purpose from both major parties. The coalitions keep forming and breaking up as their purpose is achieved. Moving on to new objectives, the President must develop a new combination of support. To make his way, the President must know when to spend and when to hoard his influence, and how to build it. He must realize, as Richard Neustadt has suggested, that the essence of his persuasive task is to convince the legislators whose support he courts "that what the White House wants of them is what they ought to do for their sake and on their authority." In playing the political game, the President occupies certain of the best vantage points in the political system. His power of publicity, his veto, his power over budget and expenditure, his power of appointment are means that exist nowhere else in the political structure. For all the limits upon his power, he is the supreme unifying force in our diffuse political system and pluralistic society. He better than anyone else can act affirmatively and flexibly. But his great rival, Congress, also enjoys distinction. No other body can cast the negative so readily, so conclusively, and in so many ways.

But the President, if he shall write his name large on the pages of history, must do more than excel at practical politics. He must use political power to advance great ends. His shining hours occur in the Fourteen Points of Wilson, in the social purposes of Lincoln and the Roosevelts, and in the assertion of principle of Grover Cleveland against the test of events. He must rise to moments as Cleveland did when pressing the House Speaker to support an administration measure; Cleveland found him hesitant and fearful of the consequences to his future. "Mr. Speaker," Cleveland exclaimed, "what is your political future weighed in the balance against the fortunes of the country? Who are you and I compared with the welfare of the whole American people?" The Speaker surrendered. But the President who, like Cleveland, chooses to enter the roaring furnace where political necessity and principle converge, subjects himself to the burning anguish that reaches its highest intensity in the Presidency itself. One day Cleveland invited a visitor, Dr. Wilton M. Smith, to listen to the draft of a speech. Cleveland, as he read on, worked up into a high pitch of emotion. He exclaimed, turning suddenly on his visitor,

> Doctor, I suppose at times you won't approve of many things I do, but I want you to know that I am trying to do what is right. . . . Sometimes the pressure is most overwhelming, and a President cannot always get at the exact truth; but I want you to know that I am trying to do what is right. *I am trying to do what is right.*

Tears welled in the big President's eyes; he blew his nose hard, and paced the room.

◊

THE President wears many chains. Since there are no more hours in the President's day than in any other man's, he needs aides and assistants for the massive affairs of the executive branch. Upon their information, skill, initiative, and loyalty much of his administration's success depends. But the vast executive bureaucracy, as Presidents have found, can be a slumbering giant, slow to act, unimaginative and uncreative, and disloyal to his purposes in its alliance with pressure groups which oppose him. Aides who earn his confidence acquire in time influence of their own, and become, to a degree, independent of their chief.

In the far reaches of foreign affairs, the President faces problems and trends he cannot control that are not running in his country's favor: the rising strength of its enemies, the independence of its allies, the recalcitrance of new nations, the spread of nuclear weapon capability. With the horror of general war at his elbow, he must conduct foreign affairs with a restraint unknown to his predecessors. President Kennedy acknowledged the weight of these realities when he declared,

> We must face the fact that the United States is neither omnipotent nor omniscient, that we cannot always impose our will on the other 94 per cent of mankind, that we cannot right every wrong or reverse every adversity, and that therefore there cannot be an American solution for every world problem.

In domestic affairs the President seems destined to struggle indefinitely with intractable problems: a steadily expanding hard core of unemployment, adjustments to the new technology which may require redefinitions of social attitudes toward work and leisure, a complex of adjustments in relations between the races which compose American citizenry, a deepening dependence of society, government, and therefore the Presidency upon intellectuals. His power ends where their knowledge stops.

Certain of the machinery of the Presidency has had little or no repair since the Founding Fathers originally constructed it in 1787. The electoral college is a creaky affair from whose capacity for disaster the country has already had narrow escapes, and given the law of probabilities we are due for further crises. Presidential inability is a problem the Founding Fathers left unsolved, and the nation, in continuing to neglect such incapacity, invites disaster. The succession law is rightly a subject of constant complaint.

The President and the Presidency, in a word, are in a race without letup against change and emergency. The office has indeed adjusted, too, and remarkably so, but the nice question remains: Has it been adapted sufficiently to stay with the race; can it give the nation, the world, and mankind creative and forceful responses for the towering problems of the 1960's?

◊

WITHOUT undue violence to history, it is possible to divide the Presidents the United States has had into three recurrent types with a view to assessing their suitability as models for the contemporary chief executive in all his rugged circumstances.

The most numerous type is one that might be styled a "literalist" President. James Madison, James Buchanan, Taft, and, to a degree, Eisenhower are of this school. The mark of the "literalist" President, as his title suggests, is close obedience to the word and letter of the Constitution. Taft, who with Buchanan is the most literal of the Presidents, formulated its operative belief:

> The true view of the Executive function is . . . that the President can exercise no power which cannot be fairly and reasonably traced to some specific grant of power or justly implied and included within such express grant as proper and necessary to its exercise. Such specific grant must be either in the Federal Constitution or in an act of Congress passed in pursuance thereof. There is no undefined residuum of power which he can exercise because it seems to him to be in the public interest.

The Taft-like President tends also to live by the Whig assumption that the legislative power is popular and the executive monarchical. He is respectful, even deferential, to Congress. "My duty," James Buchanan was prone to say, "is to execute the laws . . . and not my individual opinions." When Congress did nothing in the face of gathering rebellion, Buchanan too did nothing. In a later day, President Eisenhower is reported sometimes to have remarked privately to his aides that he felt called upon to "restore" to Congress powers that Franklin Roosevelt had "usurped." In public pronouncement and personal act, Eisenhower was respectful of Congressional prerogative and the doctrine of separation of powers. "Our very form of Government," he declared to the Convention of the National Young Republican Organization in 1953, "is in peril unless each branch willingly accepts and discharges its own clear responsibilities—and respects the rights and responsibilities of the others."

The Taft-like President makes little use of his independent powers or prerogative (his powers, for example, as commander-in-chief and as implied in the executive power clause). He exerts political pressure sparingly. Symptomatic of his approach is James Bryce's observation that the typical nineteenth-century President's communications to Congress were so perfunctory that "the expression of his wishes . . . in messages has not necessarily any more effect on Congress than an article in a prominent party newspaper."

The Taft-like President has little taste for innovation in social policy. He is nostalgic for the past and urges it be used as a blueprint for the future. He feels, as Taft did, that the bane of government is "ill-digested legislation" and that "real progress in government must be by slow stages." It is a view that Theodore Roosevelt found upheld in society by "most able lawyers who are past middle age" and "large numbers of well-meaning, respectable citizens."

The Presidency in the manner of Taft and Buchanan is, on its face, inadequate for the necessities of the contemporary Presidency. The past, which it venerates, can be only a partial and imperfect guide to the present and future. It excessively neglects the President's independent powers, which again and again have been a mighty sword in times of crisis and change. Its neglect of politics abdicates action to passivity and, as the experience of several nineteenth-century Presidents proves, can thoroughly reduce the President from leader to clerk. The best proof of the inadequacy of the "literalist" model is the abandonment of its key concepts by Presidents who once had taken them up. Cleveland at first proposed to be a "literalist" President, spurning to use patronage and pressure upon Congress and declaring, "I did not come here to legislate." But when Congress blocked the bills he was driven to sponsor, his attitude changed, and he went furiously to work to win votes by promising jobs. Dwight Eisenhower, for all his professed deference to Congress and distaste for politics, in time did push his legislative program, and his campaigning in the 1954 Congressional elections was on a scale comparable to Franklin Roosevelt's.

At the opposite end of the spectrum from the "literalist" President is the "strong" President, typified by Lincoln, Washington, Jackson, Wilson, and the Roosevelts. He generally, although not exclusively, flourishes in times of crisis—during a war or a depression—and when political movements such as liberalism or social progressivism are at their crest. He interprets his powers with maximum liberality; he is a precedent-maker and -breaker to the point where the legality of his acts is questioned and attacked. His legal bible is the "stewardship theory" of Theodore Roosevelt, who felt that it was the President's "duty to do anything that the needs of the nation demanded unless such action was forbidden by the Constitution or by the laws." "I acted for the public welfare," Roosevelt said, "I acted for the common well-being of all our people."

The strong President provides leadership, in Franklin Roosevelt's words, "alert and sensitive to change," which in the Jefferson-Jackson tradition means that the government must act positively in promoting a good life, and in the Wilson tradition means that the nation cannot shun or escape its obligations of world leadership. The strong President is, on the historical record, assertive and masterful in times of crisis and change. His orientation is less to the past than to the future, which he approaches with hope and plan. He is skillful politically and is concerned more with substance than with form. When necessary, he resorts to bold action, whether economic, social, or military, which he does not shun for the sake of lowering the national debt. He accepts and abides a strong Congress, but purposefully uses the lawmaking process. He has the gift of inspiring and rallying the people with messages that mix practicality and prophecy. In his view, the President as a person must dominate the Presidency as an institution. He, a fleeting political figure, must bend, divert, and lead the cumbrous bureaucratic executive branch according to his purpose.

Between the "strong" and "literalist" Presidents is a middle ground which many chief executives have occupied; it unites elements of both extremes. This middle ground need not now detain us. The urgencies of the 1960's and beyond make emphatically clear that only one of the three available Presidential types is suitable for the future. The United States's world responsibilities and domestic urgencies require a Presidency that is continuously strong. The great, if not the foremost, task of American politics is to convert the strong Presidency, which has appeared only intermittently, into an assured and constant feature of our government. To be sure, particular actions of past strong Presidents have to a degree been institutionalized over the years. Theodore Roosevelt's "stewardship" in the 1902 coal strike is regularized in the Taft-Hartley Act; Wilson's and Franklin Roosevelt's venturings into world affairs set precedents for our many routine commitments to alliances and especially to the United Nations. But, as John Kennedy's experience as chief executive testifies, many pieces in the mosaic of the strong President lack a coating of permanence. The President is weak rather than strong as party chief, legislative leader, and general manager of the executive branch. His weaknesses there spawn further weaknesses in his capacities as chief diplomat, commander-in-chief, and decision-maker. Charles de Gaulle, beholding the American Presidential system in 1963, concluded that it was functioning in a limping way. Our task is to see where weakness eats upon strength, to discover what combination of arrangements will satsfy our most urgent governmental need: a Presidency that has continuous strength in all its parts.

CHAPTER

2

Creation of the Presidency

———

A YEAR before the Constitutional Convention of 1787, John Jay, in a
letter to George Washington recounting the inadequacies of the existing
government, moved boldly to the inevitable question: "Shall we have a
king?" It was indeed a question stirring in many influential minds, but
few men dared ask it openly. The country had had enough of kings. The
Revolution had freed it from the ill-remembered George III and, hopefully, from every future form of monarchical tyranny. The general revulsion from monarchy had produced in the states a prevailing pattern of the
weak executive and in the Articles of Confederation almost no executive
at all. But the weak executive was maintained at a high price. The event
that drove Jay to his writing desk was Shays's rebellion in Massachusetts,
an upheaval exposing the impotence of government and foreshadowing
for the young nation a desperate existence of anarchy, confiscation of property, possible military dictatorship, and foreign intervention.

Hard questions pounded like hailstones upon responsible men's
thoughts. How could the strong executive, which circumstances required,
be best provided? Should there be a monarch, as Jay suggested? Or could
some other form of strong executive be discovered or created, untainted
with the tyranny the country dreaded, while yet endowed with sufficient
authority? In the interlude before the Convention, men carried on the
search and at Philadelphia they struggled with it under the pressure of
decision.

THE states, and before them the colonies, provided the major domestic experience with executive power. The colonial governor initially was a strong executive: commander-in-chief of the provincial forces and representative of the crown, embodying the several kingly prerogatives. He was the fountain of honor and privilege and thus created offices and filled them. With little exception he shared power with a council, usually of twelve members appointed by the crown at the governor's recommendation. The council functioned as the legislative upper house, advised and influenced the governor, and was his ally in local political struggles.

As relations with the mother country deteriorated, the governorship passed under the increasing influence and direction of the assembly, the lower and more popular legislative house. Particularly in the French and Indian War, when the governor was constantly in need of money for the army, the assemblies employed their control over supplies to pare down the governor's power. The American view of George III as the tyrant over Parliament spurred the hostility against his agent, the local governor.

The animus against executive power carried into the early state constitutions of the Revolutionary period. Power rushed to the legislature. The governor, or president as he was called in several states, was reduced almost to a cipher. His term was for one year, except in South Carolina where it was two and in Delaware where it was three. His re-eligibility was strictly limited. He was chosen by, and was therefore the creature of, the legislature. The executive branch was deliberately disunified. The governor was saddled with a council chosen by the legislature, except in Pennsylvania. Most of the enumerated executive powers and functions were subject to council control. In Maryland the council was a "board" in which the executive had one vote "for the transacting of business." In Virginia Governor Edmund Randolph viewed himself as "a member of the executive." The power the legislature did not have by direct grant it could get by bold assertion against the other branches, which were endowed with little power to defend themselves. Thomas Jefferson observed of the Virginia as he might have of most state constitutions, "All the powers of government, legislative, executive and judiciary, result to the legislative body."

The governor's drab plight was relieved only in Massachusetts, where he possessed the veto power (subject to overriding by two-thirds of the legislature) and was indefinitely re-eligible, and in New York, where he could fairly be termed a strong executive.

◇

THE New York constitution was established late, in 1777, sometime after the creation of other state constitutions, and it profited from their imperfections. The folly of the weak chief executive characteristic of those constitutions was daily revealed in the urgencies of the Revolution, which demanded the summoning of effective executive power. New York's situation, exceedingly roughened by the onmarching British, made strong executive power imperative. The state convention which drafted the constitution was literally chased up the state by the British army. It was a convention on the run, which moved from Harlem to Kingsbridge and then successively to Philipse Manor, Fishkill, Poughkeepsie, and finally Kingston, as the British pressed relentlessly northward.

The New York constitution rejected the ascendancy the legislature enjoyed in other state constitutions. In language instilled in the future federal Constitution "the supreme executive power and authority of the state" was vested in the governor. The New York governor, in contrast to the governors of other states, served a substantial term—three years—with no limit upon his re-eligibility. He was chosen not by the legislature, the prevailing pattern elsewhere, but by a constitutionally identified electorate, a popular suffrage that for the time was generously defined. His electoral independence from the legislature was a giant step toward making the governor the strongest officer of his kind in the Confederation.

His further powers all foreshadowed the Presidency. The governor was commander-in-chief and "admiral of the navy," he could convene the legislature on extraordinary occasions, and he could grant reprieves and pardons. His duty was to inform the legislature of the condition of the state, recommend matters for their consideration, and take care that the laws were faithfully executed. He did not escape altogether the restraints commonly imposed upon other governors. His power of appointment was shared with a Council of Appointment of four senators elected by the assembly from each of the four senatorial districts. The governor was president of the council and possessed a casting vote. The governor shared his otherwise strong veto power with a Council of Revision, consisting of the governor, the chancellor, and the judges of the Supreme Court. They, or any three of them, always including the governor, could veto legislative measures inconsistent with the spirit of the constitution or the public good. A two-thirds vote in both houses could override the veto.

But the offices a constitution creates cannot live on the written document alone. They thrive upon skilled and vigorous incumbents. The New York governorship, by rare good fortune, had as its first occupant a skillful and courageous chief executive, George Clinton. Clinton's reign was rich and memorable; he used fully his store of power and became the dominant political figure of his state. Particularly impressive to the federal Founding Fathers was Clinton's ability, as a strong executive, to maintain public order. He put down the savage Doctors' Riots in New York City with the militia and routed out the remnants of Shays's men who fled to

New York after springing their rebellion in Massachusetts. The New York governorship's influence was further assured by the circumstance that a Founding Father who was most influential in creating the Presidency was a principal draftsman of the New York constitution: Gouverneur Morris engaged in this double enterprise.

◇

THE Constitution-makers who gathered in Philadelphia in 1787, hailed by Thomas Jefferson as "an assembly of demi-gods," organized themselves by electing George Washington their "president" and Major William Jackson their secretary. Rules of procedure were adopted and precautions taken to keep the proceedings secret. In the weeks of lengthy, intense, and often disheartening deliberations, no single problem was more perplexing in building the new government than the office of President. He must be endowed with impressive powers, but yet not appear to the people as another king and incipient tyrant. He must have sufficient but not dangerous independence. He must be dependent, but not, as state governors commonly were, the mere creature of the legislature.

The Convention began its hard grapple with specifics when it resolved itself on May 29 into a Committee of the Whole to consider several competing plans and proposals submitted by state delegations and individual members. Each plan dealt with the whole structure of a federal government, including the question of executive power.

The Virginia plan, which had been prepared chiefly by James Madison before the Convention assembled, was presented by Edmund Randolph. As it was presented, the plan called for a "national executive" to be chosen by the "National Legislature." The executive would be eligible only for a single term and "besides a general authority to execute the National laws, it ought to enjoy the Executive rights vested in Congress by the Confederation." The Committee of the Whole at the Convention added certain features to the Virginia plan: the term of the executive would be seven years, he could make appointments "in cases not otherwise provided for," and he would be removable "on impeachment and conviction of malpractice, or neglect of duty." He could "negative" any legislative act unless overriden "by two third parts" of each branch of the legislature. With certain "members" of the judiciary, he could exercise the veto power. The Virginia plan was bold in conception. Instead of simply revising or altering the Articles, it aimed to enlarge them and proposed a national executive, legislature, and judiciary to do what was done, or should have been done, by the Continental Congress.

The New Jersey plan, offered by William Paterson on June 15, was the response of the small states to the power of the large states that would have resulted from the Virginia plan. Whereas the Virginia plan undertook to replace the Articles with a truly national government, the New Jersey plan merely revised them. It would endow the central government with powers to levy import duties and regulate foreign and domestic trade. The states were to collect taxes, but Congress could act if the states defaulted. The New Jersey plan called for a plural executive chosen by Congress, removable on the application of a majority of the state executives, ineligible for a second term, and empowered to direct all military operations though in no case to take command in the field.

In addition to the rival plans of the large and small states, comprehensive plans of two Convention members dealt with the executive. One plan, by Alexander Hamilton, presented in a five-hour speech on June 18, was the most extreme proposal to be offered at the Convention for a strong executive and central government. Hamilton announced himself as "unfriendly" to both the Virginia and the New Jersey plans, terming the former, the stronger of the two, "pork still, with a little change of the sauce." The severity of the crisis required a central government of highest competence. "The general power whatever be its form if it preserves itself, must swallow up the State powers, otherwise it will be swallowed up by them." For the substance of the new government, Hamilton's probing gaze fell upon the British structure, "the best in the world"; he doubted "whether any thing short of it would do for America." Monarchy and Parliament he unreservedly admired. No good government could exist without a good executive, and no good executive could ever be established "on Republican principles." The hereditary monarch, endowed with great wealth, was above corruption from abroad and was "both sufficiently independent and sufficiently controuled, to answer the purpose of the institution at home."

The Hamilton plan called for a monarch and nobles, a single executive and a Senate for life or good behavior, and an inferior popular house. The states would have no powers except over local affairs. So extreme was the plan that it was supported by no other delegate and was not even discussed. Days later, on June 29, Hamilton left Philadelphia, despairing that the Convention would fail to recommend a strong central government and would "let slip the golden opportunity of rescuing the American empire from disunion, anarchy and misery. No motley or feeble measure can answer the end or will finally receive the public support." The Virginia plan was "motley" and the New Jersey plan "feeble."

Still another plan was advanced by Charles Pinckney of South Carolina, member of a Congressional committee charged with recommending amendments to the Articles. His plan, most of it now lost, seems from its several surviving parts to have attempted a revision of the Articles rather than supplanting them. In drawing his executive, Pinckney relied heavily upon the New York constitution. The powers and duties of the executive and the contingencies of his death and removal all followed the New York arrangement. His election and term, however, did not. Pinckney's executive would be elected by Congress annually.

◇

THE Committee of the Whole debated the several plans with their conflicting conceptions. The issue of Virginia's proposed single executive versus New Jersey's plural executive quickly came to a head when James Wilson of Pennsylvania moved and Charles Pinckney seconded that the executive consist of one person. In the debate the principal argument made against the single executive was that it would constitute a standing invitation to the very kind of monarchy that the Revolution was intended to overcome. Randolph typified this opinion, according to Madison's *Journal*, when he "strongly opposed a unity in the Executive magistracy. He regarded it as the foetus of monarchy. We had he said no motive to be governed by the British Government as our prototype." Randolph also objected that a single magistrate could never evoke confidence, and that the appointment would generally be in favor of some inhabitant near the "center of the Community," and the "remote parts" consequently "would not be on an equal footing." He preferred an executive department of three persons "drawn from different portions of the Country."

James Wilson answered. Randolph, he contended, was less concerned with merit than with the popularity of the Convention's handiwork. Wilson, for his part, believed that the people well knew that "a single magistrate is not a King." All thirteen states, although agreeing upon almost nothing else in their constitutions, had established a single head as governor or president. "The idea of three heads," which promises neither "vigor" nor "tranquillity," "has taken place in none." Other Fathers viewed the single executive not as an "absolute" monarch like George III, but as a kind of "limited" monarch, the most desirable of all executives. "A firm Executive," as John Dickinson of Delaware put it, "could only exist in a limited monarchy."

While the Convention analyzed the monarchy, stories circulated in the world outside that the Fathers, in their love for that brand of executive, were bent upon importing a Hanoverian bishop to be king of the United States. The bishop in question, according to report, was Frederick Augustus, Duke of York, second son of George III. A Connecticut citizen added fuel to the flames by issuing a circular letter proposing "to send to England" for the bishop, aged twenty-three, and "have him crowned King over this continent." The letter was heatedly discussed in the press and two of George Washington's former aides, Alexander Hamilton and David Humphreys, investigated the mystery, but without conclusive result. Humphreys believed that the proposal and the circular letter had been "manufactured" by Connecticut loyalists longing for reunion with Britain.

Meanwhile, at the Convention a lengthy struggle centered upon two further questions, viewed as inseparable: the source of the executive's election and the length of his term. Three major types of election were advanced. James Wilson and Gouverneur Morris, friends of a strong executive, urged election, as Morris put it, "by the people at large, by the freeholders of the Country." When practical administrative difficulties were cited, Morris retorted that these had been overcome in New York and could be likewise in other states. The people, the doubters said, would be uninformed and misled by designing men. Morris preferred to be optimistic. "If the people should elect, they will never fail to prefer some man of distinguished character, or services; some man, if he might so speak, of continental reputation." A second method was election by the legislature. That body's handling of the task, Morris contended, would be the work "of intrigue, of cabal, of faction." The final method, and the one ultimately adopted, was choice by electors. Advocates of an electoral system felt that it would best give effect to the dominant popular choice whose direct expression was barred for practical reasons. Many Fathers feared that citizens would blindly favor local candidates and would be ignorant of able men in other states.

Linked with method of choice were the questions of length of term and re-eligibilty. Elbridge Gerry of Massachusetts argued that the longer the term the less would the executive depend upon the legislature which chose him. Oliver Ellsworth of Connecticut likewise proposed a long term of six years. If elections were too frequent, the executive would not "be firm enough." ("There must be duties which will make him unpopular for the moment.") Without a long term (seven years), Hugh Williamson of North Carolina argued, "The best men will not undertake the service and those of an inferior character will be liable to be corrupted."

Proposals of six- or seven-year terms were predicated upon the assumption that the legislature would choose the President. A long term plus ineligibility for re-election, a common feature of such proposals, appeared the best means to safeguard executive independence of the legislature. Re-eligibility would prompt the executive to court the legislature to win another term. The alternative of a shorter term and re-eligibility came to the fore when selection by electors was ultimately settled upon.

The Fathers considered long and anxiously the question of annexing a council to the chief executive. A council would diminish the monarchical tendency and the danger of tyranny. Collective advice was deemed safer and more competent than the assorted individual advice that might befall the President. Various kinds of councils were proposed. The Pinckney plan vested in the executive "a Right to advise with the Heads of the different Departments as his Council." Oliver Ellsworth, fearful of personal government, would add to the council the President of the Senate and the Chief Justice. George Mason preferred a council representative of the chief sections of the country, the East, the Middle States, and the South. James Madison, a strong exponent of the council, proposed that it possess initiative to advise the President and to record its sentiments. But the floor discussion proved inconclusive, and ultimately the council idea was dropped. The prospect that the venerated Washington would serve as first President drained much of the interest from the council proposal. Indeed, many Fathers feared that a council of some power might harass the position of future President Washington.

In its final draft the Constitution not only failed to provide a council, it did not even call for the "cabinet" which appeared early in Washington's Presidency. The Constitution merely specified that the chief executive could require the "opinions of the heads of his departments in writing." Hamilton, for one, considered even this provision redundant as the right "would result of itself from the office." Other critics were haunted to the very end by monarchical fears. George Mason, crying doom, warned that a Presidency without a council was an "experiment" which even "the most despotic governments" had never undertaken. Benjamin Franklin, ordinarily optimistic, beheld a melancholy prospect, seeing only "caprice, the intrigues of favorites and mistresses, etc." in the absence of a council.

The Fathers debated a score of issues in establishing the substantive powers of the executive. These were resolved with a tendency toward generosity to the executive, sparked by the prospect that Washington would become President. The veto power, remembered as an arbitrary instrument of the royal governors, was critically scrutinized. The Declaration of Independence's first indictment of George III was his refusal to "Assent to Laws, the most wholesome and necessary for the public good." But excesses by the state legislatures since Revolutionary days made the Fathers receptive to a strong veto power. The Virginia plan's coupling of the judiciary with the executive in the veto was dropped. The variant proposals for a Council of Revision met a like fate, and the President emerged as the solitary executive possessor of the veto power.

The appointing power was one of the knottier issues. James Wilson, constant friend of a strong Presidency, opposed the eventual arrangement, a power shared between the President and the Senate. "There can be no good Executive," he argued, "without a responsible appointment of officers to execute." Responsibility was impaired by involving the Senate. Wilson's view was respected to a degree when the President was given an exclusive appointing power "in all cases not otherwise provided for."

Treaty and war powers and the President's pay, removal, and disability also evoked considerable discussion. "What is the extent of the term 'disability' and who is to be the judge of it?" Dickinson asked, questions which remain unanswered to this day. Debate waxed over the respective powers of Congress and the executive to "declare" and to "make" war. One motion on the subject shocked Gerry, who "never expected" to hear in a republic a proposal to empower the executive alone to declare war. Madison contended that the war power could not be safely entrusted to the President or the Senate. He was for "clogging" rather than "facilitating" war.

◇

THE work of the Committee of the Whole was supplemented by two drafting committees, the Committee of Detail and the Committee of Style. After discussion of some weeks the Convention established the Committee of Detail—the members being Edward Rutledge (South Carolina), Randolph (Virginia), Nathaniel Gorham (Massachusetts), Ellsworth (Connecticut), and Wilson (Pennsylvania)— to reduce the delegates' ponderings to a systematic Constitution draft. The work of the Committee of Detail, a long stride toward the strong Presidency, was aided by Convention-adopted resolutions providing for a single executive empowered to execute national laws, to veto national legislation, and to appoint to offices in cases not otherwise provided for. The executive was also made subject to impeachment. The Committee of Detail adapted these resolutions to its draft, and, with an eye on the New York constitution, further elaborated the President's powers. The committee made it the President's duty to give information to the legislature, to recommend measures, to convene Congress into extraordinary session, and, in disagreement between the two houses on the subject, to adjourn them. The President would also receive ambassadors, grant pardons and reprieves, and act as commander-in-chief.

The Convention debated intensively for five weeks, section by section, the draft of the Committee of Detail. On September 8 a Committee of Style headed by Gouverneur Morris was appointed to "revise the style of and arrange the articles which had been agreed to by the house." This committee too was innovative. It installed the plan for choosing the President through electors and empowered him to make treaties, provided two-thirds of the Senators present concurred, and to nominate, and with the advice and consent of the Senate appoint, ambassadors, other public ministers and consuls, and justices of the Supreme Court. The President's term was put at four years with indefinite re-eligibility. The Presidential Article II began with a sentence, attributed to Morris, of vast future significance: "The executive power shall be vested in a President of the United States of America."

On September 13 the Committee of Style presented a Constitution draft in the handwriting of the committee's chairman, Gouverneur Morris. Two days later the Constitution was adopted, and in another two days the Convention adjourned. The Presidency, as it finally emerged, admirably fulfilled the ideal of a strong but responsible chief executive. The President would be a single, not a plural, executive, with no council but presumably heads of departments, although these were not specifically provided for. His election and identity were distinct and separate from Congress. His term of four years was longer than the state governors' and he was re-eligible for an indefinite number of terms. His powers were generous, and both specific and general. The opening language of Article II, "The executive Power shall be vested in a President," was clearly broader than the investiture of Article I, "All legislative Powers herein granted shall be vested in a Congress," or Article III, "The judicial Power shall extend to all cases, in Law and Equity, arising under this Constitution, the Laws of the United States, and Treaties."

◇

IN ANY listing of Founding Fathers who played a heroic part in creating a strong chief executive, the name of James Wilson of Pennsylvania would take an honored place. Forty-five years of age, Wilson was a Scotsman by birth and education, tall, large-featured, and afflicted with nearsightedness, which with his glasses added a touch of sternness to his appearance. Endowed with a tough, perceptive mind, Wilson contributed more than anyone else to the concept of the Presidency: he laid it persuasively before the Convention and was an instrumental member of the Committee of Detail that worked out the final revision. Wilson's success, although impressive, was not total. His chief defeat was the rejection of his proposal that the executive be chosen by the people.

Gouverneur Morris, chairman of the committee that wrote the final draft of the Constitution, is another hero. Draftsman of the New York constitution, member of the Continental Congress, and hardy *bon vivant*, he illuminated the Convention's deliberations with insights from the instructive New York experience. Eloquent, caustic, dynamic, and aggressive, Morris steadily championed the strong executive. James Madison spoke afterward of the "brilliancy of his genius." Madison too stands among the heroes. He began conservatively on the question of executive power, but gradually came around to Wilson's views.

The indispensable presence at the Convention was the presiding officer, the nation's future first chief executive, George Washington. Elected unanimously to his Convention post, his tall, heavy, ruddy presence, grave mien, his very embodiment of the young country's agony and triumph, marked him as the most conspicuous and the most influential delegate. Although he spoke but once, his commitment to strong central government was well known. "My wish is," he wrote to Madison, prior to Philadelphia, "that the convention may adopt no temporizing expedients, but probe the defects of the constitution to the bottom, and provide a radical cure, whether they are agreed to or not." The prevailing assumption, candidly articulated in the Convention, was that he would become the first President. Pierce Butler of South Carolina expressed Washington's significance in the creation of the Presidency when he wrote, "Entre nous, I do [not] believe they [the executive powers] would have been so great had not many members cast their eyes toward General Washington as President; and shaped their Ideas of the Powers to be given the President, by their opinions of his Virtue."

◊

THE making of the Presidency adhered to two overarching structural concepts: the separation of powers and checks and balances. Mutually contradictory, one posed division and independence, the other interaction and dependence.

The separation of powers was a basic principle in the works of several major political writers well known to the Fathers. Although the writers differed in the ways these powers should be separated, they shared a common view of the nature and purpose of separated powers. John Locke's *The Two Treatises of Government*, probably the most powerful philosophic influence at the Convention, Montesquieu's *Esprit des lois*, and William Blackstone's *Commentaries on the Laws of England* all viewed the concentration of power as an invitation to tyranny. Liberty was best preserved if power were distributed between several branches. Locke, for instance, divided governmental power between the legislative or law-making power, the executive or law-enforcing power, and the "federative" power of war and peace, leagues and alliances, and other foreign relations. Locke did not specify the judicial power, but presumably intended to safeguard its independence by the Act of Settlement.

Although the Founding Fathers repeatedly and reverently invoked separation of powers, the doctrine fared unevenly at their hands. As Charles C. Thach has rightly observed, few governments exceed the functional overlapping of that created by the American Constitution. Lawmaking is shared between the two-house Congress and the President, treaty-making and appointments between the President and the Senate, and so on. The Fathers did meticulously observe the doctrine in the sense of arranging a personal separation of powers in contrast to functional separation. The memberships of the three branches, executive, legislative, and judicial, were separated. An officer of one could not serve in another, except for the Vice President, who had minor duties in the Senate but a general identity with the executive.

Checks and balances, the second overarching doctrine, was also well articulated by influential writers. The theory of balanced government reached back to the Greeks and enjoyed vogue in the eighteenth century among English and continental writers. Montesquieu and Blackstone interpreted the English Constitution as a complex of checks: the Lords against the Commons and both against the crown. Government was viewed not as a cooperative enterprise between its several parts, but as an enduring conflict of opposite interests.

The leading American exponent of balanced government was John Adams, whose *Defence of the Constitutions of the United States of America Against the Attack of Mr. Turgot* was well known to the Founding Fathers. For liberty to be preserved and property safeguarded, Adams argued, government must be poised in an equilibrium. Governments, like the populations they govern, divide into three distinct entities: the one, the few, and the many; or the leader, the aristocracy of birth or property, and the mass of people. Each part is capable of abuse—of jealousy, encroachment, and folly. The wellspring of disequilibrium, in the words of Thucydides, is "thirst of power, from rapacious and ambitious passions." The art of constitution-making, as Adams perceived it, was the establishment of "a multitude of curious and ingenious inventions to balance in their turn, all those powers [legislative, executive, and judicial], to check the passions peculiar to them, and to control them from rushing into the exorbitancies to which they are most addicted." The stability and purposes of a government, in a word, were best achieved by a delicate balance between more or less equal powers vitalized by mutual jealousies.

The Founding Fathers were much preoccupied with the problem of balance. "It is [the] most difficult of all rightly to balance the Executive," Gouverneur Morris observed. "Make him too weak: the Legislature will usurp his power. Make him too strong: he will usurp on the Legislature." The leading analyst of balanced power was Madison, whose views are most fully stated in the *Federalist* paper No. 51. "The great security against a gradual concentration of the several powers in the same department," he wrote, "consists in giving to those who administer each department the necessary constitutional means and personal motives to resist encroachments of the others. Ambition must be made to counteract ambition."

◇

THE final phase of the creation of the Presidency is Washington's nearly impeccable workmanship as the office's first incumbent. His strong and good hands imparted to the Presidency a form and substance that have forever remained with it. In confronting his duties, Washington knew well that what he did possessed both present and future significance, that his every act was a potential precedent, and that the body of his conduct was creating an entire executive system. He wrote,

> Many things appear of little importance in themselves and at the beginning may have great and durable consequences from their having been established at the commencement of a new general government. It will be much easier to commence the administration, upon a well adjusted system, built on tenable grounds, than to correct errors or alter inconveniences after they shall have been confirmed by habit.

Washington did not take up his task gladly. In the weeks before his election he allowed himself to hope that he might not be elected and that if he were he might somehow contrive to decline. His longings were deepened by seizures of pessimism about the future. "May Heaven assist me in forming a judgment," he wrote to Jonathan Trumbell, "for at present I see nothing but clouds and darkness before me." But the electors, chosen for their probable support of Washington, unanimously met this expectation. Even the Virginia elector Patrick Henry, a resolute foe of the new Constitution, voted for Washington.

The Vice Presidency was contested. Washington interested himself in the struggle in an interval when he hoped that if he had to accept the Presidency, he might resign once the new governmental machinery had swung into operation. The Vice Presidency stirred a quick, intense party struggle. The Anti-Federalists, who accepted Washington as President, put forward one of their own, Governor George Clinton, for Vice President. Although Washington enjoyed sturdy wartime ties with Clinton, the future President was troubled by the governor's hostility to the new federal Constitution. Clinton had promoted the well-known "New York circular," urging its severe amendment, or "suicide" as Madison termed it. To avoid the danger of Clinton, Washington quietly and privately supported the Federalist candidacy of John Adams. Alexander Hamilton, the general's arranger and emissary, worked closely with Benjamin Lincoln, an Adams leader, and Henry Knox, a major political figure in Massachusetts. The emissaries did their work well. Washington was soon pleased to hear that "the votes have run in favor of Mr. Adams."

On April 16, 1789, Washington set out for New York, the national capital, with heavy heart. "I bade adieu to Mount Vernon, to private life, and to domestic felicity," he wrote in his diary, "and with a mind oppressed with more anxious and painful sensations than I have words to express." He added that he left "with the best disposition to render service to my country in obedience to its call, but with less hope of answering its expectations." Washington's distress was soon overwhelmed by the acclaim showered upon him on his journey northward. Townsfolk vied to do him honor. Dinners, addresses, fireworks, parades, salutes, escorts, and the approving shouts of thousands of his countrymen attended the eight-day journey. The most endearing display occurred in the Trenton area, a scene of desperate Revolutionary fighting. The simple bridge at

Assunpink Creek was adorned with a lofty arch of greenery and a motto hailing Washington as protector of American mothers and daughters. As he crossed, he was surrounded by ladies and little girls dressed in white with garlands in their hair, who sang odes and sprinkled flowers in his path.

On Inauguration Day, April 30, the joint committee of Congress arrived at the President-elect's temporary residence to escort him to Federal Hall. Shortly after midday the general started out in a grand coach drawn by four horses, preceded by troops and the Senators of the joint committee and followed by his secretaries, the Representatives of the committee, Chancellor Robert Livingston, who would administer the oath, the heads of the federal departments, and a handful of eminent citizens. When the procession reached Federal Hall, Washington passed with simple dignity into the building and mounted the stairs to the Senate chamber, where members of the two houses of Congress, foreign diplomats, and other dignitaries had assembled. The general passed through an arched central door leading onto a small, half-enclosed portico overlooking Wall and Broad Streets. Cheers rolled up from the vast multitude below. Samuel Otis, Secretary of the Senate, lifted the Bible reposing on a red cushion on a small table. Washington placed his hand on the Bible, Livingston pronounced the oath, and Washington repeated it and kissed the Book. "It is done," Livingston declared, and, turning to the crowd, made a broad sweep with his hand and shouted, "Long live George Washington, President of the United States." The crowd roared back Livingston's words and "God bless our President"; church bells rang, the flag was run up in the cupola of Federal Hall, and guns were fired from the Battery and a Spanish sloop of war in the harbor. The Presidency was now in being.

◇

IN TWO terms of office Washington launched the Presidency on a high note of success. Weathering times that were full of crisis, he left the republic stronger, more purposeful, and more confident than when he had begun his task. A string of measures, highly impressive by twentieth-century standards in their number and scope, steadily emerged from the Washington administration: a national currency was issued and a Bank of the United States was established to provide credit; manufacture and trade were fostered by tariffs and bounties; inventions were protected by patent and copyright laws; neutrality was preserved in the face of an enlarging European war; and the national security was enhanced by reorganization of the army and navy, the founding of West Point, and the building of fortifications in the East and West.

Washington exercised the powers of his office in a fashion that permitted vigorous and innovative administration, but he respected the necessities of legitimacy and responsibility. "The powers of the Executive of the United States," Washington wrote midway in his term, "are more definite, and better understood perhaps than those of almost any other Country; and my aim has been and will continue to be, neither to stretch nor relax from them in any instance whatever, unless imperious circumstances should render the measure indispensable." In "gray" areas, where the Constitution did not state whether Congress or the President was to act, Washington asserted executive authority. The establishment of the nation's neutrality in the Franco-British War, a cardinal foreign policy, was a Presidential rather than a legislative act. (Later in the nation's history the roles altered, and neutrality policy was one of the areas that became the province of Congress.)

Where authority was clearly his, Washington maintained his mastery. He truly dominated the executive branch. He was not long in office when he requested the heads of departments to provide "a full, precise and general *idea*" of the work entrusted to them. With few exceptions he prescribed the duties of his department heads and kept abreast of daily detail. He read incoming and outgoing communications of the executive branch and passed upon important plans and actions which the departments submitted in writing. All loan and debt transactions were subject to his approval. Each use of the seal of the United States required his consent. No lighthouse keeper, customs collector, or captain of a cutter could be appointed without his consideration. So confident was he of his mastery that he brought into the leading posts of his administration two of the most gifted department heads the nation has ever known, Thomas Jefferson as Secretary of State and Alexander Hamilton as Secretary of the Treasury.

Washington triumphed in an area where many of his successors have floundered: relationships with Congress. Washington converted his popularity into major laws without tarnishing his prestige in the inevitable struggle. In his deportment toward Congress he was the essence of Constitutional propriety. He stayed officially aloof from most major struggles, leaving the heat and dust of battle to his subordinates, chiefly Hamilton.

Washington was careful to respect Congress. Following his Annual or State of the Union Address, the Senate and House prepared addresses in response. The great throng of lawmakers of both chambers, led by the Mace and Speaker, gathered before the President. The Vice President and the Speaker spoke for their respective houses. The President, for his part, was attentive to Congress with social and ceremonial gesture. Shortly before the inaugural, he visited the members of Congress, and his manner was agreeable. "He made us complaisant bows," Senator William Maclay of Pennsylvania noted, "one as he mounted and the other as he went away on horseback." He regularly tendered dinners with a dozen and more guests from the Senate, the House, and his own administration.

The close work of researching and drafting legislative proposals and the chores of advocating them, rallying votes, and working out compromises were left to his lieutenant, Alexander Hamilton, Secretary of the Treasury and field leader of the Federalist party. Hamilton drafted the Great Reports, presenting with detail and justification the major legislation of the administration—public credit, the Bank, manufactures, and the like. Washington engaged in no public advocacy of these measures. He seems, however, to have been a behind-the-scenes influence when Jefferson and Hamilton arranged their famous compromise, the location of the future capital in Washington in exchange for federal assumption of state debts. The observant Senator Maclay confided to his diary,

> The President of the United States has (in my opinion) had a great influence in this business. The game was played by him and his adherents . . . his name goes to wipe away blame and silence all murmuring.

Washington was a resolute defender of the integrity of Presidential power against all trespass, even when Congress was the offender. A most momentous challenge was the call by the Republican-controlled House of Representatives for the instructions and pertinent papers of John Jay's mission to negotiate the treaty bearing his name. The House's bold intrusion into an enterprise allotted by the Constitution to the President and the Senate gripped the capital with tension. "Anxiety is on the tiptoe . . . our galleries have been crowded," Representative Francis Preston of Virginia noted. Washington's response was strong and forthright. Foreign relations by their very nature, he wrote, required secrecy; disclosure of the requested papers would be "impolitic" and "a dangerous precedent." The fundamental law did not require the House's assent to a treaty. "A just regard to the Constitution and to the duty of my Office . . . forbids a compliance with your request." The House opposition thundered and maneuvered, but all in vain. "What firmness does this great man display!" Senator William Plumer rejoiced.

Washington was no slave to literal Constitutional prescription, but a resourceful innovator. The Constitution said little of how the President might secure advice in the daily business of decision- and policy-making. Washington exploited the freedom this silence permitted and instituted practices that Presidents since his time have followed. He founded the cabinet. In the autumn of 1791 he began bringing his department secretaries Jefferson, Hamilton, Knox, and Randolph together for a joint consideration of policy. The cabinet meeting was a timesaver over individual consultation of the secretaries and permitted the testing of the opinions of his counselors in the presence of their peers. Washington believed that advice should be competitive, that one man's views should be checked against other sources. Repeatedly he ranged beyond the cabinet for counsel, to Congressman James Madison, for example, and Chief Justice John Jay, from whom he invited "ideas . . . not confined to matters judicial, but extended to all other topics which have occurred, or may occur to you, as fit subjects for general or private communications." Washington also believed that advice should be broadly representative. He recruited his cabinet from the three principal sections of the country, the North, the South, and the Middle States. A close student of grass-roots opinion, he maintained correspondents in all the sections and instituted the grand tour, traveling the length and breadth of the republic to gather impressions at firsthand.

Washington prized and jealousy maintained the intrinsic dignity of the Presidential office. He wanted, he said, to make the Presidency "respectable." His natural taste for regal display was freely indulged. He ventured forth in a handsome coach drawn by six cream-colored horses or on a white steed mounted with leopard-skin housing and saddlecloth with gold binding. The Presidential household operated on a large scale, with fourteen white servants, seven slaves, and frequent elaborate dinners done with a high formality conveyed by the presence of powdered lackeys in the entrance hall. The President conducted two levees a week and made no visits. His birthday continued to be, as it had been since the Revolution, the occasion of celebrations in the larger towns. Inevitably these practices provoked criticism. "Even Cincinnatus received no adulation of this kind," the *National Gazette* observed. "Surely the office [the President] enjoys is a sufficient testimony of the people's favor, without worshipping him likewise."

Throughout this period the Presidency was sustained by the unfailing magnificence of Washington's character. Judgment, vision, skill in managing men, integrity, infinite patience, self-discipline—all were his marks. He "always walked," his biographer Douglas Southall Freeman observed, "on a straight line." "Let honor and probity be your polar star," the President counseled his nephew Bushrod Washington. The President valued "the candid and cautious line of conduct" and abided by the principle "that without virtue and without integrity, the finest talents or the most brilliant accomplishments can never gain the respect or conciliate the esteem of the truly valuable part of mankind." In 1794 Washington perhaps was too cautious, however. He gave Hamilton precious little backing when the Anti-Federalists, who had wrested control of the House of Representatives, drove the Secretary of the Treasury, by a process of studied harassment, from the administration. Yet Washington's virtues were steadily seen by his contemporaries. "His integrity was most pure,"

Thomas Jefferson observed, "his justice the most inflexible I have ever known. . . . He was indeed, in every sense of the words, a wise, a good and a great man. . . ."

◊

B u t the Presidency was not all strength, achievement, and glory; it also harbored weakness. Ironically, it was the leading American theoretician of checks and balances, the second President of the United States, who provided the earliest illustration of the weakness his ideas had helped create. John Adams was not long in the Presidency when he demonstrated where the provision for the strong executive left off. He proved by his own experience the far depths of trouble in which the President can wallow as party chief, as legislative leader, and as general manager of the executive branch. For the first of these the Founding Fathers had made no provision; for the others, very little. The Presidency was in several large particulars an unfinished office.

Adams the President was only the nominal leader of his Federalist party; its real leader was an outsider who held no public office, the talented, driving, ubiquitous Alexander Hamilton. The contrast was exaggerated by a growing break between the two men. Thomas Jefferson, leader of the Anti-Federalists, noted that the Congressional Federalists were only "a little less hostile" to the President than to himself. The Jefferson men and disaffected legislative Federalists were unstinting in demonstrating the President's weakness as legislative leader. When relations with France crumbled and war threatened, Adams, anxious to maintain peace, recommended to Congress a defensive policy based upon expanded naval power. Hamilton, the covert influence, reputedly eager to drive the French out of North America, instructed his Congressional followers to vote appropriations for an expanded army, which they did. Congress, in another defiance of Presidential leadership, passed in succession the Alien and Sedition Acts, which Adams neither requested nor wanted.

But Adams drank his bitterest draught as chief administrator of the civil and military affairs of the executive branch. Yielding to Congress's enthusiasm for an army in an act designed to win the popular acclaim he so badly lacked, he drew George Washington out of retirement to command the provisional forces. This seemingly splendid triumph was suddenly jeopardized when Washington requested the appointment as his generals the following in order of rank: Hamilton, C. C. Pinckney, and Henry Knox. Adams disputed the order, holding that Knox rightfully should come first, followed by Pinckney and then Hamilton. Ironically, Washington, creator of the strong Presidency, now became the agent of its degradation. In a forceful letter to Adams he insisted upon his listing; otherwise, he strongly implied, he would resign. The President, in all his political feebleness, could hardly afford the storm of Washington's resignation. The commander-in-chief yielded to his commanding general. Adams staggered on through a full agenda of woe. When upon his own initiative he nominated W. Vans Murray to be Minister to the French Republic, his cabinet displayed unconcealed resentment at his failure to consult it. Other times they concentrated upon their major preoccupation of leaking secrets to Hamilton to assist his campaign against the President. Adams, the man of large talents and rich public experience, ultimately crowned his failure and abandoned his misery by sustaining defeat for re-election.

The Founding Fathers, the Washington-Adams experience reveals, had created a Presidency of both strength and weakness. The first two Presidencies were the beginning of a continuing dilemma in American history between the people's fear of executive power and their confidence in its necessity and capacity for good.

CHAPTER

3

Selection

———

ONE of the stronger parts of the American Presidential system is its method of choosing the chief executive. No other nation making this choice shows keener sensitivity to public opinion. Nowhere else do the candidates campaign so hard at carrying their word into the far corners of a land continental in size. Nowhere do so many voters turn out to cast their choice in a free election.

It is not altogether clear when the selection of a President actually begins. In a sense he selects himself; in a sense the party selects him; in a sense—and here the final decision lies—the people do the selecting themselves. To win the Presidency the aspirant must travel a long, hard, treacherous road abounding in bumps and quicksand and divisible into three distinct segments: the pre-convention build-up, the national nominating convention, and the post-conventional electoral campaign.

◊

THE pre-convention phase is the longest, often the severest, part of the journey, and it may engage the candidate in fiercer struggles with his rival contenders for the nomination than his later race with the opposing nominee. In this phase the candidate surrounds himself with an entourage of helpers of assorted skills. The entourage has expanded from less than a handful in the nineteenth century to well nigh a score for the serious modern candidate. Several standard types of helpers are distinguishable. There are the early sponsors and supporters, the launchers of the candidacy. The founding fathers of the Woodrow Wilson-for-President movement were two editors, George Harvey of *Harper's Weekly* and Henry Watterson of the Louisville *Courier Journal*, who began work two years before the 1912 convention. Three years before the 1896 convention William McKinley's indefatigable sponsor, Mark Hanna, wisely rented a house in Thomasville, Georgia, imported the William McKinleys for a three-week visit, and invited prominent Southern Republicans to meet the rising Ohio governor. The Southerners enjoyed the social approach, at which McKinley shone, and Hanna took a long first step toward lining up the Southern delegations.

Some early supporters, such as Wilson's George Harvey, fall by the wayside; others, like Hanna, become the managers of the long campaign. The managers are political craftsmen who supply broad leadership to the entire enterprise. If they are victorious, they are hailed as "kingmakers." Managers are of various backgrounds; they differ greatly in the quality and extent of their political experience. Franklin Roosevelt's managers in 1932, James A. Farley and Louis McHenry Howe, were both, as Farley put it, "virtually unknown and inexperienced in the vast field of national politics." They were put in charge even though several Democrats of national reputation had clasped Roosevelt's candidacy and would have jumped at the opportunity to become his campaign manager. Farley came with long and successful experience in New York State politics. Howe, a gnomelike ex-newspaperman five feet five inches tall and frail in health, had perceived in the youthful Senator Roosevelt, as early as 1910, the promise of a brilliant public career. Howe went to work as secretary and assistant to Roosevelt, and when "Franklin," as he called his hero, was seized with infantile paralysis, "Louie" stayed by his side and kept his political ambition alive. In 1932 Howe awed Farley with his "uncanny faculty for accurate judgment of individuals."

John Kennedy's pre-convention staff demonstrates the lengths to which specialization is resorted to in staging the candidate's effort. His brother Robert was general manager of operations. Lawrence F. O'Brien, placid, stocky, and hard-working, commanded the organizational base, a great phalanx of young men who had done their political teething in the Senator's home state of Massachusetts. Kenneth O'Donnell, a taciturn former Harvard football captain and veteran of Kennedy's Massachusetts wars, was Kennedy's link with the organization and transmitted Kennedy's reflections and directives to O'Brien. Theodore C. Sorensen was the candidate's "idea man" and star draftsman—"my intellectual blood bank," Kennedy called him. Stephen Smith, the candidate's brother-in-law, discreet and business-trained, opened the Washington headquarters for the Kennedy staff and eventually became the general manager in charge of mobilizing scores of thousands of volunteers and employees. Pierre Salinger, a former California newspaperman, Congressional investigator, and big-cigar man, presided with joviality and shrewdness over press relations. Louis Harris, public opinion analyst and market research entrepreneur, was the candidate's personal poll-taker. His findings were the basis of key campaign decisions. John Bailey, Connecticut Democratic chairman, coordinated the Northeastern bosses.

Unless the candidate is blessed with personal wealth, his managers and supporters must beat the brush for dollars to sustain the grand effort. Woodrow Wilson's initial needs were provided for by several well-heeled old Princeton friends. Cleveland H. Dodge, banker and merchant and Wilson's friend on the Princeton Board of Trustees, contributed $51,300 and extracted large amounts from fellow businessmen. Wilson's manager, William F. McCombs, often repeated a dazzling politico-economic sleight of hand. He excelled at collecting large sums from Wall Street contributors while simultaneously crying, whenever Wilson was attacked, that "Wall Street" was behind the dastardly deed.

The Wilson camp, in their quest for wherewithal, faced the devil's worst temptations. Early in the pre-convention campaign, Wilson's managers pressed him to accept a contribution, and a big one it presumably would be, from Thomas F. Ryan, the Virginia utilities czar. Ryan informed the managers at his Nelson County estate that he would support Wilson "because he was a native Virginian." The joyous managers now sounded out Wilson, proposing that he meet with Ryan to accept what they were confident would be a big slice of the latter's fortune. To their great distress, Wilson summarily rejected the offer, said some "uncivil things" about Ryan, and lectured his managers sternly that a contribution from such a source would do immeasurable harm.

◇

THE pre-convention campaign is a time of hard choices between alternative strategies. Franklin Roosevelt and his managers at the outset of his pre-convention candidacy perceived a choice between two major and opposite courses. They could sit back and conduct a passive campaign, limited to building friendly contacts and issuing press statements extolling Roosevelt's virtues. The risk of antagonizing the rather numerous favorite son candidates would be avoided, at least until the campaign began in earnest. Or the pressure could be turned on immediately, Roosevelt's candidacy announced, and the job begun of rounding up delegates to clinch the nomination. History provided not a few grisly illustrations of the outstanding candidate who declared early and subsequently was trampled into the dust by opponents who ganged up on him. Democratic candidates in Roosevelt's day, because of the party's convention rule requiring a two-thirds vote to nominate, were highly susceptible to the deadly danger. Another risk was that a candidacy begun too early might wither and die from public apathy. This species of political blight is known in the trade as the "morning-glory" candidacy. Roosevelt ultimately decided to run early and to run fast, notwithstanding the risks.

Candidates as a rule back away from the Roosevelt pattern by carefully avoiding any announcement of their candidacy for as long as possible, all the while, however, pursuing the grail with might and main. William McKinley's candidacy, although its formal announcement was stretched to maximum postponement, was in high gear as early as 1892, four years before his nomination. In the 1892 national Republican convention he was a central figure, hailed with booming ovations, pursued by crowds of admirers, and elected permanent chairman. Amid this heady adulation, disaster suddenly threatened. Delegates began rebelling against the renomination of President Benjamin Harrison and moved to enter McKinley's name in the balloting. To stem this terrible threat to bring his candidacy into the open ahead of schedule, and to use it as the means of revolt against the incumbent President, McKinley, as presiding chairman, challenged the votes for himself from the chair. Unfortunately he was overruled with wild acclaim. Harrison was renominated, but McKinley's votes tied the grandiose James G. Blaine for second place. Afterward as McKinley, his mentor Mark Hanna, and H. H. Kohlsaat, a Chicago editor, stretched out in their hotel suite to rest from their ordeal and the merciless summer heat, Hanna exclaimed, "My God, William, that was a damned close squeak."

The whirligig of McKinley's unannounced candidacy four years hence spun briskly from 1892 on. He undertook a far-flung speaking tour from Maine to Iowa for the Republican ticket, not without profit for his future. In the 1894 Congressional elections, his speech-making presence was entreated by state committees eager to bask in the sun of his popularity. In all, he moved through sixteen states, making 371 speeches and converting thousands of voters to his cause. As late as the spring of 1895 he spoke before the "McKinley-for-President" club in Hartford, Connecticut, a part of the country he visited infrequently and whose support he cherished, all the while writhing in private agony at this circumstantial acknowledgment of his candidacy. And so it went.

Tours, visits, and speeches—the chief pre-conventon activities—involve basic strategic and tactical choices. Woodrow Wilson was so impressed by the potentialities of the tour that in his first eight months of serious pre-convention campaigning he made a nine thousand-mile transcontinental journey and campaigned besides in New York, Pennsylvania, Virginia, North Carolina, South Carolina, Georgia, Texas, and Wisconsin. Tours not merely display the candidate to the populace, but enable him to visit, and hopefully to impress, key local leaders and personalities.

Wilson, in one rewarding sojourn in Atlanta, Georgia, met the leading progressive Democrats of the state, converted the editors of the Savannah *Evening Press*, the Atlanta *Journal*, and the Atlanta *Georgian* to his cause, and conferred at length with Governor Hoke Smith, who became the first important political figure to support Wilson's candidacy openly.

Tours and speeches lead the candidate onto some of the most treacherous terrain of his pre-convention effort—taking a stand on issues. Worst of all is the unavoidable issue on which any position the candidate takes will alienate support he needs. Franklin Roosevelt in 1932 was bedeviled by a momentous question he could not avoid: his attitude toward United States membership in the League of Nations. Almost anything he said on this burning subject would offend supporters on which his success at the convention depended. His foes, of course, trumpeted the League issue constantly. William Randolph Hearst in his transcontinental newspaper chain attacked the candidate unmercifully as an "internationalist," quoting abundantly in front-page editorials his pro-League statements in his Vice Presidential campaign of 1920.

Roosevelt at first hoped to fend off Hearst by maintaining silence, but to no avail. The attacks continued; a statement was necessary. In a carefully devised release, Roosevelt acknowledged that in 1920 he had worked for American participation in the League. He said,

> But the League of Nations today is not the League conceived by Woodrow Wilson. . . . Too often through these years its major function has been not the broad overwhelming purpose of world peace, but rather a mere meeting place for the political discussion of strictly European political national difficulties. . . . Because of these facts, therefore, I do not favor American participation.

Fortunately for Roosevelt, the statement accomplished its immediate purpose. Hearst ceased his attacks. But there were costs, which presumably the candidate and his managers had anticipated and weighed. The statement stretched to the uttermost the loyalty of the Wilsonians, a compact and powerful band of associates of the last Democratic President. Colonel Edward M. House, Wilson's former confidant, wrote to Farley that Roosevelt's position "created something akin to panic among the devoted Wilson followers." Intellectuals of the school of Walter Lippmann were sore distressed. Roosevelt swabbed the disgruntled with a remedy that Louis Howe called "soothing syrup." The end, the candidate explained, justified the means. He wrote to one saddened Wilsonian,

> Can't you see that loyalty to the ideals of Woodrow Wilson is just as strong in my heart as it is in yours, but have you ever stopped to consider that there is a difference between ideals and the methods of attaining them? Ideals do not change, but methods do change with every generation and world circumstance. . . . And for heaven's sake have a little faith.

One body of opinion Roosevelt could not allay was the cynics, a not un-common breed among political professionals. Senator William E. Borah, eying Roosevelt's statement, muttered sarcastically, "Repent ye, for the kingdom of heaven is at hand."

The candidate in the pre-convention period is confronted with the pos-sibility, and sometimes the necessity, of "deals" on issues and offices. The "deals" presumably will strengthen his chances for the nomination if, on balance, they gain more support than they lose. In the fall of 1895, with the future convention well in sight, Mark Hanna sat down with two great political dictators of the day, Senator Matt Quay of Pennsylvania and ex-Senator Tom ("Boss") Platt of New York. Both ruled their respective state machines absolutely and were grand masters of the arts of venality. Hanna met with the dark, cynical Quay and the scrawny, secretive Platt to bargain for the huge electoral votes of their respective states. With these William McKinley's nomination would be assured. The bosses' terms came high. Probably more than one cabinet seat was involved, and Platt wanted the Secretaryship of the Treasury for himself, in writing, please. Hanna rushed back to Ohio to report the terms of incipient victory to the candidate. He fortified McKinley first with a choice cigar. As Hanna spoke, McKinley listened in silence, pulled on his cigar, got up, and paced the floor. "There are some things in this world that come too high," he said at last. "If I cannot be President without promising to make Tom Platt Secretary of the Treasury, I will never be President." McKinley thus took a long stride toward sainthood.

The candidate makes a major strategic decision in choosing among the several Presidential primaries in which to make his race. Kennedy, in his 1960 strategy, battled a leading rival, Senator Hubert Humphrey, in the Wisconsin and West Virginia primaries and in the latter succeeded in putting the Senator out of the race. In 1960 fifteen states and the District of Columbia held primaries which chose 40 per cent of the convention delegates. The selection of delegations to national conventions began in Wisconsin in 1905, an innovation of "Fighting Bob" La Follette, who hoped to chase away the bosses and return politics to the people. Although the Presidential primary is at best only moderately successful as a pre-dictive plebiscite, it has enjoyed bursts of importance in this century's elections. Kennedy's primary victories were indispensable for his 1960 nomination. Taft's 1952 defeat in New Hampshire, the first primary, was a disaster from which his candidacy never recovered.

A national Presidential primary is sometimes proposed to replace the national convention system. Difficulties apparent in the present limited use of primaries would be compounded on a national scale. Presidential con-tenders rightly complain of the inhuman strain of existing primaries upon their health, which forces them to wage full-scale campaigns in a succession of states. "There were days when I just didn't think I could last out until Chicago," Estes Kefauver said of his 1952 primary ordeal of fierce struggles in fifteen states. For office-holders such as governors, primaries, with their weeks of intensive effort, mean neglect of official duties. A large-scale primary campaign is enormously expensive. Eisenhower's pre-convention effort in 1952 cost an estimated $2.5 million and Taft's was even more. Given the astronomical expense and the absence of public or party financing, the well-heeled candidate enjoys enormous advantage over his poorer competitor. Hubert Humphrey, fighting the West Virginia primary in a battered bus, scraping desperately to muster the price of a half-hour's local radio time, and literally throwing the family grocery money into the breach, was a picture of pathos.

◇

THE pre-convention campaign viewed outside the candidate's own camp is a vast and jumbled scene of human beings, Aristotle's political animals, embodying ambitions and loyalties, power and influence to do good or ill for the candidate's cause. On the pre-convention landscape are several standard political types. Not the least important, of course, are the several species of opposing candidates—the serious contenders, the dark horses, and the favorite sons. Franklin Roosevelt in 1932, for example, faced a full field: dark horses such as Albert Ritchie, governor of Maryland, and Newton D. Baker, Wilson's Secretary of War; favorite sons such as Senators Harry Byrd of Virginia and J. Hamilton Lewis of Illinois; and the titular Democratic leader Alfred E. Smith and Speaker John Nance Garner of Texas, serious candidates from the start.

The landscape during a pre-convention campaign is dotted with prestigious political figures who are not candidates but whose support is cherished and whose favor is courted—governors above all, Senators, Congressmen, party patriarchs, and labor, business, nationality, and racial leaders who hover at the party's fringes. The supreme example of the latter in 1912 was William Jennings Bryan, three times the Democratic Presidential nominee. In an earlier day Woodrow Wilson had viewed William Jennings Bryan and his progressive principles somewhat contemptuously. Once his quest for the Presidency began, Wilson notably shifted his attitude and courted the Great Commoner avidly. A major triumph of Wilson's Western tour in May 1911 was his meeting with Bryan and his winning of Bryan's approval. Bryan, who had his designs too, pressed Wilson to take the progressive road. In subsequent months the Great Commoner praised the increasingly progressive tenor of Wilson's pronouncements, although he added pointedly in one letter to the candidate that he had noticed no support from his Eastern friend for the proposed national income tax. Wilson was soon sending his state legislature a strong message urging adoption of the federal income tax amendment.

Beyond Washington and into the American hinterland stretches the intricate continental tangle of party machinery, manned by a varied body of functionaries, known collectively as "organization politicians," the state and local party officialdom. Many a Presidential aspirant has run aground from want of support from the organization politicians. A formidable obstacle to Wilson's 1912 candidacy was his cold rejection by the generality of organization politicians. They have an impression of you," Wilson's manager, William McCombs, wrote with frankness, "in a large degree that you are austere and dictatorial and that you will not have a due appreciation of what is to be done for you. . . . Another thing I hear much of, particularly throughout the East, is that you are unreliable."

Not the least importance of the organization politicians is their large hand in selecting the delegates, the official decision-makers, of the future convention. Most candidates run with the delegates of their home states pledged to them. Franklin Roosevelt was denied this common privilege in 1932 when Tammany Hall and its upstate allies decided upon an uninstructed delegation. When the Presidential nomination is being seriously contested, the specific commitments of state delegations may be in great disarray. In 1932 California had seemed set for Roosevelt until Al Smith announced his candidacy and William G. McAdoo, the state's Democratic leader, came out for Garner. Ultimately Garner prevailed, walking off with the prize of forty-four delegates. Massachusetts was also a disaster. Roosevelt blundered in cooperating with James M. Curley's minority faction against the dominant organization led by Senator David I. Walsh and Governor Joseph B. Ely. Curley used Roosevelt as a Trojan horse to win back control over the state organization, pushing him on with grossly optimistic predictions of success. Al Smith, the regular organization's candidate, snowed Roosevelt under. Yet Roosevelt had his successes too, sufficient to carry him into the convention still very much the front runner. These, like the defeats, were sometimes the product of accident and idiosyncracy. Senator Joseph T. Robinson, Arkansas's favorite son, fearful of a deadlocked convention, abandoned his candidacy and most of his state's votes went to Roosevelt. In Nebraska Roosevelt won thanks to National Committeeman Arthur Mullen's skill in foiling Charles W. Bryan's ambition to be a favorite son.

Among Presidential candidates there is a high incidence of personal crises which threaten to damage or wreck fatally their chances for the nomination. The crises are sometimes the product of the candidate's foibles, more often innocent acts twisted by alert opponents. Franklin Pierce's candidacy was suddenly jeopardized when the Boston *Evening Journal* carried stories that his service in the Mexican War was stained with cowardice. Probably the worst crisis Wilson faced was the publication of a letter he had written four years before to a Princeton trustee, Adrian H. Joline. The letter, although clearly private and confidential, was indiscretion at its worst. Wilson had permitted himself to write to Joline, "Would that we could do something, at once dignified and effective, to knock Mr. Bryan once and for all into a cocked hat." His foes revealed the letter's contents, gleefully expecting to ruin his candidacy. To their chagrin, Wilson was saved by Bryan's ample understanding.

◇

THE national nominating convention itself, the final arbiter, is as uniquely American as the hot dog and salt-water taffy. Everyone knows its spirit of carnival, the marching, shouting delegates, the frothy oratory, the grating brass bands. Like most citizens, H. L. Mencken, sage and cynic, viewed the nominating convention with mixed sentiments. "One sits through long sessions wishing heartily that all the delegates and alternates were in hell," he wrote, "—and then suddenly there comes a show so gaudy and hilarious, so melodramatic and obscene, so unimaginably exhilarating and preposterous that one lives a gorgeous year in an hour."

The national convention appeared rather late on the Presidential scene. After George Washington, who was chosen by general acclaim, the next four Presidents—Adams, Jefferson, Madison, and James Monroe—were hand-picked by the Congressional caucus. "King Caucus," as it was popularly called, borrowed from the state legislatures, was a joint session of party members from both houses of Congress to nominate their candidates for President and Vice President. "King Caucus" was later extended to include special delegates to represent Congressional districts held by the opposition party. Andrew Jackson, who fared badly in the caucus in 1824, proceeded to undermine the caucus system so thoroughly that in 1828 he was nominated by the combined force of "State legislative caucuses, public meetings, and irregular conventions of the people." After the example of the Anti-Mason party, which held the first national nominating convention in Baltimore in 1831, some 243 Democratic delegates with 103 alternates came to the same city the following year to renominate Jackson.

The convention poses for the top contending candidate and his managers two vitally important tasks, failure in either one of which might spell the difference between victory and defeat. The first is to keep the bloc of pledged or promised delegates "nailed fast" to prevent their straying "off the reservation" to another candidate. The second is to control the convention machinery to permit its manipulation for, rather than against, the candidate. In a contested convention these undertakings are a high-tension ordeal. Jim Farley wrote of the 1932 Democratic convention,

> The nervous strain during this period of suspense was very close to the limit of physical endurance. . . . I was working eighteen or nineteen hours a day, conversing with hundreds of people, constantly consulting with other leaders, receiving reports from every delegation, and meeting at least twice daily with several hundred newspapermen. I . . . slept a few hours just before dawn if the opportunity offered. . . . Hundreds of other men were caught in the same dizzy whirl and were trying to keep up the same maddening pace.

In facing their convention tasks, the managers of the modern candidate resort to specialization, as they did in the pre-convention phase. In 1932 Farley operated the main Roosevelt reception center at Chicago, where he greeted the Roosevelt delegates and tried mightily to win others over from the opposition. One of Farley's props was a huge map of the United States on which the Roosevelt states were blocked out in red. So vividly and convincingly did the map demonstrate that Roosevelt was the choice of a big majority that the worried opposition took pains to deride it as "Field Marshal Farley's Map." In negotiations with delegates in his hotel suite, Ed Flynn, the suave and astute Bronx boss, supplemented Farley's efforts to build Roosevelt's strength. Louis Howe too wooed the delegates, and he had installed in his suite a microphone attached to a direct wire from Albany. Roosevelt's exhilarating voice would come booming into the room full of visitors, "My friends from Iowa," and launch into a personal message. Roosevelt would expound his views, answer questions, and delight and impress the delegates. Thanks to the direct wire, Roosevelt, remaining at home, could electioneer and share in nearly every important decision at Chicago. The Roosevelt floor manager was Arthur Mullen of Nebraska, an old hand at conventions and one well-liked by all factions.

The managers of a serious modern candidate coordinate their far-flung effort through an internal communications network at the convention itself. The most elaborate of these was Kennedy's in 1960. From the Kennedy liaison post, a cottage outside the Los Angeles Sports Arena, ran a net of direct communication lines to special telephone posts fixed on the chairs of friendly delegations. Eight of Kennedy's forty "state shepherds" who roved the convention floor carried duo-com walkie-talkie sets that were linked to a communications control at the cottage. From there the floor managers, Governor Abraham Ribicoff and Robert Kennedy, directed the whole body of shepherds. Another set of lines ran to Room 8315 at the Biltmore Hotel, the strategic center of the candidate's top command. Other lines were connected with Kennedy's private hideaway in Hollywood and his public Presidential suite.

To control the convention machinery, the candidate and his managers must concentrate upon several key parts. Much of their effort occurs before the convention begins and centers upon the national committee and the national chairman who decide when and where the convention is to be held and make the local arrangements. The national committee selects the temporary chairman of the convention, who delivers the "keynote address." Since the tone and tendency of this oration shape the convention's initial and sometimes decisive mood, the selection of the temporary chairman may touch off a fierce struggle. His further power to hand down parliamentary rulings helpful to the candidate he favors adds zest to the combat.

In 1932 the Roosevelt camp had to maneuver forcefully to prevent Jonett Shouse from becoming temporary chairman. Shouse, who fiercely opposed the Roosevelt candidacy, had powerful support. The Roosevelt emissaries were able to install their own nominee, Alben Barkley, for temporary chairman, when the New York governor agreed that the arrangements subcommittee of the national committee might "commend" (Roosevelt's word) rather than "recommend" Shouse for a second major convention post, the permanent chairmanship.

Well before the convention, however, the Roosevelt forces decided to oppose Shouse for permanent chairman as well and advance their own candidate, Senator Thomas J. Walsh of Montana. Following Roosevelt's agreement to "commend" him, Shouse had campaigned ardently against the New York governor in Massachusetts and Pennsylvania and had convinced the latter's managers that a loyal permanent chairman was imperative. Cries of "unfair" greeted disclosure of the Rooseveltians' decision. The fight grew so furious and the outcome so unpredictable that Charles Michelson, the party's stellar ghost writer, carried in one pocket an acceptance speech for Shouse and, in another, one for Walsh. Roosevelt's candidate, Walsh, was elected 626 to 528, the convention high-water mark for the opposition. The Roosevelt forces rounded out their control of convention machinery by installing Cordell Hull as chairman of the committee on resolutions and Bruce Kremer of Montana as chairman of the rules committee. Roosevelt chose no nominees for two other committee chairmanships to leave Farley free to dangle them before wavering delegations.

◇

THE fine art of winning and keeping delegations, like any other art, defies exact description. It is a blend of grand strategy, nice detail, human psychology, luck, and hard work. The candidate himself may take on front-line duty at the convention in the battle for delegates. Kennedy and his chief rivals all were on hand at the Los Angeles convention in 1960. He was literally in the thick of the fight. On July 11, between 8:30 A.M. and 1:30 P.M., for instance, he addressed the caucuses of Nevada, Pennsylvania, Michigan, North Carolina, Arkansas, New York, South Carolina, Florida, and Alaska. The afternoon was equally crowded. On the morning of July 12 he addressed North Carolina again, a collective New England breakfast, Wyoming, South Dakota, a nationality group, and California. On July 13, balloting day, he spoke to Indiana, a farm-state caucus, Virginia, Colorado, and Hawaii.

The amount of effort a candidate and his camp lavish upon a delegation is roughly proportionate to its importance. Franklin Roosevelt's managers concentrated heavily in 1932 upon winning over California's big forty-four-vote delegation, one of several blocs that could break the back of the opposition if they could be swung around. California was pledged to Speaker John Nance Garner, but William Randolph Hearst, the provider of Garner's victory in the state, was beginning to doubt the wisdom of opposing Roosevelt. Hearst could not bear either Alfred E. Smith, who led the opposition, or Newton D. Baker, who was emerging as a formidable dark horse candidate. The Roosevelt men fanned Hearst's doubts. Daniel C. Roper and Bruce Kremer were constantly in touch with William Gibbs McAdoo, the California leader. Jim Farley and Joseph P. Kennedy, a business associate of Hearst, telephoned the newspaper czar long-distance to stress the danger of the Baker "dark horse" movement and the urgency of a Californa switch. Hearst fiercely denounced the Baker movement, but failed to commit himself to Roosevelt.

A race's outcome is often determined by "deals" arranged by the candidates' convention representatives. Franklin Roosevelt was eventually put across in 1932 by a bargain for the Vice Presidency, which not a few times in the nation's history has determined the choice of the Presidential nominee. Farley suggested to Garner's representative, Sam Rayburn, that if Texas threw its support to Roosevelt, Garner could have the Vice Presidency. Rayburn answered crustily that he and his co-workers had come to Chicago to nominate Garner for President, although they did not want a stalemate. Eventually Garner made the decision. Fearful that an ugly convention deadlock might damage public confidence and cost the Democrats the election, Garner released his delegates and reluctantly exchanged his proud Speakership for the quietude of the Vice Presidency. Texas and California went over to Roosevelt and the nomination was clinched.

◇

THE convention can also be viewed as a series of decisions, climbing, by phases, to the climax of the Presidential nomination. The proceedings of the convention committees—credentials, rules, permanent organization, and platform or resolutions—are often the harbinger of things to come. The committees' reports to the whole convention often provide an early test of strength of the rival candidates. The credentials committee, for instance, acts as a kind of court to decide which one of two or more contesting delegations from a given state is entitled to be seated. At the Republican national convention of 1952 nearly a hundred delegates were involved in seating contests. Supporters of Robert A. Taft controlled the credentials committee and reported favorably on delegations pledged to his candidacy from Louisiana, Georgia, and Texas. The Eisenhower camp carried the fight to the convention floor, waved the banner of "fair play," won the uncommitted delegations over to their side, seated their own delegations from the contested states, and opened the way for a first-ballot nomination.

The convention's balloting may simply be a routine ratification of the candidate's success constructed in the previous months of careful effort. The first-ballot nominations of Kennedy and Nixon in 1960 were no surprise. A succession of ballotings, which is not uncommon, reflects the continuing struggle for delegates and requires adroit maneuver. As the balloting proceeds, the serious candidate must demonstrate a steadily increasing strength. To satisfy this psychological necessity, Farley at the 1932 convention held on to a meager reserve of delegates and doled them out sparingly with each new ballot to maintain the appearance of gathering vigor. He also had the task of keeping his disclosed strength intact, of preventing delegates committed to Roosevelt from abandoning him on the next ballot. Disaster almost engulfed the Roosevelt forces on the third ballot, when Mississippi threatened to crack. The delegates were polled with intense pressures beating upon them from the several camps. Roosevelt squeaked through by 10½ votes to 9½. Since the "unit rule" was operating, by which a majority of the delegation controls the state's entire vote, all twenty of Mississippi's votes went to Roosevelt.

When at last the balloting has produced a nomination, a double formality remains: the notification of the candidate and his acceptance. Prior to 1932 the notification procedure was a musty affair, done by a committee weeks after the event. Franklin Roosevelt in 1932 smashed precedent and thrilled the nation by flying to Chicago to accept the nomination and setting forth his position in confident generalities and a ringing voice. Roosevelt's innovation has since become standard practice in both major parties.

After the Presidential nomination comes the usually anticlimactic selection of the Vice President. This decision is ordinarily governed by the tradition of "balancing the ticket" geographically. (Among the exceptions is the Truman-Barkley, Missouri-Kentucky, border state ticket of 1948.) After Wilson's nomination in 1912, his manager, A. S. Burleson, telephoned to say that the convention was leaning toward Thomas R. Marshall of Indiana. "But, Burleson," Wilson remonstrated, "he is a very small calibre man." Burleson did not argue the point, but noted that Marshall was from the Midwest and from a doubtful state. His candidacy would ideally supplement Wilson's. "All right, go ahead," Wilson said, not too agreeably. Wilson notwithstanding, the opinion of the Presidential nominee is also weighty in choosing the Vice President. The degree to which the choice is specific varies. Eisenhower in 1952 wrote down five names he considered acceptable as running mates. In 1960 Kennedy induced Lyndon Johnson of Texas to become the Vice Presidential nominee, a choice that proved to be the difference between victory and defeat.

It may seem that the prize of the nomination goes to the man with the best organization and the most compelling political personality. But actually nominees are weeded out in advance to some extent; not all able men are eligible in practice. One of America's favorite candidates has been the military hero. Of the thirty men who have been elected President, twelve have been military veterans. Both parties have thrice nominated ex-military men in the same year. The Republicans tapped no less than four Civil War generals; Theodore Roosevelt was the glamorous Rough Rider of the Spanish-American War; and Dwight Eisenhower achieved international military renown in World War II. John Kennedy's valor in that war was not forgotten, either. In the past century governors have been the leading source of Presidential candidates, sixteen in all having been nominated by the parties since 1900. Nowadays being governor of any large state almost automatically puts one in the running, and for a New York governor not to crave the White House would be downright pathological. The United States Senate, once a liability, is fast becoming a manufactory of Presidential candidates. The chief Democratic contenders in 1960—Kennedy, Johnson, Hubert Humphrey, and Stuart Symington—were all Senators, and the Republican standard-bearer—Richard Nixon—was a former Senator. Television and the dominance of foreign affairs have enhanced the Senator's importance. The Mountain states have never provided a candidate, nor did the South for more than a century until Lyndon Johnson's succession as chief executive in 1963 on the death of President Kennedy endowed him with a superior claim to the Democratic nomination of 1964. Of the fifty-five men nominated by the two parties since 1856, forty-one have come from either New York State or the Middle West. Religion, race, and sex have also been selective factors for the nomination. Kennedy's breakthrough in 1960 as the first Catholic to become President may, before many more elections come to pass, throw the gates open to all. Before this only a white Anglo-Saxon Protestant male was considered eligible.

◇

T H E Presidential nominee of the mid-nineteenth century campaigned with luxurious ease and calm compared with the fiery involvement of his mid-twentieth-century counterpart. James Buchanan, Democratic nominee of 1856, tarried on his comfortable estate, Wheatland, near Lancaster, Pennsylvania, receiving visitors and answering mail with the help of a clerk.

The bulk of the work was done by the state organizations supplemented by a quartet of Congressional managers. Nearly a century later Harry S. Truman, in an unstinting "whistle-stop" campaign, traveled 31,700 miles and delivered 356 speeches over a thirty-five day stretch, once making sixteen speeches in a single day.

Radio and television, broadened press coverage, and a burgeoning transportation technology have made campaigning strenuous for the candidate and have driven him to enlarge his staff. His increased exposure reduced the utility of that ancient stand-by, the set speech. The modern candidate must make many and varied speeches respectably adorned with an array of ideas. For this phase of his needs, Franklin Roosevelt's innovation, copied and adapted by his successors, was the Brain Trust, a body of professors and researchers who dealt with policies and issues for the candidate's speeches and other statements. A second distinct group, comprising Farley, Flynn, and others who had marshaled delegates for the convention, redirected their talents to gathering popular votes in the campaign. Kennedy's post-convention campaign organization in 1960 enlarged upon the Roosevelt pattern. There were new Brain Trusters, professors again recruited largely from Harvard through Archibald Cox of the university's law school. Ideas and speech drafts spewed from the group which followed Cox to Washington. In addition, Kennedy's idea generators included his personal Brain Trust, Sorensen and Richard Goodwin, who dealt with high affairs and pronouncements.

For the political management phases, each member of Kennedy's pre-nomination entourage adapted his special skill to the new environment of the post-convention campaign. Kenneth O'Donnell handled campaign scheduling, a difficult art which allocates every minute of the candidate's time, with due regard for transportation and speech schedules, the necessities and feuds of local leaders, and the shepherding of newsmen following hard on the candidate's heels. Lawrence O'Brien became Director of Organization for the National Committee and Byron (Whizzer) White, Director of the Kennedy-Johnson Volunteers Organization. Robert Kennedy presided over the entire enterprise—idea men and political managers —aided and abetted by Richard Donahue, Ralph Dungan, and other personal Kennedy lieutenants and a half-dozen members of the Kennedy family. The vast realm of the communications media was handled by Salinger, poll-taker Harris, and a speech coach brought in to pare down the candidate's regional accent.

The post-convention campaign, like other phases of the route to the Presidency, requires a series of major strategic decisions. Strategy on one level is the selection of an array of voter entities, which when pieced together will provide an electoral majority. Kennedy's 1960 strategy focused upon nine large states (New York, Pennsylvania, California, Michigan, Texas, Illinois, Ohio, New Jersey, and Massachusetts) comprising 237 of the 269 electoral votes required to elect a President. These plus sixty more electoral votes added by Lyndon Johnson in the deep South or by several New England and Midwestern states would make victory certain.

A further phase of strategy is the welding of groups—national, racial, and economic—into a winning coalition. Negro citizens, for instance, since the elections of the 1940's, have been wooed by both parties. A powerful political fact, not overlooked, is the large Negro population in big Northern cities that are a key to capturing the states with imposing electoral votes. Both Nixon and Kennedy courted the Negro vote in 1960, the latter, as it proved in a dramatic test, more energetically. Late in the campaign Martin Luther King, a hero of the Negro struggle, was arrested during an Atlanta "sit-in," sentenced on a technicality to four months of hard labor, and thrust into the state penitentiary. The King situation coupled with the Southern white vote, which both parties were courting, put both Nixon and Kennedy in the middle of a predicament. At least three Southern governors informed Kennedy that if he supported the Reverend King, the South would be lost to the Democratic ticket. Nixon eventually chose to keep silent in the King episode and Kennedy telephoned to Mrs. King, assuring her of his concern and, if necessary, his intervention. Word of this act spread through the Negro leadership. Robert Kennedy next telephoned to the sentencing judge a plea for King's release. He was soon freed on bail, pending an appeal. Negro leaders across the nation praised Kennedy's action and his organization printed a million pamphlets recounting the episode. These were distributed on the Sunday before the election outside Negro churches everywhere. The importance of Kennedy's action in the King situation is illuminated by the electoral data of 1960. In Illinois, carried by 9,000 votes, approximately 250,000 Negroes voted for Kennedy; in Michigan, carried by 67,000 votes, 250,00 Negroes voted for Kennedy; in South Carolina, carried by 10,000 votes, 40,000 Negroes voted for Kennedy.

The candidate must also make several basic organizational choices. He can choose between relying heavily upon the regular party machinery or supplementing it with "independent" citizens' committees. In 1952 the independent "Citizens for Eisenhower" organization figured importantly in the Republican victory, particularly in drawing dissatisfied Democrats over to support the Eisenhower candidacy. A perpetual organizational problem is the relating of national and local effort. In the Kennedy campaign, local organization implemented a major strategy of voter registration. If a massive registration drive could be mounted and ten million new names added to the voting lists, the Kennedy managers reasoned, seven million more Democratic votes would result. Congressman Frank Thompson of New Jersey, an experienced hand at registration drives, directed fifty state registration chairmen, two hundred key county registration chairman, and a paid staff of eight specially trained leaders. The Kennedy drive and a counterpart Nixon effort brought the 1960 popular vote to 6,800,000 beyond the 1956 total.

Another strategic problem concerns the candidate's personal involvement in the campaign. How much of the campaign emphasis should be on issues and how much on personality? Eisenhower, national hero and international personage in 1952, was under less pressure to emphasize issues than the lesser known Kennedy in 1960, whose campaign stressed issues. Should the candidate concentrate on mass appeal via radio, television, and big rallies? Or should he do the whistle-stop routine, as Harry Truman did in 1948, with folksy talks to hundreds of small audiences across the nation? For all of the magic of radio and television, candidates still invest their time and treasure heavily in going out to the voters. Although in 1960 the four television debates supplied the candidates with an audience of unsurpassed size, both Kennedy and Nixon traveled by rail and air to give brief talks at hundreds of communities and to shake thousands of hands. A powerful inducement for whistle-stopping is Truman's extraordinary success at it in 1948 in achieving a victory unpredicted by the public opinion polls or by any reputable politician save Truman himself.

Truman made his whistle-stop speeches from the back of a reconstructed Pullman car, the *Ferdinand Magellan*, purchased in 1942 for one dollar from the Association of American Railroads. According to the 1948 routine, the local high school band blared out "Hail to the Chief" upon Truman's arrival. Then came a gift for the President, his expression of thanks, his welcome to local Democratic leaders, and compliments to the citizenry for their new highway or factory. Hereupon Truman ripped into the Republicans and the Eightieth Congress with wild ridicule. His Republican listeners heard their party brethren referred to as "gluttons of privilege" and "bloodsuckers with offices in Wall Street." ("Ridicule is a wonderful weapon," Truman told his aides.) After his political talk, Truman asked the crowd, "Howja like to meet my family?" and he proceeded to introduce Mrs. Truman as "the boss" and his daughter Margaret as "my baby" and "the boss's boss." The family bit delighted the crowds.

The opposite of the "whistle-stop" tour is the "front porch" campaign, perfected by William McKinley and the organizing genius of his manager, Mark Hanna. Instead of the candidate going to the people, as in the whistle-stop, the people, in the front porch campaign, come to the candidate. Delegations visited McKinley from all parts of the country, thanks to the low excursion rates of the cooperating railroads. The trip to Mc-

Kinley's base at Canton, the Cleveland *Plain Dealer* complained, was "cheaper than staying at home." Sporting campaign badges, caps, and neckties, the delegations poured off the trains and into the arms of committees of greeters. They marched through the town, passing beneath an elaborate plastic structure—the McKinley Arch—which supported a huge portrait of the candidate, and finally poured onto his lawn. After a short, suspenseful wait the door opened, and McKinley, appearing on the front porch, was greeted with a roar.

A spokesman of the delegation stepped forward to deliver an address of dedication to the Republican party and its illustrious candidate, mixed with acclaim for the visitors' locality or organization. Despite the seeming informality, a copy of the remarks had been cleared beforehand with McKinley, who sometimes edited them. Then the candidate mounted a chair, bade the crowd welcome, treated the campaign issues briefly, and complimented his audience. Concluding, he shook hands with his visitors in an informal reception on the porch steps.

In 1960 Presidential campaigning took a new turn when the traditional political debate of Congressional and local elections was adapted to the Presidential canvass and the idiosyncracies of television. The resulting Kennedy-Nixon TV debates had enormous impact upon the electoral outcome. An audience of 120,000,000 viewed one or more of the Kennedy-Nixon encounters. When the debates began, Nixon appeared the likely electoral winner, with Kennedy rather well behind; when they ended, the contestants' positions were reversed.

Debates between Presidential candidates will surely continue in future elections, with further evolutions of format. The debates helpfully provide the voters with a close-up of the candidates without their props of speech writers and idea men. The candidates can be seen thinking and speaking under stress, a situation that casts a great shaft of light upon character. In 1960 the debates undeniably quickened voter interest in the campaign.

But the debate system is not without flaws. The Presidency has a limited need of forensic talent; the office is far more than a great debate. No President, fortunately, is expected to formulate in a matter of seconds answers to great questions of foreign policy. The 1960 debates, while they revealed the candidates' personalities in sharp topographical relief, added little to public understanding of issues. Indeed a built-in drawback of TV debates may be over-attention to personality and superficiality on the issues.

◇

THE final stage of selecting the President—his actual election—was a knotty, much debated issue at the Constitutional Convention. Eventually the electoral college method of choosing the President emerged as a compromise. In actuality, there are fifty electoral colleges, one in each state. The number of electors in a given state equals the number of its Senators and Representatives in Congress.

Each elector has one vote, and a majority of the whole number of electors appointed is required to choose the President. If no Presidential candidate receives a majority, the Constitution directs the House of Representatives to complete the election of the President. The House is limited in choice to the three candidates receiving the greatest number of the electors' votes.

The Constitution authorizes each state to appoint its electors "in such manner as the legislature thereof may direct." In the first three Presidential elections the electors were chosen chiefly by the state legislatures. Thereafter, popular choice gradually took hold, and by 1824 electors were chosen by popular vote in all but six states, and in 1832 in all states but South Carolina, which clung to legislative election until 1864. Popular choice was registered through two main systems—election by the people in districts and election by the people of a "general ticket." Each system spawned numerous variations. In the district method, the people would vote in districts relatively equal in population, each district choosing one elector. Districts often coincided with Congressional districts. The district system was widely employed in the early days of the Constitution; indeed, according to Madison most of the Founding Fathers strongly preferred it. A divided electoral vote often resulted, and its distribution tended to follow the pattern of the Congressional elections in the House districts.

In time a political party, having gained control of a state, would sniff an opportunity to avoid the division of its electoral strength by introducing the general ticket system, which applies an ancient principle of gamesmanship—"winner take all." The party carrying the state, by however small a popular plurality, wins all the state's electors and the minority party or parties get none. Since 1836 all states have used the general ticket system, except for a brief relapse in Michigan to the district system following the 1892 election.

Although the states determine the method of choosing their electors, the timetable of a Presidential election is set by national law. On the first Tuesday after the first Monday in November, every fourth year, the qualified popular voters of the several states choose the Presidential electors. On the first Monday after the second Wednesday in December the electors meet in their respective states to cast their votes for President. On January 6 the electoral votes are counted in the presence of the two Houses of Congress and the results are announced by the presiding officer—the Vice President, if there is one. Vice President Nixon, consequently, had the privilege of declaring Kennedy's victory and his own defeat.

The Founding Fathers' expectation that the electors would exercise an element of free judgment in choosing the President was quickly crushed by the appearance of political parties, the Federalists and the Anti-Federalists, the latter soon becoming the Republican-Democratic party. George Washington's two Presidential candidacies were untouched by electoral vote politics. Following his departure from the Presidential scene, the electors took to party-line voting in choosing John Adams as President in 1796 over his chief rival, Thomas Jefferson. Thereafter, with rare individual exceptions, the electors have functioned as the automatons of their parties. Only rarely has an elector violated his pledge to vote for a particular Presidential candidate. In 1820 William Plumer voted for John Quincy Adams instead of Monroe. In 1956 a Democratic elector in Alabama, though pledged to vote for whomever the Democratic National Convention nominated, voted for a leading segregationist judge; and in 1960 an Oklahoma elector pledged to Richard Nixon voted instead for Senator Harry Byrd. None of these lapses affected the outcome.

Custom, which dictates the electors' voting conduct, has been reinforced by legislation and court opinion. State statutes range from those calling for a party nomination of electors, which itself is a presumption of pledged electors, to the laws of two states prescribing that electors vote for the party nominees, regardless of personal preference. In *Ray* v. *Blair* (343 U.S. 214, 1952) the Supreme Court gave its blessing to these arrangements, upholding a state law empowering party organizations to fix the qualifications of candidates for nomination as electors. The state law, the Court said, simply converted custom into legal obligation. Anticipating the 1964 elections, Mississippi and Georgia in 1961 passed laws permitting the election of unpledged electors. In Florida and Louisiana comparable bills are in passage, and in Alabama electors, although identified with a major party, are not required to vote for its Presidential nominee. In 1963 Governor Wallace of Alabama disclosed that his 1964 efforts would be devoted to spreading the unpledged elector movement in lieu of launching a third party. With the tendency of present-day elections to be close, these Southern maneuvers, designed to check the civil rights trends of the Democratic party, could much affect the outcome.

The selection of electors has also been altered by revisions of the Presidential ballot that confronts the popular voter in the polling booth. One is the requirement, first adopted in Nebraska in 1917, that electors be listed and voted for as a party group rather than individually. Another change brought the names of the Presidential nominees on the ballot with those of the electors. The latest evolutionary step is the Presidential short ballot, on which only the names of the Presidential and Vice Presidential nominees appear, an innovation speeded by the use of voting machines, which impose severer limitations of space than the paper ballot does.

Each popular vote cast by the Presidential short ballot counts for the elector whose name, although unknown to the voters, is on file with the state secretary of state.

Originally, under the Constitution, each elector cast two votes for President, one of which had to be for a candidate who was not an inhabitant of the elector's state. This provision, coupled with the necessity of an electoral vote majority for victory, barred even the largest state from choosing by itself a President from among its own inhabitants. The double-vote feature virtually compelled the selection of a candidate of continental reputation. The candidate receiving the second highest number of electoral votes became Vice President, a method that brought into the number-two post men of Presidential caliber like John Adams and Thomas Jefferson. The double-voting system, for all of its seeming merit, was abandoned in 1804 with the adoption of the Twelfth Amendment. The double vote crashed on the rocks in the election of 1800, when a deadlock developed between the Republican candidates, Jefferson and Aaron Burr. The election passed into the House of Representatives, where the rival Federalist party, which controlled the outcome, favored Burr but was pressured by Alexander Hamilton, its national chieftain, into backing Jefferson. The Republicans, snatched from a disaster they wished never to encounter again, championed the Twelfth Amendment, establishing separate electoral votes for the President and the Vice President.

◊

THE existing electoral vote arrangements have long been the object of heavy criticism and dire warnings. The critics hold that the electoral system violates basic tenets of democracy and that its many mechanical flaws invite breakdown and the eruption of a Presidential election into a nightmare of civil strife.

The electoral college system has been employed in forty-two elections and has failed three times to elect a President: in 1800, 1824, and 1876. Three elections are often indicted for flaunting the voice of the people, for electing Presidents who received fewer popular votes than their opponents. The suspected elections are John Quincy Adams' triumph over Jackson in 1824, Rutherford B. Hayes's over Samuel J. Tilden in 1876, and Benjamin Harrison's over Cleveland in 1888. Jackson's showing in 1824 is clouded by the fact that no popular votes were cast in six of the twenty-four states. In 1876 Tilden received 4,285,992 popular votes to 4,033,768 for Hayes. Since fraud and violence marked the popular voting in the South, North, and West, Tilden's popular margin is not unblemished. Harrison's victory by a popular minority over Cleveland cannot be gainsaid.

In *Gray* v. *Saunders* (372 U.S. 368, 1963) the Supreme Court stated that the electoral college philosophy violated the Constitutional concept of "we the people," which, the Court said, "can mean only one thing—one person, one vote." The electoral college system, by this standard, is a kind of gigantic gerrymander. It grossly exaggerates the value of the individual popular vote in the less populous states in contrast to the large states. Thus in the 1956 election each electoral vote in Illinois represented 163,235 popular voters, in Mississippi 31,018 voters.

Of all the features of electoral college practice the general ticket system has raised the severest criticism. The general ticket, as Lucius Wilmerding demonstrates, puts the Presidency on a federative rather than a national basis. It has taken "the choice of the President from the people of the nation at large and given it, in effect, to the people of the large states." The principle of "winner take all" serves to disenfranchise a substantial minority of popular votes or, even more outrageous, transfers them to the use of the candidate against whom they were cast. Charles Evans Hughes in 1916, for instance, carried Minnesota by a popular plurality of only 359, but received all twelve of that state's electoral votes. A large part of those electoral votes were made possible by thousands of Minnesotans who voted against Hughes. On a national scale, John W. Davis received six million popular votes in 1924 which earned him no electoral votes at all—or in reality were transferred to the use of his rival, Calvin Coolidge—while two million others brought him 136 electoral votes.

The general ticket system's rough handling of minority popular votes extravagantly favors the large states. The pluralities of the eleven largest states control 264 electoral votes. If these plus one other state should vote for a single candidate, he would be elected regardless of the strength of his opposition in those states and in the remaining thirty-eight states. The general ticket system, this is to say, enables the popular voter in the large states to participate in the choice of a larger number of electors than the voter of a small state. In 1960 a popular voter in New York shared in the choice of 45 electors, and in Nevada only three. The candidate of the popular majority of the nation is far from certain to prevail in an electoral college where the representation of each state is not that of its people but of its plurality. The likelihood of minority Presidents will surely increase in our present era of close Presidential elections.

The general ticket system wreaks other distortions. It prods parties into seeking out their candidates in big states such as New York and Ohio, while ignoring the small states, whose sons may be equally talented. The general ticket system has also encouraged the historic one-party solid South. The Republican party, faced with a hopeless minority position, for years maintained no serious organization in those states. The general ticket system also causes party campaigning to be concentrated in doubtful states and in large states. New York, Ohio, and Illinois are regularly showered with relatively more campaign dollars and rhetorical fervor than states such as Maine, Nevada, or Georgia, which are safe or small. In 1960 Kennedy was hailed for his political wisdom in concentrating on the large industrial states.

The general ticket system is also attacked for grossly inflating the bargaining power of pressure groups and minority parties in large doubtful states. A well-organized national, racial, religious, or economic group whose votes are concentrated upon a Presidential candidate can more powerfully exact his commitment if the group is situated in a large state.

Defenders of the existing electoral system argue that its distortions serve the cause of social justice, that it enables smaller masses of people to strike bargains that unshackle their oppressions. A more perfect system, presumably, would afford fewer liberating opportunities. Yet a standard which judges the quality of the electoral system in terms of whether the bargains struck are good or bad is of dubious merit. Wilmerding argues in *The Electoral College*,

> If the President is to be the man of the people, if all the people are to stand on the same footing, equal masses of people must be given equal votes, equal bargaining power. Their weight in the electoral count must be proportional to their numbers and not to the rightness or wrongness of their causes.

The pretension of distinguishing good groups from bad and of assigning greater electoral weight to the former than to the latter cannot be justified in democratic theory, nor can it long be asserted satisfactorily in practice.

◇

HARDLY a session of Congress passes when legislators, distressed by the flaws of the electoral college system, do not introduce proposals, embodied in drafts of Constitutional amendments, to reform it. Although differing in detail, the proposals that perennially appear can be grouped into several broad categories:

A national popular vote. The President would be chosen by the majority of the national popular vote. Electors and electoral votes would be tossed upon the political scrap heap. In the Senate William Langer of North Dakota, Herbert H. Lehman of New York, and Hubert Humphrey of Minnesota each at one time or another advocated election by national popular majority. Individual plans differ for the eventuality that no candidate wins a popular majority. Some would permit a plurality to elect; others would hold a run-off election limited to the two or three candidates polling the highest initial vote. Still others would throw the election into the House of Representatives, with each member having one vote.

The plan of national popular election offers powerful attractions. It is the only plan extant that assures against the election of a President receiving fewer votes than his opponent. Every voter, be he a New Yorker or a Nevadan, would have one vote of equal weight. Majoritarian democracy would be cleanly applied, in which 51 per cent and above would rule. The several evils of the general ticket system would be banished in one fell sweep. The principle of Presidential selection would be national rather than federative; minority votes of states would at least be counted; large states would be barred from consolidating their votes to the disadvantage of the small. The power of pressure groups and minor parties would be more nearly proportionate to their numbers. Political activity in "safe" states would rise and be meaningful.

But the national popular vote, for all of its advantages, carries several formidable defects. It would jeopardize our two-party system by encouraging minor parties by giving them a weight in the national popular vote which they lack in the electoral college system. It violates the federal principle by redistributing political power between the states. The proposal would shift power from the smaller to the larger states, from the South to the North, East, and West; from states that are politically passive to those politically active. It is inconceivable that states standing to lose will ever rally behind the Constitutional amendment necessary to establish it. This stumbling block might possibly be avoided if the amendment incorporating it were voted on by state conventions, which presumably would be less sensitive to vested political interest than the state legislatures.

Proportional voting.   The leading modern advocate of this century-old plan is Henry Cabot Lodge, who while Senator, and with Congressman Ed Gossett of Texas as co-sponsor, incorporated it into a Constitutional amendment in 1950. In 1963 its champions included Senators George Smathers, Thomas Kuchel, and Leverett Saltonstall. Under the plan, which has many variations, each candidate who polled a fraction of a state's popular votes would win the same fraction of its electoral votes. The candidate's national electoral vote would be the sum of his electoral votes in all fifty states. The President would continue to be chosen by electoral, not popular, votes. Forty per cent of the entire electoral vote would be necessary for election. Otherwise the contest would be decided between the two highest candidates by the House and Senate jointly, with each member having one vote. The state legislatures would lose their present freedom to decide the methods of choosing electors and of voting.

Former Senator Lodge and his fellow advocates contend that their plan is "fair, accurate, and democratic." The minority popular vote in each state would be accurately reflected in the electoral vote. The plan would abolish the evil of the one-party state and diminish the disproportionate influence of local pressure groups and the dread possibility that a candidate with a minority of the popular vote will win a majority of the electoral vote. The plan harmonizes with the federal structure by preserving the interests of the small states.

Proportional voting has heavy disadvantages. It would encourage the development of minor parties and would in time weaken or destroy the two-party system. The Presidential constituency would cease to be primarily geographical and would become, instead, primarily mathematical or ideological. Groups rather than areas would be the focus of appeal. The geographical constituency encourages the candidate to be moderate in view and balanced in appeal to its diverse groups. To win an ideological constituency, the candidate must tend to extremes and subordinate himself to its special purposes. Proportional voting would increase rather than reduce the danger of electing minority Presidents. If, for example, proportional voting rather than the present electoral system had operated in the elections of 1880 and 1896, their outcomes would have been reversed. In 1880 James A. Garfield received more popular votes than Winfield Scott Hancock, and in 1896 McKinley more than Bryan. The Lodge-Gossett formula, however, would have converted Hancock and Bryan from losers into victors.

The single-member district system. Modern critics have revived interest in the single-member district system, beloved by Madison and other Founding Fathers. Its contemporary sponsors include Senators Barry Goldwater, Storm Thurmond, and Thruston Morton and Congressman Thomas Hale Boggs. Each state would be divided by the state legislature into districts equal to the number of Representatives the state is entitled to in Congress. In addition, two electors would be chosen from the state at large. Ideally, the districts would comprise contiguous and compact territory and, as nearly as possible, equal numbers of inhabitants. Each district's voters would choose one elector. (Ideally, also, the electoral college districts might comprise the districts of the House of Representatives.) The candidate winning a majority of the electoral votes (some proposals require only 40 per cent) would be deemed elected. If no candidate qualified, the House and Senate would jointly choose the President.

Like other proposals, the district system would take the method of electing the President out of the hands of the state legislatures and more nearly make the President the man of the people. It would end the power of large states, or their dominant party, to override the dominant party in the country at large. It would hamper minor parties and pressure groups in doubtful states from defeating, for their own ends, the will of the nation. Finally, it would force the parties to lift their eyes beyond the big states and into the country at large in their quest for candidates.

The district system has several forbidding weaknesses. It is vulnerable to the gerrymander. Its champions face the gerrymander evil by incorporating into their proposed Constitutional amendment precise standards concerning population and territory, by which districts would be made up. These the courts presumably would enforce. The districts still would not be equal in each state; large states would have districts with more populous constituencies than small states. Worst of all, the district plan would probably convert the present system, by which the American people engage in a national act focused upon national problems, into a series of petty campaigns in local districts. The district system would encourage minor parties by giving them a stronger opportunity to choose an elector in a district than the traditional system permits in a state. In a close election, a minor party might hold the balance in the national tally of electors. The district system would decrease the power of Northern Democrats, for they would be unable to count for themselves the votes cast against them by Republican minorities. Northern Democrats would be driven to rely increasingly upon Southern votes. (This would also be the case with the national popular vote and proportional voting proposals.)

The mixture of advantage and blemish has prevented any one of these plans—whether national popular selection, proportional voting, or the district system—from seriously challenging the traditional electoral college electoral-vote structure. Barring a national electoral disaster, the country will doubtless jog along with what it has. Two other proposals, more modest in nature and clear-cut in merit, have been advanced, but these too will stir no action, except possibly in disaster.

Altering the procedures of the House of Representatives. The Twelfth Amendment specifies that if no candidate receives a majority of the electoral votes, the House of Representatives, voting by states, shall immediately choose the President by ballot "from the persons having the highest numbers not exceeding three on the list of those voted for as President." A majority of all the states is necessary for election. The present system of a single vote for each state is unjust in making one Representative from Nevada equal to forty-three Representatives from New York.

Critics from George Mason to Henry Cabot Lodge would avoid the House altogether simply by making the candidate with the greatest number of electoral votes the victor. Most proposals would have the Representatives vote by heads rather than by states, patently a fairer procedure. Still others would have the Senate and House sit jointly and vote by heads. Including the Senate would be a sop to the small states, who would lose strength if the House shifted from voting by the states as units to voting by heads.

Keeping the electoral vote, but dropping the electors. In 1801 Jefferson wrote to Albert Gallatin of an "amendment which I know will be proposed, to wit, to have no electors, but let the people vote directly, and the ticket which has a plurality of the votes of any state to be considered as receiving the whole vote of the state." Senators George Norris in 1934 and John Kennedy in 1957 proposed similar amendments geared to the general ticket system. The accompanying argument is undeniable. If the elector is faithful to the popular vote, he is useless; if he is not, he is dangerous.

◊

IN THE interest of strengthening the Presidency, several innovations might advantageously be made in its selection procedures.

1. We ought, at the very least, to abolish the electoral college, which is a standing invitation to trouble that may materialize sooner than we think. In our present era of close national elections, it would be possible for electors in certain states to tip the balance of a final outcome by voting contrary to the popular vote. Even if we abolished the college, we could retain the electoral vote, which should automatically reflect the plurality of the popular vote.

2. We ought to review periodically the question of whether we might advantageously abandon both the electoral college and the electoral vote and substitute a plan for selecting the President on the basis of a national popular vote.

A national popular vote is most in accord with democratic principle. It would apply a standard of absolute fairness of "one American, one vote," which is badly violated by the present system. It would avoid the several distortions of the general ticket method and the dread possibility, under the present electoral vote system, that the candidate winning a national popular majority will not prevail because he does not command a majority of the electoral votes.

A serious drawback of the national popular vote plan is the possible necessity of a run-off election. But this is better in the bargain than the present danger that the popular vote winner will lose in the electoral college. The difficulty of winning approval from the small states for a necessary Constitutional amendment to install the plan might be overcome if ratification were by state conventions rather than by state legislatures. There is an additional difficulty which to this writer makes prohibitive the adoption of the national vote system now. The system would encourage minor parties by affording them a recognition in the national popular vote which they do not have in the present electoral vote. The fact that their votes would count under the national popular vote plan would induce them to extend themselves nationally. Such a development would further weaken our already much too weak major parties. But if the new Conservative party makes substantial inroads into the Republican party, and if Governor George C. Wallace of Alabama and others succeed in installing in individual states a plan of unpledged electors, who presumably would vote for a local "Dixiecrat" Presidential candidate—if our major parties suffer these and other deteriorations on a growing scale in the future, then we ought to consider all the more seriously the adoption of a plan of national popular election.

3. When the House of Representatives is called upon to choose a President, it should vote by heads rather than by states. A vote by heads clearly would better approximate the popular vote than the existing system. Best of all would be a combined Senate-House vote by heads, since Senators are chosen by the states at large and therefore reflect state-wide opinion. For similar reasons the Senate and House, voting by heads, should also choose the Vice President if the electoral college fails to do so.

4. The assassination of President Kennedy should teach us for all time that the only valid criterion for choosing a Vice Presidential candidate is his suitability for the Presidency. The folly of the traditional formula of "balancing the ticket"—the North-South tandem of the Democrats and East-West one of the Republicans—is exposed by the stark statistic that four out of our ten Presidents in the twentieth century were brought into the highest office from the Vice Presidency by the death of the President.

5. The recommendations of the 1962 report of the President's Commission on Campaign Costs, aimed at broadening financial contributions to Presidential and other election campaigns, should be furthered, particularly the proposals to encourage large numbers of small gifts. This, of course, is in the interests of promoting a healthier, more democratic situation than the present arrangement, where the bulk of Presidential campaign funds available to both parties is supplied by a relatively small group of contributors.

6. Although television debates between the Presidential candidates are not without flaw, it is inconceivable that they should be discarded after their importance in the 1960 elections. The method and form of the debates can be improved so that they deal better with issues and enhance the nation's opportunities for estimating the candidates. In an era of public relations slickness that is moving rapidly into the political arena, the television debates are a strong antidote, affording the nation a better view of the real candidate than it would get in any other way.

CHAPTER

4

Tenure

═══

TENURE is power. Whether the Presidency is a center of energy and direction or of weakness and futility will depend in part on whether the President has long to serve and whether he is eligible for re-election. The Founding Fathers, aware of the importance of tenure to the strong executive, debated the President's term and his re-eligibility long and anxiously. The most formidable attacks upon the office since then have concentrated upon the same question. The worst assault—the impeachment trial of Andrew Johnson—was at bottom a question of tenure. In 1951 those who could not abide the Presidency's swift enlargement of power and function during the thirties and forties also struck at the conditions of tenure, inserting into the Constitution the Twenty-Second Amendment, limiting the Presidential incumbent to two terms.

The Founding Fathers' anxiety about the President's term of office was reflected in their adoption at successive junctures of a term first of seven, then of six, and finally of four years. If Congress chose the President, as many favored, a long term without eligibility for re-election seemed best, because a President otherwise might become a Congressional yes-man in courting re-election. But once the electoral college system had been adopted, a shorter term with unlimited eligibility was agreed upon.

The Founding Fathers expected that George Washington would become the first President and would willingly serve the rest of his days. Their acceptance of the principle of indefinite eligibility ran counter to another American political principle deeply ingrained since Revolutionary times, when George III was regarded as the symbol of monarchical tyranny: that rotation in executive office is essential to liberty.

The principle of unlimited eligibility for re-election was innocently but irreparably undermined in practice by the man in whose behalf it had been established, George Washington himself. Washington announced upon completing his second Presidential term that it was his personal wish not to serve another. Thomas Jefferson brought the weakened principle crashing to the ground when, after admiring state legislatures earnestly asked him to continue for a third term, he declared he would not. If there were no limitation on office, understood if not required, he said, the office would be held "for life" and would degenerate "into an inheritance." "Truth also requires me to add," Jefferson continued, "that I am sensible of that decline which advancing years bring on, and feeling their physical I ought not to doubt their mental effect." By the Civil War, Presidential observance had established the two-term principle in the core of American political doctrine.

The two-term practice has occasionally been under siege, however. One assault is the proposal that a President be limited to a single term. Such a doctrine was preached, for example—though certainly not practiced—by Andrew Jackson. And as late as 1912 the Democratic platform endorsed a single Presidential term, a pledge that its nominee, Woodrow Wilson, quickly repudiated. This was by no means the last to be heard of the subject. Dwight D. Eisenhower, both before and after assuming office, found the notion intriguing. Convinced that he could establish in a span of four years his cherished concepts of moderate government, a free economy, and a balanced budget and mindful of his own advanced years, he proposed to hand over the reins after a single term to a younger man. Eisenhower came within an eyelash of incorporating this proposal into his first inaugural address. At the last minute he was talked out of it, but as his term wore on he often reverted to it in private conversation.

A second major assault upon the two-term principle has been leveled by the President who seeks a third or even a fourth term. Although Franklin Roosevelt alone triumphed over the two-term limitation by exceeding it, he was far from the first to try. In the decades between Lincoln and Franklin D. Roosevelt, there was seldom a period when the third-term fever did not seize the chief executive. So menacing in fact did the third-term boom of Ulysses S. Grant become in 1875 that the House of Representatives felt duty-driven to resolve, by a vote of 234 to 18, that departure from the two-term tradition would be "unwise, unpatriotic and fraught with peril to our free institutions." Theodore Roosevelt, like Grant before him and Calvin Coolidge at a later day, took the pragmatic view that the two-term limitation applied only to a third consecutive term. He had sworn fealty to the two-term custom in the exuberance of his elec-

toral victory of 1904, a pledge his foes gleefully recalled when he entered
the Presidential race of 1912. But Roosevelt was a supreme rationalizer
and saw no contradiction between his words in 1904 and his actions in
1912. If he were to decline "a third cup of coffee," he explained, no one
would suppose he meant never to take another cup. By his 1904 pledge,
he said, "I meant, of course, a third consecutive term."

Franklin D. Roosevelt's distinction in achieving re-election to a third
and a fourth term was prevented by the Twenty-Second Amendment from
becoming more than a personal triumph. The amendment inscribes in
the nation's fundamental law the prohibition, "No person shall be elected
to the office of the President more than twice." For anyone like Ulysses S.
Grant, who after two terms and an interlude of retirement strains to
possess the office a third time, the amendment would provide a clear and
unequivocal negative. It imposes permanent ineligibility upon anyone
who has occupied the Presidency for the allotted two terms. For Presidents
like Theodore Roosevelt and Calvin Coolidge, whose incumbencies
stretched across a full and a partial term, the amendment is too clear to be
misinterpreted: "No person who has held the office of President, or acted
as President, for more than two years of a term to which some other person was elected President shall be elected to the office of the President
more than once." Admirers of former President Eisenhower, the first
casualty of the amendment, concluded after reading its text that he could
well be restored as chief executive by the route of succession after first
being elected as Vice President.

The Twenty-Second Amendment demonstrates how vulnerable the
Presidency is to stealthy emasculation by amendment. For all of its controversial character, the amendment emerged from the House of Representatives with but a single day's debate. Its four-year journey through
the state legislatures stirred a minimum of public discussion. Only by un-
tiring alertness could the diligent citizen keep up with the amendment's
progress, disclosed in microscopic news items in the back pages of the
New York *Times*. And if he read another paper even diligence would have
been unrewarded.

The Constitution provides that amendments be ratified either by state
legislatures or by special state conventions. Backers of the Twenty-Second
Amendment skillfully avoided action by state conventions—conventions
would be more closely attuned to popular opinion than the legislatures.
From the voters' repudiation of the two-term tradition by electing Roosevelt to third and fourth terms it was clear that popular opinion could not
be trusted. In sending the amendment to the state legislatures, moreover,
Congress was relying upon bodies endowed with impressive experience
in trammeling executive authority. Curbing the terms of chief executives
is old hat to state legislatures. In fourteen states governors can serve only

one term, and in six states not more than two. Of the thirty that remain, all but five that permitted their own governors to serve without limitation recoiled from according the same privilege to the President. New York and California, for example, voted for limitation of the tenure of the Presidency at a time when they had as their governors Thomas E. Dewey and Earl Warren (the Republican national ticket in 1948), both of whom were to be re-elected for third consecutive four-year gubernatorial terms in 1950.

The Twenty-Second Amendment is a mixture of political motivations, partisan and personal. It was a posthumous revenge against Franklin Roosevelt for breaking the two-term tradition. It was a desperate attempt to push back the rushing flood of executive authority. It was a psychological release for legislators who find joy in curbing the executive. And to the career politician it was an assurance that the foremost prize of American politics would be available at regular intervals.

The amendment also instills certain weaknesses into the office of the Presidency, however. It can gravely weaken the President's influence during the entire span of his second, and final, term. In 1957, the first year of Eisenhower's second term, the President was hampered by a noticeable weakening of his grip on Republican legislators and a softening of his hitherto staunch support from the press and business. Yet Eisenhower had been returned to power only a year earlier with a fresh and overwhelming mandate. Even worse is the amendment's potential mischief in a foreign affairs crisis. The nation could conceivably be deep in war, or on the brink of it, when the tenure of its chief executive was suddenly cut off. The amendment would require the nation to violate that wise old adage warning against changing horses in midstream. The electorate would be wrenched into choosing new leadership at a time when national unity was imperative, deprived of a chief executive whose experience and knowledge of the ongoing crisis could not be duplicated. The crisis of war kept Franklin Roosevelt in office because the electorate concluded that the continuity of leadership and policy could not be safely shattered midway without peril. Had the Twenty-Second Amendment then been in force, Roosevelt would automatically have been disbarred and new leadership imposed contrary to the electorate's judgment. The Twenty-Second Amendment, whatever may be said in its favor, is antidemocratic in spirit, a frustration of the will of the people out of fear that the people might choose unwisely.

◇

THE Presidential tenure can be interrupted not only by restriction on re-election but by other means—resignation, for example, a means for which the Constitution provides. No President has ever resigned, but

Woodrow Wilson came closest of all to committing that final act of voluntary separation. An admiring student of British governmental practice, which turns upon the Prime Minister's periodic resignation to seek a vote of public confidence for his party, Wilson twice as President contemplated resigning. If his rival in the 1916 Presidential race, Charles Evans Hughes, had won, he proposed to resign to avoid a lame-duck Presidency in the midst of world crisis. His plan was first to ask his Secretary of State, Robert Lansing, to resign so he could appoint President-elect Hughes as his successor. Thereupon President Wilson and Vice President Marshall would both resign, permitting Hughes's ascent to the Presidency under the existing succession law. Wilson's electoral victory rendered the novel plan unnecessary. In a later crisis, the fight for the Versailles peace treaty in 1919, Wilson briefly weighed the tactic of resigning and then immediately running again in a special Presidential election permitted by the Succession Act of 1886 then in force. His election presumably would have expressed a national desire for membership in the League and sustained confidence in him. Wilson dropped this plan. The approaching elections of 1920 seemed to him to promise to be "a great and solemn" referendum on the treaty. In 1946, following the Congressional elections in which the Democrats lost control of Congress for the first time in sixteen years, Senator J. William Fulbright of Arkansas, presumably in a spirit of helpfulness, proposed that President Truman resign. Truman rejected the suggestion crustily and marched on to reelection in 1948 and the restoration of full Democratic control of Congress.

The President can also leave office involuntarily. If he can be "hired," he can also be fired, for causes enumerated in Article II of the Constitution: "treason, bribery, or other high crimes and misdemeanors." Imitating existing state constitutions, the Founding Fathers empowered the House of Representatives to impeach the President, and the Senate, sitting as a law court, with the Chief Justice of the United States presiding, to conduct the trial. A two-thirds vote of the Senators present is necessary for conviction. The penalties the Constitution brings down upon the convicted President are removal from office, disqualification for further office, and liability to "indictment, trial, judgment, and punishment, according to law." Although the introduction of impeachment resolutions is a favorite indulgence of Congressmen embittered by the spectacle of activist Presidents, only once has the necessary support developed. Andrew Johnson enjoys distinction as the only President who has walked the impeachment gangplank. Far more important, he, and the Presidency with him, came out of it alive. By a single vote Johnson missed conviction and the Presidency was spared.

Johnson's impeachment is memorable not merely as supreme drama but as an enduring object lesson to those who, seeking to improve the American governmental system, propose to link Congress more intimately with the Presidency when, for instance, Presidential disability may be in question. Some would trust Congress to determine the factual question of whether the President is able to carry on the duties of his office. The Johnson case demonstrates the capacity of legislators to convert a solemn judicial function into what Gideon Welles, Johnson's Secretary of the Navy, termed "a deed of extreme partisanship."

The impeachment was built upon the rotten foundation of the Tenure of Office Act of 1867, which denied the President the right to remove civil officials, including members of his cabinet, without Senatorial consent. Presidents had been removing cabinet secretaries since the days of Washington. By the Act of 1867 Congress was contravening precedent and stripping Johnson of control of his administration. Convinced that the Tenure Act was unconstitutional, Johnson requested and then ordered Secretary of War Edwin M. Stanton to resign, and appointed General Lorenzo Thomas his successor. When Thomas appeared at the War Department, Stanton barricaded himself behind his office door.

On February 28, 1868, the House voted to impeach the President for "high crimes and misdemeanors." Eleven articles of impeachment were drawn, ten centering upon Stanton's removal. The remaining article, contrived from garbled newspaper accounts of the President's speeches, charged, among other things, that he used unseemly language and spoke in a loud voice. Johnson meanwhile expected to knock the props from under the impeachment proceedings by obtaining a ruling from the Supreme Court endorsing his views on the Tenure of Office law. But the court, in a spasm of "judicial restraint," declined to act.

The ensuing impeachment enterprise reeked with self-serving politics. If Johnson were convicted and deposed, the new President of the United States, owing to the Vice Presidential vacancy and the line of succession in the applicable law of 1792, would be Ben Wade of Ohio, the vulgar and vituperative president pro tem of the Senate. When Wade's participation in the trial was objected to because of his not inconsiderable personal stake, the Senator replied with simple finality that he saw nothing wrong with serving as a judge. He would do impartial justice, he said, and was sworn. Chief Justice Salmon P. Chase, who presided, also wanted to be President, having a craving for the office that Lincoln once likened to insanity. By day Chase conducted the trial and by night he wrote letters building his claim upon the next Democratic Presidential nomination. That the trial would ooze with low politics was instantly apparent when after the President's counsel requested forty days to prepare their case, with its numerous intricacies of law and fact, they were permitted ten.

The trial itself was a garish extravaganza lasting eleven and a half weeks. The thousand tickets printed for each day, and valid only for that day, were furiously competed for. Diplomats and Senators' wives and daughters, blooming with finery, crammed the galleries, along with scores of reporters, including Anthony Trollope, the distinguished novelist, who came from Britain to cover the proceedings, and Henry Adams, who described the scene as a national nightmare of unspeakable crudity.

Of forty-one witnesses, only sixteen appeared for the defense. Johnson proposed to testify in his own behalf, but in view of his tendency to outlandish statement, was fortunately dissuaded. The Chief Justice, empowered within narrowly defined limits to rule on points of law, heroically put political ambition aside and rose to the full height of his responsibilities. According to the Senate rules specially adopted for the trial, if one Senator objected to the Chief Justice's holding, the matter was voted by the entire body. The Chief Justice was overruled seventeen times, the overwhelming number of instances suppressing evidence favorable to the President.

President Johnson, for all of his reputation for wild epithet and the big blunder, was a model of decorum. He bore patiently the lengthy conferences with his counsel on tactics and fine points of fact and law. At night he read books on immortality and Joseph Addison's dramatization of the last days of Cato the Younger, who chose to die by his own hand rather than submit to Julius Caesar's dictation. At Johnson's direction, a White House secretary researched the trial and execution of Charles I of England. The President's chief act of self-assertion lay in putting his case before the people in interviews with several friendly reporters. Said the President,

> Suppose Congress should pass a bill abolishing the veto power. . . . Suppose it should pass a dozen bills of this character—would the President be constitutionally bound to execute them as laws? Would it not be his duty, as in the present instance, to seek immediately judgment in the Supreme Court?

When the President was told that the Radicals were not above using money to obtain his conviction, and that perhaps he, too, should stoop to that expedient, he refused.

The Radicals indeed were desperate. The vote on Article XI, the first impeachment article to be disposed of, fell short of the two-thirds majority necessary for conviction. To revive their wilting plot, the Radicals maneuvered the Senate into an adjournment of ten days for the known but carefully unacknowledged purpose of lining up votes for Johnson's conviction. The adjournment occurred only after the Chief Justice's ruling against it was overridden. During the ten-day interlude a massive machinery of pressures and intrigue was unloosed upon Senators who were still on the fence or who conceivably might be lured or bullied into abandoning Johnson and voting for his conviction. After some days of effort the machinators discovered from their tally sheets that the issue's outcome turned upon the vote of Edmund G. Ross, a Radical soldier-journalist of Kansas who was believed to oppose Johnson. To make certain, the Radicals swung their cannonade full-square upon the Senator. The low character of their pressures led Ross to see through the Radicals' flimsy case. But the dread consequences of resisting it gave him pause. "Almost literally," he wrote of his moment of truth, he was looking down into his "open grave." "Friends, position, fortune, everything that makes life desirable to an ambitious man," he said, "were about to be swept away by the breath of my mouth, perhaps forever." Ross's tough moral fiber ultimately prevailed. He voted for Johnson and the Presidency was saved. Senator Lyman Trumbull, who also sided with the President, captured the significance of the lamentable episode in explaining his vote:

> Once set the example of impeaching a President for what, when the excitement of the hour shall have subsided, will be regarded as insufficient cause, and no future President will be safe who happens to differ with the majority of the House and two-thirds of the Senate on any measure deemed by them important, particularly if of a political character.

◇

THE President, as the Constitution anticipates and history demonstrates, may on occasion fall victim to crushing illness or to death. Seven Presidents (one out of five) have died in office, four by assassination. A sick President may be unable to discharge the duties of his office. According to Richard Hansen's computations, the cumulative periods of actual Presidential inability add up to a full year in which the country was "without a President." Such periods unfortunately occurred during difficult times, when large issues demanded the chief executive's full vigor and skill.

The Constitutional language concerning inability is a quagmire of ambiguity. Article II reads,

> In case of [the President's] inability to discharge the powers and duties of the said office, the same shall devolve on the Vice President, and the Congress may by law provide for the case of . . . inability, both of the President and Vice President, declaring what officer shall then act as President, and such officer shall act accordingly, until the disability be removed or a President shall be elected.

Neither here nor elsewhere in the Constitution are these questions answered: Who is authorized to say whether a President is unable to discharge the powers and duties of his office? If he is unable, does the office become vacant? To what does the Vice President succeed when the President is disabled—to the "powers and duties of the said office" or to the office itself? What is the election referred to—the next regular Presidential election or a special election called by Congress?

Twice in American experience Presidents have been incapacitated for extended periods. President Garfield lay stricken after July 2, 1881, when he was shot just before leaving Washington by train for a class reunion at Williams College. The assassin's bullet struck a vertebra of his spinal column and became deeply embedded in the muscles of his back. The White House was converted into a hospital, and fans in the President's sickroom blew cool breezes over ice cubes to provide relief from the capital's broiling summer. Garfield was expected to die shortly; great crowds gathered across the land at telegraph and newspaper offices, waiting for the news and hoping and praying that Mrs. Garfield, who was away from Washington, would reach her husband before the end.

The President, a large, rugged man who faced his ordeal with unflagging heroism, rallied through most of July. In August he passed through cycles of decline and improvement. Despite several surgical probes, the President's doctors failed to locate the bullet. Alexander Graham Bell assisted in the vain search by devising a special detecting electrical device. Meanwhile the wound became infected and the bullet encysted. As the President's fever rose and fell, his great form wasted and his strength ebbed. On September 6 he was transported by rail with maximum precautions to Elberon on the New Jersey coast, where it was hoped the sea air would by some miracle rally him. But his strength only dwindled and in a few days he died.

During his entire illness, President Garfield committed only one official act. He signed an extradition paper, prepared in the State Department, after a physician read it aloud. He saw only Mrs. Garfield and his doctors and had no visitors except one day at Elberon, when members of his cabinet filed in for brief interviews. The President had been fretting over the lapse of cabinet meetings, and by prearrangement the secretaries assured him that all was well and nothing required his attention.

In reality this was not so. The Star Route frauds, inherited from the previous Hayes administration, still bedeviled the Post Office Department, and the gush of illicit dollars from the United States Treasury into corrupt hands continued. The President's isolation brought to a standstill Secretary of State James G. Blaine's effort to modify the existing Clayton-Bulwer treaty in the interest of the proposed Nicaraguan canal. (Blaine's ultimate purpose in this complex maneuver was to establish an isthmian canal under United States control.) A conference of American republics the President had called was postponed.

As the neglected problems accumulated, demands spiraled in the press, in Congress, and among the cabinet that Vice President Arthur take over the duties of the incapacitated President. The cabinet, which was most distressed by the ravages of neglect, earnestly discussed the Vice President's possible assumption of Presidential authority, a prospect that repelled them. Agitated meetings in the secretaries' offices and homes quickly revealed disagreement on a thorny issue of Constitutional interpretation. Four of the seven secretaries believed that Arthur's exercise of Presidential power would make him President for the remainder of the existing term and would immediately and permanently oust Garfield from the office. The Attorney General, Wayne MacVeagh, the chief law interpreter of the executive branch, reportedly took this view. A minority of the secretaries held that Arthur could occupy the Presidency only for the duration of Garfield's illness, and that the latter, upon his recovery, would resume the office. In time the cabinet concluded that since the decision was of such large consequence, it ought to be discussed with the President first. But as the President's condition worsened, the consultation was deferred in the fear that its shock might speed his death.

Legalistic interpretation was not the only bond joining those in the cabinet in opposition to the Vice President's assumption of Presidential duties. Arthur, in their view, belonged to a low order of politicians—the "Stalwart" Republicans—who had fought Garfield with waspish oratory and savage deed ever since the onset of his Presidency. Indeed Stalwart rancor had inflamed the President's crazed assassin, who shouted in emptying his pistol, "I am a Stalwart and now Arthur is President!" Arthur was not helped either by his friendship with the notorious Roscoe Conkling, the Stalwart leader, upon whose advice he was known to depend. Should Arthur become President, it was feared, Conkling would come along too.

Chester Arthur, for his part, was facing the question of his assumption of the Presidency with characteristic prudence. He stayed out of public view, dodged the press, and remained in New York as much as possible. When on occasion he had to venture to Washington, he avoided his own residence and found seclusion in the home of his friend Senator John P. Jones of Nevada. The most painful element in Arthur's situation was the cold suspicion with which the President's friends beheld him. Arthur felt the full bite of the frosty atmosphere when he called one night at the White House, shortly after the attack, as a courteous demonstration of concern for the stricken President. The Vice President was ushered to an office where the full cabinet sat gathered in vigil. He paused uncertainly in the doorway, waiting for an invitation to enter. None came; no one moved to greet him. The cabinet stared with unanimous hostility. Arthur was about to withdraw in painful confusion when another visitor who came along greeted him cordially and drew him into the room. Several cabinet secretaries then extended the Vice President the minimum amenities.

For all of their revulsion toward Arthur, the cabinet in the later days of Garfield's illness again considered the question of the Vice President's succession. To the harried secretaries the mounting pile of neglected problems left no choice. Postmaster General Thomas L. James was dispatched to New York to ascertain Arthur's views. The Vice President's answer was swift and categorical. Under no circumstances would he assume the responsibilities of the Presidency while Garfield was alive. The Vice President held to his point and public problems drifted. Not until his own formal investiture in the Presidency after Garfield's death did Arthur touch the power of the office.

The other occasion of extended Presidential incapacity occurred during the second administration of Woodrow Wilson, at a time immeasurably more serious than Garfield's. During the ailing Wilson's taxing western trip in September 1919, to rally the people behind the League of Nations, the President collapsed and was rushed back by train to Washington. Conflicting versions persist of the onset of the President's illness. One, by Mrs. Wilson and Rear Admiral Cary T. Grayson, the President's physician, contends that Wilson "collapsed" in the west, returned to Washington, and three days later suffered a stroke described by Mrs. Wilson as "paralyzing the left side of his body. An arm and one leg were useless." A contrasting version by Joe Tumulty, the President's trusted secretary, holds that the stroke occurred in Colorado, during the western journey. At 4 A.M. September 26 in Pueblo, where the Presidential train had stopped, Tumulty was aroused by a knock on the door of his sleeping compartment. It was Dr. Grayson with word that the President was seriously ill. Tumulty rushed to the train's drawing room where the President, fully dressed, was seated in a chair. Tumulty stood transfixed by the spectacle. "His face was pale and wan," the secretary later described it. "One side of it had fallen, and his condition was indeed pitiful to behold. . . . His left arm and leg refused to function. I then realized that the President's whole left side was paralyzed."

The White House was again transformed into a hospital. The President, who was not expected to live long, somehow clung to the edge of existence. Although his body was broken, his mind was clear. "Physically he was very weak," observed Grayson, "but mentally very alert." Meanwhile, the nation was caught up in the cumbrous transition from warmaking to peacemaking. The peace treaty, with its controversial League of Nations provision, was before the Senate at midcourse, where it faced the hostility of the President's archrival, Henry Cabot Lodge. On the autumn agenda were scheduled visits of European dignitaries with the President. Domestically the economy was demobilizing to peacetime footing. In the din and lash of public business, the President lay crippled, his true condition known only to his wife, his physician, and the little ring of medical specialists who surrounded him and desperately administered their skills. The President, in their general opinion, was hopelessly beyond recovery. A year and a half of his term stretched ahead. What was to be done?

Dr. Francis X. Dercum, the eminent nerve authority, spoke to Mrs. Wilson, "Madam, it is a grave situation, but I think you can solve it. Have everything come to you; weigh the importance of each matter, and see if it is possible by consultations with the respective heads of the Departments to solve them without the guidance of your husband. In this way you can save him a great deal. But always keep in mind that every time you take him a new anxiety or problem to excite him, you are turning a knife in an open wound. His nerves are crying out for rest, and any excitement is torture to him."

"Then," replied Mrs. Wilson, "had he better not resign, let Mr. Marshall [the Vice President] succeed to the Presidency and he himself get that complete rest that is so vital to his life?"

"No, not if you feel equal to what I suggested," Dr. Dercum said. "For Mr. Wilson to resign would have a bad effect on the country, and a serious effect on our patient."

The modus operandi suggested by Dr. Dercum was quickly instituted for the remainder of Wilson's term. Officials coming to the White House took up with Mrs. Wilson business that hitherto they had discussed with the President. The brave First Lady applied herself conscientiously to understanding the intricacies that poured upon her and to reporting them in as precise a language as possible to her husband. Mrs. Wilson said in describing her stewardship,

> I studied every paper, sent from the different Secretaries or Senators, and tried to digest and present in tabloid form the things that, despite my vigilance, had to go to the President. I, myself, never made a single decision regarding the disposition of public affairs. The only decision that was mine was what was important and what was not, and the *very* important decision of when to present matters to my husband.

Even the trusted Tumulty, the President's secretary, used to seeing his chief whenever he chose, bent to the new procedure. Colonel Edward M. House, the President's intimate adviser and confidant, was cut off from all access. He was not invited and never ventured to the White House; his several letters to the President were neither answered nor acknowledged. Only Mrs. Wilson and Dr. Grayson saw the President.

Somehow the public business limped forward. The hurdle of the State of the Union message, an annual and unalterable Constitutional requirement, was managed when cabinet secretaries, acting in accordance with the traditional procedure, submitted paragraphs reflecting their departmental concerns to the White House. There Tumulty received them and pursued further procedures for which no tradition existed. The Presidential secretary wove the paragraphs together into a single document of reasonable coherence. It was read to Wilson and, with a few changes, the President approved it. On his better days, the President read state papers or listened as Mrs. Wilson read. He signed documents and in bursts of strength dictated notes for Senator Hitchcock's guidance in the treaty fight.

But the President's dedicated helpers and his own valiant effort could not tame the mounting suspicion and unrest in the world outside. Colonel House reported that the cabinet secretaries, cut off from all direct contact with the President, were "greatly exercised over the President's inability to transact executive business." To House, Secretary of State Robert Lansing confided his suspicion that the President was not really writing the papers purporting to come from him. Senator Gilbert Hitchcock, curious and anxious for the President's guidance in the League fight, was permitted an interview of an hour and five minutes with Wilson. The stricken President was full of fight. "I am a sick man, lying in this bed, but I am going to debate this issue with these gentlemen," he said of his Senatorial obstructors, "in their respective states whenever they come up for reelection if I have breath enough in my body to carry on the fight." On December 4 the Senate, collectively overcome by curiosity, appointed Hitchcock and Albert B. Fall, soon destined for exposure in the muck of Teapot Dome, as a committee to inquire into the condition of the President. After a visit with Wilson, they reported publicly that his mind was clear and that he was recovering. The baseless and misleading character of the latter finding appalled Mrs. Wilson. Nor did the Senators' reassurances deter several sensational newspapers from contending that the President was tightly secluded because he was insane, or that he was dead and his death was being kept secret. Several Republican Senators, according to the New York *Times*, were studying Wilson's signature on Presidential communications to the upper chamber for the possibility of forgery. One of these Senators eventually declared that either two of the signatures under study were not Wilson's, or, if they were, he had been assisted in signing his name.

The cabinet secretary most concerned over the leaderless state of affairs was the head of the senior executive department, Secretary of State Robert Lansing. A responsible man of granitic integrity, he decided it was time to act. He arranged a private meeting with Presidential secretary Tumulty in the cabinet room. As diplomatically as possible, Lansing said he wished to suggest that in view of Wilson's incapacity the Vice President be called in to act in lieu of the President. To reinforce his suggestion, he cited the disability provisions of the Constitution. Tumulty was outraged at this seeming invitation to mutiny, and candidly vented his displeasure. Who, he asked, could authoritatively determine the fact of the President's disability? Those having the best information of it, answered Lansing—Dr. Grayson and Tumulty himself. Dr. Grayson, when he learned of the proposal, helped Tumulty to kill it quickly. If "anyone outside the White House," Tumulty warned Lansing, attempted to certify that the President was unable to carry on his duties, the President's physician and secretary would jointly repudiate the notion.

Tumulty's rebuff did not quiet Lansing's conscience, agonized by the drift of affairs. The Secretary of State tried another tactic. The cabinet, the President's chief body of counselors, had not met since the commencement of Wilson's illness. If the cabinet were to meet occasionally on its own initiative, Lansing reasoned, the country's confidence would be buoyed. He placed this new inspiration before his fellow secretaries. Their response was favorable, and Lansing as senior secretary began calling and holding meetings of his fellow department heads in his office. That Lansing took the venture seriously is attested by the fact that in the first four months of Wilson's illness twenty-one cabinet meetings were called. When Wilson ultimately learned of them, he promptly wrote to Lansing pointing out that under established Constitutional procedure only the President could convene the department heads into conference and no one but he and Congress was entitled to request their views, collectively or individually, on public questions. Wilson's letter blazed with implications than Lansing's resignation would not be unwelcome. It was quickly forthcoming.

Goaded by Lansing's initiative, Wilson rallied his feeble strength sufficiently some two months later to meet with the cabinet. It was a brief and sad affair. "The President looked old, worn, and haggard," Secretary of Agriculture David Houston said of the event. "It was enough to make one weep to look at him. One of his arms was useless. [In speaking] his jaw tended to drop on one side, or seemed to do so. His voice was very weak and strained. . . . He put up a brave front and spent several minutes cracking jokes." Several more cabinet meetings, each brief, were subsequently held, with Mrs. Wilson looking in regularly and signaling their close.

In contrast to the venturesome Lansing, Vice President Thomas R. Marshall was a study in monumental caution. He shrank from every suggestion that he take over any of Wilson's duties. The Vice President, according to the New York *Times*, said he would not act unless Wilson or the cabinet requested it, and then only at the express approval of both houses of Congress. When legislators proposed that a federal court writ be secured directing the Vice President to act as President, he retorted that he would "never do such a thing in a thousand years." The Vice President's instinctive caution was stiffened by ugly forebodings. If he acted as President, he told Ira E. Bennett, editor of the Washington *Post*, he would surely be assassinated and the country thrown "into civil war." In discussing the predicament with his secretary one day, the Vice President said, "I am not going to seize the place and then have Wilson—recovered —come around and say, 'Get off, you usurper.' " Marshall rode out the crisis by doing nothing, and history remembers him only for articulating an aspiration long since dashed by inflation, "What this country needs is a good five cent cigar."

In the spring of 1920 Wilson made some gain. He could sit in his wheel chair, in the White House garden or on the South Portico, dictate to a secretary, and take up business with Mrs. Wilson. But his improvement was only tentative. When James M. Cox and Franklin D. Roosevelt, the Democratic Presidential and Vice Presidential candidates of 1920, visited Wilson in the summer of that year, Roosevelt reported afterward that Wilson was unable to speak except to mumble a few broken words.

The several illnesses of Dwight D. Eisenhower, although fortunately less severe than those of his predecessors, stirred national and world concern. In 1955 President Eisenhower sustained a coronary thrombosis, in 1956 an ileitis attack and operation, and in 1957 a mild stroke. In his first and most serious illness the President was totally removed from governmental affairs for only four days, after which he initialed papers. Sixteen weeks passed, however, before the President resumed his normal workload. Scarcely had he returned to full duty when the second illness crashed upon him. Both illnesses combined left the President partially disabled for twenty-two weeks.

Eisenhower's first illness raised a question that was settled then and for his subsequent lesser illnesses. During the President's inability, full or partial, who should discharge his duties? Although the Constitution pointed to the Vice President, Richard M. Nixon, the smooth-working team of White House staff and department heads posed an alternative. So freely had Eisenhower delegated duties and authority to his aides since the outset of his administration that they could function almost autonomously in his absence forced by illness. The "team's" director was Sherman Adams, "the assistant to the President," widely viewed as general manager of the executive branch. Another member of large importance was James Hagerty, the administration's chief public relations officer, the press secretary, who stood high in the President's esteem.

Two days after the President's heart seizure, Hagerty touched off the issue of who acts for an incapacitated President by disclosing that he had asked the Acting Attorney General, William F. Rogers, "for an opinion on any action that might be necessary at any time for delegation of powers." The next day Vice President Nixon told the press, "It is quite clear, of course, that the Attorney General must give an interpretation as to how some technical details can be handled during the time the President is away. There are many legal problems involved." The Nixon-Hagerty statements were interpreted as faintly auguring a Vice Presidential takeover. Thereupon Sherman Adams arrived in Washington from a European sojourn and quickly dominated and recomposed the situation. He conferred with Nixon and Rogers. The discussion's outcome and Adams' mastery are disclosed in Rogers' statement to the press afterward that "It may not be necessary to make a formal delegation of powers." Thereafter Hagerty in press statements referred to Adams repeatedly as the President's "deputy" rather than the President's "assistant." "The announcements served to emphasize," noted the New York *Times*, "that the powers of the President still rested with General Eisenhower and no one else [and] that in the exercise of these powers, Mr. Adams, and not the Vice President, was the chief assistant to the President."

Under the emerging formula Adams and the department heads handled the regular operations of the executive branch. Nixon took on certain established, more or less ceremonial capacities. He made public addresses and appearances and presided at meetings of the cabinet and the National Security Council, as he had done during past Presidential absences. Press conferences with Hagerty were supplemented by occasional Nixon press conferences where high-level comment was indispensable.

The executive functioning was far smoother during Eisenhower's illnesses than during those of his predecessors. His administrative machinery displayed an impressive capacity for self-direction, and thanks largely to Vice President Nixon's exemplary restraint there were no struggles for power. Conducting business from his own office on Capitol Hill or by visits to the departments, he shunned the White House. His comments to the press were scrupulously noncommittal. He turned aside admonitions like Styles Bridges' "You are the constitutional second-in-command and you ought to assume the leadership. Don't let the White House clique take command."

Eisenhower's only incapacity of any duration, the heart attack, struck during a governmental lull. Congress was in recess, no international meetings or moves were afoot, public urgencies were few. In contrast, the third illness—the stroke—occurred during a critical period. The Russians had put their first Sputnik into orbit only a month before, and the prestige of America's military and technological might had become murkily suspect at home and abroad. A NATO meeting of heads of state was three weeks off. The early signs of the acute 1958 economic recession were visible. Executive-Congressional meetings to lay the coming year's legislative programs were due in two weeks. But the gathering crisis was confined by the President's quick recovery. The day following his stroke he met with aides, and on the second day he worked on executive business in his rooms. Two weeks later he was off to Paris for the NATO meetings.

◇

THE nation's several encounters with Presidential illness and its attendant Constitutional and administrative problems have stirred wide and thoughtful concern and some action. The committee hearings of Congressman Emanuel Celler in 1956 and Senator Kefauver in 1958 and 1963 tapped the thinking of public men and scholars, and Presidents Eisenhower, Kennedy, and Johnson were moved to institute special measures. Discussion and action are complicated by the multitude of proposals advanced and the dispersal of attention over several key questions.

1. What is inability? The Founding Fathers left the question unanswered in the Constitution, and wisely so. Inability encompasses literally dozens of conditions that defy exhaustive cataloguing. Professor Ruth Silva, the leading authority on the subject, concludes that the Constitution contemplates "any *de facto* inability, whatever the cause or the duration, if it occurs at a time when the urgency of public business requires executive action."

Inability is clearly not limited to physical illness, but extends to mental illness as well, and covers periods when the President is missing or captured in military operations. In an era of intercontinental missiles, when decisions on which national survival may turn must be taken in minutes, any definition of inability must be made carefully to include all contingencies. "The ever-present possibility of an attack on the United States was always hanging over us," Richard Nixon wrote of the brief period of Eisenhower's unavailability following his heart attack. "Would the President be well enough to make a decision? If not, who had the authority to push the button?" Or again, Eisenhower's ileitis seizure necessitated an operation at Walter Reed Hospital where the President was under anesthesia for two hours. "The country," Eisenhower commented afterward to Nixon, "was without a Chief Executive, the armed forces without a Commander-in-Chief."

2. Who determines inability? General agreement prevails that the President is constitutionally empowered to determine and proclaim his own inability. But what if the President refuses to proclaim it, or because of his physical or mental circumstances cannot? Although wide consensus exists that some other authority should make the finding, little agreement has been reached on its identity. A cloudburst of proposals has drenched the political landscape.

For their own administrations Presidents Eisenhower and Kennedy made special arrangements to answer the question of determination. On February 26, 1958, Eisenhower disclosed in outline, and five days later, under popular pressure, in detail, his "clear understanding" with the Vice President on inability. "In the event of inability, the President would—if possible—so inform the Vice President." If the President were prevented by inability from communicating with the Vice President, "the Vice President, after such consultation as seems to him appropriate under the circumstances, would decide." The Eisenhower plan was perpetuated in the Kennedy administration by the announcement on August 11, 1961, of an identical "agreement" between the President and Vice President Johnson.

Soon after his accession to the Presidency, Johnson reportedly concluded an agreement with Speaker John W. McCormack, next in line in the Presidential succession, with terms similar to those employed by Eisenhower and Kennedy. The fact of McCormack's membership in the House conceivably might create special difficulties in the event of Presidential disability. Since the Constitution would bar him from functioning simultaneously as President and as a member of the House, he could not become Acting President without resigning from the House. This would cause no problem if the President were disabled permanently or for a long time. If, however, the disability were fairly brief, McCormack would find himself resigning the Speakership and his House seat for the privilege of a brief tenure in the White House. When the tenure ended, his resignation from Congress could not be retracted.

The Eisenhower-Kennedy arrangement is a long stride forward that future Presidents will be wise to perpetuate. It leaves open-ended the question of whom the Vice President is to consult, permitting flexibility in response to the circumstances. The arrangement's gravest defect is its seeming inadequacy for those briefest interludes of Presidential inability that take on haunting importance in the nuclear age. If the President is incommunicado for hours or even minutes and an enemy threatens or strikes, who decides the response? If the President reposes on the operating table under anesthesia for an hour or two, if he is away from Washington and communication breaks down, even briefly—if during such interludes an enemy chooses to attack, what then? The Eisenhower-Kennedy agreement expects that the Vice President will "consult," but in reality the precious dwindling minutes will permit little, if any, time for consultation. The Eisenhower-Kennedy plan needs supplementary understandings—and these perhaps already exist—for sudden and gross contingencies.

Although Eisenhower and Kennedy confidently involved their Vice Presidents in findings of inability, an assortment of earnest Congressmen, lawyers, editors, and professors prefer to place the responsibility elsewhere in the government, and still others in flights of ingenuity would create special bodies to decide the momentous question. The principal alternatives, with something of their variations, are these:

The cabinet or the National Security Council by a simple or extraordinary majority of their members, and with or without the Vice President's approval. The cabinet, the argument goes, thanks to its daily contacts with the President, would be best informed of his plight. The department secretaries' deepest inclination would be to act loyally and fairly to the President, since their job security depends upon him. A new President means cabinet turnover.

The cabinet's critics hold that it would be too blinded by self-interested loyalty ever to certify the President's inability. The possibility that the President, when he recovered sufficiently, would retaliate would encourage cabinet inaction. Wilson dismissed Lansing, and Harry S. Truman has declared in post-Presidential utterances that if his cabinet ever declared him disabled while he was confined on the flat of his back, his first act upon rising would be to fire every culprit who had supported the finding.

The Supreme Court acting as a court or special tribunal and by a simple or extraordinary majority or unanimity. The Court appeals to those eager to minimize political partisanship and those who look to judicial discipline for fairness and public confidence. Some of the more imposing drawbacks are that saddling the Court with nonjudicial functions—in this case of mountainous political consequences—would be a violation of separation of powers, and that the Court's remoteness from an intimate knowledge of the President's circumstances might lead it to act unwisely.

Congress acting by concurrent resolution, on its own initiative or on request of the cabinet, the Vice President, or both. Congress's attractiveness lies in the fact that it is a popular body; its limitations, like the Court's, are that separation of powers would be violated and Congressmen might be ignorant of the President's true condition. In addition, dawdling committee hearings, meandering debates, and irresponsible filibusters might hopelessly deadlock Congress during a Presidential crisis. A Congress and President of opposite parties would compound the trouble.

A panel of doctors. Inability is most likely to be largely a medical question, for which authentic answers are best provided by qualified professionals. Inability is never *only* a medical question, however. It poses a tandem political question: whether the public interest at the time requires the exercise of Presidential power. Doctors have no inherent superiority over other citizens in assessing "public interest." Even in medical questions genuine professional differences hold sway in diagnostic judgment. A public dispute of doctors on the medical phases of inability would only confound the public, delay the issue, and provide grist for the mills of politics.

A special disability commission. This has as many variations as there are proposals, and they are legion. One, urged in 1958 by former President Truman, called for a committee of the Vice President, the Chief Justice, the Speaker, and the majority and minority leaders of the House and Senate, advised by a panel of doctors. Other proposals would subtract the doctors and add part or all of the cabinet. Still others would convert the House and Senate Judiciary Committees into a permanent "Presidential Inability Commission," empowered to act even when Congress was not in session. One proposal, finding inspiration in the British Regency Act of 1937, calls for a commission composed of the President's spouse or next-of-kin, the Chief Justice, the senior Associate Justice, and the leaders of the President's party in the House and Senate. Such proposals run afoul of vital differences between the Parliamentary and Presidential systems. A committee with legislators and judiciary would violate the American structure of separation of powers. The British system of Parliamentary unity and supremacy can more easily utilize a mixed commission. The monarch is a symbolic rather than an operating executive, holds office for life, and is not buffeted by the political forces of popular election. A partisan President's tenure would be rather less secure at the hands of an equally partisan legislature.

The United States Supreme Court, for its part, has bowed out from any connection with a special inability commission. On January 20, 1958, Chief Justice Earl Warren wrote to a House Judiciary subcommittee in behalf of his fellow justices,

> It has been the belief of all of us that because of the separation of powers in our Government, the nature of the judicial process, the possibility of a controversy of this character coming to the Court, and the danger of disqualification which might result in lack of quorum, it would be inadvisable for any member of the Court to serve on such a Commission.

3. If the President is disabled, to what does the Vice President succeed —to the "powers and duties" of the office, or to the office itself? Does he become Acting President, serving temporarily until the disabled President has recovered, or does he take over permanently for the remainder of the term? These troublesome questions can be blamed on the Constitution's ambiguity in Article II and on Vice President John Tyler's astute contrariness at his succession to the Presidency in 1841 upon William Henry Harrison's death. He was not merely "Acting" President, Tyler contended; he was succeeding to the Presidential office itself, and was President in the fullest sense of the word.

All six of the other Vice Presidents who have been elevated upon the President's death have clasped Tyler's precedent. Indeed Arthur and Marshall were deterred from taking over from their infirm Presidents by the wide opinion of their fellow public men that a disabled President once pushed aside could never return. The Constitution, they reasoned, did not allow for two Presidents to exist simultaneously, one acting and the other ailing.

The Eisenhower-Kennedy agreement meets the ambiguity head-on. Upon the President's inability, the Vice President "would serve as Acting President until the inability had ended."

4. Who determines when the President's inability ends? "The President," says the chorus of general opinion. The Eisenhower-Kennedy agreement provides that "The President . . . would determine when the inability had ended and at that time would resume the full exercise of the

powers and duties of the office." Presumably a deranged President would be prevented from announcing his recovery. The champions of an inability commission would empower it to determine the President's recovery. The objections to such a commission's making a finding of inability in the first place would apply with equal force to its determining the President's recovery.

5. Is Presidential inability best handled by Presidential statement, Congressional resolution, statute, Constitutional amendment, or a combination of these? The Eisenhower-Kennedy agreement, which amounted to a bipartisan consensus upon inability, deserves to be continued in future Presidencies. The agreement could be better enforced as a precedent if it were incorporated in a resolution or act of Congress. A Constitutional amendment was briefly sponsored by the Eisenhower administration to deal definitively with inability, but the necessary two-thirds Congressional majority never materialized. Amendments are also pushed by those whose proposals founder on the shoals of separation of powers. Some who would entrust Congress with supreme responsibility toil over amendment drafts, unheedful of the ghost of Andrew Johnson weeping at their folly.

◇

THE Founding Fathers, who were geniuses at spotting thorny problems and passing them on to hapless posterity to wrestle with, applied their sure touch to Presidential succession. The all-seeing Fathers anticipated the calamitous day when a double vacancy might befall the nation—when both the President and the Vice President might be unavailable because of death, resignation, impeachment, or disability. The Fathers, accordingly, posed no solution, but simply empowered Congress to enact a law "declaring what officer shall then act as President." Congress has thrice passed laws, the last in 1947, and each time its labors have provoked criticism and sent citizens scurrying for better remedies.

In its three laws, Congress has vacillated between drawing upon its own leaders and the members of the cabinet in laying the lines of sucession. Considerations of pure political science have seldom motivated Congress's actions. The first law of 1792 was no solution rooted in Olympian wisdom, but a narrow partisan act. The law's object was to prevent the succession of Secretary of State Thomas Jefferson. The conservative leaders of Congress, who abhorred Jefferson, simply by-passed him and voted one of themselves into the succession. If the Presidency and the Vice Presidency were vacant, the President pro tempore of the Senate, and after him the Speaker, would succeed. Neither officer was to become President upon the take-over, but only Acting President. If the double vacancy happened in the first two years and seven months of the Presidential term, Congress was required to call a special election "forthwith."

In 1886 Congress passed a new law, the pendulum now swinging to the cabinet. In a future double vacancy, the succession would run from the Secretary of State to the Secretary of the Interior in the order in which the departments were established. No secretary could be wafted by fate and the act into the Presidential chair if he could not satisfy the regular Constitutional qualifications for the Presidency. The 1792 act's special election feature was dropped.

During Harry Truman's first weeks in the Presidency, into which he had been catapulted by Franklin Roosevelt's death, he perceived grievous limitations in the 1886 act. He incorporated his concern and recommendations for a new succession law in a special message to Congress on June 19, 1945. The 1886 act, placing the Secretary of State, an appointed and not an elected officer, next in line for the Presidency, in effect permitted Truman to name his own successor. "I do not believe that in a democracy," the President declared, "this power should rest with the Chief Executive." In the new legislation he proposed, Truman contended that after the President and Vice President in the succession line should come the Speaker of the House of Representatives, because he "is elected in his own district" and "is also elected to be the presiding officer of the House by a vote of all the representatives of all the people of the country." After the Speaker, in the Truman plan, would come the President pro tempore, elected first by the people of his state, and then by the whole Senate. Following the President pro tempore would be "the members of the Cabinet as provided now by law."

Since Edward Stettinius, a career businessman, was Secretary of State at the time and Sam Rayburn, a career politician, the Speaker, the House of Representatives passed a bill reflecting Truman's views with vast cheers for Rayburn and a proud sense of doing something nice for one's own. When the bill reached the upper chamber, however, James F. Byrnes, a distinguished and popular former Senator and Congressman, had replaced Stettinius as Secretary of State. Congressional enthusiasm for the succession bill shriveled. It was nearly dead when the Republican triumph in the 1946 Congressional elections suddenly revived it. The bill passed in 1947 and Truman dutifully signed it, and thereby established not a Democratic but a Republican Speaker, Joe Martin, as his successor. After the Speaker, under the 1947 act, comes the President pro tempore of the Senate, the Secretaries of State, the Treasury, Defense, Justice, the Post Office, the Interior, Agriculture, Commerce, and Labor. The Department of Health, Education and Welfare, created in 1953, has not been admitted into the succession.

Like bygone succession laws, the 1947 act has stirred more reproach than praise. It tramples upon the separation of powers principle by bringing two legislative officers into the Presidential line. Truman's estimable image of the Speakership as a popular "democratic" office is open to challenge. The Speaker's electorate is local rather than national, his district a patch of a few square miles on the face of a continental nation. His elevation to the Speakership reflects not simply the "popularity" Truman valued, but seniority, parliamentary skill, party fidelity, and finesse in personal politics. Even worse, Speakers as a lot compare badly with Secretaries of State, the Treasury, or Defense as Presidential timber. As executive officers the secretaries would afford better continuity in succeeding to the Presidency than an "outsider" like the Speaker. Ironically, the 1947 act revives the Ben Wade-Andrew Johnson "temptation" by creating for the Speaker and the President pro tempore a vested interest in the President's impeachment.

The 1947 act also stumbles badly upon the imperatives of the nuclear age. The act does not face up to the possibility that in a future nuclear war one tolerably aimed bomb could destroy Washington and with it the whole company of Presidential successors.

Criticism of the 1947 act became most acute after Kennedy's assassination and Johnson's assumption of the Presidency. Under the workings of the 1947 act, Speaker John McCormack, aged seventy-one, became next in line, followed by the president pro tempore of the Senate, Carl Hayden, aged eighty-six. McCormack's advanced age and the manifestly greater relevance of his talents to the affairs of Congress than to those of the Presidency raised a considerable outcry either that McCormack take himself out of the succession or that the 1947 act be amended to eliminate him from it. But the agitations failed because of McCormack's popularity in Congress and his expressed view that the 1947 law was "preferable" to any alternatives yet advanced. The nation reverted to its "tendency," as James Reston put it, "to do nothing but pray for the President's health."

◇

THE environment of the modern Presidency makes imperative not only a rational method of succession but a smooth transition between the outgoing and the incoming chief executives. In an age when several foreign affairs crises are flaming simultaneously around the globe, when weapons systems consume an average of seven years in passing from drawing board to operation, when the economy grows ever more intricate and sensitive, a snarl or lapse in public policy invites disaster. Foreign leaders calculate their moves with an eye on the Presidential calendar. Several weeks after President Hoover's electoral defeat in 1932, Britain requested "adjustment" of her World War I debt and suspension of her payment due December 15. Other debtor European nations quickly made similar demands. The Europeans caught the United States during an interlude of governmental paralysis, with a President discredited by defeat, a Congress whose support was indispensable controlled by the opposition party, and the President-elect, Franklin Roosevelt, visibly and understandably reluctant to plunge onto a terrain full of economic and political booby-traps, without the protection of official responsibility.

Succession presents a variety of problems: The President and the President-elect may be of the same party (Coolidge-Hoover) or of different parties (Wilson-Harding; Truman-Eisenhower; Eisenhower-Kennedy); or the transition may be from Vice President to President (Harding-Coolidge; Roosevelt-Truman), a reminder of the Vice President's potentiality as the President's understudy. Of modern Presidents, Hoover was the first to seek consultations and joint policy-making with the President-elect. Both Roosevelt and Truman, when running for re-election, permitted aides to supply the opposing candidates with vital information on foreign affairs. President Truman, mindful of his own sudden and unbriefed trajectory into the Presidency, smoothed the transfer to the incoming Eisenhower administration, thus becoming the first outgoing chief executive to accept the responsibility squarely for orderly transition. President Eisenhower reciprocated by easing the Kennedy administration's advent in 1961.

Truman's and Eisenhower's transition arrangements cover two spans, one from the Presidential nominations to the November elections, the other from election to inauguration. In August 1952, just before the Stevenson-Eisenhower campaigns pulled into high gear, President Truman invited the candidates to come separately to the White House for a briefing on the world situation. Although Eisenhower declined, saying the lack of "grave emergency" made his attendance unnecessary, he accepted Truman's simultaneous offer of weekly Central Intelligence Agency reports, provided they would not "limit my freedom to discuss or analyze the foreign programs as my judgment indicates." As President, Eisenhower supplied intelligence briefings to the 1956 and 1960 Democratic candidates, Stevenson and Kennedy.

For the interlude between election and inauguration, arrangements are more elaborate. In 1952, following his electoral victory, Eisenhower visited the White House in November when Truman wisely arranged a welcoming parade to sweeten an atmosphere heavily soured by campaign invective. President Truman and President-elect Eisenhower, tense and unsmiling at first, conferred privately and then were joined by Secretary of State Dean Acheson, Secretary of Defense Robert Lovett, Secretary of the Treasury John Snyder, and Mutual Security Director Averell Harriman of the administration; Joseph Dodge, the future Budget Director, and Henry Cabot Lodge, the future ambassador to the U.N., accompanied Eisenhower. The topic discussed was foreign affairs, and it ranged over Korea, NATO, Iran, Indochina, and elsewhere. At the meeting's close Truman handed Eisenhower three large volumes prepared by the National Security Council which contained (1) a country by country summary of current United States policies, (2) an estimate of critical trouble spots, and (3) "eyes-only" plans for meeting a possible all-out Communist attack in Korea, Yugoslavia, or Iran. The White House session was followed by a briefing for Eisenhower and his aides at the Pentagon by General Omar Bradley and the Joint Chiefs of Staff.

In subsequent weeks Eisenhower's designated appointees John Foster Dulles (State), Humphrey (Treasury), Dodge (Budget), Lodge (U.N.), and Adams (chief administrative assistant) conferred with their counterparts in the Truman administration. Future Budget Director Dodge was furiously busy since the budget is one of the knottier phases of transition, aggravated by the disharmonious scheduling of the Twentieth Amendment and the Budget and Accounting Act of 1921. The act requires that the budget be submitted fifteen days after Congress convenes. The new Congress was scheduled to meet on January 3, the budget's due date was January 18, or two days prior to the inaugural date of January 20 set in the Twentieth Amendment. Dodge, an efficient advance-runner, enabled the President-elect to acquire information that would facilitate changes in the budget after the new President took office.

The mechanics of the Truman-Eisenhower transition were duplicated in the Eisenhower-Kennedy transfer. Kennedy was apparently satisfied, for he remarked just before his inaugural, "I don't think we have asked for anything that they haven't done."

For all the surface appearance of cooperation and harmony, transitions are beset with the tensions and cross-purposes of the outgoing and incoming Presidents. The outgoing President, as Laurin Henry demonstrates in *Presidential Transitions*, prizes continuity and order, the preservation of his policies, and the maturing of his half-begun projects in the next administration. The President-elect is cautious and aloof, watchful of involving his freedom and the mandate and prestige of his electoral victory in policies of the incumbent administration over which he has no control. When in its closing days the Eisenhower administration decided to break diplomatic relations with Cuba, the incoming Kennedy administration was invited to associate itself with the move. The Kennedy camp, not surprisingly, declined. "In the absence of complete information on all the relevant factors," a Kennedy spokesman declared, the new administration could not participate.

The new President's personal philosophy may be radically at odds with the incumbent President's as Eisenhower's laissez-faire preferences were miles removed from the welfare-state commitment of Truman. The new and old Presidents may differ in their view of Presidential method: Harding's Whiggery was a long way from Wilson's dynamism. The transition may also be inhibited because the new or old President sees it as a manipulative opportunity for political gain. After Eisenhower's electoral victory, President Truman included in the customary congratulatory telegram an offer to put a military aircraft at the General's disposal "if you still intend to go to Korea," a promised venture that played no little part in the election's outcome. Eisenhower's response was cooly correct. Truman gibed again at a press conference when he announced to the nation that Eisenhower's Korean trip was nothing more than "a piece of demagoguery." Truman's comment, said an Eisenhower aide, meant "the finish of any informal across-the-desk meeting" between the two. If they conferred again prior to the inaugural, said the aide further, mindful of Eisenhower's deep displeasure, "it probably would be a cold affair."

The most pressing difficulties of Presidential transitions are Constitutional rather than administrative. Although the Twentieth Amendment helpfully moved the Presidential inaugural from March to January, a yawning hiatus still stretches between the end of the old administration and the beginning of the new one. A lapse of seven weeks between election and inauguration is absurd, given the gallop of today's affairs. The dates of the two events need to be juxtaposed within not more than four weeks of each other. Likewise, the interval between the national party conventions and the election, scheduled originally in horse-and-buggy days, has become thoroughly antiquated and ill serves the nation's interests. Following the conventions in July is a lull of four or five weeks of inactivity before the campaigns begin in earnest after Labor Day. Then comes eight or more weeks of campaigning as compared with two weeks in Great Britain and Canada. The increasing efficiency of American campaign media could easily support a shorter campaign period. Our historical political calendar has plainly become outmoded. Wise compression could eliminate two months or more between the dwindling reign of a lame-duck President and his successor's arrival at the seat of power.

◇

THE debate over the several issues concerning disability, succession, and transition is apt to wax well into the future. What seems best on each of these scores for keeping the Presidency continually strong?

1. Of the methods advanced for dealing with disability, the agreements concluded by our last three Presidents with their possible successors are the most preferable. The use of cabinets, councils, special commissions, and panels of doctors is, as we have seen, fraught with difficulty. The Eisenhower-Kennedy-Johnson method has already commended itself to three Presidents of both parties, and is well on its way to becoming an established custom. The method permits a flexible adjustment to circumstance and in no way infringes upon the President's control of his office.

He could give up his duties if he became disabled, but he could resume them simply upon his own finding that he was ready to take over again.

The Eisenhower-Kennedy-Johnson kind of agreement would be more likely to be used in the future if by resolution Congress simply expressed its general approval of whatever disability arrangement the President might make with his successor. The agreement would gain political and legal strength were Congress to give it sanction. Above all, statutes of Congressional amendments that would impose a strait-jacketed procedure or encroach in any way upon the President's control of his office should be shunned. These could damage the Presidency incalculably. If the President's tenure could be challenged at whim by Congress, doctors, or another body, the office would become paralyzed with uncertainty.

2. For reasons we have explored, the 1947 Succession Act is a major mistake and it ought to be repealed. For the contingency that the Vice Presidency becomes vacant, several proposals have been discussed. One is that the act of 1886 be restored with the line of succession proceeding through the cabinet, beginning with the Secretary of State. A drawback is that if the cabinet secretary were to serve as President for more than a year, there might be political awkwardness and weakness, owing to his lack of popular election to any national office. Another proposal is that the electoral college be especially summoned to choose a new Vice President. Given, however, the well-known disciplinary weakness of our political parties, we might well fear that the electoral college, which in reality they choose, might be the scene of a considerable factional struggle whose outcome might not be harmonious either with public opinion or with the President's own preferences. Another possibility is a special popular election of a new Vice President, but this too might disrupt the President's interests and prestige at home and abroad.

The most attractive proposal, at least to this writer, is for the President himself to choose a new Vice President. Above all, it would best assure that the President would choose a successor who would provide a continuation of his policy and administration. By long-established custom, he is permitted this choice at the national nominating convention. In filling a Vice Presidential vacancy, the President would merely be repeating the same kind of choice he was permitted there. If history proves anything, it is that Presidents are responsible men, and we can well expect that they will continue to be in choosing a new Vice President.

3. In the interest of easing the transition between Presidencies, we might well cast a critical eye on our present scheduling of the national nominating convention, the duration of the post-convention electoral campaign, and the date of the inauguration. Each could be revised to shorten the transition. A three- or four-week electoral campaign should be altogether efficient and desirable. We could use a shortened campaign as a

springboard for revising other parts of the Presidential calendar. We might redress the present awkwardness which requires a new President, days after his inauguration in January, to submit a budget, by direction of the Budget and Accounting Act of 1921, which must be prepared largely by his predecessor. A rearranged Presidential calendar would give the new President more time to prepare a budget of his own for presentation in January. On the basis of these necessities, one could project the following calendar, with approximately a one-month interval between each step. April: the nominating conventions; May: the post-convention electoral campaign; June: the election; July: the inauguration; January: the new President's first budgetary presentation.

4. Let every good friend of the strong Presidency pledge himself to work unstintingly for the repeal of the Twenty-Second Amendment.

CHAPTER

5

Party Chief

⸻

ANY President suffers continuing tension between his responsibilities to his office and the claims of his party. His office, and therefore its duties and problems, presumably exceed any obligation the party can impose upon him. He is a politician who must also be a statesman. Yet the party often and insistently violates this assumption. Senate Republicans, blithely heedless of President Eisenhower's struggle with great and manifold problems of state, required him to work in harness with their chosen leader, William F. Knowland, who opposed most of his foreign and much of his domestic policy. President Kennedy was expected, at the first electoral opportunity, to stump against Senator Everett Dirksen, Republican leader, who provided indispensable support for the test ban treaty and a string of other important measures.

The tension between office and party is aggravated by the party's almost frivolous disregard of its obligations to the President. He may by splendid electoral triumph plant the party standard in the White House, carry many a legislative party colleague on his coattails across the victory line, only to see his proposals spurned, sometimes *ad seriatim*, by a Congress whose two houses his party controls. President Truman, despite his spectacular electoral victory in 1948, which restored the Democrats to power in both Congressional houses, was able to obtain in the ensuing session the enactment of only several of a score of Fair Deal measures. President Kennedy, who summoned his fellow Democrats on Capitol Hill to rally behind an ambitious and popular program, did little better. He could well transpose for his own party role the memorable instruction of his inaugural address, "Ask not what your party can do for you; ask what you can do for your party."

The major American party does well as a vehicle of power and badly as a vehicle of policy. The contemporary President needs both these ingredients of political success in steady quantity. The party serves the President well as a campaign organ to bring himself and his party brethren into office, and as a forum for broadcasting his platform to the people. The party serves him ill in transposing his campaign promises into law. American parties, unlike those of any other major nation, fail to stabilize the chief executive's impact on policy-making. His party capacity endows him with only a fraction of the strength the British Prime Minister has to transform campaign promises into established public policy.

President Eisenhower, just before his spectacular re-election victory in 1956, was questioned pointedly concerning the affinity of several old guard Senators to his own Modern Republicanism. His response suggested perceptively several limits the President suffers as party chief. Eisenhower said,

> Now, let's remember there are no national parties in the United States. There are forty-eight state parties, then they are the ones that determine the people that belong to those parties. There is nothing I can do to say that [anyone] is not a Republican. The most I can say is that in many things they do not agree with me. . . . We have got to remember that these are state organizations, and there is nothing I can do to say so-and-so is a Republican and so-and-so is not a Republican.

The President is an uncertain monarch of a loose and far-flung party empire of several satrapies and dependencies and a host of self-governing commonwealths. His sway is full over several parts; over most it is little or nonexistent. He is a chief among chiefs. The local and state party organizations are beyond his control and are subject, at most, to his influence. The major parties function as viable national organizations only quadrennially when their state and local parts more or less unite to win the Presidency and its stakes of power. Thereafter they conduct themselves with jealously preserved autonomy. The state and local organizations command a solid corps of workers and followers, assert their own discipline, control the selection of Senatorial and Congressional candidates, and possess financial resources of their own. The Senate and House of Representatives maintain a quantity of party organizations: caucuses, steering committees, campaign committees, and policy committees. Senators and Congressmen render their principal allegiance not to the chief executive, but to the state and local organizations to which they owe their nomination and election. Legislators of the President's party both help and hobble his program of legislation. The fact that a Byrd and a Humphrey march under the Democratic banner and a Goldwater and a Javits under the Republican demonstrates how undependable the party label is as a guide to how legislators debate and vote. Nowhere in the vast party structure is there a constant and effective source of power that the President can confidently turn to for support. The National Committee, where his strength is greatest, and into which the state and local organizations converge, is chiefly concerned with the choice and election of the Presidential candidate.

The unreliability of his party, the likelihood that numbers of its Congressional members may oppose him, must lead any President to ponder privately just what good his party really is to him. Indeed, if he reads the texts of Presidential history, he will discover that Presidents achieve many, if not most, of their important policies and programs, whether in domestic or foreign affairs, only with bipartisan support. The loyalty of his own party is never so dependable that it can assure a succession of program victories. This undependability makes it necessary for the President to studiously cultivate support in the opposition party. His own party's ambiguity of support promotes the President's necessary ambiguity as party leader. For his program's sake, he must not be so fiercely and devotedly the leader of his own party that he is precluded from gaining support from the opposition.

The case for the President to treat his party role pragmatically and to conduct himself in a fashion that will pick up support beyond his party can be made in another way. The President is brought into office by a popular vote that is greater than his party vote. His electoral majority, as careful research demonstrates, is a patchwork of voters from his own party, from the opposition party, and from the steadily growing body of "independents." He may have large support from big groups such as organized labor and national and racial groups. His own party may have chosen him as its standard-bearer principally because of his presumed ability to attract broad support. Ironically, the Republican party denied Robert A. Taft its nomination because he was too much a Republican ("Mr. Republican," in fact), and therefore lacking in appeal to lure Democratic and independent voters into his column. Without substantial outside support, he could not possibly have become a winner.

The President and Vice President are the only officers of our government chosen by a national popular majority. In seeking to convert his promises to that majority into policy, the President is frustrated by the skillful arrangement of the governmental structure to permit what at most can be only limited majority rule. The system of checks and balances enables Congress, which is a series of disparate local majorities, to reject what the President, the voice of a national majority, proposes. The weakness of the parties assures that the principle of checks and balances, and therefore limited majority rule, will enjoy the full play the Founding Fathers intended. Congress's local constituencies in contrast to the President's national constituency, and Congress's internal organization—its powerful committees with chairmen chosen by seniority—tend to produce a legislature and an executive of opposite policy outlooks, even when the same party controls both branches. In recent generations Congress has usually been the domain of conservatives of both parties and the Presidency the domain of progressives.

The President is forced by checks and balances and party weakness to scramble for support by a variety of expedients. He must court approval among progressives in both Congressional parties. He may endeavor as best he can to dominate portions of his own party by building alliances with state and local leaders and by discreetly influencing the choice of legislative candidates. He may rely heavily on his own personal organization—if he has one—to make his way in party affairs. He can move to change the popular base of his party by extending it to big pressure groups to whose interests his program is akin. Desperation is nowhere else so much the mother of invention as it is in the chief executive's party plight.

◇

EVEN in its most serviceable roles—selecting the Presidential nominee and conducting the electoral campaign—the party's relation with its chosen candidate is uneasy and imperfect. The party provides no assurance that the platform he runs on accords with his wishes. His ability to make his preferences prevail depends upon a complex of factors—the power of his rivals, the nature of the issues, his own general political health. Franklin Roosevelt could confidently expect that the Democratic convention of 1936 would approve the platform prepared under his supervision. "I would like to have as short a platform as possible this year," he instructed his draftsmen, "and . . . I would like to have it based on the sentence of the Declaration of Independence, 'We hold these truths to be self-evident.' " The convention approved the several parts of the Roosevelt-made platform with waves of ovations.

Grover Cleveland in 1888 had more difficulty. The tariff was the prickly issue of the day between radicals and conservatives, and the President's general political situation was not without weakness. Cleveland himself drafted the platform, carefully stating in moderate language the tariff question. For the sake of his own political necessities, Cleveland wished to provide the Republicans with no opportunity to charge the Democratic party with free-trade principles. At the St. Louis convention, unfortunately for Cleveland, the low tariff men unshackled their bonds. They and Cleveland's emissaries of moderation were about evenly divided on the platform subcommittee on the tariff. The subcommittee met at dusk in a steaming room of the Southern Hotel and fought over the issue all night. The free-trade men, led by Henry Watterson, the Kentucky editor, ultimately prevailed.

Many a Presidential nominee views the available party organization as an enterprise of limited dependability and feels it the better part of wisdom to build a personal organization to conduct much of the post-convention campaign. John Kennedy relied upon an elaborate personal organization, consisting of his brothers, his brothers-in-law, a cadre of aides from his earliest political campaigns, and several members of the Harvard faculty, among others. His brother Robert was in general command, and the large role of his other brother, Edward, was stated by the President in a press conference of June 28, 1962: "He was in charge of our Western campaign in the preconvention period, which was a very intensive campaign where we secured the support of a good many delegates, and in charge of our campaign in the West in the campaign itself."

The Presidential nominee may be driven to build up a personal organization by the fickleness of state and local party organizations in providing support. Instead of devoting their resources in a substantial way to his race, they may concentrate upon local campaigns, especially in years when the Presidential nominee is deemed a likely loser. Adlai Stevenson, who campaigned under such circumstances, resorted to a trifurcated organization in 1956. In addition to the regular national party organization, a Stevenson-Kefauver Committee appeared in Washington, headed by James A. Finnegan, Stevenson's campaign director, and housed across the street from Democratic headquarters. A third organization was Volunteers for Stevenson, whose province was the independent voter. The poverty of support the regular party organization gave Stevenson made his decision in behalf of a personal organization eminently wise. The duplication of the Stevenson experience in other similar episodes raises a strong suspicion that a Presidential nominee cannot securely depend upon the regular organization unless his victory appears clear and imminent. In such a happy eventuality, when Senatorial and Congressional candidates eagerly press to ride his coattails, the Presidential nominee might be well advised to bar access to that privileged place to those whose known positions on policy promise to make them future saboteurs of his program. If the Presidential nominee distributed his support selectively at this juncture, he might gain more than when he applies gentle pressures at the midterm elections when there are no Presidential coattails and his power is consequently very much reduced. Nowadays the legislative campaign committees of the President's party insist that he hit the campaign trail in Congressional elections. His cabinet secretaries are expected to take their full turn, too.

The President works with something less than total ease and comfort with the Congressional and Senatorial Campaign Committees of his party. The midterm election is often a season for exposing divergences in the policy views of the President and legislators of his party. The lengths to which the malaise may go is suggested in a remarkable statement by the Republican Congressional Campaign Committee chairman, Richard M. Simpson of Pennsylvania, in 1958. Republican candidates, Simpson counseled, should forget about Eisenhower's favor in the 1958 elections and "make known" to voters any "disagreement with the President's policies." Simpson, a conservative Republican, often opposed the President's "modern Republicanism."

Despite the varying cordiality of the invitations he receives, the President has for some years now led the party in Congressional elections. The results, like the invitations, are mixed. Woodrow Wilson began the practice by appealing for a Democratic Congress in 1918, with disheartening result. His party lost control of both houses. Franklin Roosevelt launched his purge in 1938, for which the electorate slapped him hard. Not only did the purge fail, but the Democrats lost the incredible total of seventy seats in the House and seven in the Senate. Roosevelt tried again in 1942 with results only slightly less bad. Truman fared no better, and in 1954 Eisenhower made a lavish effort, traveling more than ten thousand miles and making nearly forty speeches. His reward was the loss of eighteen Representatives, one Senator, and control of both houses. In 1959 Eisenhower turned over the campaigning to Vice President Nixon, who also was rebuffed. Kennedy, however, brightened the gloomy history of Presidential influence in the off-year 1962 elections by gaining supporters, although he lost a few Democrats, but he was aided no little by a useful coincidence—the Cuban quarantine crisis rallied the voters behind the incumbent Democratic party.

On occasion the President undertakes a further function in Congressional elections. He may have to induce able citizens to become their party's nominees for legislative office. The national Republican chairman, Leonard Hall, concluded in 1956 that John Sherman Cooper, then ambassador to India, was urgently needed to run for the Senate in Kentucky. Cooper had triumphed in the Senate race in 1952, but in 1956 he was unwilling to sacrifice contentment in India for the travail of a Senate race. Eisenhower, who thought it inappropriate for the President to persuade anyone to run for office, was pressed to take on Cooper by both Hall and Presidential Assistant Sherman Adams, who had tried and failed. Cooper was brought to Eisenhower's office, and the President, who never did ask him to run, spoke eloquently of the opportunity for service in the Senate. Cooper capitulated, ran, and won.

◇

THE most important of a President's personal political objectives, need-less to say, is securing renomination, and this can only be achieved with the help of the party organization. Normally, the party almost automati-cally grants this Presidential wish. Even the likelihood of defeat may not bar his renomination, as it did not for Hoover in 1932. Yet a few Presi-dents, such as Franklin Pierce, Buchanan, and Arthur, were denied re-nomination, and Benjamin Harrison achieved it only after a hard struggle.

Chester Arthur, who became President upon Garfield's assassination but failed to be renominated, approached the Chicago convention of 1884 with imposing credentials. Old-line political leaders, independents, and liberals all endorsed him. George William Curtis, distinguished reformer and old-time foe, wrote enthusiastically, "I say that a President whose accession by means of a most tragical event was generally regarded as a serious misfortune, if not calamity, has not only allayed all apprehension, but his pacific and temperate Administration has gained the general approval of the country." Henry Ward Beecher declared, "I can hardly imagine how he could have done better." And Mark Twain, "It would be hard to better President Arthur's Administration."

Arthur's defeat for renomination was the product of his alienation of key factions and bosses, his consequent weakness in key states, and poor convention strategy. A Stalwart, he acted moderately toward the Half-Breeds, the faction of James A. Garfield, his Presidential predecessor. Arthur's conciliation was resented by his own Stalwarts as ingratitude and weakness. Garfield men in Ohio, for all of Arthur's consideration, re-mained cool. Ex-governor Charles Foster bludgeoned the Arthur move-ment by declaring that Arthur would be "a very weak candidate in Ohio." In New York, Arthur's own state, Whitelaw Reid and Thomas C. Platt, ancient foes, united in common cause against Arthur. Platt, having had small success with the Arthur administration in its dispensations of pa-tronage, now believed that Arthur's rival James G. Blaine's "turn had come." The upshot was a badly divided New York delegation. Blaine went into the convention with a plurality, but not a majority, of the delegates. Arthur's convention campaign, which with modest skill might have weaved together a victory, was badly managed. The nominating speeches in his behalf were downright inferior. His managers were dull and lag-gard in fashioning deals with rival factions. "The management of Mr. Arthur's canvass here was a botch from beginning to end," an aide wrote.

Both more formidable and more successful than Arthur's ordeal was Truman's quest for renomination in 1948, which he achieved in a steep uphill fight by a combination of pluck and luck. Before the convention

Truman's political stock was at rock-bottom. The Republican Congressional victory in 1946 foreshadowed a Republican Presidential victory in 1948. Scandals had crashed upon the administration in waves. Henry Wallace had broken off from the Democratic party and anounced his Presidential candidacy. Labor and New Deal liberals were restive and Southern Democrats stood at the brink of revolt. Truman's popularity in the opinion polls had fallen dismally. To hold back the avalanche, Truman, in January of 1948, used his State of the Union message to project a platform for his party. The message recapitulated a quantity of Fair Deal proposals with a request for an improbable tax cut thrown in. Truman's choice of theme sought to hold together the crumbling Roosevelt Democratic coalition and to forestall liberals and independents from drifting to the Henry Wallace candidacy. In June Truman made a fiery whistle-stop tour through the Middle and Far West to show local Democratic leaders his strength with the crowds before the convention began.

But Truman's ability to be renominated depended not upon his own power and enterprise, but upon the outcome of a caucus gathered in Philadelphia, shortly before the convention, to arrange his overthrow. The caucus was called by Jacob M. Arvey, Chicago Democratic leader, James and Elliott Roosevelt, the late President's sons, and sixteen other party leaders. The active coalition against Truman was a cross section of the Democratic party and the old Roosevelt coalition. It included Mayor Hubert Humphrey of Minneapolis, Chester Bowles of Connecticut, Mayor William O'Dwyer of New York, and the Americans for Democratic Action. These Northern Democrats were joined by Southern Democrats such as Senator Lister Hill of Alabama, Governor J. Strom Thurmond of South Carolina, Governor Ben T. Lancy of Arkansas, Governor William M. Tuck of Virginia, and Senator Claude Pepper of Florida. Harold Ickes and James F. Byrnes, Secretary of the Interior and War Mobilization Director, respectively, in the Roosevelt administration, both opposed Truman.

The Philadelphia caucus saw inevitable electoral defeat unless a substitute candidate for Truman could be found. Their acquisitive gaze fell upon General Dwight D. Eisenhower, then on the crest of his popularity from his European military triumphs. But Eisenhower dashed the hopes of his would-be benefactors by issuing a statement a week before the convention, saying, "I will not at this time identify myself with any political party and could not accept nomination for any political office." Leon Henderson, the ADA chairman, futilely urged the Democrats to ignore the Eisenhower statement and to go ahead with the general's nomination as "the best man the country can provide." The ADA next brought forward the name of Supreme Court Justice William O. Douglas, but many Democratic leaders balked, and Douglas issued a declining statement.

Truman was eventually renominated by default of the old coalition's failure to unite on a candidate. The vote was not unanimous as befits a President seeking re-election, but 947½ for Truman, 263 for Richard B. Russell of Georgia, and ½ for Paul V. McNutt. The New York *Post* reflected the convention's mood when it wrote, "The Party might as well immediately concede the election to Dewey and save the wear and tear of campaigning." As everyone knows, Truman went on to win in one of the most dramatic election upsets in the country's history.

◇

BUT once nominated and elected, or re-elected, a President is concerned with getting his program through Congress, a venture in which the party leadership and rank and file are as likely to fail him as to help him. Few Congressmen view their loyalties to their own careers, constituents, and party as related to their loyalty to their party's national standard bearer and his program. Eisenhower's Senate leaders were successively Senator Taft, his chief rival for the Presidential nomination, and Senator Knowland, who opposed him on a wide range of policy. In Kennedy's time, the House Democratic floor leader, and later Speaker, was John W. McCormack of Massachusetts, whose nephew contested with the President's brother Edward for the 1962 Democratic Massachusetts Senatorial nomination. President Eisenhower steadily received more support from Democratic legislators than from Republicans. In no other governmental system in the world are such oddities of party life to be found.

Creative and well-intended efforts to improve President-Congress relations in the party realm have gone awry. The Congressional reorganization legislation of 1946 founded what might fairly be called a noble experiment to build up Congressional party unity by establishing a "policy committee" for each party in the Senate. The House later also instituted such committees. The committees were conceived by their creators, Senator Robert La Follette, Jr., and Mike Monroney, as a kind of council that would meet periodically with the President to improve interbranch understanding on questions of national policy. Like many other noble experiments, the policy committees have achieved only small success. President Truman met with the Senate Policy Committee of his day only once. In the Eisenhower administration's first days, the Senate Republican Policy Committee more or less accepted his program, although it quickly turned out that the legislative party for which it appeared to speak did not. There is no record of any Eisenhower meeting with the entire policy committee. The committees have developed not as institutional organs, as their creators hoped, but largely as instruments of personal leadership. Lyndon Johnson, Robert Taft, and Scott Lucas used the committees as personal vehicles. But most important of all, the committees have become effective not for policy-making but for service and research and legislative scheduling. They do not lead in drawing up a general legislative program, and rarely do they label their decisions party policies. The policy committees indeed may take stands decidedly hostile to the President. The House Republican Policy Committee called for "substantial" reductions of approximately three billion dollars in President Eisenhower's budget for fiscal 1958, and added pointedly that it expected all Republican Representatives to support its stand at the next party caucus.

The President's party equips him with remarkably few pressures he can apply to Congress, and these are highly imperfect at best. His most ancient pressure is, of course, patronage. All Presidents are wholesale dispensers of offices, a part of their job they least like. In Lincoln's day job-seekers crammed the White House rooms, stairs, hallways, and even closets, prompting that noble spirit to cry out, "It is not the rebellion that is killing me, but the Pepperton post office." The passage of a merit law in 1883, and its later extensions, protecting the tenure of designated employees, has gradually but sweepingly reduced the relative numbers of federal jobs tagged for patronage. In 1885, the second year of the Pendleton Act, out of 126,000 federal employees, some 110,000 were political appointees. A contemporary President's patronage appointments number a mere few thousand.

Patronage enables the President to strike at the legislator in his home district, to attract or alienate local groups on whose support he depends. For the favor of his juicy patronage plums, the chief executive can exact a *quid pro quo*. Many a President, before handing out jobs, first checks the voting record of the interested Congressman on the administration's legislative program. The search may bring down the heavens upon the errant. When Samuel J. Randall, Democratic high tariff advocate, fought Grover Cleveland's grand enterprise to lower the tariff, retribution was swift and severe. Word went forth from Washington that no Randall man need expect any patronage. At Randall's political base in Pennsylvania, reaction was quick. Two key Randall organizations, the Randall Club of Pittsburgh and the Eleventh Ward Democratic Association of Philadelphia, hastened to repudiate their leader and endorse Cleveland's tariff position. When the state Democratic committee met to elect a chairman and adopt resolutions, Randall's candidate lost to a low-tariff man and the committee voted a hearty endorsement of Cleveland's tariff stand. Yet, as Presidents well know, many legislators they might strike at by withholding patronage are by no means defenseless. "It was a smart practice in government," Roosevelt's party chairman Jim Farley once said, "to avoid antagonizing the men who vote the appropriations." He could add, too, legislators of large influence on other key Congressional committees and those enjoying full sway over local party organizations.

The patronage weapon is not without flaw. Its worth rests upon the assumption that human gratitude is enduring, an assumption that sometimes falters in practice, especially in politics. Further, an appointment to one job which recognizes a local political faction may antagonize competing factions. William Howard Taft, after a wealth of experience, concluded that every time he made a job appointment he created "nine enemies and one ingrate." Virtually anything the President does in the patronage field stirs bleats of disgruntlement. For all the attention of Franklin Roosevelt and Jim Farley, complaints poured in from state organizations that not enough Democrats were getting federal jobs. After several years of the New Deal, Arthur Mullen was contending that in Nebraska 60 per cent of the federal officeholders credited to his state were not Democrats at all. President Cleveland, like many another chief executive doling out patronage, was caught in the crossfire of spoilsmen and reformers. The spoilsmen hungered infinitely for jobs; reformers like Carl Schurz and the National Civil Service Reform Association proclaimed the necessity to hold the high ground of merit appointment. Seldom, when his job is done, does the President win the plaudits of either competing faction.

◇

THE party, when it does not control the Presidency, may be expected, according to general governmental practice, to take on the function of responsible opposition. The recurrent failure to attain even a semblance of this expectation demonstrates the low capacity of the Congressional party organization to achieve party coherence. In 1950, as chairmen of the out-party, the Republicans, Hugh Scott, Jr., and his successor, Guy Gabrielson, urged some kind of national conference to develop a platform on which to base the 1950 Congressional campaign. House and Senate Republican leaders did not hide their displeasure at the suggestion, although Gabrielson managed to bring an *ad hoc* committee to draft a widely publicized two-thousand-word statement on "liberty against socialism." Hereupon the Republican Senatorial and Congressional committees reduced the statement to a ninety-word digest of their own. Senator Taft, chairman of the Senate Republican Policy Committee, quickly announced that the digest had "no official standing whatsoever."

Soon after the 1956 election of Eisenhower, Senator Hubert Humphrey proposed that Congressional Democrats adopt their own legislative program, consisting of sixteen points, including civil rights, as a responsible opposition alternative to the President's program. "If you have a platform," Democratic Mayor David Lawrence of Pittsburgh commented to reporters, "you ought to follow it up with a legislative program, not just throw it out after you are defeated in an election." Senate Democratic Floor Leader Lyndon Johnson and Speaker Sam Rayburn declared their opposition to Humphrey's step and suggested that Congress wait and act upon the Eisenhower legislative program. When later Rayburn and Johnson proved fairly congenial to the Eisenhower program, Truman, Stevenson, Humphrey, and other Democratic leaders moved to form a Democratic Advisory Committee (or Council, as it came to be called) to keep alive the spirit of creative opposition. But the Speaker and majority leader agreed only to "consult" the committee, holding that they must retain their independence of action for their Congressional responsibilities. In such a tangled situation it is difficult if not impossible to find a meaningful national party leadership. Stevenson was discredited because of his two defeats for the Presidency, and Johnson's own party-mindedness, in light of his course, was a trifle obscure.

◊

THE President's success in party affairs is a mixture of many things—his own personality, his public popularity, his skill at maneuvering, his intuitive sense. It is a game played not with rules but with a master's instinct for the shifting sources of power. Some Presidents revel in their role as party commander. Jefferson, Franklin Roosevelt, and Kennedy, for example, enjoyed the game and usually played it with skill and finesse. John Quincy Adams and John Tyler, at the other extreme, were failures. And a President like Eisenhower accepted his party leadership reluctantly, holding that the White House should be above party. The experience of each is, in different ways, instructive.

Of all the Presidents, Thomas Jefferson is unsurpassed in the authority he asserted as party leader and in the fealty he commanded from state and local party organizations. He held sway with a thoroughly formulated theory of party principles and functions and a sure grasp of the means of party action. For Jefferson, party was pre-eminently the instrument of majority rule. The party joined the executive and Congress into a majoritarian unit. The President and his department secretaries provided the legislative agenda; the party members in Congress transmuted it into law.

The Presidential program was the party program, and fidelity to it in debate and vote was a principle to be jealously guarded and enforced. Jefferson wrote critically of his Congressional party brethren,

> Our friends have not yet learned to draw well together, and there has been some danger of a small section of them, aided by the feds [the Federalist party], carrying a question against the larger section. They have seen however that this practice would end in enabling the feds to carry every thing as they please, by joining whichever section of Republicans they chose; and they will avoid this rock.

Jefferson could not abide Republican legislators who acted independently of their party. He called them "Wayward freaks, which now and then disturb the operations."

Jefferson worked through and dominated the Congressional party machinery. Caucuses of Congressional Republicans were summoned at his direction, and sometimes reportedly he presided. Secretary of the Treasury Albert Gallatin devoted no little time and skill to laying before the caucus the President's messages and requests. Jefferson, Gallatin, and other cabinet secretaries watched over the progress of administration measures in Congress at all stages until their enactment. Jefferson and his aides invented the "floor leader," a legislator, or more than one, in each house who efficiently shepherded the administration's fondest projects over the craggy terrain of votes, committee hearings and reports, and parliamentary maneuver.

At the outset of a legislative session John Randolph, House floor leader and Ways and Means Committee chairman until he fell from Presidential grace, would dine with Jefferson to go over the administration's agenda. As the session proceeded, the Congressman was in almost daily touch with executive officials. Treasury Secretary Gallatin spoke of his "free communication of facts and opinions" to Randolph. Most of Gallatin's proposals were steered through the Ways and Means Committee and onto the House floor in the manner his fastidious tastes desired. Appropriations to purchase Florida, to establish a Mediterranean Fund, and to retire the debt moved steadily under Randolph's sure hand. As floor leader, he managed such major Presidential projects as the repeal of the Judiciary Act, the reduction of civil expenditures, and the impeachment of Supreme Court Justice Samuel Chase, a loud, violent Federalist who denounced Republicanism from the bench as a mash of anarchy, atheism, and the devil.

Jefferson viewed Congressional elections as a grand opportunity to eliminate obstructors and import supporters. Although James A. Bayard, Federalist Congressman of Delaware, had by his vote finally ensured Jefferson's triumph over Burr in their struggle for the Presidency, Bayard's subsequent leadership of the Congressional opposition alienated the chief executive. The President, as he was wont to do, searched for a candidate to beat Bayard at the polls. "For God's sake, run for Congress against him," he implored Caesar A. Rodney. Bayard's "long speeches and wicked workings at this session have added at least 30 days to its length, cost us 30,000 D. and filled the union with falsehoods and misrepresentations." The President's occasional manipulations had their costs. Major lieutenants like Joseph Nicholson and Nathaniel Macon were sometimes bedeviled with rumors that he was maneuvering to throw them over. To such men he wrote what became known as his "tares" letters—"Some enemy, whom we know not, is sowing tares among us. Between you and myself nothing but opportunities of explanation can be necessary to defeat these endeavors. . . . I must therefore ask a conversation with you."

Jefferson employed patronage to induce legislators to cooperate and to assure executive loyalty to his policies. When things went awry in the party organization, he was quick with redress. Soon after John Randolph, House floor leader and Ways and Means Committee chairman, erred, he was dropped from both capacities. He managed and botched the prosecution of Justice Chase and demurred at the President's seeming tenderness to the culprits of the Yazoo land fraud and at the President's request for a secret appropriation of two million dollars to purchase Florida if circumstances warranted. Randolph announced his dissents with merciless invective on the House floor. The affronted Jefferson dropped word to Senator William Plumer that "Mr. Randolph's late conduct is very astonishing and has given me much uneasiness." Jefferson and his followers moved to depose Randolph as floor leader and to substitute Barnabas Bidwell of Massachusetts. This plan was foiled when Bidwell was defeated for re-election. Administration business that normally went to the Ways and Means Committee was routed elsewhere as long as Randolph remained chairman. In a speech on the House floor Congressman Thomas Mann Randolph, Jefferson's son-in-law, savagely attacked John Randolph as a betrayer of secrets and an inciter of clamor. From his constituency in south-side Virginia, the embattled Randolph complained that "Every engine has been set to work to undo me in the estimation of my constituents, and not without effect." The local press maintained a steady, hostile chant, and two prestigious Virginia politicians, William B. Giles and Wilson Cary Nicholas, campaigned mightily against him. Another Jefferson son-in-law, John W. Eppes, took up residence in Randolph's district, contested his House seat, and eventually won it.

◇

IF JEFFERSON achieved crowning success as party leader, John Quincy Adams and John Tyler floundered in the uttermost depths of failure. Adams won the disputed Presidential election of 1824 in the House of Representatives and then only, his enemies said, by a corrupt bargain. In return for Clay-controlled House votes to assure Adams's election, Adams promised the Kentuckian the post of Secretary of State. "The Judas of the West," Andrew Jackson, a vanquished candidate, termed Clay.

John Quincy Adams was endowed neither by personality nor by circumstance to be a party leader. Austere and principled, he faced a wretched political situation. His cabinet contained no one who had openly supported him for President. Although his party controlled the House, the opposition ruled the Senate. Key Senate committees like the Foreign Relations Committee constantly opposed him. Adams's parlous situation in the upper chamber came into sharp relief when he requested authority to dispatch a mission to the Panama Congress of Latin-American states. The Foreign Relations Committee rejected his plan with a warning against entangling alliances, but somehow he managed to squeak through the Senate by a vote of 24 to 20 despite a punishing debate.

John Randolph, master of diatribe, had a field day with the Panama Congress proposal. Charging that Henry Clay as Secretary of State had forged the invitations to the Congress, he resumed the attack upon the political partnership of the President and the Secretary of State. They were, he cried, "the coalition of Blifil and Black George . . . of the Puritan with the black leg." For Adams, the worst aspect of this rowdy day in the Senate was not Randolph's crudity, but the fact that the President's own party permitted it. Not a single Republican Senator called Randolph to order, and Vice President John Calhoun, in the chair, permitted the breach of privilege. Adams, furious at Calhoun's laxity, made a slashing attack upon the Vice President, writing under the name "Patrick Henry," in the press. Calhoun, who used "Onslow" as his pen name, reciprocated fully. The two party giants, the President and Vice President, demonstrated their rich talents for controversy in several exchanges.

Adams's personal encounters were never softened by the favors at his command as party chieftain. He conceivably could heal wounds by applying the salve of patronage. But his principles stood in the way, taking precedence over the claims of party, as General James Tallmadge, lieutenant governor of New York and Tammany chieftain, sadly learned. Tallmadge had backed Adams unstintingly in his narrow victory. In a savage fight the lieutenant governor had stopped a move by Martin Van Buren's New York machine to break up a joint session of the state legislature before the electors could be chosen. If Van Buren had succeeded, New York's electoral votes would have been wasted and Adams defeated. Van Buren and his ally, Governor De Witt Clinton, had their avenging knives poised. Tallmadge clearly needed to escape New York for a distant foreign mission if his political life was to be saved. Thurlow Weed, Tallmadge's emissary, laid the situation before the President. In a meeting that was "embarrassing and constrained," Adams quickly demonstrated his capacity to ignore political obligations. He could not appoint Tallmadge to any diplomatic post, he said, because another New Yorker, Rufus King, had just been named Minister to England, and New York could not claim more than one overseas appointment. Weed sickened when he reflected that King had opposed Adams's election and Tallmadge had risked, perhaps given, his political life to assure it.

John Tyler, like Adams, is at the bottom of the league as party chieftain, although for different reasons. A sure-footed politician, he was the victim of the relentless ambition of the Congressional party leader, again Henry Clay. The New York *Herald* wrote of Clay,

He predominates over the Whig party with despotic sway. Old Hickory himself never lorded it over his followers with an authority more undisputed, or more supreme. With the exception of some two or three in the Senate and fifteen or twenty in the House, Mr. Clay's wish is the paramount law to the whole party.

Clay coupled with his great power a fierce drive to become President. A towering obstacle was the incumbent President Tyler and his likely desire to be re-elected.

Not without reason, Clay scornfully spoke of Tyler as "a President without a party." His Whig following in Congress was so small that it was called, half-derisively, "the Corporal's Guard." In the Senate only William C. Rives supported Tyler in the heavy fighting. The President's party weakness extended to his cabinet, which he had inherited from his late predecessor, William Henry Harrison. All the cabinet secretaries except Secretary of State Daniel Webster and Postmaster General Francis Granger were allied with Clay. Even of Webster and Granger Tyler could not be certain. The President's chief sustenance in his political weakness was his personality—"approachable, courteous, always willing to do a kindly action"—and his unlimited courage.

Without a party Tyler could not well put his chief measures through Congress; with a party Clay had Congress in his hand and the President largely at his mercy. Time and again Congress rebuffed the President and the President vetoed Congress. Clay, pursuing his American system, a series of measures to promote the nation's economic development, put through a bill creating a new bank of the United States. Tyler, whose states' rights disposition was offended, vetoed it, earning plaudits from Andrew Jackson. The Clay men drenched the President with invective. "The vocabulary of the language," a witness wrote, "seems to have been ransacked for words to express their angry denunciation." A second bank bill passed, and Tyler vetoed it. At Clay's command, all his men in the cabinet resigned.

Tyler, bereft of party aid, saw many a favorite measure hacked to death in Congress. His proposed treaty with the German *Zollverein* was tabled in the Senate. His nominations to office habitually encountered rough handling in the same body. His fond project to annex Texas by treaty was lost, with every Whig but one voting against it. Eventually, almost miraculously, Tyler brought Texas into the Union by joint resolution.

Tyler's troubles lay not only in Congress. He was treated roughly in the organs of political communication, in the party press, and in the talk of the political professionals. Henry Clay was known to say that if it could have been foreseen at the Harrisburg Convention, which created the Harrison-Tyler ticket, that Harrison would die after a month as President and that Tyler would veto the Whig's bank bill, either the convention would have ignored Tyler or he would not have received a single electoral vote in the subsequent election. The Clay press re-echoed its leader's hostility. The Richmond *Whig* called Tyler "the accident of the accident," "a vast nightmare over the Republic." And when a dread influenza epidemic overtook the country, the Whig press was quick to name it "the Tyler Grippe."

◇

FRANKLIN ROOSEVELT, the most powerful of modern Presidents, was also the most assertive as party leader. Commanding unprecedented popular support, attested by his four-time election to the Presidency, he dared to attempt drastic renovations of his party: to expand its voting base by extending its commitment to programs, and to displace the Democratic Congressional foes of the New Deal with those who promised to be its friends. Bold ventures almost inevitably involve a mixture of success and failure, and they did for Roosevelt.

Roosevelt's assertions were founded upon a close and constant mastery of those aspects of party functioning that fell most within his influence. Any President's authority is foremost in his party's national headquarters. He handpicks the chairman of the national committee and runs the national office as if it were his own organization. The President and possibly certain of his executive aides superintend the national chairman, but Roosevelt assumed more authority than most. James A. Farley, for example, in discharging the chairman's large responsibility for organizing and dispensing the patronage, was frequently overridden by Roosevelt and his aides. "While I transmitted a great many recommendations for appointment to the White House and to other Cabinet officials," Farley has written, "only a small part of them actually were approved." When Roosevelt and his secretary Steve Early grew displeased with Farley's preparations for Roosevelt's second term, the approaching 1936 campaign, they began to infiltrate their own people into the national committee. Roosevelt's first recruit was Edward L. Roddan, a newspaperman who had been covering the Presidency for the International News Service. He briefed Roddan personally on how he wanted things done. After Roddan took up his task, Roosevelt sent him a flurry of notes on campaign matters, not through Chairman Farley, but to Roddan directly. White House personnel were recruits for the national committee organization, too, among them Stanley High, a talented Presidential speechwriter, and Leon Henderson, a major administration economist.

Roosevelt's superintendency in the 1936 campaign dealt not only with personnel, but with the full sweep of campaign strategy and detail. In a discussion of campaign methods with the National Emergency Council, he said, "Bring in as much as possible the simple illustrations that appeal to the average person back home. . . . Don't tell them in Georgia what is being done in Alabama; take the nearest project to where you are speaking in Georgia and tell them about that." Shortly before the 1936 National Convention, he sent to Farley a memorandum reorganizing the National Committee's activities. Let Michelson oversee speech material, High the pamphlets, and so on. He pushed Farley steadily to set up committees for independent voters, Republicans, businessmen, and other groups.

Roosevelt's close atention to detail prompted him to pounce on lapses, large and small, in campaign management. When Jim Farley in a speech derided Alf Landon, the future Republican Presidential nominee, as the governor of "a typical prairie state," a huge uproar leapt from the Middle West. The resentment of this slight was compounded by the fact that its spokesman was the worst possible kind of Easterner, a New Yorker. Handbills soon flooded the West with pictures of Abraham Lincoln and the caption, "He, too, Came from 'a Typical Prairie State.' " The Presidential reprimand was quick. "I thought we had decided," Roosevelt wrote to Farley, "that any reference to Landon or any other Republican candidate was inadvisable." In the future, the President said, no state or section should be referred to except in laudatory terms. "If the sentence had read 'one of those splendid prairie states,' no one would have picked us up on it. . . ."

A rare President may intervene not only in the elections themselves but also in his party's primaries for Congressional seats, seeking the nomination of candidates pledged to his support. Because of the grave hazards such an enterprise involves, most chief executives, such as President Eisenhower, stoutly refused to take sides in any primary of their party. Presidents who wisely keep aloof from local primaries, know all too well that the local voters resent the intrusions of outsiders. Harry S. Truman abided by this rule except in his own Congressional district, where he publicly endorsed a friendly candidate. Accordingly, he followed the normal practice in the 1950 North Carolina fight for the Democratic Senatorial nomination, when Truman's own personal friend Frank Graham, a leading Fair Dealer campaigning for "real Southern democracy," was defeated by Willis Smith. Truman was little more than a bystander while the defeat, a damaging one to his prestige in the party, was being fashioned.

Franklin Roosevelt mounted the heaviest Presidential assault yet upon the inviolability of the local primary in his attempted 1938 purge of a handful of Democratic Senators and Congressmen. If it had succeeded, it would have brought about a major revision of the Congressional Democratic party and the party's historic heterogeneity would have been displaced by loyalty to the New Deal program. The purge was sparked by the defeat of Roosevelt's court-packing plan of 1937. That defeat, the first major rebuff in five years of glittering victories, had rankled the President. Not a few Democrats who opposed the court plan, he noted, had steadily voted against his New Deal measures. Roosevelt turned a receptive ear to his aides, Ickes, Thomas G. Corcoran, and Harry Hopkins, who for months had talked of the desirablility of a purge. On a hot June night he fired the opening salvo of the purge venture in a fireside chat. He declared,

> As the head of the Democratic party . . . , charged with the responsibility of the definitely liberal declaration of principles set forth in the 1936 Democratic platform, I feel that I have every right to speak in those few instances where there may be a clear issue between candidates for a Democratic nomination involving these principles, or involving a clear misuse of my own name.

The purge took on more definite form in Roosevelt's zigzag trip across the nation. He proceeded to distinguish between those who were with and those who were against him. In Texas he beamed on liberal Congressmen Lyndon Johnson and Maury Maverick and punished Senator Tom Connally, a court bill foe, by announcing from the back platform of his train the appointment to a federal judgeship of a Texan whom Connally had not recommended. In Kentucky Roosevelt worked hard for Alben Barkley, his faithful Senate leader, embattled in a close race with Governor Albert ("Happy") Chandler, a strong campaigner with a potent machine. Roosevelt, upon reaching Kentucky, invited both Barkley and Chandler into his car for a drive to a huge political crowd at the Latonia racetrack. Roosevelt and Barkley were nettled no little when Chandler kept bowing to the right and left, acknowledging the great applause which presumably was directed chiefly to Roosevelt, and the President came roaring back with a speech heaping praise upon Barkley and dismissing Chandler as a young man who required many years to match Barkley's knowledge and experience. In a later statement Roosevelt hinted that Chandler had approached the White House with a deal in judicial appointments to clinch his Senate seat.

Roosevelt had a fitting tactic for every situation. He crossed Nebraska without inviting Senator Edward R. Burke to join his party. In Wyoming Senator Joseph C. O'Mahoney was not invited, but boarded the Presidential train at Cheyenne as a member of a citizens' welcoming committee. Roosevelt stuck out his hand; "Hello, Joe! Glad to see you," he said cheerily. At succeeding stops, he did not mention O'Mahoney, and when the Senator left the train at Casper, Roosevelt pointedly referred to politicians who paid lip service to the New Deal while frustrating its objectives. And in Colorado Senator Alva B. Adams, too, stood by uneasily while Roosevelt elaborately ignored him.

The President was spurred on by the primary victory of Barkley and of another favorite, Senator Elmer Thomas of Oklahoma. He now concentrated his fire anew on several selected purgees. High on the list was Senator Walter F. George of Georgia. George's defeat, Roosevelt reasoned, would provide a lasting lesson to Southerners in Congress who had been opposing his social legislation. Other marked men in the Senate were Democrats Guy M. Gillette of Iowa, Bennett C. Clark of Missouri, Pat McCarran of Nevada, "Cotton Ed" Smith of South Carolina, Alva B. Adams of Colorado, Millard Tydings of Maryland, Frederick Van Nuys of Indiana, and Augustine Lonergan of Connecticut. In the House the men slated for defeat by the President were Howard W. Smith of Virginia, John J. O'Connor of New York, and E. E. Cox of Georgia, all determined foes of his program.

Roosevelt personally carried the fight against his principal purgees. En route for a vacation at Warm Springs, he stopped at Gainesville, Georgia, to dedicate a public square named in his honor. Senator George introduced the President, who proceeded to ignore the Senator and beam approval upon Governor E. D. Rivers, who he hoped would run against George. When Rivers declined, Roosevelt recruited Lawrence S. Camp, United States District Attorney at Atlanta. In another Georgia visit, this time at Barnesville, and with Camp and George on the platform, Roosevelt referred to the Senator as "my old friend" and proceeded to demonstrate his inadequacy by New Deal standards. The President described his test:

> First, has the record of the candidate shown, while differing perhaps in details, a constant active fighting attitude in favor of the broad objectives of the party and of the Government as they are constituted today; and secondly, does the candidate really, in his heart, deep down in his heart, believe in these objectives?

The President proceeded to the excommunication. "I regret," he said, "that in the case of my friend, Senator George, I cannot answer either of these questions in the affirmative." Mixed boos and cheers rose from the crowd. Roosevelt shook hands with George who said, "Mr. President, I want you to know that I accept the challenge." "Let's always be friends," Roosevelt answered.

His strikes against "Cotton Ed" Smith of South Carolina were more subtle. Smith's rival, Governor Olin D. Johnston, opened his campaign in Washington after an interview with the President. In a speech in Greenville, South Carolina, Roosevelt observed, "I don't believe any family or man can live on fifty cents a day," a thrust at Cotton Ed who reportedly had said a South Carolinian could. Another chosen victim, Senator Millard Tydings of Maryland, took the heavy brunt of Presidential opposition. In a press conference, Roosevelt accused Tydings of running "with the Roosevelt prestige and the money of his conservative

Republican friends both on his side." Roosevelt bolstered his Maryland favorite, David J. Lewis, with Maryland money and politicians, and his own presence in two days of campaigning. Toward Tydings he was unsparing. At Denton, on the Maryland eastern shore, he spoke reproachfully of the Senator as one of "those in public life who quote the golden rule, but take no steps to bring it closer."

The President was supplemented by a group of New Deal aides who had been in the thick of the latest legislative fights for the court-packing and reorganization bills—Harold Ickes, Harry Hopkins, David K. Niles, Joseph B. Keenan, Thomas G. Corcoran, and James Roosevelt. Each, with varying degrees of subtlety, expressed the President's displeasure with legislators who had opposed him. Increasingly, members of this group took over the national party machinery, manipulating patronage and funds, and wrested quantities of authority from the national chairman, Farley, who opposed the purge.

For all of Roosevelt's effort, the purge ended a wretched failure. Although certain of his favorites triumphed, every Senator and Congressman he marked for defeat won except Congressman O'Connor of New York, and O'Connor's loss was attributed by New York Democratic professionals not to the President's intervention, but to O'Connor's own shortcomings—a poor campaign and a fat roster of enemies who joined together to take electoral revenge. In Georgia Roosevelt's candidate, Camp, ran a poor third; in Colorado Alva B. Adams was nominated without opposition; in Connecticut Augustine Lonergan prevailed in the Democratic state convention. "It's a bust," Jim Farley observed, as Roosevelt's political stock plummeted.

In the face of Franklin Roosevelt's grisly and unforgettable failure, no President has ventured onto the purge trail since his day. Of all post-Roosevelt chief executives, only Kennedy has dared to veer, although only slightly, toward the 1938 tradition.

Yet despite Roosevelt's failure to transfer his own power and personal magnetism into victory against Congressmen who were entrenched in their local regions, he did shake his party at its roots and transform it through his own great political talent. The traditional Democratic party, on which he performed his drastic surgery, was a classical alliance of Northern city bosses and Southern and Western agrarians, bound together by states' rights beliefs and federal patronage, and enlivened with intermittent bursts of progressivism. He replaced this old party order with a new Democratic coalition enduringly committed to positive government acting for national and group welfare. He had found the Democratic party a minority party. His graftings upon it of new group allegiances left it the instrument of the majority.

Roosevelt's vision of the new party was of one free from business domination and its debilitating effect upon political morality and public policy. He attracted into the party fold labor, farmers, racial and national groups, intellectuals, and women, all disadvantaged in the business culture. He brought in as well those businessmen who were restive under Wall Street and Eastern ascendance. Roosevelt established the new coalition by a lengthy, circuitous route. In staffing his administration after his 1932 victory, he drew talent not from the traditional Democratic organization, but from the coalition. He brought Hugh Johnson, an independent, and Donald Richberg, a progressive, into NRA; Henry Wallace, a progressive, into agriculture; another progressive, Harold Ickes, into public works; Harry Hopkins, an independent, into relief administration; John Winant, a progressive, into social security; and Joseph P. Kennedy, a new entrepreneur, and James Landis, an independent, into securities regulation.

In Roosevelt's hands lawmaking was also an instrument of party reorganization. Major laws of his administration—the Social Security Act, the National Labor Relations Act, and the like—furnished the base of a new Democratic party, Northern and urban in orientation, attractive to city-centered groups, labor, Negroes, the new immigrants, women, and intellectuals. Policy and the unifying force of Roosevelt's personality, rather than pork barrel and patronage, cemented the new party. The breadth of his success was apparent as early as the 1934 Congressional elections. The Democratic returns showed an upsurge of labor and Negro votes, and of Northern Democrats in Congress with an ebbing of the relative strength of the South. Of 69 Democrats in the Senate, only 24 were Southern; of 322 Representatives, the South had 108.

The next major stroke in the Democratic party's transformation was the infiltration of New Dealers, or coalitionists, into the party's councils and operations. New Deal emissaries Edward Roddan, Stanley High, and Leon Henderson took up stations in the National Committee. In electoral contests the party's chief campaigners were the New Deal coalitionists: Roosevelt himself, of course, and Ickes, Wallace, and Hugh Johnson. Administration policy was readily manipulated to feed the political necessities of the coalition. Roosevelt, mindful of the approaching 1936 elections, told Agriculture Secretary Wallace in February, "Henry, through July, August, September, October, and up to the fifth of November, I want cotton to sell at 12 cents. I do not care how you do it. That is your problem." When a WPA cutback in relief funds threatened the dismissal of many workers on October 1, Roosevelt instructed Secretary of the Treasury Morgenthau, "You tell Corrington Gill that I don't give a goddam where he gets the money from but not one person is to be laid off on the first of October."

The courted urban groups provided not only votes but money, organizing energy, and publicity. In 1936 organized labor created Labor's Non-Partisan League, whose wealth and manpower were consecrated to Roosevelt's candidacy. Spurred and indefatigably aided by Eleanor Roosevelt, he won the enduring loyalty of Negroes to the New Deal. J. E. Spingarn, president of the National Association for the Advancement of Colored People, said of Roosevelt, "he has done more for the Negro than any Republican President since Lincoln."

Roosevelt's experience showed that a powerful President can change the national image—and the reality behind the image—of his party. He succeeded by shrewd political finesse and also by promulgating a program with which many alienated groups could identify. And it was in defense of his new alliance, held together by a program—as well as in annoyance at the opposition—that he undertook the 1938 purge. The test of a party's success, he felt, was achievement of its program, and if a few entrenched party leaders had to go to achieve it, then this was a reasonable sacrifice. But he miscalculated local loyalties to long-time leaders and the refusal of local groups to think of the good of the party as a whole.

◇

MOST Presidents climb to their exalted office by superior political skill and, upon arriving, eagerly take up their duties of party chief. But to a few chief executives, especially to hero-Presidents like Washington and Eisenhower, party activity is unwelcome, if not distasteful. Washington gladly delegated the partisan function to Alexander Hamilton, his Secretary of the Treasury, preferring to remain above the heat and dust of party battle himself. The new country, launched in perilous circumstances, required bipartisan unity in Washington's day. There was rather less compulsion for it in Eisenhower's. During his two terms, Eisenhower resolutely, but not always successfully, shied away from partisan political duty. He immensely preferred nonpartisan and bipartisan politics to partisan. He could have been nominated for the Presidency by either party, and, indeed, a concerted effort for his Presidential services was made by both parties. His most forceful lapses into partisanship occurred on the campaign trail, most notably his attacks upon the Truman administration in the 1952 electoral struggle. He supported almost any Republican who ran, and deleted from a speech in Wisconsin, in the interests of party harmony, a defense of General George C. Marshall, whose loyalty the local Republican Senator, Joseph R. McCarthy, had impugned. Eisenhower also permitted himself to be photographed with McCarthy. His foreign policy, which he largely entrusted to Secretary of State Dulles, was also hardly bipartisan.

Eisenhower's penchant for nonpartisan or bipartisan politics was a matter partly of temperament and partly of necessity. The strongest elements of his political faith were negative: return federal activities as far as possible to the states and to private responsibility, and balance the budget. His Modern Republicanism appeared to call for federal social measures, but these he chose not to push very hard. He eschewed partisan conflict, therefore, as something neither necessary nor relevant to his program, and avoided it if possible as activity that was troublesome and petty.

Eisenhower as President faced a Congress dominated by the opposition party for a longer time and in greater numbers than any President since Zachary Taylor. Even in his first two years, when the Republicans controlled Congress, hard political reality necessitated cooperation with the Democrats. The Republicans' majority in the House was eleven, and in the Senate a mere one. Even more important was the inexperience of Republican legislators in cooperating with the chief executive. Not since 1931, nearly a quarter century, had the Republican party controlled the Presidency and both houses of Congress simultaneously. Not a single Republican Senator of the Eighty-Third Congress, which commenced on January 3, 1953, had ever served with a President of his own party. Of the 221 House Republicans, only fifteen had ever experienced a Republican President. The Republican habit of opposition did not cease with Eisenhower's advent. Indeed, it is not impossible to argue that Republicans gave Eisenhower a harder time than they ever gave Kennedy and Johnson. In the Senate Joseph McCarthy, William Jenner, Henry Dworshak, Herman Welker, Hugh Butler, and George Malone were relentless foes of the President's program in maneuver, speech, and vote. McCarthy, who was largely a gathering storm during the Truman administration, reached maximun fury during Eisenhower's first term. Most Presidents would have agreed with President Eisenhower, who decided, as he faced the Congressional session of 1953, that the coming effort of the administration and of legislative Republicans should be devoted to redeeming the 1952 party platform and his own campaign pledges. Eisenhower's State of the Union Message of February 2, 1953, diligently mirrored these party pronouncements. But in the early Eisenhower Presidency, the Senate Republican leader was William F. Knowland of California, and of Knowland Sherman Adams, the President's chief assistant, has written, "It would have been difficult to find anybody more disposed to do battle with much of the President's program in Congress." Franklin Roosevelt, in contrast, worked steadily—particularly in his first years— through a legislative party leadership that ran up a high batting average of support for his measures.

Although Presidents normally can assert a large and sometimes decisive influence in choosing their party's floor leaders, they differ in willingness to enter into the decision. When Robert A. Taft was driven from his Senate leadership by illness in 1953, Eisenhower could have replaced him with almost any Senator he chose. He scrupulously refrained, however, from influencing in the least way the selection of the new floor leader and even asked his administration colleagues not to express their preferences. Eisenhower felt that executive intrusion in this Senate affair was Constitutionally inappropriate and might well be resented by Congressional Republicans. The President's staunch abstinence was ill-rewarded. He got Senator Knowland. Eisenhower doubtless discovered that not to take a stand is, in fact, to take a stand. Two years later, in the struggle between the incumbent Joe Martin and his challenger Charles Halleck for the House floor leadership, Eisenhower took a wholly opposite stance. Martin had long displeased the administration by the mildness of his efforts in its behalf. Republican loss of House control in the 1954 elections made his continuance as floor leader highly doubtful. The administration did not hide its friendliness to Halleck's aspirations. When, after some struggle, Martin held onto the leadership and gave no place to Halleck in the leadership group, Eisenhower insisted that Halleck henceforth attend the legislative leaders' meetings at the White House. Eventually Halleck overthrew Martin as floor leader.

On April 30, 1953, a historic explosion occurred when Eisenhower, meeting with Congressional leaders, broke the news that despite severe cutting he could not balance the new budget as Robert A. Taft, Senate majority leader and "Mr. Republican," and others who were present had hoped. The President and Defense Department officials explained that part of the difficulty was that certain revisions were necessary in the nation's defense program. Suddenly Taft erupted, losing control of himself, pounding his fist on the cabinet table, and shouting at the stunned President seated opposite him. "With a program like this, we'll never elect a Republican Congress in 1954," Taft cried, "You're taking us down the same road Truman traveled. It's a repudiation of everything we promised in the campaign!" Taft went on excitedly, and when he stopped, tension gripped the room. Fortunately, several of those present commenced an aimless conversation until Eisenhower, flushed and upset, recovered himself to state in measured tones the necessities of global strategy.

Republican legislators were the most relentless foes of Eisenhower's mutual security program. Some Republicans wanted to reduce taxes at once regardless of the costs of the ongoing Korean War. Others wanted to scuttle the Reciprocal Trade Agreements Act and restore the high-tariff Smoot-Hawley Act of the Hoover era. In jest and in no little truth, Harry S. Truman declared as the 1954 Congressional elections neared, "It seems to me that President Eisenhower should be secretly wishing for a Democratic Congress . . . and hope that we can save him from the misdeeds of his own party." Not surprisingly, Eisenhower sometimes speculated privately with his aides whether he really belonged "in this kind of Republican party." He mused over the desirability of forming a new political party, internationalist, welfare-oriented, but conservative in spending and economic regulation.

Out of such experience, Eisenhower, understandably, never wore his hat as party chieftain gladly. To the Republican faithful, he denied even that he was a politician. "Everybody knew I wasn't a politician—and I'm not yet," he told a group of Republican workers on October 17, 1953. He clung to his chosen nonpartisan demeanor. He said at his news conference of February 10, 1954,

> I don't believe in bitter partisanship. I never believe that all wisdom is confined to one of the great parties, and I certainly have never in general terms criticized the other party, that is, to include its great membership. I believe there are good Americans in both parties, and I believe that the great mass of both parties is fundamentally and naturally sound.

As the 1954 Congressional elections neared, he cautioned his cabinet against an overly partisan approach, adding that he must take care himself to remain nonpartisan in using the national radio and television networks except on programs paid for by the party. When Republicans everywhere, with the eagerness of those whose bread and butter is at stake, pressed Eisenhower to stump the country for the party tickets, he refused, acknowledging at a press conference, "I am deeply interested in what happens to the complexion of the Senate and the House of Representatives, but I do not intend to make of the Presidency an agency to use in partisan elections." His administration colleagues bolstered the President's view. Henry Cabot Lodge, ambassador to the United Nations, wrote to Eisenhower in July 1954, "The basic factor is and always will be the country's confidence in you. This confidence in you can be maintained and, with it, your immense influence for good, no matter what the election results may be." And yet as the 1954 elections came closer, and the party pressures mounted, Eisenhower finally yielded and took off for ten thousand miles of travel and forty speeches. His spreading involvement never overcame his distaste for campaigning. "By golly, sometimes you sure get tired of all this clackety-clack," he remarked to Jim Hagerty, his press secretary, on election eve.

Soon after the Democrats captured Congress in 1954, Eisenhower informed his cabinet he did not see how there could be any question of the need for the White House to work with the Democratic leadership. He held bipartisan meetings with the legislative leaders and, when major happenings were afoot, diligently kept both sets of party leaders informed. Upon returning from his 1956 Bermuda meeting with Prime

Minister Harold Macmillan, for instance, he invited spokesmen from both parties on the Hill to the White House for a report on the conference. In public pronouncement, as well as in private act, Eisenhower maintained a moderate demeanor toward the Democrats. "Whenever he thought any one of us became too harsh," Sherman Adams has written, "he would remind us that we were not going to get anywhere in Congress without Democratic votes."

Each President, as party leader, is expected to assist the campaigns of Congressional candidates indiscriminately, including the campaigns of those whose election would injure his program more than their opponents' victories would. Roosevelt's attempt to flaunt this tradition had ended in failure. In the 1954 Congressional elections President Eisenhower permitted himself to be photographed with a hundred or more Republican candidates, an imposing advantage in a local campaign. He also promised to make speeches delineating his program if he happened to be in the vicinity of a candidate who supported it and invited him to speak. Asked how he chose from among the Congressmen for bestowal of his photographic and rhetorical favors, he acknowledged that there was "a little bit of a check" on the legislators' voting record. In actuality, he was not known to withhold support in 1954 from any of the more recalcitrant legislators in his party who asked for it. For the President, loyalty to party generally transcended loyalty to program during campaigns.

Roosevelt and Kennedy took the position that support for their program *was* loyalty to the party. Perhaps a strong President inevitably assumes that he and his program and the party are synonymous. The party professional, however, makes no such assumption, except for pragmatic reasons in Presidential election years.

So Eisenhower, whose temperament was bipartisan, or perhaps more accurately apolitical, was forced by circumstances into assuming a highly partisan role in election years and a bipartisan role in between in his relations with a Democratic Congress. He was a man of uncomplicated loyalties and ideological simplicity, a man for whom conflict over program or over people was uncongenial. His election-year loyalty to his party, therefore, proved nearly absolute. Is it a political paradox that those Presidents who are less party-minded can be counted on to support the party most (but with least effect) and that those who are genuinely partisan—and strong—will defy the party when a few block the fulfillment of the party's promised program?

◇

PRESIDENT KENNEDY had paid considerable heed to the lessons of both Roosevelt and Eisenhower. He was deeply concerned over the fact that a party's national program supported by its presidential candidate may falter or fail at the hands of the party's own leaders in Congress. Was the answer not to wait for the election year to initiate a purge, but to move upon the source of power ahead of time—in the state and local party organizations, where the seeds of trouble germinate?

The state party organizations are allegedly self-governing principalities, but Kennedy, who pursued his duties of party chief with zest, remorseless diligence, and ingenuity, moved upon them with aggressive enterprise. He acted principally through his personal organization—Lawrence F. O'Brien and Kenneth O'Donnell, his brother Robert and his brother-in-law Stephen E. Smith, and other associates, all of whom enjoyed close personal ties with state and local Democratic power centers in the big Northern industrial states on which Kennedy concentrated. His own organization in these states was in some ways more powerful than the regular Democratic organization. He maintained close ties with state leaders such as Jesse M. Unruh of California, city leaders such as Ray Miller of Cleveland, and local potentates such as Charles A. Buckley of the Bronx, dealing them considerable preferment. After the 1962 elections his brother-in-law Stephen Smith, a man of quiet competence, served the Democratic National Committee as a trouble shooter in the key states of New York, Pennsylvania, Ohio, and Michigan, all of which had chosen Republican governors. Smith's chief responsibility in his uneasy capacity was to prevent fractious Democrats from feuding with each other. His early assignments included the laying of olive branches on such adversaries as "reform" Senator Joseph Clark of Pennsylvania and Philadelphia "machine" leader Congressman William Green, Jr. In Michigan Smith toiled to heal the rift between the United Auto Workers and Democratic regulars, and in New York to quell the party's lengthy strife and chaos.

Kennedy did much "coordinating" himself. Soon after taking office, he worked mightily to revise the New York State Democratic leadership. He gave the cold shoulder to two top Democratic chieftains, Carmine De Sapio, New York County leader, and Michael Prendergast, state chairman. The more luscious patronage appointments credited to New York were awarded to members of a reform Democratic group dedicated to Prendergast's and De Sapio's ouster. The President appointed as ambassador to NATO Thomas K. Finletter, who with former Senator Herbert H. Lehman and Mrs. Franklin Roosevelt shared the top anti–De Sapio leadership in Manhattan. Lehman's grandnephew, Jonathan B. Bingham, was named United States Representative to the United Nations Trusteeship Council. Francis T. P. Plimpton, appointed deputy representative to the United Nations, was a resident of Suffolk County, but no endorsement was sought from the Suffolk Democratic leader. John S. Stillman, Orange County Democratic chairman, who was named assistant to the Undersecretary of Commerce, was never regarded as an ally of Prendergast.

Kennedy's "cold treatment" of De Sapio and Prendergast had a social dimension. During his inauguration ceremonies, Kennedy pointedly distinguished between New York Democrats in good and bad standing. Congressman Charles A. Buckley, the long-time Bronx Democratic leader, Joseph T. Sharkey, the Brooklyn leader, and Peter J. Crotty, the Erie County chairman, all enjoyed places in the Presidential box at the Inaugural Ball. Prendergast and De Sapio were among the fifteen thousand dancers who milled about on the floor. In a visit to New York City several weeks later, Kennedy rode with James A. Farley through the city streets, visited Lehman at his apartment, interviewed Sharkey, and talked with Buckley on the telephone. De Sapio was totally ignored and Prendergast heard only from a member of the Presidential staff. By these and other means Kennedy implied he would never deal with Prendergast and De Sapio, and encouraged lesser New York Democrats to challenge their leadership.

Kennedy resorted to several expedients to advance the candidacies of legislative Democrats he viewed favorably. To further the cause of Wilkes T. Thrasher, Jr., an all-out New Frontiersman running in the Third Congressional District of Tennessee in 1962, he picked the candidate to represent him as a special ambassador at independence ceremonies in Trinidad. The scarcity of such plums underscored the importance of the President's action. As the 1962 elections neared, Kennedy seemed to take a giant step toward Roosevelt's method when he announced that he was "going to help elect Democrats" who supported his legislative program. The incumbent Representative Leonard Farbstein of Manhattan, who was running for re-election, faced a primary contest with Assemblyman Bentley Kassal, the reform Democratic candidate. In a letter to Farbstein, Kennedy praised his "clear judgment, wisdom, dedication and energy" and expressed "my personal appreciation for your sustained support of our legislative program." Farbstein made the letter public, terming it an endorsement. His opponent, Kassal, contended that it was not, that he had been assured indeed that Kennedy would not take sides in the primary. The President said no more, and Farbstein swept on to victory. Reform groups are common casualties of Presidential party decisions, especially where the rival individual or group represents power the President cherishes or respects. Farbstein, as a member of the House Foreign Affairs Committee, had been an ardent advocate of bills favorable to Israel. In turn, the administration's attitude toward Israel is considered important by large numbers of Jewish voters in New York.

Kennedy, as other Presidents have done in by-year elections, viewed the 1962 electoral campaign not merely as an opportunity to elect Democratic legislators, but to bring his goals and programs to the people. Two years of feet-dragging by a Democratic Congress added glow to the opportunity. But while the President serves his own purposes, at least partially, his presence is cherished by the Congressional candidates and the local party organizations. Kennedy's capacity to bring out the crowds gave tremendous publicity to the campaign and a great boost to campaign enthusiasm. Thanks to the perquisites of his office, the President also has campaigning facilities which no competitor can match. While out on the trail in 1962, Kennedy had an entourage of five press assistants, a reporting service that produced texts of his speeches within minutes of their delivery, and a busload of miscellaneous aides. The transportation of himself and his group was cared for by a fleet of White House automobiles, two jet airliners, a DC-7 airliner, and four Army jet-powered helicopters. Everywhere he went he was followed by forty-four reporters, photographers, and television technicians traveling by chartered plane. His chief rival campaigner, former President Eisenhower, toured in an eight-passenger aircraft unaccompanied by press parties, mimeograph machines, or helicopters.

Like other Presidents before him, Kennedy in his attentions to the states was by no means always on the side of the reformers—if support for the regulars strengthened his own position. At a Democratic fund-raising dinner in New York City, he sent Charles A. Buckley a lavish verbal bouquet, described by a Kennedy staff member as "the most personal message I've ever known in all my twelve years' association with the President." The message, which was read at the dinner, was signed significantly, by "Joe, Jack, Bobby and Teddy Kennedy." This fulsome tribute to one of the most encrusted and anachronistic of bosses, brought the New York *Times* to protest the President's knowing recognition of a figure who needed to be "decried and deplored" rather than "promoted and protected." Not the least importance of Buckley was that as chairman of the House Public Works Committee he was admirably situated to help the administration by influencing other House Democrats to vote for the President's bills. In the Pennsylvania struggle between Senator Joseph Clark, a liberal reformer, and Congressman William J. Green, an old-style political boss of Philadelphia whose habit was victory, Kennedy veered toward Green. The President needed the Congressman for the 1964 election if the 1960 contest were a guide. In 1960 Kennedy had carried Philadelphia by a 337,000 vote majority, amply assisted by Green's machine. Yet he had carried the state of Pennsylvania by only 51.2 per cent of the vote. Green's obvious usefulness led Kennedy to shower him with attentions. The Congressman visited Kennedy in Florida, sat in his box at a football game, and accompanied him in his helicopter to the funeral of Senator Robert S. Kerr in Oklahoma. Not that Kennedy was against party reform—though many party leaders thought so—but he believed that the only way to achieve it was to win over the power centers for himself first.

Publicity is another weapon a President can employ to promote his legislative party friends, and President Kennedy moved in 1963 to co-ordinate White House publicity with the needs of his Democratic supporters on Capitol Hill. The President brought Paul Southwick, an experienced newspaperman, into the White House from the Area Redevelopment Agency of the Commerce Department. Southwick, as part of the White House press office staff, forwarded useful news and information to the Democratic legislators with suggestions of how they might exploit the President's activities for their own publicity needs.

In another publicity gambit, Kennedy moved to wrest from the Republican party one of its proudest possessions, the observance of Abraham Lincoln's birthday. He celebrated that event in 1963, the centenary of the Emancipation Proclamation, with a White House reception for Negro and civil rights leaders and a host of Democrats, chiefly legislators who supported the Kennedy program. More than a thousand celebrants were on hand, including Negroes distinguished in endeavors ranging from law to jazz. The day was ripe with suggestion of the solid harmony between Lincoln's ideals and contemporary Democratic action. Prior to a buffet, Kennedy received at a ceremony in his office a report on civil rights progress in the hundred years since Lincoln's Emancipation Proclamation. The report noted that "as the century following emancipation draws to a close, more forces are working for the realization of civil rights for all Americans than ever before in history. Government is active in every branch and at every level, if not in every region." But, it added, with a solid air of commitment, "The final chapter in the struggle for equality has yet to be written."

Kennedy's death cut short the experiment that was to have been tested in the 1964 Presidential election and probably in the 1966 Congressional election. He died in the line of duty as party leader. The purpose of his visit to Texas, which ended in his assassination, was to reduce the widening cleavage between Texan Democratic factions identified with Senator Ralph W. Yarborough and the then Vice President Johnson. It is left for future Presidents to see whether the stalemate between the party's Presidential leadership and its Congressional leadership can ever be resolved in favor of the President and the majority of the nation who support him. The Kennedy formula looked for the eventual dominance of urban politics over Congressional politics. His legislative program was heavily directed toward the urban vote, and his personal political organization concentrated upon winning and holding the allegiance of the great Democratic organizations in the Northern urban states. The combination of a program geared to urban groups and a personal political organization that mobilized local party organization conceivably could have added up to a force that Democratic legislators would have found difficult to resist after 1964.

An intriguing political question is whether Lyndon Johnson can in the future carry forward as party leader where Kennedy left off. One unknown quantity is the degree to which Johnson's switch in positions from Senate majority leader to President will influence his stand on program. In the Senate, his program orientation was relatively conservative. In his Presidency, his New Deal background has come into greater evidence than in his Senate days. To fashion a 1964 electoral victory, he must solve his major campaign problem of carrying the urban industrial states of the Northern tier: New York, Pennsylvania, Illinois, and others, and to do so he must offer a liberal economic and social program. To make his way in the big states, he must rely heavily upon the Kennedy personal staff since he has no corps of his own aides with a comparable network of personal contacts with state and local Democratic organizations.

◇

AT MOST the President can be only a quasi–party leader. A variety of forces and pressures compel him to temper and contain his partisanship. He must at times give higher priority to his calling as leader of the nation, facing needs and goals greater than those of his party. He may face a Congress one or both of whose houses is dominated by the opposition party. The body of independent voters has increased to such a degree that in several Presidential elections they have held the key to the outcome. Thanks to weak party discipline, a President knows the difference between a "paper" or party majority in Congress and a "working" majority. In many of his waking hours he is forced to be bipartisan or nonpartisan if he is to pick up needed legislative votes from the other party. Bipartisan leadership is exerted at a price. It rests upon consultation and compromise and necessarily reduces the forcefulness of policy and the President's program image.

Viewed another way, although the party system has enabled a national popular majority to choose a President, when he attempts to translate his electoral promises into policy he finds himself in a government that permits only limited majority rule, thanks to separation of powers and checks and balances, among other things. Only a rare President, such as a Jefferson or a Franklin Roosevelt, succeeds in building a strength as party leader that enables him to extend substantially the principle of majority rule. Despite the limiting realities of the party and the governmental structure, what can be done to help the strong President also be a strong party leader?

1. The formula evident in John Kennedy's labor as party leader, one which his death prevented him from fulfilling, appears the most promising. Kennedy was bent upon subordinating party and Congressional politics to urban politics. He pitched his program to the great urban groups: economic, racial, and national. In light of his proven appeal to them, he could confidently cultivate state and local party leaders who determine the selection of and the support given to Congressional candidates. The Kennedy method, had he lived to follow it through, would have lighted hundreds of bonfires under Congressmen and Senators, fueled by an urban program and maintained by urban groups and local party chieftains. The movement of social forces strongly supports the Kennedy formula: the enormous growth of urban population; its interest, as Arthur N. Holcombe long ago reminded us, in class politics and therefore program politics; and the growing sophistication of urban groups in political action—in organizing and defining their objectives on a national scale.

The urban-group formula admittedly carries weaknesses. The individual's identification is primarily with the group rather than with the party. A comparison of strong group identification with the Democratic party in the Franklin Roosevelt era and its weakening in the Truman-Stevenson era reveals its vulnerability to fluctuating events, and shifts in group and Presidential personalities. The urban-group approach has limited relevance to Republican Presidential needs because of the growing tendency of the groups to identify with the Democratic party. The Republicans must resort to a diversified appeal to the urban and suburban voter, the independent, the detachable Democrat, and a broad swath of other interests. The Kennedy recipe is good for Democrats but not Republicans.

2. Kennedy in his approach relied heavily upon a sizable personal Presidential organization to assist his party leadership by building contacts with state and local leaders. To "keep in touch" with fifty state organizations and hundreds of local organizations is a massive enterprise which a President must continously conduct or oversee. Above all, he needs loyal and capable helpers who are best assured if he recruits them himself. In the manner of Jackson and Kennedy, a President is well advised to install in the executive branch a corps of aides for party affairs who can concentrate upon them as Amos Kendall and Frank Blair did in Jackson's day and Kenneth O'Donnell and Lawrence O'Brien did in Kennedy's.

3. Kennedy was building up a technique of the "soft purge," a useful device for future Presidents. Since Franklin D. Roosevelt's ill-fated experience, Presidents had backed away from the open, concentrated purge. Kennedy, in the tradition of Jefferson, quietly encouraged his

favored candidates for Congressional office, without arousing local resentments over Presidential interference. Kennedy and his aides distributed pork barrel, publicity, campaign assistance, and Presidential blandishments in a fashion that heaped, within discreet limits, conspicuous attention upon proper voting legislators and pointedly reduced or withheld the several beneficences from offenders.

4. To strengthen the President as party leader, we might, not illogically, strengthen the parties themselves. The most comprehensive effort toward this end was proposed by a committee of the American Political Science Association in 1950, which after viewing British political parties admiringly recommended in a report, *Toward a More Responsible Two-Party System*, that several of their features be adapted for American use. The committee proposed that we revise the size and timing of our national conventions, create a national party council or cabinet, stimulate regional as opposed to state and local organizations, formulate more positive platforms, and encourage closed primaries.

Although the dream of this report has not come true, several trends are afoot agreeable to it. The Democratic Advisory Council, which has endeavored with mixed success to work out party positions on policy questions, is a substantial step toward the party council or cabinet proposed by the APSA report. The national party committee, which the APSA committee did not look upon favorably as a vehicle of policy influence, is nevertheless expanding its functions, particularly the Republican committee, in a manner potentially advantageous to the President's party influence. The national committee is the biggest collector, allocator, and spender of party money. It locates and channels patronage and is the party's dominant publicity agent in national elections. It focuses upon policy in its research, public relations, and speech-making activities. Often the committee is a catalytic in policy matters. Both the Republican and Democratic National Committees are stressing ties with pressure groups. It would be foolhardy to expect any miraculous changes in national organization that somehow would suddenly and vastly improve the President's party position. Yet the national party organization will bear watching as a flexible and fluctuating phenomenon, particularly as its relationships to pressure groups extend and deepen.

5. The gadgetry of Congressional party organization is least promising of all for future Presidential leadership. The main thrust in behalf of centralized party management are the policy committees which have proved a blunted sword. The committees' best uses are service and research, education, and legislative scheduling. Intermittently, however, they work out policy positions, significant not for their number but for the fact that they can and do materialize. The Senate Democratic Policy Committee, for example, opposed sanctions against Israel upon her re-

fusal to withdraw from the Gaza Strip. The Republican Policy Committee prepared a compromise on the Bricker Amendment, with Secretary of State Dulles and Attorney General Herbert Brownell in attendance, which won support from two-thirds of the Republican Senators. In the Eighty-Third Congress, the Democratic Policy Committee forged a party position on the proposal to tie together measures for Alaskan and Hawaiian statehood.

The Congressional and Senatorial Campaign Committees are devoted chiefly to publicity, to doling out funds for campaigning, and to research on public reactions to issues. Thanks to the separation of powers and its psychological side effects, they are jealous of their autonomy and would spurn any plan to bring them into close conjunction with the Presidentially oriented National Committee.

CHAPTER

6

Legislative Leader

—

IN a year-end 1962 interview John F. Kennedy said,

> The fact is, I think, the Congress looks more powerful sitting here than it did when I was there in the Congress. But that is because when you are in the Congress you are one of a hundred in the Senate or one of 435 in the House. So that the power is so divided. But from here I look at a Congress, and I look at the collective power of the Congress, particularly the bloc action, and it is a substantial power.

Congress's power to check and frustrate the executive has been a matter of chronic Presidential discovery from the very outset of Constitutional experience. George Washington's election as President was delayed a month until the requisite number of legislators straggled into the capital to enable Congress to organize itself and witness the electoral count. After his inauguration Washington suffered more frustration. Congress dilly-dallied in providing executive departments which the Constitution allowed for and without whose assistance the President could not function. Not until June 23, more than three weeks after the inauguration, did Congress provide the first department, a Department of Foreign Affairs.

Even a President like Dwight Eisenhower, who generally viewed Congress with good will, was sometimes seized with sensations of futility. One of his severer attacks occurred in 1955, when the administration's highway program passed the Senate but was stopped in the House, and Congress adjourned. The country faced the unhappy prospect of falling further behind in its poor race to build roads for the swelling torrents of traffic. The lack of a highway program also hurt the general economy. Eisenhower's aides, with a sense of looming disaster, urged him to call Congress into special session to act on the vital highway program. "Well," the President said ruefully, "the special session might be necessary—but calling it could be at the cost of the sanity of one man named Eisenhower." There was no sense in spending money to call them back, he added, "when I knew in advance that the result would be zero."

Eisenhower long had known the unreliability of Congressmen in transmuting the national party platform and Presidential campaign pledges into legislation. In delineating his initial program at the outset of his term, he had taken pains to remind his cabinet and legislative leaders that the Republican platform of 1952 comprised "the minimum limits of achievement below which we must not fall." Eisenhower's dedication to the platform was received with open amusement by the legislative leaders. "To my astonishment," Eisenhower has written, "I discovered that some of the men in the room could not seem to understand the seriousness with which I regarded our platform's provisions. . . . More than once I was to hear this view derided by 'practical politicians' who laughed off platforms as traps to catch voters." In his 1960 campaign John Kennedy spelled out a program by which alert and aggressive leadership might move the country forward again. He put forth several hundred specific proposals: parity for the farmer through a supply program, medical care for the aged under Social Security, full employment, equal rights for women, price stability, freer foreign trade, urban renewal, a new civil rights law, and the like. Most of Kennedy's campaign pledges required legislative fulfillment and therefore provided a ready foundation for his legislative program as President. But what came forth was a shrunken image of the earlier promises. Kennedy dropped permanent improvements in unemployment compensation and repeal of right-to-work laws, among other things; he trod softly on education, oil depletion allowances, and medical care for the aged; and he postponed civil rights. There were no radical new ideas, no great transformations of policy like those implied in the rhetoric of the 1960 campaign. In the main his items were familiar holdovers from the Eisenhower era, items that might have been passed if Eisenhower had chosen to push them. Kennedy, in a sound appraisal of Congressional realities, chose to set his sights low.

Congress follows the Presidential lead with consistency only in crisis. During the wars in 1917 and 1941 and the depression in 1933 Congress did the President's bidding. It is then that national opinion demands action, looks to the President for initiative, and brooks no denial. In the absence of crisis the President can seldom push great legislation through

Congress. Woodrow Wilson did in 1913 and again in 1916, and Theodore Roosevelt did in spurts over two terms. Wilson and Theodore Roosevelt were masters at rallying public sentiment and at manipulating in legislative encounters, and they were downright lucky in several vital particulars. Both thrived upon the nation's expanding progressive sentiment. Wilson enjoyed a large Democratic majority in the House and staunch support in the Senate. A majority of Senators in both parties were advanced progressives. No substantial rival leader flourished in the House. One hundred fourteen out of 290 House Democrats had been elected for the first time. Eager to please, their future careers depending heavily upon executive patronage and the administration's general success, they were amenable to Presidential direction.

Presidents since World War II have maintained a high batting average of success in the fields of national security and foreign affairs. Not Presidential skill or legislative acumen, but the mischief of the Russians, is the cement of union. A Truman Doctrine, a Marshall Plan, and a NATO are supported with little difficulty. Although foreign aid is an annual ordeal, the President eventually prevails. The Foreign Trade Act of 1962 and the test-ban treaty stand as Kennedy's outstanding legislative achievements. In the domestic fields the picture of Presidential achievement is ominously drab. Since 1936 only two pieces of major domestic legislation have been passed: the Fair Labor Standards Act of 1938 and the Taft-Hartley Act of 1947. The political landscape is strewn with the wreckage of Presidential proposals. The major Kennedy-Johnson planks on education and medical care for the aged remain unrealized, and civil rights finally emerged only after long delay under conditions of crisis.

◇

CONGRESS repeatedly checks and balances the President largely because they represent altogether contrasting constituencies. The President, chosen by the nation, is the natural instrument of majoritarian rule—is, as Max Lerner has written, "The greatest majority-weapon our democracy has thus far shaped." It is, to be sure, a contrived majority, one normally more difficult to maintain than to create, an association of purposeful pressure groups and the great mass of little-organized citizenry, distributed across the several sections of the country, each with its distinctive social and cultural tradition and economic organization. Congress, in contrast, is the product of local constituencies: the Senate emerging from the substantial land mass of the states and the House, except for its members at large, from the smaller Congressional districts. The validity of both the national and the local viewpoints found in the executive and legislative constituencies is affirmed by the federal principle of government incorporated in the Constitution.

Congress's relationship to the "national majority" differs in other respects from the President's. The totality of the two-house Congress is never the product of any conceivable national majority, since only one-third of the Senate is chosen in any given election. The President's national majority and the Senate's and House's local majorities have varying periods of legitimacy expressed in the terms of office allotted to the candidates they elect: the Senate for six years, the President for four, the House for two. The Senator or Congressman is identified with several kinds of majority: with the majority of his constituency, with the party majority in his house, and with the voting majority in his house. In carrying on the legislative process, the houses of Congress contain no continuing majority. A majority accumulates or emerges for limited purposes but never hardens into a durable entity. The legislative majority that passes a particular bill develops from a series of processes by which members are elected, the internal authority of the House and Senate are allocated, an agenda is selected, and procedures of debate and vote are followed. But once the bill is passed and others arise, new and almost invariably different majorities must be constructed. But Congress is also the haven for the minority—the minority party, the maverick legislator. Congress speaks with many voices. The chief executive, with his concentration of authority and use of hierarchical organization, aims to speak with one. Congress represents the rich diversity of American life, the President its necessary unity.

Despite their imposing differences, no one branch, executive or legislative, can claim inherent superiority in articulating the national or public interest. A Washington and a Wilson are shining beacons of public interest, but who can say that in the quest for the common good President Harding was superior to Senator Norris, or President Coolidge to Senator La Follette? Legislators sometimes speak with more initiative, force, and freedom on national issues than Presidents of their eras do. Webster and Clay are better remembered than most of their Presidential contemporaries. In 1964 Fulbright could undertake a candid and comprehensive review of the prevailing foreign policy in terms unthinkable, at least in public utterance, for the chief executive and his principal subordinates. Many of the nation's foremost economic and social policies were first championed by legislators well before the President was prepared to exert his influence. Thus the Federal Reserve System was preceded by the legislative spadework of Carter Glass before Woodrow Wilson took it up, the Tennessee Valley Authority by years of advocacy by Senator George Norris, and key New Deal policies by the pioneering effort of Senator Robert F. Wagner. It would be folly, in light of the historical record, to view the executive branch as the seat of omniscience and Congress as merely negative and local. For Theodore Roosevelt a strong Presidency was premised upon a strong Congress.

But distinguished legislators are more common than strong Congresses. In brutal truth, Congress is far more often weak in accomplishment than strong. However memorable a La Follette or a Norris may be, the houses of Congress are more than assemblages of individuals; they are also corporate bodies with a hearty preference for inaction and conservative leadership. Compared with the Court and the Presidency, Congress has a special distinction. It is, as Senator Joseph Clark of Pennsylvania has put it, the one branch of our federal government where twentieth-century men are not in charge.

In a series of speeches that he delivered in February 1963 Senator Clark candidly analyzed the Senate organization and found that body in the hands of a "dominant minority" rather than what he termed its "creative majority." Both the House and the Senate work with a body of procedures which have an awesome capacity either for preventing Congress from acting at all or for ensuring that it will act only after unconscionable delay. In the last year of President Kennedy's administration, his tax bill, to which he gave the highest priority, languished eight and a half months in the House Ways and Means Committee before it was reported out. The Senate Finance Committee just barely completed hearings on the measure before adjournment. At this same juncture, the civil rights bill, dispatched with the highest Presidential urgency, was becalmed in the House Rules Committee after a full six months of House attention. Of twelve appropriations bills required for the fiscal year beginning in June, only four reached the White House by the following December.

❖

CONGRESS'S internal organization and processes constitute a vast terrain of booby traps for the Presidential program. The standing committees and their chairmen, the negative power of the House Rules Committee, and the Senatorial filibuster are all potential occasions of disaster for the President. The regular center of the President's concerns is the standing Congressional committee, where party discipline is least potent.

Committees provide the money and authority indispensable to executive action. The committee chairman is a potentate presiding over a great satrapy, calling meetings when he chooses, setting the agenda, allocating time for testimony, and personally reporting the committee's measures to the floor. The sole principle by which he is chosen is seniority. He rises to his eminence not by proven excellence or loyalty to President or party, but simply by being present year in and year out. Since seniority is most easily built by legislators from "safe districts," chairmen emerge most steadily from the Old South and Northern rural districts, and with such backgrounds they prove beyond doubt that a safe seat cultivates independence both from the national party and from the President. The geographic distortion of Senate committee chairmanships is evidenced by the fact that in 1964 ten out of sixteen of these posts were occupied by Southerners. These included such crucial committees as Finance, Judiciary, Foreign Relations, Labor and Public Welfare, Government Operations, and Banking and Currency, where most of the legislation that was of major concern to the Johnson administration reposed.

Accordingly, any modern President, whether Republican or Democrat, faces an array of chairmen instinctively and philosophically hostile to his programs. Consider the chairmen of several major committees that hold the sword of fate over the Kennedy-Johnson programs. Howard W. ("Judge") Smith, the octogenarian chairman of the House Rules Committee, was first elected to Congress in 1930 from the Arlington-Alexandria district across the Potomac from Washington. When migrating federal bureaucrats rendered his tenure unsafe, Smith moved to a new and more tenable district in the Virginia interior which the state legislature obligingly created. A dedicated conservative, Smith has compiled an awesome record for killing, watering down, and postponing progressive Presidential legislation. He bottled up in the Rules Committee Franklin Roosevelt's Wage and Hour bill, battled most of Truman's Fair Deal program, and throttled education and welfare measures in both the Eisenhower and Kennedy administrations. He blocked Alaskan statehood for almost a year. In the Senate the chairmen of such key committees as Finance and Judiciary are Harry F. Byrd of Virginia and James O. Eastland of Mississippi, neither of whom supported the Democratic ticket or platform in 1960. Not strangely, the Kennedy-Johnson administration's most serious defeats have been prompted by the failure of standing committees to report out key measures.

Not only may the chairman of a standing committee be hostile to the President's program, but its members may be as well. The appointment of committees is largely in the hands of what in actuality is the ruling oligarchy of each house. In the Senate, for example, the Democratic Steering Committee, which serves as the party's Committee on Committees, exercises three vital functions affecting the standing committees. It gives Democratic Senators their committee assignments, determines the committees' size, and establishes the ratio between parties in committee memberships. In discharging its duties, the Democratic Steering Committee can discriminate against Senators who strongly support the President's program. The 1958 elections, for example, brought fifteen new Democratic Senators into the Senate. They were chiefly from the urban and industrial North, Midwest, and West, and without exception supported a legislative program strongly directed toward those interests. At the time the Senate Democratic Steering Committee consisted of fourteen members, half of them from the South. While such a distribution was reasonably in line with the body of forty-nine Democratic Senators in the previous Senate, it was hardly representative of the new total of sixty-two Democratic Senators. Soon after the 1958 election, Senator Joseph S. Clark of Pennsylvania, whose outlook was that of the urban, industrialized North, urged the then majority leader, Lyndon Johnson, to alter the Steering Committee balance "so that it would reflect not only the party within the Senate, and the will of the people as expressed in the election, but also the coming-of-age of the Senate in the modern world." But to no avail. "The Majority Leader did not agree with me," Clark has written, "and he worked his will in the caucus."

The dominance of the seniority principle—which is a custom, since it is not incorporated in any rule—is a standard, but not an inexorable Senate procedure. In 1913, for instance, it was overthrown when Senate progressives of all parties united into a majority to displace senior committee chairmen with young men, some of whom had not served in the Senate for more than two years. Meeting privately, they laid plans that enabled them to take over the Senate, reconstitute the memberships of all committees, oust the committee chairmen, and replace them with men of their own. This enterprise was indispensable for the progress of the series of legislative enactments which soon became known as Wilson's New Freedom program.

The President also may be a reforming force in the committee power structure. President Kennedy set as his first order of legislative business an assault on the most powerful of committees, the House Rules Committee, which schedules or refuses to schedule the time and conditions under which important bills come before the House. Thanks to the exertions of Speaker Sam Rayburn, the Rules Committee was enlarged by three members, hopefully a safe voting margin for administration measures. But thanks also to the behind-the-scenes bargaining over the new memberships, the administration emerged with only a precarious eight-to-seven vote advantage on liberal-conservative issues. The injection of religious, racial, or special economic factors, as events soon proved, were enough to capsize the administration's narrow majority. The committee not surprisingly stopped the administration's education bill on the parochial schools issue in 1961, stripped the scholarship provisions of the college aid bill in 1962, bottled up the urban affairs bill when the President announced that Robert C. Weaver, a Negro, would become Secretary of the new department, and stopped bills for youth employment and mass transit. In 1963 the Rules Committee was permanently enlarged, an action Kennedy encouraged by declaring that if the committee were not continued in its expanded state, his program would be "emasculated."

There is no better proof than the Senate filibuster that Congress is often more the instrument of minority than of majority. It is an ancient and favorite weapon of obstructionists—Senator John T. Morgan holding up ratification of the Colombian treaty for the Panama Canal and forcing Theodore Roosevelt to convene the Senate in special session to win the treaty's approval; the several Senators who blocked Wilson's proposal to arm merchant vessels against German U-boat attack in 1917; "Fighting Bob" La Follette's eighteen-hour marathon against the Aldrich-Vreeland Currency bill in 1908. For years, the filibuster or threat of it has been unsurpassed in blocking or paring down civil rights legislation. At the outset of the Kennedy years, legislative liberals, eager to pass a strong civil rights bill, launched an assault on the filibuster.

Kennedy, although privy to the liberals' moves, desisted from backing up the fight for fear of defeat and loss of world prestige early in his administration. The fight was resumed by the liberals in 1963 at the opening of the Eighty-Eighth Congress, equally without result. As before, Kennedy remained aloof. President Lyndon Johnson's severest legislative task in 1964 was to steer a meaningful civil rights bill past the shoals of a Southern filibuster. He prevailed, thanks to a rare imposition of closure and indispensable Republican support.

◇

THE procedures by which Congress is weighted in favor of conservative interests are reinforced by distortions in the methods by which the House of Representatives is selected. The Constitution requires that seats in the House be apportioned among the states according to population determined by the census every ten years. After each census Congress allocates to every state the number of House seats to which it is entitled according to its population. The state legislature then determines what the boundaries of each Congressional district will be and whether any of its House seats shall be subject to election at large. This political enterprise often incurs several kinds of abuses. One is the "gerrymander," by which the state legislature will carve out boundaries of Congressional districts in a fashion that will assure optimum popular voting strength for the candidates of its own party. The result is frequently a district of bizarre artistry, variously resembling a shoestring, a saddlebag, a fish, a tomahawk, and other improbable objects. In addition, since one or both houses of the state legislature has historically been weighted in behalf of rural interests, Congressional districts, in their total view, over-represent the rural population and under-represent urban and suburban dwellers. Rural-dominated legislatures are slow to adjust Congressional districts to shifts in population.

The United States Supreme Court has intervened with a two-pronged attack on the problem of unfair representation. In *Baker* v. *Carr* (369 U.S. 186, 1962) the Court ruled that the distribution of seats in state legislatures was reviewable in federal courts. In succeeding cases, federal courts have laid down standards of growing precision which will soon regularly provide fairer legislative representation within the states. A better state situation presumably will produce more equitable Congressional districts. The Supreme Court launched its second major attack in *Wesberry* v. *Sanders*, decided February 17, 1964, when it ruled that the language of Article I, section 2, of the Constitution that "Representatives shall be apportioned among the states according to their respective numbers," and that they shall be "chosen by the people of the several states" meant that "as nearly as is practicable one man's vote in a Congressional election is to be worth as much as another's." Congressional districts, accordingly, must reflect this principle. Acknowledging that Congressional districts cannot be drawn with mathematical precision, the Court nevertheless ruled that the Constitution's "plain objective" of making "equal representation for equal numbers of people" must no longer be ignored.

The *Wesberry* decision's largest significance was that it provided a legal formula to assure that the House of Representatives would reflect in its make-up the impact of population shifts, both past and future, from rural to urban and suburban areas. Since 1910 and especially during the two world wars and the 1950's, an enormous shift of population has occurred to the cities. By 1920 the balance was slightly in the cities' favor, and by 1960 it was overwhelmingly so, when 64 per cent of the population lived in counties of over 100,000 and nearly 37 per cent of these in counties of over 500,000. The forecasts are that the long-building urban trend will quicken in coming decades, a fertile development for the extension by future Presidents of the Kennedy formula of an urban-centered program, which the House of Representatives, once a stumbling block, might someday approve. The course of this development will depend considerably upon the degree to which the migrating population concentrates in urban rather than suburban areas. An Eisenhower-type program conceivably might appeal most to the suburbanite whose environment is a conservative influence, and a Kennedy-type program to the urbanite whose need of governmental services is most acute. The Presidency will surely gain by future population shifts. The hard question is how much and how fast.

In its immediate consequences, the *Wesberry* ruling brings into question most House seats. The American Political Science Association has estimated that equalizing Congressional district populations "as nearly as practicable" should put them within about 15 per cent of the average district population in each state. Only ten states which elect Representatives from districts meet the 15 per cent standard. The disposition of federal courts to apply high standards is evidenced by a ruling of March 27, 1964, holding Michigan's 1963 redistricting act unconstitutional. Districts in the Michigan plan ranged from 305,952 to 490,310. The court did not specify a maximum allowable variance.

◇

CONGRESS and the President, for all their built-in antagonisms, must somehow work together. "I am part of the legislative process," Eisenhower rightfully said in 1959. Article II, section 3, is the launching ground for Presidential leadership in legislation. The President is called upon "to give to the Congress information of the state of the Union, and recommend to their consideration such measures as he shall judge necessary and expedient." But what the President proposes Congress disposes, by defeat, delay, amendment, or approval. Congress too can initiate, and the President dispose with approval or a strong veto which Congress, needing to muster a two-thirds vote of both its houses, can seldom override.

Although in the face of an overwhelming emergency Congress may cooperate with the President, it enhances its self-image when it rejects the President or compels him to compromise. Congress can be irresponsible in its dealings with the President because with two houses, hundreds of members, powerful committees, and dispersed leadership blame cannot be readily allocated. The Senator or Representative acquires and keeps his seat not by loyally serving the President but by maintaining the approval of groups and interests in his local constituency. A labor union, a Chamber of Commerce, or a citizens' group normally has greater impact upon a Senator's or Representative's future than all the will and might of the President of the United States.

The President may have a paper majority of his party in Congress, but no working majority. Dwight Eisenhower, brought into the Presidency by the largest popular vote ever cast, and with his Republican party in control of both houses of Congress, quickly discovered the harsh realities of his new existence. A succession of hostile maneuvers were launched by his Republican colleagues on Capitol Hill, and all were directed at the White House. Not a few of the President's antagonists had been swept into office on his coattails, but neither sentiment nor gratitude dulled their purpose. Senator John Bricker of Ohio, a former Republican Vice Presidential candidate, sponsored an amendment that would have emasculated the President's power to make executive agreements and convert the treaty power, already difficult in the Constitutional arrangement, into the most cumbersome in the world. The amendment, in the full magnitude of its potential mischief, promised to do more to wreck the Union than the Confederacy ever dared to contemplate in the Civil War. Senator Joseph McCarthy was in open war with the executive branch. Daniel A. Reed, the octogenarian chairman of the House Ways and Means Committee, fought for an income tax cut that threatened to throw the budget into gross imbalance and wreck the President's program set out in his State of the Union Message. Reed's obduracy made him known, not altogether affectionately, in administration circles as "the Syngman Rhee of Capitol Hill." The President's nomination of Charles Bohlen as ambassador to Russia was severely and protractedly challenged by Senator McCarthy and other formidable Republicans. Congressman John Taber, the economy-minded House Appropriations Committee chairman, slashed nearly one billion dollars from the President's mutual security request. The President was steadily harassed by riders contrived by Republican legislators. One of the most upsetting barred any future United States contribution to the United Nations if Communist China were admitted to membership. Congress repeatedly deserted Eisenhower to cater to the hometown vote, and in that first year deferred or rejected such key administration measures as expansion of social security, amendment of the Taft-Hartley Act, construction of the St. Lawrence Seaway, conferring of statehood on Hawaii, boosting the debt limit, and increasing the postal rate. Small wonder that according to Robert Donovan's authoritative account Eisenhower after six months of office was driven almost to despair of being able to succeed in the Presidency.

The President's problem of getting voting majorities is twice compounded by the bicameral system, which provides for two legislative houses chosen by different constituencies for different terms. The Senate, the traditional "rich man's club" of the late nineteenth century, was the nemesis of Theodore Roosevelt and his Square Deal program; Franklin Roosevelt fared conspicuously better in the House than in the Senate. Eisenhower and Kennedy, in contrast, enjoyed strikingly greater success in the Senate than in the House. Measures approved by Kennedy and the Senate were rejected in the House or rewritten to its specifications. In the Eighty-Seventh Congress, for instance, the depressed areas bill sailed easily through the Senate, but the House performed drastic surgery. Kennedy's minimum wage bill swept through the Senate only to encounter trouble in the House; his public school aid bill was passed in the Senate but blocked in the House; his medical care bill for the aged was bottled up in House committee.

Why did the Senate, historic slaughterhouse of Presidential designs, give Kennedy almost everything he asked for, while the House dealt out struggle and defeat? A possible explanation may lie in the great population shifts to the cities in the forties and fifties. The Senator, answerable to a state-wide constituency, has become heavily dependent upon the great mass of urban voters for election. Kennedy's own electoral campaign and subsequent legislative programs were directed chiefly to the urban industrial United States. A basic and growing convergence of interest exists between Senate and President, extending across party lines. Representatives, in contrast, are answerable to a smaller, less complex constituency.

The vagaries of Congressional party loyalty compel the President, estimating his legislative prospects, to acknowledge two coalitions in which members of each major party are joined. One is a "conservative" coalition of Southern Democrats and Republicans who, voting together prior to the 1962 elections, comprised a majority in both chambers. This stark, imposing fact illuminated the necessity for the Kennedy administration to concentrate upon weaning away Southerners and Republicans from opposition to its bills. Notwithstanding the administration's acumen and zeal, the conservative coalition did heavy damage. In the Senate it defeated the urban affairs department and medical care for the aged. In the House it likewise killed urban affairs and the college aid bill.

When the conservative coalition lost, as it often did, it was because the administration moved sufficient numbers of Southern Democrats or Republicans over to support the rival "liberal" coalition. This coalition consists of a majority of voting Northern Democrats and minorities of Southern Democrats and Republicans. Republicans and Southern Democrats adhering to the "liberal" coalition tend to come from urban and suburban constituencies. Many of Kennedy's victories were owed to liberal and moderate Republican support. In the House, Republicans provided the margin of victory in the fight to enlarge the Rules Committee and the passage of the emergency feed grains, depressed areas, and minimum wage bills. Similar victories were won in the Senate. A de facto coalition of Northern and Western Democrats and "liberal Republicans" provided the Kennedy administration with most of its successes.

The President conducts many of his legislative enterprises through the floor leaders of each house. Floor leaders, with their split role as party leader and the President's legislative leader, vary widely in interpreting their total responsibilty. Alben Barkley considered himself responsible for Franklin Roosevelt's program, but resigned his leadership when Roosevelt sharply criticized and vetoed a tax bill. Scott Lucas served Harry Truman with absolute loyalty, even when the President, despite the Senate leader's protests, put civil rights at the top of the legislative agenda in 1949. Lucas's successor, McFarland, and Taft and Knowland in the Eisenhower administration cherished their independence and the long mile between the White House and the Hill. Taft, of course, was Eisenhower's chief competitor for the 1952 Republican Presidential nomination, and Knowland, when invited to switch California to Eisenhower to provide the general with a big victory, answered coldly, "We don't want any credit or any responsibility for *that* nomination." In true Congressional paradox, Eisenhower's best leader was Lyndon Johnson, the Democratic floor leader, whose entire distinguished service was spent under the Republican Eisenhower. Johnson consistently refused to turn Senate Democrats loose on Eisenhower at will, but worked with the President with dispassionate professionalism, supporting or opposing as he believed he should. "We prod him," said Johnson of Eisenhower, "into doing everything we can get him to do, and when he does something good we give him a 21-gun salute."

◇

THE President advances his program in Congress by means which C. P. Snow, the British novelist, terms "open politics" and "closed politics," one visible and the other covert. In open politics the President sets forth his proposals for legislation, sends appointments and treaties to the Senate, brings Congress into extra session and puts an agenda before it, and makes public statements explaining and defending his legislative actions. His chief weapon in "open politics" is his messages—his State of the Union Message rendered each January, followed since Woodrow Wilson's day by special messages which focus on single issues. These messages provide the record and delineate the scope of the administration's program. Messages bearing programs of strong appeal and stated in ringing eloquence were powerful incentives upon Congress in the hands of Franklin Roosevelt. Charles A. Beard wrote of Roosevelt in the New Deal years, "He has discussed in his messages and addresses more fundamental problems of American life and society than all other President's combined." On his second Sunday in the White House, over supper with Louis Howe, his confidential secretary, Roosevelt remarked, "I think this would be a good time for beer." Howe produced a copy of the Democratic platform, and later in the evening Roosevelt wrote out a brief message based upon its call for a modification of the Volstead Act in order to legalize beer and light wines.

Congress, too, invites messages, and therefore leadership, from the President. The Budget and Accounting Act of 1921 bids the President to submit an executive budget each January. This ponderous tome, equal in bulk to several metropolitan telephone directories, with its accompanying message, is a detailed statement of policy objectives with means of achieving them for Congress's guidance. The Employment Act of 1946 calls for an Economic Report from the President which permits him to lay out policies fostering free competitive enterprise and maintaining employment, production, and purchasing power at maximum levels.

Theodore Roosevelt began the practice of supplementing his messages with actual drafts of bills. Although Roosevelt, mindful of the niceties of separation of powers, was a trifle sheepish and clandestine about it all, Wilson did it openly. Since then all Presidents, even Calvin Coolidge, despite his strict Constitutionalism and tired blood, have drafted bills.

The Constitution endows the President with the veto, a most powerful weapon in the game of open politics. The veto's grave defect is that it is total and not partial. The President must accept or reject a bill as a whole; he cannot veto particular items and approve the rest. This permits Congress to engage with merry impunity in pork barrel in appropriation bills and to attach riders like the one Senator Pat McCarran attached to the general appropriations bill for 1951, "That of this appropriation $100 million shall be used only for assistance to Spain." Nothing at the time was more alien to President Truman's foreign policy than to provide aid to Franco, the Spanish dictator. Early Presidents seldom used the veto and then chiefly to object on Constitutional grounds. Andrew Jackson first employed the veto as a weapon of policy and of popular appeal in his war on the Second Bank of the United States. Franklin Roosevelt, who brandished the veto more than any other President, was known to say to his aides, "Give me a bill that I can veto," to remind legislators that they had the President to reckon with. Harry Truman, taking his cue from Andrew Jackson, vetoed a string of measures of the Republican Eightieth Congress, peppering his sentences with vivid expletives like "dangerous," "clumsy," "arbitrary," "impossible," and "drastic," not so much for the legislators as for the public. Truman's vetoes were no small factor in his 1948 victory.

The President plying the strong approach may, as another tactic of open politics, take his legislative program to the people. His unrivaled power to command the nation's attention and its disposition to side with him against all foes endow him with a capacity no legislator enjoys. By skillfully leading the public, Presidents have brought Congress around to actions from which, left to its own instinct, it would refrain. Theodore Roosevelt was the first of the modern Presidents to rely heavily upon appeals to the public. Gifted and joyous in public combat, Roosevelt, blocked in Congress, went to the people. Woodrow Wilson perfected what Theodore Roosevelt had begun. "He is the spokesman of the Nation in everything," Wilson said describing the President's special capacity. A spellbinder in times when oratory was admired, Wilson's lean, gripping prose and romantic moralism stirred men's better senses.

Wilson and other successful practitioners of the popular appeal follow several rules. Wilson went to the public sparingly and only when the need was strong. The issue chosen must be important to the people and one about which their feelings can be instantly rallied. There must be careful preparation; when issues are sprung, they fare badly. As Wilson well knew, the venture carries the high risk that the people will respond only fleetingly or not at all. The appealing President is laying both his own political reputation and the prestige of his great office on the line.

Worst of all, the secluded executive session of a legislative committee and the artful parliamentary maneuver, where the controlling decisions on the President's program may be made, are not directly accessible to the legions of public opinion.

John Kennedy, like other Presidents, was noticeably reticent about "going to the people." His course was rather at variance with the vision he had of his future Presidency in his 1960 campaign. "I want to be a President," he said at the New York Coliseum two days before the election, "who has the confidence of the people—and who takes the people into his confidence—who lets them know what he is doing and where we are going, who is for his program and who is against." Kennedy concentrated his addresses to the nation upon the several crises in foreign affairs and civil rights, discussing the latter at times with memorable eloquence. The test ban treaty and the tax bill highlighted his chief noncrisis appeals. He therefore did not venture before a national audience with such urgent and controversial items of his program as federal aid to education, medical care for the aged, lowering of unemployment, and improvement of metropolitan transportation. The powerful inducements which brought other Presidents to go to the people beat upon Kennedy. Congress was doing precious little, the unorganized voter sensed uneasily the need for action, Kennedy's personal popularity was climbing to extraordinarily high levels, and hostile lobbies were gathered in strength on Capitol Hill. But Kennedy did not carry the fight to the nation, sensing, doubtless correctly, with his politician's caution that however successful his popular appeal, he still could not win on Capitol Hill. His immense popularity became a wasted resource, and key planks in his program became postponed promises rather than here-and-now deeds.

Kennedy plainly eschewed the method of such forebears as Wilson, Franklin Roosevelt, and Truman, who fought for their programs both on the beaches of Congress and in the streets of national opinion. Truman highlighted civil rights in his acceptance speech at the Philadelphia nominating convention of 1948, summoned Congress into extra session, bade it to act on civil rights, and delivered a national address on the subject. Truman's reward was defeat; no legislation flowered. By ordinary standards he failed, but had he? A broader and more accurate view is that although he sustained defeat in Congress, he had altered prevailing social thought by making the nation more conscious and better informed of civil rights. He had laid the foundations for popular acceptance of the several later Supreme Court decisions, the two civil rights laws of the Eisenhower administration, and Kennedy's far-reaching innovations by executive action. Social legislation, history well demonstrates, can rarely be achieved by the effort of a single Presidential administration. It is a plant of slow growth, requiring years of careful tending by various Presidential hands. Consequently, each President has a duty to advance social causes by fighting for them even when he expects legislative defeat. In defeat he is achieving a kind of victory by educating the nation and cultivating the climate of social opinion for the eventual victory of a future Presidential administration. Such are the realities of the world of open politics.

The President in his relations with Congress also engages in the processes of "closed politics." Relatively unpublicized, unseen, and unofficial, closed politics employs the personal contact, the patronage lever, the choice viands of the pork barrel, and sundry other exertions of power and influence. The negotiation in the White House office or Congressional cloakroom, the Presidential phone call to the legislator deciding how to vote, the accommodations and compromises necessary to patch together a legislative majority for an administration bill, are the warp and woof of closed politics. The resort to closed politics is a constant testimonial to the weakness of open politics. Because the Founding Fathers made so little provision for Presidential leadership in legislation, the chief executive is driven to rely heavily upon the extraconstitutional resources of closed politics.

The President personally is, or should be, at the center of closed politics. There is no substitute for the force of his word and gesture. He therefore must explain and exhort to win backing for his program. His dealings and exertions cover the entire range from soft to hard sell. Kennedy, endowed with personal charm and a zest for closed politics sharpened in his legislative years, labored hard and sometimes fruitfully in this vineyard. He met weekly with the legislative leaders of his party and breakfasted or lunched with the Speaker of the House and the majority and assistant leader of the Senate. He also conferred systematically and individually with the chairmen of each of the standing committees of both houses, and sometimes with the entire committee when it was mulling over an item of the administration's program.

Kennedy was often found in the thick of battles on Capitol Hill. When a crucial vote approached, he not uncommonly put in long hours on the telephone, carrying his case to legislators who had not yet made up their minds or seeking to detach others from the opposition camp. Kennedy's attentions embraced Republicans as well as Democrats. Everett Dirksen, the Senate Republican leader, was the object of various blandishments, including privileged rides in the President's helicopter. When the Democratic leader, Senator Mike Mansfield, hailed Dirksen as a "tower of strength" on foreign policy, Dirksen found it necessary to deny good-naturedly, for the partisan record, that he had "gone soft on Kennedyism."

Lyndon Johnson brought to the Presidency a high reputation and rich experience in the art of closed legislative politics, with service in both houses of Congress and a record as one of the most illustrious floor leaders in Senate history. He was master of two indispensable competences in closed politics. He was ingenious at discovering politically feasible compromises and he commanded a relentless, overpowering persuasiveness at bringing those he confronted around to supporting them. His former occupancy of high Senate station provided him with an access to the centers of legislative power which Kennedy, whose Senate influence was considerably less, did not enjoy. Johnson as President seemed to range further and more insistently over legislative affairs than Kennedy ever did. "Kennedy came too late to many of his problems in Congress," said an official of both these Presidential administrations, learned in the fauna of Capitol Hill. "He would hold back, let things develop, come in at the top of the crisis. Johnson likes to stay ahead and anticipate what will happen and how to meet it." But Johnson's method also has its dangers. By intruding persistently in a wide range of Congressional details, he is spending freely his limited supply of Presidential prestige and influence. Like money, the more there is of these commodities in circulation, the cheaper becomes their value.

In dealing and bargaining with legislators, the President operates from an array of vantage points. He can dole out various degrees of help in the next Congressional elections. He manipulates the several executive beneficences like pork barrel and defense contracts. The Kennedy administration, laboring mightily to induce Southern Democrats to vote for its measures, generated good feeling by increasing price supports for Southern cotton and awarding Southern plants big defense contracts, such as the million-dollar order allotted Lockheed Aircraft of Georgia. The depressed areas bill forged ahead when its rural aid outlays were doubled. A map demonstrating how nicely the gravy would flow to Dixie under the amended bill circulated on the floor.

Not the least of the President's loaves and fishes is federal patronage, the art of bestowing offices upon legislators' protégés—with votes, hopefully, the *quid pro quo*. The President's adroit manipulation of patronage can turn the tide of legislative battle, as it did for Cleveland in his 1893 fight to repeal the Sherman Silver Purchase Act. Wilson sometimes disciplined legislators who persistently failed to support his policies by cutting off their patronage. "We not only ought to pay no attention to Senator Vardaman's recommendations for office," he wrote his Attorney General, "but we ought studiously to avoid nominating men whom he picks out." Harry S. Truman, exasperated in his futile efforts to force the repeal of the Taft-Hartley Act in the Eighty-First Congress, thundered that how Democrats voted on that matter would be weighed in handing out patronage. But patronage by Truman's day, thanks to the spreading coverage of the civil service merit laws, had been reduced to a light weapon. For all of Truman's ferocity, Taft-Hartley was intact when he left the Presidency.

Despite the weakness of his individual weapons, if the President chooses to direct his available means of both closed and open politics upon a selected objective, he can gather an imposing arsenal. An impression of the administration's diverse weaponry is provided by Congressman Otto E. Passman, chairman of the House Appropriations Subcommittee, charged with responsibility for foreign aid. A skillful, doughty foe of foreign aid, Passman offered this picture of the Kennedy administration's legislative technique in its first foreign aid fight. The administration relied heavily upon the testimony of Treasury Secretary Douglas Dillon, a Republican, Passman noted, "with his usual smile and personality." Passman continued,

> Then Democratic National Chairman Bailey sends wires to Democratic officials all over the country, trying to get them to put the pressure on Congress. . . . Then there were letters from Dillon and Rusk. . . . The program was talked up at a State Department briefing for editors. . . . There was the Ayub [President of Pakistan] pep-talk [urging foreign aid]. . . . The Citizens Committee for International Development was organized to exert more pressure. . . . McCormack [then House Democratic leader] sent letters to 2400 mayors across the United States including some in my own district. . . . Shriver [Director of the Peace Corps and the President's brother-in-law] made a personal visit to every office on Capitol Hill. Although he came for the Peace Corps, foreign aid was mixed in. . . . The White House kept contacting business groups all over the country. . . . I jotted down some figures to show my thinking [i.e., of possible cuts in foreign aid spending]. A Republican subcommittee member leaked the figures to the President a few hours before the subcommittee was to act. . . . While I was presenting the subcommittee report in the full committee meeting, administration agents continued to place phone calls to committee members in the room. In the same meeting, letters from an Assistant Secretary of State to members of the committee, all calling for more funds, were actually slipped under the door.

Yet for all the unstinting commitment of the President and his cohorts, Congressman Passman cut the foreign aid appropriation by 21 per cent, or $896 million. After the deed was done, Passman observed simply, "This is a great day for the taxpayers." President Kennedy and his aides were reported "stunned and angry."

◇

A CHIEF executive can choose between several possible "approaches" in setting the tone, pace, and pressure level of his legislative leadership. No President, to be sure, limits himself to any one approach. Like baseball pitchers, he prefers to mix his delivery, and the choice of an approach, like a pitch, depends upon how the game stands at the moment. The sheer number and variety of approaches are themselves a testimony of Presidential weakness in legislative leadership. These are some of the possibilities from which the President may choose.

"Lion" vs. "Fox."   All Presidents engage in periods of the fox-like or diplomatic approach. The Constitution's endowment of Congress with vital powers of legislation, and the President's consequent necessity of inducing its cooperation, forces him to be diplomatic in method. The President's personality and political ideology may bring him to prefer it. So also may special circumstances.

Harry S. Truman, swept unprepared into the Presidency, where the late incumbent had already been encountering trouble on Capitol Hill, took a cautious diplomatic line in his first Presidential years. There was no "must" legislation in the manner of Franklin Roosevelt; Truman limited himself to making recommendations in general terms, leaving Congress to work out the specifics unguided by executive recommendation. Truman in the meantime exerted few personal pressures upon the legislators and rarely commented on a bill until it reached his desk. He used the veto power sparingly. He filled his administration's principal posts with members and former members of Congress: James F. Byrnes as Secretary of State, Clinton Anderson as Secretary of Agriculture, Lewis Schwellenbach as Secretary of Labor, and Fred M. Vinson as Secretary of the Treasury. His communications on legislative business were discreet and deferential. He made several surprise visits to the Senate, mingling nostalgically with his old colleagues and speaking modestly and hopefully of future executive-legislative cooperation.

In the fox-like approach the President fraternizes with legislators and plies them with blandishments. Franklin D. Roosevelt excelled at the art of Congressional gratification, at giving out the easy first name, the warm handshake, the contagious smile, the intimate joke, the air of concern, the quasi-confidential interview, the picture snapped at the White House desk, the headline in the hometown newspaper.

President Eisenhower early embarked upon a practice of discussing issues in a social atmosphere with groups of Congressmen and Senators of both parties "in the hope that personal acquaintance would help smooth out difficulties inherent in partisanship." He further urged "each Cabinet member to become acquainted and develop friendly contacts with the members of every committee with which he had special dealings." Eisenhower set a Presidential record for sheer social industry by inviting all members of the House and Senate to the White House for a series of luncheons; well over five hundred legislators came. Among other things, the President sought to cultivate friendships and the impression that legislators' problems were his problems. The luncheons, in the opinion of Democratic Congressman Michael J. Kirwan of Ohio, fostered "a feeling of friendliness which will do more to bring about cooperation of mem-hers of Congress than all the testimonies presented to Congressional committees." Eisenhower fraternized with legislators at his other meals and on the golf course, and expansively invited them to drop into his office any time for a talk. To the dismay of his appointment secretary, many legislators took this invitation literally.

One Saturday afternoon in blossom time, when Senator Harry F. Byrd's friends and neighbors gathered in his Virginia apple orchard to commemorate his birthday and eat fried chicken, there suddenly burst from the azure skies President Kennedy's whirring helicopter. The President had taken time from his heavy duties to come personally to honor the Senator. The attention did not deter Senator Byrd, one year later, and in the same apple orchard, from publicly taking Kennedy to task for requiring an excessive number of airplanes, yachts, and limousines to move about, and from proposing that he "set an example by getting along with a little less."

President Johnson labors tirelessly at the diplomatic or fox-like approach. He receives Congressmen at the White House with unparalleled cordiality, dances with their wives, arranges for them briefings on world affairs by Defense Secretary Robert McNamara and Secretary of State Dean Rusk. He telephones congratulations to Congressmen for documents they have inserted into the *Congressional Record.* He showed Harry Byrd, Senate Finance Committee chairman, the budget before dispatching it to Congress, and when weighing his course in the Panama crisis, he gathered Congressional and administration leaders about him, and after discussion took a vote. Fortunately for the Presidency it was inconclusive, and Johnson retained the ultimate decision for himself.

The President who resorts to the direct or lion-like approach brandishes the veto power freely, turns on the pressures of patronage, pork barrel, and the ministrations of alert aides. He churns up public sentiment for his program to spur the legislators into support. The example supreme of the strong approach is Franklin Roosevelt's first one hundred days, when in the depths of economic crisis Congress time and again put aside established procedures in the rush to do the President's bidding.

The President is apt to be lion-like in seasons when his political prestige is riding high. Truman, after his spectacular surprise re-election in 1948, was soon giving the pressure valves a full twist. He jarred the gaiety of a Jackson-Jefferson Day Dinner of 1948 by threatening, in his address to the celebrating Democrats, to tour the country to force Congressional enactment of the party's platform pledges. Later he termed the vote on the Taft-Hartley Act's repeal a good test of party loyalty and uttered several strictures on the seniority principle and the inattention of Democratic legislators to their party's national platform.

Systematic vs. "Buckshot." President Eisenhower applied to legislative affairs the high degree of system apparent in other phases of his Presidency. His legislative program was elaborately coordinated, setting forth the President's choices and priorities in every major area of federal action. The cycle began at midyear when the Budget Bureau called upon the executive agencies to submit by September 15 a statement including "*all* items of legislation (other than appropriations) which the agency contemplates proposing during the ensuing twelve months." A month after the Budget Bureau's call in 1953, Eisenhower, looking toward the coming State of the Union Message, asked each cabinet secretary for substantive ideas based upon a "thorough rethinking of the mission of your department and the . . . means to achieve it." The response was a vast outpouring of measures, many long advocated by the career service. Sherman Adams, the President's chief assistant, and several aides spent two weeks with Budget Bureau help studying and sifting the proposals and checking with the President. Many complex and controversial measures of high policy and partisan significance—social security, taxation, agricultural assistance, and foreign aid—were tagged for presentation to the cabinet by the sponsoring department head. The White House staff previewed the presentations and gave advice. In November and December seven were presented to the full cabinet, with Eisenhower himself a leading participant, his questions and views sparking most of the changes made. In mid-December the President unveiled his program to Republican Congressional leaders in a series of carefully staged eight-hour sessions at the White House. The Vice President, the Speaker, the majority leaders, whips, most of the cabinet, and several White House aides were also present. Congressional committee chairmen participated when their subjects were discussed. When legislative leaders expressed concern over some item, the President was apt to modify it. The principal purpose of the sessions, however, was to inform the legislators and not to secure their approval or commitment.

In the three weeks between the leaders' meetings and the presentation of the President's messages in January, the several messages—the State of the Union Address (put together by the White House largely from agency submissions), the Budget Report (written largely by the Budget Bureau), and the Economic Report (largely the work of the chairman of the Council of Economic Advisers)—were coordinated for consistency and coverage by the White House staff. Meanwhile, the departments concentrated on drafting special messages and detailed bills to follow promptly each proposal advanced in the more general messages. The State of the Union Message of January 7, 1954, stated the President's program in general terms. Specifics were advanced in a series of seven special messages, delivered from January through March, on individual subjects such as social security, agriculture, Taft-Hartley, and foreign aid. An administration bill quickly followed each special message.

President Truman was addicted to the buckshot method of presenting a legislative program. His message of September 6, 1945, projecting the nation's conversion from warmaking to peacemaking, "one of the most important of my administration," contained nothing less than twenty-one points of domestic legislation, ranging from agriculture to Congressional salaries. Sixteen thousand words in all, the message was the longest since Theodore Roosevelt's marathon twenty thousand words in 1901. Nor was this all. In subsequent weeks Truman sent up special messages with additional proposals. In his legislative presentation of 1962, President Kennedy followed a similar tactic by deluging Congress with requests for civil rights, special Presidential authority to cut taxes and start public works to avert a recession, medical care for the aged, higher education, foreign aid, urban affairs, an international communications satellite, permanent unemployment compensation, and other things. Judged by its fruits, the buckshot approach is unimpressive. Only a few of Truman's twenty-one requests ever became law and Kennedy succeeded with a few. Both sets of defeats were easily predictable beforehand.

Why, then, do Presidents resort to buckshot? In both the Truman and Kennedy instances, the President was faced with an approaching election—the national elections of 1948 and the Congressional elections of 1962. Both Presidents, firing a barrage of requests at Congress that were foredoomed to failure, aimed to exploit the Republican tendency to ride the brakes, to build a record for labeling it the "do-nothing" party in the electoral campaign. The buckshot approach is usually asserted in a cantankerous style. Truman blasphemed Congress, and Kennedy, who regularly employed a sober approach puffing Congressional dignity, picked a fight on selected issues, particularly the creation of a department of urban affairs, which cast him in the hero's mold with masses of metropolitan voters. In the buckshot approach, the President invests noticeably less effort in working out compromises and patching together majorities.

Involved vs. Aloof.   Far more than most Presidents, Woodrow Wilson was deeply involved personally in the legislative struggle. As a political scientist and an admirer of British public affairs, he had long been convinced that the President must be a kind of "prime minister, as much concerned with the guidance of legislation as with the just and orderly execution of law." Wilson oversaw the development of a body of legislation promoting economic and social justice, the "New Freedom." He believed that only the President could assure an integrated legislative program. Wilson, therefore, regularly planned it, shared in the toil and sweat of drafting bills, and oversaw their progress through Congress.

Preceding each Congressional session, Wilson drew up lists of measures to be pushed, discussed them with the cabinet, and then conferred personally with House and Senate leaders, or sent his "political ambassador," Postmaster General Albert S. Burleson, in his stead. Carter Glass, chief legislative sponsor of the Federal Reserve Act, has written that Wilson "dominated" the act's preparation, and Congressman E. Y. Webb that Wilson personally drafted the Clayton Act's famous clause that "the labor of human beings is not a commodity or article of commerce," pressed legislative committees to report his bills out, watched the Congressional calendars, and scrutinized amendments to forestall damaging changes. He also managed to keep in touch with conference committee deliberations, a traditional graveyard of progressive legislation.

Wilson used his legislative influence selectively, pushing one measure at a time, but the key to his legislative approach was collaboration. The President, he said, in coming personally before Congress to promote his tariff legislation, should not be viewed as "a mere department of the Government hailing Congress from some isolated island of jealous power . . . he is a human being trying to cooperate with other human beings in a common service." Wilson put in a heavy schedule of hours on Capitol Hill. "Did you ever hear of a President occupying a room in the Capitol called 'the President's Room'? What would be thought of it," he asked the politically sophisticated Josephus Daniels, "if instead of asking Senators with whom I wished to consult to call at the White House, I should occupy that room for such conferences?" Daniels answered candidly that Senators would resent it. Wilson went ahead anyhow. When important bills were in the Congressional crucible, Wilson would see a score of legislators in his Capitol Room. At the White House he saw even more and installed a special telephone to reach Senators quickly from his office. If Congress balked, he went to the people.

In contrast to Wilson, who was intensely involved, some Presidents have scrupulously held themselves aloof from the heat and dust of legislative combat. The original progenitor of this approach was no one less than President Washington. The aloof style custom fits the hero-President by removing him from the rough and tumble that might scratch the gilt of his flawless prestige. The aloof President addresses Congress in stately, general discourse, and with a degree of deference. He avoids the specifics of issues, leaving them for Congress to determine, untutored by the chief executive. Washington's first annual message, eagerly awaited as a guide to major policy, was chiefly a general and thankful exposition of "the present favorable prospects of our public affairs." His recommendations were rendered up as innocuous generalities like "protecting the frontiers," "extension of the postal system," and the "promotion of science and literature." The last proposal was delivered in a perfect straddle: "Whether this desirable object will be best promoted by affording aids to seminaries of learning already established, by the institution of a national university, or by any other expedients, will be well worthy of a place in the deliberations of the Legislature." At every turn where controversy reared its ugly head Washington nimbly sidestepped. When his brilliant Secretary of the Treasury, Alexander Hamilton, advanced his plan for the federal assumption of state debts, Washington foresaw an embittered controversy. Both to avoid that unpleasant eventuality and in deference to Congress, he abstained from recommending Hamilton's plan to the legislators. Again, when Quaker memorials opposing the slave trade sparked a violent debate in the House of Representatives, Washington declined to comment on the issue on the ground that he might have to act officially, although personally he thought it regrettable that the question of the slave trade had been raised.

A century and a half later another hero-President, Dwight D. Eisenhower, visualized his Presidential service as a kind of unifying and moderating influence above the struggle. He was the good man above politics who eschewed conflict, reconciled differences, and healed divisions. He avoided involvement in political controversy and expressed frank distaste for partisan politics. "In the general derogatory sense," he declared in a press conference, "you can say that, of course, I do not like politics." In legislative affairs Eisenhower took on the pleasant missions and left to his colleagues, principally Vice President Nixon and chief Presidential assistant Sherman Adams, the tasks of conveying the harsh word and springing the fierce maneuver. Deeply respectful of the tripartite character of the government, Eisenhower was reluctant to assume executive leadership over a vast area which he viewed as legislative business.

Bipartisan vs. Partisan. A modern President chooses between a partisan and a bipartisan approach to legislation. In certain areas of affairs, bipartisanship is preferable, even imperative. In crisis, in much of foreign policy, and in major social legislation political realities require the modern President to employ bipartisanship to build his legislative majorities. In the depths of economic crisis Franklin Roosevelt conducted a nonpartisan administration, drawing large support from both parties. After 1936, with the crisis subsiding and with huge Democratic legislative majorities created by the elections, his administration took on a more partisan attitude.

President Eisenhower depended heavily upon bipartisan support throughout his two terms. His dependence was not less in his first two years, when the Republicans possessed a legislative majority, than in the following six years, when the Democrats controlled both houses. Eisenhower wrote to the House majority leader, Charles Halleck, early in 1954,

Because of the thin Republican margins in both Houses, both you and Knowland obviously require Democratic support in almost every tough vote. This being so, we must by all means quickly show our readiness to cooperate in every decent way, and particularly in those areas where bipartisan action is vital to the national interest.

Eisenhower's conciliatory pitch was well rewarded. From Democratic leaders Lyndon Johnson and Sam Rayburn he received, according to Sherman Adams, "more sympathy" than from the Republican Senate leader, William F. Knowland, who plagued the President with his one-track mind on the menace of Red China, and Joe Martin, the House leader, whose support of the administration was spoken of in White House circles as "uninspired and lackadaisical." Cooperation with the Democrats paid off at voting time. "Fifty-eight times," according to the *Congressional Quarterly Almanac* for 1953, the administration's worst legislative year, "Democrats saved the President . . . their votes providing the margin of victory when Republican defections or absences imperiled the happy glow." But Eisenhower paid a price for his collaboration. "This added more strain on his relationship with the right wing of his own party," Adams has written.

President Kennedy's narrow electoral victory in 1960 and his conviction that "The American people are rather evenly divided on a great many issues," spurred his administration to enlist Republican support for its program. Kennedy courted the Republican legislative leadership with good result, particularly in the Senate, where the Republican leader, Everett Dirksen, was steadily responsive in national security and foreign affairs, and agreed with President Johnson to permit the tax bill to move ahead without Republican obstruction. In the House, Kennedy and the Republican leader Charles Halleck put together a bipartisan coalition, which Lyndon Johnson perpetuated, to pass the civil rights bill. But the Republican rank and file ran up a low batting average of support for Kennedy's domestic program. In a sense, the principal reason the program did not fare better was that Kennedy was unable to bring off the colossal task of winning over a substantial number of Republicans.

But left to his own devices Kennedy preferred a partisan approach to legislation. "Legislative leadership," he said, "is not possible without party leadership." Wilson's Presidency was a telling application of this principle. In forwarding his New Freedom program, he acted true to his conceptions of the President as prime minister, party leader, and champion of a legislative program. Wilson advanced his legislative purposes through party means. He worked through Democratic legislative leaders and committee chairmen, cracked the patronage whip, and employed House and Senate caucuses in the English style. His tariff bill, for example, was taken up in the Democratic caucuses of each house at his insistence. The

Senate occasion was termed "the first caucus of Democratic Senators that anyone can remember." Wilson triumphed in both forums. The House and Senate caucuses voted to support the tariff as a party measure. When the Federal Reserve bill was advancing, Wilson again resorted to caucus with happy result. The act was passed without any Democratic Senators opposing it; in the House only three Democrats dissented.

Wilson as legislative party leader traveled a rough road, given the divisiveness of parties and the localism of Congress. He had to cut through thickets of factional differences and convert the high-tariff Senator F. M. Simmons, the Finance Committee chairman, to espouse the administration's tariff reductions. The House Democratic caucus on the tariff teetered upon collapse when seven Ohio Congressmen threatened to revolt against free wool and the Louisiana delegation fought to break the sugar schedule. But the skillful majority leader, Oscar Underwood, held his ranks, and only thirteen Democrats refused, because of pledges to their constituencies, to abide by the caucus's decision endorsing the tariff reform bill.

Withdrawal. President-Congress relations may deteriorate into such a state of futility that one or both branches may seek its purposes not through the usual channels of cooperation, but by independent action. The President, for his part, despairing at legislative obstruction, resorts to his prerogative. Theodore Roosevelt, meeting rebuff in the Senate in seeking a treaty with Santo Domingo, negotiated an executive agreement. Franklin Roosevelt, administering price controls in World War II, concluded that his efforts to hold the lid on inflation were imperiled by several farm support provisions of the existing Emergency Price Control Act. In a message of September 7, 1942, he asked Congress to repeal the objectionable provisions by October 1. "In the event that the Congress shall fail to act, and act adequately," Roosevelt added, "I shall accept the responsibility, and I will act." How could the President legally carry out this threatened self-assertion? "The President has the powers, under the Constitution and under Congressional acts," said Roosevelt rather generally, "to take measures necessary to avert a disaster which would interfere with the winning of the war." Here in slightly different guise was the "stewardship theory" of Cousin Theodore.

It is Abraham Lincoln who provides the most sweeping illustration of executive withdrawal. At the outset of the Civil War he delayed calling Congress into session, judging presumably and altogether justifiably, in light of history, that the legislators might delay and obstruct while rebellion spread. Lincoln the commander-in-chief became for twelve crucial weeks the nation's lawmaker. The normal joint legislative-executive processes were suspended, and America had its first taste of dictatorship, fortunately a benevolent one.

Executive-legislative relations can also collapse into general debacle at Congress's instigation. In two of the worst crises the nation has known, Congress discarded every vestige of cooperation with the chief executive and pursued a bitter course of general sabotage. James Buchanan, who toiled hard and prayerfully to prevent the Civil War, and Andrew Johnson in the Reconstruction era were the victims of rampant Congressional hostility. In Buchanan's case Congress denied the President nothing less than the essentials of governance. As the South continued to mobilize in spite of his entreaties, Buchanan requested more military funds. Congress responded by cutting his estimates to a fraction of their original amount and restricting the service of any additional volunteers who might be raised to the Utah territory. Buchanan justifiably asserted that the last Congress he had the misfortune to experience had "throughout the entire session, refused to adopt any measures of compromise to prevent civil war, or to retain first the cotton or afterwards the border States within the Union." Congress was derelict in other vital duties. It failed to provide for any judicial process in South Carolina following the resignation of every federal court officer. Congress declined to provide the President with authority to call out the militia or volunteers to suppress the insurrection flaming in Charleston. Even after Buchanan's message of January 8, 1861, declaring the existence of revolution and reminding Congress that it alone could muster troops, three weeks passed before a bill was introduced, only to be immediately withdrawn. Not until two months after South Carolina seceded and ten days after the Confederacy was formed was another, more modest, militia bill proposed. The House killed it with a resolution to postpone.

◊

"THERE is nothing more important for the future of popular government in America," Charles A. Beard once wrote, "than an overhauling of congressional methods and the establishment of better relations with the Executive." The problems to which Beard pointed have over the decades stirred thought in political and academic circles and have evoked a quantity of proposals for reform. The more extreme of these have urged that separation of powers and checks and balances be rigorously altered and that some variant of the British parliamentary system be adopted. The seeds of this alternative have always fallen on barren soil since it is alien to the entire American tradition. A historically assertive Congress would never bear the subordination of the legislature to the degree implied in the British system. Any changes, if they are to occur, must be in accord with the spirit of an autonomous Congress endowed with considerable power. Within such limits, what can and ought to be done?

1. The President, the Senate, and the House should be simultaneously elected for a common term of four years. Historic data establishes that we could rightfully expect that an election so administered would produce a President and two houses of Congress better attuned in party and political outlook than their present fragmented election permits. Under existing practice, the Senate, with its six-year term, is never wholly elected during a President's four-year term, and it is not until he is at his own midterm that even a majority—two-thirds—of the Senate has been chosen. Also, the House's two-year term, and consequent election at the President's midterm, subjects his administration to a severe test of its popularity at an interval that is unfair, coming when his administration has barely started. Defeat in the election can be damaging to the President's prestige in both foreign and domestic politics. All too often, either his party loses control of the House or Senate, or its majority is reduced. Despite the rare and unwanted help of the 1962 Cuban crisis, a kind of event that tends to increase the legislative strength of the party that controls the Presidency, Kennedy's Democratic strength in Congress declined in the elections of that year.

The proposal of equal legislative and Presidential terms would strengthen the chief executive's party situation in Congress, and the two branches, elected simultaneously, would reflect a common public mood precluded in the present fragmented system. The timing of election and the tenure of office would no longer be important instruments of checks and balances.

2. The President should be empowered to veto individual items in appropriation bills, as Franklin Roosevelt, Dwight Eisenhower, and others have advocated. The absence of this power subjects the President unmercifully to legislative "riders" on tax and appropriation measures. The Interior Department appropriation bill of 1948 for example, contained a rider providing that the commissioner of the Reclamation Bureau and all its regional directors should have had at least ten years of engineering experience. Neither the incumbent commissioner, Michael W. Straus, nor the regional director in California was an engineer. "This rider is designed to effect the removal of two men," President Truman cried, "who have supported the public power policy of the government and the 160-acre law which assures that Western lands reclaimed at public expense shall be used for the development of family-size farms." Truman nevertheless signed the appropriation bill. He had to. Congress had already adjourned, and a veto would have shut down the Interior Department. An item veto over state legislative appropriations has been given to a majority of state governors.

The item veto would spare the President the curse of "riders," it would regulate the pork barrel abuse, and it would promote the executive's fiscal responsibility. Most important of all, it would endow the President with a powerful new bargaining strength to assert in the arena of closed politics. He could conceivably engage in his own kind of "log-rolling," trading his acceptance of appropriations items for support of his own measures by legislators individually and in blocs. The item veto could well become the source of a new and commanding influence for the President in legislative affairs. It should preferably be adopted by amendment, although competent legal opinion holds that it might be created by a clause inserted into each appropriation bill, bestowing upon the President the power to strike out items.

3. The internal organization of the houses of Congress can be viewed as a maze of contrivances to assure inaction or minority rule. The majority is prevented from voting upon measures which by every indication it would approve, or it is able to act only after unconscionable delay. Often the thwarted majority opinion equals or approximates the President's view, and, consequently, a liberation of the legislative majority would frequently produce Congressional approval of key items in the President's program. The devices of minority rule are well known: the seniority principle in selecting committee chairmen, the method of assigning legislators to committees, the vast power of the House Rules Committee, and the Senate filibuster, to mention several of the most powerful. A concentrated attack needs to be launched in future years upon them.

The seniority principle of choosing committee chairmen, which assures that the preponderance of these eminences will oppose much of the President's program, urgently needs to be modified. Legislators and thoughful citizens have often advanced proposals to this end. The American Political Science Association, in its 1950 study *Toward a More Responsible Two-Party System*, proposed that the seniority rule be modified to permit the party leaders to name as committee chairmen senior members who are loyal to the party program. Less drastic and more feasible is the recommendation from other sources that chairmen be chosen by secret ballot of a majority of the entire committee at the beginning of each new Congress. Senator Joseph S. Clark has urged that an age limit of seventy years be imposed upon committee chairmen, the same which Congress itself has placed upon federal judges to induce their retirement. Under the Clark proposal, the over-age chairman could still continue as a member of the committee.

The importance of the age limit was evident in the incoming Kennedy administration, where the President was forty-three years old upon his inauguration and had gathered around him leading policy figures most of whom were in their thirties and forties. The age picture in the Congressional committee chairmanships at the time was altogether opposite. Howard Smith, the House Rules Committee chairman, was seventy-six; Clarence Cannon, the Appropriations chairman, was eighty; Carl Vinson of Armed Services was seventy-six; Brent Spence of House Banking and Currency was eighty-five. In the Senate Carl Hayden, the Appropriations chairman, was eighty-two; A. Willis Robertson of Banking and Currency was seventy-two; Harry F. Byrd of Finance was seventy-two; and James Murray of Interior and Insular Affairs was eighty-three. The relative youth of the Kennedy men was a handicap in their dealings with the senior Congressional leaders.

Other proposals attack the seniority problem by urging a reduction in the chairman's very substantial powers. Senator Clark, for instance, has recommended a committee "bill of rights" which would enable a majority of the committee to convene meetings, call up bills for consideration, and terminate debate after a reasonable discussion of issues in executive session. The power of the chairman or a committee minority to cause unreasonable delays in committee business and to withhold matters from vote would be overcome.

To assure that the President's program receives fair and prompt attention, several further adjustments might well be made in the standing committees. Because of their present size and memberships, many committees do not accurately reflect the majority opinion in each house, nor the strength of the apparent disposition of the houses' majorities toward the President's program. Accordingly, its items encounter delay, crippling amendment, or death in committee. Several remedies are possible. The majority party committee, which determines the ratios of majority and minority party memberships on the standing committees, might undergo a limited revision, and likewise the committee of the opposition party responsible for distributing committee places to its members. Senator Clark, for instance, has fought to expand the Senate Democratic Steering Committee, which allots committee assignments. In 1963 he also proposed the expansion of several Senate standing committees, such as Appropriations and Finance, where the Kennedy administration encountered steady trouble. Presumably, the additional members would better represent the growing urban outlook of the Senate, and therefore the President's program. The Kennedy administration and its House supporters responded to the problem of a recalcitrant Rules Committee by effecting a small increase in its size. A future Presidential administration will surely have on its agenda a further increase to reflect more accurately both the views of the House majority and the President's program.

The Senate filibuster, historic obstacle to strong civil rights legislation, has focused attention on that chamber's Rule 22, which imposes a two-thirds voting requirement for imposing cloture upon debate. Several assaults were launched in the Kennedy era to liberalize the rule, but without success. This too remains upon the agenda of the future.

A variety of other Congressional reforms can be advanced to improve the ability of the legislative majority to act and the President's program to receive its just consideration: the conference committee, which often mutilates bills with arbitrary abandon, ought to include in the majority of its members from each house only those whose votes demonstrate their support of a bill's provisions their house has passed and with which the other house disagrees. In addition, committees with an overburdening volume of business, such as House Ways and Means and Senate Finance, might have their excess redistributed to other committees, a step which hopefully might speed their work. "Super-committees," or coordinating committees, and a more extensive use of joint committees might be desirable to reduce the traditional tendency of standing committees to act independently; as Woodrow Wilson once put it, "They do not consult and concur in the adoption of homogeneous and mutually helpful measures; there is no thought of acting in concert."

4. Although legislators and private citizens have urged Congressional reform for decades, little indeed has been accomplished. What are the prospects for the sixties and seventies and what are the most promising routes of action? There are several possible approaches to Congressional reform, and they can be employed individually or simultaneously.

If the American people continue to leave the farm for the city at the rate they did in the forties and fifties—and by responsible forecasts they will—the urban vote will become more and more powerful. In *Wesberry* v. *Sanders* the United States Supreme Court has provided an adequate legal doctrine for reflecting in the composition of the House of Representatives the growing urban concentration of the American population. Urban voters require and expect more government services than their country cousins, so the growing urban pressure might bring Congress increasingly around to the President's program. How different the attitude of the suburban voter will be from the conservative tendency of rural folk is yet to be seen.

If, also, the big pressure groups, whether economic, racial, or national, can lift up their eyes to see beyond their immediate and obvious self-interest and to perceive that the highest public standards, whether in education, health, employment, civil rights, or other major social and economic policy, are good for the group as well as the nation, Presidents and legislators will both gain a far stronger support for programs which the general welfare plainly requires.

The President, too, can help in Congressional reform. Kennedy was moderately successful in tackling the Rules Committee, ancient citadel of minority obstruction to the President's program in the House of Representatives. He teetered on launching a fight on the Senate filibuster, but lacked the votes which a future President might some day possess.

Legislators themselves might take up the fight and win. Dominant Congressional groups and seemingly well-established procedures can, as history teaches, be overthrown. "Uncle Joe" Cannon, Speaker and one of the most powerful of parliamentary tyrants, was overturned and his powers were sheered. Democratic and Republican progressives united in 1913 to scuttle the seniority system in the Senate and to install new committee chairmen devoted to a progressive program. Working harmoniously with President Wilson, they were able to enact an extraordinary list of major legislation.

Finally, to study its organization Congress might again establish a joint committee comparable to the La Follette–Monroney Committee, whose work led to the Legislative Reorganization Act of 1946. Although Congress investigates sternly any suspected inefficiency in the executive branch, it displays an almost pathological resistance to improving itself. Not since 1946 has Congress tidied its operations. The sound barrier has since been broken, the space age has arrived, but Congress limps onward with methods devised in the first days of the republic. In 1963 Senator Clifford Case of New Jersey introduced a bill calling for a study commission to examine several "problem areas," such as committee functioning, floor procedure, seniority, and the scheduling of business. The President of the United States, Senator Case truly said in arguing his bill, is the man in Washington "who most needs Congressional reform."

CHAPTER

7

Administrative Chief

━━━━

THE President oversees the executive branch, the largest administrative enterprise in the free world, with its nearly $100 billion budget and 7 per cent of the nation's work force, with authority and a set of managerial tools that the head of a private corporate enterprise would deem laughably inadequate. Unlike the typical business chief, the President finds no designation in his fundamental charter, the Constitution, as administrative chief. Neither do its collective provisions confer any equivalent authority. The Constitution does grant him the "executive power," language the Supreme Court has sometimes interpreted to include certain powers normally associated with an administrative chief. He is charged to see that the laws are "faithfully executed," which suggests a general administrative responsibility, but duty is not power. He also enjoys express powers like the power to make appointments. Still other authority is conferred by act of Congress and by weight of custom.

With this gift of imperfect authority, the President engages in varied administrative activities. He shapes and determines policy, from "grand policy" to clerical minutiae, from the Monroe Doctrine to the supervision of Washington's roads. James K. Polk was harassed by laborers responsible for the capital's streets who, as Congressman Samuel Vinton said, "were in the habit of running off to the President of the United States, besieging him day after day about the little affairs of the streets, grounds, and roads of this city." In Eisenhower's day the White House staff was amused by the spectacle of scores of commissions for notaries public, spread out upon his office floor waiting for the ink of his signature to dry.

The President prepares for decisions by absorbing oral briefings and reading and pondering memoranda. Many a President would vouch for Truman's complaint that the reading is hard on the eyes and on the attention, for "Nearly every memorandum had a catch in it." The President supervises his executive subordinates with a tolerance ranging from Harding, who approved everything his Secretary of State, Charles Evans Hughes, did, to Polk, who required his secretaries, seated before his desk, to read their reports aloud before forwarding them to Congress. The President has only limited power to recruit, train, and promote the personnel of the executive branch. Most of his key appointments require the advice and consent of the Senate, and even more are subject to vagaries of Senatorial courtesy. Since the first days of the republic he has shared general personnel powers with Congress, and since 1883, when the Pendleton Act became law, with a civil service commission.

His power to make removals, a subject on which the Constitution is silent, is likewise circumscribed by the civil service laws and by the courts. In *Myers* v. *United States* (272 U.S. 52, 1926) on President Wilson's removal of a postmaster, the Court seemed to find the President's removal authority unlimited. This sweeping ruling was trimmed back in *Humphrey's Executor* v. *United States* (295 U.S. 602, 1935) Humphrey, a Federal Trade Commissioner appointed by President Hoover, was removed by President Franklin Roosevelt not for causes cited in statute but, as Roosevelt candidly disclosed, because of policy differences between Humphrey and himself. The Court, finding for Humphrey, held that Congress can protect officials such as a Federal Trade Commissioner, who wield legislative or judicial power, against Presidential removal. An "executive officer," however, or one "restricted to the performance of executive functions," the Court took pains to declare, could not be similarly protected. The distinction between an "executive officer" and one exercising "legislative or judicial power" remains blurred, although in *A. E. Morgan* v. *TVA* (115 Fed. [2d] 990, 1940) the Circuit Court of Appeals viewed a member of TVA's board of directors as an "executive officer."

The President delegates functions and authority, and, by grace of the Budget and Accounting Act of 1921, develops an executive budget—his budget—covering federal income and outgo. He coordinates the several agencies of the executive branch or, as Harry Truman has put it, he makes a "mesh" of things. Almost continuously since the Reorganization Act of 1939, a consequence of the famous Brownlow Committee, he has had a limited power to reorganize executive agencies by redistributing functions and overhauling structures.

◇

THE executive branch has not one but two managers—the President and his rival, Congress. Nearly everything the President does Congress can do, often with greater effect. The mission and structure of the departments are determined by act of Congress. Congress can give authority to subordinate officials to act independently of their department heads, prescribe specific and detailed administrative procedures, petrify the internal organization of an agency by statute, and require Senate confirmation for bureau chief appointments. Congress can establish independent regulatory commissions, like the Interstate Commerce Commission and the Federal Reserve Board, well removed from the President's direction and control. All executive agencies require annual appropriations which Congress provides as it chooses. The programs they administer Congress authorizes and amends. Congress can investigate departmental work in close detail, and its habit is not merely to query the leadership but to reach far down into the hierarchy. The stern fact of life for the department secretary is that he must respond not merely to his official superior, the President, but to the standing committees and subcommittees of the House and Senate watching over his department, aided and abetted by the pressure groups whose needs it serves.

By tradition Congress is closely involved in personnel administration. In detailed laws, Congress sets down the elements of a classification structure, rates of pay, service ratings, retirement, and the like. Although Congress gives the President the power to develop an executive budget, legislative action on its parts may be so severe that much of the document's original validity may be lost. In 1957, for example, Congress sheered off nearly 25 per cent of the budgets of the Commerce Department and the United States Information Agency. Since the early days of the Republic, Congress has made many of its appropriations in close detail, strait-jacketing administrative action. In many an appropriation subcommittee, the spirit of Representative John Sherman's nineteenth-century outcry still lingers:

> The theory of our government is, that a specific sum shall be appropriated by a *law* originating in this House, for a specific purpose, and within a given fiscal year. It is the duty of the executive to use that sum, and no more, especially for that purpose, and no other, and within the time fixed.

Some Presidents, accepting the realities, give the Congressional power centers a substantial part in the development of administrative decisions affecting program, budget, and personnel before consummating them and dispatching them to Capitol Hill. President Lyndon Johnson is of this school. However important he considered the appointment of Thomas Mann to manage Latin-American affairs, Johnson checked first with influential Senators. His elaborate budget-cutting operation in his early weeks of office was a concession to the Congressional economizers. His appointment of a public commission to reconsider the entire foreign aid program served to diminish the rising Congressional outcry.

◇

EVEN more ominous for the President's quest for dominion over the executive branch is the giant bureaucracy itself, with its layers of specialists, its massive paper work and lumbering pace, its addiction to routine and stifling of creativity, its suspicion as a permanent power center committed to program and policy of a transitory, potentially disruptive Presidential administration. The single most powerful figure in the great pyramid is the bureau chief, who in many subtle ways can frustrate the President's purposes when they diverge from his own. He cultivates ties with the pressure groups whose interests his organization serves and the Congressional committees which provide him with money and authority. Congressional committees and subcommittees welcome his attentions. The subcommittee on veterans' affairs does not wish to permit any facet of veterans' services to fall into other hands. The bureau chief may enjoy impregnable prestige with the public. John Kennedy as President-elect engaged in a clear-headed political act when he announced at the time of his first two appointments the retention of J. Edgar Hoover, a public hero, as Director of the FBI.

The remaining high-level departmental incumbents can be grouped, as Wallace Sayre has suggested, as: (1) career employees recruited under civil service regulations with permanent tenure; (2) patronage appointees chosen because of party identification; (3) Presidential appointees whose loyalties center upon the chief executive; and (4) program executives who are skillful in advancing programs which are congenial to the President's policies. The latter three groups may enter government for a limited term of service. Beyond these is the vast body of civil servants of middle and lower ranks. Between the President and the massive departments are natural antagonisms of interest. The President wants to keep control, to receive early warning of items for his agenda before his options are foreclosed, to pick his issues and lift them out of normal channels, to obtain the bureaucracy's full support for his initiatives. The great departments represent a wholly different bundle of purposes and needs. They cling to orderly routines, mountainous paper work, and time-consuming clearance procedures. They tend toward caution, and to the departments the President may represent a temporary intruder who threatens established policy. Promising career men are driven by the stifling routine and the lure of higher salaries into private callings. Able individuals in business, universities, and the professions are deterred from entering government at middle and higher ranks for fear of losing promotions and other privileges in their private career base.

At times, Kennedy and his aides despaired more over their travail in winning cooperation from the departmental bureaucracy than over their deadlocks with Congress. After one heavy interval of bureaucratic obstruction, the administration in its private comment seemed to adopt the notion that the President must contend not merely with Congress but with a further branch, a fourth branch, the bureaucracy. There were distressing signs of the force of the bureaucracy's hostile impact. Kennedy despaired of the State Department's ability to manage foreign policy effectively. The military services teamed up with the Congressional committees against the President's military policies. Treasury careerists were decidedly not helpful in their testimony on Capitol Hill concerning the tax bill. The Bay of Pigs disaster taught Kennedy, according to his own avowal, the folly of relying completely on subordinates down the lines.

To assert his influence in his uphill struggle for dominion over the executive branch, the President resorts to his White House staff, the cabinet, and the cluster of agencies composing the executive office of the President. The White House staff consists of approximately a score of assistants who bear such diverse titles as press secretary, special counsel to the President, appointments secretary, and special assistant for national security, science and technology, or a miscellany of other affairs. The staff is the President's "lengthened shadow." They help prepare his messages, speeches, and correspondence; arrange his appointments; oversee the inflow and outflow of his communications; analyze and refine the problems confronting him; advance his purposes with legislators, departments, private groups, and party officialdom. Although White House aides cherish their anonymity, they cannot escape importance. Only a few cabinet secretaries can rival leading White House staff members in influence and authority. Collectively, the staff is more powerful than all other groups in the executive branch, including the cabinet and the National Security Council.

The White House staff harks back to President Washington's appointment of his nephew and a former aide-de-camp of the Revolution as his secretaries. Until McKinley's time assistants were paid largely by the President out of his own pocket. Congress's parsimony in allowing the President assistance was purposeful: the President was not expected to play a creative role in the administrative system. Those Presidents whose pockets were not so well lined managed to carry their aides by allotting them a salaried sinecure in some department. Until the Franklin Roosevelt era, the chief White House aide was the secretary to the President, who handled a large miscellany of duties distributed nowadays among several White House staff members. Consider, for example, the regimen of James B. Henry, Buchanan's secretary and nephew. (Since the President was footing the secretarial bill, he tended to be nepotistic.) Henry attended the President in his office from 8 A.M. until 5 P.M., when Buchanan took a daily walk. Henry kept records of the receipt and disposition of correspondence. "Such letters as the President ought to see," Henry said explaining his duties, "I folded and briefed and took them to him every morning at eight o'clock and received his instructions as to the answer I should make." Once a day he sent to each department a large envelope containing letters for its attention. In addition, Henry oversaw arrangements for state dinners, managed the library fund, paid the household staff, and kept the President's private accounts.

The cabinet, founded by Washington early in his Presidency, has seldom been a source of advice upon which the President continuously relies. It exists by custom and functions by Presidential initiative, and is therefore largely what the chief executive chooses to make of it. Presidents such as Wilson, Franklin Roosevelt, and Kennedy used it very little. Quick and hard-driving, they chafed under extended group discussion. Truman and Eisenhower resorted to it more, but with uneven result. Johnson appears rather more inclined than Kennedy to employ it, but in no Presidential administration of the past three decades has the cabinet emerged to the forefront of influence in Presidential policy-making.

Unlike the British Prime Minister, who brings into office a team of ministers or department heads who have long been associated in common legislative and party enterprises with houses of Parliament, many of the President's department secretaries come into office with no acquaintance with each other and indeed little with the President himself. The two principal appointees of the Kennedy administration, Secretary of State Dean Rusk and Secretary of Defense Robert McNamara, were both total strangers to the President until the moment he interviewed them for their respective jobs. Historically, all sorts of considerations have governed the selection of department heads. Geography, to a degree: the Interior Secretary is ordinarily a Westerner. The Secretary of Agriculture is hardly apt to hail from an Eastern metropolis, but more likely from corn, wheat, or hog country. The Secretaries of Commerce and the Treasury are apt to emerge from the business and financial worlds. Franklin Roosevelt's choice of Harry Hopkins, his relief administrator, as Secretary of Commerce and Harry Truman's choice of Henry Wallace, a liberal-minded farmer, for that post, were hardly calculated to strike joy in the business community. The Secretary of Labor, Martin Durkin in the Eisenhower administration and Arthur Goldberg in the Kennedy administration, may be picked from the organized labor movement. Ordinarily the major party factions must be represented. Eisenhower dealt out recognition to protégés of Robert A. Taft, his rival for the Presidential nomination, by appointing George Humphrey and Ezra Taft Benson Secretaries of the Treasury and of Agriculture.

The executive office of the President includes the National Security Council, patterned after the British Committee of Imperial Defence and created by the National Security Act of 1947. It advises the President on national security objectives and commitments and the integration of national security policy. The NSC's top-level membership comprises the President, the Vice President, the Secretary of State, the Secretary of Defense, the Director of the Office of Emergency Planning, and the statutory advisers—the Chairman of the Joint Chiefs of Staff and the Director of the Central Intelligence Agency. The President can invite such other officials as he chooses to attend NSC sessions. In the Truman and Eisenhower administrations the NSC included a substructure of several working levels that was dropped in the Kennedy administration. The Bureau of the Budget, whose Director may be involved in a wide range of Presidential concerns, was created by the Budget and Accounting Act of 1921. In the President's behalf the bureau prepares a single executive budget or consolidated financial program, although Congress has not committed itself to pass a consolidated appropriation bill. The bureau also clears and coordinates legislation for the President and promotes management improvement in the executive branch. The Council of Economic Advisers, a child of the Employment Act of 1946, thinks, plans, and reports on the maintenance of economic prosperity. The Office of Emergency Planning oversees the mobilization of civilian resources for national security.

The executive office also includes the Office of the Special Assistant to the President for Science and Technology. This office was born in the Eisenhower administration when the Russians launched their Sputnik. The office has steadily grown in size and influence because of the emergence of science as a major claimant upon the President's attention. The office is a staff enterprise that sifts issues and opportunities in the fast-changing world of science. The office is a link between the President and the scientific community and a modest symbol of science's new status and vast responsibilities in forming national policy. Yet because it is a staff activity, the office is largely unseen. Neither it nor any other office stands in open view, its leaders accountable to the public for expressing the nation's goals for using its scientific resources. No single spokesman exists in the national government to articulate the synthesis of science and public policy, to explain and defend science to Congress and the public. Science's importance in national life makes wholly plausible the creation of a Council of Science Advisers of highest technical competence, paralleling the Council of Economic Advisers.

The Vice Presidency, whose first incumbent, John Adams, termed it "the most insignificant office that ever the invention of man contrived or his imagination conceived," has, after dormancy through most of the nineteenth century, acquired a special usefulness in the twentieth. Vice Presidents of the past three decades have participated increasingly, although unevenly, in the President's administrative enterprises. Henry Wallace, as Vice President in the Franklin Roosevelt administration, took on important administrative duties during World War II. Alben Barkley in the Truman administration became a statutory member of the National Security Council. Richard Nixon in the Eisenhower administration presided over the cabinet and the National Security Council in the chief executive's absence, was chairman of the interdepartmental government contract committee, and undertook good-will missions abroad. He did not, however, discharge any important executive responsibilities. Vice President Johnson in the Kennedy administration continued in the Nixon pattern, with assignments overseas and chairmanships of several interdepartmental committees concerning space and government contracts important for civil rights policy. That Johnson also held a substantial place as a counselor in the Kennedy administration is suggested by his membership in the "Ex Com" of the National Security Council, an *ad hoc* group of a dozen top administration officials who aided the President in working out his responses to the 1962 Cuban crisis.

In all, the Vice President has been chiefly useful to the President by relieving him of ceremonial duties and making good-will journeys abroad. A President prefers to have as his principal subordinates men of his own choosing, whom he can work easily with and discard if he wishes. The Constitution also makes the Vice President the presiding officer of the Senate, a duty which, although light, makes difficult his assumption of large and fixed executive responsibilities.

The acute question facing any contemporary President is: how best can he harness the administrative resources of the executive branch to his purposes—how can he transmute goal and plan into program and policy? How best can he awaken a sense of urgency in the bureaucracy, bestir its creativity, and command its loyalty against the blandishments of his Congressional and group interest competitors? Presumably his best ally in these causes is the Presidential staff, which after small and slow beginnings has since the New Deal era, and especially since World War II, burgeoned into a substantial bureaucracy itself, with more than one thousand employees occupying two buildings plus the east and west wings of the White House. Will the Presidential bureaucracy succumb to supreme irony and itself assume the very qualities of the greater bureaucracy it is designed to combat? The contemporary President must deploy his own aides and assistants in a fashion that will make his rule more effective and will avoid the pathologies of the greater bureaucracy. Each President responds to these challenges in his own way.

◇

FRANKLIN D. ROOSEVELT reigned as chief administrator by a highly unconventional system that gave the utmost play to his influence and enabled him to retain great power in his own hands. In pursuit of this supreme good he resorted to means that time and again violated the most sacred canons of efficient administration that are taught with unflagging zeal in our schools of business and public administration. For Roosevelt, organization blueprints were often scraps of paper, and the rules by which good executives, according to the texts, delegate authority were honored by their breach.

The textbooks warn that duplication must above all else be avoided in administration. Roosevelt went out of his way to indulge in it. He instituted the New Deal and its revolutionary changes, notwithstanding the bureaucracy he inherited from the previous Republican era. Roosevelt triumphed over the established bureaucracy with its elephantine pace and resistance to change partly by ignoring it. He established his own bureaucracy to adminster much of the New Deal. The job of regulating stock exchanges was given not to the Treasury or Commerce Departments but to the newborn Securities and Exchange Commission. The Wagner Act, enhancing labor's opportunity to organize and engage in collective bargaining, was consigned not to the Labor Department but the National Labor Relations Board. The bold new Tennessee River Valley project fell not to the Interior Department but to a special Tennessee Valley Authority. Before the normal pathologies of bureaucracy could mature, the New Deal was a going operation.

Roosevelt as administrator drew freely upon a large bag of tricks to get what he wanted done. He had little regard for the administrative niceties that are observed in most organizations. He was given, for example, to end-running his department heads and dealing directly with their subordinates. Frequently he would telephone J. Edgar Hoover at the FBI about something he wanted done quietly and in a hurry, and Hoover would promptly and wisely report the conversation to his superior, the Attorney General, Francis Biddle. Hoover knew of Roosevelt's habit of saying afterward, "By the way, Francis, not wishing to disturb you, I called Edgar Hoover the other day." When department secretaries, resentful of being undercut, sometimes protested, Roosevelt looked sheepish, apologized, and repeated the offense after a decent interval.

Roosevelt applied a competitive theory of administration, which kept his administrators unsure, off balance, confused, and even exasperated. With ambition pitted against ambition, the power of decision remained more securely in his own hands. Roosevelt at times deliberately kept the lines of authority blurred and jurisdictions overlapping. The administration of work relief thus was divided vaguely between Harry Hopkins, successively the Federal Emergency Relief Administrator and Works Progress Administrator, and Harold Ickes, the Public Works Administrator. Secretary of the Treasury Henry Morgenthau was given, with Presidential approval, such large powers of interference in the expenditures of WPA that Hopkins nearly resigned. "There is something to be said," Roosevelt observed in behalf of his method of planned disorder, ". . . for having a little conflict between agencies. A little rivalry is stimulating, you know. It keeps everybody going to prove that he is a better fellow than the next man. It keeps them honest too."

Roosevelt's devotion to the competitive principle and checks and balances led him often to prefer boards, commissions, and other variants of the plural executive to the single administrator. One of his more bizarre creations in World War II was the Office of Production Management, charged with administering much of the economy's mobilization. For this intricate and massive task, he resorted not to the leadership of a single administrator but to a biheaded authority consisting of William Knudsen of General Motors as Director General and Sidney Hillman of the CIO as Associate Director General. Although Knudsen's and Hillman's titles differed slightly, their authority, Roosevelt disclosed at a press conference, would be equal. But suppose, an incredulous reporter queried, Knudsen and Hillman disagreed, an altogether likely prospect given the conflicting premises of their respective worlds of management and labor. Might not the war effort be imperiled by dissension and impasse in OPM's biheadship? There would be no trouble whatever, Roosevelt answered confidently. If Knudsen and Hillman disagreed, he would simply lock them up in a room and not let them out until they could agree.

In maintaining competition, Roosevelt was adept at cutting down or building up his aides as situations might require. He disciplined them by withholding honors and distinctions, by assigning new authority and programs to someone else. He rewarded administrators with his intimacies. Harold Ickes, a sore and troubled administrator, suffered his most distressful period when a year elapsed in which he never saw his chief alone. In Roosevelt's hand the simple small White House luncheon became a mighty sword of reward and fear. If Ickes or Henry Wallace lunched with the President, every other member of the official family instantly knew of the event and speculated anxiously about what had been discussed and its consequences for their interests.

If Roosevelt sometimes had to knock an administrator down, he was quick to help him up. If Ickes had been shorn of a coveted jurisdiction and Hull had lost an interdepartmental dispute, Roosevelt would favor the losers with attentions days later. The building-up might take the form of an elaborate compliment in cabinet for the way the vanquished secretary had handled what was described as a difficult and sensitive matter. Another restorative was "hand-holding," as Roosevelt called it, a process of consolation at which his talent, in the discerning judgment of William Phillips, was "rare" and which took up, according to Grace Tully, the President's secretary, "hours and days" of his time.

Roosevelt, in the interest of competition, filled his administration with human opposites. His original Secretary of the Treasury, Will Woodin, was a conservative, respectable, trustworthy financier, and his first Budget Director, the economy-minded Lewis Douglas, viewed New Deal spending as "the end of Western civilization." Yet Roosevelt could also import a free-spender like Harry Hopkins and legions of young lawyers schooled in the progressivism of Louis Brandeis and Felix Frankfurter. The philosophical pluralism of his administration enabled Roosevelt to play off not merely men against men but dogma against dogma. It was a kind of double insurance for Roosevelt's own retention of the power of decision.

He loved to employ *enfants terribles* who would flay their fellow administrators and outsiders such as legislators and pressure group leaders who occasionally chose to interfere in the processes of the executive branch. General Hugh Johnson, the National Recovery Administrator, freely indulged his talent at brassy invective in violent denunciations of fellow administrators and the critical press. When told that Johnson had overstayed his usefulness, Roosevelt simply remarked that every administration had to have a Peck's Bad Boy. The bellicose Harold Ickes exchanged batterings with a similar breadth of foes, and Leon Henderson starred in the same capacity during World War II.

The crown of the formal organization, the department secretaries, were individuals of initiative and drive, and deep in their commitment to program. Roosevelt permitted them great scope. Their collective organization, the cabinet, however, he restricted to a modest role. He did not value the cabinet as a source of collective wisdom, and its meetings were apt to be hollow affairs. The President began typically by engaging in a monologue of pleasantries, recounting stories and joshing selected secretaries. He would then throw out a problem, usually one that he had been considering just prior to the meeting. Discussion rambled and was inconclusive. Roosevelt's next move was to turn to the Secretary of State and say, "Well, Cordell, what's on your mind today?" The same query continued around the table in order of the secretaries' precedence. They responded usually with items of minor importance, preferring to take up larger matters privately with the President just before or after the meeting. Large matters, the secretaries feared, might be excessively mauled or leaked to the Hill or to the gossip columnists.

Roosevelt steadily employed a free-roving assistant who shepherded the President's fondest projects over the assorted hurdles in the executive branch and outside. The assistant, acting for the President ("This is the White House calling"), made short shrift of departmental hierarchy and red tape in expediting action. He was a major tool by which the President might prevail against the vast, sluggish executive branch. Originally, Louis Howe, shrewd and devoted, a soldier of Roosevelt's political fortunes for nearly a quarter century, seemed destined for the assignment of general assistant. But illness and then death intervened. Howe, while he still could work, brought the optimistic Roosevelt to see occasionally the darker side of issues and was his only aide whose candor stretched to the point where, confronted by a Presidential note, he could snort, "Tell the President to go to hell." Howe was followed by a series of general assistants, including Raymond Moley, Rexford Tugwell, Thomas Corcoran, and Harry Hopkins. Corcoran in his day was a stellar administration lobbyist on Capitol Hill, a Presidential speech-writer, a channel to Roosevelt for those with ideas, a trouble-shooter who would rush to New York City and rescue the PWA housing program bogged down in an internecine brawl, a hirer and firer of personnel, and doyen of a vast body of young lawyers catacombed in the departments—his "chicks" he called them—a government within a government whose hallmark was action.

In World War II Harry Hopkins was Roosevelt's number-one troubleshooter. Known as "Generalissimo of the Needle Brigade," he prodded industry to speed war production, harassed laggard military administrators, and oversaw the distribution of supplies to the fighting fronts. Hopkins was Roosevelt's personal liaison with the war overseas. In conferences with Churchill and Stalin and military chieftains he did the legwork on which Roosevelt's central decisions were founded.

The Roosevelt method is the surest yet invented for maximizing the President's personal influence and for asserting his sway over the executive branch. It spurred the flow of information and ideas into his possession and magnified his impact on policy. It released the energies of men from confining bureaucratic routine. For the sixties and beyond, however, the Roosevelt method has a large although limited relevance. The new costliness of error in foreign affairs makes the Rooseveltian system of haphazard consultation, by which some departments may be left out, unthinkable. The internecine strife which marked the system is also barred by the necessity that the national executive appear before the world with the face of unity. Roosevelt enjoyed a luxury his successors are doomed never to know. He could create much of his own bureaucracy, first in the New Deal and then in the war. His successors must work with an inherited bureaucracy.

◇

AT A far opposite extreme from Franklin Roosevelt's highly personal managerial method is Dwight Eisenhower's preference for institutionalizing Presidential relationships with the executive branch. The Eisenhower method was a product of his military experience and several long-entertained convictions concerning White House practice. "For years I had been in frequent contact in the executive office of the White House," Eisenhower has written, "and I had certain ideas about the system, or lack of system, under which it operated. With my training in problems involving organization it was inconceivable to me that the work of the White House could not be better systemized than had been the case in the years I observed it."

Eisenhower's key tactic was to delegate duties, tasks, and initiatives to subordinates. After their study and formulation of decision, he as chief executive might ultimately accept or reject. "The marks of a good executive," he advised his department heads, "are courage in delegating work to subordinates and his own skill in coordinating and directing their effort." Eisenhower's subsequent illnesses speeded his inclination to delegate.

The vehicle of his delegations was the staff system. At its apex was the assistant to the President, Sherman Adams, a former Congressman, governor of New Hampshire, and early organizer of Eisenhower's Presidential candidacy. Eisenhower, Adams has written, "simply expected me to manage a staff that would boil down, simplify and expedite the urgent business that had to be brought to his personal attention and to keep as much work of secondary importance as possible off his desk." Any issue, no matter how complex, Eisenhower believed, could be reduced to some bare essence. "If a proposition can't be stated in one page," he declared, "it isn't worth saying." Impatient with the torrential paper work of the Presidency and not one who took to reading gladly, Eisenhower insisted that his subordinates digest lengthy, involved documents into one-page summaries, "which," said Adams, "was sometimes next to impossible to do."

Except in the singular case of Secretary of State John Foster Dulles, cabinet secretaries approached the President through Adams. Policy proposals were made in writing, the fruit of staff study and recommendation. Adams's task was to see that every expert in the executive branch who could contribute to a proposal had his opportunity to do so. Many final decisions were made not by the President but by Adams. Eisenhower was brought in only if the matter was very important or if the executive experts disagreed. The President, according to Adams, wasn't bothered very often. "I always tried to resolve specific differences on a variety of problems before the issue had to be submitted to the President," Adams has written. "Sometimes several meetings were necessary before an agreement was reached. But with a few exceptions I was successful."

Eisenhower kept the system on its toes by his own close knowledge of governmental detail mastered in a long military career, and a capacity to put sharp, piercing questions that could reduce premises and argument to a shambles. He could not bear flawed performance, a sentiment conveyed at times by fierce outbursts of the Presidential temper.

Adams was an ubiquitous influence. When a caller or official sprang a new proposal, Eisenhower was prone to say, "Take it up with Sherman." If a paper came to the President, he would run his eye over it for the familiar notation, "O.K., S. A." If it was missing, Eisenhower was sure to ask, "Has Governor Adams approved this?" Although each cabinet secretary had an ivory telephone connecting directly with the President's line, the connection—except for that of Secretary Dulles, who consulted Eisenhower constantly on foreign policy—was seldom used. Cabinet secretaries found it wise to call Adams instead. For the several specialists constituting the White House staff—the press secretary, the appointments secretary, the staff secretary, and the cabinet secretary—Adams was a coordinator. Though all these colleagues enjoyed direct access to the President, only Adams by dint of the breadth of his responsibilities could speak with the President on broad, general affairs. Adams dealt with policy in sweep, his colleagues in chunks. The major staff positions interlocked smoothly with Adams's undertakings; his controls extended over the communications system running to and from the President. The appointments secretary, for instance, in setting up the President's daily list of visitors, routinely checked with Adams, enabling him to veto prospective callers or fit others in. Adams also could arrange his own schedule in order to be on hand, if necessary, when Eisenhower met with visitors. The staff secretary, who presided over a system installed under Eisenhower's supervision, was a great boon to Adams. He kept records on hundreds of papers, many of high import and secrecy, dealing with national security and domestic affairs. Within minutes, Adams, thanks to the staff secretariat, could track down the location and status of reports, memoranda, and letters which had come into the White House or gone out for clearances in the far reaches of the executive branch. He could tell who had prepared a given document, the concurrences received and objections encountered, who was dragging his feet, and other essential facts of paper-work life. Adams was no mere merchant of dry-as-dust routine. He uplifted some of the administration's finest achievements in their wobbliest beginnings—the Atoms for Peace plan, the civil rights program, and the Refugee Relief Act.

The ancient institution of the cabinet also felt Eisenhower's reforming hand. Shocked that the department secretaries, the government's principal executives, should gather without any preconception of the business to be considered, Eisenhower created the post of cabinet secretary. This new official arranged an agenda for cabinet meetings, circulated it beforehand among the members, oversaw the preparation of "cabinet papers" presenting proposals for the President's action, and recorded the results of cabinet discussion. Keenly aware of the gap between Presidential decision and departmental reliability in carrying it out, Eisenhower had his cabinet secretary meet after a session of the cabinet with "cabinet assistants," a group of assistant secretaries and departmental executive assistants with responsibilities for implementation. Every several months a cabinet meeting was converted into "Judgment Day" on the "Action Status Report," in which each department head revealed how much (or little) he had honored his obligations to take actions called for by the President's decisions in cabinet.

In adapting the military staff system to the Presidency, Eisenhower viewed his cabinet secretaries essentially as theater commanders. Like field generals, the several secretaries were invested with broad initiative and responsibility for their allotted sectors of operation. In the wake of unsettling exposures by the McClellan Committee on Improper Activities in the Labor Management Field, for example, Eisenhower was asked whether he considered new legislation necessary to cope with the problems typified by Dave Beck, Jimmy Hoffa, and the Teamsters' Union. "Well," the President answered in a press conference, "I have merely been told by the Labor Secretary they are watching this very closely and see whether we have any responsibility or anything we could do reasonably." In the Eisenhower administration the cabinet secretary typically chose his own assistants. There was no Raymond Moley or Sumner Welles, who in secondary positions in the departments in Roosevelt's day trafficked directly with the President over the head of the secretary. Eisenhower backed up his department secretaries even in the face of heavy political cannonade. When a score of midwestern Republican Congressmen, with elections in prospect, grew restive over Agriculture Secretary Benson's hard line toward farm price supports and suggested it would help politically if he would resign, Eisenhower, controlling his fury, answered at a press conference that "for any group of Congressmen, either informally or formally, to raise a question concerning my appointment to the Cabinet would not seem to be in order."

One of the more complex and important elements of Eisenhower's institutionalized Presidency was the National Security Council. Eisenhower, who utilized the NSC heavily, often met with it two or more times a month, with an agenda of intelligence reports, policies to be innovated or revised, and reports on progress in fulfilling established policies. Backstopping the council proper in the Eisenhower administration was the Planning Board, considered the most influential part of the NSC system and consisting of representatives and observers from member agencies, usually at the assistant secretary level. The Planning Board provided an unremitting flood of documents with each drop painstakingly considered. "The Planning Board normally does not send a paper forward without meeting three or four times on it," said Gordon Gray, Eisenhower's National Security Affairs assistant. Planning Board members, according to report, debated not merely high policy but the subtleties of idiom and terminology. Hours of anxious effort were invested in clearance procedures, with intensive review and interdepartmental negotiation of words and phrases. Critics hold that papers worked out in such proceedings were highly watered down, lowest-common-denominator-of-agreement affairs, and there were snide remarks about this being "the century of the comma man." Defenders of the stress on paper work hold that such exercises foster exactitude in an area of utmost sensitivity and complexity.

Another NSC offshoot was the Operations Coordinating Board, created by the Eisenhower administration, which was made up of deputy-level officials who tackled the job of getting things done, of devising ways to put into operation, at home and overseas, NSC policies ranging from psychological and economic warfare to international cooperation in science. Like the Planning Board, the OCB reveled in paper work and meticulously negotiated detail.

Eisenhower, anxious to avoid the noisy administrative altercations of the Roosevelt era, relied upon several expedients. Sherman Adams was a one-man peace-keeping constabulary, practicing his coordinating arts with rugged firmness. Eisenhower himself preached the gospel of teamwork and the secretaries responded, aided by their general lack of profound convictions about public affairs. The several who entertained strong beliefs either fought for them only sporadically or lacked talent to make them persuasive. Political ambition, a disturbing force in Franklin Roosevelt's cabinet, was slight in Eisenhower's. Most of his secretaries were businessmen, eager to return to lucrative careers.

The attraction of the Eisenhower system is the assurance it promises that the President will have the benefit of coordinated counsel in an age when major problems require the best expertise of several or more departments. Adams's operation strove systematically to include every relevant department. The omission of skill and information, given the world's dangers, could be severely costly.

The Eisenhower system can be viewed as purporting to provide a security that is unattainable, given the vastness of the executive branch, the interminable Niagara of executive transactions, and the severely limited timetable imposed by events. The Eisenhower experience indeed bears instances of human and organizational failure in spite of all the elaborate safeguards. As the Dixon-Yates contract episode, a major political disaster, was building, Republican Senator John Sherman Cooper of Kentucky, whom Eisenhower highly esteemed, called at the White House to lay before the President his several objections to carrying the project forward. Sherman Adams refused to grant the Senator an appointment. When the Budget Bureau and the Atomic Energy Commission prepared chronologies of the principal facts of Dixon-Yates for the President's use and for distribution to the press, an essential detail was omitted: that Adolphe Wenzell, a Budget Bureau consultant for the contract, was simultaneously an official of the First Boston Corporation, which was financing the Dixon-Yates group. Eisenhower's staff left him helpless and exposed while the administration's foes leaped with full cry upon the error.

The Eisenhower system appears to afford the President both too little initiative and too little total impact upon policy. He depends overmuch upon others to discover and assess the magnitude of problems. He enters into policy-making only in the final stage of decision, when his area of choice is small and his dependence upon his staff great. To the ailing Eisenhower, the staff was at times a kind tranquilizer, comforting the chief executive with a therapeutic but unwarranted calm and optimism. The President was apparently allowed to assume that the 1957-1958 recession was less serious in its early stages than it really was. Remedial public measures were delayed and the recession deepened, to the harm of the administration politically and the country economically.

❖

PRESIDENT KENNEDY'S administrative method lay between the polarities of Eisenhower and Franklin Roosevelt, and veered decidedly toward Roosevelt. Like Franklin Roosevelt, Kennedy aimed to carve out a maximum personal role in the conduct of the Presidency, but without some of the more jagged methods and much of the dinful turmoil of the Rooseveltian model. Kennedy clearly visualized his Presidential role when he declared in his 1960 campaign that as President he would want to be "in the thick of things." Kennedy the President was true to the promise of Kennedy the candidate. He put in abundant hours at desk-side conferences and on the telephone, pursuing details well down the line of departmental hierarchy, and took a constant hand in coordination, its weight laid not merely upon top-level endeavor but upon minor affairs as well.

Kennedy's intensive involvement was more than an applied philosophy of the Presidency. It was a reflection of his personality, aptitude, and body chemistry. Kennedy personally comprised a bundle of restless curiosity, a high quotient of vigor, and an extraordinary spongelike capacity to absorb the daily torrent of government data.

To carry forward his administrative view of the Presidency, Kennedy relied upon several operating principles and expedients. Unlike Eisenhower, who stressed institutional structure, Kennedy placed great store in personal relationships. The person—his talent, perception, and reliability—counted more than his organization. Kennedy's person-centered approach reflected his pre-Presidential career, passed chiefly in legislative politics and in political campaigning, in both of which working relationships are highly personal. Accordingly, in dealing with department secretaries and White House staff members Kennedy insisted upon direct relationships, unhampered by organization and hierarchy. He, for his part, remained highly accessible to a large circle of colleagues. "You've got one of the most accessible Presidents in history," one cabinet secretary said. "I must talk with him in person or on the phone twenty times a week," said another secretary. "I don't hesitate to call him if something important comes up—even at night or on Sunday." "I can pick up the telephone and call him at any time," said still another. "I'll call up the White House and say, 'I want ten minutes tomorrow or the next day.' "

Kennedy, dealing with the departments, did not stop with the department head but reached down the hierarchy to lesser levels. A loud, clear hint of this practice was sounded in the preinaugural period in the manner of the President-elect's selection of his foreign policy aides. He designated an Assistant Secretary and an Undersecretary of State and the Ambassador to the United Nations before selecting his Secretary of State. To underscore the principle implied in the sequence of these appointments, of direct Presidential superintendency of foreign affairs, Kennedy for his first three foreign affairs nominees, and for others after them, accompanied the public announcement of their selection with a phrase hailing the "post" as "second to none in importance." The President-elect's pointed tribute signified his intention to deal directly with second- and third-echelon subordinates. Kennedy's own assessment of his experience in the Presidency affirmed the wisdom of this tactic. In a year-end television interview in 1962, he was asked, "Is it true that during your first year, sir, you would get on the phone personally to the State Department and try to get a response to some inquiry that had been made?" "Yes," Kennedy replied, "I still do that when I can, because I think there is a great tendency in government to have papers stay on desks too long. . . . After all, the President can't administer a department, but at least he can be a stimulant."

Kennedy injected himself at any point along the decision-making spectrum from problem-selection to final judgment. Whereas Eisenhower wanted decisions brought to him for approval, Kennedy wanted problems brought to him for decision. Eisenhower preferred a consensus to be laid before him, stated briefly and in general terms. Kennedy eschewed consensus; he wanted to know a problem's facets and alternative answers, keeping decision for himself in consultation or "dialogue," as the administration called it, with advisers. Kennedy's keen nose for detail took him far into the interior of problems. Although interested in general principles, he was essentially a pragmatist and had, as a colleague said, "a highly operational mind." Policy separated from operations, in his view, was meaningless. His desk, not surprisingly, was piled high with reports and memoranda which he read closely. Conferring with an official, he would reach into the pile, pull out a memorandum, and resort instantaneously to a paragraph to make a point or raise a question. "President Kennedy," a colleague said, "is a desk officer at the highest level."

In another burrowing tactic, Kennedy early in his term requested each department to supply his office with twice-weekly reports on its current problems and impending decisions. The procedure was intended to enable the President to inject himself into problems before they crystallized and to further his conviction that the pathways to his desk should lay open to any important official, including those several rungs down. The reports provided the departments the rare gratification of airing complaints about each other. Hence, sometime after the procedure commenced, the Housing and Home Finance Agency complained to the President that several proposed urban renewal projects that lay partially on military land were being held up in the Defense Department. The President previously had ordered all such projects speeded up to quicken the economy's slowing pace. A White House aide, seizing the report, confronted the Defense Department with the complaint. Within forty-eight hours, that department cleared proposals that had been slumbering for months in one of the Pentagon's remoter recesses.

Kennedy's appetite for detail could not be satiated by the mere resources of Washington. He prepared himself for budget-making for fiscal 1964 by going forth from the capital for several days of intensive on-the-spot surveying of major military and civilian space installations. His itinerary took him to the Redstone and Saturn projects at Huntsville, Alabama, and a new manned-space flight center at Houston. In St. Louis he inspected the plant of the McDonnell Aircraft Corporation, producer of the Mercury space capsules.

Kennedy's technique pulled innumerable matters, major and minor, out of the regular decision-action line. Officials from State, Defense, and Treasury and other agencies were constantly summoned to the White House where policy was hammered out at his desk. He launched actions on his own initiative, sometimes even without advance notice to the agencies most concerned. He startled the State Department by disclosing, in answer to a news conference question in his first year, that he planned to discuss the balance of payments problem with Heinrich von Brentano, the West German Foreign Minister, who was soon to appear in Washington.

This was news to the State Department as well as to the press. Dr. Brentano was not coming in an official capacity, although he was expected to have conversations at the department. The department knew of no plan for a meeting with the President.

Kennedy entertained well-defined views of the proper role of the individual department. His tactic was to devolve upon individual department heads and on identified subordinates the responsibility for recommending policy initiatives and overseeing the execution of decisions. He took a stern view of a luxuriant bureaucratic phenomenon, the interdepartmental committee, beholding it as an intruder upon departmental responsibility and therefore something inherently bad, to be extirpated if at all possible. After several months in office he abolished a lengthy list of interdepartmental committees and reassigned many of their functions to department secretaries and other officials. Committees, being hardy administrative plants because they serve vital purposes, cannot be eliminated by mere Presidential prescription. They are an inevitable bureaucratic routine for establishing interdepartmental collaboration at the working levels. Seldom do problems of any significance appear that are not interdepartmental in their contours. The committees that Kennedy killed, not surprisingly, did not stay dead. Many on his list resumed a more or less surreptitious existence after a decent interval.

In lieu of committees the Kennedy administration resorted to "task forces," a name appropriately suggestive of vigor and purpose. Task forces, which consisted of departmental representatives and usually one or more White House staffers, were not merely committees by another name. "They operate with a consciousness of having a mandate, often from the President himself," a participant explained. Task forces carried a sense of the importance of getting things done, which often stirred bureaucracy to faster, more constructive effort. The attendant White House staff member was a powerful reminder of the chief executive's need and interest, a bearer of his influence upon decision, not merely in the moment of final choice but along much of the journey of its formation. Departmental participants in the task forces were not altogether enthusiastic about the contribution of their White House colleagues. "When the President's man says something, you don't know whether he is speaking for himself or for his boss," a department man exclaimed. "The effect can be, and often is, to cut off discussion too soon."

Kennedy, like Roosevelt, viewed the White House staff as a personal rather than an institutional staff, a vehicle for maximizing his influence rather than its influence throughout the executive branch. Impressed that the larger a staff is the more apt it is to become institutional, Kennedy tried heroically to cut back the sizable staff he had inherited from the Eisenhower administration, but with small success. In meting out staff assignments, Kennedy put his staff on action-forcing rather than program tasks, and gave it a mixture of fixed and general-purpose responsibilities. These expedients likewise were intended to reduce the advance of institutionalization and to keep the staff personal.

Kennedy's White House staff, unlike Eisenhower's, was not organized by hierarchy or pyramid, but like a wheel whose hub was the President and whose spokes connected him with individual aides. Five aides occupied major functional posts. The staff assistant to the President, Kenneth O'Donnell, ex-football captain and war hero, handled appointments and Presidential trips and was an omnibus "chief White House official for party politics," in touch with the Democratic National Committee and local party figures. The special counsel, Theodore C. Sorensen of Nebraska, whose association harked back to Kennedy's Senate days in 1953, had responsibilities running across the board. His office, comprising two assistants, focused Presidential objectives, planned programs, broke impasses, and passed judgment on timing. Sorensen drafted Presidential messages and speeches with high artistry and a capacity that Richard M. Nixon once hailed as "the rare gift of being an intellectual who can completely sublimate his style to another intellectual." Sorensen sat with department secretaries formulating their budget and legislative programs and attended the President's meetings with legislative leaders and pre-press conference briefings. Sorensen had an acquisitive, cosmopolitan intelligence, which, as a colleague put it, "can understand anything from sugar subsidies to bomb shelters."

McGeorge Bundy, a former Harvard graduate dean, was special assistant for national security affairs. Bundy, aided by a small band of assistants ("the Bundy group"), kept watch for weakness and trouble in defense and foreign policy administration and saw to remedies and repairs. In the President's behalf he occupied a central place in the stream of intelligence. He received copies of virtually all the incoming cables to the Secretaries of State and Defense and the Director of the CIA. He sorted these out and put the most important before the President.

Other key aides were the assistant for Congressional relations, Lawrence F. O'Brien, a long-time Kennedy associate, the press secretary, Pierre Salinger, and Ralph Dungan, who was responsible for personnel, or "head-hunting," as he put it. Dungan maintained a permanent list of talent available for government posts, checked job recommendations from legislators, the Democratic National Committee, and the departments. Beyond this, Dungan took on roving assignments—he was Presidential overseer of foreign aid and of African and Latin-American policy. The assignments of Arthur Schlesinger, Jr., the Harvard historian, were even more diverse—he acted as a liaison between the President and United Nations Ambassador Stevenson and between the White House and the

State Department on Latin-American policy, and he occasionally gave assistance with Presidential speeches.

The White House staff reaped a steady harvest of influence from Kennedy's habit of entrusting important responsibilities to individuals in whom he had confidence. Staff members, therefore, oftentimes performed functions traditionally handled by departments and diplomatic representatives. Arthur Schlesinger, Jr., of the White House staff—and not high-level State Department officials—traveled through Latin America to survey the area's requirements, gathering data and impressions that became the basis of the future aid program. Press Secretary Salinger, and not the State Department or the United States Information Agency, negotiated in Moscow an agreement for the exchange of information. The attendant publicity of such assignments stripped many of the White House staff posts of their traditional anonymity.

Kennedy deployed his White House staff as critics of departmental performance and as emergency repair crews when departmental undertakings went awry. He restored direct work-flows between departments and himself and made his staff responsible for "monitoring," but not "obstructing," departmental access to him personally. With such solid mandates, the White House staff at times became overexuberant, as suggested by a "ruling" Kennedy issued after six months in office. The White House staff, Kennedy directed, was not to "interfere" in the operations of departments or agencies. The ruling was apparently triggered by a quiet crisis in the State Department's Inter-American Division. For several months the post of Assistant Secretary of State for Inter-American Affairs lay vacant, creating a power vacuum into which the President's staff quickly moved, to the bitter resentment of State Department career men.

A key function of the White House staff was to spot political and policy weaknesses in departmental proposals. Staff members played a decisive part in heading off a tax increase which may have made sense economically, but not politically, in the Berlin build-up of July 1961; they delighted liberals by implanting several public-ownership features into the Communications Satellite bill; they knocked down a State Department proposal that action on the Trade bill be postponed for more than a year, until 1963. There was wide agreement that a large advantage of the Sorensen-Bundy service was penetrating analysis. "When Sorensen gets into something," a Budget Bureau career man said, "it gets a thorough scrubbing." It was also the lack of such a scrubbing that plunged the staff to the far depths of its worst failure, the abortive Cuban invasion in the young administration's fourth month. The staff was admittedly timid about raising questions that should have been asked. "At that point," a White House aide confessed, "we just didn't have the confidence to tell the veterans of the bureaucracy, 'Look, you're crazy.' "

In another blow at the institutionalized Presidency, Kennedy performed drastic surgery on the most advanced expression of that phenomenon, the National Security Council. He abolished the NSC's nerve- and work-center, the Planning Board, and its organ for implementing decision, the Operations Coordinating Board. Most important of all, he shunned the NSC by seldom bringing it into session. He sought counsel for major crises like Berlin of 1961 and Cuba of 1962 by bringing together an *ad hoc* group of advisers in whom he had special confidence. In lieu of the Planning Board and the OCB was the Bundy offiice, which greatly scaled down the former mountainous paper work.

Kennedy also largely dispensed with cabinet meetings, holding that the entire body of secretaries should be assembled only for matters of full breadth and significance. He saw no reason for the entire cabinet to ponder matters affecting only three or four departments. The cabinet, consequently, met infrequently. In the summer of 1962 various department heads, then occupied with the political campaign, happened to converge upon Chicago. There they laughingly acknowledged that what had not transpired in Washington for some months was at last happening in the Midwest, a cabinet "meeting"!

The Kennedy technique clearly maximized the President's involvement and imprint upon policy, breathed vitality into sluggish bureaucracy, and extended the reach of a highly knowledgeable President and his staff into the departments. Yet there were also disadvantages. There was feeling that Kennedy was too accessible to operating personnel, too much "in the thick of things," over-immersed in minor policy and small detail, with too little time for major business. Or again, that Kennedy's emphasis on swiftness—terse statement, quick strides from one problem to the next—resulted at times in inadequate consideration of alternatives. Much public business, like reducing the arms race or overhauling the tax system, does not permit quick, concise expression. "The system now," a frequent participant said, "favors people who know exactly what they want to do. It is tough on people who have dim misgivings—even if those misgivings happen to be very important."

One strength of the Kennedy system may also have been a weakness. His method rested upon the realistic view that the executive branch, lacking the apparatus of collective responsibility found in Great Britain, depended heavily, for action and decision, upon the President's judgment. Yet what ordinarily was plausibly realistic may have caused at times an overdependence upon the time, energy, and talent of the President. The great risk of the Kennedy method is that no single mind, even a Presidential mind, can absorb the information or muster the wisdom necessary for sound judgment of many intricate issues pouring upon the President.

The problems with which American statesmanship must deal have acquired a complexity that render them no longer fit for individual insight and judgment, no matter how perceptive. To be dealt with adequately, they must at some stage be subjected to collective study involving diverse technical skills, specialized knowledge, and organizational viewpoints. Decision without collective study is apt to be founded on inadequate information and to lack roundness of judgment.

❖

PRESIDENT LYNDON JOHNSON's method is a blend of elements of the Franklin Roosevelt-Kennedy, President-centered style, on the one hand, and the Truman-Eisenhower tendency to system and institutionalization on the other. From Franklin Roosevelt, Johnson borrows a lively penchant for employing a Brain Trust of many faces drawn from outside the government. He turns frequently to a corps of Washington lawyers and former New Dealers: Abe Fortas, Benjamin Cohen, Thomas Corcoran, and James Rowe; a fellow Texan and former Treasury Secretary in the Eisenhower administration, Robert Anderson; and from the Truman administration the former Secretary of State, Dean Acheson, and the White House counsel, Clark Clifford. Johnson may use a Brain Truster for a special project. Fortas, for instance, pulled together the commission to investigate the assassination. Chiefly, Brain Trust folk are a sounding board with shrewd and sensitive political antennae. By testing their reactions to his instincts, Johnson senses the more general public reaction.

From Franklin Roosevelt also, Johnson, in setting up his "war on poverty" program, borrowed a well-worn page from World War II: the "czar" that Roosevelt loved to create to hold in harness the efforts of several departments in behalf of a common program. Sargent Shriver, Johnson's designee as director, is, as Johnson has put it, to be "in charge of coordinating the program between the agencies who already are working in that field." Departments such as Agriculture, Labor, and Health, Education and Welfare will take direction from the "czar." As in Franklin Roosevelt's day, the "czar" presumably will help keep the program's reins well within the President's reach.

But President Johnson, a highly cautious man, also displays a strong streak of administrative orthodoxy. He employs the established administrative institutions more than Kennedy did. Johnson resorts more to the National Security Council, whether for the crisis in Panama or for the war in South Vietnam. He has accorded new recognition to the department secretaries. Secretary of Defense McNamara quickly achieved an influence exceeding his considerable status under President Kennedy. McNamara's gain is partly a reflection of Johnson's disposition to interfere less in details of defense policy and operations than Kennedy did. President Johnson was not long in office when he declared to a gathering of Foreign Service officers his "profound confidence" in Secretary of State Rusk.

But Johnson's caution also leads him at times to violate administrative orthodoxy. He is a strong believer in the double check. When trouble boiled over in Panama, he did not rely on the local United States officials, but dispatched his Assistant Secretary of State for Latin-American Affairs, Thomas C. Mann, to the scene. In the same manner he sent Defense Secretary McNamara to Panama and Undersecretary of State George Ball to Cyprus. Faced with the decision of providing public help to finance and build a costly supersonic air transport plane, Johnson did not simply rely for advice upon the Federal Aviation Authority but also resorted to the Defense Department and private banks.

Because of the circumstances of his accession to the Presidency, Johnson has had a severely restricted freedom to create and deploy a White House staff. The short span between his assumption of office and the next election, and the political necessity of maintaining links with the previous Kennedy administration, compelled Johnson to use the inherited Kennedy staff as much as he could. He averred, with a large measure of truth, in a televised interview after his first hundred days in office that "basically the staff is the same, the duties are the same." But Johnson inserted his own cadre of long-standing associates into the White House staff: Bill D. Moyers, George Reedy, Walter Jenkins, Horace Busby, and others, who by all appearances fitted in amicably with the Kennedy holdovers. The rare spectacle of a dual White House staff, the old and the new, was abbreviated by the departure of such Kennedy men as Sorensen, Schlesinger, and Salinger. Johnson's methods most approximate Kennedy's in his use of the Bundy group. Unlike Kennedy, however, who preferred oral counsel, Johnson prefers propositions for decision to come to him on paper, a choice bound to have large effects on staff method.

Several elements in Johnson's operating methods augur a reduced role for the White House staff. The President's steady resort to a large roster of outside counselors shrinks the staff role, particularly in the area of supremely important political advice. Even more formidable is the expanding capacity Johnson is allotting the old-line departments in program development and control. The State Department made off with the Alliance for Progress in the administration's early months. The Labor Department, rather than the Council of Economic Advisers which originated it, dominated the antipoverty program, at least in its first stages. Interior took control of oil policy previously administered in the White House. All this bespeaks less involvement of the White House staff in program development, a trend which also may be fostered by the fact that the talents of Johnson's own staff men tend more to expediting, arranging meetings and appointments, and forcing out the paper work.

Against the trend of heavy, possibly dangerous, dependence upon the old-line departments is the nature of Johnson the administrator himself. He approaches policy issues with strong convictions rooted in his New Deal beginnings. His favorite tactic with those whose advice he seeks is, "I want to do this, you tell me why I shouldn't." Above all, Johnson's own cyclonic activity in eighteen-hour workdays, his talent at forcing the pace in meetings and in a hundred phone calls a day, and his overwhelming energy and persuasiveness may prove a mighty energizing influence on all the departments.

◇

T H E activist President, bent upon extracting as much mileage as possible from his resources as general manager, must plainly commit great quantities of his own personal energy and talent fully to the task. The Presidency is no place for semi-retirement. The President does best with a small cadre of assistants, with flexible assignments and responsibilities of both action-forcing and program-building nature. Yet he must be watchful that his immediate staff do not, intentionally or no, exercise their enlarging authority for their own purposes rather than his. The competitive principle of advice and action has been successfully used by activist Presidents since the days of Washington. It is the surest means yet devised for extending their influence and control.

But no contemporary President can live by personal assistants alone. He must make large use of the Presidency's institutions such as the Budget Bureau, the NSC, the CEA. Given the enormousness of his problems and the dangers of the times, he can no longer reign with the informal splendor of a Franklin Roosevelt of the 1930's. The institutionalized Presidency is the best available guarantee that the multiple specializations a major problem requires will be addressed to that problem.

In actuality, the contemporary President requires a dual organization. One is institutional, which is largely inherited and is a major link for the President with the operating departments. If its leadership is closely attuned to its purposes, it can be a mighty host for producing departmental action responsive to his needs. The other organization is a personal staff, flexible, versatile, and fast-moving, competent to exploit departmental resources and hammer out policy as the President finds it necessary. In a word, the President must have a formal structure capable of handling the great stream of business and a modifying, informal mechanism capable of intervening in and adjusting executive processes responsively to his purposes.

Four distinguished study groups, the Brownlow Committee (1937), the first and second Hoover Commissions (1949 and 1955), and the current Subcommittee on National Policy Machinery, headed by Senator

Henry Jackson, provide in their reports a mine of recommendations for strengthening the President's position as general manager. Some of them have been acted upon, and others would be immensely helpful if they were. The Brownlow Committee urged that the Civil Service Commission, which is largely independent of the President, be abolished and replaced by a civil service administrator, appointed by and responsible to the President. The recommendation assumed that personnel policy ought to be centered in the chief executive, in preference to its present diffusion between the President and the commission. The commission, as the traditional watchdog of the vast merit system, has been primarily a regulatory body alert to shut out spoils, a mission that also fosters red tape, routine, and impersonality. This is the very opposite of the first Hoover Commission's proposed "positive" personnel policy, one that would promote a working environment and career development opportunities to attract and keep the best available younger talent. The federal service suffers a heavy loss of such talent after some years of training have been invested in it, owing to the superior attractions of private employment.

The President's natural interest, the Brownlow group assumed, would be to develop the strongest possible personnel system, both for his own operating convenience and for his administration's public image. The second Hoover Commission recommended a strong mobile career corps, a "senior civil service," chosen from upper level civil service employees for leadership, judgment, adaptability, and promise for assignments in the highest civil service grades. Witnesses before the Jackson Subcommittee on National Policy Machinery advocated the adoption of an array of measures, by both government and private employers, to ease the transfer of top talent in business, the universities, and the professions for limited-period service in government at middle and higher level positions. The Washington bureaucracy could thus be regularly infused, more than it is now, with new blood, new ideas, and zest for accomplishment.

The first Hoover Commission and its Task Force on Departmental Management offered an array of proposals designed to strengthen the position of the chief executive. Congress was urged not to break his line of command by delegating authority directly to bureau chiefs. Congress's habit of requiring Senatorial confirmation of designated bureau chiefs was criticized in the same vein. The commission proposed the consolidation of the outrageous number of agencies the President is called upon to supervise—some two score and ten—to a number that a mortal can reasonably be expected to manage. The Brownlow Committee urged the redistribution of all independent commissions and government corporations to the existing departments. Consolidation is desirable only if the departments can be made responsive to the President. The first Hoover Commission's Task Force on Departmental Management and Paul Appleby in writings, informed by experience in the Department of Agriculture, pro posed arrangements of departmental undersecretaries and assistant secretaries in a fashion that would strengthen departmental leadership vis-à-vis the bureau chief and orient departmental policy-making more directly to the needs of the President. The Hoover group outlined a top command of management and policy-making aides, and Appleby formulated a blend of political, career, and program appointees whose breadth of view and combined skills might be an effective counterpoise to the bureaus.

The United States Supreme Court, which in rulings on civil rights and Congressional districting has befriended Presidential power, may well come in some future day to strengthen his power as administrative chief. The necessary judicial ingredients are at hand in the sweeping "executive power" clause. A friendly court ruling might reduce Congress's administrative scope and invest the President with authority he sorely lacks and which every good business executive fully enjoys. He would then have a clear, legal warrant for becoming the boss of the executive branch, the administrative chief which the nation so badly needs.

CHAPTER

8

Publics

———

OUR system of government tends toward paralysis except when a strong President is on hand, capable of rallying public sentiment behind his policies at critical intervals. The built-in conflict between the President and Congress, assured by checks and balances, leaves the President dependent upon broad public support as his most powerful means of bending Congress to his will. Fortunately, with the stakes so high, the Presidential office is endowed with superior opportunities for reaching the public.

But the President's relation with public opinion, for all its importance and potential for good, has a darker side. It is also difficult and uncertain, something that he must deem at times, in his private thoughts, an onerous liability. Some of the most tragic moments in Presidential history have been those when the public has spurned proposals the chief executive has advanced in the careful and honest conviction that the nation's interest, and even mankind's, required them. Woodrow Wilson, despite valiant effort, could not get enough public support to win Senate approval of the Versailles treaty and American entrance into the League of Nations. In his final term President Truman failed steadily to maintain public support behind the war in Korea.

The contemporary President faces problems which he can discuss with the American public much less freely and effectively than was possible in bygone decades. Automation and the balance of payments, which rank in the forefront of national problems, are so complex that it is difficult to see how they can be reduced to meaningful simplicity to rally the public support which is so important. Present-day foreign affairs are so hazardous that the President must treat them with a caution and reticence that remove him from large areas of public discussion of them.

The President's most agonizing encounters are those where public opinion holds tenaciously to views which he, by his own best information, knows are wrong and contrary to the nation's interest. It was public opinion that forced the President to engage in a rapid and sweeping demobilization of our armed forces promptly after World War II to the resulting advantage of the Soviet Union, which quickly launched a campaign of expansion. Although the President and his counselors well knew the folly of "bringing the boys back home" so quickly and in such large numbers, they bowed to public opinion. A rare President may choose to defy it.

George Washington is one who did, in the war Revolutionary France levied against Britain in 1793. Citizen Edmond Charles Genet was dispatched as France's minister to the United States, and his eloquence and the ideological sympathies of the American people developed an overwhelming demand for an immediate declaration of war upon the British and George III. Washington, in a shining hour of greatness, rejected the popular will and issued his memorable proclamation of neutrality. His reward for sticking to his view that the nation must not squandor its precious strength in war was unmerciful villification in the press and in public meetings. Even his safety was in jeopardy. "Ten thousand people in the streets of Philadelphia," John Adams reported, "day after day threatened to drag Washington out of his house, and effect a revolution in the Government, or compel it to declare war in favor of the French revolution and against England."

Few Presidents can resist public opinion in the manner of Washington. The first President had the advantage of a matchless personal prestige capable, as it was in the neutrality fight, of withstanding majority public sentiment. The real choice that Presidents since his time have faced is whether to convince the public or yield to its will. Contemporary Presidents have traveled both courses. In 1947 President Truman faced an enormous Soviet army massed and seemingly poised to subjugate western Europe. The President and his executive aides brought the country to take up the Marshall plan and a new North Atlantic alliance and watched over Europe's safety with nuclear weapons. Thanks to United States aid, western Europe regained its strength and the Communist threat subsided.

But the President may also be disadvantaged by the public will. In the 1960's a restored and prosperous western Europe entertains the distasteful impression that the President is an instrument of an American opinion which assumes that the United States knows what is best for others and expects full support from its friends in crises it magnifies. The President likewise lives with a domestic public opinion which views Red and Nationalist China in a manner almost incomprehensible to western European opinion. American public opinion has long assumed that the Nationalists might return to power on the mainland, that the Red Chinese can never establish their regime securely, and that, at most, they are merely pawns of the Soviet. The President has had to assert these views to allies and in general the allies have had to accept them despite their own contrary opinion. In 1964 President de Gaulle publicly broke away from the American view, however, and the American President of the middle sixties and beyond faces the dilemma that he must either change American public opinion on the China question or face a growing allied revolt.

◇

THE President of today has many publics whose will holds the key to his policies' success and his political future. His most vital public is, of course, his "bread and butter" constituency, the national electorate, upon whose favor his re-election depends. Because of this incomparable gift, the electorate is exceeded by no other in its importance to the President. He deals daily with lesser but powerful publics—the pressure groups—that characteristically are informed, articulate, and efficient. The contemporary President's increasing projection onto the international plane brings within his concern a series of publics abroad situated behind the foreign leaders with whom he deals. These further publics range from the general population to specialized groupings, just as his several American publics do. British Prime Minister Macmillan absorbed an object lesson in the President's relationship with the British public in his 1962 Bermuda conference with President Kennedy, who induced the Prime Minister to accept the submarine missile Polaris in lieu of the missile-bearing aircraft Skybolt. The agreement evoked such general disapproval among the British public that the Conservative government's chances were gravely weakened for the coming national elections.

On occasion Presidents, particularly twentieth-century Presidents, have heeded world opinion. In his address of January 25, 1919, to the Paris peace conference, Woodrow Wilson declared, "We are assembled under very peculiar conditions of world opinion . . . we are not representatives of governments, but representatives of peoples. It will not suffice to satisfy governmental circles anywhere. It is necessary that we should satisfy the opinion of mankind." During the 1962 Cuban crisis, the Kennedy administration responded to the force that Wilson invoked in 1919. In deciding to refrain from invading Cuba, the administration was moved in no small way by fear of an adverse world opinion.

The President's deepest and most continuous relation is with the American people, who not merely award the prize of his election, but are at once the source and affirmation of his policies and program. When the people are behind him, he can prevail against any of the lesser publics— the pressure groups with their lobbyists and their Congressional spokesmen who dare oppose him. Woodrow Wilson called the President's mammoth capacity the "Voice of the People" when he wrote:

> His is the only national voice in affairs. Let him once win the admiration and confidence of the country, and no other single force can withstand him, no combination of forces will easily overpower him. His position takes the imagination of the country. He is the representative of no constituency, but of the whole people. When he speaks in his true character, he speaks for no special interest. If he rightly interpret the national thought and boldly insist upon it, he is irresistible; and the country never feels the zest for action so much as when its President is of such insight and calibre.

In bidding for general public favor, the President can choose among several leadership roles. One leadership role that all Presidents play is that of "conservator." In this role the President is guardian of the existing order, of its social, economic, and political parts. He maintains programs and policies founded by his predecessors or at most extends them, but in a fashion consistent with hallowed patterns of the past. He reveres precedent and established procedure. Presidents who stress this role have administrations characterized by little controversy, and are popular and even "beloved" figures. Their popularity, however, remains a largely unused resource; they treat the day's problems cautiously and neglect ones likely to be significant in the future.

A second Presidential leadership role is "protective." The chief executive provides security against external danger to society's survival and well-being and protects its members from bodily harm and physical destruction. He familiarizes the people with their peril and maintains their confidence in his measures. If their confidence is shaken, as it was when Kennedy attacked the Eisenhower administration's military stewardship in the 1960 Presidential campaign, the administration's candidate suffers losses of popular votes.

A third leadership role is "innovative," stressing that the Presidency abides in a world of change, whether in the stirrings for popular rights and social justice, in the economy's transition from an agricultural to an industrial base, or in the emerging need for the creation of an international community. A President who responds to the forces of change undertakes novel action and revises the existing economic, political, or social order by enacting new laws and establishing new accords and arrangements among the nations. To make innovations he must sustain controversy and even risk political defeat. Although the innovative President, like any other President, prizes popularity, he will occasionally give higher priority to securing objectives.

All three types of leadership will, if successfully applied, evoke ultimate approval, for as Thomas Hobbes long ago noted, mankind will respond to anything that promises to secure him his basic human wants. Men want security against violence and death, they want the comfort of an established order, and they have a creative urge to conquer new worlds.

◇

THE President commands the nation's attention as no one else can. Whatever he says, does, or thinks is big news. The front page, the television screen, and the magazine cover are his for the taking. The continually expanding audiences of the mass media increase the impact of any contemporary President blessed with talent and charm.

The Kennedy administration plainly surpassed all others in exploiting these possibilities with relentless enterprise and success. Consider, for example, the communications scene of the first days of May 1962. The President himself dominated the political news on television and in the press. Simultaneously, he and his wife were featured in the big circulation magazines. The cover of *McCall's* bore a picture of Mrs. Kennedy and her children and the *Saturday Evening Post* featured "A Feminine Chat with Jackie." The main article in *Harper's Magazine*, according to its cover, was "The Kennedys Move in on Dixie." Meanwhile, in personal appearances at widely separated geographical points and on television, the President reached vast audiences. Some 85,000 citizens turned out for his speech at the University of California, and a few days earlier in New Orleans at least 200,000 gathered to see him. His apearances were followed by a nationally televised address at Atlantic City, a Presidential press conference, and a gigantic Presidential rally in Madison Square Garden in New York City with a generous assortment of stars from Hollywood and Broadway in the supporting cast. Kennedy's cumulative publicity well exceeded that of the most skillful of his predecessors in public relations—Franklin Roosevelt, who lacked the advantage of television, and Theodore Roosevelt, who never knew the intriguing possibility of instant communication with an entire continent. The President's powers of publicity are impressive compared with those of his fellow chief executives of the western world. His coverage well exceeds the French President's and is more even than that of the Prime Minister and queen of England combined.

While the President's image beams away at maximum wattage, the opposition's becomes weaker. In the Kennedy year of 1962, the opposition Republican party waged an uphill struggle to extend local or regional reputations of its principal state governors to a national dimension. In Congress the opposition could fight the administration, but only before small audiences on the floor or in committee rooms, while the President freely commanded his national audience of millions, an unhealthy state of affairs either for maintaining the delicate balance of the two-party system or for providing a voice to the indispensable opposition.

The formidable public relations position of President Kennedy was by no means representative of Presidential history. In seasons past, when the fortunes of the office were comparatively parlous, the chief executive was sometimes overshadowed by his powerful competitors for public attention. Tyler and Taylor were Presidents, to be sure, but they are little remembered. The historical period they straddled is symbolized by the towering personages of Daniel Webster and Henry Clay. The leading figure in the presidential years of Franklin Pierce was not the rather hapless chief executive, but the shrewd and competent Senator Stephen A. Douglas. Similarly, the worthy Rutherford B. Hayes was overshadowed by the far less worthy but more spectacular Roscoe Conkling and James G. Blaine. Even modern Presidents may be hard pushed by competitors of formidable talent. In 1916 Woodrow Wilson could view from the White House the spectacle of Theodore Roosevelt in the East calling upon the nation to intervene in the current World War, and William Jennings Bryan in the West, thrice a Presidential nominee, going up and down pleading for peace.

To communicate with his publics abroad, the present-day chief executive profits from the spreading international dimension of the communications media. His global projection has been speeded by the growing number of American periodicals, led by *Time* and the *Reader's Digest* which developed foreign editions as early as the 1940's. The cheap transistor radio is rapidly expanding the foreign audiences the President reaches over the Voice of America's facilities. The launching of the communications satellite Telestar in 1962 gives the President access to a worldwide television audience.

In his first year of office President Kennedy engaged in a wide-ranging review of American policy on a taped British television interview program with the editor of *Izvestia*, Alexi Adzhubei, Khrushchev's son-in-law. The Voice of America beams the President's words to vast audiences on several continents. In the 1962 Cuban crisis, for example, the President's address on the evening of October 22 was relayed around the world in English and thirty-seven other languages. As the President spoke, 102 United States Information Agency posts overseas were receiving the full text by radio teletype and quickly translating and reproducing his remarks for delivery to local government officials and newspaper editors.

◇

THE President invests quantities of time and ingenuity discovering and estimating the opinions of his publics. He needs to know what his publics want, how his program is being received, what the folks are saying at the grassroots. Because of the amorphous, fragmented character of opinion, the task of discovery is not simple, particularly when it is conducted largely in the peculiar isolation of Washington. Difficulty, however formidable, does not deter most Presidents from working hard at the job, and a President such as F. D. Roosevelt develops such expertise that he amazes his associates with his "complete and precise knowledge" of opinion.

In flushing out public opinion, Presidents rely heavily on "scouts," literally packs of them, who traverse numerous parts of the political landscape. William McKinley extracted invaluable intelligence from his cabinet members traveling about the country, from legislators of both parties returning after visits with their constituents, and from leading citizens, chiefly businessmen, in widely scattered communities. Franklin Roosevelt profited enormously from the extensive and observant traveling of Mrs. Roosevelt. Harry Hopkins, his administrator of public works, had informative subadministrators posted across the land who reported local sentiment. Once when knowledge of Midwestern agricultural opinion was most vital, Harry Truman dispatched his trusted and perspicacious friend Leslie Biffle, the Secretary of the Senate, to the region, where, disguised as a farmer, he learned the authentic opinion of the wheat and corn country.

Most Presidents read the newspapers closely to learn what is being said both for and against their administrations. McKinley regularly put in two hours after breakfast scanning the papers. From his hometown paper, the Canton, Ohio, *Repository*, he proceeded to "five or six New York dailies, the Washington evening and morning papers, one or two from Chicago, and perhaps a half dozen others from large cities." When Franklin Roosevelt entered the White House, his secretary, Louis McHenry Howe, compiled a daily digest of editorial opinion from 750 newspapers representing every city of more than 25,000 population. Thanks to the press, Roosevelt reputedly was convinced that he possessed an infallible method of knowing whether he was right or wrong on an issue. If certain newspapers opposed him, he felt that he must be generally correct. If they were with him, he became suspicious.

Presidents since Franklin Roosevelt's day can keep their eyes on the public opinion polls, those conducted both by private sources and by governmental departments. Presidents also look to their mail and to visitors for soundings of opinion. In Harding's time letters numbered about four hundred a day and in Franklin Roosevelt's they soared to an average of four thousand. The mail of his successors is similarly heavy, requiring a considerable staff to answer, digest, abstract, file, and index it. Roosevelt, it appears, seldom read the general mail, but watched the abstracts. Visitors, as Truman has said, are "valuable to the President, for they help him keep in touch with the cross section of American interests and opinion." Truman's predecessor, Franklin Roosevelt, regularly saw a diversity of people from many sections of the country, from whom he skillfully extracted information, often without their knowing it. Truman, for his part, closely systematized the considerable time he devoted to visitors. By setting aside an average of four hours each work day, he could take on ninety-five appointments a week, in the course of which he might see two hundred and fifty persons.

◊

PRESIDENTS with knowledge or even a bare inkling of opinion may choose to act. Their aides set to work to amass ideas for new policy. They may appoint study commissions of experienced and esteemed citizens to investigate a chosen problem. They may direct the great departments to act. If it is a matter of significance, the President personally may speak on it in his press conference, in a special White House statement, in any or all of his messages to Congress, and, if it is worthy of a grand effort, in an address by television and radio to the nation. A President may choose to champion not one or several proposals of policy, but a quantity, linked more or less into a program. Such were Franklin Roosevelt's New Deal and Woodrow Wilson's New Freedom, essentially collections of proposed legislation to which the President's leadership was committed.

Presidential success in popular leadership rests upon a dual foundation of personality and opportunity. If the country is floundering in economic depression or gripped in war or the threat of it, Presidential leadership will not only be welcomed, it will be demanded. There is, happily, a lesser range of problems and situations upon which innovative Presidential leadership can be bestowed, as the Theodore Roosevelt administration attests in its economic and social policies. The second major underpinning of presidential leadership, the human personality, although infinitely varied, must have certain traits if it is to be successful. Three of the most pre-eminently successful practitioners of popular leadership from the high place of the Presidency have been Theodore Roosevelt, Woodrow Wilson, and Franklin Roosevelt.

Each was a man of courage, firmness, and hope. Each was blessed with gifts of charismatic power, radiating a dynamism that stirred hearts and inspired minds. All three were forceful moral teachers who exposed social and economic evil and pointed the way to constructive reform. They had the demagogue's ability to simplify the complex world for their fellow man and to convince him of their fervent concern for his problems and their high resolve to do something about them. All three Presidents, whether by word or by gesture, were superbly articulate. Wilson was the most moving and exact in his use of words, the master of a lean and force-ful style. Each was adept in providing the memorable phrase. T. R.'s "malefactors of great wealth," Wilson's castigation of "a little group of willful men," and F. D. R.'s "We have nothing to fear but fear itself" live in memory. All were "characters" in the best sense of the word, adept at focusing attention upon themselves and at converting the Presidency into a kind of venture in dramaturgy. T. R., whose talent in this regard is unrivaled, is aptly conveyed in the cartoons of the day depicting him as a huge creature with enormous clenched teeth, a thick spiked club and a belt full of pistols, all adding up to a blustering, roaring, swashbuck-ling ruffian who wowed the electorate.

As part of his showmanship, the popular leader communicates a sense of mastery and confidence, even when the situation confronting the nation little warrants it. F. D. R.'s ringing avowal of faith in the future was hardly justified in his 1933 inaugural, in the face of the soaring unemploy-ment rate, the failing banks, and the swaths of mortgage foreclosures. One shudders at what a more literal interpretation of the facts would have done to the status of the new administration in the national psy-chology.

Great popular Presidents such as Wilson and the Roosevelts excel at manipulation; they are flexible and even opportunistic. One of the most intriguing, as well as fruitless, pastimes is to speculate on the individual political alchemies of these Presidents, on how much of their official conduct represented an idealistic concern to improve the lot of their fel-low humanity, and how much of it a desire to pick up large blocs of votes among the discontented. Franklin Roosevelt's admonition to one of his subordinates, a chafing reformer, that an administration must take care in "picking its fights," suggests that not blind idealism, but a concentra-tion upon the attainable is an inevitable preoccupation of the President when he makes strategical and tactical choices.

◇

TO REACH their publics, most contemporary Presidents rely upon the press conference, a young institution that harks back only to the adminis-tration of Woodrow Wilson. Soon after his inauguration, reporters gathered by general invitation in his office for a question-and-answer exchange on the administration's business. The reporters assembled with lofty expectations encouraged by Wilson's solemn invocation of "pitiless publicity" for public business in his pre-Presidential writing on political science. The new practice of the press conference replaced the old arrangement by which Presidents had granted interviews only to selected reporters, a tactic permitting favoritism and penalization. In the press conference, reporters enjoy equal footing.

Unfortunately, the sessions under Wilson and his early successors fell far short of the initial optimism. Wilson's glacial reserve inhibited interchange. He was often irritated by the reporters' habit of speculating about the news and of persisting with questions before he was prepared to release information. He considered the reporters' cross-examining a reflection upon his honesty. Wilson's successor, Warren G. Harding, a trusting, genial former newspaperman, took the press freely into his confidence until a Presidential misstatement during the negotiation of the Four Power treaty brought such painful diplomatic repercussions that henceforth reporters had to submit all questions beforehand in writing. Calvin Coolidge continued the practice of written questions, and by drastically sifting them and selecting only a few to answer, by laconic, noncommittal remarks, he quickly reduced the press conference to a drab and fruitless exercise. Under Hoover the press conference continued to be a stilted, meager source of news.

The advent of Franklin Roosevelt finally brought the little-tried institution into its own. Roosevelt set up two press conferences a week, canceled the requirement of written questions, and with his facile charm turned the sessions into lively occasions on which he provided the public with a running account of what he was doing and what he proposed to do and why. Truman's sessions, although numerous, were briefer, less sprightly, and more staccato. On several occasions he made statements that constitute a monumental lesson on how easily and how thoroughly a President can put his foot into his mouth. Once when asked if the atomic bomb was under active consideration for possible use against Red China in the Korean War, he replied that use of the bomb was always under active consideration. This seemingly ominous announcement stirred a flurry of anxious protests in Congress and the press until the "White House" issued a "clarifying" statement.

Eisenhower's penchant for a balanced statement which permitted him to avoid taking a position reduced the newsworthiness of his conferences. His further habit of freely delegating tasks and decisions to subordinates sometimes left him shy of details when facing queries. Eisenhower permitted the innovation of televising his press conferences and presenting them, with minor editing, to the public. With Kennedy there was no editing; the televised presentation was made exactly as his encounters with the reporters occurred.

Kennedy's press conferences were highly effective, his responses to questions revealing an almost photographic memory for detail and a gift for keeping abreast of policy development from incubation to implementation. His brisk assurance and his opening statements charged with newsworthy content lent zest and excitement to his administration. Despite his success, he used the news conferences erratically. Three and four weeks would pass without meetings with the press. The longest lapses occurred in the Berlin and Cuban crises, when the President apparently concluded that a public discussion would not be helpful and that some chance and unstudied remarks might be greatly harmful.

Kennedy's news conferences took place in the vast State Department auditorium, with about three hundred newsmen on hand. Millions of citizens later took in the half-hour's proceedings on television and radio. Although superficially the press conference appeared informal and off-the-cuff, Kennedy, like his predecessors, did considerable preparing beforehand. He and his aides engaged in intensive pondering to anticipate the questions. His wide reading of newspapers and magazines and his listening to broadcasts apprised him of the mental stirrings of the journalists and therefore of what they were apt to ask. On the afternoon before the conference, the President's press secretary, Pierre Salinger, summoned the information chiefs of the executive departments to his White House office to share their experiences of the past week with press inquiries. On the day of the news conference Salinger, with his sundry notes, breakfasted with the President. Also partaking of the meal were Secretary of State Dean Rusk; Walter Heller, chairman of the Council of Economic Advisers; Theodore Sorenson, the President's counsel; McGeorge Bundy, assistant for national security affairs; and Myer Feldman, deputy counsel. The breakfast group canvassed the news questions that occurred to them and supplied Kennedy with data for answers.

In his early months in office President Lyndon Johnson, who excels more in conversation and in encounters with small groups than in large, formal presentations, groped for the most suitable forum for his news conferences. He tried such places as the vast, windowless, international conference room of the State Department, the office of the White House press secretary, the cabinet room, the LBJ ranch, and the East Room, the White House's largest and most formal room, where reporters sat on gilt chairs in a semicircle around the President, who stood in front of a golden drapery flanked by huge portraits of George and Martha Washington. A talker rather than a performer, Johnson fares best in a setting where he is most natural.

Presidents may open their news conferences with a prepared statement to put an opinion or decision on public record. A cooperative reporter may achieve the same result by asking a question requiring the information. The President may know beforehand who the reporter is and be careful to recognize him. This is the planted question, an old productive device.

For all of its slow start, the Presidential news conference occupies a vital place in American political life. It is the only regular occasion on which the nation can view the chief executive in an active interchange with people outside his administration. Notwithstanding the President's preparations, there is still much spontaneity, owing to the unpredictable twists reporters often give their questions. The sessions are also invaluable opportunities for the President to present his opinions and raise trial balloons. Nevertheless, press conferences are sometimes unproductive. The President can easily dodge and parry questions; no mere reporter can nail an incumbent of the awesome office to the wall. Many of the questions are not keen. The prolixity with which they are sometimes put may produce a question substantially longer than the President's answer. Some queries have no other merit than to gratify the urge of reporters to appear on television. Since the advent of television, reporters have asked more and more questions of a regional or minor character that titillate the folks back home but lack the national quality the press conference deserves.

◇

I N T H E estimation of Arthur Krock, the distinguished political analyst, the Kennedy administration practiced the art of news management "boldly," "cynically," and "with the utmost subtlety and imagination." The reward of this effort, Krock contended, was a portrayal of the administration in the press with a radiant aura of approval which neither its achievement nor the country's circumstances warranted. In the Kennedy era as in other eras, many critics voiced concern for the continued integrity of Thomas Jefferson's dictum that the people have a right to "full information of their affairs thro' the channel of the public papers."

News management, which is a craft of many tricks, cultivates the image of the President as infallible even in the face of flagrant error. If things go wrong, blame is placed upon others, usually his subordinates. A major tool of news management is the use of selective personal patronage, whereby those reporters who "behave," or write favorably of the administration, are granted privileges unavailable to their fellows. Thus Stewart Alsop and Charles Bartlett, co-authors of a widely noticed magazine article on the 1962 Cuban crisis, which could not have been undertaken without the unparalleled privilege of access to National Security Council proceedings, were candidly referred to by the President in a news conference as "old friends." Another plum was a 1961 year-end informal televised interview of the President by three cooperative reporters covering an extraordinary range of subjects and witnessed by a vast audience. A contrasting and less selective Kennedy tactic was the use of "social flattery," by which a succession of groups of editors and publishers were feted at the White House. In May 1961, for example, the President had to luncheon eight editors from Florida; in October a throng of New Jersey publishers followed by twenty-four publishers and news executives from the state of Washington; and in December twenty-five Minnesota news executives. The pattern was used even more extensively in 1962 and 1963. Kennedy reached reporters and editors on a large scale in occasional intimate, far-ranging background briefings. The press participants emerged, Krock observed, "in a state of protracted enchantment evoked by the President's charm and the awesome aura of his office." The mood carried over into the news columns and editorials.

The Kennedy administration's news policy had a reverse side, a regulatory aspect that did not gain favor with the press. In the 1962 Cuban crisis Assistant Secretary of Defense Arthur Sylvester declared, in a moment of mismanaged candor, that the administration's management of the news was "part of the weaponry" of government in the cold war, and that "the results justify the methods we use." Presumably, concealment and distortion were permissible when necessity required. The perils of official fabrication were glaringly revealed some weeks later when Senate Republican leader Everett M. Dirksen of Illinois revealed that four Americans had been killed in the 1961 Bay of Pigs invasion. The disclosure was especially upsetting because two months earlier Attorney General Robert F. Kennedy had denied emphatically that any Americans had been killed at the Bay of Pigs. The Attorney General's statement reinforced a pledge by the President, uttered just five days before the invasion, "to make sure that there are no Americans involved in any actions inside Cuba."

News management was not a creation of the Kennedy administration, however. It is an ancient and common practice of the Presidency. Management assumes a variety of forms, from the complex to the simple little expedient Chester A. Arthur employed to present to his critics the appearance of being busy. Having a large reputation for indolence, Arthur maintained a "property basket" filled with official-looking documents which a secretary would carry into the President's office when he was with visitors to create the impression of industry.

Earlier Presidents, indeed, applied managerial strokes that no contemporary chief executive would dare consider. At the height of his battle to secure legislation to establish a Bureau of Corporations, for example, Theodore Roosevelt, knowing all too well that John D. Rockefeller's Standard Oil empire was massively pressing legislators to vote against the measure, resorted to a desperate move. The company was sending quantities of unsigned telegrams to numerous members of Congress bearing the terse and imperious message, "We are opposed to any anti-trust legislation—it must be stopped." Looking for advantage in the grim struggle, T. R. declared in a public statement that the author of the reprehensible message was no one less than John D. Rockefeller, reigning monarch of the Standard empire. T. R.'s enemies gleefully spread out for public view incontrovertible evidence that the author was in fact John

Archbold, Standard Oil president. Totally bereft of rebuttal, T. R. subsided, for once, into silence. "The last thing in the world that John D.
Rockefeller would have done," wrote Ida M. Tarbell, biographer of
Standard Oil, with headshaking resignation, "was to send such a telegram to anybody."

Flattery and favors are old Presidential tactics. John Tyler treated the
New York *Herald*'s Washington correspondent, Parmly, as a confidant.
A rival and less fortunate journal observed that Parmly enjoyed

> the run of the presidential kitchen, and is favored with copies of his messages
> and other public acts before they have been submitted to his cabinet ministers.
> For these high privileges and distinguished favors, he, of course, evinces his
> gratitude, and does his share of the dirty jobs about the palace, by abusing in
> the most gross and vulgar language, the members of the late cabinet. . . .

Some Presidents also bestow disfavor upon certain papers and their
Washington reporters. Theodore Roosevelt was a busy feuder whose
worst war was with the New York *World*. The conflict reached a point
where the paper solemnly informed its readers that the President was a
madman soon destined for an asylum. Roosevelt's several countermoves
included a large attempt to put Joseph Pulitzer, the *World*'s publisher,
behind bars.

Occasionally, Presidents have distributed a considerable largess to
awaiting journalistic hands. In the Republic's early decades the piecework
and job-printing of the executive departments were awarded to struggling
journals that trumpeted the administration's accomplishments with loud
adulation. Abraham Lincoln, who greatly respected the power of the
press, appointed several influential journalists to responsible posts in his
administration. Gideon Welles, the Secretary of the Navy, was a former
editor of the Hartford *Times*, and the Assistant Secretary of War was
Charles A. Dana of the New York *Tribune* and later of the *Sun*. William
Dean Howells, the Ohio newspaperman and author of a Lincoln campaign
biography, became consul at Venice, John Bigelow of the *Evening Post*
minister to France, and James Watson Webb of the New York *Courier
and Enquirer* minister to Brazil. At least a half-dozen other major appointees were journalists, and in the early weeks of the administration no
fewer than four employees of the New York *Tribune* were named to posts
abroad. This prompted the rival *Herald* to notice acidly, "It is evident
that Mr. Lincoln has determined upon an evacuation of the New York
Tribune office, if he has not decided about Fort Sumter." The transplanted
journalists were normally expected to continue writing in their own
papers and to cultivate those of the country in which they were residing,
with a view to influencing public opinion.

In confronting the ways and wiles of the chief executive in managing
the news, the press is not without defenses. If the press is alert and pro-

fessionally responsible, it should easily be able to cope with the President's slickest manipulations. News management is a game in which the President is by no means the only player. The newspapers can, with ingenuity and enterprise, do their share of "managing" as well. They can, if they choose, put before the public an impression of the chief executive that is utterly contrary to reality. They converted the dour, colorless, withdrawn, futile Calvin Coolidge into a forceful, red-blooded, two-fisted, strong, silent "sage of Vermont," a man who never was. They can oppose and harass the President with little regard for truth and overlook every shred of merit his administration possesses. Many of the most powerful press organs of Lincoln's day, for example, fought his administration without letup. The New York *World*, the New York *Daily News*, the Chicago *Times*, the Baltimore *Exchange*, and the Columbus *Crisis* all contended against him. Among the heaviest crosses Lincoln had to bear was James Gordon Bennett, Sr., of the New York *Herald*, a fast-growing, widely influential paper. Toward Lincoln, the *Herald* vacillated between the far extremes of praise and condemnation. In certain seasons the President was "a sorry joke," "a standing joke," "a broad joke," "a solemn joke"; other times he was "master of the situation." The *Herald*'s mercurial tendencies seemed to depend upon the administration's willingness to give Bennett the high office and social recognition he wanted. He was given invitations to the White House for himself and his wife and son, and then he was appointed minister to France, whereupon the *Herald* finally settled down. "Mr. Lincoln deemed it more important to secure the *Herald*'s support than to obtain a victory in the field," explained Thurlow Weed, the administration's principal intermediary with the newspaper.

Some chief executives, instead of influencing the press, have been utterly laissez-faire in their demeanor toward it. Their appoach is one of blunt and artless candor in public statement. Unfortunately, history repeatedly demonstrates that these same Presidents also have committed the most costly political errors in putting the record of their administrations before the public. President Taft, a forthright man, was remote from the press, was annoyed by its constant criticisms, and freely expressed his contempt of it. Indeed, in his uncalculating way, Taft went to war with the press when, in the face of a $17.5 million post office debt, he declared in a State of the Union Message that newspapers and magazines were not paying enough postage and that magazines indeed were receiving a government subsidy of $50 million annually. Hereupon Taft went on to an observation so gross and impolitic that it clinches the case for managed news. "If we wish," he said, "to contribute a subsidy of $50 million to the education of the country, I can find a good deal better method of doing it than by the circulation of *Collier's Weekly* and *Everybody's Magazine*." In the Congressional elections following his message, newspapers and pe-

riodicals widely and ferociously attacked the administration, and its legislative supporters were so badly defeated at the polls that the Republicans
lost control of Congress. In subsequently analyzing the debacle, Taft
attributed it to journalistic resentment of his postal measure.

◇

MOST Presidents reach their publics by engaging in "grand tours," a
tradition that George Washington founded in a two-month journey
through the South in 1791. Then, as now, the peregrinating President
ordinarily has a dual purpose: to discover popular sentiment and, by his
presence and word, to rally support for his administration. Washington's
original precedent-setting journey involved two thousand miles of travel
in a new light chariot, in the company of his secretary, Major Jackson,
and a servant. In planning his trip, the President wisely allowed eight
days for "casualties." Of these, the worst occurred in the crossing of the
Occoquan, when a horse fully harnessed to the chariot fell into the stream
and created such general excitement that the entire team followed him.
Only the quick and expert work of all hands, especially the President's,
prevented a fearful loss.

Washington's itinerary was crowded with ceremony and business. His
two-day stop at Richmond included a parade, a civic dinner, an illumina-
tion, an address and answer, and a formal leave-taking. He briefed himself on local sentiment in a lengthy conversation with Colonel Edward
Carrington, his appointed United States marshal for the district of Virginia. His further stops included Tarboro, a hamlet where, he noted,
"We were received . . . by as good a salute as could be given by one piece
of artillery." The ceremonial climax of the journey, which led through
North and South Carolina, occurred at Charleston, where Washington
survived tests of gastronomic and physical endurance that no future
President has exceeded. He weathered three receptions, two breakfasts,
and seven sumptuous formal dinners, listened and replied to four addresses, was the honored figure at two assemblies and a concert, rode
through the city, went twice to church, observed a display of fireworks,
visited the scenes of military operations, and drank sixty toasts. Perhaps
the most cheering interlude Washington experienced in this unremitting
onslaught upon his well-being was the governor's ball in his honor, where
the coiffures of nearly all the ladies contained a bandeau or fillet on which
was painted the President's head or a patriotic and sentimental reference
to his career.

For all its rigors, Washington considered the trip enormously rewarding. He was impressed with the improved state of trade and industry and
was surprised and gratified to find his government as popular in the
South as in Federalist New England. "I am much pleased that I have

taken this journey," Washington wrote to David Humphreys, friend and
aide-de-camp, "as it has enabled me to see with my own eyes the situation
of the country thro' which we traveled and to learn more accurately the
disposition of the people than I could have done by any information."

The contemporary President must not only pass before the view of the
American public; he must also appear periodically before foreign publics
whose approval his administration values. Although various Presidents
have traveled abroad, Dwight D. Eisenhower was the first chief executive
to do so on a large scale to reach his multiple publics. In 1959 Eisenhower
made a journey of 22,370 miles to visit eleven nations from Italy to
India, conferring with his fellow chief executives and shaking the hands
of thousands of people. On occasion the junketing President may be
caught up in a kind of popularity contest involving both himself and his
policies. Kennedy's visit to West Germany in 1963, for example, was
watchfully compared for the size and response of his crowds with those
drawn in an earlier visit by General de Gaulle. The sizably more demon-
strative display Kennedy attracted, it was hoped, would show German
leaders that the West German people preferred the American President's
vision of the future Atlantic Community to the French President's.

Presidential travel is costly. Although Eisenhower's 1959 journey
was heroic in the face of his illnesses, perhaps he might better have employed his time and strength for the sake of world peace by remaining in
Washington to grapple with knotty foreign policy problems, instead of
placing himself before the clamoring multitudes. In leaving Washington,
the traveling President removes himself from vital tasks which only he
can do and which may be crucial to the success of his policy projects. At
a crucial juncture when the House Rules Committee was deliberating on
his school aid proposal in 1961, President Kennedy, who might have
slowed or stayed a rapidly deteriorating situation if he had conversed
with several committee members, was in Paris conferring with President
de Gaulle.

In taking up travel, the President may have more momentous purposes
than consultation with his fellow executives and bringing himself before
the people. He may take to the road, in full armor, to do battle for his
basic policies. Confronting obstruction from Congress and group interests
to legislation incorporating his program, the President may choose to "go
to the people." By adroit and moving appeal, he aims to stir the masses
into a state of such general and intense approval that the opposition will
crumble and his measures will prevail. Although certain chief executives
have moved mountains in such undertakings, the loud clear warning of
history is that "going to the people" is a perilous venture that can succeed
only in an exceptional combination of circumstances.

Franklin Roosevelt, the Presidency's foremost master of the art of popular appeal, made his way thanks to the happy coincidence that the nature of the times called for the play of his formidable political talents. His principal achievements of popular leadership occurred in the first "hundred days" of his administration in the pit of the depression. Goaded by chaos and despair the people demanded action, and Roosevelt provided it. By skillfully maintaining public opinion in a state of general approbation, he could indulge in the political luxury of making short shrift of Congress. He relied chiefly upon his twice-a-week press conference, supplemented by his inimitable "fireside chats," speeches over the radio by which he projected into millions of homes his intimate, informative reports on his stewardship. The President's oratorical skill and the prevailing public mood made his demands upon Congress irresistible. The President's least intimation that Congressmen were balking would unloose a torrent of mail upon the legislators insisting that they do whatever the President wanted.

For all his success, Roosevelt was keenly aware that the tactic of public appeals was not without weakness. He knew it could easily be overdone; the public's attention and enthusiasm were limited. Even in his balmiest political season, the first hundred days, he presented only four fireside chats. The following year he offered two, and only one in each of the next two years. Roosevelt himself once explained his rigorous selectivity. He wrote,

> The public psychology and, for that matter, individual psychology cannot, because of human weakness, be attuned for long periods of time to a constant repetition of the highest note in the scale . . . people tire of seeing the same name, day after day, in the important headlines of the papers and the same voice, night after night, over the radio.

Presidential appeals have also known disastrous and humiliating failure. Andrew Johnson's "swing around the country" in 1866 to bring off the election of a Congress favorably disposed toward his policies, and Woodrow Wilson's 1919 western tour to evoke popular support for the peace treaty he had negotiated and United States membership in the League of Nations, are monumental reminders to future Presidents that to entrust their political fortunes to the turning wheel of public opinion is to engage in a highly uncertain gamble.

Long before he became President, Wilson had entertained a high, almost romanticized regard for the constructive potentialities of public opinion in governmental affairs. In 1908 he wrote in *Constitutional Government*, "Opinion is the great, indeed the only coordinating force in our system." The President, of all the officers of government, was the people's chosen instrument, owing to "his close and special relation to opinion the nation over."

Wilson's twenty-two-day trip in September of 1919 was not born of the aggressive optimism of his earlier writing. It was an act of desperation. The Republican majority of the Senate Foreign Relations Committee was pressing ahead with plans to amend the peace treaty drastically. Such Republican personages as William Howard Taft and Elihu Root, who had once supported the League, now failed to come forward in its behalf. Worst of all, there were ominous indications of betrayal by Wilson's own Senatorial followers. "I ask nothing better," he declared in the face of rising obstacles, "than to lay my case before the American people." Hopefully, an aroused people would bring the Senate into step with the President. The state of public opinion, or what was known of it, made Wilson's course seem altogether plausible. Every available gauge of public opinion—polls, resolutions of state legislatures, mass meetings, speeches, editorials, and letters to the press—revealed that the mass of people demanded some kind of league to forestall the horror of war again.

His fighting blood in a high boil, Wilson mapped out a plan of speechmaking rigorous enough to stagger an athlete. Approximately forty formal speeches were arranged for the twenty-five-day tour, plus innumerable unscheduled appearances on the rear platform of the Presidential train. The formal speeches delivered—in stadiums, opera houses, tabernacles, and tents—were a great strain in an era which did not know the microphone, particularly upon a man of Wilson's declining health. Obviously ill before the trip began, his twitching facial muscles and gray color worried his friends.

Although by sheer heroism Wilson completed twenty-two days of his journey, he ultimately collapsed in Pueblo, Colorado, the victim of a stroke. To compound the tragedy, there was not even a flicker of compensating political gain from this noble effort. Although the President drew large and sympathetic audiences, the hard truth was that those who came to see and cheer him never felt committed to follow him through fire and water. Far from welling up in a great directing shout upon the Senate, they returned quietly to their daily concerns. "We are so busy making money that we haven't time to worry about the Peace Treaty," confessed a leading Omaha businessman who, like so many of his fellow citizens, came to see Wilson merely out of curiosity.

Even if Wilson's trip had rallied opinion to a pitch that exceeded his highest expectations, it is impossible to see how he could have forced the Senate into speedy and unreserved approval of the peace treaty. The majority of Senators had no reason to be fearful of aroused opinion. The next Senatorial elections were far distant—fifteen months away—and even then only one-third of the Senate would face re-election. The remoteness of the next election, the lengthy Senatorial term of six years, the public's short memory, the likelihood that new issues would arise and distract in the meantime, the prospect that if a Senator was "right" on local issues he would not have to fear the remote League—drained all force from Wilson's impact. As Thomas A. Bailey has suggested, it would be difficult to prove that a single Senatorial vote was changed by Wilson's unstinting journey. Its enormous personal cost encourages the speculation that Wilson might have done far better to remain in Washington where he could have shepherded his health and perhaps converted the reservations that would inevitably be made to the treaty into acceptable compromises.

◊

ALTHOUGH the President is normally his own best publicity agent, he is assisted by a large and growing staff of communications experts. Presidents got along with a press secretary and a speech-writer or two earlier in this century, but it is possible for a present-day chief executive to become an enclave surrounded by communications specialists.

Dwight D. Eisenhower knew something of this experience as President. His press secretary, James Hagerty, was a former reporter and press secretary for Governor Thomas E. Dewey. A Presidential administrative assistant, Emmet Hughes, on leave from *Life* magazine, was a leading speech-writer. The President's economics assistant, Gabriel Hauge, was a former editor of *Business Week* and member of the executive committee of the McGraw-Hill publishing company. Hauge was a ghost-writer in Dewey's 1948 and in Eisenhower's 1952 Presidential campaigns. In the early Eisenhower years C. D. Jackson of *Fortune* doubled as a speech writer and research director. The associate press secretary, Anne Wheaton, had previously been assistant publicity director for the Republican National Committee. Elsewhere in the Presidential staff, Frederic Morrow, administrative officer for "Special Projects," was a former field secretary for the National Association for the Advancement of Colored People and public relations officer of the Columbia Broadcasting System. Howard Pyle, deputy assistant for "Intergovernmental Relations," had public relations experience as announcer, writer, and program director, and numbered among his professional achievements the production of the Grand Canyon Sunrise Easter Service. Robert Cutler, the assistant for national security affairs, was a distinguished fund-raiser for the Community Chest and other projects in his home city of Boston. The President's "television coach," Robert Montgomery, was a Hollywood star and producer.

Although public relations is not a new profession, only recently have its practitioners come into high estate in both politics and private affairs. They have climbed from secondary status as technicians to participation in top policy councils. Where once they were fund-raisers, publicity men, and press secretaries, now they are often dignified by the designations "social engineers" and "practicing social scientists." The public relations man's ascent in politics is a by-product of the burgeoning mass communications technology and the steady enhancement of the "power of public opinion" in democratic society: the universalization of suffrage, the advent of mass education, and the galloping rate of population growth. The vast electorate can be reached efficiently and economically only by the mass media. The technician who can conceptualize policy problems so they can be presented on television, on the radio, in the press, and in specialized publications becomes indispensable. In the stress he places by professional necessity upon unity of image, the public relations man is a potent centralizing force in administration and politics. He deplores dissent and irregularity because they blunt his impact. Like other professional people, he serves, and therefore tends to identify with, the established interests rather than with new ideas and less privileged groups that also have social importance.

The public relations man uses the communications apparatus not merely to distribute information, but to exert social control. As Edward L. Bernays, the public relations pioneer, has written, "He helps to mould the action of his client as well as to mould public opinion." In politics the public relations expert strives to "market" his client in a favorable image, and, in the case of the chief executive, to establish and maintain him as a figure beloved, and perhaps idolized, by the masses. Policy, as it is formed and asserted, is subordinated to the necessities of image. Controversy and risk are avoided, and the taint of failure shunned. Actions attributed to the chief executive are selected and staged to reinforce his image of virtue and infallibility in the popular mind. Thus President Eisenhower was marketed as the war hero, the beloved nonpartisan, noncontroversial figure who stood above the political battle. When, therefore, in certain seasons, the Democrats had to be lashed, the task fell not to Eisenhower, but to subordinates such as Richard Nixon and Sherman Adams. When the civil rights issue gathered in the ugly clouds of the Little Rock crisis, Eisenhower's involvement was carefully minimized. His duty as President, he said, was only to enforce, not to make, the laws. By thus circumscribing his own role, he endeavored to avoid hard political choices and to disassociate himself from currently unpopular policies.

A prime illustration of the career possibilities of the public relations expert in the contemporary Presidency is provided by the press secretary of the Eisenhower administration, James Hagerty. Like other press secretaries before him, Hagerty handed out news releases, answered reporters' questions, excelled as an advance man on the President's trips, and was in general a buffer between the President and the public. But Hagerty was more than the efficient press secretaries preceding him. He was the President's confidant and enjoyed full status in top-level policy

councils. Of all the members of the White House staff, he had the warmest
personal relations with Eisenhower, regularly accompanied him on trips,
and shared in his golf, bridge, and fishing. Hagerty was a trusted counselor in Eisenhower's most personal political decisions. The press secretary was among the dozen friends who gathered with the President at a
White House dinner on a January evening in 1956 to consider the advis-
ability of his candidacy for a second term.

Hagerty regularly attended cabinet meetings and the President's
weekly sessions with Congressional leaders and is reputed to have spoken
forcibly. "Probably more than anybody in the President's official family,"
Sherman Adams once said, during his term as Presidential assistant, "he
relies on Jim for the testing of the new idea. He looks to him as the man to
mirror the public reaction and in a large majority of cases would dispose
of the matter then and there and on the basis of Jim's judgment."
Hagerty's privileged status had an international dimension. At the Big
Four Conference in Geneva in 1955 he mingled with foreign diplomats as
a member of the United States delegation. No press officer of the other
participating nations enjoyed such status. While Hagerty took in the proceedings at the close range of the conference table, his fellow professionals
had to be content with viewing them from afar. Hagerty reached the
pinnacle of his importance in the crises of Eisenhower's illnesses. In the
face of the most trying circumstances, the press secretary mastered the situation and presented the country and the world with a reassuring image
of confidence and calm.

More than any press secretary in the past, Hagerty was the authentic
voice of the White House. In intervals between the President's speeches
and press conferences, during his vacations and illnesses, Hagerty was the
daily source of Presidential pronouncement. The press secretary excelled
at rendering up the minutiae of administration happenings of interest to
most newspapers, in lieu of concentrating on policy. When the President
in extemporaneous statements floundered in error, it would be Hagerty
who picked up the pieces by issuing statements "clarifying" the President's meaning. If Hagerty provided most of what the world learned about
the President, he was also the source of most of what the President learned
about the world. Since Eisenhower was not given to reading the newspapers, Hagerty kept up with an array of publications, culling from them
the information which, he believed, warranted the President's attention.

In an administration that prized harmony and teamwork, Hagerty was
a public relations chieftain of great power. His controls over news and
statements emanating from the departments were unprecedented. He met
regularly with departmental press officers, scanned departmental news
bulletins prior to their release, and ably rescued departmental secretaries
whose loose talk plunged them into the briny depths of trouble. Cabinet

members learned the value of checking their speeches beforehand with Hagerty, and the Republican national chairman, Leonard Hall, found it advantageous to consult with him on many matters.

The Hagerty pattern raises several kinds of criticism. His concentration on the operational convenience and necessity of the newsmen and the incidental minutiae of the Presidency tended to diminish his attention to interpretations of the administration's purposes. His close rein on departmental sources prevented reporters from getting fuller expositions of policy and perhaps contrasting views directly from department spokesmen. The number of informal background briefings by leading administration officials declined substantially. They began to feel a widespread distrust of reporters and left the field to Hagerty. On occasion, the President seemed inadequately informed of the activities of his administration. In press conferences his comments upon such critical and controversial episodes as the Dixon-Yates contract and the inflamed situation at Little Rock betrayed an astonishing ignorance of basic fact. How much of this is attributable to Eisenhower's personal disinclination to become entangled in administrative detail and how much to Hagerty's over-efficiency in shielding the chief executive from official problems remains a mystery.

The Hagerty instance invites the question of whether the public relations function was excessively important to the inner councils of the Eisenhower administration, whether its centralized controls over the departments and its dominance in the President's illnesses constitute a reach of power that is altogether harmonious with democratic processes.

◊

THE strong President has the gift of rallying public opinion, of bringing it to perceive the nation's problems and interest and the rightness of his measures. In a world of great change that the nineteen sixties and seventies and beyond promise to be, his gift becomes ever more valuable. The President's task is made all the more difficult by the tendency of public opinion to lag behind change. The American public mind in the mid-nineteen sixties appears overcommitted to long-established conceptions in domestic and foreign affairs. In foreign affairs the public holds views acquired in the Roosevelt and Truman eras which are unsuited to changes that have since transpired in the world. The possibility of spreading unemployment, speeded by growing automation, may require bold innovations in employment policies not a little alien to our economic traditions. How are future Presidents to be strong in their high task of educating and rallying the public?

1. They might restore the fireside chat of Franklin Roosevelt, or some adaptation of it, which would enable them or their aides to inform the people periodically on topics for which their preconceptions may be out-

moded. Cooperative relations with Yugoslavia, Poland, and other countries bearing the Communist label, the place of Red China in the international community, the needs of our educational system, and the plight
of the aged in our society are a sampling of items that the President in
years ahead might well take up with his domestic public. Like certain
of Roosevelt's fireside chats, these might be background presentations,
without specific request for public support. The public would simply be
"educated."

2. In addition to informative presentations, Presidents can "go to the
people" to solicit their support on a specific issue, admittedly a hazardous enterprise. As both Roosevelts demonstrated, it can be a formidable
weapon if used with careful timing and in reasonably promising situations. "Going to the people" must be done sparingly, on issues which interest the public and in circumstances where the tide of events will command
general attention for them.

3. Issues nowadays are so numerous and complex and change so
rapidly that the President needs more help than ever in building public
sentiment from thoughtful and responsible private spokesmen. Leaders
of religious, business, and labor organizations, racial and national groups,
and the artistic and academic world must become better social critics
than they have been. They must expand the missions to which their
efforts are committed and become aware that in a changing environment
a narrow view of their self-interest is one of the surest ways toward decline
and extinction. The chief executive in a pluralistic society, that is, has a
right to expect creative thought and effort addressed to public problems
by private leaders and spokesmen.

4. If the President wants to communicate effectively, he will need
speech writers and other aides of whom at least some are not public relations professionals. The professional's attachment to the status quo and
his tendency to subordinate policy to image mean that the President will
need a representation of communications people of altogether different
backgrounds—men like Samuel Rosenman, a lawyer of wide public
experience who was a draftsman for Franklin Roosevelt; Malcolm Moos
of the academic community who served Eisenhower; or Theodore Sorensen, Kennedy's draftsman, whose background combined law and politics.

5. To maintain his far-flung foreign constituencies, the President requires several kinds of staff assistance. As Richard Nixon and Lyndon
Johnson proved in the Eisenhower and Kennedy administrations, the
Vice President is an invaluable emissary in representing the President
before his foreign publics. As the number two executive leader, the Vice
President is well fitted by the prestige of his rank to relieve the President
from large and strenuous duties. Above all, the President needs aides
whose gifts with ideas and words will infuse his public statements with
intellectual and moral vigor and with phrases that are memorable.

CHAPTER

9

Chief Diplomat

═══

From his superior vantage point on the Senate Foreign Relations Committee, J. W. Fulbright maintains that "for the existing requirements of American foreign policy we have hobbled the President by too niggardly a grant of power." The contemporary President, Fulbright contends, performs his mammoth diplomatic toil with powers laid in the eighteenth century by men who assumed that the nation's external affairs would be few and insignificant.

The Founding Fathers applied to foreign affairs, as they did to domestic, the principle of checks and balances born of distrust of power. Much Presidential activity in foreign affairs is subject to Senatorial or Congressional checks. The contemporary trend toward a dependence of foreign policy on domestic affairs has enlarged the importance of domestic affairs. What the nation can do abroad depends upon its economic strength and growth at home and upon the quality of its people—the levels of their education and health. How the nation is reflected in the world mirror turns no little on what it does and leaves undone in its own backyard concerning its domestic problems, such as Negro civil rights. All these subjects are much in the grasp of Congress. A contemporary foreign policy of vast military and economic aid programs requires appropriations granted by Congress, at the initiative of the House of Representatives. The joining of Congress and the President in foreign affairs, which the Founding Fathers so carefully arranged, has deepened rather than diminished.

Yet there is powerful, even unimpeachable, authority that the President is "chief diplomat." No one less than Thomas Jefferson once termed the conduct of foreign affairs "executive altogether." Harry S. Truman, discoursing on his office one day to a visiting body of the Jewish War Veterans, declared flatly, "I make American foreign policy." The perceptive authors of the *Federalist* papers viewed the chief executive as possessing certain intrinsic qualities peculiarly suited for the management of foreign affairs: unity of office, capacity for secrecy and dispatch, and superior sources of information. Jefferson and the *Federalist* writers seem impressed with the President's autonomy in the conduct of foreign policy, and Truman seems impressed with his autonomy in the making of it. Do the Constitution and executive-legislative practice treat these two phases of foreign policy alike, assuming for the moment that they are identifiable and separable? Is Senator Fulbright's concern valid for either or both?

◇

THE Constitution is most explicit concerning the administration or conduct of diplomacy. Article II, section 2, provides that the President "shall have power, by and with the advice and consent of the Senate, to make treaties, provided two-thirds of the Senators present concur." Significantly, this language associates the President with the Senate throughout the course of treaty-making. President Washington, interpreting the Constitution literally, understandably felt constrained to secure the advice of the Senate on certain questions arising in the course of negotiations of a treaty with the Southern Indian tribes. But the Senate chose to respond churlishly, resolving to consider the questions privately, without the chief executive present. Washington, incensed by this treatment, withdrew, according to Senator William Maclay, "with sullen dignity." This little set-to finished Washington, and for that matter all future Presidents, on consultations with the full Senate. Not, however, with individual Senators. Although the executive negotiates treaties, he has deemed it wise on occasion to involve key Senators in the enterprise. Senators Tom Connally and Arthur Vandenberg were members of the United States delegation to San Francisco to construct the United Nations Charter or treaty. Negotiations of the 1963 test ban treaty were conducted in the presence of a panel of Senators. Some historians blame Wilson's League of Nations defeat on his failure to include Senators in the United States delegation to the Paris peace conference.

In practice, the Senate can approve or reject a treaty outright or impose conditions or reservations which may or may not be acceptable to the President. When the test ban treaty was in the Senate's hands, President Kennedy, at the urging of Senator Everett Dirksen, the Republican minority leader and a supporter of the treaty, sent a letter to the Senate carrying "unqualified and unequivocal assurances" that the treaty would not deter him from maintaining a vigorous weapons program. Kennedy gave other explicit assurances, including one that the treaty would never be amended by executive action, but only by treaty procedure. The President's action headed off possible Senatorial reservations.

The Constitutional requirement that two-thirds of the Senate give its advice and consent establishes for the President the unavoidable and sometimes difficult test of winning support from the opposition party. Wilson's failure to attract sufficient Republican backing wrecked United States membership in the League of Nations. Franklin Roosevelt, anxious to avoid the Wilsonian disaster in his quest for a United Nations organization, took elaborate precautions to win both Republican and Democratic cooperation. While the European war was yet proceeding, a Joint Advisory Committee on Postwar Foreign Policy was established, chaired by Secretary of State Hull and comprising various executive officials and leading legislators of both parties. The principles on which the future world organization might be constructed and the nature of the United States affiliation were thoroughly canvassed. Hull was often in touch privately with key Senators such as Connally, George, and Vandenberg. Connally, Fulbright, and others sponsored resolutions approving United States participation in an international peace organization. Not merely Republican Senators, but the national Republican party organization voiced its support. The Republican Mackinac Island declaration of 1943 endorsed the tenor of the legislative resolutions, as did the 1944 Republican and Democratic platforms and Presidential campaigns. Finally, Senators of both parties were members of the United States delegation to negotiate the United Nations Charter. Again, the 1963 test ban treaty could never have passed without Republican votes in the Senate and the skillful cooperation of Senator Dirksen, the Republican leader.

The President sometimes disregards the treaty procedure and resorts to "executive agreements." These entail no Senatorial review, and may stem from several types of independent Presidential authority—the executive power clause or his power as commander-in-chief—and from statute or treaty. These agreements are not mentioned specifically in the Constitution. The exchange of United States destroyers for British bases in World War II was founded upon the commander-in-chief power and executive power clauses and a statute permitting the transfer of "obsolescent" military materiel. Presidents have used executive agreements for nearly every conceivable diplomatic subject: fishing rights, boundary disputes, the annexation of territory, and so on. In *United States* v. *Curtiss-Wright Corp.* (299 U.S. 304, 1936) the Supreme Court seemed to contemplate an almost limitless variety of matters for executive agreements. Yet what the President can do in law he may be unable to do in politics. Some, indeed most, executive agreements depend for their effectiveness upon support from Congress. The legislators are not loath to exploit their leverage. When Congress in 1951 put up money for President Truman's emergency agricultural aid to Yugoslavia, several strings were attached. Aid, for example, was to be distributed "without discrimination as to race or political or religious belief." Legislators critical of Yugoslavia's penchant for collective farms required that nation to pledge itself "to take all appropriate economic measures to reduce its relief needs, to encourage increased production and distribution of food stuffs. . . ." In a word, Congress was instructing the President's negotiators to require the Yugoslavs upon entering an executive agreement to partake of its benefits not by their accustomed dictatorial, but by democratic, means; not by Communist economics, but by free enterprise.

The President, the Constitution says, "shall nominate, and by and with the advice and consent of the Senate, shall appoint ambassadors, other public ministers and consuls. . . ." Ordinarily, the Senate raises no objections to the President's nominees for diplomatic posts, but trouble is by no means unknown, and President Eisenhower drew a full draught of it early in his term when he nominated Charles E. Bohlen as ambassador to the U.S.S.R. A leading expert on the Soviet Union, Bohlen numbered among his experiences service as Franklin Roosevelt's Russian language interpreter and adviser on Russian affairs at the Yalta conference. Bohlen's presence there made him a renegade in the eyes of many Republican Senators. His prospects did not improve when he testified to the Senate Foreign Relations Committee that he saw nothing wrong with the Yalta agreements. Senators Joseph R. McCarthy and Pat McCarran questioned Bohlen's loyalty, compelling Eisenhower to come out strongly for Bohlen in a press conference. Senator Taft, the Republican leader, backed up the President and the Bohlen nomination finally prevailed. Mopping his brow, Taft got word to Eisenhower that he did not want to carry any more Bohlens through the Senate.

The Constitution empowers the President to receive the diplomatic representatives of other nations. The power to receive or exchange ambassadors enables the President to recognize new governments without consulting Congress. Congress, however, can pass resolutions expressing its wishes and intent. The President indeed may welcome the step. After France fell in World War II, the Senate and House passed companion resolutions reaffirming a policy to which the United States had been committed at the earlier Havana Consultative Meeting of pan-American foreign ministers agreeing not to permit the transfer of sovereignty of any European possession in the Western Hemisphere to another non-American power. Congress's action signified the unity of the two political branches in policy. By implication, the President's power to receive diplomatic representatives also enables him to demand their recall. Washington began the latter practice when he could bear no more the extravagantly undiplomatic deportment of Citizen Genet, representative of the new France of the Revolution.

Although the Constitution vests in Congress the power to declare war, Presidential initiative in military action has long been an arm of foreign policy. Jefferson on his own initiative dispatched naval frigates to chase the Tripolitan pirates, McKinley sent troops to China to subdue the Boxer rebellion, and Kennedy flung a naval blockade around Cuba. The President finds authority for involvement in violence or potential violence as commander-in-chief, as custodian of the executive power, and on certain occasions since World War II under Article XLIII of the United Nations Charter. Congress does not ordinarily begrudge the President the use of his initiative. If anything, one or both of the legislative houses may fret because the President seems to be moving too slowly. Within a space of two weeks in 1962, for instance, the House of Representatives adopted resolutions expressing determination to use all means, including force, to defend United States rights in Berlin, and a similar resolution was adopted for the Cuban missile crisis. In neither case had the President yet given signs of making a strong response.

But Presidential military initiatives can be hazardous politically. Dwight Eisenhower, who well appreciated this fact of Presidential life, in order not to use his rightful power to the full, evolved an ingenious tactic to couple Congress with his Chinese policy. In 1955, in the face of Red China's menacing activity in the area of Formosa, Eisenhower dispatched a draft resolution to Congress authorizing the use of armed forces to protect Formosa and the Pescadores Islands against invasion. As enacted by Congress, the resolution "authorized" the President "to employ the Armed Forces of the United States as he deems necessary for the specific purpose of securing and protecting Formosa and the Pescadores against armed attack." In his request, Eisenhower was careful to say that the "authority for some of the actions which might be required would be inherent in the authority of the Commander-in-Chief." His purpose, of course, was to stifle any inference that he was yielding to Congress his Constitutional power to employ force upon his own responsibility. In seeking the resolution, Eisenhower had two discernible motivations. He believed that by associating Congress with his effort, his declaration of his readiness to fight for Formosa would have greater impact on Peiping. Equally, Eisenhower did not want to repeat what he considered Truman's mistake in sending air and naval forces into Korea in 1950, and later the army, without consulting Congress. When, eventually, the Korean conflict became politically unpopular, President Truman took the brunt. Eisenhower invited Congress to share any similar liability in a drawn-out Formosan struggle. The technique of the Formosa resolution, known as the "Eisenhower Doctrine," was renewed in the 1957 Middle Eastern crisis. With Communist maneuvers stirring, Eisenhower again brought Congress to authorize the President to resist "overt armed aggression" by "any nation controlled by international Communism" in the "general area" of the Middle East.

◇

HARRY S. TRUMAN notwithstanding, the President and Congress together make foreign policy. The President, to be sure, as commander-in-chief and head of the executive, has impressive power to make policy. But if his policy requires legislation, and some important policy does, then he must act jointly with Congress. Thus President Kennedy set as his highest legislative goal in 1962 the passage of the Trade Expansion bill, in which he was pre-eminently successful. But Congress, if it chooses, can also amend and thwart the President's proposals. Kennedy also in 1962 proposed that Congress adopt legislation permitting the President to grant to Yugoslavia and Poland the "most favored nation" treatment given non-Communist trade partners. Congress rejected the request, urgently recommended by the United States ambassador to Yugoslavia, George F. Kennan, who remonstrated that "without the support of Congress it was impossible to carry out an effective policy there."

Hostile blows, whether parliamentary delays, headline-hunting investigations, or crippling amendments, can fall from many places. Power is widely scattered among autonomous committees run by chairmen with little, if any, political attachment to the President, and they can act with minimum detection and maximum effect. The Mutual Program of military and economic assistance, a keystone of United States foreign policy, involving billions of dollars of annual expenditure, demonstrates the lengths and hazards of Congressional policy-making. The Program runs the gauntlet of six committees: the foreign affairs, armed services, and appropriations committees of each house. It presents an annual suspense drama, in which the President's proposals are subject to drastic cuts, partial restorations, and great delays, and the eventual result is usually well below his original request.

Foreign aid's worst troubles have been suffered at the hands of hostile Congressmen such as Otto E. Passman, Democrat of Louisiana, Chairman of the Subcommittee on Foreign Aid Operations of the House Appropriations Committee. Passman, who delights in referring to himself as a "country boy," though he is modestly wealthy and indulges a fondness for snow-white silk suits, applies his "countryman's axe" to the President's foreign aid requests. Although there is some redress elsewhere in the legislative review, the net damage is severe. In one of Passman's more effective years, a Presidential request for a $4.9 billion foreign aid appropriation was chopped to $3.9 billion. President Johnson, however, repulsed Passman's attack.

To counter his legislative hazards, the President resorts to two major strategies. He resists chiefly by mobilizing bipartisan support for the aid program. He goes along by deferring to Congress, indulging in expedients that silence or win over the legislative critics. In his bipartisan campaign for his 1961 foreign aid request, President Kennedy was backed by the nation's two leading Republicans, Eisenhower and Nixon. When Passman, in a single flourish of his axe, severed 21 per cent of the administration's request, Eisenhower from his Gettysburg farm cried out that "these slashes are incomprehensible to me, especially in light of present world tensions." Later, both Eisenhower and Nixon issued statements in behalf of foreign aid, and an amendment by Congressman Gerald R. Ford, Jr., Republican of Michigan, restored half of Passman's cut. More restorations were made by a Democratic-Republican coalition in the Senate Appropriations Committee. These were accomplished with help from further prestigious sources. Governor Rockefeller sent telegrams to each Republican of the House. A citizens' committee, composed largely of leading international-minded businessmen, contacted legislators and poured out publicity. Kennedy spent hours talking to legislators by telephone. The legislative representatives of the White House, the State Department, and the AFL-CIO descended on Capitol Hill. President Ayub Khan of Pakistan, who was in town, was hustled over to a joint sitting of Congress for "a pep talk," Passman called it, on the urgency of foreign aid.

In his acts of deference toward Congress, in the hope of winning votes and silencing critics, the President may subject his aid program to the hard scrutiny of figures whose word presumably carries weight with Congress. Eisenhower, soon after coming to office, dispatched teams of businessmen to observe foreign aid operations abroad and make recommendations. Kennedy in 1963 received a report from an advisory committee headed by Lucius Clay, hero-general of the Berlin air lift and businessman, which was candid but not comforting. With a tough-mindedness that must have impressed hostile legislators, the Clay committee reported that the existing aid program was a half billion dollars too big. The President is also given to a drastic reshuffling of foreign aid administration, a hopeful by-product of which is a resurgence of Congressional confidence and support. He may, as Kennedy attempted, turn to the business community for his foreign aid administrator. Upon the establishment of his new Agency for International Development, Kennedy moved to bring to its headship George D. Woods, chairman of the First Boston Corporation, a leading financial enterprise. But the connection between First Boston and the Dixon-Yates contract episode of the Eisenhower administration throttled the appointment. Kennedy next reached into another hopper of respectability by nominating Fowler Hamilton of a large, distinguished Manhattan law firm.

Choosing foreign aid administrators is a busy task for any contemporary President. Since Paul G. Hoffman took over direction of the Marshall plan in 1948, ten different administrators with an average tenure of eighteen months have guided the aid program. Eisenhower had four aid administrators, Kennedy three; and one of Lyndon Johnson's early acts was an overhaul of aid to Latin America. Each new administrator is accompanied by a busy reshuffling of functions, promises of saner working principles, and even a change in the agency's name. While these deeds are committed to build Congressional confidence, they also have certain costs: a slowdown of effectiveness as the program adjusts to the new structure, an erosion of employee morale, and an impairment of public, if not Congressional, confidence in the validity of foreign aid.

President Kennedy held something of a record for the lengths he went to in order to create a bipartisan administration in foreign affairs. He handed over much, if not most, of foreign affairs administration to Republican appointees, presumably to stifle Congressional criticism. One of his first acts was to announce the retention of a Republican, Allen Dulles, as director of the Central Intelligence Agency. When Dulles resigned after the Cuban invasion debacle, he was replaced by another Republican, John A. McCone, who in the Eisenhower administration had been chairman of the Atomic Energy Commission. Two members of Kennedy's cabinet were Republican, and both were in major posts: Douglas Dillon, Secretary of the Treasury, and Robert McNamara, Secretary of Defense. McGeorge Bundy, another Republican, was special assistant for national security affairs. A Republican, John J. McCloy, was the President's first disarmament chief, and McCloy's successor was another Republican, William C. Foster. These Republicans—and there were others—were responsible for certain of the most important foreign policy areas: defense, intelligence, finance, and disarmament. Each area, at one time or another in the decade before Kennedy's advent, had been a source of political controversy, a focal point of legislative investigation and discussion. They represented some of the most fruitful areas of Kennedy's own attack on the Republican record in the electoral campaign of 1960. Yet, upon coming into office, Kennedy proceeded to appoint Republicans to administer these very areas. In return, legislative discussion regarding them was less hostile than it often is.

✧

GIVEN the high moment of foreign policy to their administrations' success, many Presidents have become, as the cliché goes, "their own Secretaries of State." The Roosevelts, Wilson, and Kennedy are rightly remembered as such. A President–Secretary of State closely involves himself in major problems, sets high policy, intrudes upon routine, and engages heavily in diplomatic negotiation. He is both general commander and front-line soldier. But an activist President by no means requires a passive Secretary of State. The dynamic Theodore Roosevelt successively retained two eminent secretaries, John Hay and Elihu Root, whose distinction increased with their tenure.

At another extreme are the Presidents who delegate freely to their Secretaries of State, as Harding did to Hughes and Eisenhower to Dulles. John Foster Dulles enjoyed an unparalleled gift of authority as policy formulator, negotiator, and chief spokesman in foreign affairs. Indeed Dulles's sweeping power brought Senator J. W. Fulbright to protest that "Secretary Dulles seemed at times to be exercising those 'delicate, plenary, and exclusive powers' which are supposed to be vested in the President." A hazard whenever the Secretary of State assumes a large role is that he will pursue policies reflecting his own well-considered convictions rather than the President's. The Dulles-Eisenhower enterprise, however, was conducted within certain ground rules. Dulles abided by Eisenhower's rejection of a "Go It Alone" philosophy pressed by isolationist Republicans. Eisenhower himself contends that Dulles never made a major decision without Presidential knowledge and approval. In the judgment of Sherman Adams, chief Presidential assistant, "Far from relieving Eisenhower of the burden of foreign problems, this unique partnership required him to spend more time in consultation with Dulles than he did with other department heads." Dulles, according to Adams, had from six to ten hours a week of private conversation with Eisenhower. The secretary reported faithfully as situations and policies were developing and relied heavily upon the President's estimates of consequences. They worked by little notes, telephone calls, and late evening conversations, sometimes held in the White House Trophy Room. Eisenhower was well impressed with the secretary's knowledge and skill in world affairs, hailing him as the best Secretary of State since Jefferson.

Eisenhower, as Adams has written, "delegated to Dulles the responsibility of developing specific policy, including the decision as to where the administration would stand and what course of action it would follow in each international crisis." Dulles ranged far and wide over the foreign affairs spectrum. He was a familiar on-the-scenes figure at the world's trouble fronts. When trouble boiled at the Suez in 1953, Dulles journeyed there, spent five hours in anxious conference with the Egyptian leader, General Naguib, and visited eleven other Middle Eastern countries concerned with the gathering crisis. When Suez affairs reached the forum of the United Nations, it was not the resident United States ambassador, but Secretary Dulles, who presented the nation's case. Or again, when the European Defense Community faltered in attracting national support in 1953, Dulles executed a trouble-shooting itinerary through seven capitals: Rome, Paris, London, Bonn, The Hague, Brussels, and Luxembourg. In all, Dulles traveled farther, visited more countries, and personally got to know more statesmen than any other diplomat before his time. His secretarial career is a monument of dedication to his country and his President.

The extent of his influence is evidenced by the fact that when Eisenhower chose spasmodically to assert leadership himself, he promoted policies rather milder than Dulles's usual firm line. Eisenhower, who cherished world peace, welcomed reasonable ventures to reduce tensions and foster disarmament. He proposed at Geneva in 1955, for example, the Open Skies plan to reduce the likelihood of large-scale surprise attack. Dulles, according to Sherman Adams, viewed the plan with "skepticism." Eisenhower's other major contributions, such as his Atoms-for-Peace proposal, designed to promote "peaceful discussions" and "a new approach to the many difficult problems that must be solved," were all "mild line."

Those Presidents who have suffered most from their Secretaries of State suffered almost invariably if the latter were major political figures. A chief executive who imports eminent politicians to find favor in Congress or in party quarters sometimes does so to his grief. The least promising appointee is one who believes the higher office should have been his. Lincoln's Secretary of State, William H. Seward, had expected to win the 1860 Republican nomination and regarded the victorious Lincoln as an upstart. Ability was now serving mediocrity. Seward in his rationalizations began thinking of the President as monarch and the Secretary of State as Prime Minister, and the train of these quaint ideas led to a memorandum entitled "Thoughts for the President's Consideration," probably the most extraordinary document ever presented to a chief executive by a subordinate. "We are at the end of a month's administration," it read, "and yet without a policy, domestic or foreign." Further delay will "bring scandal on the administration and danger upon the country." Seward generously offered to take on the great task of policy-building himself. Lincoln's reply, fortunately, was an unsparing squelch. "If this must be done," he said, "I must do it."

Benjamin Harrison suffered even worse when he brought in as Secretary of State his eminent rival for the 1888 Presidential nomination,

James G. Blaine, in an obvious act of pacification. They had hardly settled down to work when Blaine asked that his son Walker be made First Assistant Secretary of State. Harrison refused. "All first propositions are rejected," wrote Mrs. Blaine. "It is a most uncomfortable twist in the make-up of the man." Relations quickly deteriorated into a state of general mistrust. It all ended with Blaine's cold, formal request for relief from his duties, with Harrison acceding in an equally hostile reply. Blaine, it was widely surmised, was deeply disappointed by Harrison's impending renomination, having expected the honor for himself.

Later Presidents who have brought in erstwhile political rivals as Secretaries of State have fared no better. Wilson chose for his secretary the perennial Democratic Presidential nominee, William Jennings Bryan. His stubborn pacifism and neutrality eventually collided with Wilson's drift toward involvement and its risk of war, and the nation was rocked by the secretary's resignation. Harry S. Truman appointed as his Secretary of State James F. Byrnes, his rival for the 1944 Vice Presidential nomination, the route to the Presidency upon Roosevelt's death. Truman indeed had nominated Byrnes for the Vice Presidency. After the convention chose, Truman wrote that "Byrnes, undoubtedly, was deeply disappointed and hurt. I thought that my calling on him at this time might help balance things up." Again the relationship did not work.

◇

POWER for the President reflects among other things the quality and usefulness of his staff. When Presidents choose to assert themselves in foreign affairs, as when Eisenhower on occasion chose to circumvent Dulles, he turns to the White House staff. Time and again, Eisenhower used his staff to generate creative spark and produce bold ideas for hard problems. The important Atoms-for-Peace proposal was handed over to a White House special assistant, C. D. Jackson, an executive on leave from Time-Life. Jackson made it ready and single-handedly bucked it through the Atomic Energy Commission, State, Defense, and elsewhere, against objections, evasions, and indifference. The Open Skies proposal was the province of another White House assistant, Nelson Rockefeller, and a special group, and disarmament was the bailiwick of still another assistant, Harold Stassen. Of both enterprises, Secretary Dulles was suspicious and skeptical.

A regularly potent force, too, in foreign affairs is the President's speech-writers. Dean Acheson, while Secretary of State, felt behooved to join White House speech-writing groups as often as he could, however odd such activity seemed for an already overburdened Secretary of State. "But this is often where policy is made," Acheson wrote, "regardless of where it is supposed to be made."

President Kennedy regularly used the White House staff to maximize his own involvement in foreign affairs. He relied heavily upon his national security assistant, McGeorge Bundy, and a small band of aides to monitor foreign policy and national security problems and the progress of decisions throughout the executive branch. Kennedy turned over great chunks of Latin-American policy to members of his White House staff— Adolf A. Berle, Jr., a special Presidential coordinator of Latin-American affairs; Arthur M. Schlesinger, Jr., a special assistant to the President; and Richard N. Goodwin, assistant special counsel to the President. Berle served in a split capacity, since his office was in the State Department, but he headed a Presidential task force on Latin America. Goodwin and Schlesinger toured Latin America, and the latter drafted a manifesto on Cuba. Although the special handling of Latin-American affairs was patently founded upon Kennedy's dissatisfaction with the State Department, Latin-American diplomats complained that the division of authority was confusing. They did not know, they said, whether to take their problems to the White House staff, thus breaking out of regular diplomatic channels, or to resort to the State Department, whose officers in the general obfuscation were understandably reluctant to assume authority. The United States representative on the Inter-American Economic and Social Council of the Organization of American States, Harry R. Turkel, eventually resigned, and in his letter to the President voiced his distress over the diffusion of responsibility between the White House staff and the State Department's Bureau of Inter-American Affairs.

President Lyndon Johnson early chose to wrestle with the slippery problem of Latin-American Affairs. His eventual administrative solution, like Kennedy's, was idiosyncratic. He appointed his close friend and fellow Texan, Thomas C. Mann, Assistant Secretary of State for Latin-American Affairs, and, in addition, special assistant to the President. "As special assistant to the President," Johnson explained, "he will be dealing with many other American agencies. We expect to speak with one voice on all matters affecting this hemisphere. Mr. Mann, with the support of the Secretary of State and the President, will be that voice." The tenability of this explanation remained to be tested.

Presidents are restless and easily dissatisfied in their use of staff. They have, to be sure, a wealth of assistance: the Central Intelligence Agency, the cabinet, the National Security Council, the Joint Chiefs of Staff, and the like, whose diligence and lapses bear mightily upon his administration's fortunes. The cabinet originated in the diplomatic crisis of 1793, when it charted United States neutrality in the Franco-British war. The cabinet's role has been erratic. It reached the height of its influence in fashioning the Monroe Doctrine; in the two world wars its activity was slight. The fortunes of the National Security Council, which has largely displaced the cabinet in foreign affairs, have also wavered. Truman and Eisenhower resorted regularly to the NSC, but Kennedy used it infrequently, preferring instead meetings with administrators individually and in small groups. Modern Presidents throw together *ad hoc* groups to provide counsel in diplomatic crises. To weigh the American response when Israel invaded Egypt in 1955, Eisenhower summoned to the White House Secretary of State Dulles, Admiral Arthur Radford, chairman of the Joint Chiefs of Staff, Secretary of Defense Wilson, CIA Director Allen Dulles, and Sherman Adams, the President's chief assistant.

For counsel and action the President turns also to the Department of State, home of a vast assemblage of specialists and a distinguished career organization, the United States Foreign Service. Many activist Presidents have become disenchanted with the State Department and the Foreign Service, however. Woodrow Wilson and Franklin Roosevelt for example, held them in low esteem. Kennedy was distressed by the seeming super-caution and lack of imagination of many career diplomats and the department's laggard response to policy issues. He grabbed hold of the situation by perpetrating the "Thanksgiving Massacre" of 1961, a drastic shake-up of the State Department's top echelons, with the principal new talent injected from the White House staff. Walt W. Rostow, deputy special assistant to the President for national security affairs, became counselor of the State Department and head of its policy-planning staff; Richard N. Goodwin, the President's assistant special counsel, became deputy to the Assistant Secretary of State for Latin-American Affairs; Frederick G. Dutton, a special Presidential assistant, Assistant Secretary of State for Congressional Relations. In additional moves, Kennedy appointed a new Undersecretary of State, an Undersecretary for Political Affairs, and an Assistant Secretary for Far Eastern Affairs. In the spirit of reciprocity, Kennedy took several displaced department officials into his White House organization.

Presidents enjoy almost limitless freedom to employ special agents on high missions abroad if for any reason they prefer not to use the regular ambassadors. Unlike ambassadors and ministers, special agents are appointed solely by the President, without referral to the Senate; they are not mentioned specifically in the Constitution, although their employ is implied by the treaty power and the all-purpose "executive power" clause. George Washington dispatched John Jay to England to negotiate the treaty bearing his name. Thomas Jefferson sent James Monroe to the court of Napoleon to help Robert Livingston arrange the Louisiana Purchase, and Lyndon Johnson had Attorney General Robert F. Kennedy go to Sukarno to induce the Indonesian President not to fulfill his threat to crush the new country of Malaysia.

Special agents command the President's confidence and trust, whereas the ambassador most logically concerned may not always. Special agents know better than anyone else the latest intentions and objectives of their chief executives. They radiate prestige because they come directly from the White House, and at their approach the gates of foreign ministries open wide. But special agents are at best a mixed blessing. They undercut the resident ambassador, whether intentionally or not, and often they are totally unemcumbered with relevant diplomatic training or experience.

They are most often employed by strong Presidents and achieve their fullest potential in time of war. In World War I Colonel Edward M. House and in World War II Harry Hopkins, as special agents, conducted major negotiations of United States foreign policy. Indeed, so momentous were their activities that the United States, in those intervals, had in reality two foreign offices: the State Department, which concentrated on voluminous lesser policy, and the special agent, who concentrated on making and implementing top-level policy.

Edward M. House, a modestly wealthy Texan and a dilettante in public affairs, brought off the awesome accomplishment of ingratiating himself, for the better part of two Presidential terms, with Woodrow Wilson, never an easy executive to work with. House's diplomatic endeavors began with a trip to Europe in 1914, a frantic effort to preserve peace against threatening war. In further missions abroad House built a confidential rapport with Prime Ministers and Foreign Ministers, with leaders of opposition parties, and with influential private citizens.

House was intensely pro-ally and longed to see the United States enter the war, even as Wilson was constrained by instinctive pacifism and the neutrality of the great mass of the American people. Not deterred from taking an independent line, however, House in conferences with British officials discounted the President's official complaints against the Royal Navy's violations of American rights upon the high seas as a sham to soothe a befuddled public. When at last the United States entered the war, House headed the United States War Mission overseas to build the machinery to dovetail the United States miltary and industrial effort with the allies. He represented the United States on the Supreme War Council, expedited war loans to Britain, and while Wilson was absorbed in the daily urgencies of warmaking, focused upon the long view of the impending peacemaking, including a future world organization. At the Paris Peace Conference, House was a fellow negotiator with Wilson and headed the United States delegation in his absence. But House too used his trust in ways in which his chief executive did not intend. Upon returning to Paris and viewing the concessions his deputy had made, Wilson, deeming these excessive, felt "betrayed."

Harry Hopkins, a former social worker and New Deal administrator, was Franklin Roosevelt's chief liaison with foreign affairs and the war overseas. "His was a soul that flamed out of a frail and fading body," Winston Churchill said of Hopkins, who was often ill. "He was a crumbling lighthouse from which there shone the beams that led great fleets to harbor." Hopkins negotiated with Churchill and Joseph Stalin their needs in armaments and munitions that the United States might supply. He sat in on White House sessions of the Joint Chiefs of Staff and on meetings in London and Washington of the Anglo-American Combined Chiefs of Staff. He was in the thick of sessions, thrashing out the decisions and details of the North African and Normandy invasions and the alternative Mediterranean campaigns.

As chairman of the Munitions Assignment Board, he allocated materiel to American forces, to the Allies, and to all the theaters of war. His protégés occupied the principal production and diplomatic posts. Donald Nelson as chairman of the War Production Board and Edward Stettinius, first a lend lease administrator and subsequently Secretary of State, owed their appointments chiefly to Hopkins. Stettinius got word of his lend lease position not from the President but from Hopkins. "Does the President want to talk it over with me first?" Stettinius asked, incredulous that Roosevelt should not personally confer the seals of an office so vital to the war. Hopkins assured him that this was not necessary. Several days later Stettinius received a letter from the President. "Harry Hopkins," it blandly read, "is, of course, familiar with the administration of Lend Lease, and I hope you will consult with him and with me where matters of major policy arise." Stettinius maintained the same consultations with Hopkins in his tenure as Secretary of State.

◇

FOR the President, power in foreign affairs lies in the ability to persuade foreign leaders, whether friend or foe or neutral, to back his policies. Our leadership of the western alliance, our infinite cornucopia of foreign aid, our military might have made rapport with the American President an important concern of other national executives. His chief policy objectives such as keeping nations out of the Communist orbit have led him to pursue these contacts diligently with meetings and correspondence. Kennedy's foreign visitors in his first year are countable by scores.

His letters to a wide circle of foreign leaders were no mere puffs of good will but dealt with major problems. At the height of the 1962 Cuban crisis, the Kennedy-Khrushchev exchanges opened up an understanding that averted general war. An essential feature of the arrangement was the secrecy both countries threw about the exchange. Personal communication permitted greater privacy and was less susceptible to leaks than regular channels, and, unlike formal diplomatic notes, custom does not require their publication. The Soviet news media did not mention the exchange at all. The White House kept secret the number of letters involved, the content of most of them, and the channels used. Top-level communication was also nicely attuned to Khrushchev's preference for personal diplomacy and to that of his Foreign Minister, Andrei Gromyko, who functioned as a technician rather than a policy-maker. Nevertheless, the Kennedy-Khrushchev notes were not a substitute for normal diplomatic endeavor, but a supplement, resorted to when the diplomats were unable to agree or when the problem exceeded the bounds of the forum in which they were negotiating.

To help in keeping up contacts in his global constituency, the President may send forth his own special emissaries. Soon after taking office, Kennedy snatched Dean Acheson from private life and sent him off to Adenauer to review the future of NATO. West Germany had become increasingly uneasy that the new administration would withdraw Eisenhower's offer to equip NATO forces with atomic missiles. Vice President Johnson was a busy emissary for President Kennedy, dispensing assurances on all the continents. In effect, he had to convince his foreign hosts that United States foreign policy did not mean altogether what it seemed. To Iran, Greece, and Turkey, all economically troubled allies on the Soviet-bloc periphery, he stressed in 1962 that the United States would continue its full-scale support despite its shift to a self-help policy for foreign aid recipients. When the Berlin wall was thrown up, he journeyed to the scene for the not very easy task of giving assurances that despite the absence of major action, the United States was staunch behind that beleaguered city.

A President's relationship with world leaders may be harassed by the vagaries of American domestic politics. Nehru was moved to withdraw his request for United States assistance to help India build a state-owned steel plant at Bokaro after the House of Representatives, objecting to the project because it would use large United States loans to spread socialism in India, prohibited the administration from proceeding with the venture. Nehru's offer was taken up by Kennedy, however reluctantly, and administration officials gave a collective sigh of relief to be rid of a grave political embarrassment.

The domestic politics of foreign countries too may be a jarring influence. The President has at times to shore up other chief executives whose perpetuation in office suits his purposes. When the 1953 West German elections left Konrad Adenauer's Christian Democratic Union party with a majority of one in the Bundestag and dependent upon votes of several smaller parties, cries went up for the Chancellor to step down as Foreign Minister, the first presumably in a series of steps to curb his large powers. Faced with this serious political crisis, Adenauer badly needed a success in foreign affairs to bolster his imperiled fortunes. President Eisenhower, who viewed the Chancellor with great favor, moved to provide it by personally superintending the admission of Germany into the NATO alliance. Adenauer's long campaign for a rearmed German Federal Republic was now realized, and his political stock for a time resurged. Then his political strength again declined, placing the American President, particularly Kennedy, in a full predicament. The official leadership was on the way out, and the identity of the future leadership was not yet clear. Kennedy played both sides of the street. He fortified Adenauer and widened his contacts with the rising German leaders. His Washington visitors included Dr. Erich Mende, leader of the Free Democratic party of West Germany which from 1962 onward controlled the balance of power in the Bundestag; Dr. Gerhard Schröder, also of that party, Foreign Minister and possible successor to Adenauer; Willy Brandt, mayor of West Berlin and leader of the Socialist opposition, another possible successor; and Ludwig Erhard, who eventually prevailed. Each, as well as Adenauer, trekked to Washington in an effort to create in the West German public mind his image as the best guarantor of good relations with the White House.

Fortunately, the President's foreign visitors can redound to his political profit too. In his early Presidential weeks, Johnson displayed Erhard to the German-American voters of Texas and entertained President Segni of Italy with an imposing Italian-American night at the White House.

◇

THE President as chief diplomat often engages in diplomatic ventures himself, notably the summit conference. From Franklin D. Roosevelt onward, the summit, a rare experience prior to World War II, has become standard Presidential fare: Roosevelt at Yalta, Truman at Potsdam, Eisenhower at Paris, Kennedy at Vienna.

Presidents have, in general, displayed no great enthusiasm for summitry. Roosevelt journeyed to Yalta reluctantly to meet with Churchill and Stalin. Reports that the area was unhealthy and unsanitary troubled the President, and its far removal from Washington, exceeding the capabilities of direct mail communication, threatened harm to public business. Truman did not go to Potsdam gladly, holding that the State, War, and Navy Departments should negotiate with their foreign counterparts instead. Kennedy early in his administration pointedly expressed appreciation for the quiet, normal diplomatic channels. President Johnson, soon after taking office, uttered the friendliest Presidential statement extant for summitry when he declared his readiness to meet with any world leader, including Premier Nikita Khrushchev, should such a meeting contribute to his loftiest goal, achieving "peace and prosperity." But in actuality,

Johnson, anxious to spend his new Presidential months at the most promising endeavors, has nimbly avoided summits.

Pressures for summit meetings beat most insistently upon the President in great crisis. Indeed an almost invariable Soviet tactic in such moments is to propose a chief executives' meeting. Khrushchev did so in the 1962 Cuban crisis and at several junctures when Berlin issues were at their crest. For the Soviets, the move is a fruitful propaganda stroke and a brake on the momentum of the President's moves. Presidents, for their part, have found that summits work best when dealing with questions well prepared at lower diplomatic levels. Sometimes they unfreeze disagreements which regular diplomacy cannot resolve. Kennedy, meeting Khrushchev in Vienna, was eager to size up the Soviet leader. Although De Gaulle, Adenauer, and Macmillan had briefed him on the subject, he thought he had better see for himself in the interest of informed decisions. Even more, Kennedy said afterwards, "The direct give and take was of immeasurable value in making clear and precise what we consider vital." But the sizing up of Khrushchev was also a grim experience, as Kennedy made clear in reporting to the nation. The U.S.-U.S.S.R. quarrel over Laos, then at high flame, was "not materially reduced," and his hopes for a nuclear test ban agreement had received "a serious blow."

Summit meetings score low on policy achievement and high on general failure. They force the President to negotiate issues that deserve to be mastered well beyond the point where the chief executive merely reads papers that aides put before him. Not surprisingly, no President has brought off at the summit a negotiation comparable to Philip Jessup's handling of the first Berlin blockade, Dulles's Japanese Peace Treaty, and Llewellyn Thompson's Austrian settlement. Summits can create moods of optimism which the realities of policy hardly warrant. Eisenhower could note "the new spirit of friendliness" which the 1955 Geneva meeting seemed to burst upon the world. Yet a scant three months later the high hopes of Geneva were punctured by the Soviet-Czechoslovak-Egyptian arms deal. The 1959 Eisenhower-Khrushchev meeting produced "the spirit of Camp David," again a benevolent mood without tangible policy. Within months, the Paris meeting of the two leaders exploded into an international disaster. Although Kennedy hailed his Vienna encounter with Khrushchev for "making clear and precise what we consider vital" and for diminishing "the chances of a dangerous misjudgment," two months after Vienna the Berlin wall went up, and in the following year the Soviet was not deterred from installing missiles and manpower in Cuba.

Harry S. Truman, as a new President only briefly in office, put in a month at Potsdam, wrenched away from duties he was only beginning to master which had been suddenly thrust upon him. Understandably, in the final stages of the Potsdam conference, as Truman wrote later, he got "tired of sitting and listening to endless debate on matters that could not be settled at this conference yet took up precious time. . . . I was becoming very impatient, and on a number of occasions I felt like blowing the roof off the palace." High-level meetings can severely tax the dwindling health and strength of a President like Franklin Roosevelt, too. "The President," Winston Churchill noted at the Yalta Conference, "seemed placid and frail. I felt that he had a slender contact with life." Roosevelt, fatigued and engrossed in running the war, "had made little preparation," his aide James F. Byrnes observed. Further, summit meetings, rather than facilitating communication, may actually muddy it. At Vienna Kennedy greeted Khrushchev warmly but with deference, a gesture which in some Soviet quarters was misunderstood as personal awe rather than as a young President's courtesy toward an older man.

◇

T H E President's need to establish and manage a series of alliances has soared since World War II. Alliances or understandings exist with individual countries and with regional groupings around the globe—Europe (NATO), Southeast Asia (SEATO), Australia and New Zealand (ANZUS), the Middle East (CENTO), Latin America (OAS), and Central America (OACS). When NATO was forming, Truman promised "the support which the situation requires," backed the bipartisan Vandenberg resolution endorsing the United States' association with NATO, featured the treaty in his 1949 inaugural address, urged upon Congress a vast program of military aid to the NATO countries, and assured its passage by announcing the first atomic explosion in the Soviet Union. Presidents have led in NATO's sharper turns of direction, too. Truman pushed West Germany's rearmament and inclusion in the western European defense system. Eisenhower promoted the European Defense Community treaty to merge the armed forces of six western European nations into a "hard and dependable core" for NATO. Kennedy advocated a NATO missile fleet of surface ships manned by crews of mixed nationality. Alliances, since they weaken with age and the rising national strength of their members, are often less a source of power for the President than of woe.

The President does much of his alliance toil in "working meetings," abroad or in Washington, to transact quantities of operational business or to thrash out issues at the topmost level. A model of such enterprise was Churchill's visit to the White House shortly after Pearl Harbor. In a fourteen-day stay, Churchill and his aides staked out with their American counterparts the political-military-economic lines of cooperative war effort. The chief executive is never loath to bid such foreign allies to join his battles on Capitol Hill. Churchill addressed several joint sessions of

Congress, and he and his Foreign Secretary, Anthony Eden, appeared before the Senate Foreign Relations Committee. When Senators Joseph Ball, Harold Burton, Carl Hatch, and Lister Hill introduced a resolution in 1943, committing the United States to stipulated peace objectives and calling upon the President to summon an immediate international conference, the Britishers' remarks before the Foreign Relations Committee gladdened the Roosevelt administration, which feared the resolution's disruptive effects. Churchill and Eden usefully warned the committee against prematurely specifying peace objectives in the absence of soundings and probable agreement among the major Allies.

Presidents can reverse the trend and visit allied chieftains abroad, as Kennedy did in his 1963 tour of Germany, Italy, England, and Ireland, involving public appearances and intensive private consultations. The depth of the latter is suggested by his entourage, which included Secretary of State Rusk, Special Assistant for National Security Affairs Bundy, Special Counsel Sorensen, and a quantity of other White House and State Department aides. At each country stop Kennedy took up major business. Thus in Britain it was the test ban treaty, the NATO nuclear force, international trade, and British-American aid to India invaded by Red China. No shiny new diplomatic agreements emerged, but advances were made. Probably the main achievement was Kennedy's projection of himself and his purposes before several national European publics. In speeches before great multitudes and to national audiences by television he put his plea for an integrated Europe, attacked De Gaulle's nationalistic course, and affirmed the United States' resolve to defend Europe.

But Kennedy's 1963 "swing around" the NATO alliance also had its debit side. It removed him from Washington at a crucial juncture in the civil rights crisis, with street demonstrations nearing their peak. The President was investing great quantities of hours in negotiating with lame duck European statesmen, a chronic, unavoidable species in democratic politics. Adenauer's remaining days in office were numbered; the Macmillan government was not expected to survive beyond a few months. In Italy a scrambled political situation had produced a caretaker government little inclined to discuss major new commitments. The extravagant, intoxicating acclaim of his enormous audiences brought Kennedy to say things in speeches that were at variance with his previous policy positions. In Berlin, where a million inhabitants hailed him with wild acclaim, the President declared, "And there are some who say in Europe and elsewhere, 'We can work with the Communists.' Let them come to Berlin." This was hardly in accord with his speech at American University some two weeks before, proposing new negotiations with the U.S.S.R. to end the cold war.

Alliances can be hobbled to the point of crisis when their members engage in hot pursuit of national interest. If the damage is to be contained, much may depend upon the President. A case in point is the Suez crisis, which burst upon the Eisenhower administration in 1953 from the determination of the Egyptian government of General Mohammed Naguib to throw out the British from their vast base along the Suez Canal. The British Foreign Secretary endeavored to bring President Eisenhower into the dispute as a kind of mediator, but Eisenhower declined without encouragement from Naguib, which was not forthcoming. Eisenhower nevertheless dispatched emissaries Dulles and Stassen with a gift to Naguib, a handsome Colt revolver. The gift's symbolic import—a vast future flow of American firearms for the Egyptians—consternated the British, and Eisenhower was constrained to provide reassurances.

Dulles invested five hours of discussion with the Egyptians, but to no avail. The situation deteriorated rapidly. Israel moved into Egyptian territory on the Sinai Peninsula, and British bombers from Cyprus attacked Egyptian airfields. The move, according to Sherman Adams, "caught the President completely by surprise and the suddenness of it shocked him. He had received no previous warning from the British or the French. . . ." Eisenhower called off an electoral campaign trip, explained the crisis in a nation-wide television address, and asserted the principle that "we do not accept the use of force as a wise and proper instrument for the settlement of international disputes." Eisenhower ordered the dispute taken to the United Nations, a step which produced a strange array of bedfellows: the U.S. and the U.S.S.R. joined against France, Britain, and Israel. The Anglo-American alliance was at rock bottom.

A periodic disturbance in alliance relationships is United States policy toward Nationalist and Red China, more fixed and adamant than the dispositions of its allies. In 1954, for example, the Nationalist Chinese offshore islands and the trends of American policy put the British into a state of acute nervousness. The Chinese Communists had commenced intensive artillery shelling of Quemoy. As the Eisenhower administration debated policy, British leaders, watching anxiously, proffered advice. Prime Minister Clement Attlee wanted to "neutralize" Formosa and "get rid of Chiang," and made abundantly plain, Eisenhower has written, that he "had no enthusiasm for risking a war over Quemoy and Matsu." While the British were urging caution, a large body of American opinion led by Senator William Knowland demanded a blockade of China. The President writhed between the competing pressures of international and domestic politics. But before damage was done, the clouds of crisis dispersed, to the immense relief of the British.

Far more raucous was a dispute emerging from Kennedy's efforts to rearrange the structure of political influence of one of his allies. With the war going badly in South Vietnam, and therefore constituting a threat to his own domestic political welfare, President Kennedy sought to force the removal of Ngo Dinh Nhu, whose influence over his brother, President Ngo Dinh Diem, was apparently great and the cause of several unfortunate turns of policy. In a televised interview President Kennedy criticized the Vietnamese regime for losing touch with the people whose support against the Communists was essential in the local war. The President attributed much of the declining popularity to repressions against the Buddhists, which culminated in attacks by secret police on their pagodas. Popular support, Kennedy suggested pointedly, could be regained only by "changes in policy and perhaps with personnel." As Kennedy spoke, a Vietnamese newspaper accused the United States Central Intelligence Agency of planning a coup d'état against President Diem's government. The United States ambassador Henry Cabot Lodge was soon advising President Diem that the United States regarded the removal of Ngo Dinh Nhu as vital and that unless the regime could solve its problems mounting Congressional pressure might force the Kennedy administration to cut economic and military aid to South Vietnam. The Vietnamese regime continued intact and Mme. Ngo Dinh Nhu, President Diem's sister-in-law, journeyed to the United States in a highly publicized transcontinental tour, launching counterblasts against the Kennedy policy. Midway in her campaign, President Diem's regime was overthrown, he and his brother were murdered, and the "changes" of "personnel" proceeded.

◇

PRESIDENTS must be struck at times with the resemblances between their dealings with foreign chief executives and their encounters with Congressional committee chairmen. Both foreign executives and committee chairmen respond to local interests and constituencies, face the test of periodic election, and enjoy resources to act, if they choose, with independence, indeed defiance. They test hard the President's means of persuasion and often prove them wanting.

Syngman Rhee, President of South Korea, ardent patriot and anti-Communist dedicated to the cause of reunifyng his country, opposed President Eisenhower and Secretary Dulles, who sought to conclude a truce with the Communists to end the Korean war. Rhee refused to negotiate because he deemed it tantamount to betraying his country. As Rhee's aloofness persisted, resentment ran so high in American councils that Eisenhower had to remind Republican legislative leaders at one juncture that the enemy in Korea was still the Communists and not Rhee. The Korean President meanwhile was professing his intention to continue the fight even without American or United Nations help. The United States, Rhee was told repeatedly, could not risk world war for a reunified Korea. "I can't remember," Eisenhower said of his unavailing encounters, "when there was ever a forty-eight hours when I felt more in need of help from someone more intelligent than I am."

Midway in the truce negotiations, Rhee precipitated a grave crisis by releasing thousands of anti-Communist North Korean prisoners in his charge well before he was authorized to do so. Fearful of further excesses, Eisenhower wrote a personal letter to Rhee, but to no avail. In cabinet one day Eisenhower cried out in his perplexity, "If anybody has any ideas, for God's sake, don't hold them back." Rhee was finally corralled when Eisenhower dispatched Walter S. Robertson, Assistant Secretary of State for Far Eastern Affairs, to talk with him. The quiet, soft-spoken Robertson brought Rhee around by sitting in a room with him for several days and listening patiently to his complaints and then leading him shrewdly to accept the United States position.

If American Presidents from Franklin Roosevelt onward were asked to name the most difficult allied chief executive to work with, there is little doubt that Charles de Gaulle would be at or near the top of every list. Harry S. Truman was not long in office when the French at De Gaulle's decision, taken unilaterally, occupied parts of the Aosta Valley in northwest Italy. Despite all entreaties, De Gaulle would not withdraw until Truman threatened to stop United States supplies. Truman soon was finding "my own feelings about General De Gaulle were less and less friendly," and he breathed a loud amen to the judgment Winston Churchill cabled that De Gaulle was "one of the greatest dangers to European peace." Kennedy crossed swords with De Gaulle on major issues, including the general's thesis that in crisis the United States might not risk nuclear war to save Europe. This issue was not limited to customary political channels but passed into public forums in Kennedy's midyear trip to western Europe in 1963. In a speech at Frankfurt Kennedy endeavored to allay De Gaulle's doubts about American willingness to defend Europe by pledging that the United States would "risk its cities to defend yours, because we need your freedom to protect ours." He added the rebuke, presumably for De Gaulle, that "Those who would separate Europe from America, or split one ally from another, would only give aid and comfort to the men who make themselves our adversaries and welcome any Western disarray." But mere oratory could not budge De Gaulle from his contention.

Kennedy's most dedicated antagonist, however, was not in France but in Canada, whose friendly relations with the United States are a matter of mutual pride. In his 1961 visit to Ottawa, Kennedy, apparently through inadvertence, left behind a "working paper" intended for Presidential eyes only, for guidance in discussions with Canadian Prime Minister John Diefenbaker. The working paper suggested that Canada be pushed to join the Organization of American States and step up her aid to embattled

India. The paper came into the hands of Diefenbaker, who held onto it, personally and politically incensed. Another unsettling episode occurred at a 1962 White House dinner for Nobel Peace Prize winners that included Lester B. Pearson, Diefenbaker's rival and eventual successor as Prime Minister. Before dinner, Kennedy had a private chat with Pearson, which the latter referred to as "casual and innocuous." Coincidentally, Diefenbaker was opening his 1962 electoral campaign and, upon learning of the Kennedy-Pearson conversation, was enraged at the President's act of singling out his opponent and, in effect, intervening in the Canadian election. Diefenbaker threatened to expose the 1961 working paper, adding that it contained an insulting reference to himself in the President's handwriting. The threat fortunately did not materialize; Diefenbaker built his campaign on a strong anti-American theme, but the strategy failed and Pearson was elected. Kennedy, in a sense, had won the elections, and Canadian-American relations were quickly restored to a smooth-running track.

❖

THE contemporary President faces the jarring idiosyncracies of Communist diplomacy, involving strains and stresses which his nineteenth-century predecessors never knew. They lived in the era of the "old diplomacy," whose marks were gentility and serenity and whose pride was quiet, professional negotiation. Communist method often reduces diplomacy to a branch of propaganda and employs a variety of rough expedients, not the least of which, from the President's standpoint, is its resort to calculated rudeness. Franklin Roosevelt, who labored valiantly for constructive U.S.-U.S.S.R. relations, received shortly before his death a message from Stalin so offensive that he laid it aside in order to cool off sufficiently before answering. At Paris in 1960 Khrushchev toppled the summit conference into crashing ruins by heaping upon Eisenhower a barrage of abuse over the Gary Powers U-2 incident. President Eisenhower heroically rose to the test and made an even, effective reply. Defense Secretary Thomas S. Gates, who sat next to the President, characterized his deportment the "most remarkable performance of strength of character and dignity of any man I have ever seen." Even Jefferson, Lincoln, and Cleveland knew no test such as this.

The President's agenda for foreign affairs depends as much upon Communist initiatives as upon his own. Moscow loves to alternate between threats and acts portending doom and destruction and pleas for sweet reason and peace. By manipulating crisis and its eventual resolution, Communism supplies the President with his chief diplomatic diet. As every postwar President knows, the Soviets tend to keep agreements as long as it is to their interest. To a professional politician like Harry Truman, steeped in the mores of his craft of honoring one's word, this was the worst of faults. "No contract should be entered into lightly," he commented on the Soviet habit, "I don't give my word lightly. When I say I'm going to do something, I do it, or bust my insides trying to do it." Soviet officialdom is apt to view the United States through the unflattering lenses of Marxist ideology. They see a nation of capitalists and imperialists, a nation doomed to collapse by impending economic disintegration. They take fixed positions which the most compelling presentations of reason and fact cannot budge. Yet the President and his aides, in the face of the ominous hazard of general war in a nuclear age, must toil away at unpromising negotiation which their nineteenth-century forebears, in their simpler times, would have soon abandoned.

❖

IN SETTING his foreign policy, the modern President must reckon, of course, with the United Nations. President Kennedy, striving to alter the tone of U.S.-U.S.S.R. relations, found the UN General Assembly a useful forum in which to urge that in the future the two nations compete in "leadership and responsibility" instead of competing in a search for better methods of destruction. In Kennedy's 1962 confrontation with the U.S.S.R. over Cuba, the UN served its classic functions as a forum in which the American complaint could be ventilated and world opinion marshaled, and where machinery could be found for negotiation and conciliation. But for the President the UN may also be a hazard. Kennedy, in the agony of a Berlin crisis, was urged by certain of his counselors to lay the problem before the UN General Assembly. Charge Khrushchev, they said, with threatening the peace over Berlin and call for economic sanctions if he fails to accept the UN verdict. Kennedy quickly spurned this advice, pointing out that a UN verdict might favor Khrushchev and that the neutralist nations might be persuaded to accept his suggestions for a free city.

❖

SENATOR FULBRIGHT'S thesis that the President's grant of power is "too niggardly" must be tested not simply against the President's traditional diplomatic powers in the Constitution, but against the whole spectrum of his domestic powers as well. For the President the line between domestic and foreign affairs has become virtually nonexistent. Lyndon Johnson's associates advised him well that his prospects would be better in the courts of De Gaulle and Khrushchev if first he proved his power at home by pushing a program through Congress. Presidential power is derived from more than Constitution and statute. It depends on the quality of his staff, the competence of his allies, and their consent to his lead—in a word, on his political skill in the affairs of nations. He has less power if allies break away, if rivals outmaneuver, if they dominate the choice of the grounds and weapons of the struggle. He is chief diplomat because he has the responsibility, however imperfect is his power.

What, nevertheless, might be done to improve his situation?

1. The proposals of Chapter 6 to improve the President's position as legislative leader are fully applicable to his duties in foreign affairs. What he can do in world affairs depends increasingly upon what he is doing or has done in domestic affairs, and Congress applies to foreign affairs legislation many restrictions which it imposes upon domestic. Detail in legislation handicaps the President in dealing flexibly with Communist satellite nations. Appropriation subcommittees employ their discretion roughly against the administration. These and other jarring tendencies make it all the more urgent to strengthen the President's leadership position in Congress. He therefore needs the item veto, stronger party leadership in Congress, and a revision of committee chairmen's method of selection and powers. He badly needs appropriations for substantial periods of three, five, or ten years so that the highly *ad hoc* management of foreign aid can be replaced with the advantages of integrated planning.

2. Every forewarning of what the sixties and seventies will be like suggests the necessity of revising the nation's attitudes toward its sovereignty and toward its relations with the individual nations of the Communist bloc. It must in all likelihood extend its affinities with the regional alliances to which it belongs and speed their development as organs of political and economic union. These future tasks were heralded in Kennedy's "Strategy of Peace" speech at the American University on June 10, 1963, and in Fulbright's Senate address of March 25, 1964. Perhaps the most difficult part of this enterprise for the future President is the necessity of interpreting persuasively to the public the urgencies of the times and his prescriptions for them. He will need to wrestle with the truth, as Fulbright suggested, that "A creative foreign policy . . . is not necessarily one which wins immediate general approval."

3. The treaty power should be revised by Constitutional amendment to replace the required two-thirds approval of the Senate with one of a simple majority. If in future decades the United States is to enter into international arrangements to solidify the world community and strengthen its powers at the sacrifice of national sovereignty, the practicality of the treaty power will become crucial. The present two-thirds majority requirement imposes upon the President the necessity to secure heavy bipartisan support, in which lurks the peril of easy defeat, of which the

League of Nations fight is the classic example. The two-thirds requirement also slows down the American government's capacity to act while the huge Senatorial majority is painstakingly compiled.

4. However substantial may be the limitations the President suffers in dealing with Congress and public opinion, they must not be used as whipping boys to expiate the executive branch's own shortcomings. The President and his executive aides are far better situated than anyone else to provide creativity in foreign affairs, despite the limitations of their power. They, more than any other groups, determine the balance between principle and expediency, between clarity and contradiction in the nation's foreign policy. Thus when President Kennedy said in his June 1963 visit to Europe that United States forces would remain there as long as they were "required and desired," and Deputy Secretary of Defense Roswell Gilpatric declared four months later that an eventual reduction was planned in American forces overseas, the resulting bewilderment and outcry in western European capitals can be laid to but one source: not to Congress or public opinion, but to the United States executive branch.

5. Making and conducting foreign policy has become a vast enough task to absorb the simultaneous efforts of a strong President and a strong Secretary of State. Historical experience with special agents and White House aides does not refute the wisdom of making the Secretary of State the President's chief deputy in foreign affairs. The Secretary of State, more than any other executive aide, is entrusted with the responsibility for formulating all aspects of national policy bearing upon the national interest and security. He can best take the lead in integrating the political, military, economic, and cultural efforts of the executive branch into coherent foreign policy. To succeed he needs a high order of personal talent and sophistication in foreign affairs, the President's backing, and the ability to prove himself constantly in his daily battle with shifting world problems to win and retain the confidence of his chief and his executive colleagues. He needs help in the struggle from high caliber top officials in his department and a strong career service.

In the absence of internal reform of Congress, the President will continue to rely heavily upon the Secretary of State and his aides to win the understanding and support of Congressional committees. In the absence of reform, only executive candor and a willingness to discuss difficulties and problems, as well as accomplishments, are apt to produce Congressional support for the mountainous problems awaiting the nation in foreign affairs.

10

Commander-in-Chief

———

As COMMANDER-IN-CHIEF the President manages the huge, far-flung military enterprise of armament, manpower, and alliance, which has steadily claimed upward of 60 per cent of the budget since World War II. The commander-in-chief is the maker of key military decisions. Madison in the War of 1812 and Lincoln in the Civil War selected points of attack. Truman, at his own initiative, went to war in Korea in 1950 and Kennedy was prepared to fight in certain contingencies in the Cuban crisis of 1962. As the sole person who decides when to use nuclear weapons, the President is in reality the nation's principal field commander. As commander-in-chief he can also terminate hostilities by arranging an armistice. He can set armistice terms which provide the basis of the subsequent peace-making, as Wilson did when he incorporated his Fourteen Points into the armistice for World War I.

For all his seeming power, the President is by no means the sole master of the military enterprise. He shares power with a motley array of associates: Congress, the courts, public opinion, the nation's allies, and the professional military, among others. There are times when he may well wonder whether in truth he is the "chief," given the powers of his associates, and whether his function really is to "command." His highest task may be to "persuade" Congress and the allies, whom he cannot command, and the professional military, whose resistance is not unknown, to unite in common cause.

◇

THE Defense Department, which shelters most of the military endeavor, was created in 1947 with strong leadership and support from President Harry Truman. Certain of his proposals were not adopted, signifying the capacity of the individual services to resist the President with support from friendly legislators, and from Truman onward the President has engaged in periodic struggles with the military services. The President habitually presses for "unification" and "economy," and makes hard choices between competing proposals to develop weapons systems pressed by the individual services. They, in turn, are jealous of their traditional autonomy and vested functional interest, and are driven by professional commitment to accord military security a higher priority than fiscal "soundness."

The President's chief deputy, the civilian officer who most approximates his alter ego as commander-in-chief, is the Secretary of Defense. The National Security Council, although uneven in effectiveness, has endeavored to approximate Truman's view of it as "the place in the government where military, diplomatic, and resources problems could be studied and continually appraised. This new organization gave us a running balance and a perpetual inventory of where we stood and where we were going on all strategic questions affecting national security." The national security sector's representative on the White House staff is the Special Assistant for National Security Affairs.

The President's principal professional military advisers are the Joint Chiefs of Staff, created by President Roosevelt shortly after Pearl Harbor. The Chiefs existed wholly by Presidential fiat until 1947, when the National Security Act inspirited them with the firmer breath of statutory life. Relations between the President and the Joint Chiefs since the Roosevelt years have been troubled and sometimes stormy. The severest encounters occurred under Eisenhower, whose incomparable professional prestige lent enormous weight to his evaluation of military issues. Soon after taking office, Eisenhower announced that his administration would instill a "New Look" into military policy. The New Look relied heavily upon the new weapons of mass destruction to deter aggression, large or small, and permit reductions of conventional military forces. Since nuclear weapons were less expensive than a conventional military establishment, the New Look permitted budgetary cuts cherished by the Eisenhower administration. "More bang for the buck!" was the watchword.

Eisenhower's reverence for economy was shared, perhaps with even greater fervor, by two men of big business who towered in his military decisions: Secretary of Defense Charles E. Wilson of General Motors and Secretary of the Treasury George M. Humphrey of the M. A. Hanna

Company of Cleveland. The President, by several simple administrative expedients, placed the economy-minded businessmen in firm ascendance over the professional military. Reorganization Plan Number Six of April 30, 1953, was issued, expanding the powers of the Defense Secretary over budget, weapons, and strategic planning. The Secretary of the Treasury and the Director of the Budget, who was also economy-minded, were brought into the center of the National Security Council's work, where the military budget was scrutinized.

With his new doctrine Eisenhower brought a wholly new Joint Chiefs of Staff. His views of the Chiefs' functioning quickly emerged. They were members of the administration "team" (a favorite Eisenhower word), working for its objectives under civilian guidance. In formulating military advice, the Chiefs should weigh appreciatively their superiors' views and avoid submitting contentious recommendations. They must accept public responsibility for the administration's military policy, regardless of their personal views.

The President and his aides manipulated sanctions to nurture the team spirit. The new Chiefs were appointed for no specified term, and each appointment, it was disclosed, would be reviewed after two years. "Again and again . . ." General Ridgway, then Army Chief of Staff, has written, "pressure was brought on me, in the name of economy, to keep the semblance, but not the reality, of a fighting force overseas." Secretary of Defense Charles E. Wilson pressed continually for economy. "Why don't you reduce the strength of your combat divisions?" he would ask Ridgway in a budgetary conference, clearly implying that the President was interested in reductions of unit strength. General Maxwell Taylor, in his tour of duty as Army Chief of Staff, was invited to a White House stag dinner with his fellow Chiefs and the Service Secretaries. Their fellow guests included the Budget Director, the Secretary of the Treasury, and the Secretary of Defense, all disciples of economy. Taylor and the Chiefs ventured to the dinner with the understanding that issues of the new military budget would be discussed with the President. After dinner Eisenhower led his guests into the library for talk over coffee. That year's budget was not taken up specifically. Discussion centered instead on general economic conditions, problems facing the Treasury, the general importance of a balanced budget and a stable dollar, and the necessity for greater "team play" by the military in the budget enterprise.

But as the budget further developed, the participation of the Chiefs remained only peripheral. "The Joint Chiefs of Staff as a body took no part in the formulation of the 1960 budget—nor had they in previous years," Taylor has written. The exclusion was simply contrived; since the Chiefs' budgetary role had never been officially defined, they could easily be ignored. Individual Chiefs, to be sure, made recommendations concerning their individual services—a procedure, however, of limited value. Ridgway bridled at higher directives slashing the uniformed forces from 1,500,000 to 1,000,000 and Army expenditures from $16.2 billion to $8.9 billion. The Army, he argued, would be so weakened that it could no longer perform its missions. Although Ridgway persisted in his dissent, it was to no avail. His distress was compounded when he came upon the following in the President's State of the Union message for 1954: "The defense program recommended for 1955 . . . is based on a new military program *unanimously recommended* [italics supplied] by the Joint Chiefs of Staff." The General's resulting state of shock was worse, he said, than he had hitherto suffered from ambush, aerial bombardment, or any other unsettling experience in his professional career. Ridgway was not long in retiring as Army Chief of Staff. General Taylor too fell out with the Eisenhower administration on budgetary issues.

Although John Kennedy's advent to the Presidency was a great day for the advocates of conventional weapons, relations between the Joint Chiefs and the chief executive lost none of their turbulence. The debacle of the attempted invasion of Cuba in 1961 brought the Chiefs into the ill graces of the new President. In the months following the debacle, Kennedy and his high aides criticized the Chiefs, sometimes caustically and by name. The Chiefs' chairman, General Lyman Lemnitzer, was shifted to Europe as commander of United States forces and was replaced by General Taylor, whose return from retirement into private life seemed a reflection upon the military. Trouble again fell upon the Chiefs when certain of the incoming Taylor's views proved sharply at odds with those of Admiral George W. Anderson, Chief of Naval Operations, and General Curtis E. Le May, Air Force Chief of Staff. Not the least of these differences were Taylor's proposals of an expanded army and the abolition of the Joint Chiefs and their replacement by a single chief.

In less than a year the forces of conflict were resolved thanks to forceful Presidential intervention. President Kennedy failed to reappoint Admiral Anderson as Chief of Naval Operations and hence to the Joint Chiefs. General Le May was not reappointed for the standard two-year term but only for one year. The drastic maneuver against Anderson shocked the Naval officered community where both his reappointment and his eventual rise to the chairmanship of the Chiefs were generally expected. Anderson had earned himself black marks by criticizing semi-privately a reorganization of the Navy's command structure that the President was to recommend to Congress, limiting the province of the Chief of Naval Operations. The Admiral had publicly opposed the administration's position on two other key issues, the TFX contract and the military pay bill. General Le May had also been critical, but less pointedly. Both officers were widely influential on Capitol Hill, able to summon with their own dissents a sizable chorus of legislative opposition to administration policies. Ultimately, President Kennedy removed Admiral Anderson some distance from Capitol Hill by appointing him ambassador to Portugal. Anderson's successor as Chief of Naval Operations, Admiral David L. McDonald, was little known in Congressional circles.

◇

As COMMANDER-IN-CHIEF the President appoints and removes his field generals. In wartime the responsibility is especially important because of the consequences of the President's choice for the nation's survival. Several Presidents have faced major crises either in bringing their field generals to engage in battle or in keeping them within bounds, not simply on the battlefield but within the framework of Constitutional government. General George B. McClellan, the most lagging of field generals, was a great trial to Abraham Lincoln. Bold in his strategic conceptions, McClellan nevertheless dreaded execution. His standard tactic was to demand more reinforcements after overestimating the enemy's strength and deprecating his own. He was a wonderfully imaginative procrastinator. If he had Lee at a disadvantage, he almost invariably failed to exploit it. He must wait, McClellan would report to his impatient superiors at Washington, until the Potomac rose to be sure that Lee would not recross it; he must finish drilling new recruits, reorganize his forces, and procure more shoes, uniforms, blankets, and camp equipment. McClellan also passed some of his battle-idle time pouring his innate arrogance into a letter to Lincoln of July 7, 1862, pointing out that it was high time the government established a civil and military policy to cover the full canvass of the nation's troubles. The general generously offered to inform the President of what it should be.

The McClellan question became critical with his failure to exploit his victory at Antietam by pursuing Lee's fleeing army. Lincoln worked mightily, as his secretary Nicolay put it, at "poking sharp sticks into Little Mac's ribs." When the general included among his ingenious excuses one that an epidemic had afflicted his army's horses with sore mouths and weary backs, Lincoln was goaded into a sharp reply. "I have just read your dispatch about sore tongues and fatigued horses," he telegraphed. "Will you pardon me for asking what the horses of your army have done since the battle of Antietam that fatigues anything?"

Lincoln and his administration were now at a critical juncture. Winter was approaching and would assure that except for Antietam the long record of Eastern defeat and stalemate would remain intact. Congress, restive with this state of affairs, was soon to convene. Governors were nervous, the cabinet was divided, and the extreme war and peace men were thundering against the President. Nor was Lincoln unmindful of

McClellan's personal softness toward the South, and the presence on his staff of some who advocated a waiting game to prolong the war until both sides were exhausted and the Union might be preserved with slavery intact. Replace McClellan? The available generals were a sorrowfully undistinguished lot, many already well scarred with failure, and others abysmally inexperienced.

After heavy deliberation, Lincoln cast aside the adverse factors and on November 5, 1862, relieved McClellan and appointed General Ambrose E. Burnside in his place. Upon reading the President's order, McClellan exclaimed, "Alas for my poor country!" Certain of his officers urged him to disobey. He later wrote that he might have marched his troops into Washington and taken possession of the government. Instead, he handed over his command of 120,000 men in an elaborate ceremony. But this was by no means the last encounter between McClellan and Lincoln. In 1864, two years after his removal, McClellan met Lincoln on a new terrain—as the Democratic nominee for the Presidency.

In another day, President Harry S. Truman experienced a confrontation with a field general prone to do too much rather than too little. General Douglas MacArthur, commander of the United Nations forces in Korea, possessed a military career of rare distinction—peerless hero of the Pacific theater in World War II, successful viceroy of postwar Japan, and a widely mentioned potential Republican Presidential nominee. His handsome, erect presence and majestic eloquence were marks of an imperious figure.

Truman's difficulties began when the general, midway in the Korean War, visited Chiang Kai-shek at Formosa. After their meeting, Chiang declared, "The foundation for Sino-American military cooperation has been laid." Since these words were both obscure and potentially expansive, and the administration was anxious to keep Formosa neutralized, Truman dispatched Averell Harriman to review with MacArthur the entire Far Eastern political situation. Harriman's apparent success was shattered when MacArthur released a statement to the commander of the Veterans of Foreign Wars urging a more dynamic United States-Formosa partnership. The President himself now went forth to see MacArthur in a hastily cleared-out Quonset hut on Wake Island. There were two meetings, the first between the President and the general, and the second between the two with their advisers. The latter meeting was surreptitiously recorded by the secretary of Philip Jessup, United States Ambassador at Large, who sat in the shadow of a door that was ajar and took shorthand notes. According to these, which were released to a subsequent Senatorial investigation, the whole Eastern policy was broadly and congenially discussed. The part of Truman's visit that the public saw seemed entirely happy. The President pinned the Distinguished Service Medal on the general and presented a five-pound box of candied plums to Mrs. MacArthur. The general reciprocated by declaring, through the President's press secretary, "No commander in the history of war has had more complete and admirable support from the agencies in Washington than I have during the Korean operation."

MacArthur pressed the war forward, routed the North Koreans, and received approval from the United Nations General Assembly to pursue the fleeing foe across the 38th parallel, the division between the two Koreas. Hereupon Communist China entered the war. The struggle proceeded to seesaw between MacArthur's forces and the enlarged enemy. On March 17, 1951, in a public statement issued from his United Nations headquarters, MacArthur lamented the "abnormal military inhibitions" upon his command and pointed to the necessity for "vital decisions—yet to be made." These presumably should incorporate his proposals to the Joint Chiefs for broadened military action against Red China, including a blockade, air bombardment, and ultimately invasion. MacArthur's public statement coincided with efforts of the President and the State Department to end the Korean conflict by re-opening diplomatic negotiations.

MacArthur made other public statements, not the least of which was a reply to Joseph W. Martin, the House minority leader, who had asked the general for his views on the use of Chinese Nationalist troops. MacArthur indeed believed they should be employed, and added, in words implying that it was necessary to vastly expand the Korean conflict, "Here we fight Europe's war with arms while the diplomats there still fight it with words; . . . if we lose the war to Communism in Asia the fall of Europe is inevitable." Congressman Martin read MacArthur's letter on the House floor.

Anxiety flowed like wine in foreign capitals. Kenneth Younger, British Minister of State, typified the mood of America's allies in lamenting "irresponsible statements . . . from highly placed quarters, without the authority of the United Nations, or indeed of any member government." President Truman now concluded that decisive action was unavoidable if Presidential authority, civil supremacy, and established policy were to be preserved. He wrote to a friend, "I reached a decision yesterday morning after much consideration and consultation on the Commanding General in the Pacific. It will undoubtedly create a great furor but under the circumstances I could do nothing else and still be President of the United States." On April 11 the President announced MacArthur's removal from his command.

Truman explained his decision in an address to the nation. MacArthur, returning to the United States, addressed Congress and advanced his policy tenets with superb oratorical skill. Several legislators moved to impeach Truman, and the Senate Armed Services and Foreign Relations

Committees commenced a joint investigation. The top military unqualifiedly supported the President.

Presidential power was eventually vindicated by Truman, as it had
been earlier by Lincoln. In both episodes, civil supremacy had been maintained over the professional military, a cardinal arrangement of the democratic state. Both Presidents in their self-assertion faced grave political
risks: the possibility that the successors of the deposed generals would
compile a less favorable military record, that public opinion would feel
affronted, and that legislators would exploit the situation for personal
political gain. But both Presidents clung to duty and brushed aside political expediency and the temptation not to act. The military rallied
around them, the public understood, and ultimately the chief executive
prevailed.

◊

THE President, functioning as he does in a democratic state, requires
legal authority to pursue his military purposes. In wartime, of course,
the need and the quest become most compelling. Presidents in the nation's
major wars have invoked two contrasting patterns of legal justification
for their acts. One, the Lincolnian, asserts an expansive view of the President's independent authority based on the commander-in-chief clause in
Article II, section 2, of the Constitution and on the duty "to take care that
the laws be faithfully executed" expressed in section 3. In the ten weeks
between the outbreak at Fort Sumter and the convening of Congress in
special session on July 4, 1861, Lincoln employed these two clauses to
sanction measures whose magnitude suggests dictatorship.

In the ten-week interval, Lincoln added twenty-three thousand men to
the Regular Army and eighteen thousand to the Navy, called forty thousand volunteers for three years' service, summoned the state militias into
a ninety-day volunteer force, paid two million dollars from the Treasury's
unappropriated funds for purposes unauthorized by Congress, closed the
Post Office to "treasonable correspondence," imposed a blockade on Southern ports, suspended the writ of habeas corpus in certain parts of the
country, and caused the arrest and military detention of persons "who
were represented to him" as engaging in or contemplating "treasonable
practices." He later instituted a militia draft when voluntary recruiting
broke down and extended the suspension of the habeas corpus privilege to
a nationwide basis for persons "guilty of any disloyal practice." His first
Emancipation Proclamation freed the slaves in states in rebellion against
the United States and pledged "the Executive Government of the United
States, including the military and naval authority thereof," to protect the
freedom conferred. Lincoln invited Congress to "ratify" his enlargement
of the armed forces, which it did, and it bolstered his handling of the writ

of habeas corpus. Altogether, Lincoln's actions, as Edward S. Corwin has written, "assert for the President, for the first time in our history, an initiative of indefinite scope and legislative in effect in meeting the domestic aspects of a war emergency."

The world war Presidencies of Woodrow Wilson and Franklin Roosevelt afford a contrasting pattern. The spreading character of war, its encroachment upon the economy, the involvement of growing numbers of people, and the resort to propaganda have fostered an executive-legislative partnership in war leadership. In both of the world wars statutes were passed delegating broad powers to the chief executive. Selective service laws in both wars enabled the President to administer a vast manpower draft. The Lever Act of 1917 empowered the executive to license the mining, importation, manufacture, storage, and distribution of necessities; it authorized the seizure of factories, pipelines, mines, and the like; and it fixed the prices of wheat, coal, and other basic commodities. In World War II the Lend Lease Act permitted the President and his deputies to transfer "defense articles," meaning anything from bacon to battleships, to the "government of any country whose defense the President judged vital to the defense of the United States," on any terms he "deems satisfactory."

By gift of legislation, Roosevelt managed much of the domestic economy in World War II. Through deputies he allocated "materials," fixed prices, controlled rents, settled labor disputes, and seized strike-bound plants. Like Wilson, Roosevelt as commander-in-chief created "executive agencies," such as the Office of Price Administration and the National War Labor Board, to administer delegated legislative power.

The President needs not only laws from Congress, but a variety of other cooperative deeds to assure effective military policy and administration. By grace of the Constitution, with its mechanisms of checks and balances, the chief executive shares a wide range of military powers with Congress. Congress raises the armed forces, provides for their regulation, and investigates the military enterprise; the Senate gives its advice and consent to military nominations; Congress passes laws governing military organization, appropriates vast funds for equipment and materiel, and declares war. Its powers, Presidents would gladly testify, enable it to act forcefully in military affairs. The results are not always positive and cooperative. Checks and balances, bolstered by rivalries between the armed services, sometimes bring the President and Congress into incipient or actual conflict.

In 1962 President Kennedy faced a gathering crisis which threatened to become a head-on clash simply over the merits of a military artifact, but between Congress's and the President's respective military powers. The subject of controversy was the RS-70 bomber, then in its final stages of development. Air Force leaders strongly backed the RS-70, stressing the necessity of a manned bomber program to avoid excessive reliance upon missiles. Substantial Soviet bomber advances were cited. Army and Navy leaders, and President Kennedy, like President Eisenhower earlier, opposed the RS-70, holding that great numbers of long-range missiles would be available before the new bomber could be produced in sufficient quantity. The Kennedy administration requested $180 million in 1962 to continue the RS-70 development program. The House Armed Services Committee lavishly authorized $491 million. The committee's bill "directed" that the funds it authorized be spent.

The choice of this particular word signified the beginning of a possible massive Constitutional confrontation between Congress and the President for dominion over military policy. The House committee based its wording "direct" upon Article I, section 8, of the Constitution, which vests in Congress the responsibility for raising and maintaining the military forces. In choosing its ground, the committee likened the President, or commander-in-chief, to a field general who can direct and order his forces, but must use the weapons furnished by Congress. Representative Carl Vinson of Georgia, chairman of the Armed Services Committee, a patriarchal influence in military policy, candidly admitted that his committee's maneuver was intended to force the Pentagon to respect Congressional insistence that continued manned bomber development was essential to maintaining "an adequate military establishment."

President Kennedy refrained from picking up the gauntlet of the Constitutional issue thrown down by Vinson. Instead he took the "Swamp Fox of Georgia," as Vinson is otherwise known, for a stroll one sunny March afternoon in the White House rose garden. The President and the Congressman fortunately arranged an honorable, peacemaking compromise by which the administration agreed to spend more than was originally budgeted for the RS-70 if a new review and technological developments warranted an increase.

Presidents must also reckon with a favorite preoccupation of Congress in the military realm: investigation. Harry Truman's Senate Committee to Investigate the Defense Program was a model of searching, but constructive, criticism that produced fruitful change in the administration of World War II. Success as a wartime investigator established Truman's chief claim upon his subsequent Vice Presidential nomination. A contrasting view of the investigatory power is provided by a great cross Lincoln had to bear in the Civil War, the Joint Committee on the Conduct of the War. Spotty and arbitrary, the committee concentrated upon the Army of the Potomac and selected generals—McClellan, Charles P. Stone, Fitz-John Porter, and William B. Franklin—to investigate. John C. Frémont and Benjamin Franklin Butler were its favorites and could do no wrong. The committee investigated its selected victims with preconceived notions of guilt, employed wild rumor and irresponsible publicity, and became the factional instrument of the radicals. Its busiest members were staunch anti-Lincoln men such as Zachariah Chandler, Benjamin Franklin Wade, and George Washington Julian; Chandler, in a typically unflattering estimate of the administration, wrote, "Folly, folly, folly reigns supreme. The President is a weak man." Lincoln reciprocated in his judgment of the committee. He said,

> I have never faltered in my faith of being ultimately able to suppress this rebellion and of reuniting this divided country; but this improvised vigilant committee to watch my movements and keep me straight, appointed by Congress and called the "committee on the conduct of the war," is a marplot, and its greatest purpose seems to be to hamper my action and obstruct the military operations.

◇

As commander-in-chief the President also faces tensions with the remaining governmental branch concerned with military affairs, the federal courts, with their high duty in a democratic state to protect the Constitution and the laws against encroachment. The most perplexing and consequential issues between the executive and the courts may arise during actual war, when the President is driven to curtail, or even to suppress, key liberties sanctioned in the Bill of Rights. To further the progress of war, to safeguard the nation's imperiled safety, the President has set aside political and economic liberties which in peacetime are inviolable.

The Civil War, fought within the nation's borders and jeopardizing its capital, was resented and resisted in many sectors of the North, to the point that President Lincoln promulgated several orders and proclamations restrictive of individual liberty. The most important of these was his suspension of the Constitutional privilege of the writ of habeas corpus, protecting the civilian against arbitrary arrest. Lincoln's first habeas corpus proclamation, issued in the war's early weeks, was triggered by events in Maryland. Underground resistance and open defiance were rampant in that state. Federal troops were attacked by mobs in Baltimore, communications to the capital were severed, and the mayor and police chief were unabashedly pro-Confederate and anti-Lincoln. Bridges were destroyed to hamper the passage of Union troops, and newspapers hostile to the administration fanned disunion sentiment. The state legislature was soon to convene, and a formidable bloc of its members aimed to have the state secede from the Union.

Union generals moved to nip the growing conspiracy by arresting the mayor of Baltimore, the chief of police, and several police commissioners. Even more sensational was the arrest of members of the Maryland legislature. To forestall the passage of an act of secession, Union General Nathaniel P. Banks barred the legislature from meeting and arrested nine of its members and the chief clerk of the Senate. Still other Marylanders were arrested, including one John Merryman "charged with various acts of treason." Merryman was languishing in Fort McHenry when the Chief Justice of the United States, Roger B. Taney, on circuit duty, ordered "the body of John Merryman [produced] and . . . the day and cause of [his] capture and detention" made known. A head-on clash between the President and the Court, between the war and the Constitution, was in the making. Taney, to the administration's great relief, confined himself to declaring that the power to suspend the writ, which should be exercised only with "extreme caution," belonged to Congress, and not to the President (17 Fed. Cas. 144). Taney's opinion, nevertheless, put the administration under the cloud of the likelihood of a hostile Supreme Court decision, an event the Attorney General, Edward Bates, said would "do more to paralyze the Executive . . . than the worst defeat our armies have yet sustained."

The administration's position was strengthened when Congress, after much struggle, passed the Habeas Corpus Act of 1863, affirming the President's power to suspend the writ. Despite several procedural devices incorporated to placate the courts, the act left to the executive the setting of policy concerning arrests and imprisonments. Prisoners were tried, as before, by military tribunal and punished or released under authority of the War Department. Arrests continued apace. Clement L. Vallandigham, fiery Copperhead, after his arrest, trial, and sentencing by a military commission, appealed to the United States Supreme Court to lift his case into civil court. But the Supreme Court ruled that it had no jurisdiction, since a military commission was not a "court," to which the federal judiciary was limited under existing law (*ex parte Vallandigham*, 68 U.S. 243, 1864).

Although Vallandigham never lived to see it, his legal position was ultimately vindicated in the celebrated case of *ex parte Milligan* (4 Wallace 2, 1866). Milligan too was a Copperhead, tried by a military commission for "treasonable" speeches. Condemned to hang, he invoked the habeas corpus writ. But the war was now over, and the Court was prepared to act boldly. It ruled that Indiana, where Milligan resided and spoke, was not part of the "theater of war" and that the civil courts there were "open" and therefore available to conduct his trial. Under such a combination of circumstances, the writ could not be Constitutionally suspended. The *Milligan* case, needless to say, has become the source of permanent consternation to the friends of Presidential power. It establishes the principle that the courts shall determine, even to the point of overriding the executive, what is the area of war and public danger, a principle that could well work havoc with Presidential effectiveness in actual emergency.

Despite the hazards of the *Milligan* doctrine, the Court proved tolerant of Presidential power in the two world wars. In *ex parte Quirin* (317 U.S. 1, 1942) the Court broadly construed the commander-in-chief's capacity as executor of the Articles of War, enacted by Congress to further the United States' obligations under the laws of war, a branch of international law. The Articles of War provide for their enforcement through courts-martial and military commissions. *Ex parte Quirin* concerned eight saboteurs, seven Germans and one American, who were trained in a Berlin espionage school and deposited on Long Island and the Florida coast by German submarines in 1942. They doffed their German military uniforms for civilian attire, and with their tools of sabotage set out for New York City, Jacksonville, and other points to practice their art on American war industries. Arrested by the FBI before they could get down to work, they were turned over to the provost marshal of the District of Columbia. As commander-in-chief, President Franklin D. Roosevelt appointed a military commission to try the would-be saboteurs for violating the laws of war by not wearing fixed emblems revealing their combatant status. Midway in the trial the defendants petitioned the United States Supreme Court and the District Court for the District of Columbia for leave to bring habeas corpus proceedings.

The defendants argued that the offense charged against them was not known to the laws of the United States and was not one "arising in the land and naval forces," as described by the Fifth Amendment of the Constitution. Nor was the military tribunal which was trying them, they said, constituted in keeping with the Articles of War. The Court struck down the latter contention by declining to distinguish between the powers of the President as commander-in-chief and of Congress to create a military commission. The Court rejected the other arguments, holding that cases involving enemy personnel had never been deemed to fall under the Constitutional guarantees of the Fifth and Sixth Amendments. The Court also cited the long-standing practice represented by an act of 1806 which imposed the death penalty on alien spies "according to the law and usage of nations, by sentence of general court martial." The saboteurs, accordingly, were tried and sentenced by military commission.

The most extreme application of the commander-in-chief's power to designate the theater of military operations was President Franklin Roosevelt's executive order of February 19, 1942, directed at the presumed danger of Japanese sabotage on the West Coast. In the high excitement over the Japanese bombing of Pearl Harbor, Roosevelt was pressed by the military, Congress, West Coast groups, and the newspapers to remove persons of Japanese ancestry from that area farther into the mainland. By Executive Order No. 9066 Roosevelt empowered the Secretary of War to establish "military areas" from which "any or all persons" might be excluded to prevent espionage and sabotage, and he designated military commanders to police these areas. The Secretary of War was directed to provide food, shelter, and transportation for persons evacuated. Soon the three westernmost states and a part of Arizona were declared "military areas 1 and 2" by Lieutenant General J. L. DeWitt. In a brief resolution of March 21, 1942, Congress endorsed the Presidential action by making it a misdemeanor "to knowingly enter, remain in, or leave prescribed military areas" of the Secretary of War or of the commanding officer. A War Relocation Authority was established to care for persons cleared out of the military areas. In all, some 112,000 persons were removed from the West Coast, of whom the vast majority— 70,000—were United States citizens. Both the transplanted United States citizens and the aliens were eventually placed in ten "relocation centers" in California, Arizona, Idaho, Utah, Colorado, Wyoming, and Arkansas.

The relocation enterprise was challenged several times, but never effectively. In *Hirabayashi* v. *United States* (320 U.S. 81, 1943) the Court, by the drastic surgery of legal technicalities, reduced the issue to the right of the West Coast commander to subject citizens of Japanese ancestry to a special curfew order. The Court stressed the nation's plight and the state of the war in reaching its decision. Japan was achieving striking victories in 1943, the West Coast lay exposed, defense plants were heavily concentrated there, and, in the eyes of the Court, the ethnic affiliation of Japanese-Americans with the enemy posed a danger unknown from those of other ancestry. The Court deemed relocation within the powers of the President and Congress "acting in cooperation." In *Korematsu* v. *United States* (323 U.S. 214, 1944), a United States citizen, a Japanese-American, was convicted in district court for remaining in his California home. The Supreme Court again severely narrowed its decision and reasserted the reasoning of earlier relocation cases, though Japan was now in full retreat throughout the Pacific.

The most general abrogation of civil liberties in World War II occurred in the territory of Hawaii. Soon after the Japanese bombed Pearl Harbor, Governor J. B. Poindexter of Hawaii invoked section 67 of the Hawaiian Organic Act of April 30, 1900, proclaimed martial law throughout the territory, and turned over to the commanding general of the Hawaiian Department the exercise of all normal gubernatorial powers "during the present emergency and until the danger of invasion is removed." President Roosevelt approved Poindexter's decision, and a regime of martial law commenced which remained in force until October 24, 1944, when a Presidential proclamation terminated it. Habeas corpus was suspended and the civil courts were supplanted by military tribunals in which civilians were tried for crimes by summary procedures.

The Hawaiian arrangement was challenged in 1943, when District Judge Delbert E. Metzger issued a writ of habeas corpus in behalf of two naturalized Germans interned by the Army. The Hawaiian commander, Lieutenant General Robert C. Richardson, countered by forbidding writs of habeas corpus, including those of Judge Metzger. The issue was soon settled administratively.

Finally, the Court in *Duncan* v. *Kahanamoku, Sheriff* (327 U.S. 304, 1946) cited section 5 of the Hawaiian Organic Act, which declares that the Constitution of the United States has "the same effect within said Territory as elsewhere in the United States." The war was now well past, and the Court declared that the suspension of normal judicial processes had been unlawful. The Organic Act of 1900, it found, did not authorize the supplanting of civil courts by military tribunals.

In addition to seizing persons, the President as commander-in-chief has also seized property. Six months before Pearl Harbor, while the nation was still officially at peace, President Roosevelt, citing his earlier proclamation of an "unlimited national emergency," seized the strike-bound North American Aviation plant at Inglewood, California. Roosevelt's claim of authority was sweeping and somewhat imprecise—"the duty constitutionally and inherently resting upon the President to exert his civil and military as well as his moral authority to keep the defense efforts of the United States a going concern," and "to obtain supplies for which Congress has appropriated money, and which it has directed the President to obtain." Both before and after the United States became a belligerent, Roosevelt seized other aircraft plants, shipyards, and a railroad.

The most serious legal challenge of the President's authority was levied by Montgomery Ward and Company, the giant mail-order house, with three factories, seventy thousand employees, and seventy million customers, who purchased everything from auto parts to boots and shoes. Montgomery Ward was racked with waves of labor troubles and work stoppages until the entire enterprise was seized by Presidential order. The resulting litigation had enormous implications. Montgomery Ward was not a "war industry" in the manner of the shipyards and aircraft plants previously seized. It was consumer-oriented; if the President could seize it, he could conceivably take over much of the economy.

The principal judicial pronouncement in the Ward situation occurred in the Federal Circuit Court of Appeals (*U.S.* v. *Montgomery Ward and Company,* 150 F. (2nd) 369, 1945, C.C.A., 7th). The United States contended that both as commander-in-chief and as executor of the War Labor Disputes Act, the President could make the seizure. Montgomery Ward argued that the commander-in-chief clause was strictly a military power and that the War Labor Disputes Act was not intended to authorize the seizure of plants like its own. The circuit court concluded that the act was applicable and did not choose to consider whether the President acting solely as commander-in-chief could make the seizure. A rapprochement between the government and Montgomery Ward precluded a definitive finding by the Supreme Court.

In the Korean conflict President Truman brought down the Supreme Court upon his head when he ordered the seizure of most of the nation's steel mills in the face of a threatened strike, citing "the authority vested in me by the Constitution and laws of the United States." The President ignored the Taft-Hartley Act, which established special procedures for national labor emergencies but did not give him the power of seizure. The Supreme Court in *Youngstown Sheet and Tube Co.* v. *Sawyer* (343 U.S. 579, 1952) ordered the President and his executive colleagues to stay out of the steels mills, holding that in seizing them he had seized legislative power. Only Congress could have ordered the mills seized; the President lacked power to seize them without its authorization. Like the *Milligan* case, this hastily improvised opinion throws a lasting shadow of doubt over the President's independent seizure power.

Labor too has felt the pressure of the commander-in-chief power. In World War II the President by executive order created a War Manpower Commission to manage the mobilization of manpower for employment in the war production industries. Later Roosevelt added to the commission's province the administration of the Selective Service System. The WMC was not long in issuing a "work or fight" order requiring all workers designated as "non-deferable," or those engaged in "nonessential" enterprise, to choose between induction into the armed services and transfer to war production jobs. Draft requirements were simultaneously lowered, and the nation's workers faced a categorical choice: work in a war plant or be drafted into the armed forces.

◇

IN THE era since World War II, the President's responsibilities as commander-in-chief have been compounded in urgency and complexity. International Communism asserts its formidable challenge; the United States' strength and resources thrust upon it unavoidable responsibilities of global and interplanetary dimension. The destructive capacity of military weapons has soared to almost incomprehensible extremes. The mountainous tasks implicit in these developments have fallen mainly upon the chief executive. Not the least of the novelties he has had to cope with are the unorthodox methods of warfare, infiltration, and take-over contrived by Communist operatives. He has faced large-scale "police action," or undeclared war, in Korea, civil war in Greece, guerilla war in South

Vietnam, insurrection in the Canal Zone, a Communist revolution in Cuba, and Communist infiltration and threatened take-over in other lands. Presidents have committed American forces to combat, as in Korea, and they have sent "advisers" to train loyal South Vietnamese and apparently fight side by side with them. The President oversees vast programs of military and economic aid to nations around the globe, particularly on the Communist periphery. He engages in a range of other acts of fluctuating subtlety and urgency to stem the Communist tide.

Something of the possibilities of Presidential method in the face of Communist manipulation is conveyed by President Eisenhower's moves to foil a take-over in Guatemala in 1954. In that brief drama's early stage, a ship bearing two thousands tons of small arms, ammunition, and light artillery pieces manufactured in the Skoda arms factory in Czechoslovakia, a quantity far beyond Guatemala's normal military requirements, was bound for that country. Nicaragua, alarmed at Communist infiltration from neighboring Guatemala, broke off relations. Guatemala's pro-Communist government suspended constitutional rights, made mass arrests, and killed the leaders of the political opposition. To offset the incoming Czech weaponry, the Eisenhower administration flew arms into Honduras and Nicaragua, threw up a naval quarantine around the beleaguered countries, and detained in the port of Hamburg, Germany, still another shipment of arms destined for Guatemala. Forces led by Carlos Castillo Armas, a former Guatemalan colonel, crossed from Honduras into his country and made good progress until he lost two of his three bombers. President Eisenhower, mindful of Latin-American sensitivities and taking anxious counsel, decided to replace the planes. The existing pro-Communist government was soon deposed, and a new anti-Communist ruling junta was established under the watchful eyes of United States Ambassador Peurifoy, with Colonel Armas at its head.

President Kennedy imparted some novel twists to the craft of revolutionary overthrow in the abortive invasion of Cuba in 1961. What distinguished the Cuban enterprise was that its base was on American soil and that the United States government was intimately involved in its decisions. The initial preparation of the invading force of a thousand and more exiled Cubans was undertaken by the Eisenhower administration in its twilight days. The invaders were trained under United States auspices in Guatemala and they used staging bases in Nicaragua. They were outfitted with United States aerial bombs, rockets, ammunition, and firearms. Their transports were equipped with guns and radar in New Orleans. The invasion plan was prepared by United States military experts; D-day was known in advance and approved by President Kennedy. He delimited the United States' relation to the project when he declared in a public statement, "There will not be, under any conditions, an intervention in Cuba by United States armed forces." When the invasion, in its desperate hour, faced collapse without United States cover and logistical support, it was not forthcoming. The President held to his word, and the ill-conceived venture failed.

◇

IN ANOTHER major response to the division between the Western and Communist worlds, the President is heavily engaged as a builder and custodian of alliances. He and his deputies have constructed bilateral alliances with nations around the world, committing money, technicians, armaments, and even American soldiers. He has played a leading role in the founding of such multilateral alliances as NATO (North Atlantic Treaty Organization), SEATO (Southeast Asia), CENTO (Central or Middle East), and OAS (Organization of American States or Latin America). He is a regular participant in the top-level annual NATO conference. He buoys up the alliances when their inspiration lags in seasons of Communist quiet, and enheartens them when disaster threatens. He views alliances at times as a step to world community, a vehicle for advancing objectives urgent for all mankind. He and his fellow chief executives are restrained and goaded in the common task by the pressures of their inescapable domestic political necessities. The promise and frustration alliances hold for American chief executives are illustrated by several encounters President Kennedy experienced with allies.

Kennedy included among his objectives the adoption by the United States and its allies of efficient and economical American-built weapons systems. He also worked mightily to forestall individual European nations from building their own nuclear weapons, but proposed that their development and use be integrated into the NATO alliance. Kennedy, whose keen sense of political realism extended to the international plane, took up his task conscious that "you can't possibly carry out any policy without causing major frictions."

Kennedy and his principles were severely tested in his confrontation with British Prime Minister Macmillan at their Nassau meeting in the Bahamas in December 1962. The subject of discussion was Skybolt, a thousand-mile nuclear-tipped missile launched from high-speed bombers. In a conference with President Eisenhower at Camp David in 1959, Macmillan had arranged for the purchase of one hundred Skybolts at a relatively low price for delivery in 1964. The United States Air Force's candidate for the top weapons vehicle of the next generation, Skybolt was being developed in competition with Polaris and Minuteman. Relying upon Skybolt, the British abandoned their own Blue Streak, a land-based missile, in 1960. The Kennedy administration, faced with climbing weapons costs, decided to abandon Skybolt and concentrate upon other weapons systems. The land-based Minuteman, tests proved, could reach any Skybolt target from underground launching silos in the United States. The administration felt that Minuteman plus Polaris, a submarine-launched missile, would satisfy both American and allied needs for long-range weapons. Abandoning Skybolt would slow the big weapons drain on the United States budget, a major consideration with the Presidential election of 1964 approaching, and, if the British could be induced to accept Polaris, Kennedy could advance another valued objective: the vesting of nuclear weapons not in individual nations, but in the trust of alliances to which the United States belonged.

At Nassau, Kennedy gave Macmillan the tidings that Skybolt would be no more and proposed instead that Britain adopt Polaris within a framework of NATO control. Macmillan apparently had little forewarning of the proposal, the President and his aides having just emerged from the engrossing Cuban crisis. The Skybolt cancellation was a hard blow to the Royal Air Force and its manned bomber. It was bad budget news for Macmillan because Skybolt, coupled with existing British bombers, was the cheapest possible way of maintaining an independent British deterrent. The cancellation also had implications for British domestic politics. Several days before venturing to Nassau, Macmillan had been a supplicant at the court of Charles de Gaulle, seeking entry to the European Common Market. The Prime Minister suffered the political ignominy of rebuff. At Nassau, with Kennedy's sudden confrontation, he was threatened with a second major political defeat. His party's fortunes were already badly in eclipse at home and an election was impending. Looming political disaster brought Macmillan to drop his accustomed Edwardian gentility and roar back at his Presidential antagonist. But Kennedy held fast and offered Polaris to the British at the lowest possible price, with the proviso that although the missiles would operate under NATO, they would pass under British command in "supreme national" emergency. Macmillan ultimately acquiesced, enabling Kennedy to improve his budgetary position and advance his purpose of internationalizing nuclear weapons.

Kennedy's policy of nuclear interdependence fared less well with another traditional American ally, France. His careful and reasoned arguments were repulsed by the imperial personality of President Charles de Gaulle. Bent upon restoring French grandeur and perhaps upon asserting his own, De Gaulle was not one to work easily in alliance. Kennedy meanwhile pushed his policy to the point of withholding American aid for French nuclear ambitions. But the Kennedy policy was not all of one piece. His administration delivered to the French an atomic-powered submarine, promised by the Eisenhower administration, and a dozen aerial tankers of the KC-130 type, capable of refueling French bombers that could be armed with nuclear weapons. The Kennedy administration termed these concessions "peripheral" (its standard term for retreats from major objectives) and a sensible recognition of France's commitment to an independent nuclear policy.

As leader of alliances, the President has the unhappy task of prodding laggard member nations to honor their obligations. President Kennedy had several sharp encounters with the Diefenbaker government of Canada over its failure to act upon commitments under the American-Canadian military alliance. Canada had never fulfilled a 1958 agreement with the United States to install nuclear warheads on Bomarc missiles at two sites on Canadian soil. Canada likewise had not acted upon her NATO obligation to equip her interceptor squadrons in Europe with nuclear weapons. Canada's lapses brought Kennedy to permit hostile expressions from his own State Department and the NATO commander, General Lauris Norstad.

But if the President gives criticism, he is also the object of it and the suspicions and resentments of his country's allies. West Germany, fearful of any weakening of western military defenses in Berlin, was privately distressed and required considerable reassurance in mid-1963 after the United States removed six hundred troops from its West Berlin garrison. The United States' Asiatic allies are often critical that it overconcentrates upon Europe to the neglect of the East. Pakistan openly charged in 1963 that the United States was indifferent to CENTO, in contrast to NATO, upon which it showered its treasure and concern.

◇

T H E President bears the awesome responsibility to our allies, to his own people, indeed to all mankind, of deciding when if ever to use the vast arsenal of American nuclear weaponry. Under law only he, the commander-in-chief, can give the order. He has done so on but one occasion—near the end of World War II, when Truman ordered atomic bombs to be dropped on Hiroshima and Nagasaki in 1945. Later Presidents have threatened to use nuclear weapons. In 1953 President Eisenhower threatened Communist China with nuclear attack unless she supported a truce in Korea. In his 1962 confrontation with the Soviets over their emplacement of offensive missiles in Cuba, President Kennedy put the Strategic Air Command and Air Force missile crews on maximum alert. One hundred fifty-six intercontinental ballistic missiles, based in the western part of the nation and with flight ranges of at least six thousand three hundred miles, were readied and pointed presumably at the Soviet Union, if the President's speech to the nation on October 22 is a guide. Kennedy then warned, "It shall be the policy of this nation to regard any nuclear missile launched from Cuba against any nation in the Western Hemisphere as an attack on the United States requiring a full retaliatory response upon the Soviet Union."

In facing his responsibility for nuclear weapons, the chief executive has been absorbed in two concerns. One is keeping the ultimate decision in his own hands. "I don't want some young Colonel to decide when to drop an atomic bomb," President Truman was known to say. The other is the avoidance of the dread possibility of an "accidental" nuclear war. Both problems thrust the President well into a complex of mechanisms and procedures regulating the release of nuclear weapons.

The complex begins at BMEWS (Ballistic Missile Early Warning System) in Thule, Greenland, where radar screens are poised to pick up Soviet missiles, if they are ever launched against the United States. BMEWS intelligence is simultaneously flashed to NORAD (North American Air Defense Command) in Colorado Springs, Colorado, for interpretation; to the SAC (Strategic Air Command) command and control post near Omaha, Nebraska; to the Joint War Room of the Joint Chiefs of Staff in the Pentagon; and to the President. Several kinds of radio systems, telephones, teletypes, and television link these points. Alternate locations; multiple routings, frequencies, and circuits; verifications by senders and recipients that the messages actually come from their presumed source; procedures to challenge and counterchallenge the verifications; hundreds of men to pass the word to the button-pushers, who also number in the hundreds, all contribute to the vast effort to find safety.

The policy-makers, generals, psychologists, sociologists, and physicists charged with tightening the safety factor must deal with several types of possible human failure. Elaborate testing and "redundancy" procedures help thwart the kind of situation which arose in 1958 when a berserk sergeant threatened to fire a pistol at a nuclear bomb, but was fortunately talked out of it by a supervisor. Suppose the President of the United States "goes ape," as the military say? Or suppose he singlehandedly decides to reverse national policy and launch a preventive war? The President too is subject to checks. Even he cannot simply pick up his telephone and order "go," nor does he know the one signal for a nuclear strike—the "go code." In an emergency he would receive intelligence via the "gold phone circuit" which connects him with the offices, action stations, and homes of the Secretary of Defense, the Joint Chiefs of Staff, the SAC commander, and others, all of whom could assist in his decision. An agenda with key questions concerning the probable emergency has been prepared, which could be administered quickly and in code.

Time is a slight safety factor. In the existing state of weapons systems, the President has a possible thirty minutes after the report of launched enemy ICBM's to consult and await further information before unleashing a full, irrevocable "go" order.

Suppose the President is out of reach, dead, or believed dead? Moments after President Kennedy's assassination, the Pentagon put into effect a system by which, law or no law, the "go" order could have been issued by the Secretary of Defense or the Joint Chiefs of Staff.

Chief executives have been concerned with several species of non-Presidential safety factors. President Kennedy asked for more funds from Congress to speed movements across the whole gamut of warning systems. He pushed construction of the Polaris and hardened Minutemen capable of withstanding surprise attack, thus reducing the need for a hair-trigger response to enemy actions. Kennedy arranged the "hot line" to Moscow to deal with breakdowns and miscalculations of the kind featured in the novel *Fail-Safe*. The Kennedy administration also instituted a new lock system for the nation's huge and far-flung nuclear weapons arsenal. Through remote-control devices comparable to those used on ordinary television sets, officials at central locations can control the many thousands of United States nuclear warheads around the world that are in stockpiles or attached to weapons maintained in a continuing alert status. In his further notable efforts to reduce the risks of nuclear war, Kennedy consummated the 1963 test ban treaty with the Soviet Union and labored tirelessly, although unsuccessfully, to dissuade the French from building their own nuclear forces.

❖

A MAJOR by-product of the President's preoccupation with nuclear weapons is his deepening relationships with the scientific community. The capability of his military establishment depends increasingly upon the efficiency of their research; in hard decisions he looks for their counsel. Scientists were consulted when President Truman weighed how he would use the newly developed atomic bomb. Then, as they often have been in facing momentous Presidential issues, the scientists were divided. Some advocated a purely technical demonstration, others a military application best designed to induce Japanese surrender.

Scientists, like the President they serve, have lived in the coils of a continuing predicament. They spend their lives improving the United States' weapon capability, but they feel conscience-bound to reduce the possibilities that the terrible weapons will ever be used. Scientists counseled the President when he took his first steps toward committing the United States to the international control of atomic weapons. The Truman-Atlee-King declaration of November 15, 1945, resulted, which called upon the United Nations Organization to establish a commission to develop proposals to promote peaceful uses of atomic energy, eliminate nuclear weapons, and foster an open world. The declaration was prepared by Vannevar Bush, Director of the Office of Scientific Research and

Development, with the help of Niels Bohr, Leo Szilard, and other scientists.

The Soviet's development of an atomic bomb in 1949 hurtled the scientists and the President into a formidable new issue. Should the United States, in the face of the Soviet achievement, forge ahead in the race by developing a hydrogen bomb? The President again received divided scientific counsel. One sector of scientific opinion deemed the bomb both feasible and necessary to the nation's security. Another opinion urged the President "to tell the American public and the world that we think [it] wrong on fundamental ethical principles to initiate the development of such a weapon." America's abstention, these scientists also argued, would set an example which might limit the extent of war and raise the hope of mankind. President Truman ultimately ordered the development of the hydrogen bomb.

The Soviet's atomic achievements also thrust the President into a difficult and at times agonizing new relationship with scientists. He had to determine at times whether particular scientists were "security risks" and therefore should be barred from access to classified government information. After 1949 the suspicions of legislators and administrators of the loyalty of scientists rose markedly. Late in 1953 William L. Borden, a former executive staff director of the Congressional Joint Committee on Atomic Energy, wrote to FBI Director J. Edgar Hoover that it was his "own exhaustively considered opinion, based upon years of study, of the available classified evidence, that more probably than not J. Robert Oppenheimer is an agent of the Soviet Union." An FBI report on Dr. Oppenheimer was prepared and ultimately forwarded to President Eisenhower. "This report," he has written, "jolted me." The President, after consultations, directed that sensitive agencies were to erect at once a "blank wall" between Dr. Oppenheimer and classified information. With the President's approval, a three-man board headed by Gordon Gray, president of the University of North Carolina, was appointed to conduct a hearing. The hearing drew upon forty witnesses and produced three thousand pages of testimony. By a vote of two to one the Gray board found Dr. Oppenheimer a security risk, although a loyal citizen. The Atomic Energy Commission, Dr. Oppenheimer's employer, approved the Gray board's finding by a vote of four to one. President Eisenhower concurred in the finding and Dr. Oppenheimer's clearance was not reinstated.

But the President not only taketh away; he also giveth. Shortly before his death President Kennedy concluded plans for a White House ceremony for the presentation of the Enrico Fermi award to Dr. Oppenheimer for his "outstanding contributions to theoretical physics and his scientific and administrative leadership." When Kennedy's assassination intervened, President Johnson made the presentation in an early act of office-holding, to the satisfaction of many in the scientific community, who had long been seeking a symbolic clearance of Dr. Oppenheimer's name.

Before the Soviet's launching of Sputnik, the President, for all of the importance of science in national life, had no regular, full-time scientific staff in his White House organization. In the wake of Sputnik the post of Special Assistant to the President for Science and Technology was created, with James Killian, President of the Massachusetts Institute of Technology, as the first incumbent. The existing Science Advisory Committee was brought to the White House level. President Eisenhower was soon turning to his scientific associates for alternative advice to the views of the Pentagon and Atomic Energy Commission. In Eisenhower's closing Presidential years, his scientific counselors debated intensively the scientific feasibility and the political desirability of a nuclear test ban. Ultimately Eisenhower, spurred by certain scientific advisers and Secretary of State Dulles, embarked upon negotiations for a nuclear test ban agreement, a major reversal in American nuclear policy which was finally consummated in the test ban treaty of President Kennedy.

In the test ban venture scientists served Presidents Eisenhower and Kennedy as both negotiators and counselors. Eisenhower dispatched a scientific delegation to Geneva in mid-1958 to meet with their British and Russian counterparts and consider methods for policing a nuclear test ban. Out of their work emerged Eisenhower's proposal on August 22, 1958, that the three nuclear powers negotiate a treaty for the permanent suspension of nuclear weapon testing. To provide himself with continual advice on test ban problems, Eisenhower appointed a Committee of Principals—outside the National Security Council, interestingly—whose membership included the Special Assistant for Science and Technology plus the heads of State, the CIA, Defense, and the AEC.

Although the Eisenhower disarmament effort ended in an impasse, President Kennedy, upon entering office, resolved to try again and convened a panel of scientists under James Fisk, President of Bell Laboratories, to evaluate the American position and recommend modifications. Out of Fisk's panel and the work of the President's Disarmament Adviser, John J. McCloy, came a draft treaty. The awakening hopes were crushed when the Soviet resumed its testing program and soon, at Kennedy's order, the United States did likewise. For this new situation the President again needed scientific counsel. Had the self-imposed moratorium on American testing enabled the Soviets to overcome the American lead in nuclear weapons? The finding that the American lead was intact although reduced encouraged Kennedy to pursue the test ban treaty. As the negotiations advanced, Kennedy like Eisenhower was faced with absolute cleavage within the scientific community on the technical feasibility of a control system to monitor a nuclear test ban. Ultimately, Kennedy drove himself to choose between the conflicting schools. Presidents, with their ample experiences of the fifties and sixties, would readily concur with C. P. Snow that decision-making in the modern scientific world is "one of the most intractable that organized society has thrown up." Although scientists have not provided neat, reassuring guideposts in Presidential policy-making in the field of nuclear weapons, they have achieved a full partnership with political administrators and the military.

◊

IT IS debatable whether President Lyndon Johnson, for all of his riches in terrible weapons, has more self-determining military power than such predecessors of his as Theodore Roosevelt and James K. Polk. The contemporary President suffers limitations of power unknown to nineteenth- and early-twentieth-century incumbents. He must work with allies whose good will must be courted and whose favor fluctuates. His acts are challengeable in an ongoing world organization, the United Nations. Earlier Presidents suffered neither of these fetters. Because of the sheer horror of nuclear weapons, the contemporary President is conscience- and duty-bound to leave nothing undone to avoid general war. This solemn obligation requires him to protect national security by toiling diligently even at unpromising negotiations and to resort to force only in the most extreme urgency. He lives with the haunting realization that the merest local incidents can escalate into situations of worldwide importance. His predecessors worried little over such subtleties. Theodore Roosevelt could truthfully boast, "I took Panama." Lyndon Johnson, facing civil disorder in the Canal Zone that Theodore Roosevelt would have quashed by sending out troops, put his main reliance upon discussion, restraint, and judicious criticism of Canal Zone Americans. The students at Cristobal High School, he said, should not have run up the American flag.

As commanders-in-chief, future Presidents will face the test of the adequacy of their powers and their adaptability to fast-changing world realities as never before.

1. The commander-in-chief must now and hereafter be both strong and restrained. His most solemn duty is to maintain his nuclear power and the general military establishment in a state of strength that will effectively deter the rival camp. Not only must he possess this strength, but he must communicate its true degree intelligibly and convincingly at home and abroad. But his companion duty is to keep his nuclear power in check, to avoid the appearance of bomb-rattling, and to press simultaneously for the settlement of international differences through diplomatic negotiation.

2. The President will face the continuing question of "How much is enough?" in developing the nation's armed strength. His answers to this question involve him with Congress, the allied powers, and his own scientific and military communities. It is the weightiest question our political system imposes upon the fragile structure of President-Congress relations. The question admits of no single answer, but evokes many responses. At one extreme is the tendency of Presidents of the nuclear age to appreciate that missile production too has diminishing returns; President Johnson has expressed the view that nuclear defense expenditures can never be justified as a grand relief project for the economies of local communities and the states. At an opposite extreme is Secretary of Defense McNamara's 1964 testimony to the House Foreign Affairs Committee that Congress had jeopardized the nation's security in cutting the foreign aid program of the year before by 30 per cent. Both Democratic and Republican committee members were understandably stung by the secretary's implication that Congress had acted irresponsibly and could not be relied on to provide an adequate military program.

3. It has never been more urgent for the President to demonstrate to our allies and competitors that the President is truly the commander-in-chief, supported by the vast Department of Defense, by a Joint Chiefs of Staff of high competence, and by the houses of Congress. Only a strong President can rise to and hold such dominance. To be strong he clearly requires a strong Secretary of Defense, his chief deputy, whose powers have steadily increased since the office began in 1947. The JCS have seen a limited increase in the powers of their chairman, though their relations with the President have been uneven. Any tendency toward a still more powerful chairman, even perhaps a single chief of staff, would sizably strengthen the President's position as organizer and director of the armed forces. Likewise would the reduction of the Army, Navy, and Air Force from their present departmental status to the status of services within the Defense Department, much as the Marine Corps functions at present within the Navy Department.

4. The Pentagon's power to issue the "go" order for nuclear war in a situation like the first minutes following Kennedy's situation, when the Presidency is briefly disorganized, needs to be revised in the interest of sound democratic procedure. The memorandum of understanding, discussed in Chapter 4 between Presidents Eisenhower, Kennedy, and Johnson and their next-in-line successors in cases of Presidential inability, should be extended to cover the "go" order problem when the President is out of reach, dead, or believed dead.

5. The limitation of the arms race through international agreement will remain a large preoccupation of the President. Only a strong chief executive can press the case upon Congress and the people that a spiraling

arms race is a threat to the nation's security. The individual services and the Congressional committees to which they are allied will provide a fierce resistance that only the chief executive can overcome. He alone can keep alive useful proposals that at first are rejected and assure that new possibilities are considered. The commander-in-chief does not simply conduct war or stay prepared for the threat of it. He has a further mission upon which the nation's and the world's future depends: the commander-in-chief also keeps the peace.

CHAPTER

11

The Economy

———

THE President is head of the economic administration of the country.
He applies quantities of laws promoting, regulating, and planning economic affairs. The Employment Act of 1946, a grand codification of his
responsibilities, broadly charges him to lay before Congress each January
an economic report on levels and trends of production, employment, and
purchasing power, and to recommend ways to stimulate them. He col-
lects taxes to provide roads, airports, research, and other services vital
to industry. Thanks to its military needs, the executive branch which the
President manages is the nation's largest purchaser. The aircraft and
shipping industries would indeed be in a parlous state were not the United
States government their best customer. Through loans and guarantees
administered by the Commodity Credit Corporation, the Federal Housing Authority, the Federal Deposit Insurance Corporation, and other vast
agencies the President reduces or erases the risk to private enterprise. As
administrator of the Social Security programs, he softens the cruelties
of unemployment, illness, and old age. In the nearly two centuries of his
office's existence, the chief executive has in fact presided over a variety
of economies, including simple agricultural, industrial, financial, and
state capitalism. He has lived through the scientific and technological
revolution of the mid-twentieth century, and its crowning feature, automation, may well require him to face basic changes in social attitudes
toward work and leisure. In that great and difficult event, the President
will rightly be expected to provide leadership.

As head of the nation's economic administration, the chief executive possesses only limited power. He presides over a pluralistic economy in which private enterprise makes the key decisions of what and how much to produce, when and at what price, and how profits shall be used. The extent of private decision is evidenced by the gap which may exist between what the President tries to do and what he accomplishes. The President can toil, plan, and hope for prosperity, but there may be only depression. He can thunder against the trusts, but big enterprise grows apace. He can come into office pledged to get the country "moving again," but for all his exertion the economy only lags.

The several administrative agencies of the executive branch dealing with the economy differ widely in their responsiveness to the President. A Bureau of the Budget and a Council of Economic Advisers are *his* agencies and behave accordingly. The great operating departments—Treasury, Commerce, Labor, and Agriculture—are part of his cabinet family and partners to large and intimate decisions of his administration. An array of independent regulatory commissions—the Federal Reserve Board, the Securities and Exchange Commission, the Interstate Commerce Commission, and the like—make basic decisions in vital economic areas such as banking and credit, transportation, communications, the sale of securities, and the conduct of the stock exchanges. The independent commissions are carefully removed from the President's line of command. He has influence but lacks authority over them.

The limitations of his economic powers enthrone the President on the jagged prongs of a predicament. His authority over the economy does not equal his responsibility for its condition. Legally and administratively, he has important but severely limited means to influence its health and growth. As Martin Van Buren and Herbert Hoover would gladly have testified on the election nights of 1840 and 1932, the voters hold the chief executives responsible for the plight of their jobs and their pocketbooks above all else.

◇

PRESIDENTS as a lot assume that harmony and confidence between government and business are profitable to both. This benign assumption burns weakest in economic depression and brightest in war, when the nation's survival depends upon coordinated public and private economic effort. Presidents, for all their good intentions, differ widely in their individual dispositions toward business. Calvin Coolidge's worshipful dictum "The business of America is business" bespeaks his administration's total dedication to facilitating business. No President can be said to be anti-business. Franklin D. Roosevelt, who waged fierce struggles to reform the worst business malpractices and said harsh things about "economic royalists" and "unscrupulous money-changers," accepted the basic structure and premises of the business community. "I am certain," his Secretary of Labor, Frances Perkins, well observed, "that he had no dream of great changes in the economic or political patterns of our life." Roosevelt limited his rejection of private enterprise to TVA and several sister projects in the belief that popular and business power needs could not be adequately supplied by private means. He apparently never wished government to take over the railroads, the coal mines, or any other basic industry. He considered government ownership both clumsy and unnecessary.

Republican Presidents view business fondly and their modern Democratic brethren tend to be critical, but John Kennedy fell somewhere in between. His treatment of business was studiously conciliatory. His angry confrontation of the United States Steel Corporation in the 1962 price crisis and his antitrust prosecutions of steel companies in 1963 were exceptions. In lieu of innovating tough regulatory policies in the New Deal tradition, the Kennedy administration concentrated upon objectives calculated to make the generality of business rejoice and thrive. In 1962 Kennedy focused upon balancing the budget and pushing through the Foreign Trade Expansion Act. His foremost economic priority for 1963 was reducing corporate and personal income taxes. Kennedy scrupulously abided by his 1961 pledge that the federal government would not undertake new electric power projects without compelling reason, a policy more akin to Eisenhower's than to Truman's or Franklin Roosevelt's.

The President's relations with the components of the business community may differ widely at any one time. The community is not a monolith but a sprawling, continental, indeed intercontinental, pluralism whose members' interests differ markedly by region (Wall Street and the East versus the West), by size (big, intermediate, and small business), and by function (manufacture, wholesale, and retail). A single industry may contain both "liberal" enterprises which are public-minded and public-relations conscious and "conservative" enterprises whose self-interest blinds them to national necessity and who habitually fight governmental regulation in Congress and the courts. Presidents are wily enough to exploit business differences. The easiest and most commonly employed tactic is to pursue policies that appeal to the many and offend the few in the business community. In launching his famous antitrust suit against the Northern Securities Company, a giant consolidation of the James J. Hill, J. P. Morgan, and E. H. Harriman railways, which embraced nothing less than the Northern Pacific, the Great Northern, and the Chicago, Burlington, and Quincy systems, Theodore Roosevelt scored a ten-strike in the esteem of the majority of the business world. They hailed Roosevelt's crusade joyfully because the Northern Securities Company was the outcome of a massive struggle between Morgan and Harriman on which most businessmen blamed the panic of 1901.

By word and deed the business community bestows its approval or disfavor upon the Presidents. The United States Steel Corporation abstained from raising its prices in the eight Presidential years of Dwight Eisenhower, but boosted them twice during the three years of John Kennedy. The New Deal's cleansing and chastising of business created a lasting embitterment. No President has been more widely hated in the upper economic stratum than Franklin Roosevelt was. Visitors to J. P. Morgan in New Deal days were forewarned against mentioning the Roosevelt name lest it launch the mighty financier into apoplectic rage.

◊

PRESIDENTS hankering to rouse business confidence in their administrations apply a variety of old and proven nostrums. A standard remedy is the appointment of businessmen to responsible administration posts. Even Presidents like the Roosevelts, with large reputations for ferocity toward business, carefully provided "balance" in their administrations by including prestigious businessmen in them. Franklin Roosevelt counted heavily upon Jesse H. Jones, chairman of the Reconstruction Finance Corporation, to maintain an image of respectability in the eyes of the business community. A wealthy, monumental Texan who had built a fortune in the grand manner in banking, real estate, and newspapers, Jones was a paragon by business standards. The price of his services came high, but Roosevelt cheerfully paid it. "Whenever we did anything of importance, that was on the borderline of our authority," Jones said once in explaining the ground rules at RFC, "I would try at first opportunity to tell the President about it, but after the fact. He was always interested, and he never criticized." Roosevelt, in turn, never failed to appreciate the usefulness of Jones's gilt-edged prestige with business and Congress. "Your conservatism is a good thing for us in this Administration," the President would reassure the great Texan.

Several officials in the Kennedy administration approximated Jones's role with Roosevelt. One was C. Douglas Dillon, the Secretary of the Treasury, a Republican board chairman of the distinguished Wall Street investment house of Dillon, Read & Co. and Undersecretary of State for Economic Affairs in the Eisenhower administration. Dillon's appointment gave joy and comfort to the business community even as it brought pain to Senator Albert Gore, progressive Democrat of Tennessee. Dillon's nomination, Gore wrote anxiously to Kennedy when it was contemplated, "would be a signal that you had given up the goals of a truly Democratic Administration in domestic affairs and, consequently, the progress necessary to restore United States position and prestige abroad."

It "would mean . . . that . . . economic policies would not be very different from the present [Eisenhower] administration."

In cultivating business confidence, Presidents work hard at tilling an image of fiscal responsibility. When national circumstances force the budget into imbalance, Presidents, with the aid of wizard-technicians of the fiscal arts, resort to elaborate hocus-pocus to maintain at least the window-dressing of fiscal respectability. For example, in his early Presidential years Franklin Roosevelt could face the nation with a balanced budget by the simple expedient of putting his costly recovery programs into a separate account. Even Democratic Presidents with solid reputations as big spenders put in hours of anxious cogitation in choosing between launching a costly program and suppressing it in the interest of fiscal soundness. The President's attention to economy may be as much a reflection of personal conviction as it is of deliberate public relations. Franklin Roosevelt was viewed by several of his colleagues as perpetually torn between two contending forces in his Presidential psyche. His natural instinct tended to fiscal tidiness and a balanced budget; he wished also, during the depression's depths, to do right by the unemployed. As plans were laid for work relief and social security, the question he was most apt to ask with unfeigned anxiety was, "Will it ruin us financially?" Invariably he included among his counselors those whose lives represented an unbroken consecration to conventional fiscal policy. Lewis Douglas, Director of the Budget, chanted the virtues of the balanced budget and a Hoover-like program of subsistence relief, with wages, hours, and prices shaped by natural economic forces. When Douglas eventually departed, Henry Morgenthau, as Secretary of the Treasury, made temperate public spending his special cause.

A President may keep business confidence at high flame by fraternizing with leading businessmen conspicuously more than with any other species of citizenry. The guests most frequently invited to President Eisenhower's stag dinners, a social function with incidental discussion of the administration's purposes, were businessmen. In his hours on the golf course Eisenhower's favorite companions were George E. Allen, a puckish corporation director; William E. Robinson, president of Coca-Cola; and Clifford G. Roberts, a New York banker. William Howard Taft had a similar hankering for businessmen, particularly those of the uppermost echelons. Taft once spent a golfing vacation with a procession of partners, beginning with Henry C. Frick, chairman of the Carnegie Steel Company, who was followed by J. P. Morgan, the peerless magnate; Nelson W. Aldrich, big business's ambassador plenipotentiary to the United States Senate; and other tycoons. Not surprisingly, political progressives around the country began to mutter darkly that the President and the ultraconservatives were uniting in common cause.

A President and his aides may seek to rally the business community behind their cause by wooing it with speeches. During his first year in office Kennedy waged a campaign of proportions unequaled in Presidential history to induce industry's cooperation in his efforts to maintain stable prices, without which he could not hope to secure labor's vital support in paring down its wage and fringe demands. Business could swallow the bitter price medicine more easily if it were sweetened with evidences of the administration's general concern for its interests. This was no small order for a latter-day Democratic Presidency, but the Kennedy administration met the challenge head on. In the single month of October 1961, for example, the President dispatched his aides far and wide for speeches before management gatherings to demonstrate that his administration was not antibusiness but brimmed with sympathetic understanding of business problems. Interlarded with these most gratifying expressions was the administration's price message. Within a single week Treasury Secretary Dillon in San Francisco renewed the promise of a balanced budget for 1962–63 and at Hot Springs reaffirmed the administration's good will to a gathering of top-drawer corporation executives. In Chicago Commerce Secretary Hodges prophesied a series of government actions long clamored for by the business and financial worlds. To the Illinois Chamber of Commerce in Chicago Labor Secretary Goldberg explained that the administration's recent extension of unemployment benefits was not really to be interpreted as "pro" or "anti" anything but only "pro" the national interest and incidentally providing money "to help keep alive many businessmen in stricken communities." In New York Undersecretary of the Treasury Fowler assured the American Retail Federation that business's long yearnings for better depreciation allowances under the tax laws would soon be realized.

Presidential speeches to business organizations are a kind of barometer of the state of relations between the two camps. Franklin Roosevelt's addresses to the United States Chamber of Commerce in his early Presidential years accurately charted his deteriorating standing with the business community. In 1933, when the National Recovery Act was in high gear to the general satisfaction of business, the Chamber gave Roosevelt a rising ovation. By 1934, when administration policies had assumed a sterner aspect, the Chamber's delegates felt so alienated that the President wisely decided not to address them in person, but sent a not unfriendly message. In 1935 there was no Presidential appearance, no Presidential message, not even a Presidential greeting.

A President may cultivate business by consulting it on problems and policies of mutual concern. In 1962, following his head-on collision with the United States Steel Corporation over its rising prices, which had resulted in part at least from a failure in business-government communications, Kennedy moved to avoid any similar lapses in the future by establishing a Business Council. The President took up with the council, composed of the presidents and chairmen of large corporations, such knotty problems as the balance of payments and the outflow of gold. One year after the steel price encounter, Kennedy could view with high satisfaction the testimony of corporate executives at the council's meetings at Hot Springs that they were less nervous about business-government relations than they had been at any time since his inauguration.

◇

MUCH of the President's economic policy may advance both the President's and business's purposes. The income tax, established by amendment in 1913, is not merely an enormous producer of revenue but a reflector of an administration's underlying economic philosophy and a means of slowing or quickening general economic activity. Presidents Harding, Coolidge, and Hoover were more or less the spokesmen for the view of their Secretary of the Treasury, Andrew Mellon, that "the prosperity of the middle and lower classes depended upon the good fortunes and light taxes of the rich." Taxes that were too high, Mellon believed, would prevent the rich from saving and would make them reluctant to invest. If they failed to save and invest, the economy would ultimately falter. When Mellon took office in 1921, the income tax's top rate was 73 per cent; in 1925, thanks to Mellon's pressure, it was down to 25 per cent. A broader distribution of stimulants was arranged by the Kennedy-Johnson tax-reduction bill enacted in 1964. It was expected by both its Presidential sponsors to stimulate consumer demand and business investment, which in turn would promote increased employment and production, sustain the growth of the economy, and hopefully avert recessions.

Not all taxpayers take the view of Justice Holmes, "I like to pay taxes. With them I buy civilization." The Presidential administration is also the dispenser of special treatment to selected taxpayers (invariably the influential big ones), notwithstanding President Eisenhower's contention that "Every real American is proud to carry his share of the burden." He "doesn't ask for favored protection or treatment." Dispensations, or tax relief based on influence, were a favorite recourse of Secretary Mellon, beginning with his own tax situation. In time he permitted himself such lavish deductions that Senator George W. Norris of Nebraska was brought to exclaim that "Mr. Mellon himself gets a larger personal reduction than the aggregate of practically all the taxpayers in the state of Nebraska." In his first eight years in the Treasury, Secretary Mellon dispensed $3.5 billion in the form of cash refunds, credits, and abatements, while appealing to the generality of citizens to pay their taxes.

The most pervasive of all taxes—the tariff—can also advance or ob-

struct a broad sweep of the President's economic policies. When in 1921
the Republican Congress pushed through an emergency tariff bill raising
the rates to protect the United States against the produce of depressed
European labor, President Wilson declared in a veto, "If there ever was a
time when America had anything to fear from foreign competition, that
time has passed. If we wish to have Europe settle her debts, governmental or commercial, we must be prepared to buy from her." But Wilson's wish was in vain and the Fordney-McCumber Tariff Act of 1922
boosted rates to new highs. Although Presidents Harding and Coolidge
employed their discretionary authority under the act to adjust rates, they
tended to raise them even further. The Fordney Act and its administration fostered the concentration of domestic economic power, prevented
Europe from paying her obligations to the United States in the form of
goods, and brought reprisals from foreign countries.

But discretionary Presidential authority to adjust rates may also promote trade, as demonstrated by the Reciprocal Trade Agreements Act
of 1934, which authorized the President to negotiate with various countries trade agreements altering United States tariffs by not more than
50 per cent. The Trade Expansion Act of 1962 goes even further. It
authorizes the President to cut tariffs in general as much as 50 per cent,
to eliminate tariffs on goods of which the United States and the European
Common Market account for 80 per cent of the free world trade, and
to cancel tariffs on tropical products on which the tariff is no more than
5 per cent of the value. Never before has the President possessed so much
power over foreign trade. The act was designed to help the balance of
payments problem and to open up the Common Market and other countries to American goods, especially farm products.

◊

T H E President's dialogue with business takes on a tougher weave when
he endeavors to persuade the business community to come around to
some action which although vital to national welfare does not altogether
square with business's self-interest. One of the more emphatic passages
of Presidential discourse with private enterprise occurred in 1916, when
a major railroad strike confronted the nation. President Wilson summoned the railroad owners to the White House and eloquently appealed
to them to accept a compromise he had devised to resolve the dispute.
Wilson's formula called for an eight-hour day, no raises, and time and a
half for overtime. For all Wilson's exhortation that his plan was fair and
that the national interest required its acceptance, the railroad owners
were negative and adamant. The President was butting his head against
the rock of Gibraltar. Upon reaching this conclusion, Wilson, not a man
of any great patience, rose from the conference table. His face twisted

with anger, he exclaimed, "I pray to God to forgive you; I never can," and left the room.

A President may also negotiate with individual titans of industry with great consequence to the economy. The most fabulous of these negotiations took place in 1905 between Theodore Roosevelt and the unsurpassed presence J. Pierpont Morgan. Morgan was building his empire with no-holds-barred fury; the administration had mounted its trust-bursting policy; a head-on collision was a matter of time. Morgan decided to talk to Roosevelt. In the lengthy interview Theodore Roosevelt was bemused by the mighty Morgan's notions of the character and status of the United States Presidency. "Mr. Morgan," Roosevelt noted afterward, "could not help regarding me as a big rival operator, who either intended to ruin all his interests, or else could be induced to come to an agreement to ruin none."

The Morgan way of dealing with the United States Presidency came into full play on a January day in 1905 when an official of the Bureau of Corporations of the Department of Commerce and Labor appeared in the offices of Judge Elbert Gary, board chairman of the United States Steel Corporation, a Morgan enterprise, to discuss the bureau's impending investigation of the company. With Morgan's encouragement, the astute Gary, a suave erstwhile judge, arranged a meeting at the White House with Secretary of Commerce Victor H. Metcalf, Commissioner of Corporations James R. Garfield, and Theodore Roosevelt. Gary opened the session by amiably declaring that he would not challenge the constitutionality of the Commerce Department's request that U.S. Steel open its books and records. In return for this benevolence, Gary tactfully invited the administration to pledge that any information gleaned from U.S. Steel's files would be used not by subordinate government officials, but "by the President alone for his guidance in making such suggestions to Congress concerning legislation as might be proper, expedient, and for the actual benefit of the general public." If questions should arise over the use of material that Gary deemed confidential, he, Garfield, and Metcalf would seek agreement, and that failing, the President would decide. A memorandum of the conference was prepared to Theodore Roosevelt's satisfaction.

The Gary-Theodore Roosevelt concordat was put to a test one year later when the administration brought International Harvester, another Morgan company, under scrutiny. Would International Harvester be satisfied with whatever the Commerce Department's findings were, Theodore Roosevelt teasingly asked George W. Perkins, the Morgan representative. Perkins responded uninhibitedly. The company expected, he said, "the Department frankly [to] come to us and point out any mistakes or technical violations of any law; then give us a chance to correct them, if we could or would, and . . . if we did, then we would expect the Attorney General not to bring proceedings." Although Theodore Roosevelt, in ensuing brass-tacks discussions, was somewhat more demanding than Perkins anticipated, International Harvester pretty well passed muster at the White House.

In making secret deals with Morgan and his men, Theodore Roosevelt risked raising the hackles of progressives who surely would interpret his behavior as a betrayal of the people. But Theodore Roosevelt was not merely doling out approval to the Morgan interests. The President was playing a game, too. In arranging secret pacts Theodore Roosevelt was achieving a cherished peace with Wall Street at a juncture when its aid was critical to the advance through Congress of the topmost item of his economic program, the Hepburn railroad bill. Roosevelt also aimed to achieve in the Morgan consultations new and mutually more rewarding government-business dealings than the barren negativism of the Sherman Act had thus far permitted.

◇

WHEN business fails to cooperate or openly fights the President, he may resort to an armory of diverse and potent weapons. A most important one is the whiplash of adverse publicity. When Standard Oil was charged with secretly eliciting lower shipping rates from the railroads to the utter grief of its competitors, Roosevelt accompanied the ponderous government report in which the finding was made with a lusty personal blast at Standard Oil. The President's remarks took on an extra surge of vehemence from his discovery that a glaring national disclosure of Standard's sins would greatly enhance his chances for securing his precious Hepburn railroad bill. President John Archbold of Standard Oil, after several applications of the shrillest Presidential criticism, concluded that "Darkest Abyssinia never saw anything like the course of treatment which we experienced at the hands of the Administration."

At his beck and call the President has scores of statutes enacted over the decades by which he can prod business toward behaving as he wants. One of the President's favorite weapons in moving upon recalcitrant industry are the antitrust laws, beginning with the Sherman Act of 1890. Kennedy, for example, busily used these laws to hold back prices in his fight against inflation. His administration brought case after case against the price-fixing of bakery products, milk, moving vans, building materials, and the like.

The President can also regulate business by drawing upon his "prerogative," or power directly granted him by the Constitution. The most enriching provisions for the prerogative-minded President are the opening clause of Article II ("The Executive power shall be vested in a

President of the United States of America") and his designation as "Commander-in-Chief." Prerogative is usually exerted in crisis, in war or economic decline, and it is often buttressed by statutes delegating broad powers to the President. From World War I on, industry's growing involvement in warmaking has made it the frequent object of Presidential prerogative. On June 7, 1941, six months before the Pearl Harbor attack, for example, Franklin Roosevelt, citing his earlier proclamation of "unlimited national emergency," seized by executive order the strike-bound North American Aviation Plant at Inglewood, California. The executive order pointed to the "duty constitutionally and inherently resting upon the President to exert his civil and military as well as his moral authority to keep the defensive efforts of the United States a going concern" and "to obtain supplies for which Congress has appropriated money, and which it has directed the President to obtain."

The employ of Presidential prerogative in labor-management disputes was set back badly in the Supreme Court's review of President Truman's seizure of the steel industry midway in the Korean "police action" in 1952. In *Youngstown Sheet and Tube Co.* v. *Sawyer* (343 U.S. 579, 1952), the Court struck down the President's action as unconstitutional. The President, in moving upon the steel strike, had relied upon "prerogative" and ignored the Taft-Hartley Act passed by a Republican-controlled Congress in 1947, subjecting Presidential intervention in labor-management disputes to a specified procedure. Truman had vetoed the bill, holding partly that his prerogative was sufficient for labor-management crises. Congress, in turn, overrode his veto and Truman solemnly avowed he would observe the new law. When a steel strike loomed in April 1952, however, the President ignored the Taft-Hartley Act and its eighty-day no-strike provision and, brandishing his prerogative, seized the steel mills. Pointing to the mountainous military requirements of the nation and its allies, he invoked "the authority vested in me by the Constitution and laws of the United States."

The central proposition of the Court's opinion was that since Congress could have ordered seizure of the steel mills, the President lacked the power of seizure without specific legislative authorization. This altogether novel doctrine was unsupported by reference to previous decision or practice. The Court also blithely overlooked innumerable historical instances of Presidential pioneering in territory eventually occupied by Congress, in the manner of President Washington's issuance of the first neutrality proclamation in 1793 and Congress's enactment, a year later, of the first neutrality statute.

In addition to statutes and prerogative, the President can summon a variety of "pressures" to encourage industry's "cooperation." Glimpses into the character of these pressures are provided by President Kennedy's sharp encounter with U.S. Steel in 1962. Eager to hold the steel price line against inflation, the Kennedy administration, by energetic persuasion, had brought the steel union to curb its wage and fringe demands and agree to a two-year compact with the United States Steel Corporation. The administration emerged with the blissful expectation that the steel industry in reciprocal sensitivity to the nation's welfare would make no price increases. Suddenly U.S. Steel raised its prices and other big steel companies quickly followed its lead.

Kennedy and his aides, deeming the steel companies' action nothing less than a double-cross, unloosed a barrage of pressures. Hopefully, the few steel companies that had not raised their prices could be induced to refrain from doing so. Several administration aides even dared to surmise that if only a few companies held out, market forces would induce the giants to drop their price increases. The administration gave the pressure faucets a quick full turn. In a nationally televised news conference, the President questioned the patriotism of the "tiny handful of steel executives—whose pursuit of power and profit exceeds their sense of public responsibility." The President asked Senator Kefauver, Democrat of Tennessee and chairman of the Senate Anti-trust subcommittee, to express publicly his "dismay" over the price rise and consider an investigation. These the Senator gladly did. The Justice Department and the Federal Trade Commission announced that the price action would be closely scrutinized for possible violations of the antitrust laws. The President, Secretary of Defense McNamara, and leading officials of the Treasury and Commerce Departments and the Council of Economic Advisers put in friendly low-key telephone calls to contacts in the steel companies that had not raised prices, gently suggesting the wisdom of continued abstinence.

At Democratic National headquarters calls were made to Democratic governors across the nation inviting them to make public statements supporting the President and encouraging local steelmakers to hold the price line. When it appeared that the proceedings of a stockholders' meeting of Bethlehem Steel Corporation, held shortly before the price rise, might be relevant in possible antitrust prosecutions, the Justice Department moved to secure the potential evidence. In the middle of the night overzealous FBI agents routed out for questioning three newspaper reporters who had covered the Bethlehem meetings. In testimony on Capitol Hill administration officials unloosed alarming analyses of the impact of the steel price rise upon military and economic foreign aid and the nation's relationship to the Common Market. In the Defense Department, Secretary McNamara ordered military agencies to shift their buying to the few steel companies that had not raised their prices. The Kennedy administration's "divide-and-conquer" strategy ultimately paid off when the several hold-out companies announced they would not raise prices. Fearful of a disastrous loss of sales, U.S. Steel and all other companies that had followed its lead quickly canceled their rises. But U.S. Steel and other companies bounced back, nearly a year later, by raising prices, this time without administration opposition.

◇

BUSINESS too has an abundance of sinewy strength it can flourish in encounters with the Presidency. Not the least element in business's potency is money, which takes on an added allure when elections are approaching. The iron baron and political boss Mark Hanna dexterously intertwined the national Republican organization and a coterie of top-level businessmen into a working alliance. By assessing the magnates shrewdly, Hana assured a perpetually well-stocked campaign fund and, to gladden his generous donors, a respectably conservative program. Hanna's crowning success was handpicking William McKinley for the Presidency and installing him.

McKinley's death, Theodore Roosevelt's ascent, and Hanna's departure did not extinguish the wondrous system. J. P. Morgan and other business luminaries contributed lavishly to Theodore Roosevelt's 1904 campaign on the theory that any Republican President would be more tolerable than a Democrat. Theodore Roosevelt's campaign manager, George B. Cortelyou, gave the Hanna technique an added twist by employing methods approaching blackmail in enlisting contributions from the large industrial trusts. When Alton Parker, the Democratic Presidential nominee, began charging that the trusts were underwriting the Republican campaign, Theodore Roosevelt was put upon to denounce the accusations as "unqualifiedly and atrociously false."

Businessmen or their proven servants may fill strategic elective and appointive offices of government whence they can exert a channeling influence upon the President. Theodore Roosevelt, for example, bent upon a progressive program, was faced by the "Big Four" Republican leaders in the Senate—Nelson W. Aldrich of Rhode Island, John C. Spooner of Wisconsin, Orville H. Platt of Connecticut, and William B. Allison of Iowa. Time and again Theodore Roosevelt, in inescapable reckonings with these hard-line conservative leaders, had to trim his progressive measures. In the executive branch, businessmen may dominate the cabinet secretaryships, lesser departmental posts, and the independent regulatory commissions. President Eisenhower's original cabinet, for example, was described, not without exaggeration, as a "millionaires' corporation." So captive were the millionaires to their traditional economic doctrines that Eisenhower had the steady chore of lecturing to his cabinet on the importance of avoiding actions lending credence to critics' epithets that his was a "business administration." The administration, Eisenhower would say, must never fail to demonstrate its concern for the little man.

Business's political attention is constantly focused on the independent regulatory commission—the Federal Trade Commission, the Securities and Exchange Commission, the Federal Reserve Board, and the like. These are the principal regulators of the economy, and their policies can do much to curb the practices and profits of business. The best insurance against inconvenient regulation, business has found, is to fill the commissions' positions with its own men. Undoubtedly, the most complete take-over of the commissions was engineered by the Harding-Coolidge appointments to those bodies. John J. Esch, a Harding nominee to the Interstate Commerce Commission, had long and amply proven his deep love for the railroads as a former member of the House Commerce committee. The Esch appointment, Senator Robert La Follette thundered, was "a travesty on justice." President Coolidge's nomination to the Federal Trade Commission of William E. Humphrey, an efficient, dedicated counsel to great corporations, goaded Senator George Norris into branding the nominee "a fearless advocate of big business in all lines." Coolidge's naming of T. O. Marvin, secretary of the Home Market Club of Boston and editor of *The Protectionist*, to the U.S. Tariff Commission drove Norris to exclaim, "It seems to be the idea of those in control that the Tariff Commission should be composed of men whose whole lives disclose the fact that they have always advocated an exorbitantly high tariff."

Business may resort to more savage actions, when occasion demands, to take care of a President whose behavior has become downright unbearable. A league of mighty businessmen, for example, toiled hard but, as it happened, futilely, at lining up delegates to the Republican national convention of 1904 to quash Theodore Roosevelt's renomination and to replace him with one of their own, Mark Hanna. When Theodore Roosevelt grabbed the nomination, big business abandoned its seditious enterprise and put their dollars behind his race. Probably the most haunting fear of any President is of economic disaster, with its attendant dire political consequences. The business community, a complex of production schedules and buying and selling patterns, with the stock market as its symbol and nexus, rests upon a tenuous foundation of confidence. The foundation easily quavers, as history demonstrates, in times of political change. But in the eyes of many Presidents, natural economic fluctuations have been deliberately aggravated by the machinations of business leaders.

Presidents who champion progressive social programs are both sensitive and vulnerable to economic pressures from the business community. Theodore Roosevelt was visited with two economic "panics," as they were known, each a large threat to his political fortunes. In the late spring of 1903, when his nomination and election appeared certain, economic panic suddenly struck. The stock market fell into deep decline, wiping out $2 billion in security values; credit tightened and business failures soared. The high priests of finance, in their analytic incantations, attributed the disaster to a single and simple cause: Roosevelt's harassment of business. Only a few business spokesmen mentioned the contributing factors of an inflexible monetary structure and the over-capitalization of trusts like U.S. Steel. Roosevelt's own analysis of the ominous events, confided to his Secretary of State, Elihu Root, was that "certain of the big men" in Wall Street were not reluctant to see the panic get worse to discredit the administration and "to force the Republican party back into the path of conservatism." Mark Aloysius Hanna, waiting in the wings, was a tailor-made conservative candidate, in fact. Root, for his part, brought the President corroborative intelligence that a pro-Hanna, anti-Roosevelt campaign among "the substantial men" of New York was blooming in the Union League Club of which Root was president. When the further bludgeon of the 1907 panic smote his fortunes, Theodore Roosevelt made no bones about articulating his suspicions in a public statement charging that "certain malefactors of great wealth" had combined to intensify the panic "in order to discredit the policy of the government."

◇

THE second member of the great economic tandem—labor—like other groups attracted significant attention from the President of the United States only after it attained major political strength. Samuel Gompers, president of the American Federation of Labor, was not given the privilege of visits with Presidents until the late nineteenth century, and even then the occasions were few and brief. Gompers first extracted sustained Presidential interest from Theodore Roosevelt. Roosevelt invited the labor leader to the White House socially, consulted him on a wide range of subjects, and meted out honorific recognitions. Upon receiving the Nobel prize, for example, the President set up an industrial peace foundation and named Gompers to its board of directors.

Of all Presidents, Franklin Roosevelt maintained the most extensive relations with labor leaders. With labor he employed the same technique he applied to other private organizations. Viewing the nation's politics as essentially group politics, Franklin Roosevelt was wont to approach groups whose support he cherished through their leaders. Roosevelt's dealings with labor leaders ran the gamut from intimacy to mortal enmity. Dan Tobin of the Teamsters' Union was such an exalted favorite that Roosevelt made his "labor speech" of the 1944 campaign at a Teamsters' dinner, after rejecting entreaties of a dozen other unions for his presence.

Roosevelt's most intimate and profitable rapport was with Sidney Hillman, president of the Amalgamated Clothing Workers and vice-president of the CIO, a Lithuanian émigré whose sensitivity and appreciation of social workers, intellectuals, and others outside the labor movement set him apart from rougher hewn colleagues. Hillman served in responsible government posts in the New Deal and World War II, on NRA's Labor Advisory Board, on the National Defense Advisory Council, and as Associate Director of the Office of Production Management. To Roosevelt, Hillman was one of "the longest-headed individuals I have ever met." A constant visitor at the White House, Hillman enjoyed the rare privilege of a right-of-way by telephone to the chief executive. By the mid-thirties, a CIO official could plausibly assert that "A whisper from Sidney Hillman of the Amalgamated is louder than the loudest shout of almost anyone in the national Cabinet." And CIO president John L. Lewis, even when he was beholding the CIO vice president with a critical eye, declared, "Sidney Hillman was after all the driving force behind many of the measures attributed to the New Deal. If it had not been for him there would probably have been no Fair Labor Standards Act." Probably Hillman's thorniest assignment in the middle thirties was smoothing the troubled waters that kept churning up between his superior, John L. Lewis, and Franklin D. Roosevelt. Hillman's busy diplomacy was made doubly difficult by Lewis's resentment of his aide's privileged closeness to Roosevelt. The ordeal ended when Lewis finally broke with Roosevelt in 1940.

The Hillman-Roosevelt nexus, although resting upon a sturdy underpinning of personal regard, was mutually advantageous. For Hillman an unrivaled access to the White House meant speedy advancement in his labor career. For Roosevelt Hillman was a constant friend in the court of labor who could cushion the blows of unwelcome policy decisions like the administration's proposed labor draft in World War II. In the New Deal and the early war years Hillman was a kind of auxiliary Secretary of Labor at the White House's beck and call on myriad problems. Indeed Roosevelt seems to have seriously considered making Hillman his Labor Secretary at several junctures, but was dissuaded by Mrs. Roosevelt, who did not like having her old friend, Secretary Perkins, the only woman in the cabinet, superseded.

With John L. Lewis, the leonine, bushy-browed master of ornate rhetoric, Franklin Roosevelt's relations were unceasingly tempestuous. Lewis, like Roosevelt, loved power and position; when they met, giants clashed. A stickler for the amenities for himself and his office, Roosevelt was offended by Lewis's spiny arrogance. The President, who had a large talent for noncommittal generalities, would be brought up short when Lewis would stop him in mid-sentence to ask, "Well, will it be yes or no?" Roosevelt was also distressed by Lewis's occasional crudity in exploiting his White House access. Soon after section 7a of NRA went into effect, for example, a provision defined to encourage union organization, Lewis's United Mine Workers organizers raced through the coal fields shouting, "The President wants you to join the Union." This unseemly and wholly unauthorized use of the Presidential office put Roosevelt squarely on the spot. Politically, he could not disavow the organizers' activity, but could only writhe in private anguish. By 1936 Lewis was referring to Roosevelt as "my man." Roosevelt conveyed his own estimate of the labor leader in an interview with Max Lerner. "You know, Max," said the President, "this is really a great country. The framework of democracy is so strong and so elastic that it can get along and absorb both a Huey Long and a John L. Lewis." Lewis, when he heard the remark, growled, "The statement is incomplete. It should also include 'and Franklin Delano Roosevelt.' "

In 1940 the fragile Roosevelt-Lewis connection was snapped asunder by the coming of the war and Roosevelt's third-term candidacy. During a White House visit in January 1940, according to Frances Perkins, whose report of the interview is corroborated by Philip Murray, a later CIO president, and denied by Lewis, the Mine Workers chief made a startling proposal. He suggested to the President that he, Lewis, should run for Vice President of the United States on the third-term ticket. A strong labor man, Lewis argued, would ensure full labor support plus the support of all the liberals who, he added pointedly, would be a little troubled by the Constitutional irregularity of a third term.

The rebuff of Lewis's Vice Presidential aspirations launched a train of bizarre events that widened the chasm between himself and the President from miles to oceans. After weeks of intensive wooing by the camp of Wendell Willkie, the Republican Presidential candidate, Lewis abandoned Roosevelt. "He is not an aristocrat," Lewis said, endorsing Willkie in a labor-oriented statement, "He has the common touch. He was born to the friar and not to the purple. He has worked with his hands, and has known the pangs of hunger." In a radio address Lewis urged the workers of America to vote against Roosevelt. In a flourish that left his fellow labor leaders gasping with disbelief, Lewis declared he would consider Roosevelt's re-election a vote of no confidence in himself and would thereupon resign from his CIO presidency. The labor rank and file, forced to choose between Roosevelt, beloved as their President, and Lewis, their adulated leader, chose Roosevelt at the polls. Honoring his threat, Lewis resigned from the CIO leadership.

Under Kennedy labor leaders again enjoyed easy access to the White House, a privilege they have come to expect from Democratic Presidents. Although Kennedy, mindful of the President's responsibilities to all the people, held labor and its aspirations at arm's length, abundant good fellowship reigned. Indeed the President accorded a new privilege withheld by his predecessors. George Meany, Walter Reuther, David J. McDonald, and other distinguished union presidents were invited to the White House socially. On the guest list for the select Mount Vernon gala honoring the President of Pakistan, for example, were Mr. and Mrs. Walter Reuther.

Differences cropping up between Kennedy and the unions were handled with scrupulously quiet decorum. When the AFL-CIO politely criticized the Kennedy antirecession program in 1961 for not going far enough in the face of burgeoning unemployment, the President's reply took no specific note of the criticism, but resorted to a high incontrovertible ground of noble sentiment. All groups, he wrote to the union leadership, should concentrate upon finding points of unity instead of "belaboring those problems which divide us." The unions, too, employed the soft manner. When the AFL-CIO executive council concluded in 1963 that the President was not doing enough to stimulate the economy, it voiced its criticism on so vital a matter not in hostile resolution or public outcry. It authorized its leaders, George Meany and Walter Reuther, to bring its views quietly and privately to the President. Labor's absolute commitment to Democratic Presidents well nigh mutes, for the duration of their administrations, public discussion of labor problems in an era of cataclysmic economic change.

Lyndon Johnson's early months in office were devoted to building up good relations with labor's top leadership. This was something of a task, since his nomination as Vice President in 1960 was not gladly received in the labor community. The first liberal voice to be heard publicly in behalf of Johnson's Vice Presidential candidacy was that of an old and warm friend, David Dubinsky, president of the International Ladies Garment Workers Union who deserves watching as a possible future Sidney Hillman in the Johnson administration. Like other Democratic Presidents, Johnson in his relations with organized labor faces a conflict between personal political necessity and the requirements of national economic policy. Politically he needs labor's support in the great industrial states, where his fortunes for the 1964 Presidential race are weakest: states like New York, Pennsylvania, Michigan, and Illinois. While the top labor leadership could be expected to endorse Johnson for the Presidency, it was not certain how enthusiastically union officials at the local level would regard his candidacy. If they pitched in to get out the vote, both for registration and for election, they could be of great help to him as they were to Kennedy. If local leaders held back, labor's most reward-ing help would be lost where Johnson needed it most. Meanwhile, like Eisenhower and Kennedy, he proclaimed guideposts for noninflationary wage and price behavior. Wage increases, he has said, should be limited to the amount by which economic productivity rises each year. Walter Reuther, president of the United Automobile Workers, served notice that he, for one, did not intend to be bound by such a limitation in his 1964 negotiations with the automobile industry. A major Johnson task has been to juggle his political and economic necessities without offend-ing local labor leaders to the point of indifference toward his electoral and legislative future.

Although most union leaders are steadily committed to support Demo-cratic Presidential candidates, Dwight Eisenhower, upon his accession to the office, numbered among his earlier callers Walter Reuther, then the CIO president, and David J. McDonald, head of the United Steelworkers. "Eisenhower," the administration's biographer Robert Donovan has written, "was very curious to know more about the kind of man Reuther was, and he listened with great interest as the CIO president expressed his views on how labor-management relations could contribute to the cause of peace in the world." Afterward Eisenhower remarked on how impressed he was with Reuther's "moderation and sincerity." As the ad-ministration proceeded, labor leaders conferred occasionally with Eisen-hower and several, particularly McDonald, enjoyed more than cordial footing with the President.

◊

TWENTIETH-CENTURY Presidents, particularly those of Democratic vintage, perform various functions to further labor's interests. Annually on Labor Day the President of the United States, be he Republican or Democrat, will make a speech, preferably in Detroit, full of praise for labor's contribution to the Republic. At other times in messages, press statements, and letters he will approve of labor's goals and sterling achievement. Since 1933 all Presidents, Republican and Democratic alike, have promoted new legislation beneficial to labor. The removal of obstacles to the effective exertion of labor's economic power, the increase of labor's legal rights, and the enlargement of the government's welfare services are areas of legislation that vitally interest labor. Since labor legislation ordinarily is not passed without a long and impassioned strug-gle, a President proposing it sets the agenda not merely of his own ad-ministration, but often of future administrations. In 1905 Theodore Roosevelt proposed that Congress "regulate" the "procedure" for granting labor injunctions. Not until twenty-seven years after his initiative, in the Norris-La Guardia Act of 1932, did Congress finally do it.

Although most of the laws promoting labor's fundamental interests were enacted in Franklin Roosevelt's administration, and he of all Presidents is the most revered in the labor community, the truth of the matter is that Roosevelt was not an eager champion of labor's causes, but a reluctant hero. In the enactment of each of the three basic labor laws of his administration—section 7a of NRA, the Wagner Act of 1935, and the Fair Labor Standards Act of 1938—his participation was cautious and half-hearted. Section 7a was included in the National Recovery Act not because Roosevelt rushed to put it in, but because John L. Lewis insisted on it. Roosevelt's principal involvement in NRA's preparation was to order the industrialists and labor leaders who drafted individual bills to "get into a room and weave it all together." In the ensuing Congressional phase of NRA, Lewis was fearful that 7a, blessed with little Presidential support, might be dropped, so he entered into an intrigue with a labor-minded White House assistant. Lewis would write to the President, and the compliant assistant, who drafted Franklin Roosevelt's reply, would slip in a dash of exhortation for 7a. The tampering, according to Lewis, passed unnoticed. With the letter in hand, the labor leader spread the word among fence-sitting legislators that Roosevelt really wanted 7a.

Roosevelt's commitment to the Wagner or National Labor Relations bill, which enhanced labor's right to organize and obliged employers to engage in collective bargaining, was also mild. In 1934, indeed, a Presidential decision had sidetracked the Wagner bill. The Senator was encouraged to reintroduce his measure the following year not by the President but by the labor movement. Franklin Roosevelt, to Wagner's dismay, despite expressions of mild approval the year before, now took a hands-off attitude. Even in the bill's late stages, Secretary of Commerce Daniel Roper was predicting a Presidential veto. After the bill had passed the House, and just before the Senate's final action, Roosevelt convened a White House conference where Senator Wagner and Donald R. Richberg, the administration's labor adviser who opposed the bill, debated its merits at the President's invitation. Midway in the discussion, Roosevelt, whose position still was unknown, finally made clear that he wanted the bill. On the Fair Labor Standards bill of 1938, Franklin Roosevelt likewise engaged in belated, feet-dragging decision. It was not the President or his administration, but Sidney Hillman, the CIO Vice President, who rallied the labor bloc of legislators and worked out the minimum wage of twenty-five cents an hour in a hard-wrought compromise with the Southern Democrats. Roosevelt, ever skeptical of the bill's chances, gave help only when its success was assured and political prudence required that he quickly identify himself with it.

Why was Roosevelt so chronically reserved and reluctant? For one thing, born into comfortable gentility, he had no first-hand understanding of labor problems. Instinctively and intellectually he sympathized with labor's objectives, but he had little grasp of its needs and feelings. On setting the priorities of his administration, he gave labor's objectives a secondary place. In the depression years of 1934 and 1935 and in the recession of 1938 his primary interest was economic recovery. Time and again he seems to have been impressed by the argument that production might climb faster in the depression-bound economy if labor decisions could be postponed until business was on its feet again. Labor's most drastic weapon, the strike, sometimes annoyed him, especially when it obstructed his own political and economic purposes. In the main, he envisioned himself not as labor's champion but as a balancer and adjuster between labor and management in which he approached both sides with a good measure of judicious detachment.

In the post-Franklin D. Roosevelt era the fate and substance of labor legislation have varied strikingly between the Republican Eisenhower Presidency and the Democratic Presidencies of Truman and Kennedy. Eisenhower's personal preference for state action and his apparent lack of philosophical sympathy with labor's aims wrought results considerably below labor's aspirations. Twice Eisenhower vetoed legislation providing federal aid to depressed areas with severe unemployment. When the AFL-CIO proposed amendments to the Fair Labor Standards Act, raising the minimum wage from $1.00 to $1.25 an hour and adding some 5 million employees not covered by the act (chiefly in retail trades), the President recommended an increase of 10 to 15 cents an hour and the extension of coverage to some 3.2 million employees. Consistent with Eisenhower's avowed preference for state action, his administration achieved a major extension of the state-oriented Social Security Act, the largest in the act's history.

Kennedy, in contrast, stressed national action in labor matters. Kennedy pushed through legislation for depressed areas, which Eisenhower had vetoed, and the $1.25 minimum wage, which Eisenhower had resisted. Kennedy also won liberalizing amendments to the Social Security Act which increased minimum benefits and lowered the eligibility age. He won legislation extending unemployment compensation for up to thirteen additional weeks and giving special benefits to the children of the unemployed.

Since the days of Franklin D. Roosevelt, labor has expected Presidents, particularly Democratic Presidents, to resist legislation hostile to its interests. The noisiest and most politically profitable instances of Presidential jousting in labor's behalf was Harry S. Truman's veto of the Taft-Hartley bill of 1947. An omnibus measure passed in the wake of a large upsurge in strikes, Taft-Hartley aimed to equalize employer-employee responsibilities by regulating union organization and practices. After polling the Democratic National Committee and the state Democratic chairmen and vice chairmen for advice, Truman delivered a fiery veto which was overridden by the Republican-controlled Congress. For Truman the defeat was merely the beginning of a long, implacable, politically rewarding crusade. In the 1948 Presidential campaign and after, he lost no opportunity to identify the legislation with Republican conservatism, though a majority of the Democrats in both Houses had voted for it.

From Franklin D. Roosevelt onward, Democratic Presidents have sometimes been preoccupied with building peace and harmony between the American Federation of Labor and the CIO. The contrasting philosophies of the two labor giants provide a built-in conflict: the AFL is devoted to the craft principle and has a historic preference for nongovernmental action; the CIO is oriented to the plant and industry-wide labor group, to skilled and unskilled workers alike, and to governmental intervention. Their philosophical differences are aggravated by the personal values of the union leaders and inter-union jurisdictional disputes. Although the CIO and AFL merged into a single organization in 1955, their traditional divisiveness has not evaporated. From 1938 onward every message Franklin Roosevelt dispatched to the annual AFL convention urged inter-union peace. In 1939, in identical letters to the AFL and CIO leaders, he proposed that a committee be instituted to negotiate a reunion of the two federations, and to speed the project he brought William Green and John L. Lewis, the AFL and CIO presidents, to the White House for discussions. Franklin Roosevelt's busy interest in labor unity was not unalloyed. Although he had not yet decided on a third term, Roosevelt hoped that through AFL-CIO peace he or his Democratic successor might capture a larger share of the workers' vote.

The President may bring labor into his official family by appointing as his Secretary of Labor a figure from the organized labor movement. Woodrow Wilson inaugurated the practice when he made William B. Wilson of the United Mine Workers his Secretary of Labor in 1913. The precedent was renewed not by his Democratic successors Roosevelt and Truman, but by the Republican Eisenhower, who named Martin Durkin, president of the plumbers' union, Secretary of Labor. The appointment proved ill-fated; after eight months Durkin resigned, vexed because the White House rejected his views on amending the Taft-Hartley Act. Kennedy's first Secretary of Labor, Arthur Goldberg, general counsel to the United Steel Workers' Union, did not, like Durkin, hail from the workers' ranks, but from labor's growing professional wing.

In appointing a non-labor man as Labor Secretary, a contemporary President will make a selection that is inoffensive to the labor movement.

Eisenhower's choice as Derkin's successor was James P. Mitchell, a figure highly regarded in professional labor-management relations. Democratic Presidents scrupulously sound out labor's views before launching the appointment. Minutes before President Kennedy notified W. Willard Wirtz of his appointment as Goldberg's successor, George Meany, the AFL-CIO president, had pronounced his blessing in a White House visit.

◇

Since the 1930's the great bulk of organized labor has made a clear and absolute choice in Presidential politics, in casting its lot with Democratic candidates and opposing the Republicans. When a Republican occupies the White House, labor constitutes a major opposition force second only to the Democratic party. If the Democratic party is divided and dominated by moderates and conservatives, as it was in Eisenhower's first term, organized labor "plays a role of *the* major loyal opposition within American politics," as James Tracy Crown has put it.

For the Democratic chief executive, labor is the major interest group in the American polity supporting his domestic program, and, to a large but lesser degree, his foreign policy. In seasons when his foreign aid legislation encountered rough sledding in Congress, President Kennedy could count on help from a squad of expert and experienced lobbyists of the AFL-CIO and its constituent unions who descended upon Capitol Hill. Before he launched his foreign trade bill, Kennedy emphatically invited labor's support in an address to the 1961 AFL-CIO convention. "Don't worry about us," George Meany replied. "We will cooperate 1,000 per cent." When labor's cooperation slackened to unsatisfactory percentages, Kennedy did not hesitate to call the union chiefs to account. In 1961 he let the word go forth that he was disappointed and displeased at some unions' failure to lobby more strenuously for his minimum wage bill in the House of Representatives.

From Franklin D. Roosevelt onward labor has played a central part in selecting Democratic candidates for the Presidency. Indeed no Democratic candidate during that time has been named without its approval. There was truth in Kennedy's jest when he acknowledged in a 1961 speech to the AFL-CIO convention that he was "one whose work and continuity of employment has depended in part upon the union movement."

Labor has displayed an almost equal interest in the selection of Democratic Vice Presidential candidates. In the fateful selection of Harry S. Truman for the Vice Presidency in 1944, labor had at least as great a part as the incumbent President, Franklin Roosevelt. The latter's frail health, a fact well known to the labor leaders, lent urgency to their task. Roosevelt himself contributed only confusion by recommending no less than four candidates for the Vice Presidency. Robert E. Hannegan,

Franklin Roosevelt's representative embarking for the Chicago convention, beseeched his chief for instructions on the Vice Presidential question. Before making a final selection, Roosevelt was heard to say Hannegan and his aides must first "clear it with Sidney" (Sidney Hillman), the CIO vice president. The union leaders, after rejecting James M. Byrnes and expressing indifference toward Henry Wallace, the incumbent Vice President, settled upon Truman. "Clear it with Sidney" quickly took its place in the national lexicon and raised a drumfire of conservative indignation. Cried Westbrook Pegler, "How came this nontoiling sedentary conspirator who never held American office or worked in the Democratic organization to give orders to the Democrats of the United States!"

Since Franklin Roosevelt's day, Democratic Presidential campaigns have counted heavily upon labor's contributions of treasure and leg-work. "The election of John F. Kennedy is Labor's number one job," proclaimed George Meany in 1960. Union halls across the nation were tuned in to Kennedy campaign centers, and union registration drives in the cities were indispensable to his success. Franklin D. Roosevelt cemented labor and the Democratic Presidency into close bond in the embittered election of 1936, when he courted the aid of AFL and CIO leaders. They responded lavishly in the conviction that for labor's fortunes and future everything turned on Roosevelt's re-election. Lewis's United Mine Workers made cash contributions and loans by its own count of $486,288.55 to the Democratic party and a nearly equal sum to Labor's Non-Partisan League, labor's own campaign organization zealously devoted to Roosevelt's cause. Hillman's Amalgamated Clothing Workers added $100,000 to the Roosevelt coffers and a further $400,000 to the League's. In all, labor committed a full $1 million to Roosevelt's re-election.

That labor expected something of a *quid pro quo* Sidney Hillman made plain in a telegram to Franklin Roosevelt after Amalgamated pledged its treasure. "Labor anticipates your support," Hillman wired bluntly, "for decent labor legislation . . . the guarantee of the right to organize and the enactment of minimum labor standards." Roosevelt in a telegram to Amalgamated and a letter to "Dear Sidney" expressed gratitude and blithely ignored the suggestion of a bargain, saying merely that Amalgamated's action had given him "new strength and courage." Following the electoral victory, when Lewis began growling that Franklin Roosevelt had better start reciprocating, the labor leader expressed impatience with those who were shocked by his temerity in demanding a dividend on labor's $1 million investment. "Is anyone fool enough to believe, for one instant," asked Lewis, "that we gave this money to Roosevelt because we were spellbound by his voice?"

The Lewis-Hillman technique of direct financial contributions was banned by law in 1943 and again by the Taft-Hartley Act in 1947, which also prohibits direct union expenditures for candidates for public office. Similar restrictions apply to business corporations. Both unions and corporations freely circumvent the laws, however, with Congressional and Presidential acquiescence.

◇

TWENTIETH-CENTURY Presidents have regularly become entangled in labor-management disputes over union recognition, collective bargaining, and "bread and butter" issues of wages, hours, and general working conditions. The President's participation ranges from leadership in labor-management negotiations—personally or through deputies—to the seizure of struck properties and the use of the military to maintain law and order. In his earliest interventions in labor-management disputes, the President used military force under acts of Congress of 1792, 1795, and 1807 to enforce national laws in local disorders and to guard the states against domestic violence as guaranteed in Article IV, section 4, of the Constitution. In the 1877 railroad strike in ten states, Rutherford B. Hayes furnished state authorities with arms from national arsenals and, as commander-in-chief, transferred troops from remote posts to the scenes of trouble. In the Pullman strike of 1894, President Cleveland, against Governor Altgeld's strenuous protests, dispatched troops to Chicago to protect United States property and "to remove obstructions to the United States mails." The Supreme Court upheld Cleveland in *In re Debs* (158 U.S. 564).

Theodore Roosevelt reversed the Presidency's pro-management tendencies in resolving the anthracite coal strike in 1902, the largest work stoppage up to that time. The severity of approaching winter, the popularity of the miners' cause, and the anthracite industry's membership in a close-knit trust drew Roosevelt actively into the crisis. He ordered his commissioner of labor to investigate the strike and make recommendations, which furnished the basis of a compromise solution Theodore Roosevelt proposed to the operators and miners. When the operators rejected it, Secretary of War Elihu Root rushed to New York to confer with J. P. Morgan, and together they drafted an agreement to submit the dispute to an arbitration commission. The imperious Morgan pressed the agreement upon George Baer, president of the Reading Railroad Company and the operators' chief negotiator. Morgan's achievement approaches the awesome, for Baer had sprouted a bad case of self-righteous intransigence. "The rights and interests of the laboring man," he maintained, "will be protected and cared for not by the labor agitators, but by the Christian men to whom God in his infinite wisdom has given the control of the property interests of the country, and upon the successful management of which so much depends."

Acting on the Root-Morgan agreement, Roosevelt appointed an arbitration commission. To assure that the award would not go too decidedly against the miners, Theodore Roosevelt took pains to include a cleric and a union official, the latter filling the place designated for an "eminent sociologist." The commission's findings were made and accepted by both sides, and the strike ended. It remains a landmark of Presidential innovation in labor policy. For the first time in a labor dispute, representatives of both capital and labor were called to the White House, where Presidential influence induced a negotiated settlement. For the first time, both sides promised to accept the decision of a Presidentially appointed arbitration board. If the board had failed, Theodore Roosevelt in an equally innovative step, was prepared to "put in" the army to "dispossess the operators and run the mines as a receiver."

Succeeding Democratic Presidents have elaborated on the patterns originated by the Republican Roosevelt. In the Colorado coal strike of 1913–14, Woodrow Wilson employed federal troops not to protect strike breakers, but to protect the property and safety of both labor and management while they negotiated a settlement. The theme of equality persisted in legislation passed in the Wilsonian era which established the Department of Labor, with a Division of Conciliation to handle labor disputes, with the bargaining parties, labor and management, enjoying identical status.

Franklin D. Roosevelt clung to his preference for keeping out of specific labor-management disputes even in the most ruinous confrontation of his time, the sit-down strikes of 1936. Both the sprawling General Motors organization, the focus of the strikes, and the CIO pressured Roosevelt to intervene. His personal political interest was to end the conflict quickly without becoming involved in the specifics of its settlement—a purpose calling for fine maneuver. At one juncture Roosevelt called the CIO leaders to the White House and asked them bluntly to "get the men out of the G.M. plants." John L. Lewis, the CIO president, would only promise that the men would leave "when the company begins to bargain with them or even with me, in good faith." To balance the scales, Franklin Roosevelt publicly spanked Alfred Sloan, the General Motors president, for breaking off negotiations. In a characteristic tactic, Roosevelt forced negotiations to proceed at lesser levels of authority—between the disputants themselves and through the good offices of the Conciliation Service and Governor Frank Murphy of Michigan, where the strikes were heaviest. Roosevelt viewed the Presidency as a supreme arbiter, to be held jealously in reserve and used only as a last resort. Ultimately, Roosevelt brought General Motors to begin what it had never done before—negotiation with union representatives and the CIO to end the strikes.

In World War II strikes were few, thanks largely to the Roosevelt-

Truman insistence that labor-management disputes must not hamper war production. When strikes erupted in vital war industries, both Presidents seized and operated the struck industries. In the Truman era of postwar reconversion, with labor meaning to hold its wartime gains, strikes soared. A corporation-wide General Motors strike, national steel and railroad stoppages, the CIO Electrical Workers strikes against General Electric, General Motors, and Westinghouse, and several coal strikes hobbled the economy and blanketed the nation's cities with "dim-outs" and "brown-outs."

The embattled Truman resorted to fact-finding boards, and his principal assistant, John R. Steelman, was not for nothing plucked from the directorship of the U.S. Conciliation Service. Much of Steelman's time was devoted to White House conferences with the disputants in key labor-management impasses. In addition, Truman instituted a general labor-management conference in Washington in 1945, and when restrictive labor bills began stirring on Capitol Hill, he rushed to beat Congress to the punch by advancing labor-management legislation of his own. For his provident action Truman was accused by Philip Murray, the CIO president, of yielding "in abject cowardice" to Congressional pressure. Eventually Truman's proposal was submerged by the harsher Taft-Hartley Act.

Truman's stormiest involvement in labor-management relations occurred in 1946 when the Brotherhood of Locomotive Engineers and the Brotherhood of Railway Trainmen struck first against management and then against the government after it seized the railroads. The striking brotherhoods had rejected a compromise formula worked out by Truman and Steelman. Thousands of railroad workers struck, ignoring the President's nationally televised appeal that they stay at their jobs. The general debacle brought Truman personally before Congress to request temporary emergency powers to break strikes against the government, including the authority to draft strikers into the armed forces. The severity of the request and Congress's booming ovation to the President brought the Brotherhoods to terms. Meanwhile the opposition that quickly formed against Truman's extraordinary request constitutes the strangest combination of bedfellows in twentieth-century politics. Senator Claude Pepper, whose persuasion was to the left, said he would resign before supporting the President. From the right, Senator Robert A. Taft cried that the proposal was recreating "involuntary servitude" in America. At a CIO rally Truman was christened "the number one strikebreaker of the American bankers and railroads." "Pay no attention to the calamity howlers," Truman advised the graduating class of George Washington University. "When the President of the United States, by one speech, can get Senators Pepper and Taft and *The Daily Worker* and *The Wall Street Journal* together, then the country is perfectly safe." Truman's proposal was eventually strangulated by a combination of conservative Republicans, Southern Democrats, and pro-labor Senators.

Eisenhower and Kennedy both avoided Truman's raucous embroilments in labor-management disputes. Truman's successors have benefited from increasing labor-management stability and by labor's marked shift in tactical emphasis from the strike to the bargaining table. In contrast to Truman, Eisenhower and Kennedy had no Steelmans, but kept labor-management issues largely locked up in the Labor Department. James P. Mitchell, Eisenhower's Labor Secretary, and Arthur Goldberg and Willard Wirtz, Kennedy's Labor Secretaries, were the chief engineers of administration labor policy. Kennedy, although personally more involved than Eisenhower, worked chiefly behind the scenes. When he did act publicly, Kennedy preferred a moderate decorum.

Like his predecessors in the contemporary Presidency, Kennedy moved most forcefully when labor-management disputes impaired the nation's military needs. When in 1962 a strike threatened at Boeing Aircraft, a prime contractor for the Minuteman intercontinental missile and other key defense items, Kennedy turned on the full force of his personal persuasion to bring the union to postpone the strike. When the International Association of Machinists walked out of two California plants of Aerojet-General Corporation, supplier of essential components of Polaris, Minuteman, Titan II, and other weapons, administration officials responded with acrid comment and instant action. Defense Secretary McNamara termed the strike "a callous disregard of the national and public interest," and Labor Secretary Wirtz and the Mediation Service worked massively upon the issues in dispute. Like other Presidents, Kennedy used special boards, under the Taft-Hartley Act and other authority, to find facts and recommend terms of settlement. Professors George W. Taylor of the University of Pennsylvania, Nathan Feinsinger of the University of Wisconsin, and David L. Cole, a leading arbitrator, are representative of a small body of men who served on such boards in Democratic and Republican administrations alike. Their technical skill and reputation for impartiality take on growing importance as an appendage of the Presidency. Presidential boards are also utilized in disputes in vital national industries such as transportation. Ordinarily Kennedy backed up the board's findings with public statements urging their acceptance for the sake of the national interest.

For all of Kennedy's invocations of a labor-management duty to heed national interest, his own conduct was not always free from the taint of expediency. Indeed a double track was sometimes discernible in the Kennedy administration's approach to labor-management relations. Two labor disputes of 1962 illuminate the contrast. In the first, strikes loomed at

North American, Ryan, General Dynamics, and Lockheed, manufacturers of missiles and aircraft. A special Presidential board recommended union-shop elections to resolve the dispute. The two powerful unions involved—the United Automobile Workers and the International Association of Machinists—welcomed the board's recommendation, but the employers cold-shouldered it. Kennedy backed up his board in a strong statement holding that if the employers rejected the peace plan, the country should blame them for the ensuing trouble.

In a second dispute, where labor, rather than management, rejected a Presidential board's findings, Kennedy's course was altogether different. A strike of the Chicago and North Western Railway which inflicted severe economic injury upon nine midwestern states, commenced when the Order of Railroad Telegraphers rejected a Presidential board's recommendation that the union abandon its demand for a veto over job reductions caused by new technology and other factors. The Presidential board proposed a formula to cushion lay-offs through liberalized unemployment, retraining, and severance benefits. Kennedy, departing from his accustomed procedure, pronounced no words of personal endorsement of the board's report, nor censure for the union. Wholly ignoring the railroad's readiness to negotiate a contract reflecting the board's proposals, the President entreated "both sides" to make "sufficient concessions" to find accord.

In contract negotiations of key industries, the Kennedy administration looked over the shoulders of capital and labor at the bargaining table and insisted that agreements reached respect the "national interest." By the latter phrase, the Administration apparently meant that excessive wage demands and price rises that wither economic growth, weaken employment, and speed gold outflow were to be shunned. To lend substance to the Presidential view of national interest in the steel contract negotiations of 1962, the Council of Economic Advisers concluded from its researches that improved labor productivity and retention of the forty-hour week permitted a rise in labor costs of up to 3 per cent without necessitating a price increase. When the negotiated contract entailed a labor cost rise of 2½ per cent, Kennedy hailed the contract as "noninflationary." While it was being negotiated, Kennedy and Labor Secretary Goldberg pressed the steel union leaders in telephone calls and conferences to hold down their demands. When the contract was concluded with such a happy result, Kennedy telephoned a message of high praise to President McDonald of the Steel Workers Union that was relayed by loud speaker to a vast assembly of the rank and file at union headquarters.

◊

THE gap between the President's authority and his responsibilities concerning the economy has widened since World War II, and there is every prospect that it will continue to do so. The President will be expected to hold down inflation and to jog up economic growth to rates that are appropriate in light of the growth of the Soviet and western European economies. He must maintain a high degree of industrial peace, and at the very least avoid repetitions of anything like the long steel strike of 1959–1960. There is widening recognition that ours is an "affluent society" and an "age of high mass consumption," and more and more people are questioning whether more of the new-made wealth ought not be used for purposes other than personal material gratifications, and therefore for constructive public purposes—for schools, hospitals, recreation facilities, and the like.

The sixties and seventies may conceivably bring revolutionary changes in the economy. One may be the cybernetics revolution that promises to increase unemployment to such a degree that the traditional link between jobs and income will be badly broken. The electronic computer and the automated, self-regulating machine may largely invalidate the general mechanism that undergirds people's rights as consumers. A companion development may fulfill the forecast of Roswell L. Gilpatric, former Deputy Secretary of Defense in the Kennedy administration, that if the growing *détente* with the Soviet Union continues, the defense budget can be cut back 25 per cent by 1970. The consequences of such a cut for the economy would be vast. What is the President, whose economic responsibilities far exceed his economic authority, to do in light of these gathering demands for policy?

1. He must, of course, seek new statutory authority. He must resume the fight that Kennedy lost, to gain the power to raise and lower income taxes within limits, in response to general economic conditions. He will need new laws to extend the fight against poverty begun by President Johnson and to strengthen the economic opportunities of Negroes, nearly 45 per cent of whom are living in poverty—that is, they have yearly incomes of less than two thousand dollars. With the growing cybernetics revolution, the day may not be far when the President will have to urge upon Congress legislation guaranteeing every American an adequate income as a matter of right.

2. The President can ask for new statutory authority, but whether he will get it, given separation of powers, checks and balances, and weak parties, is highly problematic. Kennedy asked for legislation to combat poverty but did not win it. Johnson, although persisting with the request, is wisely relying for part of his needs upon extant authority. It is on economic questions that the President's weakness as legislative and party leader is most debilitating. The fifties and sixties have been especially barren of major domestic economic legislation, producing nothing com-

parable in importance to the Taft-Hartley Act and the Employment Act of the forties. As the New Deal of the thirties demonstrates, the President fares best in securing economic legislation during severe and dramatically evident crises. But the economic crisis of the sixties and seventies is apt to be a quiet one—an undramatic, although steady and substantial increase in unemployment—a crisis unlikely to stir Congress and the nation the way the depression did.

3. The President's most promising recourse in the face of a balky Congress and a quiescent public opinion is to urban groups—to organized labor and to racial and national minorities lacking access to ordinary economic privileges. The Kennedy formula of linking program and urban groups to influence Congress will face its hardest test and, if it succeeds, will gain its finest achievements on economic issues.

4. Presidential politics based upon group politics will be complicated by drastic alterations in the nature of the groups wrought by economic change. Unlike F. D. Roosevelt, who thrived upon a growing organized labor movement, future Presidents face a declining movement. Between 1960 and 1962, according to the U. S. Bureau of Labor Statistics, AFL-CIO affiliates lost 220,000 members of a membership of fourteen million, representative of a rather steady decline since the 1950's. Structural changes in the economy, the shift in the national job pattern toward more white-collar workers, the absence of the organized spirit of the thirties and forties, all contribute to union decline. The weakening of organized labor may require the President to rely more heavily upon racial and national groups and to direct his appeal more pointedly to consumer interest.

5. The President will need to become increasingly the champion of groups whom the economy has alienated or excluded from its privileges. These are, above all, the unemployed, among whom are numbered a growing body of youth, and the aged. They lack organization and money to assert themselves. Their plight is a fit and urgent object of the President's concern as the spokesman of our social conscience.

6. In the absence of adequate statutory authority, the President will need to rely all the more upon executive means to forward his economic policies. He and his aides can use the conference method more widely to spread information and to help form opinion as, for example, among industry and union leaders on issues of price and wage stability. The government contract and the manipulation of government spending, the several pressures that Kennedy employed in the 1962 steel price crisis—all these and more constitute richly varied executive means to further the President's policy and the public interest.

CHAPTER

12

Social Justice

———

PRESIDENTS face the struggle that goes on in our society, as in any other society, between those who have wealth and power and are loath to share them and those who do not have wealth and power and seek to get them. The disadvantaged want to improve their condition and the advantaged to hold to their privileged position. A dynamic democracy makes no lasting arbitration between the contestants, and their conflict is an enduring feature of politics. The Presidency, as the principal elective office of American democratic society, has made no enduring and unqualified commitment to either the advantaged or the disadvantaged. Particular chief executives have been heavily committed to one of the sides; others have remained largely indifferent or have been distracted by other problems of their administration. Nineteenth-century Presidents were uneven and chiefly negative in their attention to social justice; in the twentieth century unevenness still prevails, but positive actions have become far more numerous and more forceful.

Social justice has a dimension beyond social rights and social welfare. It includes the civil liberties of the individual and their protection against encroachments by government. In this sense government is conceived of not simply as the promoter of social justice, but as the perpetrator of social or individual injustice. Government and the individual are linked in a basic tension which Lincoln expressed in his message to Congress on the newborn Civil War on July 4, 1861: "Must a government of necessity be too *strong* for the liberties of its own people, or too *weak* to maintain its own existence?" In the deepest sense, Lincoln was expressing a fundamental problem of democratic society: finding the proper balance between the individual's liberty to live his life as he will and government's authority to protect and enhance the welfare of its people.

◇

ALTHOUGH Thomas Jefferson is rightly placed at the forefront of our chief executives who have championed human justice, his finest achievements occurred rather less in his Presidency than elsewhere. As chief executive his concerns centered largely upon foreign affairs and partisan politics: the Louisiana Purchase, the embargo, war on the Barbary pirates, the impeachment of Federalist judges, the repeal of the Federalists' Judiciary Act. His inaugural address viewed government as essentially negative: let it keep men from injuring their fellows; otherwise leave them to regulate their own concerns. He spoke against special privilege, rejected the Hamiltonian view that government should encourage manufacture, but instead conceived of agriculture and commerce "as its handmaid." An exponent of states' rights, he circumscribed a limited role for the federal government, chiefly in foreign affairs, and proposed to leave local affairs to the states. But Jefferson demonstrated the capacity of the President and of government to promote individual liberty. Turning to the Alien and Sedition laws of 1798 of the previous Federalist administration, granting the chief executive summary power to deport any alien "deemed dangerous to the public peace or safety," and making it a crime to publish false, scandalous, or defamatory writings with intent to discredit the government, Jefferson pardoned all persons imprisoned under the legislation, and Congress, following his cue, ultimately ordered all fines returned.

Andrew Jackson, despite his military affinities and contrasting intellectual endowment, was an extension and adaptation of his great Republican-Democratic forebear, Jefferson. Jackson too indulged a large, although somewhat erratic, devotion to states' rights. His position on two major issues of his administration—his opposition to federally developed internal improvements and his war upon the Second Bank of the United States—reflected a strong surge of states' rights sentiments. His war upon the Bank, which he did not begin, was the product of many forces, including the anti-Bank persuasions of his advisers, Amos Kendall and Martin Van Buren, and the Bank's own ill-advised heavy-handed tactics which encouraged Jackson's view of it as a monster of concentrated economic power and potential tyranny. But most of all whether he altogether deserved to be or not, Jackson was a rallying point for the common man.

Yet the chief curative for those who were restive under the heel of privilege was not government reform, but the opening of new territories, the push of human settlement westward. If one became dissatisfied with his lot in society—his income, his rights, his prospects—he could journey westward to the new country, start over again, and hope to do better. The frontier was America's magic medicine for social injustice until it too eventually failed as a healer of the most divisive issue in society—slavery—and the Civil War erupted. To wage it, Lincoln, relying upon Presidential authority, imposed drastic restrictions upon civil liberty: without legislative authorization he suspended the privilege of the writ of habeas corpus and subjected those who discouraged enlistments, resisted the draft, or engaged in other disloyal practice to martial law and trial by military commissions. Newspapers were suppressed by military order. To some, although not to most, the Civil War was a fight for social justice. The war produced the foremost blow yet struck by a President in behalf of any massive class cursed with injustice. The Emancipation Proclamation was limited, indeed, in scope. But Lincoln's document was only a beginning, and the progress of its ideals, entrusted to other hands and eras, has been an enduring issue, sometimes relegated to the background of national affairs and other times to their forefront.

Lincoln's successor, Andrew Johnson, a Southerner and states' righter, assumed a contrary position toward the Negro cause that was aggravated by his titanic struggle with Congress leading to his impeachment trial. He vetoed the extension of the Freedmen's Bureau and the Civil Rights Act designed to guarantee to freedmen, through federal courts, certain rights from infringement by state law. He vetoed the Reconstruction Act, which, among other things, required individual Southern states to accept Negro suffrage and to ratify the Fourteenth Amendment before they might again secure representation in Congress. The act was passed anyway. But there was another side to Johnson. In the conviction that well-to-do Southerners had led the humbler classes of the South into secession, in his special procedure for alloting pardons he required those whose estimated value of taxable property exceeded twenty thousand dollars to subject themselves to a rigorous review.

The remainder of the nineteenth century is a glorious saga of national growth, although it is not an era of notable advance for social justice. The Presidency became the preserve of the Republican party, save for the two intrusions of Grover Cleveland. Republicans could claim that their party had saved the Union and Democrats were tainted with the odium of secession. With but one exception every Republican Presidential candidate between 1868 and 1900 had been an officer in the Union army. A country engrossed in flinging railroads across mountain barriers, felling forests, ravishing the earth of its riches, enlarging their cities beyond count, and bestowing mansions upon the rich whose ornate display breached into vulgarity, had neither time nor inclination to erase social evil.

Wealth dominated commonwealth. The President was little more than titular leader. Hayes, Garfield, Arthur, and Harrison made no enduring contribution to social policy, or for that matter to public policy. Hayes, to be sure, made limited motions in behalf of reform. He included the egregious political reformer, Carl Schurz, in his cabinet, and vetoed a popular Chinese exclusion bill, not on social but on legal grounds.

Politics was an annex of business. Politicians like Blaine and Aldrich were deputies of such masters of capital as Morgan and Gould and such captains of industry as Carnegie and Rockefeller. The ethics of business was the ethics of politics. The major political parties seldom divided along economic lines and straddled important issues. Railroad and trust regulation ostensibly were favored by both parties, but neither lent it meaningful support. Labor was anything but a courted political object. Hayes in the railroad riots of 1877 and Cleveland in the Pullman strike of 1894 countenanced the use of the injunction and sent federal troops to protect business interests. The land laws, tariff reform, and the money question, each bearing powerful social facets, notwithstanding the eloquence of party platforms, Presidential pronouncement, and sharp legislative conflict, produced results little distinguishable from one Presidential administration to the next.

If the history of social justice possesses turning points, one indeed is the ascent of Theodore Roosevelt to the Presidency. The talents and instincts of that extraordinary man and the climactic momentum of forces that had gathered great speed in the final decades of the nineteenth century combined to produce an epoch of Presidential social achievement. The forces were many and diverse. The two great groups most injured by big industrialism—agriculture and labor—were well astir. Declining farm prices and soaring costs had produced the Granger movement of the seventies and the Populists of the nineties. Both championed broad programs and taught the farmer the value of political action against specific abuse. The Populists, with farm and labor support, pressed for a flexible currency, free silver, a graduated income tax, an eight-hour day for labor, and public ownership of railroads, telegraph, and telephones.

The churches' consciousness of the urban poor evoked a growing guilt in sensitive parishioners. Walter Rauschenbush and others propounded a "new theology." The individual, it held, was so enmeshed in the social environment that the human soul could not be saved unless society were saved first. Akin to the organized churches was the social justice movement—the intellectuals, ministers, lawyers, and especially women, who agitated for public regulation to diminish the toll of industrialism upon urban labor. Through the National Consumers League, the National Child Labor Association, the National Labor Association, and other organizations, the humanitarians worked to secure protective labor laws. In the new profession of social work, Jane Addams, Lillian Wald, Florence Kelley, and Julia Lathrop concentrated their great and merciful talents more upon the causes of poverty than upon cold dispensations of charity.

The way for reform was also prepared by a legion of social novelists, preachers, philosophers, and researchers. Novelists like Frank Norris, Brand Whitlock, Alfred Henry Lewis, David Graham Phillips, and Winston Churchill levied searing indictments of social conditions that shocked a vast reading public and sparked political investigation and action. The most sensational of the social writers were the "Muckrakers," a corps of early twentieth-century journalists such as Ida Tarbell, biographer of Standard Oil; Lincoln Steffens, whose baring of public corruption in St. Louis became a national sensation; Upton Sinclair, whose novel *The Jungle* was a nauseating description of the business of the Chicago stockyards. Others of high talent such as Ray Stannard Baker, Mark Sullivan, and Samuel Hopkins Adams swelled the torrent of revelation. The Muckrakers' handiwork appeared in the new, cheap, mass circulation magazines, *McClure's*, *Munsey's*, *Cosmopolitan*, *Collier's*, and *Everybody's*.

Laissez-faire individualism, the philosophical base of the competitive and exploitative system, was challenged by Henry George, Lester Ward, and Henry Demarest Lloyd. William James and John Dewey, apostles of pragmatism, taught that if man used his mind creatively, adventurously, and with moral sense, little was impossible. By 1900 the new discipline of "social science" had appeared and soon poured forth data, theories, and manpower to prepare Presidential reports, draft reform programs, and staff governmental agencies.

The first reform wave hit the cities, flushing out the political hirelings of corporations, railroads, and utilities. From 1889 onward, a series of new mayors, morally committed and politically gifted, came into power and rescued their cities from grasping economic tentacles—Seth Low in New York, James D. Phelan in San Francisco, Hazen Pingree in Detroit, Samuel M. ("Golden Rule") Jones of Toledo, and Tom Johnson of Cleveland. The backwash of reform struck the states, and eventually the nation.

Theodore Roosevelt's assumption of the Presidency was prophetically acknowledged by a plunge in the stock market. The first President to wage large-scale war upon economic abuse, he viewed his office as a "bully pulpit." Endowed with moral fervor and oratorical gifts, he awakened Congress and the people to the urgency of reform. The curbing of railroad rate discriminations, the pure food and meat inspection laws, the brassy warfare upon the trusts, and the federal employers' liability act typify his trail-blazing achievements. Certain of his proposals were so far-reaching they were not adopted until the distant day of the New Deal.

Theodore Roosevelt was spurred by his own large capacity for social initiative and moral fervor and the play of forces about him. Progressive sentiment was at a crest. If social reform tends to come when economic power becomes too concentrated too fast, when disparities between wealth and poverty become too glaring, the times indeed were right. Huge corporate profits and the lack of graduated income or inheritance taxes had created at the economy's apex a set of fabulously wealthy people. Their princely mansions and splendid yachts contrasted starkly with the squalor of the city tenement. No American group has enjoyed so much power as the top ten industrialists and financiers of 1900. Its king of kings, J. Pierpont Morgan, was thrice called upon by Presidents of the United States to save the country from financial disaster.

Theodore Roosevelt was also goaded by the two great evangelists of western progressivism, of whom he was ever wary, the Democrat William Jennings Bryan and the Republican Robert La Follette. To counteract the Bryan-La Follette preachings that the size of the trusts should be rigorously curbed, Roosevelt trundled out a competing doctrine that size in itself was not evil and that the trusts consequently should not be broken up. Roosevelt proposed that the trusts be regulated by making their operations public and outlawing dishonesty.

Although he profited greatly from the Muckrakers' skilled endeavors, Roosevelt knew interludes of moderation in which he by no means altogether welcomed their contribution. It was he indeed who coined the name "Muckrakers" as a term of disrepute. Fearful that the Muckrakers were driving the American people into socialism and stirring revolution abroad, Roosevelt in a violent speech once lowered the boom on the valiant writers. They dwelt only upon the "vile and debasing," he cried, like the man with the muck rake in Bunyan's *Pilgrim's Progress*, who with his eyes on the ground raked incessantly "the straws, the small sticks, and dust of the floor." Conservatives joyfully took up the Presidential epithet.

In his later Presidential years, Roosevelt veered sharply to the left, fearful of Democratic liberalism and the opposition of union labor in the approaching Congressional elections of 1906. Roosevelt's leftward swing was evident in his special attentions to eminent Senatorial progressives— La Follette, J. P. Dolliver, and A. J. Beveridge. These men he favored with general notes and summonses to the White House for chatty visits. The conservative Senate leaders, once an object of Presidential solicitude, were doused with Presidential criticism; playing the bull in the conservative china shop, Roosevelt moved on to harsh words about "plutocracy" and stepped up his requests for reform legislation. A powerful, perhaps indispensable, force to keep the chief executive moving down the road of social justice is the pressure of political rivals. His competitors for the Presidency in his own and the opposition parties, and legislators, especially Senators, who command national publicity and large followings can jog the President onward.

Woodrow Wilson could hardly have gained his New Freedom's social and economic reforms without William Jennings Bryan's thunderous schooling of the Democratic party in progressivism in three races for the Presidency. Wilson also prospered from the progressive's infiltration of Midwestern Republicans. A majority of both Democratic and Republican opinion demanded tariff, tax, and currency reforms; increased federal aid to farmers, workers, and other disadvantaged groups; and national controls over banking and industry. Wilson did not have to create a progressive public outlook in 1913; it was already there. He came to power at a time when social reform was in its ascendancy and the elections of 1912, with their overwhelming progressive sentiment, produced a President's dream of opportunity. With good working majorities in both houses of Congress, Wilson swept through a bulging social program. The time of maximum achievement in social legislation is apt to fall just after a decisive national election. It tends to fare least well in the final years of a President's term. With his political days numbered, his influence dwindles.

In his struggle to secure tariff reform, a venture that brought a legion of lobbyists to Washington, Wilson remarked, fight glinting in his eye, "A brick could not be thrown without hitting one of them." Those with superior economic advantage meant to keep what they had. Even mild economic change, which conceivably might benefit the economy, may require quantities of behind-the-scenes soothing and salving to contain the wildly escalating fears of the business and financial community. As the Wilson administration's plans for a Federal Reserve system proceeded, the President's intimate adviser, Colonel E. M. House, put in heavy hours reassuring such egregious and sophisticated financiers as Henry C. Frick, Henry P. Davison, and Otto Kahn that the future Federal Reserve would not wreck the economic system and that while the President "was a progressive, at the same time there would be no measure enacted into law, over his signature, which was in the least degree demagogic." After several intensive sessions of his ministrations, House sighed that the banking tycoons were "like a lot of children whose fears must be quieted. They must be told that there are no bears around to hurt them."

The closer the United States drew to involvement in World War I, the more strenuously Wilson campaigned to ease tensions between government and business. He cut back his antitrust prosecutions as a first step and petted the business community with soothing deeds and honeyed words of confidence. War or threat of it smothers the ardor for reform. War again was damaging to the civil liberties, the chief offender this time being Congress, whose espionage, sedition, and other laws seriously curtailed freedom of speech and press and other liberties. "Once lead this people into war," Wilson predicted, "and they'll forget there ever was such a thing as tolerance." His Attorney General, A. Mitchell Palmer, proved the force of these words by employing private spies, making lawless raids on private homes and labor headquarters, rounding up several thousand aliens holding them incommunicado, and subjecting them to drumhead trials. Eventually a few hundred were deported.

Wilson's trio of Republican successors—Harding, Coolidge, and Hoover—were as solidly aligned with the interests of business as any nineteenth-century President of their party, not excepting Benjamin Harrison and William McKinley. Coolidge clung to the status quo, admired business, and distrusted progressivism. His principal policies were high tariffs, tax reduction, and government support to industry. The reward for his steadfast partiality to business was the nation's soaring prosperity. Although Hoover preached doctrines of economic self-government, his administration, prodded by the Great Depression, undertook positive measures to bestir business activity.

Franklin Roosevelt, more than any other Democratic President, identified his party with social and economic reform and with the desires of major disadvantaged groups, such as labor and the Negro, to better their position. The New Deal, like the "deals" of other reforming Presidents, implied that in the game of life a beneficent superintending government can deal out a better playing hand to the great mass than does the unregulated market place of society. In the breadth and number of its innovations, the New Deal stands at the head of the list. Relief for the jobless, insurance against unemployment, pensions for the aged, help for labor to organize, aid to the farmer, protection for the Negro against discrimination in employment, regulation of securities and the stock exchanges, the Tennessee Valley Authority—the list is lengthy. The depths of the Great Depression provided Roosevelt with a magnificent opportunity to act. Social justice, paradoxically, advances most in times of misery.

It is in the New Deal that the advantaged have made their fiercest resistances in behalf of their imperiled privileges. Consider the utility company lobby that fought the administration's Wheeler-Rayburn bill in 1935, designed to cleanse utility holding companies of malpractices that had brought on some of the grosser financial scandals of the 1930's. Roosevelt called the lobby "the most powerful [and] dangerous . . . that has ever been created by any organization in this country." According to one authoritative computation, the lobby had more representatives in Washington than there were members of Congress. Senator Harry S. Truman was swamped with thirty thousand messages, hundreds identical in wording, urging him to oppose the bill. Congressional debate on social measures can evoke the dankest predictions of doom. "No, Mr. Speaker," said Congressman Joe Martin of Massachusetts in the debate on TVA, "I think I can accurately predict no one in this generation will see materialize the industrial-empire dream of the Tennessee Valley." "This bill, and every bill like it," added Representative Charles A. Eaton of New Jersey, "is simply an attempt to graft onto our American system the Russian idea." For all the furor, TVA quickly became law.

Like other reform Presidents before him, Roosevelt's most productive period fell in the first half of his first term, marked by the election of a new President and Congress, both Democratic. With the coming of World War II his revelation that old "Dr. New Deal" was henceforth superseded by new "Dr. Win-the-War" signaled the primacy of military victory and a shutdown on social legislation for the duration. Restraints upon civil liberties again took over, although on the whole the Justice Department functioned with commendable moderation. The wartime administration's worst offense to civil liberty was the relocation of the persons of Japanese descent residing in West Coast areas at the war's outset. The Smith Act, or Alien Registration Act, outlawed various activities knowingly designed to foster the government's violent overthrow.

The post-Roosevelt administrations have undertaken, in varying degree, extensions and adaptations of the New Deal. Truman ventured further into civil rights, championed a vast program of national health measures, and gave social justice an international dimension through his "Point Four" program by making "the benefits of our . . . industrial progress" available to "underdeveloped areas." The Truman era also witnessed the maturing of international Communism into a major challenge and the initial American restrictions upon domestic civil liberties. Congress passed over Presidential veto the Internal Security or McCarran Act, requiring "Communist-action" organizations and their members and "Communist-front" organizations to register with the federal government. Previous laws on espionage, sabotage, and assassination remained in force. Federal employees were tested for their loyalty.

Eisenhower shifted the emphasis of the employee test from "loyalty" to "security," thus reaching an employee who might be loyal but nevertheless a security risk because, for example, of his indulgence in personal indiscretions that might invite blackmail from enemy agents. The Eisenhower administration made several restrained assertions in the social field. It brought off the largest extension of social security coverage since the law was first established. Eisenhower trod cautiously on civil rights, preferring to leave responsibility for that troubled field to the states and the private citizen. Yet his administration also witnessed the passage of the first civil rights laws since the post-Civil War era. The Eisenhower administration exhibited at least a limited recognition that the general disposition of the Coolidge-Harding-Hoover era opposing federal assertion in behalf of the disadvantaged has become obsolete in the practice of the Presidency. It alienates too many voters to make the Presidency attainable. The Republican party can no longer be simply the party of business.

It must cast its appeal more widely to catch up disadvantaged groups without whose votes the Presidency cannot be captured.

John F. Kennedy's "New Frontier" program in the 1960 campaign was a large-scale program of social services and reforms pointedly addressed to the great urban groups. Kennedy's narrow popular victory, however, and his lack of a "working majority" in Congress led him to lower his sights. His major social proposals were a rise in the minimum wage, medical care for the aged, the liberalization of social security benefits, aid to education, aid to depressed areas, and an omnibus housing bill. Some of these were familiar holdovers from the Eisenhower era which might have been passed in some form if Eisenhower had chosen to push them. Civil rights, a large subject in the 1960 campaign, was treated vigorously and imaginatively by the executive. Kennedy, meanwhile, held back his civil rights legislation because of his wobbly Congressional strength, until the Negro civil rights demonstrators pried it loose in mid-1963. Many of Kennedy's advisers and supporters were waiting for the 1964 elections to provide a firmer platform of popular and legislative votes on which to launch the far-reaching social program heralded in his 1960 campaign.

Lyndon Johnson's program is largely a continuation of his predecessor's unfinished business. Johnson named as his major domestic objective the passage of the civil rights bill and attached an equal status to his own new program dedicated to attacking the causes of poverty.

◇

SOCIAL reform depends upon more than a set of special circumstances; it also requires the vital ingredient of the man—the President. Without his talent and involvement, circumstances, however favorable, will be wasted. If circumstances are not advantageous, we may well wonder whether a President endowed with conviction and creative gifts can bring off major achievement in the face of limited opportunity. Those Presidents who have wrought the greatest social achievements—the two Roosevelts and Woodrow Wilson—were all endowed with certain personal qualities. However much they differed otherwise, each possessed a strong sense of right, a confident faith in man's capacity for progress, and an aristocratic heritage of *noblesse oblige*. Wilson, the Calvinist, *knew* what was right and faced public questions with bristling faith in his predestined ability to find righteous solutions with God's help. "Talking to Wilson," Clemenceau once said, "is like talking to Jesus Christ." Theodore Roosevelt, morally, was rather different. He had a strict sense of personal morality that he followed impeccably in private life and held others to in public life. In pursuing public or political ends, however, Theodore Roosevelt often forgot his moral code in choosing means. Gifford Pinchot once told Roosevelt that he had either to be a great politician or a great moral teacher; he couldn't be both. But as John Blum has pointed out, Theodore Roosevelt had to be, and he was, both.

The Roosevelts and Wilson were all, in their way, aristocrats—Wilson by dint of his Calvinistic faith; the Roosevelts by birth and fortune. They were men apart from the usual run of aristocrats who evidence no particular sense of responsibility for others. The Roosevelts each bore a hard vein of benevolent paternalism; Theodore Roosevelt often articulated his conviction that superior station meant superior responsibilities to the less fortunate and to the state. Wilson was inspired by the ideal of service as man's highest endeavor. By grace of their aristocratic condition, all three Presidents enjoyed detachment from the existing economic order. Neither their material sustenance nor their moral tenets depended upon it. They were free to be its critics. Franklin Roosevelt's limited experience in business—he dabbled briefly in law and insurance—his lack of understanding of the importance of making a profit, Frances Perkins, his Secretary of Labor, deemed all to the good. "It gave him freedom to think," she was convinced, "in fields in which common people need their leaders to think."

All three Presidents were cosmopolitan, endowed with a sturdy intelligence and curiosity to seek out new and provocative ideas. They were not rigid and inflexible in their sympathies and associations, as aristocrats tend to be, but were eager to know the world about them and excelled as assimilators of ideas. They represented, in a word, the aristocratic tradition at its best. No modern President has brought to the office a more enterprising or cosmopolitan intelligence than Theodore Roosevelt. At the age of forty-three, when he assumed the Presidency, his far-ranging interests had established him as a naturalist, a discoverer of rivers, and a prolific author. Scientists, labor leaders, corporation executives, and religious chieftains numbered among his friends, and for them, as indeed for anyone of distinction, the welcome mat was always out. The White House calling lists in Theodore Roosevelt's day read like an occupational encyclopedia.

Woodrow Wilson began his gubernatorial candidacy as a spokesman of Democratic conservatism, the viewpoint of his sponsor, boss James Smith, Jr. Quickly learning the issues that were agitating the people, Wilson displayed his capacity for assimilation by cutting loose from the Smith machine and supporting the reforms that progressives of both parties had been pressing for a decade.

Franklin D. Roosevelt was also a great assimilator. "He was easy of access to many types of mind," Frances Perkins noted. The roots of his social philosophy, nourished by many sources, reached far back into his life. "One who is trying to discover the economic origins of New Deal," Rexford Tugwell has written, "cannot ignore the Harvard class of 1903." There Franklin Roosevelt took in W. Z. Ripley's strictures on corporate finance and the lectures of O. M. W. Sprague, a future New Deal adviser, on the merits of central banking and credit control as devices for economic stability. Certainly one of his foremost teachers in the elements of social justice was Eleanor Roosevelt. Observant and reportorial, especially after his illness, Mrs. Roosevelt excelled at bringing to her husband persons expert and stimulating in social subjects. Among Mrs. Roosevelt's importations were Rose Schneiderman and Maude Schwartz of the Women's Trade Union League, who subtly tutored Roosevelt in the mission of trade unionism. He habitually preferred to assimilate background from conversations rather than from books. "I doubt," acknowledged Frances Perkins, "that he had ever read any of the standard works on trade unionism." It was during his Albany days that Roosevelt, with the encouragement and guidance of his counsel, Samuel I. Rosenman, founded his Brain Trust of Raymond Moley, Rexford Tugwell, Adolf Berle, and other Columbia professors. In gubernatorial seminars with his university friends, Roosevelt, as Tugwell put it, was brought "to grapple with the complex realities of industrial life, and to move beyond his oversimple reactions which were insufficient as guides to policy."

Wilson and the Roosevelts all had a faith in man's capacity for progress and in government's ability to help achieve it. All had a vision of Presidential leadership that was positive and assertive. They discovered what the people wanted or needed and rallied them with great gifts of oratory. Social justice requires in large degree the passage of legislation, and all three possessed a dynamic philosophy of the Presidential role as legislative leader and a sturdy knack of success. Indeed, they exploited the full legal and political potentialities of the Presidential keyboard. "I believe in a strong executive," Theodore Roosevelt exclaimed, "I believe in power." To this Wilson and Franklin Roosevelt would add a firm amen.

◇

THE President's political necessities take priority over ventures in social justice. No matter how lofty the cause or how intense the chief executive's dedication, he obeys a higher law of political survival. He must win the next election and carry on his coattails his fellow party candidates on national and local tickets. One day Franklin Roosevelt, pressed by the impatient idealism of several youthful aides, discoursed on the realities of the political world in which he and they worked. Roosevelt began,

> You know, the first thing a President has to do in order to put through good legislation? He has to get elected! If I were now back on the porch at Hyde Park as a private citizen, there is very little I could do about any of the things that I have worked on. So don't throw away votes by rushing the gun—unless there is some good sound reason. You have to get the votes first—then you can do the good work.

The subordination of ideology to politics means that even those Presidents whose achievements of social justice are monumental often make their way by a course that is bafflingly erratic. Their social undertakings evolve according to no master plan but piecemeal, with quick, and not too costly, visible results preferred. The President's course is full of half-steps, forward and backward, covered with smoke clouds of obfuscation.

Theodore Roosevelt's State of the Union Message of 1902 demonstrates how a President of strong political and social instincts can mix his gestures to produce a common bewilderment. The message, a thirty thousand-word affair, was widely hailed as "safe," a result he doubtless hoped for. For assassins and anarchists Roosevelt had harsh words, which surely pleased the general citizenry. He titillated a broad swath of the more privileged population by advocating economic and educational tests for future immigrants. He said the things the business community liked most to hear: that big corporations were "natural," that foreign trade should be expanded, and that the merchant marine should be subsidized. Camouflaged in profuse and cautious verbiage were three references of large importance for Theodore Roosevelt's future Presidency: a request for national conservation of natural resources, reciprocal tariff treaties, and national supervision of corporations. If the message's real intent was obscure, its underlying political necessities were not. Theodore Roosevelt had read several handwritings on the wall. Unless he cooperated with the conservative Republicans of the Senate, led by Nelson W. Aldrich, he could expect precious little legislation. His most sacred political objective, his renomination in 1904, required protection. Not surprisingly, he invited the men who he felt had the greatest influence upon his renomination, Senators Aldrich, J. C. Spooner, W. B. Allison, O. H. Platt, and Mark Hanna—the Senate Republican leaders, all conservatives—to go over his message in draft before he sent it to Congress.

Like any other political leader, the President can at most push his ideas only a little beyond the tolerance of his constituents. As Rexford Tugwell has written, he must balance "the risk of alienating support against his conviction about what must be done and his desire to put it into practice." Franklin Roosevelt thus had to find a broad base of support and gain the specific consent of powerful groups he had to work with—labor, national and racial groups, and the like. He had to impress them that no matter what happened, he cherished their interests at heart. Yet he also had to carry a Congressional majority. He could not alienate articulate groups such as business, the press, the lobbyists, or vote-rich groups like the several immigrant bodies and the Catholic Church. Or, more precisely, he must not alienate enough of them at once to bring real trouble.

No President of the United States has been or is ever likely to be a social zealot. The political system which selects him for the great office precludes it. To win election, he must cast the net of his promises wide; the more he can offer to more people of diverse economic interests, geographic sections, and national and racial groups, the more likely he is to triumph. The balancing effect of promise upon promise keeps the President from extremes. Indeed, the political system sifts so finely that it has invariably produced Presidents who are "safe" not merely in public utterance but in personal conviction. When Franklin Roosevelt spoke of himself as "a little left of center," he was both accurate and candid, for all of his opponents' fierce characterizations of him as a "socialist" and a "Bolshevik." Woodrow Wilson, architect of the New Freedom, bore the stamp of a Southern upbringing. He remained at heart a states' rights Democrat who conceived that federal power should sweep away special privilege and other restrictions on individual energies. In his view, tariff legislation should be sheared, credit liberated from Wall Street, and the antitrust laws invigorated to restore competition. In turn, he opposed direct federal aid to depressed groups and would not fortify the natural economic power of workers and farmers. This too was special privilege.

Theodore Roosevelt likewise was a safe man. He is well described by George E. Mowry as an orthodox heretic, a respectable agitator, an intellectual Philistine, and a conservative revolutionist. "At times I feel an almost Greek horror of extremes," Theodore Roosevelt once said. He abhorred "the dull, purblind folly of the very rich men, their greed and arrogance." At the other extreme, he possessed an almost morbid fear of socialists and social violence. To Theodore Roosevelt, the Populist William Jennings Bryan and the Socialist Eugene Debs were the monstrous American replicas of Marat and Robespierre. His own high and solemn function, as Roosevelt saw it, was to bring balance between the greedy rich and the violent poor.

◇

DESPITE the caution and balance of Presidents, their administrations tend to show a predominant concern either for the advantaged or for the disadvantaged. Since the Civil War Republican Presidents have been largely disposed to favor business and Democratic Presidents labor and Negroes. The Republican party of Coolidge is the party of business; the Democratic party of Franklin Roosevelt is the party of the disadvantaged groups. Roosevelt remains enshrined in business's embittered memory. He and at least two of his Democratic Presidential successors—Truman and Kennedy—were involved in severe altercations with business. Kennedy's outcry upon discovering the steel price rise of 1962, "My father always told me that all [steel] businessmen were sons of bitches," is memorable not only for its unbridled candor but as a display of viscera not uncommon among Democratic Presidents.

Yet there is substantial evidence that since the Eisenhower era our political parties and Presidential administrations have reached a point where they can no longer be overwhelmingly disposed either toward the advantaged or toward the disadvantaged. Neither party, this is to say, can any longer afford to be labeled probusiness or antibusiness. They must appeal to both. The pressures producing this circumstance are a blend of economics and politics. For any Presidential administration, prosperity is good politics. Prosperity turns no little on business confidence in the existing Presidential administration. If Kennedy lost his temper over steel prices, he quickly recovered it, and in his subsequent deeds and words sought to mollify the business community. Lyndon Johnson tirelessly endeavors to convince business of his good will and his commitment to governmental economy and fiscal sanity. Business confidence and a healthy economy are all the more vital in what many analysts perceive as a coming era of close Presidential elections, in the manner of Kennedy's narrow triumph in the popular vote in 1960.

An historic distinction of the Eisenhower Presidency is its break with the Republican tradition of overriding favoritism for business exemplified by Coolidge, McKinley, and Benjamin Harrison. Eisenhower's "modern Republicanism" called for a retention and in some instances an extension of the major social programs of the New Deal, including improvements in the social security system. How else could the Presidency be won and kept? But social changes were not made simply to win votes. As many of Eisenhower's counselors appreciated, they were also the key to general economic well-being. What is good for the country as a whole—to borrow and adjust Charles E. Wilson's famous adage—is ultimately good for business.

The Kennedy administration bore witness to the same discovery in another way. At the peak of its experience with the civil rights crisis, the administration, seeking to promote both calm and progress, found, according to the New York *Times*, that of all the many Southern groups it conferred with, "the business group . . . proved to be among the most cooperative." Social justice is not simply sound public morality; it is good economics, good business.

The President ordinarily is regarded with suspicion and even with disapproval by the progressives or liberals whose reform convictions are more advanced than his. Tension regularly prevailed between Wilson and the advanced reformers. To them he loomed a slippery rhetorician whose heart belonged to small businessmen and manufacturers. Advanced progressives gagged over his devotion to states' rights and his simple faith that regulated competition could solve the big business evil and bring to pass a fairer distribution of wealth. Inevitably, Wilson was compared to his disadvantage with such urban-Democratic reform mayors as Tom L.

Johnson of Cleveland, an apostle of Henry George, and John Purroy Mitchel of New York City, who cleansed city hall of corrupting business influence, combatted urban squalor with enlightened social services, and brought mass transportation under public ownership. The cautious Wilson seemed oceans removed from the mayors' tradition when he vetoed legislation prohibiting child labor and easing farm mortgages. Franklin Roosevelt, in his day, was widely regarded by progressives as a chameleon who spurned progressivism in 1934 and embraced it in 1935. Roosevelt, who cherished acceptance by the progressives, courted their favor with mixed success. John Kennedy, in his turn, experienced a frequent questioning of his social course by a major political organization to the left of him, the Americans for Democratic Action.

The reform President also views uneasily the rare elements of the extremists who achieve major political strength. Franklin Roosevelt's adoption of a program of old age assistance was encouraged by the rise of the Townsend movement, named for Dr. Francis Everett Townsend, an unemployed physician who, looking out his bathroom window while shaving one morning, saw in an alley below, cluttered with rubbish barrels and garbage cans, "three haggard, very old women, stooped with great age, bending over the barrels, clawing into the contents." Angered by this indignity to his generation, Dr. Townsend launched a plan for old age pensions calling for two hundred dollars a month for everyone over sixty, a sum which in those deflated days seemed outrageous. Eventually other economic lures were embroidered onto the movement. By 1935 its membership and impact had mounted so that Raymond Moley was calling it "easily the outstanding political sensation as this year ends," and Edwin Witte was writing, "The battle against the Townsend Plan has been lost, I think, in pretty nearly every state west of the Mississippi, and the entire Middle Western area is likewise badly infected." With the Townsend fever burning high, Franklin Roosevelt, moving with a decisiveness he never showed for unemployment compensation, directed that an old age insurance plan be incorporated into the Social Security bill.

◇

WHEN the President's reform proposals require legislation, they must traverse a labyrinthian course filled with obstructions and quicksands. They must run the gauntlet of committee hearings and floor debates, parliamentary motions and conference committees, where a reversal at any time may be fatal.

The President's cherished social projects are highly vulnerable to sly parliamentary maneuver. Some of the more acute perils besetting a President are disclosed in the difficulty Theodore Roosevelt had trying to strengthen the Interstate Commerce Commission's rate-control powers over the railroads. That deep trouble was in store was suggested when Senator Stephen B. Elkins, Chairman of the Interstate Commerce Committee, who normally would sponsor such a bill, declined to do so. Worse trouble rolled in from the hand of Nelson W. Aldrich, the Senate Republican leader, a marrow-deep conservative and unstinting dispenser of government favors to business enterprise, who could not bear to increase the government's financial burdens. In a cute maneuver, Aldrich, who was also a member of the Commerce Committee, placed Senator Benjamin Tillman in charge of the Hepburn bill, as it was known. Tillman was not even of the President's own Republican party. He was a Southern Democrat, whose nickname "Pitchfork Ben" accurately suggests a tempestuous personality. Even worse, he was at this very moment thoroughly disliked by the President. After Theodore Roosevelt had entertained the distinguished Negro Booker T. Washington at the White House, Tillman had shrieked in racial protest and declared he would never set foot in the executive mansion again. Roosevelt had promptly taken the Senator at his word by withdrawing a previously issued invitation for a dinner honoring Prince Henry of Prussia, and the cornerstone of a lasting feud seemed to have been securely laid. A solid ray of hope suddenly pierced the shambles when Tillman voiced enthusiasm for the Hepburn bill. This was enough for the pragmatic Theodore Roosevelt. Through an intermediary Roosevelt let Tillman know the White House latchstring would henceforth be out for the Senator. Theodore Roosevelt's unpredicted rapprochement with Tillman opened the gates to eventual victory.

It is not uncommon for a President to do well with social legislation in one house of Congress and encounter hard trouble or even a rebuff in the other. The worst of fates, the predisposed negativism of both houses, was a common ordeal for Theodore Roosevelt. In the Senate the "Big Four" Republican leaders, all intractable conservatives, ruled with a firm hand and a granitic hostility to change. In the House a tyrannical Speaker, "Uncle Joe" Cannon, held sway. Cannon controlled committee appointments and rules of procedure and acted as a crusty, unsleeping, self-appointed watchdog over the federal treasury. He greeted every proposal of social reform with the cry, "This country is a hell of a success." Cannon and the Big Four stacked the key committees with members whose conservative instincts, they knew, would prompt them to nip Theodore Roosevelt's measures in the bud.

By uncommon good fortune, a President may discover a legislator whose prestige, committee assignments, parliamentary skill, and ideological convictions all harmonize with executive necessities. By these criteria, Senator George Norris's service in the cause of Franklin Roosevelt's fond dream of a Tennessee Valley Authority is almost idyllic. Prestigious progressive and chairman of the Senate Agriculture Committee, Norris for years had pushed for public power development in the Tennessee region. In 1933 Franklin Roosevelt and Norris drove through the shabby, eroded countryside along the Tennessee River in the President's open touring car, happily devising plans for a millenium of cheap electric power, flood control, soil conservation, afforestation, diversified industry, retirement of marginal farm land, and general developmental planning there. Roosevelt's message to Congress broadly delineating the bold new idea of TVA, Norris hailed as "the most wonderful and far-reaching humanitarian document that has ever come from the White House."

When a Norris is lacking, a President may aggressively go out and find one by encouraging selected legislators to support social measures which the administration will be pushing. Woodrow Wilson waged a large-scale effort to build bridges between his administration's purposes and interested influential legislators. On November 20, 1913, the President invited all Democratic legislative leaders to recommend to him new legislation which might well be included in the New Freedom. The overwhelming response calling for interpretive amendments to the Sherman Antitrust Act did much to thrust Wilson into a campaign that materialized in the Clayton Antitrust Act and the Federal Trade Commission Act. The acts thrived under legislative sponsorship that was well nigh Presidentially handpicked. Early in 1933 Franklin Roosevelt, a full two years before launching his social security proposal, encouraged Senator Robert Wagner and Congressman David Lewis to build momentum for their respective bills for unemployment compensation.

One of the more formidable hazards a social measure must survive is the appropriation process, easily manipulated by the foes of reform. After the Social Security Act was passed, when its advocates were rejoicing in the afterglow of victory, the wily Huey Long launched into a Senate filibuster to forestall any appropriation for the new program. Coming near the close of the legislative session, the filibuster was successful. The President had a new program but no money to run it. The chagrined devotees of social security implored Roosevelt to foil Huey Long by summoning Congress into special session. "We shall have a riot on our hands if we call them back for an appropriation," laughed Roosevelt. Then, goaded by the spectacle of his crestfallen colleagues, he put to work his genius for improvisation that saved many a social measure in its evil hours. His colleagues watched entranced as he spun out a solution to unbind their new program. "Well, the N.R.A. is being liquidated," he mused. "There has been an appropriation from Congress to enable them to liquidate. You can take the people laid off there." In another Roosevelt-contrived gambit, the Labor Department asked the WPA to start a "research project" on the ways and means of administering social security.

The WPA in actuality supplied personnel to operate the program. "The President was always willing to try even a risky technique to accomplish things," Frances Perkins noted appreciatively.

John Kennedy, in his key social proposals, was bedeviled by the delaying tactics of hostile legislative committees. His plan for medical care for the aged, presented within a month after his assumption of office, was bottled up in the House Ways and Means Committee for the duration of his Presidency. Although the Committee heard a long parade of witnesses on both sides of the issue in 1961, it failed to report out the bill and chalked up a major defeat for the administration. In 1962 and 1963 the committee placed the bill behind the President's tax proposals. Since the latter received interminable review, the bill for the aged remained immobile and, like many other languishing bills, magnificently reinforced the reputation of the committee chairman, Wilbur Mills, for cautious and unhurried deliberation.

A second major New Frontier project, a vast proposal of aid to education, encountered fatal opposition in committee and from the House leadership. The battle was touched off by Kennedy's unequivocal opposition to federal aid to parochial elementary and secondary schools. The principal strategist for the concerned Catholic interests was Democratic Majority Leader John McCormack of Massachusetts, the evident chieftain of a large bloc of Catholic-oriented Representatives. In the school aid fight, McCormack unofficially stepped out of his role as majority leader to operate independently of the regular Democratic organization headed by Speaker Rayburn. The fatal blow to Kennedy's 1961 education proposal occurred in the House Rules Committee, which by a vote of 9 to 6 decided not to clear the administration's education bills until it had in hand a bill to aid private and parochial schools. Rayburn informed the President, with accurate prophecy, that the public school bill was "as dead as slavery."

The Senate, which earlier this century was known as "the millionaires' club" and a citadel of hostility to social legislation, has undergone something of a transformation well evident in President Kennedy's experiences. His administration enjoyed conspicuously greater success in the Senate than in the House, where measures approved by the Senate were rejected or drastically revised. Kennedy's 1961 education program was approved in the Senate only to be rejected in the House. The Senate passed his depressed areas and minimum wage bills; the House severely amended them.

Kennedy's greater success in the upper chamber than in the House is largely explained by the mounting population shifts to the cities in recent decades. The Senator, answerable to a state-wide constituency, depends increasingly upon the great mass of urban voters for election, a happy coincidence for Kennedy's legislative program, which was directed heavily to the cities. The Representative, in contrast, responds to a smaller, less complex constituency. Rural voters, who tend to look askance at social legislation except for agriculture, possess a powerful voice in the House, owing to the lag in the redistricting of House seats to reflect the swelling population shifts from rural to urban and suburban areas. The Supreme Court's 1964 decision in *Wesberry* v. *Sanders* promises to compel a more equitable districting for the underrepresented areas. Likewise, if population shifts to those areas live up to predictions for future decades, the Court's decision may provide the basis for an improved capacity of the federal government to enact social legislation. Much will depend upon the suburban voter's attitudes, whether he will be more tolerant of federal social action than his country cousin.

Social legislation in the Kennedy era faced a coalition that reaches back to the Franklin Roosevelt administration. In the Eisenhower administration Southern Democrats and conservative Republicans repeatedly had played a decisive part in defeating or modifying social legislation for civil rights and medical care for the aged. The same coalition flourished in Kennedy's time. (As defined by the *Congressional Quarterly Weekly Report*, the coalition exists in a house when a majority of the voting Southern Democrats and a majority of the voting Republicans oppose the position of a majority of the Northern Democrats.) In what Kennedy styled as his "Big Five" programs of 1961—medical care for the aged, aid to education, aid for housing, a higher minimum wage, and aid to depressed areas—the only item on which the coalition did not operate in the House of Representatives was housing. The coalition's single absolute victory was on federal aid to education, and the medical care bill, bottled in committee, did not come to a vote. In the Senate the coalition appeared in the voting on four bills—depressed areas, minimum wage, housing, and school aid. On none of these was the coalition victorious. Despite the coalition's eclipsed influence, Kennedy was consistently wary. He withheld civil rights legislation until late in his term, anxious not to alienate Southern Democrats not simply on civil rights, but on other social proposals as well. In a bow to Southern Democrats in the House, the Kennedy administration agreed to eliminate 140,000 laundry and 15,000 cotton gin employees, mostly Negro, from the minimum wage bill's coverage. The concession weaned away from the opposition a sufficient number of Southern Democrats to provide the margin for victory. These, it happened, were Southern Democrats who really wanted to vote for the bill but were under heavy local pressure to keep out the workers finally exempted.

Kennedy's successes against the conservative coalition were vitally assisted by the rise of an offsetting bipartisan liberal coalition. Most of the administration's victories where opposition was strong were indebted to liberal Democratic and Republican support. In the House this species of Republican provided the votes for victory for the depressed areas bill and the minimum wage bill, and the battle to enlarge the Rules Committee, at the administration's outset, to brighten prospects for social measures. The conference report on the depressed areas bill, which prevailed by thirty votes, was supported by thirty-one Republicans. In the Senate, Republican help enabled the administration to push through the temporary extension of unemployment benefits, the minimum wage bill, the school aid bill, and housing. Time and again the practical problem facing Kennedy and his strategists was putting together a bipartisan liberal coalition to defeat the conservative coalition.

In the Senate the liberal Republican bloc consisted of eight to thirteen members and in the House about twice that number. Republican bloc members of both houses tended to come from urban industrial states and explained their frequent siding with administration positions on the ground that Kennedy had pre-empted the middle of the road and left them no alternative but to go along or yield the center and with it their grip on their constituencies. The result was a de facto coalition of Northern and Western Democrats and "liberal Republicans," the source of most of Kennedy's victories on social issues.

◇

VICTORIES won in social legislation can be lost in the selection of the administrative agency to carry it out. Since the President initiates the selection of the agency's leadership, he is sometimes the perpetrator of defeat. In reality, he is yielding to conservative pressures. To the newly established Federal Reserve Board, Wilson appointed an array of leading bankers and businessmen, a stroke that put the progressive community into a state of shock. "Why, it looks as if Mr. Vanderlip [president of the National City Bank of New York] has selected them," sputtered one dazed progressive. When Wilson, in a similar tactic, loaded the ICC with devoted friends of American railroads, Senator Robert La Follette exclaimed, "What an inspiring spectacle to the millions who voted for Wilson as a true Progressive." The newly created Federal Trade Commission was not long at work when Louis Brandeis, who had envisioned it as a dynamic force to relieve the economy of strangulating monopoly and to restore competition, was driven to dank despair. Wilson, he said, had ruined the FTC by his choice of commissioners. A typical Wilsonian choice was Edward Hurley, a Chicago industrialist and an ardent disciple of business-government cooperation.

◇

THE executive branch, with its wealth of talent, data, and organizations, provides the President with vital resources of social reform. His success in social enterprises depends in no small way upon his skill in exploiting these resources, particularly his stable of human talent. Within its stalls are specialists in the branches of political labor whose common effort is required to transmute the President's reform agenda into reality.

Advisers.   To make social innovations, the President requires advisers with ideas and access to his attention. Advisers may do their most fruitful toil well before their chief takes office. Woodrow Wilson, facing his 1912 Presidential campaign and looking about for a vivid and solid issue, conferred hopefully with Louis D. Brandeis, then a distinguished private lawyer with defined views on policy. The Wilson-Brandeis meeting of August 28, 1912, was fraught with consequence for the subsequent New Freedom. A champion of regulated competition, unhampered enterprise, and economic freedom for the small businessman, Brandeis guided Wilson into the conception that the worthiest issue his future administration might take up was the preservation of economic freedom in the United States. Business, by grace of government action, was to be freed from the shackles of monopoly and privilege. The Brandeis proposal fitted very precisely the necessities of the campaign. Its approach to the trust problem differed markedly from that of Theodore Roosevelt, Wilson's chief rival in the 1912 race. Theodore Roosevelt would legalize "good" monopolies. Wilson, taking his cue from Brandeis, argued, in contrast, that competition should be regulated and safeguarded so that all monopoly and its potential for evil would eventually be destroyed.

Some Presidents resort not merely to solitary advisers but to whole teams of them like Franklin Roosevelt's Brain Trust. John Kennedy preparing for the Presidency, recruited "Task Forces" to study and report on foreign and domestic problems. From his nomination until shortly after his inauguration, Kennedy established twenty-nine of these task forces in such fields as education, health, social security, and natural resources. The task force members exuded diverse viewpoints, enabling Kennedy to choose between alternative policies, and the task force reports, some of which were published and others of which remained confidential, were trial balloons testing legislative and public reactions to proposals the President hoped to embody in his future program.

Presidential advisers hail from all sorts of nooks and crannies of the executive branch and of society itself. Andrew Jackson's principal counselor in his war upon the Bank of the United States was Amos Kendall, fourth auditor of the Treasury. The President's adviser may be a general counselor whose attention to a social justice is but one of a host of assignments. Colonel Edward House, whose main beat was foreign policy, worked mightily in the service of Woodrow Wilson to bring about the Federal Reserve system. House harried the nation's professors of economics for the cream of their theory and data and conferred with bankers of varying viewpoints on the issue. Or again, the President's chief adviser may be, as plain logic suggests, the cabinet secretary whose department bears most closely upon the social reform at stake. Franklin Roosevelt's Secretary of Labor, Frances Perkins, for example, made the social security program her special cause. A social worker and Roosevelt's New York Industrial Commissioner, Miss Perkins, before accepting appointment in the national cabinet, had laid before the governor a program, including unemployment and old age assistance, she would insist on if she came to Washington. Franklin Roosevelt told her to come along.

Experts. Since projects of social justice are founded upon the conceptualizations and data of social science and its several branches, experts and technicians play leading roles in Presidential ventures. The chief expert toiling for the creation of the Social Security Act in 1935 was Edwin E. Witte, Executive Director of the Cabinet Committee on Economic Security. With this lordly bureaucratic title, Witte oversaw quantities of outside experts, a technical board of government experts, an advisory council, and a national conference. Prior to these responsibilities, Witte had served as secretary to the progressive Congressman John M. Nelson, statistician and secretary to the Wisconsin Industrial Commission, and chief of the Wisconsin Legislative Reference Library. In the latter capacity he drafted pioneering social legislation for which Wisconsin is distinguished. He taught at the state's university, served as acting director of the Wisconsin unemployment compensation law, and studied social insurance methods in Europe.

To launch his new Washington job, Witte made a month's grand tour of the American social security world, conferring with knowledgeable Washington officialdom, professors, mayors, and state legislators, business executives, and social workers. "Very contradictory advice was given me by the people consulted," he noted, "but I still regard these conferences as having been distinctly worth while, as they served to rapidly acquaint me with the widely varying views entertained within the Administration circle and the difficulties to be overcome." At the behest of Professor Raymond Moley, then a leading Presidential adviser, Witte prepared a lengthy statement on the problems of economic security for inclusion in Franklin Roosevelt's scheduled speech at Green Bay, Wisconsin. Although only two of Witte's sentences were eventually used, their effect was electric. The stock market dropped five points. Appalled high Treasury Department officials sprang forth to demand that social security be soft-pedaled at once. In his lesser concerns, Witte oversaw the handling of the voluminous mail on social security pouring upon the President, the executive committee, and its members. Much of the mail, which climbed to one thousand five hundred letters a day, concerned not the administration's social security project but the wild and booming Townsend plan.

Witte's most trying task was to find and hire social security experts willing to subordinate their professional predilections to the necessities of the executive committee and the President. Working under severe time limitations set down by Franklin Roosevelt, Witte had to badger the specialists into putting aside their accustomed standards of perfection so their reports would be finished on schedule. The executive committee's report, which emerged from the specialists' reports, Witte had to shepherd through agonizing rounds of negotiations. Several committee members refused to sign the report without having every word in it and the accompanying draft legislation scrutinized by subordinates in whom they had absolute confidence. Witte's worst hours were spent in the Treasury where two groups opposed social security, one conservative, bent upon holding down expenditures and avoiding any stir that might alarm business, the other radical, which felt that given the deep economic morass in which the country was wallowing the proposals had little value. Witte's ordeal was topped off with four days of testimony on the technical phases of social security before the House Ways and Means Committee and three days before the Senate Finance Committee. His experience illuminates a common fate of Presidential experts. Their talents are useful at both ends of Pennsylvania Avenue.

Promoters.   Social justice measures, taking the form of legislation, have touched off the most violent battles that Congress has witnessed. Among the most enflamed of these scenes was the Franklin Roosevelt administration's public utility bill, with its "death sentence" provision, designed to outlaw some of the grosser abuses of the holding companies of gas and electric utilities. To guide his cherished legislation through the pending strife, the President turned to a lieutenant with proven talent for the rough and tumble of legislative politics, Thomas G. Corcoran, a youthful, cherub-faced protégé of Professor Felix Frankfurter of the Harvard Law School and former law clerk of Justice Oliver Wendell Holmes.

Nominally a counsel of the Reconstruction Finance Corporation, Corcoran with his partner in several New Deal enterprises Benjamin V. Cohen, the counsel of the Power Policy Committee, had drafted the utilities bill they were now promoting. To touch off his campaign, Corcoran prepared a Presidential letter of fitting exhortation to accompany the bill to Capitol Hill. He provided full-time, all-around assistance to the bill's sponsors, Senator Burton K. Wheeler of Montana and Congressman Sam Rayburn of Texas. Corcoran and Cohen coached the sponsors and a parade of government witnesses on the bill's many intricacies. For Senators and Congressmen friendly to the bill, they ghostwrote letters addressed to legislative colleagues and influential constituents, entreating their support. Corcoran negotiated compromises on hostile amendments and lobbied frantically in cloakrooms and hallways, lining up votes. The juggernaut of influence the utilities were wheeling through Congress lifted his effort to a high and steady pitch.

The President's youthful promoter was faring tolerably well until an explosion of ominous publicity was touched off by Congressman Ralph O. Brewster of Maine. At the height of battle, Brewster rose in the House to declare,

> During the consideration of the "death sentence" clause in the Holding Company bill, Thomas G. Corcoran, Esquire . . . came to me in the lobby of the Capitol and stated to me with what he termed "brutal frankness" that, if I should vote against the death sentence for public utility companies he would find it necessary to stop construction on the Passamaquoddy dam in my district.

(The dam was a huge work relief project established primarily to develop public power. "Quoddy," situated across from Campobello, Franklin Roosevelt's summer home, was a pet enterprise of the President.) Promptly after Brewster's disclosure, Corcoran was faced with two inquiries. One, a cryptic request from Franklin Roosevelt, read "Please send me as promptly as possible a complete statement of all your dealings on governmental matters" with Congressman Brewster. The second was a House committee investigation of the incident. Corcoran passed both tests with flying colors. In putting his case before the House committee, he had the advantage of a witness, a fellow official of the executive branch, while Brewster was handicapped by having no corroborator. Meantime the utility bill was passed.

Administrators. The administrators of the great departments and agencies, at both the highest and lesser levels, do the vital work of carrying out reform polices and of proposing their revision and extension. In selecting administrators even those Presidents most closely identified with causes of social justice do not load the departments with chiefs of that philosophy. If anything, the cabinets of Wilson and the two Roosevelts were, in their majority sentiment, at least middle-of-the-road and even conservative in disposition toward social questions. The state of the cabinet partly reflects the mixed sentiment of the body politic itself regarding social reform and partly the unsettled attitude of the President. Franklin Roosevelt's original Budget Director, Lewis Douglas, and his Secretary of State, Cordell Hull, were devoted to sound money, fiscal orthodoxy, and tariff reduction. Old-line progressivism was embodied in Harold Ickes, a Bull Mooser, and the preferability of government-business collaboration in Raymond Moley on the right and Rexford Tugwell,

Assistant Secretary of Agriculture, on the left. These and other philosophical schools scored successes, although the predominant image that emerged was of social reform.

It was part of Franklin Roosevelt's administrative genius that he encouraged his diverse administrators to ride and expand their own programs vigorously and never think of sparing him. "Thus a very energetic set of people were stimulated by their leader to develop programs of reform and action," Frances Perkins noted. The pressures unloosed upon the President were often exerted in secret collusion by his several administrators. In the early New Deal, for example, those who wanted a gigantic public works program to relieve the misery of the unemployed and to bestir general economic activity continuously pressed the chief executive. Secretary Perkins would bring up the matter at one session of the cabinet; Jim Farley, the Postmaster General, at the next; and then Ickes at the one after that. The object of this unceasing harassment was to keep the subject stirring in the President's mind. The allied secretaries had a sense of special urgency thanks to the chief opponent of large-scale public works, the Budget Director, Lewis Douglas, who attended cabinet meetings where his skillful argument raised doubts in Roosevelt's mind and forestalled him from acting at once. Eventually, however, Roosevelt chose to establish a mammoth public works program.

◇

THE President may advance or retard social justice by employing or neglecting the abundant resources of executive action. Of all social fields, civil rights for the Negro has evoked the most various and sometimes the most enterprising executive responses. It has also been frequently ignored by Presidents.

Despite the beacon light of Lincoln's Emancipation Proclamation, Presidents have dealt gingerly with Negro civil rights since his time. Of modern Presidents, Theodore Roosevelt is the first to act assertively, at least by the standards of his day. His entertainment of Booker T. Washington, the eminent Negro educator, has been noted. Early in his administration, Roosevelt appointed Dr. William Crum customs collector at Charleston and Mrs. Minnie Cox postmistress at Indianola, Alabama. Both were Negroes. Although Theodore Roosevelt's moves seemingly championed the Negro cause, they were not unalloyed. His eye was fixed upon the 1904 Presidential nomination and his considerable rival, Mark Hanna. The latter's awesome strength at past Presidential nominating conventions was founded no little upon unswerving Southern delegations of "lily-white" Republicans. To counterweigh Hanna, Roosevelt had to enlist the "black and tan" Republicans, and for this high enterprise Booker T. Washington was his staff and reed.

Theodore Roosevelt's good progress was suddenly jeopardized by the Brownsville affair, when Negro soldiers, angered at their treatment by local folk of Brownsville, Texas, made a shooting sortie into the town, killing a citizen. Efforts to lay responsibility for the slaying failed; the soldiers would not talk. Theodore Roosevelt, the commander-in-chief, conscious of his duty to maintain discipline, meted out punishment by discharging "without honor" every man of three Negro companies. Republican politicians, mindful of the traditional Negro vote for their party, grew fearful, and Theodore Roosevelt redoubled his attentions.

Although Woodrow Wilson appealed openly for Negro support in the 1912 elections, he and his principal administrators quickly exhibited the predominant Southern background of his Presidency. Civil service workers were rigidly segregated in offices, shops, restrooms, and lunchrooms. Negro political appointees, including those with civil service status, were widely dismissed. Herbert Hoover, despite his Quaker roots, evidenced little interest in the Negro's plight. He made, said W. E. B. Du Bois, "fewer first-class appointments of Negroes to office than any President since Andrew Jackson." Franklin Roosevelt accomplished the awesome feat of transferring the Negroes' traditional loyalty from the Republican party, cemented by Lincoln, to the Democrats. The New Deal was, by contrast to the barren Democratic past, rich in its dispensations to the Negro. The National Industrial Recovery Act tended to set a single standard for Negro and white wage earners in the South. Relief funds, housing projects in the wake of slum clearance, rural resettlement, land-utilization schemes providing parks, picnic grounds, and beaches for the Negro, and growing federal attention to education and health were a great boon to that race, which suffered more than any other part of the population in the depression. Roosevelt's successor, Harry Truman, created a Commission on Civil Rights whose distinguished report, *To Secure These Rights*, charted a wide ground for future action. He accepted the 1948 Presidential nomination with a fiery speech, broadcasting his future call of Congress into special session to act on civil rights. Truman tarnished his promising record by never mentioning civil rights again in his ensuing campaign until a wind-up speech in Harlem. Otherwise Truman moved to establish a permanent Fair Employment Practices Commission, fought the Senate filibuster by prodding Democratic leaders to bring about an amendment of the Senate rules, attacked racial discrimination, and backed the United Nations' Declaration of Human Rights. His strong stand on civil rights was diminished by the occasional fluctuating character of his support for legislative and administrative action, and by off-the-record comments he made on several occasions after his Presidency that were hardly in keeping with his administration's record.

Negro civil rights first assumed crisis proportions, in the Presidential view, in the Little Rock school episode of the Eisenhower era and boiled over into the multiple crises of the Kennedy administration. The two Presidents differed radically in their views on civil rights, particularly on public school segregation. The several Supreme Court rulings of 1954 striking down segregated public schools as a violation of the Fourteenth Amendment's requirement of equal protection of the laws were followed by widespread resistances in state and local government, to the point where activity in the South toward integration came almost to a halt. President Eisenhower made little effort through federal policy to support the Supreme Court holdings, leaving the question of compliance to voluntary action and local lawsuits. He intervened personally only after Governor Orval Faubus of Arkansas defied a federal court order and employed the National Guard to prevent Negro school children from attending the Little Rock Central High School. In addition, the governor failed to prevent a mob from blocking the Negro children from entering the school. Eisenhower, stung by the governor's defiance, federalized the Arkansas National Guard and called out Regular Army units to enforce the court order and protect the Negro children. Eisenhower, nevertheless, refused to declare that he personally favored elimination of segregation from public schools, holding that policy on the question was the province of the Supreme Court and not the President. He sometimes remarked that race relations could not be effectively regulated by law, but depended upon voluntary action.

President Kennedy, in contrast, became the first chief executive to place himself at the head of the Negro civil rights movement. He publicly asserted his support of the Supreme Court's rulings in the school segregation cases. He enforced the enrollment of James Meredith at the University of Mississippi and of Vivian Malone and James Hood at the University of Alabama, quelled the raging strife in Birmingham, Albany, Jackson, and other cities, North and South, and quietly encouraged or at least failed to discourage the march on Washington. Kennedy was faced with social revolution and had to act. That it was congenial to his own nature to act made his stand more consistent and more forceful. In meeting the civil rights issue, whether in its more subdued stage earlier in his administration or in its later critical phase, Kennedy and his aides wielded, with skill and enterprise, a variety of executive tools.

Litigation. The 1957 Civil Rights Act authorizes the Justice Department to sue in federal courts or to seek injunctive relief where the right to vote is denied or threatened. In its first year, the Kennedy administration initiated twice as many cases as the Eisenhower administration did in three years. Although the latter administration commenced the first exploratory cases under the Civil Rights Acts of 1957 and 1960, the Kennedy administration displayed greater litigious vigor and resourcefulness. Kennedy's Justice Department stepped up the tempo of school segregation cases and forged a major innovation by casting itself as plaintiff in the Prince Edward County, Virginia, case. The Kennedy administration's law arm also struck in other urgent civil rights situations. When the city of Albany, Georgia, sought an injunction banning further Negro protest demonstrations in that city, the Justice Department filed a friend-of-the-court brief in opposition. Likewise, when Governor Ross Barnett of Mississippi interposed obstructions to the enrollment of James Meredith at the University of Mississippi, the Justice Department petitioned the Fifth Circuit Court of Appeals to levy a fine of $100,000 upon the governor.

The Presidential constabulary. The United States Code authorizes the President to suppress domestic violence stemming from unlawful assembly and a state's inability or unwillingness to protect a Constitutional right. To keep order, the President is assisted by a tri-part constabulary: the Regular Army, the federalized National Guard, and the United States marshals. In the severe rioting in Birmingham in May 1963, Kennedy vowed before the nation, "This Government will do whatever must be done to preserve order, to protect the lives of its citizens and to uphold the law of the land." Even as the President spoke, units of the armed forces specially trained in riot control moved into military bases near Birmingham. The President simultaneously ordered the taking of all "necessary preliminary steps" to call the Alabama National Guard into federal service. James Meredith's presence and safety at the University of Mississippi depended, at least in its early season, upon units of the Regular Army and the federalized Mississippi National Guard. The busiest unit of the President's constabulary are the United States marshals, called upon to protect variously the freedom riders and demonstrators in Albany, Georgia. When a mob took over the bus station in Montgomery, six hundred marshals moved in to fill the law enforcement vacuum.

The government contract. Presidents since Franklin Roosevelt have employed the government contract as a weapon to clear pathways for civil rights progress. The one hundred largest defense contractors and their subcontractors employ approximately ten million persons. Countless other workers are employed under federal contracts or aid. From Franklin D. Roosevelt onward, interdepartmental committees composed of the departments contracting most heavily have existed to overcome job discrimination by private employers performing government contracts. Congress's disinclination to establish a Fair Employment Practices Commission has made reliance upon the interdepartmental committees all the heavier. Through the committees, Presidents have insisted upon anti-discrimination provisos in government contracts, heeding their implied duty as executors of the Constitution, with its affirmation of equal rights, to see that federal money is not tainted with racial prejudice.

In the Kennedy administration Vice President Johnson headed a Committee on Equal Employment Opportunity, whose enforcement powers were broadened by a March 6, 1961, executive order. Its impact was deepened by his persuasive talent and vigorous administration and Kennedy's strong support. Under the executive order employers must pledge, in taking on a government contract, to act against discrimination in hiring and on the job. The Johnson committee required employers to file regular reports, an innovation to prove their compliance with the executive order. More than a score of major contractors signed "Plans for Progress" agreements with the committee, pledging steps against employment discrimination. Militant civil rights groups pressed to cancel the contracts of gross violators, particularly in the textile industry, but the commitee rejected this counsel.

The civil service.   The United States government, as the nation's largest employer, has its own house to put in order. Legal authority to do so is abundant. The 1883 Pendleton Act established merit as the primary test for federal employment, and from 1940 onward various statutes prohibit discrimination "on account of race, creed, or color." The President's official oath and responsibility as chief administrator impart further authority. The Kennedy administration's personnel policies put new stress upon the appointment and upgrading of qualified Negroes. Complaint procedures concerning discrimination were liberalized and the Committee on Equal Employment Opportunity investigated agency compliance.

The Kennedy administration's emphasis upon Negro recruitment was reinforced symbolically by Kennedy's exercise of the Presidential appointment power. The selection of Robert Weaver as head of the Housing and Home Finance Agency, of Andrew Hatcher as White House associate press secretary, and of Carl Rowan (appointed USIA director by President Johnson), as Assistant Secretary of State for Public Affairs and later ambassador to Finland, were indicative of the administration's commitment. In 1961 Cecil Poole and Merle McCurdy became the first Negroes to serve as United States attorneys in the continental United States. Kennedy's judicial appointments stand as equally innovative. Wade McCree and James B. Parsons became, in 1961, the first Negroes ever to be appointed District Judges in the continental United States. Kennedy, wielding the appointment power, also reached up to the next judicial level, where Thurgood Marshall, former counsel of NAACP's Legal Defense and Educational Fund, was named to the United States Circuit Court.

Administrative regulation.   The freedom riders' visitations in Southern territory spurred the Kennedy administration to petition the Interstate Commerce Commission to desegregate facilities in terminals serving interstate bus travel. After months of delay and insistent Justice Department pressure, the desegregation order was issued. The administration lacked power to move similarly upon airports under the Civil Aeronautics Act. To foster desegregation in various Southern airport facilities, the Justice Department relied upon court action and private persuasion.

Federal funds. The expenditure of federal funds is a Presidential weapon of vast potency in the civil rights struggle. Few aspects of American life are untouched by the incessant outpouring of federal money. In many states and localities, the federal wherewithal has, in actuality, supported rather than checked racial discrimination. Housing, education, job training, the National Guard, recreation facilities, hospitals, libraries, university research, agricultural extension, state employment services, vocational rehabilitation, school lunches, and highway and airport construction are objects of federal largess and occasional sources of racial discrimination.

In his 1960 campaign, Kennedy flayed the Eisenhower administration for not blotting out racial discrimination in federally supported housing, holding it could be achieved merely by "a stroke of the pen." After long delay and much pressure by racial groups, the President finally issued an executive order of November 21, 1962, barring discrimination in the sale or rental of housing financed through federal assistance. The executive order's seeming breadth was badly sheared by administrative interpretation. "Conventional" or private financing, houses "already built," houses that are not in commercially developed neighborhoods, and FHA-insured loans for home improvements were ruled to be not covered.

President Kennedy was insistently pressed to issue a blanket order prohibiting discrimination in all federal programs. Indeed in Kennedy's encounters with Governor Barnett of Mississippi to enroll James Meredith in the state university, the Civil Rights Commission urged that Mississippi be barred from all federal funds. "I don't have the power to cut off the aid in a general way as was proposed by the Civil Rights Commission," Kennedy responded, adding that "I think it would probably be unwise" to grant the President that power.

Public appeals. In the major civil rights crises, Kennedy as a regular tactic made radio and television addresses, pleading and lecturing to the nation, stressing the moral aspects and local responsibilities. In the University of Alabama episode of 1963, Governor George C. Wallace stood in the doorway of a University of Alabama building to prevent the registration of two Negro students, Vivian Malone and James Hood. The governor, in his chosen stance, was both fulfilling a campaign pledge and violating a court order rendered to assure the students' registration at the university. The students eventually embarked upon their studies with the help of the National Guard. In his television address on the Alabama episode, Kennedy termed the rising tide of Negro discontent "a moral crisis," which "faces us all in every city of the North as well as the South." The problem of the Negro's place in American life, the President declared, "must be solved in the homes of every American across the country." In an address to the 1963 National Conference of Mayors, he urged increased local responsibility in coping with disturbances in Northern and Southern cities; the establishment of local biracial human relations committees to spot developing tensions and push for the revision of local segregation laws; and the adoption of equal opportunity ordinances for housing, public accommodations, and employment.

Kennedy's public appeals were also put to individuals and specific local communities. His most eloquent appeal in behalf of civil rights was his televised address to the nation in the crisis of James Meredith's enrollment in the University of Mississippi. Kennedy appealed to the students and people of Mississippi to comply with court rulings and therefore with federal law to bring the crisis to an end. "The eyes of the nation and all the world are upon you and upon all of us," he said, "and the honor of your university and state are in the balance." As rioting spread and Negro houses were bombed in Birmingham in 1963, the President implored that community to restore peace. Kennedy's public expressions included an appeal to Governor George C. Wallace of Alabama to stay away from the campus of the state university at Tuscaloosa. This rare proffer of advice from a President to a governor was sparked by Wallace's threat to bar physically the admission of two Negro students to the university. The governor's plan, the President stated candidly in a published telegram, was "the only announced threat to orderly compliance with the law." In addition, Kennedy pointed the finger of national opprobrium at local malfeasance. The burning of Negro churches near Albany, Georgia, in September 1963, he termed "cowardly as well as outrageous." When a general civil rights impasse seized that unhappy city, Kennedy declared in a news conference that he could not see why city officials could not sit down with Negro citizens to work out racial problems. In the New Orleans school integration crisis, he reminded segregationists that the Supreme Court's school desegregation decision was both Constitutionally and morally unassailable.

Private persuasion.   To head off brewing civil rights crises or to steady them at a low boiling point, President Kennedy, the Attorney General, and their aides counted heavily upon the arts of private persuasion. President Kennedy met at the White House with whole delegations of Southern businessmen, theater owners, and newspaper editors to put the case for voluntary desegregation and warn of the danger that Negro extremists might gain power should the moderates fail. Cabinet secretaries sometimes joined the effort. Secretary of Commerce Luther Hodges, a North

Carolinian, wrote letters of encouragement to fellow Southerners; the Attorney General telephoned friendly and unfriendly local officials, encouraging, persuading, or scolding, as required. The Justice Department in private, unpublicized talks helped some Southern communities desegregate their schools without incident. The Justice Department quieted several violent intervals in Birmingham by negotiating agreements between the contending groups, and as tensions mounted in Jackson, Mississippi, in June 1963, a peace-building meeting transpired in the local Masonic Lodge between John Doan, Assistant Attorney General for Civil Rights, and Negro representatives. In its discussions with white Southern leaders, the administration stiffened its language with appeals to party loyalty and used higher and lower forms of political inducement. The administration also engaged in dialogue with Negro civil rights leaders, including an intensive discussion in New York at the peak of the 1963 crisis when Robert Kennedy reviewed with the leaders both what they were seeking and what the administration could do.

President Kennedy and his aides invested many hours in White House discussions with Negro leaders to plumb their views and to convey the administration's intentions and a sense of the political realities it faced. Soon after taking office, Kennedy invited the emissaries of several Negro groups to outline what they would consider a good administration civil rights program. A sixty-one-page memorandum resulted, and, midway in discussing it with Roy Wilkins and Arnold Aronson, chairman and secretary, respectively, of the Leadership Conference on Civil Rights, Theodore Sorensen, the President's Special Counsel, let out the bitter news that the administration would not push civil rights legislation, at least in its first year. This disclosure bathed the 1961 conference of the National Civil Liberties Clearing House in Washington in gloomy lamentation. Tempers were somewhat smoothed when Harris L. Wofford, Jr., a special assistant to the President, candidly reviewed the pressures necessitating the administration's course. Because of his own eminence in the Negro civil rights movement, Wofford's good faith could not be questioned, and his acceptance of the President's position lent it plausibility. Kennedy himself salved the feelings of Negro leaders when his administration was politically unable to give them what they wanted. When Martin Luther King, after declaring to the National Baptist Convention that Negroes "cannot wait any longer" and that he would go to the President for a "new Emancipation Proclamation," called at the White House to make his request, Kennedy had a ready response. "Let me show you where the first one was signed," he said, leading the way to the Lincoln bedroom. The King-Kennedy talks proceeded by mutual consent not on the basis of a proclamation, but on specific areas of future concrete action.

Like other Presidents who, because of political restraints, could give social groups only a part of what they wanted, Kennedy sustained public criticism from Negro civil rights leaders. In the administration's first years, when it held back civil rights legislation and shunned a futile fight to throttle the Senate filibuster, NAACP secretary Roy Wilkins sadly declared that an "atmosphere of super-caution" had "pervaded" all civil rights discussions with Kennedy and his staff since election day. In a television interview in June 1963, amid the demonstrations crisis, the Reverend Martin Luther King, viewing the cheerless scene, conceded that President Kennedy "may have done a little more" than President Eisenhower, "but the plight of the vast majority of Negroes remains the same." In the spirit of constructive criticism, Dr. King urged the President to forego a trip to Europe scheduled later in the month, and remain, instead, in Washington to push his civil rights program. The President, Dr. King said, in a further pointer, should revive "fireside chats" to explain civil rights to the nation.

The Negro civil rights revolution throws a sharp, unflattering glare upon the limitations of Presidential power as an instrument of social change. It is one thing for the President to issue executive orders and proclaim high policy; it is quite another to transmute policy into action and orders into compliance. In the acid test of performance, the President depends upon a vast federal bureaucracy and far-flung field organizations staffed heavily with local personnel. The President's housing order, for example, sweeping and well-intentioned on its face, was softened by administrative interpretation—the sweeping exemptions and the stress upon "persuasion" rather than enforcement. The unacknowledged motivation behind such choices is the fear that vigorous executive action will alienate Southern legislators situated on strategic committees.

Civil rights is also vulnerable to fluctuations in its capacity to command the President's attention. In June 1963, when Negro rights demonstrations gained their peak, the President could, for a time at least, give civil rights a maximum priority on his agenda, even above foreign affairs and the cold war. But as weeks passed, civil rights clung to its topmost position only fitfully, falling below the claims of foreign affairs at one time or another. Civil rights, like any other government business, must compete for the President's attention, priorities, and action. For all the heat of the street demonstrations and Dr. King's criticism, President Kennedy went off to Europe. Similarly, the administration, dispatching its civil rights legislation to Capitol Hill, hailed the event by proclaiming that this bill would be given the "highest priority" in future political effort. Yet only a month later the administration rather downgraded civil rights by declaring that its privileged priority would henceforth be "shared" with the tax cut bill. Still later President Kennedy, in one of his last major pronouncements on civil rights, gave his tax bill a higher priority than his rights bill, holding that a rising economy was indispensable for the better-ment of Negro rights.

But Kennedy and his administration continued to fight hard for civil rights legislation until his assassination. In few places did that tragedy evoke more grief than in the Negro community. On a Washington, D.C., street corner, a blind Negro woman plucked at the strings of her guitar, half singing and half weeping a dirge—"He promised never to leave me. . . ." In the Negro part of a Southern city, people rushed into the streets moaning, and one little girl, asked by a bystander what had happened, replied, "Jesus has died." Effort for civil rights legislation was lent a new urgency by a growing view of it as a kind of "memorial" for the late President. President Johnson accorded the bill the highest priority. In time it passed the House of Representatives, escaped the snare of the Senate filibuster, and, with strong bipartisan support, became law.

◊

SOCIAL justice brings the President, Congress, the parties, and the nation to grips with the most urgent and difficult choices in public affairs. It is a continuous testing of the capacity of men and institutions to adjust to change. It provokes struggle between those, on the one hand whose self-interest weds them to the status quo or fills them with nostalgia for the past, and those, on the other hand, who are disadvantaged in present society or are troubled in conscience by the severe inequities dealt by economic and social forces to their fellow men. The exponents of social justice are not only alive in conscience; they believe progress is possible and look confidently to the future.

To compound the difficulties, social justice is itself wrapped at times in obscurity, its substance and meaning anything but clear. When does government welfare stray into paternalism; when does public authority unjustifiably intrude upon private initiative and private right? Since social justice is a human enterprise, those it involves can err. It is dispensed by no omniscient, infallible source, and the men, groups, and sections of the nation associated with it have no monopoly on wisdom and rectitude. A Theodore Roosevelt fights splendidly for conservation of natural resources, but acts with questionable judgment and severity against the Negro regiments in the Brownsville episode. Franklin Roosevelt champions the New Deal, a vast mission of mercy for the downtrodden, but countenances the uprooting of Japanese-Americans in World War II, one of the most flagrant mass injustices in the nation's history. The South, although the stronghold of racial injustice, produces for the United States Senate a Lister Hill or Claude Pepper whose political toil played no little part in identifying the New Deal with the Negro's cause. The East is the stronghold of traditional business resistance to social change; yet it also produced

three Presidents—the Roosevelts and Kennedy—who perceived its character most acutely and acted on what they saw. The Middle West can look
askance at "do-good" internationalism, but produce a Bryan or a La Follette whose influence upon the Presidency's commitment to social reform
is enormous.

The strong Presidency of the future will need to be continuously and
deeply involved in furthering social justice. The ambitions and resentments of disadvantaged peoples at home and abroad have long passed the
point where Presidential attention to social justice can be a part-time concern, or predominantly the pursuit of one major political party rather than
the other. The Eisenhower Presidency, representing as it does a limited
break with the Republican Harding, Coolidge, and Hoover tradition of
identification with the advantaged, must be carried forward and enlarged
by any future Republican President in his attentions to the disadvantaged.
The Democratic President has the easier, but no less vital, task of building
upon an impressive heritage.

The President of the future, unless he keeps the enterprise of social
justice continuously in high gear, may well face a series of formidable
social revolutions. If 1963 was the year of the Negro Revolution, 1965
could well become the beginning of the Revolt of Youth—demonstrations
and marches protesting high unemployment, denial of opportunity, and
discriminatory treatment. For the remainder of the sixties some three million new young workers will be entering the labor force each year. Unless
the economy performs radically better than in the fifties, youth's unemployment will soar. In that decade, 840,000 new jobs were created annually; in the sixties, a million and a half jobs are needed merely to keep
the present youth unemployment rate from rising beyond the already high
figure of 11 per cent. And there may be other revolutions. The time is
fast fading when the President dispenses social justice because it will win
votes or bespeak conscience. The forces of revolution will require that he
be of a mind suggested by Robert Kennedy, in the Negro civil rights crisis
in mid-summer 1963, when he conceded that relevant policies of his
brother's administration might be losing votes and hurting his chances of
re-election. "I think we have to do it," the Attorney General said. Future
Presidents will need to master this perception.

Decision-Making

———

THEODORE SORENSEN has written in his *Decision-Making in the White House*, "Each President has his own style and his own standard for making decisions—and these may differ from day to day or from topic to topic. . . . The man affects the office as the office affects the man." Decision-making is a point where the strong Presidency depends most upon the strong President—upon the caliber of the man, upon his talents, prudence, and resolution. His choices point up the issues of his Presidency and the means and success of their disposition. Decision-making is a continuous process of the President's existence, his choices tend to be difficult, and the end-products often have great consequences. "There are no easy matters that will come to you as President," Eisenhower counseled the incoming President Kennedy. "If they are easy, they will be settled at a lower level."

The President determines what choices or decisions are possible. His choices are influenced not only by his personal ideals but by his knowledge of what has worked in the past, his estimate of the response of his adversaries, his judgment of what his publics at home and abroad will bear, of whether the bureaucracy will comply, and whether his party will go along. No one else in American government or society has a sweep of duties, and therefore of decisions, like his.

The situations on which the President's decisions are based may develop spontaneously or he may somehow contrive them. If fate had wafted Franklin Roosevelt into the Presidential chair in 1880, the serenity of that age would have presented only a miniature opportunity for decision. The President is a creature of his environment, and yet one of the factors of the environment is the man himself. The lights and shadows of his personality, the state of his political fortunes, his self-image and his view of his role in history, his foibles, his miscalculations—all influence his decisions.

Some of his decisions come in response to emergencies, but more are called for automatically at established intervals by a network of fixed deadlines which he does not set and cannot change. He faces the catalysis of the electoral calendar—the next Congressional or national election. His State of the Union Message, his Economic Report, his budget, which together are a massive compilation of decisions embracing the full sweep of policy, are all rendered up to Congress in January. Each of these documents has an extended subcalendar for its preparation. Budget ceilings are set in April; departments prepare their estimates in the summer; the Budget Bureau reviews them in the fall; the President dispatches the great tome of the budget and his accompanying message to Capitol Hill in January. His fixed schedule heightens the tyranny of events. In Monroe's day, the surge of revolutions in Latin America and the opportunistic stirrings of the imperial European powers lent special force to the President's oncoming State of the Union Message. Since it would have been unthinkable for the President not to discuss in its paragraphs relations between the hemispheres, his Union Message posed, in actuality, a deadline by which he was forced to formulate his historic doctrine.

Not only must the President make a decision according to a timetable, but it must be a decision picked from among a circumscribed variety of possibilities; only certain alternatives will be available to him. He can delegate some of his tasks: the selecting of problems for action, the fashioning of alternative solutions, and even the making of sound minor choices. But the ultimate decisions are his own to make, and he cannot choose to ignore them.

Sometimes a President has time to study and consider his decisions; sometimes he must act immediately. President Monroe acted on a tight time-budget at a dinner he tendered one night for the resident diplomats. Sir Charles Vaughan, the British minister, was seated opposite Count de Serurier, the French representative, and, as always in this era, relations between their countries were edgy. So indeed was the deportment of these diplomats. Vaughan in time noticed, to his great annoyance, that whenever the French minister spoke, he bit his thumb. Finally, unable to contain his irritation any longer, Vaughan inquired, "Do you bite your thumb at me, Sir?" "I do," replied the count. Both instantly left the table, withdrew into an adjoining hall, an unsheathed their swords. Monroe, who had followed them, made a split-second decision which conceivably saved two nations from war and his own from possible involvement. With an expert flourish, he forced up the ministers' crossed swords with his own, called his servants, consigned the battling ministers to separate rooms, and ordered their carriages.

Time is a help and boon when it is available. After the 1962 Cuban crisis President Kennedy expressed his thankfulness for the length of time—some fourteen days—the situation permitted him to take to determine the nation's response. "If we had had to act in the first twenty-four hours," Kennedy observed, "I don't think . . . we would have chosen as prudently as we finally did." When the *Maine* blew up and a great outcry for war, fanned by the yellow press, swept the country, McKinley declared to his young friend, Senator Charles W. Fairbanks of Indiana, "I don't propose to be swept off my feet by the catastrophe. My duty is plain. We must learn the truth and endeavor, if possible, to fix responsibility. The country can afford to withhold its judgment and not strike an avenging blow until the truth is known." But McKinley used his gift of time less competently than Kennedy, and the country was pushed into war.

◇

SCORES of aides in the executive branch earn their daily bread by anticipating situations and events well before they occur, preparing possible responses when they do. Some of this preparation is "contingency planning"—preparation for emergencies that might happen—a process applied since World War II to the world's most likely trouble spots, especially, in the Eisenhower, Kennedy, and Johnson periods, to Berlin. The planners have built up crowded files of events likely to take place in Berlin and the appropriate responses. Ironically, none of these plans anticipated the wall the East Germans threw up in 1961.

So, too, in Korea. In the balmy June days of Washington in 1950, Harry S. Truman and his most sapient military and diplomatic aides basked in the assumption that the tiny republic of Korea, which was little on their minds, stood in no danger of aggression from the Communist North Korean People's Democratic Republic. Indeed, on June 24, 1950, President Truman, dedicating a new international airport near Baltimore and exuding the then existing global serenity, voiced "his faith in a peaceful future" and flew away to Independence, Missouri, to visit his mother and brother. His sojourn was suddenly collapsed by a telephone call from his Secretary of State, Dean Acheson. A telegram, Acheson reported, had just been received from American Ambassador John J. Muccio at Seoul, the South Korean capital. "North Korean forces," Acheson read, "have invaded the Republic of Korea. . . ." The force of this sudden intelligence rushed Truman back to Washington and for weeks the events it heralded took a full toll of his effort.

In making choices, the President must be heedful not to commit more resources than he needs to secure his objectives. His resources—whether popularity, legislative favor, military weapons, or whatever—are all limited and must be used prudently and with maximum effect. President Kennedy, faced with a string of Soviet provocations in Berlin in 1961, warned his aides of the danger of the "false climax"—of going all out for a Soviet-contrived challenge that would not finally materialize. It was important, Kennedy stressed, not to commit everything you had at once, but to keep something in reserve. His subsequent decisions illustrated his point. In January 1961 he ordered an increase of airlift capacity, thereby enhancing the mobility of American forces; his March defense message to Congress outlined steps to be taken to prepare for conventional war. In May he appeared before Congress offering five recommendations to strengthen conventional forces. In late summer he called up troops to expand the base of the enlarged conventional army.

In foreign as in domestic affairs, the President's course may be largely determined by the nation's previous commitments and his own past policies. For example, elements of the Monroe Doctrine had been stated some years earlier by Clay and Jefferson. Of the incipient South American revolts, a key event in the Doctrine's development, Jefferson said in 1808, "We consider their interests the same as ours, and the object of both must be to exclude all European influence in this hemisphere." The roots of the great doctrine reached back before Jefferson and Clay, to the formative years of the republic, to the pronouncements of Washington, particularly his Farewell Address. In an important sense Monroe's decision had been made for him.

The political risks of decision either way can be great. Whatever a President does faces the hostile scrutiny of the opposition party bent upon dragging him from his great office at the next election. Unfriendly factions in his own party may manipulate against him. Some of the most formidable pressures upon the chief executive may be unloosed from Congress, where legislators may harass the President with speeches, investigations, parliamentary maneuver, and public outcry.

In putting forward his Supreme Court packing plan in 1937, Franklin Roosevelt risked no little of the prestige of his smashing electoral victory the year before which had lifted him to the crest of his influence. In arranging the sale of wheat to the U.S.S.R. in 1963, President Kennedy assumed the risk of offending sectors of American opinion and probably losing votes if he had lived to run again in 1964. His stand on civil rights appeared to alienate millions of white voters—yet to have refused to take it would have alienated millions of Negroes and damaged his country in the eyes of the world.

Since Dwight Eisenhower's second term, Presidential risks have ac-

quired a new and forbidding dimension. Eisenhower became the first
President to live with the Soviet Union's possession of a substantial nuclear delivery capability. The mutual nuclear capacities of the U.S. and
the U.S.S.R. give the decisions of their chief executives the quality of
"irreversibility." Decisions based upon miscalculation cannot be called
back nor can actions once taken be revised. If by miscalculation the American or Soviet leadership should bring on war between their nations, the
resulting holocaust would have irremediable consequences. Nothing that
the erring chief executive might do subsequently could compensate for
the costs levied upon mankind.

◇

Presidential decision-making is both an intellectual endeavor and
an organizational enterprise. The President chooses his advisers and determines how they shall render their counsel—their roles and relationships
to each other and to him. His solicitation of advice can be perfunctory or
genuine. He may ask their views only of that part of the problem representing their special competence or invite them to comment on the problem as a whole.

"Insiders," who are on the payroll of the executive branch, and "outsiders," who are not, are both called upon to give advice. Among the
insiders are the heads of departments, keepers of the vast storehouses of
information, ideas, and drafting skills indispensable to Presidential decision-making, the undersecretaries and assistant secretaries, the bureau
chiefs, and the great company of civil servants. The department secretaries themselves may be men of special talent, as was the case in the
Monroe administration when preparation of the Monroe Doctrine benefited from the diplomatic knowledge, drafting skill, and acumen of Secretary of State John Quincy Adams. President Eisenhower, in his turn,
depended heavily upon the experience of his own Secretary of State, John
Foster Dulles.

The insiders include also those quiet figures who compose the official
White House entourage. From Andrew Jackson's day to Franklin Roosevelt's, the chief officer of the entourage, the secretary to the President,
was a far-ranging adviser and assistant. Jackson's nephew, Andrew Jackson Donelson, was a stalwart of the "Kitchen Cabinet" and a skilled draftsman whose well-defined policy convictions seeped into leading Presidential
papers.

From Franklin Roosevelt onward the White House staff has become
larger and more specialized. One of the more important of the specialists
is the special counsel to the President. Samuel Rosenman, who occupied
the post in the Franklin D. Roosevelt era, was more than a legal craftsman
devoting his skill to the President's necessities. Like many of his succes-

sors, Rosenman was much involved in decision-making as an idea man, trouble-shooter, and speech-writer. In World War II Franklin Roosevelt employed as special assistant Harry L. Hopkins, a confidant who covered the war effort, poking into every nook and cranny of the executive branch, gathering facts, spotting problems, and resolving interagency conflicts. In many particulars Kennedy relied upon Theodore Sorensen as his alter ego. Still, not all helpers really help. McKinley, for example, was burdened with a wholly unsatisfactory secretary, J. Addison Porter, foppish and pompous, whose eyeglass ribbon trailing down his plump cheek was a standing joke to reporters and clerks. Porter hurt the President by writing patronizing letters and botched his duties of office management. When, periodically, burdens became unbearable, his chief weapon was a burst of temper. A kindly man himself, McKinley could not fire Porter but treated him with unbroken tolerance. The ill-served President relied increasingly upon his assistant secretary, George Cortelyou, lavished leaves of absence upon Porter for reasons of health, and fostered Porter's interest in Connecticut's Republican gubernatorial nomination.

When the President wants advice, he has many resources at his command. Department heads and others may gather with him as the cabinet or the National Security Council. *Ad hoc* groups may assemble at his direction. The more routine the decision the more constant the group; the more innovative, the less constant. The decisional unit for the Monroe Doctrine encompassed the President; his cabinet, including Secretary of State John Quincy Adams; Minister to London Richard Rush; and ex-Presidents Jefferson and Madison. Monroe accomplished the feat of keeping such spirited charges as Secretary of State John Quincy Adams and Secretary of War John Calhoun in harness. Adams, who could not bear the criticisms Calhoun heaped upon his drafts of papers on the Monroe Doctrine, was able to accept them from a tactful President whose judgment he respected.

In deciding whether to sign or veto the Taft-Hartley bill, President Truman supplied himself with an exhaustive analysis of its provisions prepared by a team of advisers and assistants. Secretary of Labor L. B. Schwellenbach did an over-all analysis; Attorney General Tom Clark studied the legal aspects, Secretary of Commerce Charles Sawyer the industrial implications, and Secretary of the Interior Julius Krug, who was managing an array of seized coal mines, the bill's effects on the coal strike. NLRB chairman Paul Herzog reported on administrative problems; Presidential counsel Clark Clifford guided the group and studied the legislative history of the bill and the many committee reports. Truman ultimately decided to veto the bill upon the recommendation of a dozen of his closest advisers and with the final unanimous support of his cabinet.

Agents in the field also are available to gather facts and negotiate ques-

tions upon which Presidential decision is based. General Douglas Mac-
Arthur's findings initiated the use of American ground troops in Korea
in 1950. His tour of the fighting fronts and observance of the broken and
fleeing South Korean forces convinced his superiors that American troops
were necessary.

"Outsiders," free from the confinement of daily responsibility for policy,
may offer the President the advantage of a fresh perspective when he is
faced with important decisions. They have no axe to grind for the status
quo—and they are more easily gotten rid of than insiders. James Monroe,
struggling to formulate the great doctrine bearing his name, turned instinctively to his mentor, the ex-President, the sage of Monticello. In response Jefferson proposed a two-part doctrine: "Our first and fundamental maxim," he wrote, "should be never to entangle ourselves in the
broils of Europe. Our second never to suffer Europe to intermeddle with
cis-Atlantic affairs. America, North and South, has a set of interests distinct from those of Europe and peculiarly her own. She should therefore
have a system of her own, separate and apart from that of Europe."
Lincoln, in fashioning the Emancipation Proclamation, consulted Senator
Charles Sumner of Massachusetts. William McKinley read the draft of
his message to Congress on the explosion of the *Maine* to his brother Ab-
ner, a White House visitor at the time, who suggested alterations for the
concluding paragraphs which William accepted. Raymond Robbins, a
free-lance adviser to Presidents, was one of the earliest to propose the
purge to Franklin D. Roosevelt, urging him to serve notice "that in 1938
he will try to elect his friends and defeat his enemies."

The breadth of the world the President understands and values is a
measure of the richness of the advice available to him. "Why is it that
your White House guests are limited to men of business?" Calvin Coolidge
was asked one day. The questioner cited Morgan, Firestone, Atterbury,
Stotesbury, Giannini, Baker, Rosenwald, Young, and other great names
of American industry and finance. "Why don't you have artists, musicians,
actors, poets around the White House as Wilson and Roosevelt did, and
sometimes Taft and Harding?" "I knew a poet once, when I was in
Amherst," Coolidge drawled, "class poet, name of Smith." A pause, and
then, "Never have heard of him since."

◇

EACH President has his own style of decision-making. Eisenhower preferred to be calm and composed. "Boy, there's just one thing I really
know," he once said, "You *can't* decide things in a *panic*. Any decision you
make when you are panicked, you can be sure of only one thing. It will be
a bad one." He placed great store in the slow, gradual power of persuasion.

Franklin Roosevelt's style was, as Arthur Schlesinger, Jr., has described it, "involved and inscrutable." Roosevelt weighed a basket of factors in a typical major decision: political timing, consequences to his personal public fortunes, interest group reactions, partisan advantage, impact on Congress and the public. He permitted situations to develop and crystallize, he let competing forces pull in conflict, and then through some system of "unconscious calculation," as Rexford Tugwell termed it, the decision finally emerged. Roosevelt's method, Tugwell observed, made it seem that "no choosing had taken place" and forestalled discovery of his "governing principle." Decision and policy were not thought out; rather, the President's intuitions seemed to coalesce and initiate a result. That his decisions were sometimes untidy never troubled the President. Clear-cut administrative decisions, he felt, worked only if they reflected clear-cut political realities. If they did not, the decisions would prove hollow and weak. He was devoted to final objectives and flexible means. Roosevelt, like many another President, valued procrastination. Wait long enough for clamoring forces to settle, for the momentum of events to slacken, and the imperatives of today will be gone tomorrow. Time he considered a great corrective, one that spares the President many hard choices. Viewed collectively over time, Presidential choices appear wavering and inconsistent, and Roosevelt, therefore, seemed alternately to advance upon and then to back away from a progressive line. He began with an isolationist economic policy and shifted to an internationalist trade policy. He turned from cooperation with business to regulation of it. In reality, he was responding to changing events and situations, to the necessity of winning and holding a broad base of support. He loved to make minor choices in a dramatic way that shocked and surprised the public. "I'm going to spring a bombshell," he delighted to announce, and then stunned his gaping audience with a novel proposal such as changing the date of Thanksgiving or imposing national daylight-saving time the year around to aid the war effort. "He delights in surprises—clever, cunning and quick," Hugh Johnson observed, "He likes to shock friends as well as enemies with something they never expected."

A President's non-decisions may be as exacting and important as his decisions. President Kennedy, faced with Castro's refusal to permit on-the-spot inspection for the presence of missiles and launching sites in Cuba, made several protests, and then apparently relegated the thorny matter to the limbo of nondecision. But some Presidents specialize in non-decisions; Warren Harding smiled and maneuvered his way out of difficulty until his whole kingdom of neglect tumbled down upon him.

A President may be forward-looking, hopeful of a better society, and confident of progress, but he may also look backward, as Buchanan did, longing to restore a past for whose beneficence he is nostalgic. Buchanan set the theme of his future administration upon his election to the Presidency, when the students and faculty of nearby Franklin and Marshall College in Lancaster, Pennsylvania, trudged out to congratulate him. He told them his object as President would be "to destroy any sectional party—North or South—to harmonize all sections of the Union under a national and conservative government as it was fifty years ago." Suspicious and distrustful of mankind, Buchanan insisted upon overseeing all details, great and small, within his charge. Except for Howell Cobb, Secretary of the Treasury, he held his cabinet at arm's length. He spent endless hours of heavy toil over quantities of papers which he insisted pass over his desk. He would work far into the night in a favorite old dressing gown and slippers, chewing his cigar, as he read his way through a pile of correspondence.

A President who chooses to concentrate upon adaptive or routine procedures sacrifices the opportunity to make major or innovative decisions. Franklin Pierce, in his first Presidential years, sat two hours each day with his assembled cabinet engaged in the hard business of dispensing patronage. Together they read recommendations, weighed qualifications, and estimated political consequences. He proclaimed lofty standards to guide the task—"If a man who has attained [this] high office, cannot free himself from cliques and act independently, our Constitution is valueless." But a President like Pierce who concentrates so heavily upon such choices neglects the big decisions. Pierce loved detail and injected himself into an ever shifting miscellany of petty problems. He visited the departments regularly, heeded minor matters, encouraged his secretaries to bring him a full store of middling business; tracked down all manner of complaints pouring in from his mail; and kept his door open to the public. A disgruntled humanity, bearing paltry complaints, streamed in. The incessant puttering with trivia was, in actuality, Pierce's kind of compensation for his inability to handle major policy. The larger problems slid by little touched by Presidential power—trouble in Cuba, Mexico, and Central America; ailing relations with England; Kansas torn and bleeding.

Programed decisions, repetitive and routine, following established rules, precedents, and strategies, are part of any chief executive's day—the hour when he starts work, his choice of tasks, the distribution of his time, what he reads or ignores. But some Presidents are controlled by routine. Calvin Coolidge is the supreme example of Presidential subordination to programed decision. His inviolate schedule was breakfast at eight, to work at nine, lunch at twelve-thirty, back at his desk at three, and at four he called it a day. This admittedly mild routine, contrasting shockingly with the hours of the average factory worker, he clocked from minute to minute. So, in fact, did he regulate the time of his retirement at night. William Allen White, the journalist, made this discovery during a festive outing aboard the Presidential yacht, the *Mayflower*. The conversation was gay and voluble, with everyone joining in but the chief executive, who was proving his large reputation for silence. "Literally," noted White, "we forgot him." At the stroke of ten Coolidge rose, walked across the room to his wife, and stood in silence. Mocking his Yankee accent, she laughed, "Time tur go tew bed!"

Coolidge also excelled in getting others to make the hard choices. As revelations of the Teapot Dome corruptions of the previous Harding administration unfolded in his own young Presidency, Coolidge resisted counsel, urgently pouring upon him, that he fire his Attorney General, Harry Daugherty. Even when the prestigious progressive leader, Senator William E. Borah of Idaho, proposed the step, Coolidge demurred. "I am here to carry out the Harding policies," he said. "I am here as a Republican President. Daugherty was Harding's friend. He stands high with the Republican organization. I do not see well how I can do it." The importunities from many sides to dump Daugherty continued, but the President would not act.

At last, when a Senate resolution was introduced calling upon the President to dismiss Daugherty, Coolidge summoned Borah to the White House one night for "urgent business." After several minutes of Presidential silence, Borah was still puzzled about what the urgent business was when Daugherty came up the grand stairway to Coolidge's study, "his jaw set," according to a White House secretary, "and his eyes like flint." Coolidge tersely introduced his visitors, adding, "Well, don't let my presence embarrass you!" This instruction was superfluous. Borah and Daugherty went at it for an hour of shrill debate. Coolidge sat by, slumped in his chair smoking. In the din of the exchange, Borah exclaimed that it was not for him to tell the Attorney General to resign; it was the President's duty. Coolidge said not a word. When at last the antagonists finished, the little President, standing to hurry his parting guests, quacked, "Senator, I reckon you're right!" Daugherty, "white with rage," according to White House secretary Mary Randolph, who witnessed the encounter, stomped "angrily down the stairs and out of the White House." He soon resigned. Yet Coolidge did not hesitate to deny requests of others. "It took courage to ask Mr. Coolidge for a favor," his secretary declared.

Some chief executives limit themselves as far as possible to the pleasant decisions. They leave the dispensing of the hard negative to subordinates. Harry Hopkins in his day established himself securely in the craw of many a defeated decision-seeker as Franklin D. Roosevelt's abominable no-man. Sherman Adams excelled in his day in the same role for Dwight D. Eisenhower. Indeed Adams's eventual departure from the Presidential scene was hastened by the large and ever growing body of the disgruntled created by his capacity to say no.

President Eisenhower eschewed personal criticism of others and the entire terrain of political counterattack. Tormentors could lose their salvos; Senator McCarthy could apply the torch of insinuation and unsupportable charge with full confidence that Eisenhower would not retaliate. The President said to aides who urged sterner measures, "I simply do not believe it does a damn bit of good wasting time answering the other fellow. All you do is double the audience he had the first time when he proclaimed whatever it is you are trying to answer." Or again, when President Truman launched his "Give 'em hell, Harry!" attacks upon the Republican ticket in the 1952 campaign, Eisenhower brushed aside all suggestions that he counterattack. "I'm sure they would like me to get down to *their* level," he declared. "Well, that's *one* satisfaction they will *never* have."

More than any other contemporary President, Eisenhower relied upon subordinates to define situations and present alternative approaches to them. The President's own contribution was largely one of choosing between alternatives in whose formulation he had had little part and with whose substance he may have been unfamiliar. The Eisenhower method places a premium on "presentations" and "briefings," on charts and one-page summaries. Eisenhower also made heavy use of committees of Presidential aides drawn from departments and the White House staff. Such committees may select problems for study, develop alternative solutions, and choose between them, leaving the President the simple task of ratification. Critics of the committee system contend that it rewards the wrong qualities by stressing fluency and "averageness," promoting agreement but discouraging creativity. They contend that Eisenhower was often kept ignorant of alternatives his subordinates rejected and therefore never laid before him. Eisenhower's defenders point to a considerable body of "split decisions," or alternatives which his subordinates could not decide between themselves and did lay before the President for his choice.

President Kennedy, eschewing the Eisenhower method and vowing to put himself into "the thick of things," expended great quantities of energy and time spreading himself all across the decisional spectrum. The President, he thought, should hover constantly over the quest for alternatives, and if he does not, he is a prisoner of the choices which his aides finally put before him. Kennedy consulted with many advisers both outside the executive branch and inside, at various ranks in the hierarchy, at desk-side conferences and over the telephone. Professor Hans J. Morgenthau argues that the Kennedy method exposed him to too much advice, steeping him with all shades of opinion, engendering a state of mind that makes timely and forceful decision difficult. He cites the Cuban invasion fiasco of 1961 and the delayed response to the rise of the Berlin wall as case studies of Presidential irresolution. Kennedy's reaction when the Russians threw up the Berlin wall in 1961 was characterized, Morgenthau noted, by a duality. Kennedy responded with a "hard" line in what he said and how he said it. His style was truly Churchillian. But what he did was something else. He acted "flexibly," or, less euphemistically, he did little and he did it late. His deeds were reminiscent not of Churchill but of Chamberlain. The contradiction, this analysis concluded, confused the American public, the nation's allies, and probably the U.S.S.R. Yet Morgenthau's critique came in 1961, shortly after Kennedy had taken office. Later Kennedy achieved widely hailed results by using the broad consultation method—in the Cuba crisis of 1962, the controversy over the admission of James Meredith to the University of Mississippi, and U.S. Steel's price rise.

◇

SOME Presidents are compelled to make choices that change the entire direction of their administration or indeed of the country itself. Not always does a President make these momentous choices wisely. It may be instructive to look at some of the major decisions which Presidents have made in the context of their time. One of the first of the great choices was Jefferson's decision on the Louisiana Purchase.

Jefferson's political career had long been given to cultivating amity with France. He had served with distinction in her court and had been her unstinting friend in his years as Washington's Secretary of State. His party was traditionally attached to France. Still, as President he deemed it necessary to sacrifice his attachment in the face of the new and ominous situation. France, led by Napoleon, that incomparable maker of empires, had recently acquired the vast province of Louisiana and loomed threateningly at the American border, superceding Spain in North America. Jefferson deemed it "impossible that France and the U.S. can continue long friends when they meet in so irritable a position." The Jefferson administration stressed that it was in the interests of inland communication for the United States to possess New Orleans and the Spanish Floridas. "The United States," said Secretary of State James Madison, in explaining his government's point of view to Louis Pichon, the French chargé, "had no interest in seeing circumstances rise which should eventually lead their population to extend itself on the right bank of the Mississippi." The extensions, said Madison, could not but "weaken the state," and perhaps lead to dangerous separatist movements.

When Jefferson tried to negotiate with France the annexation of the Louisiana Territory, he first encountered French recalcitrance. The most hopeful message his emissary could send to his chief was, "Do not absolutely despair." His faltering plan was dealt still another blow when Federalist Senator James Ross of Pennsylvania introduced a resolution in Congress advocating the immediate seizure of Louisiana by force. The chief executive was to be entrusted with five million dollars and fifty thousand men sufficient to do their task before the French could arrive. Ross's project was thoroughly discussed in both houses in secret session. Jefferson, a strong, skillful leader of his party in Congress eventually defeated this challenge to his authority—but only after suffering acute embarrassment in his dealings with the French.

Fortunately, however, Napolean was vexed by a wasteful military campaign in Santo Domingo whose success was necessary to the retention of Louisiana, and was struck as well by the prospect of a strong United States as a counterpoise to British sea power. He called his ministers into conference. "I renounce Louisiana," he said, "It is not only New Orleans that I will cede; it is the whole colony, without any reservation," and turning to his minister, François de Marbois, he added, "I direct you to negotiate this affair with the envoys of the United States."

In his 1803 move to purchase Louisiana, Jefferson knew full well that he was supplying the rival Federalist party with invaluable political capital. The Federalists, who had been shouting for a war of conquest, greeted his decision with the cry that he was bankrupting the Treasury to buy a desert. But in Jefferson's own party the purchase was a huge political success. The Republican factions scrambled madly to claim credit for it. Northern Republicans, sniffing hungrily for a strong candidate to rid them once and for all of the "Virginia succession" to the Presidency, aimed to establish one of their own as the hero of the Louisiana conquest, and a lavish campaign was launched to prove that Robert Livingston of New York, who with James Monroe negotiated the purchase, deserved entire credit for its success.

A Presidential decision of magnitude may lead to bitterness or it may touch off national exultation and create a mood rich with political promise. All acts, all decisions, have consequences. When a horseman rode into Washington from New Orleans on January 15, 1804, with the news that Louisiana had been peaceably delivered to the United States three weeks before, the nation rejoiced. Congress gave a great dinner, with the President and the cabinet as the honored guests, to celebrate the gain of a new empire. French representative Pichon, informing his government of the jubilation, well observed that "The acquisition of Louisiana and the peaceful manner of possession have raised Jefferson and his friends to a high point of popularity and regard. His re-election must be considered as assured."

◊

ANOTHER great decision was Lincoln's proclamation of emancipation. Here, too, there were pressures to meet and alternatives to face. In Congress voices had clamored long and insistently for Negro freedom. The rebellion had hardly commenced when Charles Sumner, the blunt, un-compromising Senator from Massachusetts—"the conscience of the Senate," as Emerson called him—began to urge outright emancipation upon the President. Sumner never faltered in championing his idea. After the first and disastrous battle of Bull Run, he pressed Lincoln to deliver a counterstroke by proclaiming emancipation. On July 4, 1862, he was back at the White House to lay a new temptation before the President. "You can make this day more sacred and more historic than the Continental Congress," he said and urged that emancipation be proclaimed on that great national holiday. But Lincoln, fearful of the effects of such a step upon enlistments, troop morale, and the border states, would not act. "He is hard to move," the exasperated Sumner noted. "He is honest but inexperienced." Behind Sumner was an equally insistent Congressional majority. Time and again it put upon the statute books acts building the foundation for emancipation.

Lincoln was also besieged by many groups among the electorate, as all Presidents are. Among the abolitionists no one stressed more earnestly to Lincoln the necessity of converting the war into a crusade against slavery than Frederick Douglass, the distinguished Negro leader. In speeches, in his newspaper, and in letters to influential friends Douglass, according to historian John Hope Franklin, insisted that the "Union cause would never prosper till the war assumed an Anti-Slavery attitude, and the Negro was enlisted on the loyal side." In a speech at Cooper Union he lamented the government's "uncertainty and vacillation and hesitation in grappling with the great question of the war-slavery." Lincoln was also petitioned repeatedly by religious groups. In June 1862 a delegation of Progressive Friends waited upon him to urge emancipation. The President was not encouraging, saying only that "if a decree of emancipation could abolish slavery, John Brown would have done the work effectually." A committee of the Synod of the Reformed Presbyterian Church presented resolutions urging abolition. Lincoln assured his visitors that no difference lay between them concerning the immorality of slavery. The problem was how best to get rid of it.

> Were an individual asked whether he would wish to have a wen on his neck, he could not hesitate as to the reply; but were it asked whether a man who has such a wen should at once be relieved of it by the application of the surgeon's knife, there might be a diversity of opinion, perhaps the man might bleed to death, as the result of such an operation.

But the demands of pressure groups may conflict with other demands upon a President. The alternatives he ponders may be mutually exclusive: to choose one is to preclude the others. Or they may be mutually reinforcing; he then does not choose among alternatives but determines how many possible paths of action to combine into a single decision or policy. In weighing his intention to free the slaves, Lincoln believed the alternatives were complementary rather than exclusive. Plagued with doubts that whites and freed Negroes could live together peaceably, he at first studied the possibility of achieving emancipation through colonization. He was impressed also with the legal necessity of compensating the slave owners, and in November 1861, he drafted two bills for compensated emancipation in Delaware. In that experiment, which, if successful, might have been extended to other states, Lincoln proposed to emancipate Delaware's slaves through federal financing, or $700,000 of 6 per cent bonds to be retired in five years. Less than a year later Lincoln was urging Congress to underwrite emancipation in all states that freed their slaves. His eventual Emancipation Proclamations—there were two, one a preliminary notice heralding the major document which quickly followed—did not incorporate or even refer to these choices.

A President not only chooses among alternatives; he must also consider how to prepare for and how to time the announcement and excution of the policy he has chosen. The decision must be revealed neither too late nor too soon. Not surprisingly, Presidents withhold their decision until the time is ripe. Lincoln had composed and firmly decided upon his Emancipation Proclamation some weeks before he finally issued it. He bided his time, waiting for a Union victory on the battlefield to enhance the historic document's importance and reception. Union victories were not easily come by at this stage in the war, and weeks passed. While he waited, one of his most formidable critics, Horace Greeley, editor of the New York *Tribune*, took him to task in a moving, widely read editorial, "The Prayer of Twenty Millions." The President's followers, Greeley charged, were "deeply pained by the policy you seem to be pursuing with regard to the slaves of rebels. . . . We think you are strangely and disastrously remiss in the discharge of your official and imperative duty with regard to the emancipating provisions of the new Confiscation Act."

But Lincoln, considering the realities that would make the issuance of his Emancipation Proclamation a plausible act, gave great weight to a victory on the battlefield. Without a victory, the Proclamation would be a hollow gesture, he believed. Finally, the battle of Antietam came, and though the Union's claim of victory was disputed, Lee had been checked. This was enough for Lincoln, and he hurried off to the quiet of the Soldiers' Home to put the finishing touches on his Emancipation Proclamation. He issued it within days.

In great decisions it is ordinarily not the President's fate to receive the lavish approval that befell Jefferson, but mixed praise and censure. The Emancipation Proclamation evoked large doses of both. Democratic Governor David Tod of Ohio endorsed "every word and syllable of it." Sumner of Massachusetts exulted, "the skies are brighter and the air is purer now that slavery has been handed over to judgment." Frederick Douglass was "greatly encouraged." The New York *Times* declared, "No more important and far-reaching document ever issued since the foundation of this Government." But doubt was expressed in much of the press that any real good would come from the proclamation. Lincoln acknowledged that his expectations were

> not as sanguine as . . . those of some friends. . . . While commendation in newspapers and by distinguished individuals is all a vain man could wish, the stocks have declined, and troops come forward more slowly than ever. . . . The North responds to the Proclamation sufficiently in breath; but breath alone kills no rebels.

A President's own mood and gesture can enchance the force of his decision, just as diffidence can drain a strong decision. Lincoln added immeasurably to the force of the Emancipation Proclamation when he declared, upon signing it, "I never, in my life, felt more certain that I was doing right than I do in signing this paper."

The attitude of President Eisenhower on the civil rights issues that faced his own administration was, in contrast, hesitant. At a news conference on July 3, 1957, he spoke candidly of the administration's civil rights bill then afoot in Congress in words that revealed his feelings better than a previous terse official statement accompanying the bill did. "I was reading part of that bill this morning," he told the newsmen, "and I— there were certain phrases I didn't completely understand. . . . I would want to talk to the Attorney General. . . . Naturally, I am not a lawyer." In three sentences the President had punctured the status of a bill drafted in his Justice Department and offered to Congress as a major part of "the President's program." The bill's champions on Capitol Hill were further disheartened several weeks later when the President, again in a press conference, applied more cold water. "If you try to go too far too fast," he reminded the nation, ". . . you are making a mistake."

◇

IMPORTANT decisions can lead to apparent failure, as well as to the success of the Louisiana Purchase and the Emancipation Proclamation. Such was the case with Franklin Roosevelt's decision to try to pack the Supreme Court.

Over many exasperating months Roosevelt had developed a variety of alternatives for dealing with the Supreme Court's mounting tendency to strike down New Deal laws as unconstitutional. He would not take the Court action lying down, he told his aides. The country was with him and not the Court, and he would bring the Justices into line if he had to "pack" it or "deny it" appellate jurisdiction. As his bitter encounter with judicial review wore on, Roosevelt fashioned other possible alternatives. Remembering the experience of Andrew Jackson, also a forceful chief executive who suffered from the judiciary, and anticipating a hostile decision from the Court in the famous gold cases, Roosevelt prepared the draft of an address which borrowed Jackson's famous defiance of the Court: "You have made your law, now enforce it." The Court held for the government in the gold cases, however, making the address unnecessary. But subsequently the justices struck down the New York minimum wage law, a decision that boded ill for a great swath of labor legislation, national and state. The eminent progressive, Senator George Norris, urged Roosevelt to center his approaching 1936 electoral campaign upon the Court issue. Between the alternatives of electoral campaigning and packing, Roosevelt eventually chose the latter.

A President's commitments and past decisions and promises often herald his future policy. Roosevelt's frame of mind in the Supreme Court packing plan had long been evident. As early as the 1932 campaign, in an off-hand remark in a speech at Baltimore, he had characterized the Court as a mere annex of the Republican administration. When the Court struck down the National Industrial Recovery Act, nearly two years before the packing plan was launched, Franklin Roosevelt, in a fighting mood, called in Professor Felix Frankfurter of the Harvard Law School and Hugh Johnson, administrator of the deposed program. He would bring the Court into line, he insisted bitterly. He would either pack it or cut back its appellate jurisdiction. His visitors, appalled by the Presidential ferocity, attempted to dissuade him. Their arguments were futile, and when Roosevelt finished with his visitors, he went on to a press conference where he charged the Court with taking the country back to "horse and buggy" days.

The operative ideas of many a great Presidential decision may emerge from the researches and findings of the bureaucracy. The idea of how to pack the Court seems to have come from Roosevelt's Justice Department. The Attorney General, Homer S. Cummings, a lanky, elderly politician, had been given an important secret assignment from Roosevelt. His task was nothing less than to contrive a plan which would thwart the Court's tendency to rule unconstitutional many of the most sacred laws of the New Deal. As he mused over this delicate assignment in his lavish office, pince nez in hand, Cummings was picking aimlessly through a pile of books one day when he came upon a volume, *Federal Justice*, that had been written by Carl McFarland, a departmental aide. The book, a study of the ills of the lower federal courts, posed a most intriguing solution. Let "worn-out" judges be retired on respectable pensions, the author argued. If after a reasonable interval an eligible federal judge did not retire, let the President add a judge to the court. McFarland's prescriptions for lower federal courts were joyfully taken up by Cummings for the Supreme Court. He spread his handiwork before the President. Roosevelt was enormously pleased. Cummings was Roosevelt's rock of comfort in both devising and forwarding that epitome of convoluted indirection, the Court-packing plan. He supported the President fanatically in the midst of seemingly unanimous denunciation.

Roosevelt loved symbolic rituals. Fresh from his decision to launch the Court-packing plan, he tendered the annual Presidential dinner for the judiciary. All the high court justices appeared at the White House except the aged Louis D. Brandeis, who never ventured out in the evening, and Harlan F. Stone, who was ill. Approximately eighty notables gathered, and those seated at the President's table presented a spectacle tinged with an irony that Roosevelt relished. At his table were all but two of the justices he was about to subjugate, and at the table also were Attorney General Cummings and several other faithful helpers who had prepared the artifacts for the subjugation. When soon the packing plan would be sprung, the justices would recall, and presumably with not a little awe, the President's droll finesse.

Franklin Roosevelt also loved to instill surprise into the execution of his policy, for in addition to satisfying a puckish streak in his own nature it threw the opposition off guard and added momentum to his decision. He sprang his court plan with elaborate precautions to keep it a surprise, a feat not easily accomplished in an executive branch whose officials practiced to the hilt freedom of speech in dealings with the press. For all the obstacles, Roosevelt kept the court plan a secret by personally supervising the details of its launching. The afternoon before the well-guarded event commenced, Roosevelt instructed the White House secretarial staff to report promptly for work the next day at 6:30 A.M. At that hour the mimeograph machines turned out the several Presidential papers announcing the plan. The papers were distributed to the cabinet, hastily assembled in a mid-morning meeting, with Joseph T. Robinson of Arkansas, the President's loyal floor leader in the Senate, and Speaker William B. Bankhead also present. Roosevelt, with a hurried and distracted air, informed the company that he had very little time, since he had to attend a press conference in less than half an hour. The men around the table read on; no one spoke; the President did not ask for comments. It was all over in a few minutes.

At the moment when Roosevelt launched his plan to pack the Supreme Court he was at the crest of his political power. His grand victory just fashioned in the 1936 elections seemed an almost limitless mandate to move in any direction he chose. His principal advisers, Harry Hopkins and Thomas G. Corcoran, encouraged this view of the mandate. No challenge seemed too great. But the plan to pack the Court launched Roosevelt into a season of political decline. For all of his political genius, he made a series of mistakes.

Priority of action was vital to Roosevelt's Court-packing strategy, and so he directed his legislative leaders to place his Court bill ahead of the farm bill, the wages and hours bill, and the "little T.V.A." bill on the Congressional calendar. The precedence of the Court bill would communicate to farm and labor leaders and to liberals the loud, clear message that the quickest way to secure their cherished legislation was to put their shoulders behind the President's Court bill. The faster it was passed, the faster would their measures advance.

But the dream far exceeded the reality. Weeks passed in the Court fight before Roosevelt regarded as credible the grim daily reports his lieutenants brought him of voting prospects on Capitol Hill. Impressed with his recent massive electoral victory of 1936 and the long string of major political triumphs compiled since the outset of his administration, he was unaccustomed to the possibility of defeat. When his Court fight wallowed inconclusively for weeks in Congress, Corcoran and his Secretary of the Interior, Harold Ickes, noticed a marked shrinkage in their chief's aggressive leadership. The President, Ickes noted in his diary, "has acted to me like a beaten man."

Though his Court fight was going badly, the proud and seemingly invincible political warrior refused, at least for a season, to compromise. Several potential compromises, which Roosevelt's advisers implored him to accept, gleamed through the dust of the struggle. At one juncture Senator Burton Wheeler of Montana, who led the opposition, offered to add two new justices to the Court and to induce Justice Sutherland's resignation through Senator Borah. These, with the vacancy brought by Justice Van Devanter's resignation, already submitted, would have given the President four appointments sufficient to assure a friendly Court. Roosevelt proudly spurned the offer. An aide next suggested that the President might well drop the Court bill temporarily and push his other legislation. But Roosevelt held to the fight. Retreat or compromise? Never! Not until eight more weeks of bitter, fruitless struggle passed did he finally signal Vice President John Nance Garner to arrange as graceful a withdrawal as possible. Garner worked out with Senate leaders on both sides the recommittal of the Court bill to the Senate Judiciary Committee, which soon reported an emasculated and meaningless substitute whose quick passage was assured by its innocuousness.

On no other issue except that of the third term did the cry of dictatorship rise so sharply in the Roosevelt era. The defeat of the Court-packing plan proved merely a battle that Roosevelt lost in the course of winning the war. Justices opposed to the New Deal continued to resign and within a few years the Court was remade. Roosevelt appointed Justices Black, Reed, Frankfurter, Douglas, Jackson, Murphy, and Byrnes, and the weight of the Court's decisions shifted to support the views of the executive branch. But Roosevelt's prestige had dimmed. He had achieved his purpose of a tolerant Court, but he might have done so with less damage to his personal political fortunes.

◇

SOME decisions have no opportunity to develop slowly over a period of time. Some situations call for immediate solutions. Such was the case in the Truman administration in 1950, when South Korea was invaded. On the plane which carried him back to Washington, President Truman came quickly and solitarily to a fundamental decision: North Korea's aggression across the 38th parallel must be countered by force. The Communists had launched a challenge that could not be sidestepped: "An outlaw was terrorizing the world community"; to ignore him meant risking "a third world war." At a meeting with his military and diplomatic aides that evening for dinner and discussion at Blair House, Truman apparently did not even consider the possibility of a nonviolent response. An implicit decision that American armed forces must be committed provided the operating premise; from it other necessary decisions and their alternatives would follow—what kind of force, how many men, and within what territorial confines should the Americans fight?

Each department head and each member of the Joint Chiefs of Staff was urged to speak his mind on any aspect of the entire problem. The advisory group took no vote but developed an evolving consensus in a Quaker-meeting style of discussion. In his later testimony before a Congressional committee, Secretary of Defense Louis Johnson threw doubt on the administration's unanimity, but Secretary of State Dean Acheson avouched to the same committee that the Korean decisions represented "the unanimous view of the political and military advisers of the President." The President more than anyone else establishes the atmosphere of a discussion. Truman's "resolve" and "determination" inspirited the entire Korean deliberations. The Secretaries of State and Defense had also been called back to Washington. A group quickly formed at the State Department, among them Ambassador at Large Philip Jessup, Assistant Secretary of State for Far Eastern Affairs Rusk, Assistant Secretary of State for United Nations Affairs John Hickerson, Deputy Undersecretary of State H. Freeman Matthews, and Secretary of the Army Frank Pace. This group quickly set down a key provision of subsequent American policy—to bring the threat to world peace to the attention of the United Nations.

The President and his aides canvassed the possible courses of action.

These had to be invented, formulated, and analyzed, pursuits which Herbert Simon calls "design activity." The raw information about the crisis had to be gathered and interpreted first, and interpretation, at its best, is an inexact enterprise. President Truman and his counselors started with the plausible assumption that the heavy hand of the Soviet Union was behind the venture, and faced the question of the Kremlin's motive and purpose. General Omar Bradley, chairman of the Joint Chiefs of Staff, contended that the North Korean attack was a diversionary gambit preparatory to a major Soviet blow, possibly against Iran, and urged that few American troops, therefore, be committed to Korea, since they would be needed elsewhere. George Kennan, a premier authority on Soviet behavior, argued that the Communists were engaging in "soft spot probing" and advised that "situations of strength" be created wherever the Soviet thrust came, even in Korea. Others believed that the Soviets were testing the will of anti-Communist nations to resist open aggression, as Hitler did when he reoccupied the Rhineland. Still other counselors advanced a "demonstration" theory—that the U.S.S.R. expected to make Korea a show of their strength and of Allied impotence, with worldwide repercussions. Finally, there was the view that the Soviet was promoting a general "Far Eastern strategy." For example, John Foster Dulles, then negotiating the Japanese peace treaty, saw the Korean attack as a Soviet thrust to block American efforts to bring Japan into the free world.

Heretofore unchallenged assumptions are often destroyed when a crisis comes. The unanticipated war in Korea smashed an assumption generally embraced by top American military authorities and sanctioned by Presidents Franklin Roosevelt and Truman: United States ground forces, the view went, should never be engaged on the Asian mainland lest they be needed elsewhere. Least of all should they be committed to an area like Korea, slight in military value and difficult to defend. This assumption was an early casualty of the Korean War; its violation intensified as the conflict dragged on, until eventually some 250,000 American troops were dispatched to that unhappy land.

The ultimate conclusions of Truman and his counselors were that the entire Far East was in jeopardy, that a line had to be drawn at once, and that the United States must do it. The security of the United States, world peace, and the future effectiveness of the United Nations, which was the principal architect of the South Korean government, were all at stake. The risk of a bold response had to be taken, and other UN members might be invited to share in it as they saw fit. The United States laid the Korean conflict before the UN Security Council, which, with the Soviet delegate absent, called upon the North Koreans to withdraw at once to the 38th parallel and upon the UN members "to render every assistance to the United Nations in the execution of this resolution." The UN Security

Council subsequently adopted a stronger resolution requesting UN members to "furnish such assistance to the Republic of Korea as may be necessary to repel the armed attack." Truman committed United States forces to the Korean conflict in support of the Security Council resolutions and in accordance with the United States' obligations under its membership in the UN. Among Truman's further decisions was one not to ask Congress for any formal expression of concurrence with his Korean policy.

◇

THE President's method in decision-making has something of the quality of fire. It can serve for good or ill; it can be a virtue or a vice; at one time it can succeed, at another it leads to abysmal failure. There is no available body of absolute directives like the Ten Commandments to assure correct decision-making. "Don't put off unto tomorrow what can be done today," the adage says. But, according to another: "Sufficient unto the day is the evil thereof." A Franklin Roosevelt can long postpone a key decision, and, endowed with a kind of charmed political life, manage to get away with it. William McKinley on the eve of war with Spain, a peace-minded man eager to avoid conflict, delayed so in his bewilderment at events that war-minded legislators and the yellow press grabbed the initiative and with it the issue of war or peace.

The President does well to consult, but he does ill to consult too much. Truman and the Democratic party paid dearly for his failure to involve Congress substantially in his early Korean decisions. Later, when the Korean war became unpopular, he could not share the resulting political liabilities with a Congress shut out from his original decisions. But consultations also can be too wide, productive of such contradictory counsel and excessive information that decision is delayed and weakened. Decision is a blend of fact, thought, incisiveness, and vigor; to stress one ingredient is to diminish others.

When the occasion requires a decision, the President must communicate his will clearly and not create havoc, as Wilson did in proclaiming, "We are too proud to fight," a well-intentioned moral standard for the nation, which the allies understandably misinterpreted as an evidence of cooling ardor toward their cause. Yet the President will also need an instinct for ambiguity in his daily grapple with petitioners and their pressures for his favor. For others to know his will too clearly and too soon may bring him political trouble and grief.

There are discernible in the world of the President several principles that seem far more often right than wrong. Above all, the President must keep the initiative in decisions that are his, and not permit it to be grabbed off by Congress or private groups. He should not decide in anger, or grief, or other high emotion, but only in composure. Presidents by this standard have been remarkably successful. As a lot they have not been hotheads or desk-pounders. The magnitude of the chief executive's power and responsibilty and his need to maintain to the outside world an image of self-confidence, require that he appear to be "in charge," that he speak and act with assurance, hold his subordinates in rein, and comprehend the problems they are struggling with. Decision is more than the creation of policy. It reveals the President as a person.

14

Crisis

═══

SOMETIME in the first hundred days of the New Deal, Norman Davis, a distinguished roving ambassador of that era, encountered Raymond Fosdick outside the White House. "Ray," said Davis, "that fellow in there is not the fellow we used to know. There's been a miracle here." Wrote editor Oswald Villard of the *Nation* during the same period, "Many of us who have known him long and well ask ourselves if this is the same man." Crisis had thrust the man, Franklin D. Roosevelt, as it has other Presidents, up to a level of effectiveness that hitherto he had never achieved. Crisis is a crucible in which a President and his administration are tested as nowhere else. No other event tries so rigorously the physical endurance, self-confidence, and prudence of the President and his aides. At no other time are the stakes so high. The consequences of his actions are enormously magnified; his decisions may determine nothing less than national safety and survival.

Most great Presidents have been crisis Presidents. Lincoln brought the nation through the holocaust of civil war, Wilson through World War I, and Franklin Roosevelt through the depression and World War II. But the brilliant success of Presidents in crisis cannot blind us to the debit side of the balance sheet, to the substantial failures. James Madison, administrator of the War of 1812, suffered defeats and retreats and the ignominy of having the White House burned from under him. Lincoln was preceded by Buchanan's administration, which failed to stay the onrush of civil war. Under Hoover the nation sustained almost four years of Jobean torment from soaring unemployment and unrelieved despair.

Contemporary Presidents are surfeited with opportunities for greatness, facing as they do crises of a scale unknown to their predecessors. Since the end of the American nuclear monopoly, the Presidency has existed in a state of perpetual crisis in its enforced vigil to prevent some incident or issue from escalating into general war. Presidents since World War II have chronically been caught up in multiple crises, thanks to the Soviet Union's capacity to strike on many fronts and our domestic society's to churn up big trouble. For Kennedy 1962 was a year of crisis. The Soviets emplaced missiles in Cuba and lunged in Berlin and Laos. Civil rights crises exploded in Mississippi and Alabama, and a price rise in steel threatened to smother the administration's foremost economic goals: curbing inflation, bettering the balance of payments, speeding economic growth, and relieving unemployment. Lyndon Johnson, in his first hundred days as President, faced violence in Panama, upheaval in Zanzibar, civil war in Cyprus, threatened war over Malaysia, a coup in Vietnam, and churning trouble in Laos, among other worries.

No nation can endure to live in a state of maximum commitment in crisis after crisis, and so a President must assign priorities. In 1961 Kennedy accordingly rejected the recommendation that he declare a full-scale national emergency over the Berlin wall, because he recognized that a resort to ultimate powers and public commitment had to be used selectively. Presidents may be betrayed by subsequent events into a posture of overreacting to a situation seemingly bearing all the marks of crisis. In Lyndon Johnson's first months in office, Cuba suddenly launched a radio campaign for the "return" of the Guantánamo base, and her fishing boats began intruding into United States waters. The boats were seized, whereupon Castro shut off the Guantánamo water supply. The United States, sensing crisis and mindful of the 1962 confrontation with the U.S.S.R. over Cuba, announced that most of the several thousand Cubans commuting daily to the base would be dismissed unless they spent their earnings there. Just after this stern measure was announced, Castro pulled his reverse lever and poured out conciliatory words. The President was left with a strong public stand but no crisis.

Crisis distorts relations between the branches of government. It may drive Congress and the President far apart, as Buchanan and Hoover learned, and shut out even the most elementary cooperation. Or it may be an overriding force for unity as the normal divisions and rivalries between the legislative and executive branches are abandoned and partisan skirmishing is put aside. Congress, which ordinarily does not delegate the President authority gladly, may do so with a lavish hand. In the hundred days after his inauguration in 1933, Franklin Roosevelt was showered with matchless gifts of statutory authority. "Since March 4, 1933,"

Lindsay Rogers wrote in those incredible days, "Presidential government has been stronger than at any previous time—even during the War. The powers granted to President Roosevelt are considerably in excess of those which Congress allowed President Wilson to exercise and the popular support at present manifest is immeasurably greater."

Crisis spotlights the inadequacies of the existing order and opens wide the opportunities for creating sweeping new policy. The exigencies of World War II brought the first large modern strides for Negro civil rights in permitting the federal Fair Employment Practice Committee. The grave economic crisis of 1933 invited the government to stimulate and control a vast economic revolution. The central question fiercely debated in New Deal councils was, How big a revolution should it be? To some, the changes accomplished were awesome. "Never was there such a change in the transfer of government," Supreme Court Justice Harlan Stone wrote to Herbert Hoover after two months of the Roosevelt administration. "To judge by the rapidity of changing events, as many decades might have passed." But there was also disappointment that the President did not exploit his opportunity more fully, that he had not attacked unemployment with more basic solutions, that he had not reconstituted the entire banking system rather than merely saving the banks. "I think back to the events of March 4, 1933, with a sick heart," Senator Bronson Cutting later wrote. "For then . . . the nationalization of banks by President Roosevelt could have been accomplished without a word of protest."

Four historic situations provide a panorama of crisis: the Great Depression during Hoover's administration, the depression during Roosevelt's first hundred days, the rush of events preceding the Civil War, and the Cuban crisis of 1962.

◇

I T W A S Herbert Hoover's lot to confront the severest economic depression the nation has known, which commenced with the great stock market crash seven months after his inauguration. The whole economy was clawed and gouged; no worker, farmer, or lofty business executive escaped the infinite, invisible adversary.

In October and November 1929 stocks listed on the New York Stock Exchange fell over 40 per cent in value, a loss of twenty-six billion dollars. Although President Hoover bravely announced, "The fundamental business of the country, that is, production and distribution of commodities, is on a sound and prosperous basis," events soon slashed the President's optimism. Commodity prices, freight-car loadings, pig iron and steel production, coal output, and automobile production, the crucial economic indicators, fell sharply. But the most fearsome aspect of the collapse was the soaring unemployment which at its peak numbered one-fourth of the labor force. Men eager to work found factory gates shut, so they sat home, their spirits rusting. In those times the unemployed were maintained by private and local public resources, and support was scanty. In Allegheny County, Pennsylvania, according to Benjamin C. Marsh, executive secretary of the people's lobby, "There are families who have not even salt in their homes. It is a matter of beans, week after week." Waves of foreclosures of farms and workingmen's homes swept the country.

The creaky, jerry-built banking system passed through a vale of utter darkness. Bank failures, which had been building up in the twenties, rocketed at the spark of the depression. In all, 5,102 banks went under from 1929 through 1932. Depositors marched on banks and thousands of veterans of World War I with their wives and children marched on Washington to press Congress to award immediately a bonus for World War I veterans not due until 1945. Commander Walter W. Waters of the marching veterans spoke of them as the vanguard of a general revolt of the unemployed. Men in high places did strange things and appeared in odd lights. Samuel Insull, emperor of a vast public utilities network, resigned his eighty-five directorships, sixty-five chairmanships and eleven presidencies and abruptly departed for Europe. J. P. Morgan, it was later revealed, did not pay one cent of federal income tax in 1930, 1931, or 1932, nor, in the last two years, did any of his partners. The Great Depression had an international dimension. The failure of Austria's largest bank, the Credit-Anstalt, precipitated a general panic in central Europe that swept rapidly westward.

The general economic ruin fell upon Herbert Hoover, a solemn and wealthy engineer. He had become a household symbol of merciful efficiency as relief administrator in World War I, and then as Secretary of Commerce and strong man of Harding's cabinet. Because of confusion over his party affiliation, important Democrats had boomed him for the Presidency in 1920. "He is certainly a wonder," Franklin D. Roosevelt had said, "and I wish we could make him President of the United States."

On March 4, 1929, Hoover took the Presidential oath. The new Bible used for the ceremony was then turned back to Proverbs 29:18, which read, "Where there is no vision, the people perish; but he that keepeth the law, happy is he." Seven months later, however, the stock market crashed and the holocaust of the Great Depression, which had long been gathering in the Harding and Coolidge administrations, struck with total fury. In responding to the disaster, Hoover was controlled by a personal philosophy which he believed had forged the nation's past extraordinary economic growth while simultaneously preserving the basic liberties.

"It is not the function of the [federal] government," he said later on August 11, 1932, in accepting renomination for the Presidency, "to relieve individuals of their responsibilities to their neighbors, or to relieve private institutions of their responsibilities to the public, or of local government to the States, or of State governments to the Federal Government." At most, the federal government might employ "reserve powers" in behalf of citizens and communities, but only after insisting that "all of them assert their responsibilities in full." Man's responsibility to his neighbor was "God-imposed," he declared in his inaugural address of March 4, 1929, and the cooperation of man with his fellows and of private organizations with one another was "an advance toward the highest conception of self-government." The choice between local and federal activity was a choice between liberty and tyranny. And in 1931 in a radio address he told the nation:

> Where people divest themselves of local government responsibilities they at once lay the foundation for destruction of their liberties. . . . At once when the government is centralized there arises a limitation upon the liberty of the individual, and restriction of individual opportunity . . . can lead but to the superstate where every man becomes the servant of the State and real liberty is lost.

The depression's root cause, in Hoover's view, was not material or political, but psychological—the erosion of confidence and the spread of fear. "The courage and enterprise of the people still exist," he wrote to Senator Simeon D. Fess, "and only await release from fears and apprehension." The federal government could best restore confidence by balancing its budget. "The government no more than individual families can continue to expend more than it receives without inviting serious consequences. . . ." A balanced budget meant less spending and lower taxes. "It is the relief of taxes from the backs of men which liberates their powers."

Hoover, true to his doctrines, stressed public works by states and municipalities for the unemployed. He stepped up federal construction and halted immigration, but would go no further. When Senator Robert F. Wagner introduced legislation calling for advance public works planning by a Federal Employment Stabilization Board, a strengthened employment service, and improved statistical data on the unemployed, Hoover supported only the last proposal. Unemployment relief belonged to the states, local charitable organizations, and the employer. Federal action would open the way to evil "politics," and the time required to train a suitable bureaucracy could not be spared.

In Hoover's view the federal government might "indirectly" help the unemployed, the farmer, the bank depositor, by aiding employers and banks. Rising production and cheaper credit would diminish the misery of the hard-hit groups. As bank failures soared, Hoover proposed that the leading banks pool their funds to provide a credit reserve for their weaker fellows. When this proved to no avail, he proposed to Congress on December 8, 1931, the creation of the Reconstruction Finance Corporation to make loans to shore up credit, check inflation, expand employment, and bolster the badly wobbling banks and railroads. He modeled the RFC after the War Finance Corporation of World War I and believed it would accomplish its mission within two years. But as the depression worsened, the RFC, his principal contribution to recovery, continued to be needed. By March 31, 1933, the RFC had lent $1,785,315,120 to 7,411 institutions, principally banks and railroads. Eventually the RFC provided loans for unemployment relief. Belatedly and grudgingly, Hoover took this long step away from his philosophical hostility to federal action. With equal tardiness and reluctance, he tried to improve the credit facilities of the farmer and the home owner. As the international economic picture deteriorated, Hoover, pushed inexorably by events, proposed a moratorium on intergovernmental debts.

Hoover was chronically opposed to increases in Presidential power to cope with the emergency. When revival of the wartime Council of National Defense was proposed to widen the attack upon the depression demon, he scotched the idea, holding that it was more important to balance the budget. When the Democratic-controlled Congress, in the face of the deepening misery, moved to empower the RFC to make loans "for any conceivable purpose on any conceivable security to anybody who wants money," he vetoed the legislation.

Few, if any, Presidents have worked as hard on the job as Herbert Hoover. "Work is life," was his motto. Up at six and at his desk by eight-thirty, he drove his staff ragged by relentless application. His own life was incessantly preoccupied with the crisis. "A repairman behind a dyke," he described himself. "No sooner is one leak plugged up than it is necessary to dash over and stop another that has broken out. There is no end to it." His mastery of the situation's facts was dazzling. "He has the greatest capacity for assimilating and organizing information of any man I ever knew," said his Secretary of State, Henry L. Stimson. "To Hoover's brain facts are water to a sponge," noted Bernard Baruch, "They are absorbed into every tiny interstice." But Secretary Stimson lamented the President's habit of "seeing the dark side first" and likened their conferences to "sitting in a bath of ink." Although Hoover fought hard, his darkling views drained his zest.

However much Hoover valued public confidence, his administration was a monumental failure in public relations. Shy and sensitive, he considered political polemics alien to the dignity of his office. "This is not a showman's job," he would say, "I will not step out of character." When on occasion he resorted to the radio, he read from a manuscript in a dull monotone that quickly lost his audience.

The Hoover era was more than a failure of the uses of Presidential initiative and power; it was, of course, a failure also of society to use its own alternative sources of leadership. The businessman who in 1925 had been rightly characterized as "the most influential person in the nation" lay prostrate in failure. The imperious J. P. Morgan might take to the radio in 1932, but the heavens opened not a crack. The grand academic economists, Taussig, Ely, Commons, Mitchell, and Seligman, were almost totally unprepared for the collapse. Organized labor was in the hands of little men. Except for the thirty-hour week, their pronouncements were barren of concrete proposals. Congress, which passed into Democratic control with the 1930 elections, tended to reject the President's proposals. Democratic measures, in turn, calling for more vigorous action than Hoover's ideology could bear, were vetoed time and again. And the President-elect, Franklin D. Roosevelt, chosen by the people in a massive rejection of the Hoover leadership, treated gingerly Hoover's invitation to a kind of joint leadership in the four-month "lame-duck" interlude between the election and the inauguration. With only a few minor exceptions, Roosevelt chose not to act until his formal investiture in the Presidential office.

◊

ON MARCH 4, 1933, Franklin D. Roosevelt was sworn into the Presidency before a hundred thousand spectators crammed upon forty acres of lawn and pavement before the east front of the Capitol, while millions more gathered at their radios. The nation was gripped in tension. For weeks devastating runs on savings banks had continued unslackened. When Roosevelt took the oath, every bank in the nation had locked its doors.

Roosevelt's inaugural pronouncements set the themes of his approach to the crisis and his operation of the Presidency. "This nation asks for action, and action now," he declared. "This great nation will endure as it has endured, will revive and will prosper." He quickly provided action. He called Congress into special session and proclaimed a national banking holiday from March 6 to March 9. In that interval his administration worked out plans to revive the banks. The convening of Congress on March 9 signaled the beginning of the "one hundred days," in which the President literally engulfed the legislature with proposals for economic recovery and reform. At the top of the list was legislation to regulate the resumption of banking. "I cannot too strongly urge upon the Congress the clear necessity for immediate action," read the President's message. Congress needed no urging. In less than forty minutes the House of Representatives passed unanimously the administration's bill, which few of its members had seen. It swept through the Senate and reached the President for signature less than eight hours after its introduction.

The next day Roosevelt sent over his message on economy in government, curiously reminiscent of Hoover's strictures on the subject. On March 16 the President asked for agricultural legislation, the first of a series of proposals to reorganize the nation's economic processes. The central feature of the administration's agricultural bill was the provision of a price subsidy to the farmer who pledged to limit his output. Hopefully, these procedures would help restore the farmer's badly eroded purchasing power. The administration's bill eased the farm mortgage crisis and increased the value of farm loans. On March 21 the President tackled the problem of unemployment by asking for federal grants to the states for direct unemployment relief, a step the Hoover administration had grudgingly begun in its twilight days. He next called for a civilian conservation corps, consisting eventually of a quarter million of the youthful unemployed, who built dams, planted trees, improved streams, fought forest fires and diseases, and cleared beaches and camping sites. On March 29, spurred by the revelations of abuses in the stock markets, he asked for supervision of the sale of investment securities in interstate commerce. On April 10 came the New Deal's most monumental achievement, the plan for a Tennessee Valley Authority with responsibilities for planning the "proper use, conservation and development of the natural resources of the Tennessee River drainage basin and adjoining territory." Power development, flood control, soil erosion, reforestation, the retirement of marginal lands, industrial development, indeed planning for the entire watershed were on the TVA agenda. On April 13 the President urged legislation to save small home mortgages from foreclosures that were averaging a thousand a day; on May 4 came emergency legislation to improve the ailing railroads; and on May 17 a National Industrial Recovery bill to foster "a great cooperative movement throughout all industry in order to obtain wide reemployment, to shorten the working week, to pay a decent wage for the shorter week and to prevent unfair competition and disastrous overproduction." The President also requested a vast three billion dollar program of public construction to spur employment.

In these hundred days Roosevelt sent fifteen messages to Congress and shepherded fifteen laws through to enactment. He made ten major addresses, held press conferences and cabinet meetings twice a week, received innumerable visitors and delegations, conferred with the heads of other nations, and made all the important executive decisions. In the months after the one hundred days Roosevelt's further policies unraveled in an atmosphere of urgency. In 1934 the stock exchanges were regulated, a new labor policy was inaugurated facilitating union organization and imposing upon employers a duty to engage in serious collective bargaining. A social security system was installed to cushion the hardships of old age and unemployment. To push the economy, Roosevelt engaged in "pump-priming," chiefly through an elaborate program of public works. He dabbled briefly in the intricacies of a commodity dollar, contrived to raise the price level, and went off the gold standard. Periodically, he stoked business confidence by retrenching public spending and balancing the budget. The New Deal's frantic activity succeeded. The banks reopened, their health vastly improved, the United States government guaranteed their deposits, and the rain of failures ceased. Employment rose, the farmer kept his home and bettered his land, business failures dropped; the sun shone again.

How had Roosevelt reversed the plunge of crisis into enheartening upturn? His administration indeed was, as his inaugural promised, action-oriented. Crisis, in his view, could not be coped with merely by hopeful public pronouncement and private hand-wringing, or by defensive response to the depression's newest attack. The hundred days and after witnessed a grand offensive. Roosevelt made his way by taking a sweeping view of his powers and of Presidential leadership. In his inaugural address he asserted a well-nigh limitless vision of Presidential authority. "Our Constitution," he declared, "is so simple and practical that it is possible always to meet extraordinary needs by changes in emphasis and arrangement without loss of essential form." He went on to reveal that if the nation's worsening plight or a laggard tendency of Congress required it, "I shall ask the Congress for the one remaining instrument to meet the crisis—broad Executive power to wage a war against the emergency, as great as the power that would be given to me if we were in fact invaded by a foreign foe." As his administration proceeded, Roosevelt commanded his legal counselors to tell him not what he could not do, but what he could do.

His conception of Presidential leadership was formed by the models of Woodrow Wilson and Theodore Roosevelt, which teach that the people respond to vision and moral purpose. For Franklin Roosevelt, the models illuminated weakness as well as strength. Theodore Roosevelt, he discerned, lacked Wilson's "appeal to the fundamental" and capacity to stir "the truly profound moral and social convictions." Wilson, in contrast, failed to raise, as Theodore Roosevelt did, "people to enthusiasm over specific individual events." Franklin Roosevelt, setting his own performance in the economic crisis, endeavored to combine the best of Wilson and Theodore Roosevelt by appealing to underlying convictions, by stirring the nation over specific events, and by making government the positive instrument of the people.

The New Deal, he said, "implied a new order of things designed to benefit the great mass of our farmers, workers, and businessmen would replace the old order of special privilege. . . ." In countless ways he expressed his administration's commitment to the welfare of all the people.

When the banking community lay sprawled in utter helplessness, Roosevelt noticed, not without amusement, how bankers who once had objected so high-mindedly to federal assistance for farmers and the unemployed now cried for it for themselves. It was more important to save the people, Roosevelt said, although he cast many a lifeline to bankers, too. He measured his administration's progress in terms of improvements in the people's condition. Mrs. Roosevelt, whose far travels and keen eye made her the President's star reporter, would depart with his instructions, "Watch the people's faces. Look at the condition of their clothes on the wash line. You can tell a lot from that." He greeted her return with a barrage of questions on what people she visited had to eat, how they lived, and what their homes and farms and educational facilities were like.

The hundred days and beyond was an interlude crammed with improvisation and experimentation such as the nation had never seen. Unlike Hoover, who was ruled by dogma, Roosevelt had few preconceptions and no panaceas. The New Deal was a coat of many colors, of centralization in the manner of NRA, of decentralization in the states' large role in the workings of the unemployment compensation system, in the nationalism of the United States at the London Economic Conference, and the internationalism of reciprocal trade agreements. Those mindful of the wide chasm between Theodore Roosevelt's New Nationalism, with its stress upon planning and government operation, and Wilson's New Freedom, with its devotion to regulation and the retention of private ownership, rubbed their eyes in disbelief in beholding elements of both in the hundred days. TVA was a monument to planning; regulating securities was in the Wilsonian tradition. To assure this rich diversity, Roosevelt skillfully kept about himself a circle of administrators and advisers of clashing views and backgrounds.

As befits an administration pledged to action, the qualities Roosevelt valued most in his subordinates were initiative, vitality, and vision. Most major posts of the New Deal were occupied by men with ideas and drive —chiefly lawyers, professors, economists, and social workers who were at home in the world of ideas and its workaday procedures of analysis and dialectic. The administrators were not simply specialists but generalists confident of their capacity to illuminate any social problem with positive rationality. Yet Roosevelt retained his own grip on decision sufficiently to recapture jurisdictions whenever an administrator faltered. To assure that programs would be carried out with maximum action, he entrusted their administration not to the old-line departments, as a rule, but to newly created agencies. The old departments, he was impressed, were wedded to bureaucratic routine and the policies of bygone Republican administrations. The new agencies offered the energy and enthusiasm of their youthfulness and commitment to New Deal policy.

Roosevelt's success in pushing an unprecedented quantity of major laws through Congress had something of a pattern. He outlined his proposals in brief, general messages, and followed them with bills or detailed memoranda prepared by his executive aides and introduced by friendly Congressmen. In the follow-up, Roosevelt excelled at face-to-face persuasion with legislative leaders and at coordinating them and his administrative aides in common cause. The stock exchanges law, for instance, was the joint product of James M. Landis, Benjamin Cohen, and Thomas Corcoran of the executive branch, who coached witnesses and prepared data for the legislative committees; Congressman Sam Rayburn and Senator Duncan Fletcher of the legislature; and Ferdinand Pecora, who brilliantly investigated the malfeasance of bankers and brokers.

Roosevelt's progress was speeded by his tactic of bipartisan or nonpartisan appeals, which won strong Republican support. "The house is burning down, and the President of the United States says this is the way to put out the fire," the House Republican whip, Bertrand Snell, cried when the emergency banking bill came up for debate. Roosevelt, enheartened by the constancy of Republican support, held rigorously to a nonpartisan approach throughout his administration's first year. When an exuberant Democratic organization man invited the President to the party's celebration of the birthday of its founder, Thomas Jefferson, Roosevelt indignantly refused. "Our strongest plea to the country in this particular year of grace," he replied, "is that the recovery and reconstruction program is being accomplished by men and women of all parties—that I have repeatedly appealed to Republicans as much as to Democrats to do their part."

Roosevelt's approach to the crisis was a massive venture in public relations. Like Hoover, interestingly, Roosevelt considered the root cause of the depression to be psychological, but where Hoover crumpled in ineptitude in his public relations, Roosevelt gloriously mastered them. "The only thing we have to fear is fear itself," he said memorably in his inaugural. He perfected two techniques to bathe the country regularly in the ointments of hope and optimism—the press conference and the fireside chat. He transformed the press conference from an interlude of dour secretiveness, which it was under Hoover, into a vehicle of lively and informative interchange between the President and the press. After a week in office, on Sunday evening, March 12, Roosevelt gave his first "fireside chat," a radio address to the nation on the banking situation. The President, said Will Rogers, the humorist, made banking clear to everybody, even the bankers.

To associates and to the country at large, Roosevelt shone with confidence. His flashing smile, his cigarette holder set at a jaunty angle, his ready humor and booming laugh were the trademarks of his self-possession against the pressures of crisis. A brief exposure to Roosevelt was enough to repair the panicky, quiet the agitated, and inspirit the downhearted. No adversity could quash the President's ever soaring mood. To Anne O'Hare McCormick of the New York *Times* he was "apparently the least worried man in the country." Said his aide Rexford Tugwell, "Roosevelt was a man with fewer doubts than anyone I had ever known." Various explanations have been offered of the President's impregnable serenity. "F. D. R. was very tough," said Francis Biddle, "He had got on top of life. Nothing could touch him." Tugwell put it more strongly: "He had a source of detached exaltation which could not be touched by the outcome."

◊

THE contrast in method and skill between two Presidents—Buchanan before the Civil War and Kennedy in the 1962 Cuba missile crisis—who faced the threat of war reveals how much individual talent and personal judgment determine a President's style and effectiveness in crisis and his standing in history.

"Blessed are the peacemakers," say the Scriptures, but politics takes a different view of this quiet breed. Often the search for peace seems like appeasement, and "appeasement" has become a term of scathing political reproach. James Buchanan, the President who more than any other in American history practiced conciliation and moderation—appeasement—against tremendous odds, is remembered with derision and falls well toward the bottom of the list in ranking of chief executives by their success and failure. Buchanan, ironically, has been dealt this ignominy even though he prevented war from breaking out between the North and South in his Presidential term. Five weeks after he left office, the fratricidal explosion occurred. (Lincoln, who carried the nation into war, is remembered as one of the greatest Presidents.) Ironically, too, Buchanan's peace policy seems to have been supported by the public opinion of the day. The country, North and South, wanted caution and delay, and Buchanan strove as hard as he could to provide them.

Buchanan worked for peace against crushing obstacles. Nowhere was the brewing holocaust more evident than in the unbridgeable divisions of his cabinet. Three of his secretaries, Cobb, Thompson, and Floyd, defiantly espoused the right of secession, and three, Cass, Holt, and Black, denied it. Congress was also hopelessly divided. The Senate was Democratic and the House Republican, and each house split into numerous factions on questions of secession, compromise, and force. Worst of all, Buchanan was a repudiated President, denied renomination by his party, the titular head of an organization that the Republican Lincoln defeated in his race for the Presidency. In Northern political circles, Democratic and Republican alike, Buchanan was an outcast, the suspected ally of the secessionists, a potential betrayer of the Union to the promoters of rebellion.

Not the least of Buchanan's handicaps were his own personal limitations. True, he came into the Presidency with gilt-edged training and experience. Congressman, Minister to Russia, Senator, Secretary of State, Minister to England, Buchanan was a rarity with three decades of service in the nation's most responsible posts. But he came into the Presidency at a ripe age and in ill health, despite the contrary impression created by his tall figure and his ruddy face crowned by a pile of gleaming white hair. In 1859–60, when the slavery crisis came to a head, he was seventy years old, afflicted with heart trouble, a glandular difficulty in his neck, polypus growth in his nasal passages, myopic vision that induced a squint, and general infirmity which prevented him at times from moving outside his upstairs rooms. His head was tilted and drawn askew by scars from an operation, and he tried to cover these blemishes with a large collar and an expansive neck cloth, which gave him the appearance of being perpetually dressed for cold weather. In addition to his physical torments, Buchanan suffered from psychological stresses. A broken romance of his youth still burned in his bachelor's memory. Religion tormented him. Seeking anxiously the "experience of salvation," he engaged in intensive private devotion and constant church attendance. In 1859, a year of grave national crisis, he pursued a series of discussions with the Reverend William M. Paxton of the First Presbyterian Church of New York City on the intricacies of regeneration, atonement, repentance, and faith.

Buchanan's political style was diplomatic rather than combative. His forte was not the hustings and debate but conference and negotiation. Patient and meticulous in procedure, he shunned irretrievable commitment and was infinitely willing to yield matters of minor advantage. He bore his terrible burdens by clasping and repeating such maxims as "Sufficient unto the day is the evil thereof" and "It is better to bear the ills we have than to fly to others we know not of." By converting these maxims into a kind of political rosary, he resigned himself to bad situations, dodged decision, and surmounted failure. The brilliant stroke, the gamble, the sudden move were not for him. He considered political discussions of moral principles and abstractions futile and dangerous. "The Bible for Heaven, the Constitution for earth," he would say. "You cannot legislate morality." Mutual accommodation, the avoidance of extremes, and the majority's forbearance toward the minority were the cement of lasting union in his eyes.

Buchanan's Presidency was strongly Southern in coloration. Indeed he sided with the radical slavery men on every issue except the revival of the slave trade. He opposed any bar against slavery in the territories, against expansion in Cuba and Mexico, against new slave states. Slavery, he believed, should be treated not in moral terms, but as a question of Constitutional law. He was closely tied to the Southern Democratic wing and permitted Howell Cobb of Georgia, Jefferson Davis of Mississippi, John Slidell of Louisiana, and Henry A. Wise of Virginia to dominate his administration. At heart he considered Southern grievances valid and Republicans guilty of sectional excess.

Late in 1859, the final year of Buchanan's Presidency, the long-gathering crisis broke. In October John Brown raided the federal arsenal at Harpers Ferry, turning the slavery issue into a soaring flame and pulling the Democratic party hopelessly asunder. In November Lincoln was elected President, although with only 39.8 per cent of the popular votes cast. In South Carolina, which long had threatened to secede if Lincoln were elected, the wheels of disunion began to turn. The federal grand jury at Charleston and the federal district court resigned. No one could henceforth be charged with breaking federal law, since no federal courts existed to try offenders. South Carolina's Governor William H. Gist asked his compatriot, Assistant Secretary of State William H. Trescot to ascertain Buchanan's intentions concerning the four federal forts at Charleston: Forts Sumter, Moultrie, Johnson, and Castle Pinckney. The President, in fact, pacing in his library and passing sleepless nights, was quite baffled. The forts were hopelessly weak, only a sergeant at Pinckney, seventy-five officers and men at Moultrie, and a handful at Sumter, which was still under construction. The cabinet, debating the wisdom of reinforcements, was hopelessly divided. By late November the federal commander at Charleston, Major Robert Anderson, was calling urgently for reinforcements. South Carolina would soon leave the Union and seize Fort Moultrie, he reported, and nothing could better prevent bloodshed than to strengthen the forts to the point "that it would be folly and madness to attack us."

Buchanan had little hope of deterring South Carolina from her expected next step, adopting a secession ordinance. Rather, he aimed to dissuade other Southern states from joining her. This happy result might be best achieved if the federal government demonstrated, by scrupulous behavior, how little cause any state had to secede. Then, if South Carolina took the step, it would appear in its solitude foolish and precipitate. The President, accordingly, must avoid any menacing posture or unconstitutional action which might provoke or justify secession.

While mulling over his position, Buchanan received a lengthy statement of "Views" from his general-in-chief, Winfield Scott, aged seventy-four and in ill health. Scott's "Views" largely ignored the Charleston forts, conceded a right of secession to the states, detailed the probable horrors of civil war, and beheld as "a smaller evil" the Union's dissolution into several confederacies. Buchanan dismissed the "Views" as imbecilic and improper.

Scott's weakness seemed to goad the President into action. He instructed Secretary of War Floyd to supply the forts with all necessary men, arms, and provisions. He next took up with his cabinet a plan he was evolving to preserve peace and union. Buchanan envisioned a convention of the states, authorized in Article V of the Constitution, to devise some plan of adjustment. A Constitutional convention, he believed, would congeal and express popular sentiment, override a hopelessly divided Congress, and avert disunion. The cabinet split on the proposal.

The President received more helpful counsel in calling upon his Attorney General, Jeremiah S. Black, for a statement of available legal powers in several possible contingencies of the crisis. Federal law, the Attorney General wrote, required the President to collect import duties and protect federal property. An act of 1795 empowered the President to enforce United States laws when opposed "by any State, by combinations too powerful to be suppressed by the ordinary course of judicial proceedings." But the 1795 act contained a flaw. The President was duty-bound to employ it not merely against South Carolina, but against various Northern states as well whose Personal Liberty Laws had undermined enforcement of the federal Fugitive Slave Act. The Northern states had committed overt acts of defiance; South Carolina as yet had only talked. The President could not march against a state that merely threatened while ignoring others that had long and actively opposed federal law. Black regretfully rejected the supposed precedents of the Whiskey Rebellion and the 1832 nullification crisis, in which federal forces moved to local trouble spots at the President's command. In contrast to the earlier instances, Black pointed out, no state or federal officer in the present crisis had asked for help or complained that a law had been violated.

On December 3 Buchanan dispatched his anxiously awaited State of the Union message to Congress. The document reflected his aspiration to stand between the quarreling sections as a moderator "with my hand on the head of each, counseling peace." The message, aimed to pacify everyone, pleased no one. It irritated the South, incensed the Radical Republicans, and frustrated the Douglas Democrats. Secession, Buchanan said, was unconstitutional, but Congress and the President were without power to compel a state to remain in the Union. Turning to the North, he blamed its antislavery agitation as primarily responsible for the crisis. Turning to South Carolina, Buchanan said that although the President was duty-bound to enforce the laws, he really could not do so because no machinery now existed in South Carolina to administer the laws. No statute empowered the President to use force against South Carolina. He followed this confession of executive helplessness with a specific proposal. Let Congress call a Constitutional convention to add an explanatory amendment to the Constitution affirming the right of property in slaves in states and territories where it now existed or might in the future exist. Let the title of masters to fugitive slaves be reaffirmed, and all contravening state laws be declared null and void. Hopeful that his message would arrest the secession movement, he dispatched an advance copy to Governor Gist of South Carolina.

But there was only disappointment. South Carolina elected delegates to its secession convention and the state's legislators in Washington called on Buchanan seeking understandings to avoid future bloodshed. The President upbraided his visitors for their state's "ingratitude" and precipitation in leaving the Union before suffering any injury. He would collect the revenues "at all hazards," he said. The vigor of this statement was diluted minutes later when he was asked whether he would use force to execute the laws. "I will obey the laws," he answered. "I am no warrior—I am a man of peace—but I will obey the laws."

Troubles now fell upon Buchanan in whole battalions. Secretary of the Treasury Howell Cobb resigned, signifying Georgia's impending swing into the secession movement. The South Carolina delegation brought Buchanan, reeling under Georgia's blow, to declare that it was not his policy to reinforce the Charleston forts. The President's shift prompted his Secretary of State, Lewis Cass, to resign in protest. The radical Northern press interpreted the step as the refusal of a patriotic statesman to remain any longer in the house of a President flirting with treason. Buchanan reconstituted his cabinet by shifting Black to the State Department and preserved the ideological balance by appointing Philip F. Thomas of Maryland and of Southern sympathies to the Treasury. The new Attorney General was Edwin M. Stanton of Ohio, a hard-core Unionist.

Ugly rumors and reports concerning the President were circulating widely. "Buchanan is today as truly a traitor as was Benedict Arnold," Lincoln was warned. Horace Greeley's New York *Tribune* declared that the President was insane; other reports said he was a coward, sick with terror, and alternated between praying and crying. Anti-Buchanan conspiracies were stirring. Senator Louis T. Wigfall approached Secretary of War Floyd with a plan to kidnap Buchanan and install Vice President Breckinridge in the Presidency. Floyd, to his credit, angrily rejected the scheme.

The crisis climbed to new intensity when Major Anderson, taking the initiative into his own hands, brilliantly maneuvered his forces from Fort Moultrie to the more defensible Fort Sumter. A Southern delegation carried the first news of the development and their protests to the White House. "My God," cried the President, standing at the mantelpiece of his bedroom and crushing a cigar in his hand, "are misfortunes never to come singly? I call God to witness, *you*, gentlemen, better than anybody, *know* that this is not only without, but against my orders. It is against my policy." Yet when his Southern visitors pressed Buchanan to repudiate Anderson and restore the status quo, the President refused to act until he consulted the cabinet and had Anderson's report. Ultimately, Anderson held fast. Secretary Floyd, now under the clouds of gross scandals in the War Department, used Anderson's move as the pretext for an honorable resignation. South Carolina, for its part, countered by seizing Fort Moultrie, Fort Castle Pinckney and the U.S. Custom house. Adversity leaped from still another quarter. Buchanan's intermediaries who journeyed to Springfield, Illinois, to induce Lincoln to back up the proposed Constitutional convention were flatly rebuffed.

As the new year 1861 dawned, Buchanan still wrestled with the question of reinforcements to Major Anderson. South Carolina lent urgency to the Presidential deliberations by seizing the lighthouse in Charleston harbor, by blocking mail service to Fort Sumter, and by announcing that all United States ships were henceforth to be excluded from Charleston's vicinity. Buchanan, after much anguished temporizing, decided to reinforce Anderson by dispatching the U.S.S. *Brooklyn*. General Scott, fearful that a heavy vessel might ground upon a bar near the fort, insisted upon chartering the *Star of the West*, a side-wheel merchant steamer. On January 5, the *Star* quietly sailed from New York, loaded with foodstuffs and troops below deck. Two cabinet secretaries who were Southern in their sympathies and who had not been informed of the maneuver resigned. The *Star of the West*, alas, was driven off by shore batteries as it entered Charleston harbor. New denunciations of Buchanan rang to the heavens from both sides of the Mason-Dixon line. During the din, Buchanan re-aligned his cabinet by appointing John A. Dix of New York as Secretary of the Treasury and Moses Kelly, chief clerk of the Interior Department, to the Secretaryship. The cabinet was now entirely Northern and in general harmony with the President's outlook.

On January 8 Buchanan sent Congress a special message on South Carolinian affairs. "The prospect of a bloodless settlement fades away," he warned. He intended "to collect the public revenues and to protect the public property" to the point that existing laws permitted. His province was "to execute" the laws and not "to make them." Congress alone could authorize the use of troops, declare war, or legislate the removal of grievances. He again appealed for a Constitutional convention. "In Heaven's name," he pleaded, "let the trial be made before we plunge into armed conflict upon the mere assumption that there is no other alternative." But Congress did nothing. The Senate refused to confirm his nomination of a revenue collector at Charleston and thereby deprived him of his only means under existing legislation of calling up the militia.

(Only if a collector had appealed for aid could the President act, Buchanan felt, without special law.) Senate Republicans buried his Constitutional convention proposal in committee.

The deterioration rushed on. Georgia elected a pro-secession convention and seized Fort Pulaski at Savannah. Florida and Alabama occupied federal properties, and in Washington Southern Senators charted the creation of a confederacy. At no point in the spreading debacle did Congress gird the President with new authority to call out the militia or raise volunteers to suppress insurrection. Why did he not act boldly on his own, without waiting for Congress, Buchanan was asked. To do so, he replied, would be to make war not only upon South Carolina but upon Congress, which was resolved to do nothing until Lincoln's advent. On March 4, 1861, the scepter finally passed. "My dear sir," Buchanan greeted Lincoln, "if you are as happy in entering the White House as I shall feel on returning to Wheatland, you are a happy man indeed."

◇

KENNEDY's style in handling the threat of nuclear war with the Soviet Union was altogether different, though it too was based upon a desire for peace. The Cuban crisis of 1962 began in the whirring camera of an Air Force U-2 reconnaissance plane high over San Cristobal on October 14. Analysis of the developed films the next day struck the Kennedy administration with massive impact. Soviet medium-range missiles, a mobile type used by the Red Army, were in place near San Cristobal, 100 miles west of Havana. Every American city was potentially only a few minutes away from them. The revelation set off fourteen days of diplomatic maneuver and military build-up which brought the United States to the threshold of nuclear war.

The U-2's October discovery was the climax of a Soviet build-up commencing in July. Soviet technicians and instructors, surface-to-air missiles, patrol boats with missiles, and MIG-2 fighters, according to U.S. intelligence sources, were pouring into Cuba. The executive branch was not alone in its watch. Republican and Democratic legislators alike followed and exclaimed upon the ominous developments.

A frequent Republican critic of Kennedy's Cuban course was Senator Kenneth B. Keating of New York. On September 2 he urged that an Organization of American States mission investigate reports of Cuban missile bases. If the OAS failed to act, the United States should blockade Western Hemispheric waters against vessels carrying armed forces personnel or materiel. In early September, at the instigation of Democratic Senator Richard B. Russell of Georgia, chairman of the Armed Services Committee, Congress passed a resolution invoking the Monroe Doctrine against foreign intervention in the Western Hemisphere and the 1947

Rio pact for joint Western Hemispheric defense. The United States, the resolution declared, was determined to prevent, by "use of arms" if necessary, any Cuban military build-up threatening American security. The resolution's backers, who hailed from both parties, had a double purpose: to warn Khrushchev and Castro, and to invigorate certain administration policy-makers who seemed to them to be taking too detached a view of the Cuban developments.

The administration appeared to accept Khrushchev's characterization of the weapons imported into Cuba as "defensive," although the President stated publicly on September 4 that "Were it otherwise the gravest issues would arise." The close surveillance the United States intelligence community was simultaneously maintaining upon Cuba was spurred by reports from Cuban refugees in Florida that surface-to-surface missiles with nuclear warheads, capable of reaching American cities, were on the island. In a speech at Albuquerque, New Mexico, on October 6, Vice President Johnson brushed aside the critics' proposal of a blockade by declaring that "The stopping of a Russian ship is an act of war." Answering a call by Senator Homer Capehart, Republican of Indiana, for more action on Cuba, President Kennedy in a campaign speech at Louisville, on October 13, hit at those "self-appointed generals and admirals who want to send someone else's sons to war."

The momentous news of the U-2 discovery was conveyed to the President at 8:45 A.M. October 16 by his assistant for national security affairs, McGeorge Bundy, who had learned of it the night before. Bundy later explained, when Kennedy himself inquired, that nothing could have been done that night and that to call advisers in from dinners about town would have touched off alarmed public speculation. The possibility remains, however, that the President could have been informed personally, without disturbance of his aides at their dinners. The question lingers whether Bundy had such a right of choice, and whether in making it he was not, in a limited way, superseding the President. Kennedy was immediately aware of the atomic danger, and was outraged at Khrushchev's barefaced duplicity. The President ticked off to Bundy a list of officials he wished to see. These included his brother, Attorney General Robert Kennedy, and Treasury Secretary Dillon, upon whose judgment he often relied.

The implications of the Soviet move were clear enough. By placing medium- and intermediate-range missiles in Cuba, Russia was narrowing its gap with the United States. Missiles of such range in Cuba would provide the Russians with immediate power without the long wait necessary for equivalent increases in her intercontinental missiles arsenal. A missile fired from Cuba promised far more accuracy than an ICBM from Russia. Cuba-based missiles would reduce the United States' attack-warning time to virtually seconds. The Strategic Air Command would have to be dispersed on a more or less permanent basis.

At 11:45 A.M. on October 16 Kennedy met with a group later known as the Executive Committee (Ex Com) of the National Security Council. The President presided, and his fellow conferees included Vice President Johnson, Secretary of State Rusk, Secretary of Defense McNamara, Dillon, Robert Kennedy, Undersecretary of State Ball, Deputy Secretary of Defense Gilpatric, CIA Deputy Director Carter (CIA Director McCone was away from Washington in the crisis's first days), Assistant Secretary of State for Inter-American affairs Martin, General Taylor (chairman of the Joint Chiefs of Staff), and Theodore Sorensen, Presidential counsel and principal speech writer.

The atmosphere of crisis clung thickly over the group as they canvassed the possible responses to the Soviet thrust. If the United States did nothing, its prestige would tumble and the credibility of its pledges would be destroyed. Latin America might fall into the Soviet basket. If, as a second possibility, the United States bombed or invaded Cuba, its moral position would be tainted, its alliances would be disarrayed, the neutral nations would burst into great cry, and the Russians might make a countermove in Berlin or elsewhere. A third possibility was a blockade, but it too might stir a Soviet response and offend our allies, particularly the maritime powers. The meeting produced two immediate decisions. One was that air surveillance over Cuba should be intensified and the other that any action the United States took should come as close as possible to the United States' public disclosure of the Russian bases.

The vast departmental machinery began to turn. The Defense Department estimated the kinds of units, numbers of men, and time factors necessary for various military actions. The State Department explored the possibilities of Latin-American and European support, and its most sophisticated analysts of Soviet behavior began mulling over the probable effects of various actions on the Russians. United Nations Ambassador Adlai Stevenson was brought into the discussions.

The President had other commitments in addition to the crisis. The Congressional electoral campaign was in full swing, and Kennedy set out for Connecticut to honor long-established speaking dates. The discussions on Cuba were to be kept secret—Khrushchev did not know that Kennedy knew about the offensive missiles, and the secret could best be kept by maintaining a normal Presidential schedule. During his absence, the Ex Com met day and night in Undersecretary of State George Ball's conference room, or "think tank" as it was dubbed, a windowless chamber furnished with a long table, pumpkin leather chairs, prosaic water decanters, and Dixie cups. The meetings were informal, the participants wandering in and out to keep up simultaneously with their regular duties.

Further incoming U-2 reports of new discoveries of medium- and intermediate-range missile sites compounded the situation's urgency. Former Secretary of State Dean Acheson was brought into the meetings.

Upon returning to Washington from the Connecticut hustings, the President took up a varied schedule of regular business, ceremonial duties, and crisis management. He met often with the Ex Com, brought former Defense Secretary Robert Lovett into the discussions, and deliberately absented himself to encourage his aides to express their views uninhibitedly. In moments away from the Ex Com, Kennedy received the Crown Prince of Libya, conferred with a former Finance Minister of Japan, discussed a new threat to Berlin with the West German Foreign Minister, lunched at the Libyan embassy, vetoed a Tariff Commission recommendation to raise duties of self-closing coin purses, and rejected a proposal for the exclusion of foreign-made nails. Although poised on the knife's edge of incipient decision that could long determine the fate of the nation, the West, the world, and mankind, Kennedy bore up with his accustomed composure even in his severest test, a White House meeting with Andrei A. Gromyko. The visit of the Soviet Foreign Minister had been arranged prior to the crisis. In his two hours and fifteen minutes with Kennedy, Gromyko reaffirmed previous assurances that Soviet activity in Cuba was defensive only. Kennedy repeated to Gromyko his belief that the Soviet effort in Cuba was defensive and his warning that any change in this estimate would have grave consequences. The President refrained from confronting Gromyko with the damning truth because the administration had not yet decided what action to take, and the Russians, faced with exposure, might resort to an evasive counterthrust to blunt the eventual decision.

Gromyko dined that evening with Secretary of State Rusk and other officials on the eighth floor of the department. On the floor below, in the "think tank," the planning group continued its crisis discussions. In mid-evening they piled into a single limousine, sacrificing comfort for security, and journeyed to the White House. In this meeting the President seemed to be moving toward a blockade. Ambassador-at-large Llewellyn Thompson, Jr., stressed the need for the solid legality of any action taken. The Russians, he said, had a feeling for "legality," and well grounded legal action would impress world opinion. The State and Justice Departments began work on the legal justification for a blockade.

On October 19 Kennedy resumed his political campaigning, partly to quiet press suspicions that great happenings were afoot, with stops at Cleveland, Chicago, and at Springfield to lay flowers on Lincoln's tomb. Before departing, he expressed approval to the Ex Com of the trend of decision toward a blockade. In the continuing Ex Com discussions, advocates of an offensive air attack vigorously pressed their case, but the blockade attracted the dominant support, even with its admitted danger that, in Vice President Johnson's words, "stopping a Russian ship is an act of war." Staff work proceeded on each alternative to preserve the President's choices to the very moment of decision.

The next day a telephone call from Robert Kennedy brought the President back from Chicago to Washington. Time was running out and secrecy was crumbling, said the Attorney General. The White House informed the press that the President was forced to return by a slight infection of the upper respiratory tract, with one degree of fever. In actuality, the President's cold, which was mild, did not require his return, but it was necessary to mislead the reporters by some contrivance in the interest of security. Kennedy, arriving at 1:37 P.M., went over a speech Sorensen had prepared upon the assumption that a blockade would be imposed. The final speech emerged after five drafts. The President all but clinched the decision for blockade and directed the relevant operations to proceed, subject only to his final word the next day. The State and Defense Departments drafted a blockade proclamation, the chief of Naval Operations made the plans necessary to enforce it, the State Department laid out an approach to the Organization of American States, Acheson prepared to embark for Paris to confer with De Gaulle and the NATO council, and Alexis Johnson, Deputy Undersecretary of State for Political Affairs, worked up a "master scenario" depicting every necessary preparation prior to the President's speech—briefings, orders to embassies, ship movements, and the like. A military helicopter picked up former President Eisenhower at his Gettysburg farm and flew him to Washington for a briefing by the CIA. Vice President Johnson dropped his election campaigning in Hawaii and flew back to Washington.

The next day, October 21, the scenario was converted into action. Kennedy, after conferring again with numerous key officials, definitely decided upon the blockade. In the afternoon he met with the statutory National Security Council. The State Department drafted forty-three Presidential letters to the heads of government of all the alliances and to Willy Brandt, Mayor of West Berlin. A Kennedy-to-Khrushchev letter was prepared to accompany a copy of the TV speech announcing the blockade. Instructions were readied for distributing the speech to sixty embassies. On October 22 Lawrence O'Brien, the President's Congressional liaison assistant, telephoned twenty Congressional leaders of both parties for a meeting with the President. The Soviet ambassador at Washington, Dobrynin, was called to the State Department. General Lauris Norstad, the NATO commander, was alerted. In the meeting with Congressional leaders, Senator Russell, supported by Senator Fulbright, the Foreign Relations Committee chairman, who interestingly enough had opposed the Bay of Pigs attack, bluntly asserted that a blockade was too slow and therefore involved great risk, but the President was not to be dissuaded. At the State Department, Undersecretary Ball and Intelligence and Research Director Hilsman briefed forty-six allied ambassadors in the State Department's International Conference Room.

At 7 P.M. in a calm but intense and blunt eighteen-minute television report, the President delivered his speech alerting the public for the first time. He blamed not Cuba but the Soviet Union for the crisis, which, he said, had violated its leaders' most solemn assurances that only defensive weapons were going to Cuba. The President said he had ordered a "quarantine"—a word he had substituted for "blockade"—on all offensive weapons for Cuba. Ships carrying them would be turned back. Furthermore, he said, the preparation of the missile sites must cease, and if it did not, "further action" would be taken. He was ordering the surveillance continued and he called upon Chairman Khrushchev to withdraw "all offensive weapons" from Cuba.

While the President was speaking, his vast administrative machinery was in full motion. At the State Department the forty-six allied ambassadors watched the speech on a large screen, Assistant Secretary Martin gave a further private briefing to Latin-American ambassadors, Secretary Rusk and Director Hilsman briefed the neutral nations, including Yugoslavia, Undersecretary Ball briefed the diplomatic correspondents, and Defense Secretary McNamara the military correspondents. "Whatever force is required"—even striking—said McNamara, would be employed to enforce the blockade. At the United Nations, Ambassador Stevenson requested a special meeting of the Security Council.

Thirteen hours after Kennedy's speech came the Soviet's first reaction, a long, rambling, published statement of accusations and warnings of thermonuclear war, plus a letter from Khrushchev to Kennedy. These the administration interpreted as betraying that the Kremlin was caught off guard and playing for time to think out its moves. Developments elsewhere were encouraging despite protest marches in various world capitals. In Paris marchers carried placards reading "Kennedy the Assassin" and "Peace in Cuba," and in London two thousand demonstrators screamed "Long Live Castro" and "Down with Kennedy." British Prime Minister Macmillan telephoned his full support. In a meeting with Acheson West German Chancellor Adenauer was equally positive. At the United Nations the NATO countries supported a United States resolution calling upon the Soviet Union to withdraw the missiles and dismantle the sites under United Nations verification, after which the United States would end the quarantine. Citing the Rio pact of 1947, Secretary Rusk offered the Organization of American States a resolution authorizing the use of force, individually or collectively, to enforce the blockade. The OAS Council adopted the resolution 19 to 0. The NATO and OAS unanimity surprised both the United States and the Soviet Union and apparently added to the latter's confusion.

There were less gratifying developments, however. U Thant, Acting Secretary General of the United Nations, urged several weeks' suspension of the blockade and arms shipments to Cuba while negotiations were held. Khrushchev accepted with alacrity, but Kennedy, anticipating the disarming of his powerful diplomatic and military initiative and doubting that they could ever regain momentum if negotiations failed, as they were expected to, turned down Thant's request. "The existing threat," the President replied, "was created by the secret introduction of offensive weapons into Cuba, and the answer lies in the removal of such weapons."

On October 25, twenty hours after the blockade began, the United States Navy made its first interception, a Soviet tanker, the *Bucharest*. It was allowed to proceed without search because the Navy was satisfied it carried only petroleum. Two days later the Lebanese freighter *Marucia* was stopped, boarded, and searched by a five-man party from the destroyers *Joseph P. Kennedy, Jr.*, and *John R. Pierce*. The *Marucia* also was allowed to proceed after it was ascertained that she carried nothing but peaceful cargo.

On October 26 and 27 Khrushchev dispatched two letters to Kennedy. Embedded in the first, although not explicitly stated, was an offer to withdraw the offensive weapons under United Nations supervision if the United States would lift the blockade and promise not to invade the island. The President heard the transcription of this letter with great relief. Then a second Khrushchev letter came clattering over the wires bearing another catch. The Soviet Union would trade its bases in Cuba for the NATO missile base in Turkey. In a National Broadcasting Company telecast of February 9, 1964, McGeorge Bundy stated that the Soviet offer also proposed that the United States pull its missiles out of Greece as well. As Kennedy and his aides pondered a reply, incoming intelligence reports disclosed that Soviet technicians were building away furiously at the Cuban sites. It was estimated that the sites would be ready for missile launchings within a mere five days. Kennedy decided to write again to Khrushchev, saying that if he understood the Premier correctly—that the offensive weapons would be removed in return for an end of the blockade and a promise of no American invasion of Cuba— then it was a deal. It could now go "either way," the President remarked grimly to his aides.

If it should go the bad way, the United States armed forces were ready. The Tactical Air Command's 19th Air Force had moved into the sprawling base outside of Homestead, Florida. By October 23 nearly one thousand attack-fighter and fighter-bomber aircraft were poised in Florida, with a conventional airborne firepower rivaling that in England prior to the Normandy invasion. Army divisions from Fort Bragg, North Carolina; Fort Campbell, Kentucky; Fort Riley, Kansas; and Fort Benning, Georgia, were on full alert. These divisions plus Marines at sea, in Florida, and at Guantánamo, formed a one hundred thousand man force the United States stood ready to hurl into Cuba. Drop-zones in the Cuban interior had been carefully designated for paratroopers of the 82nd and 101st Airborne Divisions. Globemaster transports poured into the Key West naval base with soldiers, sailors, marines, mobile radar units, photographic gear, trucks and jeeps, and weapons of all types. The Association of American Railroads was alerted and 2,418 flatcars and 299 equipment cars from as far distant as Denver and Minneapolis began rolling to Fort Hood, Texas, to take on Honest John Rockets and rocket-launcher vehicles, Patton tanks, self-propelled howitzers, and other cargo. Bases at Miami, Canaveral, Orlando, and Homestead were mushrooming with fighter and fighter-bomber aircraft.

The United States military preparations indeed were proceeding on a global scale. U.S. Navy ships and submarines in the European Atlantic, Pacific, and Mediterranean were hurrying out to sea. Three Polaris-firing submarines scurried to sea from their berths at Holy Loch, Scotland. The Strategic Air Command was on Defcon 2, or full war footing, from which it needed but one signal to go to Defcon 1, which puts it at war. For the first time in history, SAC's medium-range bomber force of B-47's were ordered to disperse. ICBM firing crews, spread in complexes throughout the United States, were brought to full alert and missiles were raised. The Navy's Fleet Ballistic Missile submarines were on station, carrying 128 Polaris missiles, within range of major Soviet targets. The United States had made full preparations to lay the explosive equivalent of more than thirty billion tons of TNT upon the Soviet Union. The United States was also maintaining close air surveillance over Cuba. On October 27 Major Rudolf Anderson, Jr., one of two U-2 pilots whose photographs touched off the crisis, was shot down over Cuba.

In cryptic comment during a speech at Columbia, South Carolina, reported in the press on April 25, 1963, six months after the crisis, Attorney General Robert Kennedy said that Major Anderson's death "led the President to notify Mr. Khrushchev that strong and overwhelming retaliatory action would have been taken unless he received immediate notice that the missiles would be withdrawn." United States officials connected with the crisis believe that this Presidential message, whose text has not yet been revealed, coupled with the open movement of American military power, were the factors that really brought Khrushchev around to his ultimate decision in the immediate crisis. "What got the message through to Khrushchev was action," one official said. "The message was clear that something was going to happen and happen soon."

October 28 brought Khrushchev's answer, the fifth Premier-President exchange in seven days. Khrushchev said that he had ordered work on the bases stopped and the missiles crated and returned to the Soviet Union. Representatives of the United Nations, he promised, would "verify the dismantling." In return, the President's no-invasion pledge would be trusted. After hurried consultations with his aides, the President issued a statement welcoming Khrushchev's "statesmanlike decision," and the blockade was lifted.

In the months following the crisis, the United States and the Soviet Union handled the Cuban question with high caution, neither side appearing to contemplate any drastic action so long as the other kept the October "gentlemen's agreement." Senator Keating remained attentive to Cuba, declaring on the Senate floor on January 31, 1963, that "there is continuing, absolutely confirmed and undeniable evidence that the Soviets are maintaining the medium-range sites they had previously constructed in Cuba. . . . Without on-site inspection, it is hard to see how we will ever know for sure the true missile situation in Cuba." In a press interview, Keating said he would be glad to disclose his information, but not his sources, to the President. Senator Strom Thurmond, Democrat of South Carolina, made similar charges. But intelligence estimates one year after the crisis disclosed that the Soviet force in Cuba was down to ten thousand from twenty-two thousand at the peak of the crisis. The remaining personnel were believed to be devoted to training the Cuban armed forces.

◇

THE Cuban crisis was the first confrontation of its kind since the onset of the age in which the two great nuclear powers possessed the capacity to destroy each other and much of the world. The decisions that Kennedy was called upon to make were therefore the most delicate and the most perilous that any President has ever faced. Not only the welfare of the American public, but the fate of peoples everywhere who had no voice in his selection, of unborn generations, of western civilization itself, depended upon his choices.

The stressful decision-making of the Cuban crisis—the pattern of action by which the President mastered the tangled skein of intense events— was a nightmarish experience. The President is often spoken of, to the point of cliché, as a lonely figure. He has never appeared more solitary than in nuclear confrontation. Surrounded though he is by aides and data and counsel, he must decide alone. His choice cannot be delegated. It is a cruel test of self-confidence which has undeniably removed the Presidency for all time as a refuge for the faint-hearted.

Kennedy followed several elementary procedures in facing up to the nuclear showdown. He rightly insisted that before publicly according the Cuban events the status of crisis, he needed "hard intelligence" and could not act simply upon rumor and report. He held to his course despite the revelations and criticisms of legislators of both his own and the opposition party, and despite the hostile Congressional resolutions. To be careful and responsible, as Kennedy had to be, is neither easy nor popular. Political outcry was perhaps not the worst of the afflictions he had to bear. The atmosphere in which the President acted was charged with danger and uncertainty, with inexorable climax and with scores of opportunities for surprise. For all their knowledge of the Soviet Union, American officials could not predict what the Soviet leader would decide to do—especially since he delighted in surprise as a source of strength in foreign affairs. The Russians took advantage of seasonal fluctuations in our political system, launching their gambit during an election campaign. They expected that the President would be eager to postpone the prickly Cuban issue until after the election, and by that time it would be too late.

In the Cuban crisis the President sought always to leave Khrushchev with an option or choice. Above all, the aim of Kennedy and his advisers was to avoid backing him into a corner, where his only recourse would be military. A military attack of any kind upon Cuba, a Communist power, would have posed to the Soviet Union the necessity of either a military response or a humiliating surrender, badly damaging to their prestige around the world. The blockade afforded the advantage of giving Khrushchev a choice. He did not need to have his ships approach the blockade and be stopped and searched, but could divert them, as he did. The blockade, therefore, left an acceptable way out for the Soviet Union, a cardinal principle of decision-making in the nuclear confrontation. Equally important, Kennedy carefully preserved the United States' own options: that is, he did not rely wholly upon the blockade, but simultaneously speeded the full-scale alert of American forces, a procedure which Robert Kennedy and others felt did more than anything else to bring Khrushchev to agree to remove the missiles from Cuba.

Another cardinal principle is evident in the effort of the President and his aides to slow down the escalation of the crisis to permit Khrushchev time to consider his next moves. Deliberation, hopefully, might produce a more measured and less drastic response than fast-moving exchanges. Hence the value of notes and ambassadorial visits, and the preferability of a blockade, a relatively gradual procedure compared with the precipitous engagement of an invasion or an airstrike.

The President was limited to choices that were morally defensible. Democracy, by its nature, requires such a limitation upon its officials. Equally does a regard for world opinion, to which the administration policy-makers were attentive. The air attack alternative would have looked

like "Pearl Harbor" to the rest of the world, an incongruous action for a
nation which once had protested memorably against it. Linked to the
"moral defensibility" of his decision is the President's "usable power," as
Secretary of Defense McNamara has termed it. Particular kinds of power
could not have been used in the Cuban situation without reflecting ad-
versely upon the United States in world eyes.

Kennedy took the fullest precautions to keep the decisions in his own
hands, both the initial decision settling upon the blockade and the further
critical decisions required to implement it. When a United States Navy
reconnaissance plane spotted the *Marucia* headed for Cuba, the information was sped to the President, and it was he who gave the order to board
and search it. Other procedures assured that control of the blockade operation remained in his hands. Kennedy was resolved that the issue of
peace or war should not turn upon the decision of a local commander.

In making his choices, the President must be mindful of several "constituencies" but still keep decision in his grasp. He must be willing to act,
as Kennedy was, notwithstanding the express disapproval of certain of
these constituents. Kennedy accordingly convened members of his legislative constituency, or leaders of both parties. Paradoxically, his party's
leading legislators in the fields of foreign affairs and national security held
that his decision was inadequate for the situation, and urged him to do
more. The House Republican leader, however, Congressman Halleck, declared, "I'm standing with the President." The dissent of several of his own
party leaders did not deter Kennedy. He sought and won the approval of
another great constituency: the leaders of the nation's great allies—Macmillan, De Gaulle, and Adenauer—and the member countries of the major
alliances, NATO and the OAS. Kennedy was fortunate enough to win an
approval from his foreign constituency extending well beyond his expectations. But it is also clear that he was prepared, as a President in a nuclear confrontation may need to be, to carry forward his decision even
without allied endorsement. In choosing his course, the President must
weigh and balance factors which no ally can know or perceive, owing to
the simple circumstance that only he occupies his Presidential place, and
only he, therefore, holds the responsibility.

Nuclear crisis is more than an intensive exercise in decision-making.
Equally, if not more important, it is an enterprise in communication. The
evidence is impressive that a major cause of the crisis was a misreading
by Khrushchev and his colleagues of the Kennedy administration's attitude and intentions. In their Vienna meeting, Khrushchev reportedly
found Kennedy somewhat deferential, conduct attributable to their difference in age rather than to any weakness in Kennedy, as the Soviet leader
apparently presumed. The fiasco of the Bay of Pigs and Kennedy's restrained response to the Berlin wall may well have encouraged a Soviet

impression of American softness. The strength of this impression was conveyed in Khrushchev's remark to Robert Frost that the United States was "too liberal to fight."

A nuclear confrontation involves a desperate resort to various communications channels and an intensive scrutiny of the opponent's act and word for clues of his intent and meaning. Kennedy and his counselors were heavily occupied in the dangerous and difficult task of estimating the probable Soviet reaction to possible United States moves. Equally to be anticipated was the effect upon our allies, upon trouble spots around the world, whether Berlin or Turkey, which held our bases that the Soviet Union was discussing, or the Formosa straits, where the Chinese were preparing for belligerent action. Likewise the effect upon Latin America: if the United States responded strongly, would the Latin countries become alarmed? Would they be even more alarmed if we did too little? For Kennedy and his aides, the crisis was a rigorous introspective experience in determining American purposes, in anticipating what our reaction might be to the Soviet reaction, and so on, until each possible course that might be chosen was followed to its ultimate conclusion.

The Cuban crisis is a good model for any future nuclear confrontation because of the administration's recourse to almost every conceivable channel of communication between the opposing powers: the letters between Kennedy and Khrushchev, the proper reliance upon the American and Soviet ambassadors, the visit to Moscow of the American businessman William Knox, chairman of Westinghouse Electric International, to whom Khrushchev conveyed the dire warning that if the United States Navy stopped and searched Soviet vessels on the high seas, it would be piracy, and that after several such incidents, Soviet submarines would be ordered to sink American vessels. But according to available evidence, the most effective channel for communicating American intentions was the open, full-scale mobilization of our armed might.

◇

THE four Presidents in the four crises described above were not free agents, let alone "dictators," as demagogic critics sometimes portray them. The President in crisis is bound by a web of restraints, institutional, social, and personal. In a government of laws he must act within the Constitution and other statutes; in foreign relations he must act in accordance with his country's commitment to international law. But in a crisis law is not merely confining; it is also a means of conciliation and conflict resolution. Buchanan, in setting his course, chose to walk a legalistic tightrope to convince the South of national good will and thereby weaken the case for secession. Kennedy's counselors valued legality for itself and as a means of impressing the Russians and world opinion.

The President must reckon with the nation's past commitment to principle and his own and his predecessors' pronouncements and decisions. Significantly, at the outset of the Cuba crisis Kennedy sent for copies of all his earlier statements on the situation. He and his aides were driven to reject an air strike on military installations in Cuba in large part because the United States had taken a strong stand against invasion of a sovereign country, however serious the provocation of self-defense. An attack on Cuba could be regarded as Pearl Harbor in reverse. Franklin Roosevelt's memorable label of that 1941 event as a "day that will live in infamy," was an invisible barrier—moral and pragmatic—between hard-pressed Kennedy officials and the choice of a surprise offensive.

In facing a crisis, the President can be either helped or hampered by his personal ideology and opinions. Hoover was a prisoner of ideology; it narrowly channeled his conduct for three long years while the nation sank ever deeper into economic despair. He fought the economic enemy with clichés about "rugged American individualism" and the nobilities of localism and private charity, which proved to be paper weapons. What the President does in crisis is also governed by his view of his office. Franklin Roosevelt was instructed by the models of Theodore Roosevelt and Woodrow Wilson, impressed by the Presidency's resources for moral leadership and its potential for making government the instrument of the people. He viewed the Constitution as a simple, adjustable document which vested in the President the equivalent of a wartime power to combat the economic depression.

Much of a President's effectiveness in crisis depends upon his image of himself. Nearly as important as his policy is the self-confidence he projects to the country. If Franklin Roosevelt displayed political genius in 1933, it was not in offering solutions to the economic puzzle, for he had none, but in projecting confidence that the nation soon would be restored. The ringing voice, the flashing smile, and the cigarette holder set at a jaunty angle portrayed an impressive confidence that obscured the slender reed of reality on which it perched. In contrast to Franklin Roosevelt, handsomely at terms with himself, is the unfortunate Buchanan, indecisive, troubled in spirit, the object of bizarre tales and hostile rumor.

If the past be our guide, Americans prefer that in crisis their Presidents be men of action, calm but confident. Hoover, putting his store in private resources, vetoing acts of Congress that would have broadened his powers, taking the defensive rather than the offensive, was overwhelmingly voted out of office at the first opportunity. Activist Presidents who slay the dragons of crisis are the nation's folk heroes—Jackson, Lincoln, the Roosevelts, and Woodrow Wilson. They attack problems frontally and aggressively, interpret their powers expansively, and radiate confidence. In contrast to the activist or "doer" President is the negotiator or "talker" who relies primarily not upon deed, but upon discussion. He seeks to talk out with his adversary the issues threatening terrible conflict. He values procrastination to cool off issues and allow events to settle into a less perilous state. He holds closely to the law. Buchanan, a negotiator, was forever consulting his Attorney General, and his basic solution for the slavery crisis was legal, his Constitutional amendment, from which he expected so much. At most, the "doers" and the "talkers," as we are using the terms, are mere types. No President is wholly one or the other.

In crisis, Congress may prod the chief executive, preferring to move at a faster pace than he deems wise. In the New Deal, individual legislators time and again championed social and economic measures toward which the President was unenthusiastic or downright opposed. Roosevelt showed little ardor for the proposed Federal Deposit Insurance Corporation pushed by Arthur H. Vandenberg and other legislators. Or again, when Senator Robert F. Wagner led the way for the legislation bearing his name, enhancing labor's opportunities for organizing and engaging in collective bargaining, Roosevelt regarded Wagner's whole enterprise with doubt and suspicion. Senators of both parties demanded action on Cuba more than a month before Kennedy acted. "A member of Congress or the press," his aide Theodore Sorensen has written, "can achieve some measure of fame by reporting rumors or stating problems or raising questions. But that is not enough for a President."

Crisis exacts its own distinctive patterns of decision-making and administrative organization. Crisis heightens the President's dependence upon his staff, yet it is more vital than ever that he keep the reins of decision in his own hands. As long as he can, he must make decisions in a manner that will permit him to make further decisions. Kennedy, mindful of the enormous hazards in confronting the Soviets over Cuba, made certain that his early moves did not close out all his options or all of theirs. Franklin Roosevelt, Frances Perkins noticed in the early New Deal, "rarely got himself sewed tight to a program from which there was no turning back." A President can more easily control decision by keeping in his stable of counselors representatives of the principal alternative responses to the crisis. Buchanan had in his cabinet Southerners and New Englanders, or human replicas of the views dividing American society and his own deliberations. In the Cuban crisis Kennedy maintained conflicting groups of counselors, some advocating an air strike, others a blockade, the "hawks" and the "doves," as some chose to label them. He did not fear controversy, rather he welcomed it as a corrective to impulse.

In crisis the President must improvise his staff into new combinations and arrangements to gain the speed and concentration of effort that events demand. Crisis may force the President to disagree with his most prestigious experts. Buchanan proposed to dispatch a gunboat to Charleston; his commanding general, Winfield Scott, insisted upon a merchant steamer. To his eventual grief, Buchanan yielded. His burden in crisis was aggravated by his subordinates' initiatives and indiscretions. Major Anderson's transfer of forces from Fort Moultrie to the more defensible Fort Sumter was a brilliant maneuver, but it vastly complicated Buchanan's conciliatory approaches to the Southerners. Kennedy's creation of the Ex Com, a supple extract of the larger, slower, procedure-bound National Security Council, gave him a working staff of experts.

On the scale of a modern international crisis such as Cuba, the President must orchestrate a massive staff effort—diplomatic approaches to traditional European allies, the several alliances, NATO and the Rio nations, and the forum of the United Nations; the Defense Department must administer the blockade and ready itself for possible more drastic measures; the U-2 air surveillance of Cuba must be maintained and its photographic product interpreted; the legal documents and justifications for the blockade must be prepared, key legislators apprised, and the public informed via television and radio. Even the views of the outsider can be useful, for they bring experience, skills, and a challenging detachment from ongoing policy and can be valuable to the President as a counterbalance, an aid to perspective.

Although Kennedy and Franklin Roosevelt were men of action, and therefore a breed of President that is most admired, they were not, in any degree, creatures of impulse. The latter type, installed in the contemporary Presidency, would be disastrous for the nation and mankind. An activist President triggered by emotion, who neither consulted advisers nor pondered consequences, would be both decisive and wrongheaded, a type who would keep the nation, so long as it survived, quaking in high alarm. Kennedy and like chief executives root their actions in thought and validated evidence. They are decisive and forceful only in response to reason tested by qualified opinion.

The Presidency Compared

THE strength and weakness of the American Presidency may be better perceived if we examine the chief executive of other major nations. We may find in the experience of others clues for eliminating the flaws from our own system, for keeping up better in the race every nation is running against the forces of change. Possibly too, we may take some small comfort if we find that weaknesses which afflict our own chief executive are bedeviling other major nations, be they our allies or our foes.

◇

No MAJOR nation can boast a method of selecting its chief executive that assures a choice from among the proverbial "best men available" by means that are assuredly democratic. Because of the enormous stakes, the contest is almost universally a great scramble to which the arts of pressure and maneuver are fully committed. It is an enterprise in which democratic values and procedures are vulnerable. The United States prefers its Presidents from large states and therefore arbitrarily excludes worthy contenders from the small. It requires long primary campaigns, thus loading the dice for the candidate with money. The creaky electoral college machinery is a standing invitation to disaster in opening wide the gates of chance that a Presidential candidate with a minority of popular votes may be elected.

In Great Britain, if the Prime Minister is selected fresh after a national election, the procedure follows a well-regulated routine. The voters have elected a new House of Commons, and the leader of the majority party is automatically made the new Prime Minister. Following the election, the queen requests the leader of the winning party to form a government, in effect ratifying the electorate's choice. But the selection of the party leader in the first place, prior to his appearance before the electorate, is largely a matter of intraparty maneuver. The magic key is the building of support among the factions. Harold Wilson bested George Brown in their contest for the Labor leadership in 1963 as a kind of middle-of-the-roader who had least offended the factions whose support was vital.

Just as the American system can produce a Lincoln and a Harding, the British processes of selection may elevate a Churchill and a Baldwin. The latter is generally considered one of the most mediocre of twentieth-century chief executives. In a burst of candid self-appraisal Baldwin once termed himself "no use to God or man." His pre-ministerial career in the House of Commons was shrouded in silent obscurity—in six years he spoke only five times—and he rose to the Prime Ministership by the art of giving little offense—"One of the nicest fellows in the House," Asquith said of him—and by the affection the incumbent Prime Minister, Bonar Law, had for Baldwin's late father. Even when his name was tendered to the monarch as one who might form a government, his sponsor acknowledged that his public career had been "more or less uneventful and without any signs of specific gifts or exceptional ability."

The American President, once elected, enjoys relative stability of tenure, rather greater than the British Prime Minister's and rather less than that of the President of the French Fifth Republic and the established Soviet leader. The sole legitimate means of removing the American President, impeachment, is constructed to operate only in the utmost extremity. Neither Congress nor public opinion can remove him. A Buchanan or a Hoover persist in office even though the majority of public opinion is set against them. To be sure, the Twenty-Second, or two-term, Amendment is a severe hobbling of Presidential power. This enactment not only imposes an absolute deadline on Presidential tenure but cuts deeply into his effectiveness in his second term. President De Gaulle, in contrast, who came into power in 1958 as the last Prime Minister of the Fourth Republic, made known in 1963 his earnest intention to retain office until 1970, the year the North Atlantic Alliance comes up for revision. De Gaulle's associates say he is not particularly concerned with the way in which he prolongs his stay in power, although it will be "constitutional," given the full and flexible power the fundamental law gives him.

Although the British Prime Minister enjoys a term of five years, his retention of power over that span is less assured than the American President's is during his established four-year term. In his five-year interval, the Prime Minister can be toppled if he loses the support of his majority in the House of Commons. In actuality, however, the historical record shows that the twentieth-century Prime Minister is no longer in any real danger of losing the majority support of his highly disciplined party colleagues. The Prime Minister's fall occurs not by lack of majority support, but with a touch of subtlety. Neville Chamberlain was deposed in World War II not because, in a vote of confidence, he lacked the support of a majority of those voting, but because ninety-three of his followers failed to support him, principally by not voting. This large minority in Chamberlain's party, who presumably reflected general public dissatisfaction, brought down his government by withdrawing their consent to his leadership.

The fact that a Prime Minister can be pulled down by fiat of his party in the House of Commons makes him vulnerable to plots against his political security, particularly in seasons when policy may go awry and the country's fortunes dip, common occurrences in the present stage of Britain's historical experience. Nineteen forty-seven was just such a bad year for the Prime Minister. A general economic decline was aggravated by the ill luck of a terrible winter, the worst since 1880, which touched off a fuel crisis and temporarily brought all industry to a stop. Sir Stafford Cripps, a member of the cabinet, let it become known that in the sudden crisis the country required greater inspiration than the mild-mannered Prime Minister Clement Attlee could possibly provide. Cripps proposed that Attlee step down and permit the Prime Ministership to be handed over to Ernest Bevin, whose toughness he admired. Attlee, Cripps generously suggested, could take over the Foreign Office in place of Bevin. Alternatively, if Bevin did not want to leave foreign affairs, to which he was extremely devoted, Attlee could go to the Treasury while Cripps himself took over the Prime Ministership. Newspapers to which the plan was carefully leaked and right-wing Labor M.P.'s, who opposed Attlee's left-wing faction, rallied behind Cripps's plan. Attlee nevertheless held fast by several adroit maneuvers, including a sudden reshuffling of his cabinet, not the least part of which was the installation of Cripps in the new post of Minister of Economic Affairs with more extensive powers over the economy than any minister in peacetime had ever before possessed.

The tenure of Soviet leadership is vulnerable to palace revolution. Stalin's death remains a mystery and suspicions persist that his departure was hastened by human agency. Malenkov was pushed out by an intense and secret oligarchic struggle. Khrushchev faced his severest known test in the crisis of June 1957. He seemed doomed when the majority of the party Presidium called an extraordinary session and by a vote of seven to four elected to remove him from his party post as First Secretary. The anti-Khrushchev majority comprised the older members and former associates of Stalin: Voroshilov, Molotov, Kaganovich, Bulganin, and Malenkov; and, from the newer generation of leadership, Pervuklin and Saburov. The hazardous maneuver was apparently born of fear of Khrushchev's ambition and growing doubts of his capacity to rule. But the power of the rebelling group was limited. Khrushchev controlled the parent body of the Presidium, the Central Committee. He dominated the vast party apparatus across the Soviet Union, and his impregnable influence blocked his foes' access to the means of physical force, the political police and the armed forces. With such enormous strength, Khrushchev could counter with swift and bold measures. He quickly mobilized the Central Committee members who were then in Moscow, summoning them into a meeting where they reversed the Presidium's decision and expelled the anti-Khrushchev factions from both the Presidium and the Central Committee. In the ensuing recriminations, the conspirators were alleged to have temporarily barred Central Committee members from access to the Kremlin. Bulganin's bodyguard was credited with accomplishing this brief miracle.

◇

WHEN the Vice Presidency is filled, the American Presidency clearly holds the advantage over other chief executives in handling the problem of succession. If the Vice Presidency is vacant, the Succession Act of 1947 comes into play, with an arrangement that is, for reasons we have seen, undoubtedly the worst in the world.

President Kennedy's assassination, for all its rending tragedy, was also the occasion of a remarkable demonstration of the velocity and assurance with which executive power can be transferred in the American system. Within minutes after Kennedy's death the Presidential oath was administered to Vice President Johnson, with Mrs. Kennedy by his side, herself a brave witness to the continuity of the American system. No other major government affords such quick and automatic transfer.

Nearly a month before the catastrophe in Texas, a succession occurred to the British Prime Ministership. The procedure took all of eleven days to consummate, with lengthy passages of farce and satire. Through much of this anguished interlude, the effort to find a successor to the ill and hospitalized Prime Minister Harold Macmillan foundered upon the deadlock of two intractable and opposed groups in the Conservative party. To the left were the liberal revisionists, headed by R. A. Butler, Deputy Prime Minister in the Macmillan cabinet and the man who, according to party and public opinion polls, enjoyed the greatest backing. Prime Minister Macmillan reportedly wished above all else to bar Butler's succession. A second major contender was Viscount Hailsham of the Conservative right wing. Several lesser contenders made up the field. Early in his quest for an heir, Macmillan pressed Sir Alec Douglas-Home, the Foreign Secretary, to enter the lists, but Home declined.

A polling that Macmillan ordered taken of the cabinet revealed that Home was running strong as a second and third choice. Soundings were likewise made among the fifty junior ministers, the 350 M.P.'s, and the active Conservative peers. The party whips were instructed to gather answers to three questions: 1. Whom would you like to see in office? 2. Do you want to choose *possible* runners-up? 3. Is there anybody you would rather *not* see in office? Home emerged with a slight majority of first preferences and a clear margin of second choices, but the column most in his favor was "against": few opposed him. Martin Redmayne, chief whip and poll supervisor, also weighted the votes according to each M.P.'s status in the party, a process that Home's opponents later disputed. A Butler man said: "Redmayne could have weighted Home's votes and tied little balloons to Rab's."

Buttonholing and telephoning proceeded intensively. Hailsham's candidacy began to sag with Home's advance, although Butler's held strong. Meanwhile Home, notwithstanding heavy pressure from Macmillan, would not declare his candidacy. With more time, he told Macmillan, either Butler, Hailsham, or a third candidate, Reginald Maudling, might come through. Maudling, who might have thrown in with Butler, thereby establishing a majority for the latter, made no move. Macmillan, bound to his sickbed, dreaded a deadlock that would entitle the monarch to send for Harold Wilson, leader of the opposition Labor party, who would have then formed a government, dissolved Parliament, and called an election. Macmillan again appealed to Home, who now acquiesced. The Prime Minister called the poll-takers to his bedside to arrange an updated tabulation of Conservative Parliamentary opinion. Butler was now revealed to have gained strength, although he was outnumbered by combined Hailsham and Home first preferences. The blackball again provided the clearest impression. So many interviewees opposed Butler and Hailsham that the double negative in a sense produced Home as a positive. Macmillan wrote out a lengthy, complex assessment of the balance of opinion.

Hours before Macmillan resigned and presented Home's name to the queen, an emergency cabal led by Iain Macleod, co-chairman of the Conservative party and leader of the House of Commons, and Enoch Powell, Minister of Health, met with Redmayne, who was requested to inform Macmillan that both Hailsham and Maudling were prepared to support Butler. Sir Michael Adeane, the queen's link with the party, was telephoned and told that, irrespective of what Macmillan might say, Butler could now form a government. Butler telephoned Macmillan at King Edward VII's Hospital, but the call was not accepted. Macmillan resigned, presented his written estimate to the queen, with supplementary oral comment. The queen sent for the Earl of Home. In the aftermath, critics assailed Home's elevation "on the heap of blackballs cast against his three rivals," and the "tricky maneuverings" of Macmillan and Redmayne, and called for "modernization" of the selection procedure.

Succession goes little better in other lands. Chancellor Adenauer marred an otherwise luminous career with the ungainly procedures by which he eventually yielded power to the successor he did not want, Ludwig Erhard. It is impossible to see how any other Frenchman can fill the spacious Presidency of De Gaulle. Soviet Russia, like all dictatorships, cannot solve the problem of succession. The transfer of power, for which the Soviet Constitution makes no provision, is the occasion of numbing uncertainty, subterfuge, terror, and violence.

Stalin's death and its aftermath disclose the jagged course of dictatorial succession. The announcement of his demise was withheld for six hours and ten minutes. A statement accompanying the eventual disclosure declared that the "most important task of the party and the government is to insure uninterrupted and correct leadership . . . the greatest unity of leadership and the prevention of any kind of disorder and panic." As Bertram Wolfe has well observed, admonitions against "disorder and panic" are inconceivable in an American transfer. When power passed from Roosevelt to Truman and from Kennedy to Johnson, there were, needless to say, no comparable warnings from high places.

With Stalin's passing, a reshuffling of state and party positions proceeded, with Malenkov, in the intra-factional bargaining, emerging as the head of government and First Secretary of the party. But the bargain did not stick. After nine days Malenkov asked to be "relieved" of his duties as party First Secretary. Two years later, again at his own request, he abandoned the Premiership as well. Malenkov's degradation continued in the Soviet manner when he confessed to "errors" in agricultural policy which could only have been committed by his rival Khrushchev. Another major figure, Lavrenti Beria, head of the secret police, was arrested, shot, and made an "unperson." Meanwhile Khrushchev took over the post of First Secretary and consolidated his power to the point where, in an extraordinary address to the Twentieth Party Congress, he denounced the memory of Stalin, depicting him as a tyrant, a sadist, and a glutton for adulation. Among the interpretations placed upon this grotesque performance is one that Khrushchev, in effect, was pledging not to employ his new-won power according to Stalin's example.

◇

MANY a critic of the Presidency gazes admiringly upon the British Parliamentary system and proposes to engraft upon the American structure some of the better elements of the British. Woodrow Wilson, both as a youthful political scientist and as a practicing President, longed to introduce the British method into American politics. He would greatly have preferred to have been a Prime Minister rather than a President, and indeed tried manfully during his incumbency to nudge the office into the ways of the British model. Such legislators as George Pendleton of the nineteenth century and Estes Kefauver of the twentieth doggedly proposed to borrow from British practice to bring executive and legislative effort into purposeful cooperation. A study committee of the American Political Science Association in 1950 emerged with an ingenious plan for adapting the British party system to the circumstances of American parties. Is the British Parliamentary system better for the United States than the existing Presidential system?

The leading attractions of the Parliamentary system are unity and coherence of policy. It encourages the executive to tackle the major problems of the day, to propose bold plans and broad programs. The British executive has every assurance that everything he asks for will be enacted, not the 40 or 50 per cent the American President is likely to secure, but 100 per cent. The secret weapon of the Parliamentary system is tight party discipline.

The Prime Minister's party, be it Conservative or Labor, provides him with a majority of legislators whose obedience is granitic, "solid masses of steady votes," Walter Bagehot put it, for policy and program. The Conservative party leader, who is ordinarily the Prime Minister or leader of the opposition, possesses powers that are well nigh autocratic, and against which the American President's party powers are limp and pallid. Once elected, the Conservative party leader, for example, need not submit to periodic re-election. He is not obligated to report in any formal way concerning his activity as leader to the party in Parliament or to the National Union. He has the sole ultimate responsibility for formulating policy and an electoral program. The party's annual conference "conveys" its resolutions to him "for his information"; they are not binding upon him. The party secretariat or central office is his personal machine. He appoints the principal officers and thereby controls propaganda, research, and finance. The Conservative leader is vested with lordly power over his party followers in Parliament. With rare exception, an M.P. who quits or is expelled from his own party has no political future. An M.P. can incur the dread wrath of higher authority by any one of several offenses, whether challenging, criticizing, or publicly differing with his party. No M.P. who has crossed the floor, or aligned himself with the opposition, by these means has won re-election since 1945. All this, needless to say, is a far cry from the American President's circumstances. Franklin Roosevelt was the only President to launch a substantial purge upon recalcitrant Democrats, with results so inglorious that no successor has dared repeat the venture.

The Conservative party leader somewhat tempers his autocratic power by taking advice and seeking information. Although he is not required to report on his work to party organizations in Parliament or outside, he appears periodically at party meetings to discuss policy. He does not attend the annual conference of National Union, but he customarily addresses a mass meeting of delegates promptly after the conference adjourns. The resolutions of the conference come to him, and although he is not bound to support them, he reads closely their revelations of the mood of his followers. He enjoys exclusive responsibility for formulating party policy, but he wisely consults key leaders, watches the resolutions of party organs, and yet remains "the main fountain and interpreter of policy." The amount of his consulting and heeding depends upon his showing in the last elections and the current state of his fortunes with public opinion. An electoral defeat and sagging public opinion polls bring down undeniable pressures upon him to share his policy-making responsibilities.

The vulnerability of the Conservative leader to overthrow when party fortunes dwindle is disclosed by the startling statistic that of seven leaders since Disraeli, three have been driven from office. A. J. Balfour and Austen and Neville Chamberlain were unlucky enough to be pulled down by their own followers. Stanley Baldwin waged a bitter fight to remain as leader. Only Salisbury, Bonar Law, and Churchill were spared concerted moves to drive them from office. Law and Churchill were aided no little by the coincidence of their leaderships with the two World Wars, when internal party conflict was reduced to a minimum. Labor party leaders have been less susceptible to overthrow than their Conservative brethren. Despite certain variations in detail, the roles of Labor and Conservative Prime Ministers as party leaders have no significant difference. Unlike the American President, who faces state and local organizations of imposing autonomy and power, the Prime Minister presides over a national party structure in which local units are thoroughly meshed.

In the selection of candidates for American national legislative office, state and local organizations dominate the decisions. The result is a goodly crop of Senators and Congressmen opposed to the President of their own party on principal policy questions. In Britain the local choice of the candidate must win central approval. The Labor party's constitution provides that a candidate's selection "shall not be regarded as completed until the name of the person has been placed before a meeting of the National Executive Committee, and his or her selection has been duly endorsed." Often the real choice is made by the national Labor or Conservative leaders. The Labor constitution clearly stipulates the conditions of approval: the candidate must conform to "the Constitution, Programme,

Principles and Policy of the Party" and "act in harmony with the Standing Orders of the Parliamentary Labour Party." Noncompliance unlooses a fierce array of pressures. The party label and financial support may be withdrawn from the candidate. The party leader will not send the customary formal letter of endorsement to the voters and no major party figures will venture into the constituency to help the campaign.

British party discipline depends not simply on organization and gadgetry. It also reflects the lesser role of pressure groups in national life. The United States, in contrast, is a land where pressure groups flourish, where regional differences are vast, and their influence is divisive, preventing the tight integration of opinion and leadership in the major parties. Above all, differences between the British and American peoples are an influence, the latter's heterogeneity forcing the parties to be broad and flexible in method. British party methods in the areas of finance, selection of candidates, and platform-development, however, deserve close study for possible borrowings and adaptations to the United States.

◊

JUST as the American President's weakness as party leader earns him unreliable Congressional support for his program, the British Prime Minister knows the luxury of enduring legislative backing. The President, viewing his ally, the British executive, across the Atlantic, must see him as abiding in a political utopia which assures that whatever he asks for the legislature will provide.

In theory, the President is more powerful than the Prime Minister in legislation. Head of the executive branch, he is the coequal of Congress. He is not responsible to Congress in the sense that the Prime Minister is to Parliament. To become Prime Minister Sir Alec Douglas-Home had to surrender his seat in the House of Lords and be elected to the House of Commons, where he answers daily for the actions of his government. In British constitutional theory he, his cabinet, and other ministers are a committee of the House of Commons. They hold their place by grace of the House's majority; they can be deposed if the majority withdraws its sanction. But this dread eventuality has never occurred in the twentieth century, thanks to the iron discipline of British parties.

Although in theory the Prime Minister and his government are the servants of the House of Commons, they are in fact its masters. The government, not the House, legislates. The government plans and controls the House's time. The introduction of legislation is almost completely the government's monopoly. A rule requiring that all legislation involving expenditure bear the crown's, or in actuality the government's, approval invests the government with a sweeping control, since virtually all legislation of significance requires money. This order of things is supported by an implicit democratic rationalization: parties contest elections on platforms; upon winning a popular, and therefore a legislative, majority a party should command priority for its program in the House.

The government is normally certain that any bill it introduces will pass without significant change, in good time. Although the cannonade of brilliant oratory and merciless jibes may beat upon its program in House debate, the government ultimately prevails. It knows no evil like the committee bottleneck and the crippling amendment which kills or damages beyond recognition the President's requests. At most, Parliament can only influence the government's future course. Flaws exposed in legislative debate presumably will not be prolonged or repeated. If House criticism reflects public opinion, the government, most likely, will mend its ways. No government, Neville Chamberlain would testify, can afford the unremitting criticism of a substantial body of its supporters. And ever in the background is the ultimate, if unused, weapon: the House's power to overthrow the government.

Yet in his daily legislative life the Prime Minister sails a smooth sea compared with the American President. Sir Alec Douglas-Home confidently committed his government to twenty-four specific bills at the outset of his first Parliament. In addition, the queen's speech opening the session promised that "other measures will be laid before you." The government's program called for major enactments concerning national housing, the reorganization of the Defense Ministry, industrial training for youth, and the redefining of central police powers. The Prime Minister, introducing his proposals in the fall of 1963, could rightfully expect their full enactment by late spring or early summer. President Johnson, in contrast, taking up where President Kennedy left off, struggled to advance a tax bill languishing in Congress for more than a year, a medical care bill for more than two years, and a civil rights bill that after eight months of legislative deliberation faced stoppage by a Senate filibuster. The tax and civil rights bills eventually passed, considerably amended. On financial and tax legislation, the Prime Minister enjoys marked advantages over the President. New taxes become effective in Britain from the moment the Chancellor of the Exchequer discloses them to Parliament.

The Prime Minister, unlike the President, has the constant and assured support of his legislative party. If it has a working majority in the House, he need have no fear for his legislative program. A working majority, allowing for illness, unavoidable absence, and other happenings, is about thirty. A government with a majority of seventy-seven out of 630 members has an open road.

The Prime Minister, unlike the President, shares power with fellow executives, the ministers, and particularly those who comprise the cabinet. The Prime Minister, however, enjoys powers his fellow ministers do not have. In Constitutional practice all ministerial offices derive from him and depend upon him, since he can make and unmake ministers. Meeting with his ministers shortly after their selection in 1945, Prime Minister Attlee announced that they were all on trial; he would not hesitate to replace any who were found unequal to the task. The Prime Minister can prompt the dissolution of the entire government simply by resigning. No minister has such power. The Prime Minister alone can make certain great decisions without cabinet approval. His fellow ministers have small choice but to back him. To repudiate him is to split the party and deliver the government to the enemy.

Yet for all his seeming power the Prime Minister is subject to constraints the American President does not suffer. The gravity of the issue, the political weakness of his government, the fact that his cabinet is a coalition of parties, may bring him to consult his fellow ministers faithfully and fully prior to decision. When Franklin Roosevelt and Winston Churchill negotiated the Atlantic Charter in their meeting at sea of several days, Harry Hopkins noted that Roosevelt was willing and able to commit the United States, exercising his independent authority conferred by the Constitution. Churchill, in contrast, seemed hardly able to take a step without getting in touch with his War Cabinet, which rested upon a coalition government, and particularly its second-in-command, the Labor party leader, Clement Attlee. Hopkins estimated that in three days more than thirty communications passed between Churchill and Whitehall. Churchill clearly operated within the confines of a "collective leadership," to which the President was not subject.

In choosing his cabinet, the Prime Minister faces ground rules far more restrictive than any confronting the President. The Prime Minister is literally forced to work with certain associates; the President is not. Kennedy could choose a cabinet in which not a single major legislative figure of his party was represented. In Franklin Roosevelt's there was only one. The President, it is true, must pay heed to geography in constituting his cabinet—give Interior to a Westerner, and Labor, Agriculture, and perhaps Commerce to appointees acceptable to the clienteles of those departments. But these are generalized frameworks within which the President can select among scores, if not hundreds, of individuals. The Prime Minister's choices, on the other hand, are definite and particular.

To form a government, the Prime Minister must build upon the support of the principal factions of his party. Factional allegiance requires a *quid pro quo*, a seat for the factional leader in the cabinet. Accordingly, Lord Home brought into his cabinet each of his rivals for the Prime Ministership. His principal opponent, R. A. Butler, came in as Foreign Secretary, Reginald Maudling as Chancellor of the Exchequer, and Viscount Hailsham as Lord President of the Council and Minister of Science. Home also offered posts to Ian Macleod and Enoch Powell, who had led the last-minute revolt against him, but both declined to serve.

◇

THE supreme attractiveness of the Parliamentary system is the ease and assurance with which it produces policy. The executive has charge of legislation, guided by public opinion as it is expressed by interest groups, the press, and in the House of Commons. Administration, whether it concern organizational structure, program, finance, or personnel, is the secure province of the executive. The House votes the funds the cabinet requests. The House lacks constitutional power to vote more money for any purpose than the cabinet asks for, a situation that is the bane of budget-minded Presidents, who often prefer less money than Congressional Armed Service Committees, goaded by the military, rush to provide. Thanks to iron party discipline, the cabinet can count not only on a majority but regularly on the same majority. Parliament's orientation, like the cabinet's, is national rather than local. The lack of a tradition that the legislator reside in his own district, the common incident of an M.P. elected from a district he has never visited, the party's intolerance of any local deviation from national policy, give Parliament an orientation as resolutely national as the consciousness of Congress, and particularly of the House of Representatives, is local.

But the Parliamentary system, for all its undeniable excellence as a vehicle of national policy, also carries weakness. It is immediately suspect because it is not employed today by any major nation on the rise. England's own decline in power and place in the family of nations, although a product of many factors, strongly suggests that the Parliamentary method smacks excessively of the past and has not adjusted sufficiently to modern change. There is indeed much that is anachronistic in the British Parliamentary model, much that once was meaningful but that time and change have reduced to hollow pretense. What was constitutional political fact in that nation in the nineteenth century, as Don K. Price has put it, has become constitutional fiction in the twentieth. The House of Commons in bygone days did control the government and could, when it chose, dismiss it. Nowadays, however, public opinion rather than the House determines cabinet tenure.

The House of Commons has been reduced to a passivity which even the most resolute critic of Congress would not wish upon it. In its tightly restricted capacity, the House resembles the American electoral college, registering the popular will in choosing a government and then automatically ratifying its program and voting the funds it asks for. The House lacks means of initiating policy; unlike Congress, it has no standing committees to investigate and recommend, deprivations which preclude any legislative capacity to take an independent line and exercise meaningful control. More than three decades ago Stanley Baldwin rightly observed that House members widely felt they had "nothing much to do of a responsible nature."

In the 1960's outcries are rising in Britain against Parliament's general ineffectuality. In 1963 Professor Brian Chapman of Manchester University voiced the wide concern of responsible Britons when he wrote, "We need a state in which Parliament is an effective partner in the process of government, and not simply an ineffectual appendage employed to make noises of approval or discontent." Seeking a rearranged governmental structure enabling Parliament to "play a vital role in the formulation of policy," Chapman looked admiringly upon the American Congress, with its subject matter and joint committees, and urged that the House of Lords be reconstituted by regions.

The administrative features of the Parliamentary system are also questionable. The minister, the equivalent of the American departmental secretary, is primarily a legislative leader and not an administrator. He is chosen not so much for administrative ability as for his command of House support and his skill in defending party policy. He makes his way by shining in debate and by leadership in party affairs. Accordingly, if Robert S. McNamara, generally hailed as a distinguished Secretary of Defense in the Kennedy and Johnson administrations, were to live and work as a Briton, chances are slight that he would achieve the place and make the contribution permitted him in American public affairs. Mr. McNamara, by general consensus, is not a politician in the usual sense. He has something of a reputation of being a "human IBM," which grates at times in personal relationships, a fatal flaw in political life.

Finally, much of the criticism that Britons themselves have levied against their governmental system has fallen upon the civil service. Long and rightly hailed as a model career system for other nations, including the United States, to emulate, the British civil service is handled roughly by its critics of the 1960's. It is viewed as ingrown, uninspired, uncreative, and out of step with the fast pace of Britain's problems. In essence, the administrative class, or policy-making career service, is recruited at a youthful age, when its members complete their university education, after which they pass all their working lives in governmental service. Except for specialized employment, it is difficult, almost unheard of, to bring into the civil service those midway and beyond in a business, academic, or professional career.

The British ministerial system reinforces the tendency of large bureaucratic organizations to be cautious and safe, and therefore unenterprising. A minister progresses in his political career if the civil service keeps him out of trouble. The civil service reads the handwriting on the wall, which instructs that they will gain more by caution (which avoids trouble) than by initiative (which invites it). Furthermore, the civil servant figures that even if the initiative succeeds the minister will receive most of the credit. Britons looking for reform take their cues from American practice. They propose a generous use of a "brains trust" to be attached to the Prime Minister's and each minister's office, an injection of new blood into the civil service at many levels from the untapped talent of the professions, business, and local government.

◇

ALL nations have donned increasingly the trappings of the administrative state. Managing the economy, providing welfare services, and maintaining the military force and weaponry have compounded executive tasks, resources, and power in society. In most of the nations of the world, administration has gained in power and autonomy at the expense of the legislature. The United States, however, for all the expansion of its governmental responsibilities, displays far less of a shift of power from the legislature to the executive. The American Congress exerts controls over administration that other legislatures do not possess. Its legislation is more detailed, its controls over administrative structure, finance, program, and personnel are far tighter than those exercised by other legislatures of the world.

In Great Britain Parliament practices a relationship with the executive in matters of administration which, were it followed in the United States, would immeasurably strengthen the President's position as administrative chief. Although Britain has a unified political system, with both legislative and executive power concentrated in Parliament, administration is treated altogether differently. Administration is accorded the full benefit of the doctrine of separation of powers. Paradoxically, the United States claims to observe a separation of powers, but Congress freely breaches it in matters of administration. The British, applying separation of powers, leave to executive discretion the employment of the basic means of administration. The organizational structure of departments, which Congress provides for in close detail, Parliament delegates to executive decision. Personnel policy, for which Congress has compiled a thick volume of close legislation, the British leave to the executive. The executive budget, which Congress can deal roughly with when it chooses, remains fully intact in the hands of Parliament. If even one of these instances of legislative self-denial were adopted by Congress, the President's situation as administrative chief would be vastly improved.

Another British practice equally instructive for the United States is the technique of delegated legislation. Parliament often passes laws in skeletal form, setting forth only major principles and leaving the details to the departments to work out. The practice permits great flexibility in administration. A common additional arrangement is that many administrative rules and orders are not valid until the legislature expresses consent either by positive action or by lack of action. A minority of orders must be affirmed by Parliament; others must lie before the House for forty days and are considered approved if no nullifying action has been taken against them. Delegated legislation specifies the limits of executive discretion, sets forth guiding standards, and requires publicity when the administrative regulations are in preparation. A special House committee investigates such regulations as it chooses and elicits any necessary information from departmental officials.

The British practice might be preferable to the independent regulatory commissions in the United States that trespass so badly upon the President's economic powers. Relative to British practice, the commissions represent a reverse trend by Congress. Whereas Parliament views economic regulation a fit subject for increased executive discretion, Congress resorts to its own commissions, free from ordinary executive control and reporting to the legislature.

The Fifth French Republic of Charles de Gaulle is the ultimate in the democratic administrative state, veering as it does in certain seasons into constitutional dictatorship. As a model of the continuously strong chief executive in a more or less democratic setting, it is too extreme for adaptation to the United States. In the previous Fourth Republic a well-nigh powerless executive was subordinate to an all-powerful lower legislative house, the Chamber of Deputies. In the De Gaulle Republic much of the Deputies' power has been transferred to the executive, chiefly to the President and to a much lesser degree to the Prime Minister in subordination to the President. The President controls policy-making in foreign affairs and national security, and he can, when he chooses, extend his powers by revising constitutional practice at will and ruling under emergency powers for periods extending well beyond the actual emergency. The Prime Minister and his cabinet wield so many powers not subject to the approval of the Assembly, the lower legislative house of the Fifth Republic, that they can confidently anticipate the enactment of most of their vital policies for the low price of occasional minor changes in program and personnel shifts. Parliament's lawmaking powers are limited to specific subjects set out chiefly by the constitution. The administration, in turn, wields a rule-making power over all matters not specifically reserved to Parliament.

French Parliamentary lawmaking is subordinate to administrative necessity. Article XXXVIII of the constitution provides that "for the execution of its program" the executive may ask Parliament for power temporarily to take measures by ordinance that constitutionally are among the subjects reserved to the legislature. The French Senate, which belongs to the administrative tradition of French politics, works as an ally of the executive. A Constitutional Council tests the constitutionality of laws enacted by Parliament. The Council too is an auxiliary of executive dominance, watchful that Parliament remains within the confines of its inferior position. De Gaulle conducts his Presidential office as a crisis executive, and under Article 16, which provides unlimited emergency powers in external and internal crisis, he enjoys authority that largely subjects the government and its policies to Presidential control.

The United States, an executive-legislative state, faces in its great competitor, the Soviet Union, a monolithic administrative state. The Soviet is in the hands of party admininstrators, a political bureaucracy or "new class," as Milovan Djilas terms it. The new class members enjoy special privileges and economic preferences derived from their administrative monopoly. Unlike bureaucracies in the non-Communist world, which are subject to political authorities, "the Communists," as Djilas has written, "have neither masters nor owners over them."

The Soviet's top leadership is produced by the party administrative system. Stalin was himself the epitome of the party administrator, rising not as a charismatic leader but as one skilled in the ways of the party apparatus, who outdid competitors who excelled as orators or theoreticians. Stalin neither preached nor inspired, but made decisions, spoke without ardor or color, and stressed the concrete administrative tasks of industrializing the Soviet Union and collectivizing its agriculture. To retain power, he incorporated a system of relentless terror into the administrative apparatus.

Stalin's successors, Malenkov and Khrushchev, are both party administrators who climbed the career ladder. The ascent to the top is by apolitical means; it is done without a struggle for votes or an assertion of new ideas for program and policy, but rather depends upon one's usefulness and docility to the incumbent dictator and upon choosing the right protectors.

◇

PRESIDENT JOHNSON'S commitment to an eighteen-hour workday, President Eisenhower's extensive overhaul of his top-level staff machinery, and President Kennedy's overhaul of Eisenhower's overhaul evidence a restless dissatisfaction with the means and processes of decision-making. Is Khrushchev similarly troubled? Does internal, top-level executive decision-making differ substantially in method in the monolithic Soviet Communist system from that in the pluralistic Presidential system? Is Soviet experience at all relevant and instructive for American needs?

In the Soviet monolith, supreme authority is vested in Khrushchev, First Secretary of the party and Chairman of the governmental Council of Ministers. The use of joint party and governmental decrees attests to the integration of the lines of command.

The top policy organ, over which Khrushchev presides, is the Presidium of the party, comprising fourteen full, or voting, members and ten candidate members, who participate to varying degrees in decision-making. Djilas provided insight into the functioning of a top-level Communist policy group when he wrote, "In the Communist system, exclusive groups are established around political leaders and forums. All policy-making is reduced to wrangling in these exclusive groups, in which familiarity and cliqueishness flower. The highest group is generally the most intimate."

Although little is known of the party Presidium's internal functioning, it includes Khrushchev's confidant, Mikoyan, and Party Secretaries Kirichenko and Aristov. These, with Party Secretary Suslov, whom Khrushchev appears to value more for his political and professional qualities than as an intimate friend, comprise the inner circle of top policy-makers for both domestic and foreign affairs. Thus the highest policy decisions are taken in a relatively small group bearing government and party authority. The Presidium appears to meet frequently and to work out many decisions on the spot. Whereas the Soviet structure is vertical, with the neat simplicity of the straight line, the American is horizontal and diffuse. The American President does not work with any single group as regularly as Khrushchev does. The President distributes his consultations among larger groups such as the cabinet, the National Security Council, and *ad hoc* groups thrown together for such critical situations as Cuba in 1962 and Panama in 1964. The President, unlike the Soviet Premier, may feel behooved to touch base with figures outside the executive branch, such as legislators, private group leaders, and ex-Presidents. The Presidium seems to have nothing of the elaborately prepared and negotiated papers that characterized Eisenhower's National Security Council. Yet Soviet departments have access to the Presidium through its members and the Secretariat, the party's principal administrative apparatus over which Khrushchev presides. Agencies like the Ministry of Foreign Affairs report to the Presidium directly.

The party Presidium is Khrushchev's cabinet and its prerogatives are subject to his discretion. Since he is by nature gregarious, extroverted, and garrulous, he often modifies the severe simplicity of the monolithic structure. He seems disposed to delegate responsibilities to subordinates, to place confidence in them, and to weigh their opinions. Although he possesses supreme power, his lieutenants seem to play major roles in policy-making and administration. In actual decision-making, Khrushchev, like Lyndon Johnson and other Presidents, prefers to employ competing sources of information and advice. Regular reports on scientific and military developments, the economy, and foreign policy are supplied by government and party agencies. A Central Committee staff prepares a secret, uncensored, and unslanted coverage of the foreign press. The mass of data flowing from various sources and the participation of each Presidium member in both party and government organs enables top leaders to judge independently proposals arising from below, and to initiate policy on its own. Thus Khrushchev's initiatives in Soviet agricultural policy—his championing of the cultivation of virgin lands in Kazakhstan and Eastern Siberia and his sponsorship of the cultivation of corn. On at least one known occasion, he revised upward certain planned goals contrary to his experts' advice. He reportedly initiated the Presidium's support for the Austrian treaty and dictates *in camera* important foreign policy pronouncements.

Presidium decisions appear concerned with great quantities of trivia as well as major issues. Questions like the wages of minor functionaries or the ideological qualities of a slight literary piece may crowd the Presidium docket. In Stalin's time the press almost daily carried over the dictator's signature a lengthy, solemn decree covering a banal task or duty, like the currying and shoeing of beasts of burden and the gathering of potatoes and beetroot. The top officialdom's immersion in trivia is forced by their need to prevent subordinate bodies from inserting themselves into the line of authority and to keep open the channels of information from the lower echelons. The Presidium, therefore, must invite a constant inundation of memoranda and reports from the lower levels. Khrushchev understandably complained in a public speech of the "many tomes" of official documents he had to read.

The Communist administrative system is an elaborate mechanism of control from the top. There are no departmental bureaus with the autonomy of an FBI and an Army Corps of Engineers. In Soviet practice the party, which dominates the government apparatus from top to bottom, leaves nothing undone to assure that the orders of the top command are carried out. The Soviet leader can act with a rigor toward his administrators and ministries that no American President would dare consider even in his fondest dreams. The leader, whether Stalin or Khrushchev, must appear infallible despite the treachery of events and human error. If he falters, others must bear the blame. A high privilege of dictatorship is the free and constant power to effect administrative reorganization at will or whim. When the Central Statistical Department annoyed Stalin, he suppressed it, because, as his press put it, "statistics cannot be neutral" and "class statistics are necessary." When the director of the Marx-Engels Institute made an irreverent remark, Stalin passed it off with a joke which shrouded a threat, "Riazanov is homesick for Turkestan." The arctic ice and Central Asia's burning sands were not the worst of Stalin's punishments for offending administrators.

◇

THE Presidency is America's foremost political export. The Philippines, France to a degree, and most of all Latin America have engrafted onto their governments elements of the American Presidential model. At one time or another all the Latin-American countries have adopted the strong Presidency. It is instructive to study what they have borrowed, added, or left out in their adaptation of the American prototype because it reveals what they believe to be the strengths and shortcomings of our Presidential institution.

The powers of the Latin-American president invariably exceed those of the United States chief executive. The Latin president's appointment power is stronger. He can fill most offices on his own authority, referring relatively few for Senatorial or Congressional approval. He sends messages and appears personally before Congress to request action. In Venezuela he can even introduce bills, a power treated somewhat ambiguously in several other constitutions, which assertive presidents have interpreted to their own advantage. He presents the budget in the form of an appropriation bill, enjoys a broad and strong veto power, including an item veto for appropriations, and has a sweeping power to issue decrees and administrative orders. Laws are passed in far more general terms than the American Congress would ever tolerate, affording the president broad discretion. He enjoys extraordinary powers to cope with civil disorder, invasion, or other crisis and to intervene in the provincial governments.

Latin experience abundantly demonstrates, however, that in spite of all his impressive power the president must dominate the army and build a political party or following of "interests," especially the organized urban workers, if he is to succeed. Even the best presidents have indulged in what is termed "exaggerated presidentialism," by which they assume dictatorial powers for brief or substantial periods. Bolívar, for one, was convinced that exceptional executive powers must be readily available to counter the demagogic exploitation of racial-cultural tensions. The spectacle of the presidency transformed into an outright military dictatorship is all too common. Although the United States' transplant has not proved to be the means to good government, it is reassuring that each departure from legitimate government for some variant of dictatorship has been marked by an eventual return to the presidential form.

As is the fate of merchandise, not every potential foreign buyer who has looked at the American Presidential system has bought it. Charles de Gaulle, beholding the American Presidency in 1964, turned aside clamors in certain domestic quarters that France repattern its own Presidency along American lines. De Gaulle would have nothing of it. The American system, he declared in a press conference, was functioning in a limping way, and, if it were applied in France, he foresaw only "a chronic opposition" between the executive and legislature, leading to "general paralysis." Presumably De Gaulle had in mind the breakdowns in Presidential-Congressional cooperation which provide the American nation with a steady diet of political futility. The American Presidential system, De Gaulle contended, had thrived in the peculiarly favorable environment of the United States:

> it is in a country which because of its technical make-up, its economic riches, its geographical position, never knew invasion, and which for a century has known no revolution; in a country where, moreover, there are only two parties that are divided by nothing essential in any field, national, social, moral, international; in a federal country where the Government assumes only general tasks—defenses, diplomacy, finance—while the 50 states of the union are entrusted with all the rest.

The American Presidency was not transferable, at least not to France.

◇

WHETHER De Gaulle's estimate of the American Presidential system will be true in the future will depend upon our success or failure in dealing with the three great revolutions of our time: the human rights revolution, the automation revolution, and the weaponry revolution. Coping with the first two will require bold new legislation and administrative action in the fields of education, health, civil rights, and national resources. Social attitudes toward work and leisure will have to be redefined. No less initiative will need to be asserted in foreign affairs to make reason prevail over the unthinkable alternative of the terrible weaponry. Congress must be moved, peoples aroused, the bureaucracy stirred. Only the President can do it.

The President's greatest weakness is Congress. The Senate filibuster, the seniority principle of selecting committee chairmen, the power of the House Rules Committee, the flourishing of so many power centers that responsibility is lost—all this and more give the President's role as legislative leader the assurance of a leaky sieve. His ancillary role as party leader too is ridden with weakness that enfeebles him with Congress, and his Congressional malady spreads into his functioning as diplomat and commander-in-chief.

In the executive branch he faces the mammoth bureaucracy, slow in responding to his purposes, unimaginative in the face of momentous problems, laboring mightily to bring forth a mole. Not a little of its recalcitrance is rooted in Congress.

In the face of these formidable obstacles to the maintenance of a Presidency that is continuously strong, several responses are possible. One is to substitute an altogether different form of government, such as the Parliamentary system, but our tradition, the variety of our national life, and the intermittently good record of the Presidency preclude such a departure. Furthermore, the Parliamentary model is not flourishing at the moment anywhere and is under a shadow in its own motherland, England.

A second response is to reorganize the government in a limited way. The nation's most vital renewal project is the overhaul of Congress to bring it out of the nineteenth century, to which its organization and working methods cling, and enable it to address itself positively and responsively to the problems of the twentieth. A limited reorganization, much of it inspired by the strong British party model, can be usefully applied to the major American political parties. Reorganization, too, is promising medicine for the ills of bureaucracy.

A third response is to exploit more than we have certain resources of the Presidency and certain trends and changes in society. John Kennedy taught us vividly the effectiveness of the President's independent powers for advancing civil rights. They can be used to advance other social and economic measures the times require. The full dimensions of the executive power clause are yet to be explored, and, by creative interpretation, they could become a great boon for strengthening the President as administrative chief. The United States Supreme Court, in its civil rights rulings and its requirement of a wholesale revision of the districts of the House of Representatives, has clearly befriended the cause of the continously strong Presidency. The Court, altogether logically, could take up the executive power clause with results equally favorable to the Presidency.

Profound changes are afoot in society on which the strong Presidency can capitalize. The great population shift from rural to urban areas continues apace, and forecasts agree that the trend will quicken. The Supreme Court's reapportionment decisions promise that the House of Representatives will in the future more accurately reflect the growing urbanization of society. Urban society requires a greater quantity of public services, and the city, although not the suburbs, has been, historically, a staunch constituency of the strong Presidency. It is in urban society that most of the great contemporary revolutions have been concentrated. The Presidency that is continuously strong will be urban-centered.

If the American people agree that a strong Presidency, a better Congress, and a more meaningful party system are essential to the well-being of their country, they can achieve them within the contours of the Constitution and the nation's tradition. There are solid indications that pressures are building to see that they are achieved.

Presidents of the United States

Constitutional Provisions
Relating to the Presidency

Sources

Index

Presidents of the United States

	PARTY	TERM
1. George Washington (1732–99)	Federalist	1789–1797
2. John Adams (1735–1826)	Federalist	1797–1801
3. Thomas Jefferson (1743–1826)	Democratic–Republican	1801–1809
4. James Madison (1751–1836)	Democratic–Republican	1809–1817
5. James Monroe (1758–1831)	Democratic–Republican	1817–1825
6. John Quincy Adams (1767–1848)	Democratic–Republican	1825–1829
7. Andrew Jackson (1767–1845)	Democratic	1829–1837
8. Martin Van Buren (1782–1862)	Democratic	1837–1841
9. William Henry Harrison (1773–1841)	Whig	1841
10. John Tyler (1790–1862)	Whig	1841–1845
11. James K. Polk (1795–1849)	Democratic	1845–1849
12. Zachary Taylor (1784–1850)	Whig	1849–1850
13. Millard Fillmore (1800–74)	Whig	1850–1853
14. Franklin Pierce (1804–69)	Democratic	1853–1857
15. James Buchanan (1791–1868)	Democratic	1857–1861
16. Abraham Lincoln (1809–65)	Republican	1861–1865
17. Andrew Johnson (1808–75)	Union	1865–1869
18. Ulysses S. Grant (1822–85)	Republican	1869–1877

19. Rutherford B. Hayes (1822–93)	Republican	1877–1881
20. James A. Garfield (1831–81)	Republican	1881
21. Chester A. Arthur (1830–86)	Republican	1881–1885
22. Grover Cleveland (1837–1908)	Democratic	1885–1889
23. Benjamin Harrison (1833–1901)	Republican	1889–1893
24. Grover Cleveland (1837–1908)	Democratic	1893–1897
25. William McKinley (1843–1901)	Republican	1897–1901
26. Theodore Roosevelt (1858–1919)	Republican	1901–1909
27. William Howard Taft (1857–1930)	Republican	1909–1913
28. Woodrow Wilson (1856–1924)	Democratic	1913–1921
29. Warren G. Harding (1865–1923)	Republican	1921–1923
30. Calvin Coolidge (1872–1933)	Republican	1923–1929
31. Herbert Hoover (b. 1874)	Republican	1929–1933
32. Franklin Delano Roosevelt (1882–1945)	Democratic	1933–1945
33. Harry S. Truman (b. 1884)	Democratic	1945–1953
34. Dwight D. Eisenhower (b. 1890)	Republican	1953–1961
35. John F. Kennedy (1917–63)	Democratic	1961–1963
36. Lyndon B. Johnson (b. 1908)	Democratic	1963–

Constitutional Provisions
Relating to the Presidency

SECTION 3

6. The Senate shall have the sole power to try all impeachments. When sitting for that purpose, they shall be on oath or affirmation. When the President of the United States is tried, the Chief Justice shall preside; and no person shall be convicted without the concurrence of two-thirds of the members present.

7. Judgment in cases of impeachment shall not extend further than to removal from office, and disqualification to hold and enjoy any office of honor, trust, or profit under the United States; but the party convicted shall, nevertheless, be liable and subject to indictment, trial, judgment, and punishment, according to law.

SECTION 7

2. Every bill which shall have passed the House of Representatives and the Senate shall, before it becomes a law, be presented to the President of the United States; if he approve he shall sign it, but if not he shall return it, with his objections, to that house in which it shall have originated, who shall enter the objections at large on their journal and proceed to reconsider it. If after such reconsideration two-thirds of that house shall agree to pass the bill, it shall be sent, together with the objections, to the other house, by which it shall likewise be reconsidered, and if approved by two-thirds of that house it shall become a law. But in all such cases the votes of both houses shall be determined by yeas and nays, and the names of the persons voting for and against the bill shall be entered on the journal of each house respectively. If any bill shall not be returned by the President within ten days (Sundays excepted) after it shall have been presented to him, the same shall be a law, in like manner as if he had signed it unless the Congress by their adjournment prevent its return, in which case it shall not be a law.

3. Every order, resolution, or vote to which the concurrence of the Senate and House of Representatives may be necessary (except on a question of adjournment) shall be presented to the President of the United States; and before the same shall take effect, shall be approved by him, or being disapproved by him, shall be re-passed by two-thirds of the Senate and House of Representatives, according to the rules and limitations prescribed in the case of a bill.

ARTICLE II

SECTION 1

1. The executive power shall be vested in a President of the United States of America. He shall hold his office during the term of four years, and, together with the Vice-President, chosen for the same term, be elected as follows:

2. Each state shall appoint, in such manner as the legislature thereof may direct, a number of electors, equal to the whole number of Senators and Representatives to which the State may be entitled in the Congress; but no Senator or Representative, or person holding an office of trust or profit under the United States, shall be appointed an elector.

3.* The electors shall meet in their respective states and vote by ballot for two persons, of whom one at least shall not be an inhabitant of the same state with themselves. And they shall make a list of all the persons voted for, and of the number of votes for each; which list they shall sign and certify, and transmit sealed to the seat of the government of the United States, directed to the President of the Senate. The President of the Senate shall, in the presence of the Senate and House of Representatives, open all the certificates, and the votes shall then be counted. The person having the greatest number of votes shall be the President, if such a number be a majority of the whole number of electors appointed; and if there be more than one who have such majority, and have an equal number of votes, then the House of Representatives shall immediately choose by ballot one of them for President; and if no person have a majority, then from the five highest on the list the said House shall in like manner choose the President. But in choosing the President the votes shall be taken by states, the representation from each state having one vote; a quorum for this purpose shall consist of a member or members from two-thirds of the states, and a majority of all the states shall be necessary to a choice. In every case, after the choice of the President, the person having the greatest number of votes of the electors shall be the Vice-President. But if there should remain two or more who have equal votes, the Senate shall choose from them by ballot the Vice-President.

4. The Congress may determine the time of choosing the electors and the day on which they shall give their votes, which day shall be the same throughout the United States.

5. No person except a natural born citizen, or a citizen of the United States at the time of the adoption of this Constitution, shall be eligible to the office of President; neither shall any person be eligible to that office who shall not have attained to the age of thirty-five years, and been fourteen years a resident within the United States.

6. In case of the removal of the President from office, or of his death, resignation, or inability to discharge the powers and duties of the said office, the same shall devolve on the Vice-President, and the Congress may by law provide for the case of removal, death, resignation, or inability, both of the President and Vice-Presi-

---

* This paragraph was superseded by the Twelfth Amendment.

dent, declaring what officer shall then act as President, and such officer shall act accordingly until the disability be removed or a President shall be elected.

7. The President shall, at stated times, receive for his services a compensation, which shall neither be increased nor diminished during the period for which he shall have been elected, and he shall not receive within that period any other emolument from the United States or any of them.

8. Before he enter on the execution of his office he shall take the following oath or affirmation:

> I do solemnly swear (or affirm) that I will faithfully execute the office of President of the United States, and will to the best of my ability preserve, protect, and defend the Constitution of the United States.

SECTION 2

1. The President shall be Commander-in-Chief of the Army and Navy of the United States, and of the militia of the several states when called into the actual service of the United States; he may require the opinion, in writing, of the principal officer in each of the executive departments, upon any subject relating to the duties of their respective offices, and he shall have power to grant reprieves and pardons for offenses against the United States, except in cases of impeachment.

2. He shall have power, by and with the advice and consent of the Senate, to make treaties, provided two-thirds of the Senators present concur; and he shall nominate, and, by and with the advice and consent of the Senate, shall appoint ambassadors, other public ministers and consuls, judges of the Supreme Court, and all other officers of the United States, whose appointments are not herein otherwise provided for, and which shall be established by law; but the Congress may by law vest the appointment of such inferior officers, as they think proper, in the President alone, in the courts of law, or in the heads of departments.

3. The President shall have power to fill up all vacancies that may happen during the recess of the Senate, by granting commissions which shall expire at the end of their next session.

SECTION 3

He shall from time to time give to the Congress information of the state of the union, and recommend to their consideration such measures as he shall judge necessary and expedient; he may, on extraordinary occasions, convene both houses, or either of them, and in case of disagreement between them with respect to the time of adjournment, he may adjourn them to such time as he shall think proper; he shall receive ambassadors and other public ministers; he shall take care that the laws be faithfully executed, and shall commission all the officers of the United States.

SECTION 4

The President, Vice-President, and all civil officers of the United States shall be removed from office on impeachment for and conviction of treason, bribery, or other high crimes and misdemeanors.

AMENDMENT XII

The electors shall meet in their respective states and vote by ballot for President and Vice-President, one of whom, at least, shall not be an inhabitant of the same state with themselves; they shall name in their ballots the person voted for as President, and in distinct ballots the person voted for as Vice-President, and they shall make distinct lists of all persons voted for as President and of all persons voted for as Vice-President, and of the number of votes for each;

which lists they shall sign and certify, and transmit sealed to the seat of the government of the United States, directed to the President of the Senate. The President of the Senate shall, in the presence of the Senate and House of Representatives, open all the certificates and the votes shall then be counted. The person having the greatest number of votes for President shall be the President, if such number be a majority of the whole number of electors appointed; and if no person have such majority, then from the persons having the highest numbers not exceeding three on the list of those voted for as President, the House of Representatives shall choose immediately, by ballot, the President. But in choosing the President the votes shall be taken by states, the representation from each state having one vote; a quorum for this purpose shall consist of a member or members from two-thirds of the states, and a majority of all the states shall be necessary to a choice. And if the House of Representatives shall not choose a President whenever the right of choice shall devolve upon them, before the fourth day of March next following, then the Vice-President shall act as President, as in the case of the death or other constitutional disability of the President.

The person having the greatest number of votes as Vice-President shall be the Vice-President, if such number be a majority of the whole number of electors appointed; and if no person have a majority, then from the two highest numbers on the list the Senate shall choose the Vice-President; a quorum for the purpose shall consist of two-thirds of the whole number of Senators, and a majority of the whole number shall be necessary to a choice. But no person constitutionally ineligible to the office of President shall be eligible to that of Vice-President of the United States.

AMENDMENT XX

SECTION 1

The terms of the President and Vice-President shall end at noon on the 20th day of January, and the terms of Senators and Representatives at noon on the 3d day of January, of the years in which such terms would have ended if this article had not been ratified; and the terms of their successors shall then begin.

SECTION 2

The Congress shall assemble at least once in every year, and such meeting shall begin at noon on the 3d day of January, unless they shall by law appoint a different day.

SECTION 3

If, at the time fixed for the beginning of the term of the President, the President elect shall have died, the Vice-President elect shall become President. If a President shall not have been chosen before the time fixed for the beginning of his term, or if the President elect shall have failed to qualify, then the Vice-President elect shall act as President until a President shall have qualified; and the Congress may by law provide for the case wherein neither a President elect nor a Vice-President elect shall have qualified, declaring who shall then act as President, or the manner in which one who is to act shall be selected, and such person shall act accordingly until a President or Vice-President shall have qualified.

SECTION 4

The Congress may by law provide for the case of the death of any of the persons from whom the House of Representatives may choose a President whenever the right of choice shall have devolved upon them, and for the case of the death of any of the persons from whom the Senate may choose a Vice-President whenever the right of choice shall have devolved upon them.

AMENDMENT XXII

No person shall be elected to the office of the President more than twice, and no person who has held the office of President, or acted as President, for more than two years of a term to which some other person was elected President shall be elected to the office of the President more than once. But this article shall not apply to any person holding the office of President when this article was proposed by the Congress, and shall not prevent any person who may be holding the office of President, or acting as President, during the term within which this article becomes operative from holding the office of President or acting as President during the remainder of such term.

Sources

========

I. GENERAL WORKS ON THE AMERICAN PRESIDENCY

Binkley, Wilfred, *The Man in the White House* (Baltimore, 1959).
Brownlow, Louis, *The President and the Presidency* (Chicago, 1949).
Corwin, Edward S., *The President: Office and Powers*, 4th ed. (New York, 1957).
———, and Louis W. Koenig, *The Presidency Today* (New York, 1956).
Finer, Herman, *The Presidency: Crisis and Regeneration* (Chicago, 1960).
Heller, Francis H., *The Presidency: A Modern Perspective* (New York, 1960).
Herring, E. Pendleton, *Presidential Leadership* (New York, 1940).
Hyman, Sidney, *The American President* (New York, 1954).
Laski, Harold, *The American Presidency* (New York, 1940).
Milton, George F., *The Use of Presidential Power* (Boston, 1944).
Neustadt, Richard E., *Presidential Power* (New York, 1960).
Patterson, C. P., *Presidential Government in the United States* (Chapel Hill, 1947).
Rossiter, Clinton, *The American Presidency*, 2nd ed. (New York, 1960).
Stanwood, E., *History of the Presidency* (Boston, 1928).
Taft, William H., *Our Chief Magistrate and His Powers* (New York, 1916).
Tugwell, Rexford G., *The Enlargement of the Presidency* (New York, 1960).

II. SPECIALIZED WORKS

Acheson, Dean, *A Citizen Looks at Congress* (New York, 1956).
Berdahl, C. A., *War Powers of the Executive in the United States* (Urbana, Ill., 1921).
Binkley, Wilfred, *President and Congress* (New York, 1947).
Burns, James MacGregor, *The Deadlock of Democracy* (New York, 1963).

Chamberlain, Lawrence H., *The President, Congress, and Legislation* (New York, 1946).

Commission on Organization of the Executive Branch of the Government (Hoover Commission), *Reports* (Washington, 1949 and 1953).

Committee on Government Operations, Subcommittee on National Policy Machinery, *Reports*, (Washington, 1959 and after).

Dangerfield, Royden J., *In Defense of the Senate* (Norman, Okla., 1933).

David, Paul, Malcolm Moos, and R. M. Goldman, *Presidential Nominating Politics*, 5 vols. (Baltimore, 1954).

Fenno, Richard, *The President's Cabinet* (Cambridge, Mass., 1959).

Goebel, Dorothy B., *Generals in the White House* (New York, 1945).

Greene, Evarts B., *The Provincial Governor* (New York, 1898).

Hansen, Richard, *The Year We Had No President* (Lincoln, Neb., 1963).

Harris, Joseph P., *The Advice and Consent of the Senate* (Berkeley, Cal., 1953).

Hart, James, *The American Presidency in Action* (New York, 1948).

Hatch, L. C., and E. L. Shoup, *A History of the Vice Presidency* (New York, 1934).

Hinsdale, Mary L., *A History of the President's Cabinet* (Ann Arbor, Mich., 1911).

Hobbs, Edward H., *Behind the President: A Study of Executive Office Agencies* (Washington, 1954).

Holt, W. Stull, *Treaties Defeated by the Senate* (Baltimore, 1933).

Humbert, W. H., *The Pardoning Power of the President* (Washington, 1941).

Koenig, Louis W., *The Invisible Presidency* (New York, 1960).

———, *The Presidency and the Crisis* (New York, 1944).

Learned, H. B., *The President's Cabinet* (New Haven, 1912).

McClure, Wallace M., *International Executive Agreements* (New York, 1941).

Marcy, Carl M., *Presidential Commissions* (New York, 1945).

Moos, Malcolm, *Politics, Presidents, and Coattails* (Baltimore, 1950).

Nash, Bradley D., *Staffing the Presidency* (Washington, 1952).

Nourse, Edwin G., *Economics in the Public Service: Administrative Aspects of the Employment Act* (New York, 1953).

Overacker, Louise, *Presidential Campaign Funds* (Boston, 1946).

———, *The Presidential Primary* (New York, 1926).

Pollard, J. E., *The Presidents and the Press* (New York, 1947).

Polsby, Nelson W., and Aaron Wildavsky, *Presidential Elections* (New York, 1964).

President's Committee on Administrative Management (Brownlow Committee), *Report with Special Studies* (Washington, 1937).

Randall, James G., *Constitutional Problems under Lincoln* (New York, 1926).

Remini, Robert V., *Martin Van Buren and the Making of the Democratic Party* (New York, 1959).

Rich, Bennett M., *The Presidents and Civil Disorder* (Washington, 1941).

Roseboom, Eugene H., *A History of Presidential Elections* (New York, 1957).

Rossiter, Clinton, *The Supreme Court and the Commander-in-Chief* (Ithaca, N. Y., 1951).

Schubert, Glendon A., Jr., *The Presidency in the Courts* (Minneapolis, 1957).

Silva, Ruth, *Presidential Succession* (Ann Arbor, Mich., 1951).

Silverman, Corinne, *The President's Economic Advisers* (University, Ala., 1959).

Small, Norman J., *Some Presidential Interpretations of the Presidency* (Baltimore, 1930).

Somers, Herman M., *Presidential Agency: OWMR* (Cambridge, Mass., 1954).

Sorensen, Theodore C., *Decision-Making in the White House* (New York, 1963).
Stein, Charles W., *The Third Term Tradition* (New York, 1946).

1922).
U. S. National Archives, *Public Papers of the Presidents of the United States* (Washington, 1957 and after).
Waugh, Edgar W., *Second Consul* (Indianapolis, 1956).
White, Theodore H., *The Making of the President, 1960* (New York, 1961).
Williams, Irving G., *The Rise of the Vice-Presidency* (Washington, 1956).
Wilmerding, Lucius, Jr., *The Electoral College* (New Brunswick, N. J., 1958).

III. BIOGRAPHIES, PAPERS AND MEMOIRS OF PRESIDENTS

Adams, Charles Francis, ed., *Memoirs of John Quincy Adams*, 12 vols. (Philadelphia, 1875).
Bishop, Joseph Bucklin, *Theodore Roosevelt and His Time* (New York, 1920).
Blum, John M., *The Republican Roosevelt* (Cambridge, Mass., 1954).
Brant, Irving, *Madison the President* (New York, 1957).
Brown, Stuart Gerry, *The Autobiography of James Monroe* (Syracuse, 1959).
Burns, James MacGregor, *John Kennedy: A Political Profile* (New York, 1960).
———, *Roosevelt: The Lion and the Fox* (New York, 1956).
Caldwell, Robert G., *James A. Garfield: Party Chieftain* (New York, 1931).
Childs, Marquis, *Eisenhower: Captive Hero* (New York, 1958).
Chitwood, Oliver Perry, *John Tyler: Champion of the Old South* (New York, 1930).
Cleveland, Grover, *Presidential Problems* (New York, 1904).
Cresson, William P., *James Monroe* (Chapel Hill, 1946).
Donovan, Robert J., *Eisenhower: The Inside Story* (New York, 1956).
Eisenhower, Dwight D., *Mandate for Change, 1953–1956* (Garden City, 1963).
Freeman, Douglas Southall, *George Washington*, Vols. VI-VII (New York, 1954—1957).
Freidel, Frank, *Franklin D. Roosevelt: The Triumph* (Boston, 1956).
George, Alexander and Juliette L. George, *Woodrow Wilson and Colonel House: A Personality Study* (New York, 1956).
Harbaugh, William Henry, *Power and Responsibility: The Life and Times of Theodore Roosevelt* (New York, 1961).
Hoover, Herbert, *The Memoirs of Herbert Hoover* (New York, 1951–1952).
Howe, George Frederick, *Chester A. Arthur: A Quarter-Century of Machine Politics* (New York, 1935).
Hughes, Emmet John, *The Ordeal of Power* (New York, 1963).
James, Marquis, *Andrew Jackson: Portrait of a President* (Indianapolis, 1937).
Klein, Philip Shriver, *President James Buchanan: A Biography* (University Park, Pa., 1962).
Leech, Margaret, *In the Days of McKinley* (New York, 1959).
Link, Arthur S., *Wilson: The New Freedom* (Princeton, 1956).
———, *Wilson: The Road to the White House* (Princeton, 1947).
———, *Woodrow Wilson and the Progressive Era, 1910–1917* (New York, 1954).
Morgan, Robert J., *A Whig Embattled* (Lincoln, Neb., 1954).
Mowry, George E., *The Era of Theodore Roosevelt* (New York, 1958).
Nevins, Allan, ed., *The Diary of John Quincy Adams* (New York, 1951).
———, *Grover Cleveland: A Study in Courage* (New York, 1932).
———, ed., *James K. Polk: The Diary of a President* (New York, 1929).

Nichols, Roy F., *Franklin Pierce: Young Hickory of the Granite Hills* (Philadelphia, 1931).

Pringle, Henry F., *The Life and Times of William Howard Taft* (New York, 1939).

———, *Theodore Roosevelt* (New York, 1931).

Randall, James G., *Lincoln the President* (New York, 1945–1955).

Roosevelt, Theodore, *Autobiography* (New York, 1913).

Rosenman, Samuel I., *Working with Roosevelt* (New York, 1952).

Schachner, Nathan, *Thomas Jefferson: A Biography* (New York, 1951).

Schlesinger, Arthur M., Jr., *The Crisis of the Old Order* (Boston, 1957).

———, *The Coming of the New Deal* (Boston, 1959).

———, *The Politics of Upheaval* (Boston, 1960).

Sherwood, Robert E., *Roosevelt and Hopkins* (New York, 1948).

Sievers, Harry J., *Benjamin Harrison: Hoosier Statesman* (New York, 1959).

Stryker, Lloyd Paul, *Andrew Johnson: A Study in Courage* (New York, 1929).

Truman, Harry S., *Memoirs* (Garden City, N. Y., 1955–1956).

———, *Truman Speaks* (New York, 1960).

Tugwell, Rexford, *The Democratic Roosevelt* (Garden City, N. Y., 1957).

White, William Allen, *A Puritan in Babylon* (New York, 1938).

Williams, Charles Richard, ed., *Diary and Letters of Rutherford B. Hayes* (Columbus, O., 1924).

Winston, Robert W., *Andrew Johnson: Plebian and Patriot* (New York, 1928).

IV. COURT CASES

In re Debs (158 U.S. 564, 1895).

Duncan v. *Kahanamoku, Sheriff* (327 U.S. 304, 1946).

Ex parte Grossman (267 U.S., 1925).

Hirabayashi v. *United States* (320 U.S. 81, 1943).

Humphrey v. *United States* (295 U.S. 602, 1935).

Korematsu v. *United States* (323 U.S. 214, 1944).

Ex parte Milligan (4 Wall 2, 1866).

Mississippi v. *Johnson* (4 Wall 475, 1867).

Myers v. *United States* (271 U.S., 1926).

In re Neagle (135 U.S. 1, 1890).

Ex parte Quirin (317 U.S. 1, 1942).

Ray v. *Blair* (343 U.S. 214, 1952).

United States v. *Curtiss-Wright Export Corp.* (299 U.S. 304, 1936).

United States v. *Montgomery Ward and Co.* (58 F. Supp. 408, N.D., Ill., 1945; 150 F. [2d.] 369, C.C.A. 7th, 1945).

Yakus v. *United States* (321 U.S. 414, 1944).

Youngstown Sheet and Tube Co. v. *Sawyer* (343 U.S. 579, 1952).

V. CHIEF EXECUTIVES OF OTHER COUNTRIES

Adam, Thomas R., *Elements of Government: An Introduction to Political Science* (New York, 1960).

Attlee, C. R., *As It Happened* (New York, 1954).

Davis, Harold E., *Government and Politics in Latin America* (New York, 1958).

Deutscher, Isaac, *Russia after Stalin* (New York, 1949).

———, *Stalin: A Political Biography* (New York, 1949).

Djilas, Milovan, *The New Class* (New York, 1957).
Eden, Anthony, *The Memoirs of Anthony Eden: Full Circle* (Boston, 1960).
Fainsod, Merle, *How Russia Is Ruled* (Cambridge, Mass., 1963).
Hazard, John N., *The Soviet System of Government* (Chicago, 1960).
McKenzie, R. T., *British Political Parties* (London, 1955).
Macridis, Roy C., *The Study of Comparative Government* (Garden City, 1955).
———, and Bernard E. Brown, *The De Gaulle Republic: Quest for Unity* (Homewood, Ill., 1960).
Morrison, Herbert, *Government and Parliament* (London, 1954).
Rossiter, Clinton, *Constitutional Dictatorship* (Princeton, 1948).
Williams, Francis, ed., *Twilight of Empire: Memoirs of Prime Minister Clement Attlee* (New York, 1962).
Wolfe, Bertram D., *Khrushchev and Stalin's Ghost* (New York, 1957).

Index